CHRIST PROTAGONIST
or
LOGOS DETHRONED

CHRIST PROTAGONIST
or
LOGOS DETHRONED

Transforming the Symbol of Roman Power
Into Jewish Salvation
In the Slander of the Prophet of God

M. H. T. Kang

Creative Fire Press
— 2023 —

CREATIVE FIRE PRESS

Creative Fire Press is a division of The Walden Group, a Michigan non-profit educational publisher.

Library of Congress Cataloging-in-Publication Data

Kang, M. H. T.
Christ Protagonist or Logos Dethroned

p. cm.
Includes bibliographical references

ISBN 979-8986-7250-17
(pbk.: alk. paper)

1. Christianity, history of

Printing number: 9 8 7 6 5 4 3 2 1

Printed in the United States of America on acid-free paper.

DEDICATION

This book is dedicated to two people: 1. My baby brother Saleh, who was my only true supporter, editor, and the first person to read it. His confidence in me and continued encouragement is always an essential piece of anything I do. Since a baby, my baby brother Saleh has been my only student and has endured both the criticism of fake friends and the challenges necessary it takes to be a philosopher and to stand ready with the truth over and against anything that comes your way. I have no doubt that Saleh will surpass me as a philosopher and great communicator, and if anyone cannot find me to explain portions of this book, only he would make a fine replacement. What a bad credit one pays one's teacher if one only remains a student. Seek knowledge even unto China and the ends of the Earth and may you grow smarter and wiser than all your teachers.

2. My late best friend and greatest example of what a Christian was to me is Mark Sumpter. Mark was a youth minister at a Pentecostal Church in Ypsilanti Michigan who I went to school with and spent countless hours debating the meaning of the Christian doctrine. When Mark would show up to my house to talk about the various philosophical systems that attempted to explain God, it was not clear to me that he was also someone respected in his community, beloved by his parents, and working a fulltime job to get himself through school taking on twice the responsibilities that I had; and he did so always with a smile on his face and kindness for whoever he met. I never saw Mark get angry, and one day he told me to reflect on the verse "He who is slow to anger is better than a warrior, and he who controls his temper is greater than one who captures a city".

Mark was in the process of reading my book when he passed on Christmas Eve of 2020; the last text message that I received from him explained that he had bought a book on Kierkegaard for us to study together. My fondest wish is that we will study that book one day, no matter what, my dear friend, as we both were always painfully aware that death is not the end and especially not the end of a philosopher or a believer in God. Mark Sumpter is always the example of a real Christian to me and one that I will always respect, and a true philosopher of the heart.

How to Read This Book...

This book is a book about Western civilization and is a workable "introduction to philosophy" textbook, hoping to take the discipline in a new direction—one that combines theology, philosophy, and political theory into one historical or chronological progression. The central motif in this progression is the figure of Christ who is cast as a heroic figure within a false dialectic of oriental vs. occidental, and religion vs. science. Paul is cast as one that forms the main values of the west, such as: "all for one", separation of church and state, faith in the future, progressive revelation, gentiles coming into the Jewish salvation, the reversal of symbols of Roman power, salvation by faith alone, grace through suffering, and his characteristic false humility or false bragging. This is the application of the themes of "Paulinism" to the full breadth of the progress of Western civilization and even the scientific and secular worldview which developed in Europe; the result was a horror show which allows one to realize that Paul's preaching in Europe, and the Jewish diaspora in Europe, caused the formulation of what is now being termed a "Judeo-Christian" synthesis to promote a pseudo-eschatology of the coming kingdom of God.

This book is organized into four parts; it matters not in what order one begins but only that each chapter be read a coherent unit from start to finish. One should start in order of importance, relevance, salience, and/or focus first on the areas where one feels most deficient. Part one is composed of historical critiques of first century Palestine. Part two is a transition from the historical world of the experts to the historical and political narratives of the theologists and co-religionists of the Christian movement. Part three is composed of the subversive role of philosophers in spreading the Pauline synthesis or Christian message which led to the unification of Europe and therefore the development of the secular and scientific worldview. We attempt to show how some of the most relevant chapters of philosophical thought brought forward this progression in history. Finally, we look at Christianity on its own terms, focusing and narrowing in on the doctrines and teachings presented to us in the works now known as the New Testament. There we present a full exegesis of the Pauline epistles. For those who are not well-versed in Pauline theology, we recommend beginning at the exegesis located near the end of the book.

Special Thanks
A special thanks is reserved for Dr. David Skrbina for always believing in me and challenging me. It was kind words offered by the Doctor in the presence of his wife at a Jesus Hoax debate that gave me the confidence never to shrink from my task.

More special thanks are reserved for everyone that financially supported this book or has taken time to listen and consider the arguments here. I only wish we could sit together longer, my friends, even the ones who abandoned me. As a man who will never give up on anyone, I humbly wait your reconsideration.

CONTENTS

CHRIST PROTAGONIST
or
LOGOS DETHRONED

PREFACE

"Give instruction to a wise man, and he will be yet wiser:
teach a just man, and he will increase in learning."

Proverbs 9:9

"Speak not in the ears of a fool: for he will despise the wisdom of thy words."

Proverbs 23:9

In Chapter 81 of the Tao Te Ching, Lao Tzu says, "True words are not always beautiful. Beautiful words are not always true". What is the relation between beauty and truth? Plato says that Wisdom, Truth, and Beauty are divine muses for the highest semblance of human consciousness, but the truth is much stranger than either Wisdom or Beauty. While beauty is sometimes dangerous and wisdom mysterious, in reality only truth seems to guide knowledge, but knowledge can only tell us the difference between right and wrong. Wisdom, which comes by experience and cannot be rendered purely in the domain of abstract thought and imagination, not only differentiates between right and wrong but also finds out what then to do with that information in application of activity in the world and in application to projects of political organization—or to the deep-rooted questions of trust and morality associated with one's conscious and psychological engagement with other humans.

Ultimately, any philosophy that refuses to answer the question "Then what?" is doomed to failure. Hence, just as truth and imagination are superior to knowledge, which is limited by other forms of knowledge, and just as the way in which organization and rhetoric are superior to logic and argumentation, Wisdom and experience are superior to Truth and Beauty and courage is superior to knowledge.

Ultimately, the goal of knowledge is moral action. Beauty is not superior to Truth or Power. Power is not control or Justice through the rule of the righteous but can sometimes engender mistrust and fear. He who uses fear for control must rely on anger and retribution as a tool and those who play with fire may get burned or may go free, but this is for sure: Power relies on the weak, just as beauty requires ugliness by contrast, and love is part of hate. Just as form requires emptiness and space, movement and time require stillness and impermeability (ubiquity). Truth is singular like light and consciousness (sound) but falsehood (density) has many layers. Falsehood has many varieties and versions and parts and is compartmentalized into types of knowledge while the truth is whole. Truth is heard but not seen, while falsehood leads by false representation and disinterested idealism of a mass conscience and is thick like thieves in the belly of the beast.

This attunement brings us to our current endeavor. Our endeavor is not future-oriented but past-oriented. Those who know not where they come from know not where to go, and to those who know not where they are going, any road will take them to their aimless direction. These are the "Sumyun, Bukmun, Umyun" or the dumb, deaf, and blind. They know not where they go, leading each other because they are not enlivened by the traditions of the past.

Why do you not have any rites? It is because your rites were exchanged for "rights" and equality under the law. We believe history is superior to science and that philosophers should distinguish themselves from the cold and patient truth of scientists. History is superior to science because science and philosophy themselves have a history. Science is a methodology that is determined in part by past research and in part by the cultural disposition of those called scientists. Granted as such, it must function under the bounds of social agreement and is imprecise as any other tool.

Since in the modern world, social organization is itself determined by technological advance and the forms of social organization are themselves technocratic means, Science is determined on the one end by historical processes and on the other end by advancements in technology, which is the goal of science and not science itself. Hence the notion that technology is created by scientific enterprise is false. Science does not create technology, but it is technology that creates Science, both via knowledge of the past and the drive for technological advance which exists in the future. Primary to technology is Man's creation of symbols and the architectonic arts of history, religion, and philosophy. These determinations are where we situate ourselves in our quest for knowledge, dear listener. God is truth manifest; only the truth can sober us, and let the truth be all our guide and our highest allegiance.

PART I

THE MYSTERIOUS ORIGINS OF THE ARCH PROTAGONIST

Chapter 1
An Unlikely Introduction

1. According to Kierkegaard (source unknown), "When all ethical determinants of evil are excluded, and only empty metaphysical determinants are used, the result is the trivial, the comic". In an age chained by its own seriousness God is a comedian. Where people no longer believe in true human goodness and indeed no one clamors about virtue, there is also a distinct feeling that we have become desensitized to all forms of deeper emotion, and even tragedy and pain. This apparent numbness seeks to deliberate the world through the medium of either light humor or grotesque sympathy. In such an age God is an imp and a trickster just as the devil is a deceiver. Thus, while the believer sees the world as a playful prank or a subtle joke, the one who follows the devil sees that the only way to gain power in the world is by fooling others. Indeed, God is a comedian for God is one who laughs last, and whoever laughs last laughs the finest of laughs, and bears the most satisfaction. God as the trickster or the one who hides in the shade of reminiscence to ensure a more distraught yet discerning ensemble to envelop the day, is the divine that hides in plain sight. Seriousness is the enemy of truth just as propriety is the bane of virtue. We shape a dialectic between a trickster and a fool. When one spreads untruth knowingly or unknowingly, either one invents lies or is a useful idiot, but God knows the liar and the fool as one[1]. To paraphrase Rumi, they say Jesus rode on a donkey, but how could a zephyr ride on an ass?

2. A man often finds a piece of truth on the ground as it is said. Soon enough he finds the devil tapping him on his shoulder. A nice truth you have there says the devil. If you hand it over to me, I will do you the favor and save you the time by reorganizing it for you. Since the truth is barely discernible to the man, he agrees to hand it over to the devil, thinking maybe he will help make some sense of it. When the devil returns to offer the man a newly organized version of a newly found truth that is very old, it is barely recognizable to the man. He thinks and ponders to himself if it is even the same truth that was handed to the devil in the first place. The devil assures the man that he does not deceive and only works with the truth he was given. He does not lie. The devil cannot invent his own truth and the devil is in the details. Indeed, the devil is in the details and the truth is hidden in plain sight. The devil knows that organization is more important than even the logic of argumentation and

---

[1] "God knows the liar and the fool as one" is a quote by rapper Jus Allah in the song Vengeance by Blue Sky Black Death as far as I am aware.

puts reason above faithfulness and discernment of righteousness and truth[2]. Knowledge is knowing the difference between right and wrong, but wisdom is knowing what to do with that information[3]. The truth cannot simply be reorganized to one's satisfaction without the risk of error, but we must also realize that truth that is built on a lie is a faulty foundation, as well as a truth that leads us to a lie and leaves us lost. We must seek out the living truth instead of inert organization. We have indeed too often been told that the truth exists apart from us and apart from God. We wrongfully discern truth as something that exists besides us, without us, outside of us, and beyond us. When the light shines in the dark and the dark knows it not, if we are to be discerned by truth then we must find truth within ourselves. For this very reason the truth is manifest. If this is true, then only the truth can set us free and we are bound by truth. With this deeper truth we begin our inquiry. We must not be afraid where the truth leads us, because if we do not know where we come from we do not know where we are going. And without knowledge of where to go every road will look the same. Every lie is based on a truth. The lie has to stand upon a truth, but the truth cannot be brought forth from a lie. The truth is more sinister than logic just as reality is stranger than fiction.

3. In an age of rampant individualism, morality has come to mean only to be true to ourselves and since this means that everyone can only be held responsible in circumference to their own beliefs, we must endeavor to hold people responsible this way if it is our only recourse. To go against oneself is the ultimate contradiction, and the ultimate preparation to engage in sinful behavior. For a sin is a contradiction against oneself. If your right eye offends thee pluck it out and caste it from thee. Any hesitation in this is clear spitefulness and vengefulness and turning against oneself and hence turning against God. If one cannot love oneself, how successful will one become in loving anything else? The final commandment in our day and age seems to read: "do not do unto thyself which thou shalt not have done!". A second one perhaps reads: "to go against oneself is to go against God!". Shouldn't we at least hold accountable everyone for what they themselves are always preaching? Are we not to condemn each man by his own rules that he picks for himself? An old Hindu saying by Chanakya reads, "God is not present in idols. Your feelings

---

[2] Kohr, L. (1978). *The Breakdown of Nations.* Dutton. The following quote can be found on pg. 83 of this work: "the statistician is expelled from heaven. Arriving in hell, he immediately asks to be brought before Satan and, hoping for better results this time, submits a similar plan. 'Satan,' he begins, unpacking again his charts and diagrams, 'I have a plan for organizing hell.' At this Satan interrupts with laughter that shakes every rock in the fiery caves of the underworld. 'Organize hell?' he roars; 'my dear professor, organization is hell!' And so is unity, which organization creates, and from which it results!". The parable in the second paragraph is loosely adapted from this tale.

[3] This is a paraphrase of a statement made by Scholar and Shaheed Anwar Al-Awlaki in his talk entitled "The Life of Umar Bin Khattab (R.A)".

are your God. Your soul is your temple"[4]. But has our age not become infested with idols?

4. An idol is a mediation between oneself and the divine. Anything that does not afford one direct connection to the divine is a stinking idol! Idols deserve to be smashed and forlorned! Whether it be the heart or truth or even ourselves, is it not an idol? What is our relation to the divine? Since it may be the ultimate relation, it will refuse to be mediated. Organizations have caused idols to manifest in the heart of man that are mediations between himself and the divine. Are we to accept this? Have we not always claimed that man has a direct relationship with God? The primary symbol or most prominent symbol throughout the ages that represents both the mediation between Man and the divine and a direct connection between Man and the divine is Jesus Christ. In this play we meet our protagonist as the founder of the Christian religion. This character of Jesus was used by Paul, who opposes his teaching in many respects. Even though Paul practiced religious subversion of Jews, Christians, and Gentiles, many Christians are unaware that what they follow is not the teaching of Jesus but instead the message of Paul, who was a self-styled "apostle to the Gentiles". This is quite a fitting term because the message of Paul has had a profound effect on European development throughout history and moved them to accept that salvation is of the Jews. We meet our antagonist in the Apostle Paul, and the eventual synthesis in the Church and doctrine that represents a Pauline line of interpretation throughout history. If Paul is the ultimate deceiver and inventor of the ultimate idol, then his lie is based on an ultimate truth which is represented by the Christ. Hence, we draw a dialectic between the teaching of Paul and Christ.

5. Christ was not seeking to establish an antithesis to the Roman or Jewish chains of command, but it was Paul who sought a synthesis between these two disparate forms of religious and social institution through religious subversion. This was a deliberate attempt by Paul to forge a new path of salvation apart from the purely religious and purely political. While some within the Jews were seeking a political answer to their plight and subjection under Roman rule, many others sought purity through religious commands and felt the need to distinguish between spiritual and political binds within the community. Christ sought an ethical message that began on the outskirts of Judea and sought an ethical and religious reform apart from political and clerical disputes. Christ taught of the kingdom being within, while Paul taught of a New Covenant and of a worldly kingdom arriving in the future only available to those with faith. Christ sought to reform Judaism while Paul sought to establish Christianity. Analogically speaking, Buddha did not wish to make a new

---

[4] This quote is attributed to Chanakya Nitti, an Indian Brahmin philosopher who existed around the 4th century and can be found in a book entitled simply "The Philosophy of Chanakya"

religion but only wished to reform Hinduism by ending the cycle of rebirth. While maintaining the outwardly form of the Roman cult and the inwardly conglomeration of Jewish ethical principles, Paul forged a message that stood at odds with early followers of Christ. Christ attempted to take the promise of a worldly kingdom away from Jews by showing them that inward corruption was blocking the essence of their divine nature which had been made the birthright of everyman through their father Adam. Paul instead blamed Adam for the sins of Mankind (Romans 5). It is clear that while Christ challenged the existing interpretation of Judaism that existed at the time, he did not seek to establish a new religion according to the New Testament and other writings associated with the early Christian message. The coming of a judgement upon Man reverses the vision of a Kingdom of God being sought on Earth. However, this proto-Utopian Zionism that culminated in a world-rule and end of history has been reinforced in history by Pauline theology and challenged by a notion of a coming judgement. While Jesus claimed to be the Messiah of the Jews but was rejected, Paul stresses otherworldly concerns which require the bringing in of the Gentiles to the message of Jewish salvation. Finally, Luke attempts to reconcile these two disparate views, as does John. Luke expands the view by using Jewish theology, while John brings in Greek themes like the Logos in order to reconcile the Jewish and Alexandrian views.

6. Throughout history this message has become a sort of "Platonism for the masses"[5], and has imported Greek metaphysics, Roman politics, and Jewish eschatology, which has toppled the Roman system, spread to Europe, contributed in the reformation of both Jewish and Christian law, and finally led to the rise of a new secular age with its eventual implosion in the form of New Age mysticism[6] and Scientism. Consequently, Jews, Christians and Muslims have been caught up in the fervor of a Pauline synthesis, whose intellectual achievements have dwindled anything ever known, and have eclipsed the message of Jesus Christ himself. The true message of a return to simplicity has been eclipsed by one that looks to the future for salvation, and that seeks to evade the true cause of human suffering by an acceptance of our own frailty.

---

[5] This statement is a quote by Nietzsche found in the preface to his book "Beyond Good and Evil". In the last paragraph of the preface he states, "But the fight against Plato or, to speak more clearly and for 'the people,' the fight against the Christian - ecclesiastical pressure of millennia, for Christianity is Platonism for 'the people', has created in Europe a magnificent tension of the spirit the like of which had never existed on earth: with so tense a bow we can now shoot for the most distant goals".

[6] Although New Age mysticism generally differs with the Gnostic viewpoint in terms of its emphasis on utopian thinking, which clashes with the Gnostic view that no ultimate form of happiness can be sought in the material realm, it shares the view that Man must transcend his current frame and borrows from both Gnostic and Hermetic cosmology as it is a sort of perennial form of religion. When we apply this term going forward, we do so in the manner we have just described and not in the way it may be used in today's popular nomenclature.

By placing the door of salvation at the foot of Roman power embodied in the crucifixion of Jesus, Paul inverted the message of crucifixion from one of Roman justice into one of Jewish salvation. This singular act of religious subversion that colored the content of all four Gospels, whose appearance begins after the letters of Paul are in circulation, seems to be the single most overlooked fact in both religious and theological efforts pertaining to the Christian doctrine as well as their historical, political and philosophical development. We must also explore the pretentious narratives laid out by those who profess to be ambivalent to such religious beliefs as New Testament scholars. The singular genius of the Pauline message was to turn the symbol of Roman terror into one of Jewish salvation. While we applaud the efforts of such groups in their attempts to expound on religious narrative, we point out the fact that their claims do not address main questions of motive, of what role the divergence of Christian thought from Jewish thought represents, and what part Pauline theology plays in regard to the various imports of Christian theology by various groups in history. Furthermore, we address the work of our predecessors and offer a more in-depth reprisal of some of the information presented as to how the various historical, political, philosophical, and contextual developments assist in establishing our own views which seem to be at variance with the majority of those views now in circulation. The sheer magnitude of conflicting information and scholarship on the issue of what Jesus taught immediately lets one know that some great truth is being obfuscated.

Chapter 2
It is with the Beyond that One Kills Life

7. I grew up believing that Christians and Jews were people of the book that possessed knowledge, and parts of a message which I also shared. It was something in me that felt that even the Hindu ritual was a superb declaration of human artistic impulse, and that whoever wholeheartedly believed and expressed a singular will and devotion towards the supernatural object of their affection was bringing out something most sincere. I found the sincere devotion of faith to bring a most serene and joyous semblance of human potential. With a tender heart I have often felt that no matter the content of one's belief, if one sincerely believed and did not contradict their own systems of beliefs, then they were admirable at the very least by their severe intransigence and singular force of will. But I soon found this way of thinking to be far too simplistic and philosophical. Any real system of philosophy must be balanced with history so as to not lead to idealism and the somberness of traditional religious practice to not let it get lost in mysticism and perennial philosophy. I also found that the term "people of the book" meant little in its modern context. This is because the books were dictated to the prophet who spoke the books that others had written down. Not the physical book or the information contained in it is what is referred to as scripture, but rather only what God dictates to the prophets. I found further that "people of the book" meant more than the Abrahamic traditions, because included therein were the Sabaeans who reflected a Zoroastrian cosmology. Furthermore, in Chapter two of the Quran it asked if Abraham could be considered a Jew or Christian before any book such as the Torah or Gospel were actually revealed. The view that there was one religion for all mankind in the distant past that was the source of all religious differences instead of one religion being formed from the various religious traditions by combining their agreements was the opposite of the perennial philosophy. Jews and Christians today cannot be considered "people of the book" because the book they follow was changed. Indeed, the religions known as Judaism and Christianity have had different expressions throughout time lending to a "world-historical" conception of God. Sometimes the two have been chimerically linked and styled as "the Judeo-Christian Western Tradition". We will come to regard these configurations as false.

8. Later I came to see that while belief is a dead thing and the truth is inert, a heart of faith was the singular force of will that moved one to action, and a carefully honed faith is a rare and loyal spiritual device, a formidable weapon of will, as well as a trustworthy and loyal companion. God sent prophets to all nations. God makes the truth stranger than fiction. It is God who makes his grace greater than human reason and the heart more powerful than the mind. It

is God who makes the mind harder than the fist, and the broken heart harder than the mind[7]. If God is one as is often said and repeated, then should it not follow that nothing can be separated from God? We can say that we can never really be fully aware of God since we are limited, but all that we know is God as nothing can be known outside the oneness of truth. On the other hand nothing is truly equal to God. We cannot divorce knowledge from the sacred, the divine beauty from human desire, or nature from art. To do so is to lose our humanity. We must also be aware that the decadent and dualistic and ascetic modes employed as spiritual practice are mere cultural relics and grotesque idols, when compared to the solemnity and beauty of standing alone before God in perfect unity, where harmony is beauty, and both intelligence and goodness are in inextricable relation. Over 100 years before Plato, Xenophanes, thought to be the teacher of Parmenides and Zeno of Elea, declared "God is one, greatest among gods and men, not at all like mortals in body or thought". He says, "All of him sees, all of him thinks, all of him hears"[8]. He too complained that the various anthropomorphic depictions of God were a corruption of the original truth.

9. The outward expression of religious life has the tendency to become an end in itself for some who pray in order to be seen by others. This is not the true practice of religion but merely an outwardly display of cultural affectation. Others pray for an otherworldly salvation and confuse the practical message of religion with one of a withdrawn life which reinforces a view of spiritual materialism achieved through ascetic practices. Both of these methods attempt to placate or control God through various incantations and put oneself above the world. It is with the beyond that one kills life as Nietzsche has said, and we tend to agree. As Punjabi poet Bulleh Shah writes, "Tear down the mosque, tear down the church, and tear down the holy temple, but do not break anyone's heart because God lives there"[9]. No sacrifice of this world for the next in the form of ritual decadence or spiritual materialism can account for the real mission of faith, which is to teach and struggle for the poor. God demands of

---

[7] This is an adaptation from the line by Brother Ali in the song "Dial Tone" where he says "Jinn really do exist. I submit the proof is this: truth is the that the human heart is harder than the human fist."

[8] Miller, P. L., & Reeve, C. D. C. (Eds.). (2006). *Introductory Readings in Ancient Greek and Roman Philosophy*. Hackett Publishing Company. In a section entitled Early Greek Philosophy there appears a chapter entitled "Three Iconoclasts". In the part about Xenophanes his statements are numbered. These statements appear under number 6 and 7 on pg. 8 of this text.

[9] *Rebel Sufis of the Punjab — Ishtiaq Ahmed*. (2006, December 2). ApnaOrg. Retrieved April 7, 2022, from https://apnaorg.com/articles/ishtiaq7/. The transliteration of punjabi text from the poetry of Bulleh Shah reads "Masjid dha de, mandir dha de, dha de jo kucch dainda. Par kisi da dil na dhain, Rab dilan vich rehnda", which means, "Tear down the Mosque, tear down the temple, tear down everything in sight But don't (tear down) break anyone's heart because God lives there".

one to be a poor righteous teacher. Anything less is falling short of the goal of true religion. I have often felt that God has placed us here not only as a test for the next life, but also to read and study his signs and to be witnesses for others.

10. Christianity can be styled as a controlled opposition, a noble lie of elusive motives, and in a manufacturing of consent to fool the masses, a demonic crusade was launched on the world. Is this a fair claim? The most critical of dangers is hidden in plain sight. This consists of a character assassination of a prophet of God, and of a doctrine that is the mockery of the pagans. This revolutionary doctrine touted a reversal of world power and the fulfillment of a new world order. Look no further than the simple antagonism of Paul who took the message of Christ, to find the threat of an anarchic impulse whose suffering is grace, and whose contemplation is liberation from the world. Here we will examine the major aspect of the Antagonism thesis as first expounded by Dr. David Skrbina in his work "The Jesus Hoax"[10]. The act of forging lesser gods and giving them over to the people while maintaining the real doctrine of religious practice for oneself, as seen in the priestly classes of Egypt and India, was maintained. Even today religion is, and can be, used as a tool of mass subversion. While posing as a storehouse for morality and meaning the undercurrents of religious thought are like a socio-cultural virus or plague whose symbiosis can either strengthen or deplete one's civilization, if used incorrectly. Our claim is simply that the profound misuse of this tool has been seen in the Pauline line of Christian teachings and come to sublimate human evil and become a spiritual terror.

11. We believe in order for Paul to construct a wholly new message from an already existing movement within Jewish Messianic circles, he had to borrow and embellish a story already put in use but had to reconstruct certain characteristics of what the main character of that story was said to have accomplished. Through this Paul, forged a vision of a New Covenant wholly separate from the pre-existing message of salvation by monotheism preached by the prophets of the Jews whose teachings were preserved by the Jewish tribes, but not opposed to enlisting Romans, whose underclassmen were quickly swayed by a message that proclaimed the coming of the Kingdom of God and the Son of God. Paul bolstered his ranks with both Jews and Gentiles. Reimarus (1770), Baur (1820), and Strauss (1835) have all noted the Jewish origins of Christianity, as well as the distance between the Gospel materials and the life of Jesus in terms of chronology. Therefore, we must begin with the

---

[10] Skrbina, D. (2017). *The Jesus Hoax: How St. Paul's Cabal Fooled the World for Two Thousand Years*. Creative Fire Press. Our work is heavily based on the "antagonism thesis" of Dr. David Skrbina whose work we have taken great care to explain both in the opening and closing of this book. What we feel Dr. David Skrbina does is accurately portray the motives of Paul granted the various historical facts we have at hand and assign motive where others don't. In paragraphs 11, and 15-19 we share some of the information repeated in his book as it relates to the general flow of our own arguments.

history of the Jewish people around the time of the Roman Empire and the development of the Jewish religion throughout history must be seen as a natural counterpart to the Christian tradition whose growth it has paralleled within European history. While the recent cessation of power of the Hasmonean Dynasty had kept Jews on edge in 1st century Rome, the plight to seize power from Rome cannot be ignored as a motive for any and all major shifts in Jewish thought around this time. Only 30 years after the death of Jesus, we see both the disappearance of Paul, and the destruction of the Jewish temple. Then right before the beginning of the second century, we see the first appearances of the various manuscripts that have now been rendered to contain the parts of the Bible primarily in circulation today. In the second century we find various interpretations and groups of Jews that find the viability of certain texts that contain the teachings of the Jewish Messiah to provide a basis for a spiritual reformation. While some begin to formulate a more complex oral tradition, others splinter off to join the new Christian movement whose various expressions will be discussed shortly.

12. Jesus practiced Judaism (but not Judaism as it is known today). There are many references to his practice of Judaism throughout the Gospels. Jesus was referred to as a Rabbi by his followers. Jesus kept the Passover feast. Paul taught against the law and did not know Jesus during his lifetime. Peter tells us in the book of Acts 1 (20-22) that a disciple must meet the criteria of being a companion of Jesus in his own lifetime, beginning with his baptism with John, and sights the Psalms as a source of reasoning. It is clear that the followers of Jesus were a close-knit group that were not willing to go outside of the Jewish scripture to obtain justification for their beliefs. Paul not only did this but claimed to have been directly taught by Jesus himself. Paul writes both over and against, and for the Roman rulers and the Jewish Roman authorities that control the Jewish temple. He fulfills the role of an early persecutor of the Christian church. As a political conflict grew and his ministry began to reach more people, Paul knew that to function as an enemy of both Romans and Jews was the craftiest solution. He travels to a faraway place and has a "vision" mentioned in Corinthians 1:9. Paul never cites the Gospels or any of the sayings of Jesus. Paul preaches a message of the death and resurrection of God's only son as a redemption of all forms of human suffering, which would continue to plague mankind until the return of the Lord, and the establishment of the Kingdom of God. Now a new message of salvation, one size fits all, was made for the world to usher in a new age of salvation and grace. All Paul needed was Christ crucified. Christ was a "second Adam" that would make up for the curse put on all mankind by the first "son of God" Adam. Furthermore, there were two ways to be saved as one could be born circumcised in flesh, one could also have a "circumcision of the heart" brought solely by the grace of God and not by human works. As the Christian message progresses it begins to lose Jewish support and as Rome weakens it begins to assimilate Rome which accounts for the increasingly Anti-Jewish tone. Later martyrs to the Christian church, like

Polycarp, would be found among the Gentiles, and not the Jews. This indicates a shift of power between Jewish Christians, and Christian Gentiles.

13. Mark seemed to get his account of Jesus' life from secondhand sources and is widely considered to be the first appearance of a text resembling the Gospels. The earliest mention is in a hardly trustworthy source of Josephus, whose scrolls were probably edited by his benefactor Flavian and altered by later Catholic sources. Non-Jewish sources like Tacitus and Pliny mention Christians, but this is already well after the first century has passed. These are other indications that Christianity was a purely Jewish phenomenon, that became inter-dispersed after the destruction of the Second Jewish Temple. As was the period of slavery in Egypt, exile in Babylon, the Roman and Jewish war became another redefining period for the Jewish Nation. The Ancient remnants of Jewish nationalism, and the ethnos of a unique cultural identity, was formulated through the Jewish struggle. One can neither minimize, nor disavow, nor take sides with history in all of this, but the spread of Christianity to Europe also brought the scattering of Jews throughout Europe and Arabia.

14. In all times of struggle there have been those who defer to the "powers that be" and sell out their own people for a comfortable state of affairs, including being assimilated or enslaved. This message of God's chosen people was the adoption of considerable faith in the future and awaited a period of salvation. If one is chosen by God, then one has not anything to do for one's own salvation and one can resign oneself to ascetic practices. Another group would try to arrest power from the hands of destiny, to create one's own salvation, and even invent one's own laws for that purpose in a nationalistic fervor. Finally, there was invented a middle path of assurance that the world of power was a movement towards justice and security, which combined these two measures with revolutionary sensibilities. At once, both future salvation and the political stage of the world, were justified and sanctified. One could use this new ideology to justify one's laziness, pride, hostility, subjugation, and assimilation. In the midst of the struggle there are tales of Jewish Polytheism and sedition. Even today some Jews repudiate Israel for not following the laws of the Torah, while awaiting the return of the Mashiach (Messiah) and rebuilding the "Third Temple" in a dangerous game and self-fulfilling prophecy, while others clean their hands of the whole affair and seek a more direct spiritual connection with God and find irrevocable harm in the oppression of Arab neighbors.

15. The style of Rome was not to vanquish, but to expand, subdue, and assimilate Jewish power within Rome, whereby Judea would become a commonwealth as well as servant of the Roman Republic (their gods and rituals would be assimilated into the Roman cult). Since Jews would not acquiesce to this form of subjection, they chose to fight it out with Rome, as they faced either forced expulsion from Judea or a show of Roman force. While Paul was around during this troubling time, on the way to Damascus he could have very

well hatched a plan to Judaize Rome. In order to do this, he had to first convince the poor rabble that he was the disciple of God, and Christ's apostle to the Gentiles. This meant constructing a third path to salvation between Judaism and Paganism. This did not require a complex theology, and if Paul needed one then it was readily supplied by the Christians whom he was persecuting on behalf of Rome and Judea. In history many examples can be found of gods replacing the gods of their conquered people. Marduk was a replacement for Enlil. Zeus had dethroned Cronus. Akhenaten had replaced the entire Egyptian pantheon with a single deity represented by the Sun. In Homer, we find many gods, and even in other traditions, who take on half-godlike and half-human-like characteristics. Rebellion by inversion of power, and internalization of the hatred of this world, as well as an outer struggle against Rome, was all portrayed in poetic semblance. This laid down the necessary foundation for the coming Kingdom of God. The Gentiles must be used to save Israel, as Paul states in Romans 11:25.

16. Paul talks of destroying every rule and every authority and power to accomplish his ends (Romans 15:24). By what means is this to be accomplished, it remains to ask ourselves. It seems, by Paul's own admission, the purpose was accomplished by ideological subversion of the highest order. Paul states, "I have become all things to all men" (Corinthians 9:19). It is clear to us that he has done this in order to accomplish a subversive end. The end is what Nietzsche pointed out as nothing less than a brilliant task of the revaluation of values, that cannot and will not be minimized by us. Nietzsche states that the task of the revaluation of values is a task of the highest order, and one that can only be accomplished by the dismantling of Paul, who accomplished the very same task. In order to be the master one has to beat the master, and Paul was the master of ideological subversion, and a liar extraordinaire. Paul preached against marriage, against family, against society, and against the law of Moses to accomplish his ends. Some of the more warlike passages of the New Testament, about donning armor for the Kingdom of God, leaving one's family behind, breaking down nations, and disowning Jewish relations (even a decidedly anti-Jewish flavor especially in John) is accentuated by the letters and followers of Paul. We must also remember that Paul's letters and followers consist of the majority of the views of Christianity as we see them today and so if even some of what we have presented is true, it paints a significantly problematic portrait of what can be considered to be the real teachings of Jesus Christ. We are caught in the harsh predicament of trying to find who Jesus is without relying on Paul telling us who he is when most of what we know about Jesus has been seemingly altered and deformed by the message of Paul, if we are to be honest about what task lay before us.

17. Paul must have known the Roman view of Jews as Atheists, who could provide no tangible representations of their gods, and anarchists, who did not

believe in any worldly power. Now Paul saw in these decadents a will to oppose Rome, but not face Rome directly. Knowing that his task was to replace a
Roman ideology for a Jewish one, he saw that the Jews were strictly Monotheistic and would not believe his message at first. Thus, his attack was on the
Gentiles or the lower classes of Rome. This was a dual edged attack against
Romans and their Jewish counterparts, which was done by turning the symbol
of Roman violence into one of Jewish salvation. To do this he had to employ
nonviolent means and indeed "turn the other cheek" as he used more effective
subversive, and propagandistic means.

18. Not surprisingly, only a few other options exist. The first would be to
accept the Pauline story as we have it today. Here we would accept that God
was born and then died, but was resurrected, is in an intermission, and will
return. The second option is what would be a more scholarly consensus based
on historical evidence and the scientific materialistic framework. This consists
in the claim that Christianity started with the composite of a heroic and priestly
figure that was misconstrued as a Jewish Messiah, and his claim to being "king
of the Jews" was seen as a rebellion against Rome. This is known by us as the
Rumor thesis. The third and final option is finding and discovering the various
versions of mythical and metaphorical truths that existed among ancient people
and discovering reflections of the story of Christ within a plethora of framework spiritual and mythical and cultural adaptations of the archetypal fabric of
existence. We call this the Mythicist view.

19. Altogether we have four views: 1. The Antagonism Thesis, 2. The
modern Christian interpretation, 3. The Rumor Thesis, 4. The Mythicist view.
We will show, not only the shortcomings of the other three views, but also
how information provided in the other three views tends to support our own
view, that Paul preached a truly unique doctrine whose goal was political and
religious subversion. All of these groups allege that someone lied but make no
mention as to who it could be and make no theory as to the important question
of what motivated the lies. As you may have gathered, we place the blame
squarely on Paul, seeing how his doctrine of eternal salvation by faith alone is
truly unique and hardly found in the Gospels themselves. The modern Christian view puts the blame on Romans and Jews, but more so on the shoulders of
the Jewish Nation, which it has historically persecuted as a result. The Rumor
thesis puts the blame on early Christians and religious mystics who took too
many liberties expounding on doctrine by the use of lofty metaphors which
were fervently misplaced to support different versions as well as blaming the
Romans for the crucifixion of Jesus. The Mythicist view claims that Christianity stole its religion from ancient cults, pagan myths, and the mystery religions
of the Gnostics and Hermetics. While all of them claim that someone lied, no
motive is assigned, and there are certainly no directives provided on what must
be done about the lies that are now used to support a range of cultural, philosophical, religious, and political interests around the world.

20. What motive would make such a colossal lie necessary? If no motive can be established and no nefarious purposes are to be promulgated, then indeed what would be the need to construct a lie? If Christianity is nothing more than a smorgasbord of Astro-theological speculation, pseudo-spiritual gargle, archetypal myth, whose subtle emergence is nothing more than an equinoctial celebration of pan religious transcendence, as claimed by mythicist and self-help gurus everywhere, then what can explain away it's Jewish origins? This compendium of ineffectual "do what thou wilt" attitude of antinomian heresy and apostasy, as well as anthropomorphic degeneration of religious values, is nothing more than a modern heterodox appropriation of centuries of ancient myths, that are cleverly hijacked by obfuscating their more vociferous cultural achievements and are to be suited and transformed as a convenient New Age occult of themes and coming of a New Age Aquarius fantasy and or utopia. This "techno-buddhism"[11] is simply just a fashionable instantiation devoid of any substance of historical and philosophical relevance. Furthermore, since the early Gnostic traditions reflected a perennial and neo-pagan sensibility that grew from a cosmopolitan mixing of several mystery cults and deriving of metaphors from ancient myths, the claim by modern historians that one man's orthodoxy is another man's heterodoxy and that religious ideas are devoid of any stable doctrine lends itself to Gnostic and Perennial beliefs.

21. If on the other hand, as the Rumor thesis claims, these stories were morphed and changed and embellished and exaggerated to suit the progress of the times in a stale attempt to defend humanism then they can have little historical relevance. This view haphazardly suggests that the militaristic style of Rome was being opposed legitimizing claims of a noble Jewish cause. This rather mistaken view puts Christianity at the cornerstone of western progress and liberal antics and has rightfully so won the hearts and minds of European Jews and Whites around the world, who cannot but claim that their particular civilization was the basis for world peace. All this arrogant self-evaluation has shown not to live up to its talk in its grandiose promises of progress and world peace. This view simply congratulates Jews for inventing a recipe for the Christian story that was later secularized and developed in the west and tailored to fit the enterprise of science and humanism. Where they find justification for this so-called Judeo-Christian synthesis, that not surprisingly excludes Islam or anything similar as foreign intrusions, is quite a mystery, and a convenient narrative used to justify their modern reconstructions. Both views seemed to claim that, on the one hand, Christianity was constructed out of whole cloth, but on the other end, that it was somehow an organic phenomenon that spanned centuries. The tension in these views has not been consolidated. What they often forget is their own ideological bias, and modern scientific worldview, as well as hidden paradigms and themes that are the meta-

---

[11] We lay out the meaning of the term techno-buddhism which we coined in sections 611-637 of this book

physical goggles they use to view the world. They choose to abstract from a plain and accurate assessment. Some wish to take what is clearly parable and reduce it to historical realism and dogmatic naturalism. We must look at the material on its own terms, and sometimes these groups fail to give an honest listen. Why would someone blow such stories wholly out of proportion, or invent these lies from whole cloth robbing them of their historical element? Simply by inductive inference and through arriving at what has survived from centuries ago, one is not able to paint a clear picture, because all methods historians employ are only to gain a probabilistic view of what most likely occurred. Since this fact is admitted to by most historians, we should take their word for the fact that they are not telling us the complete truth, and we cannot simply rely on how many doctorates one possesses. Eventually we have to read and study for ourselves.

22. Lastly, to merely brush off how these views are affected by their historical context and effect the future scope with philosophical range and propensity for dominance, and steer clear of mentioning certain metaphysical views and constructs, and to merely suggest such studies are ethically neutral as to their political dogmas, while claiming to restrain themselves to complete objectivity, is a suspiciously arrogant claim made by these scholars. Especially in the modern climate of Jewish Zionists and Messianic Cults using Christian Zionists and Dispensationalists to form a controlled opposition against Wahabi terrorists, who are often funded and given arms to engage in proxy wars for the same groups, religious life in the West has become politically charged. Anybody who observes the movements of NATO can tell that certain Jews are using Muslims to scare European Christians into Zionist backed causes. Anybody who is not willing to admit this has an odd compliance with the predominant situation of military force in the world and are forced to take sides in this supposed "clash of civilizations"[12].

23. We obviously abhor such rhetoric and can clearly define its roots in Neoconservative[13] circles of Jewish and Christian Zionists but what we must also look much further back for a more honest view. One cannot be neutral on a moving train. Any form of pretense to objective nuance should be carefully

---

[12] The popularizing of this term was due to the 1993 article in Foreign Affairs by then leading member of the Council on Foreign Relations Samuel P. Huntington. The article castes the state of international affairs into various cultural modes and argues that a looming conflict with the Islamic world is around the corner and came to become highly influential in the coming years in Bush era policy.

[13] Although readily promoted in its most nominal sensibilities by Zionists and Christian evangelicals like those of Prager University and Turning Point USA, the term comes from those circles around the Council on Foreign Relations that drafted the Project for a New American Century documents and also the Chicago School of Economics and the University of Chicago centered around thinkers like Karl Popper, Leo Strauss, and Milton Friedman and represent a classical liberal criticism of modern liberalism.

examined and most claims of neutrality are used to support the status quo. It should be clear to anyone why there is not a concerted interest in exposing the story, and not many books written about the issue outside of Nietzsche's sections of Antichrist 58, 59 and 60[14]. There are literally volumes of books written on Nietzsche's philosophy that do not discuss this claim even once. With the interfaith mood of the day being employed by most religions to save their membership ranks in the face of a secular takeover, any mention of a doctrine that is a standard religious view would be hard to compartmentalize. In the face of Christian Zionism, indeed Christians and Jews have become strange bedfellows from a historical perspective. The linking of Christianity as a continuation of the original Western views laid out in Greek Civilization is expounded without clarity, especially as to how Greek or Roman thought makes little mention of European civilization[15]. Furthermore, the earlier influences on Greek and Roman society are dismissed, and the phenomenon of Greek and Roman civilization is itself treated with dogmatic intrigue of the worst scholarly types of infidels who wish to bridge the gaps between religion and philosophy, seeing that science has excluded theology and metaphysics from the critical fields of inquiry which now only includes neuroscience, engineering, programming, abstract math, and the arts and social sciences.

24. Since the so-called separation of Church and State which was ironically started by those who fought for religious freedom, like Lutherans and Calvinists, governments of a Western democratic style have claimed to remain neutral on religious issues. This compounds the problem of religious sects acting on the State in an unnecessary bifurcation of morals and business. Even though one is naturally inclined to not go around questioning the belief systems of others to not be openly attacked, the current air of respecting others beliefs has gone decidedly too far. Surely we can begin a conversation without either total agreement or complete assimilation of each other's viewpoints, which seems hardly necessary to preserve intellectual stimulation so cherished in the Western world as a hallmark of progress.

---

[14] As pointed out by Dr. David Skrbina, the theory that Christianity as we know it today was centered around the death of resurrection of Christ was devised by Paul to sway the Roman lower classes into a slave mentality and slave morality and was first expounded by the philosopher Friedrich Nietzsche.

[15] *Dr. John Henrik Clarke vs Mary Lefkowitz: The Great Debate (1996) | Best Quality*. (2019, January 28). YouTube. Retrieved April 8, 2022, from https://www.youtube.com/watch?v=fmei-hUQUWY. The following video is an example of a debate on topics of how much Greek or Roman society owed to European civilization which was practically nothing. Conversely, African cultures like that of Egypt exercised a vast range of influence on Greek writers like Herodotus and Plato who seemingly drew from foreign influences rather than Greek ones.

Chapter 3
The Light Shineth in the Darkness and the Darkness Knew it Not

25. Like a light that shines in the darkness, our view is hidden in plain sight. There is simply no conclusive proof by anyone that Jesus did not exist, or that he was the Son of God. All anyone has ever been able to claim is that there was a man named Jesus existing around the First Century, who was a teacher that was sent to the Jews, and whose teachings had a world altering effect on their adherents. The claim that Jesus was a "Jewish" teacher is correct in one sense and false in another. Jesus seemed to be a follower of the Law of Moses but this seems to be apparently not true for other Jews even in Jesus' own time. Modern Talmudic and Kabbalistic interpretations of Judaism were formulated after Christianity and even Islam[16]. What Jesus purportedly taught and who his adherents were will have to be determined, or at least examined, throughout our discourse. It would seem that Jesus belonged to a sect of Jews who were observant of the teachings of the Torah but challenged some of the practices of the Temple Jews and Pharisees. Christians admit that whether Jesus was God or not (there are some who maintained that being "Son of God" was not identical to being "God the Father"), he certainly resembled a man, and perished as a man according to most of the views laid out in conventional Christian teaching (while there are some who believe that Jesus never died). At the very least, no one disputes the fact that Jesus resembled a human male. Whether he is still dead, or actually died, or was a hologram as some Gnostics believed, or that he died and was resurrected, everyone can agree that Jesus was in the form of a man and appeared to most people to be in the form of a man. The symbol of Jesus represents all of humankind. While many will disagree on how this took place, there can be found a singular point of agreement (which is rare in this line of inquiry) to be had by all members of the debate. Christians who are accepting of a view of a high Christology must admit that the separate parts of the trinity possess distinct natures. In other words, they justify the fact that God came in the form of a physical human being.

26. The situation is rather strange because most Christians are not aware of such matters. They are not aware of who the twelve disciples of Jesus actually were. None of the Gospel fragments have names of the people who wrote them. And the names of the people who wrote them like Paul, Mark, and Luke,

---

[16] Modern Scholarly consensus seems to suggest that the Talmud (especially the Babylonian Talmud) and the Kabbalah were collectively complied sometime between 500 A.D and 1100 A.D and their origins have been attributed to a variety of conflicting sources.

cannot have been said to have ever known Jesus or absorbed his teachings in his own lifetime. This fact is seen mainly by their own admissions. A scholarly consensus finds that only seven of thirteen letters attributed to Paul can even be said to be written by him. On this point we give Christians the benefit of the doubt. Because we do not know who wrote them, we cannot rule out the names commonly attributed to the works in question, although as most scholars point out there is a problem of chronology in some of the attributions of names. Little mention appears about the Christians from external sources outside of the Church. Mentions by Tacitus and Pliny occur after the first century, but even more strangely the Vatican Codex, and the unified Christian movement only occur after the fourth century. What can be said over three hundred years after the fact, and after the destruction of the Jewish Temple, which would purge some of the early documents of the Church, is anyone's guess. We know that the books included in the Bible today do not consist of a full historical rendering of what was read by early Christians, but significant changes and alterations have been made in history as to what books are to be included, and what interpretation certain verses of the text are allowed to have. If it is true that the story of Jesus was edited or changed then it is equally true that some other version of events must be true.

27. It is true that the historical method uses inference to the best explanation and can only offer a probabilistic sketch of what actually took place. Apparently, the claim that Jesus was both a Rabbi, and the Son of God is no problem for Christians. The Christian claim that the Old Testament justifies Christian beliefs is confusing. Either Christianity is not separate from Judaism, and therefore is identical to Judaism, or Christians must clarify their beliefs over and against Jewish beliefs and so they are clearly separate. Adding the Old Testament to the discussion will only create more confusion, so we will avoid it for the most part but are forced to arrive at some definition of Judaism itself. For centuries Jewish scholarship has repudiated the claim that the modern version of Christian teaching can stem from any Jewish elements and regard Christianity as a Jewish heresy just as Islam is regarded as a Christian heresy, so there is no need to repeat the claims here. To lump all the three big western religious traditions in one pile is to deal dogmatically with historical facts which demonstrate that these traditions have had stark differences in their various representations in history. Another fact that bears mentioning is that the Jewish messiah is seen as a Prophet and Lawgiver like Moses but is not mentioned to be God in the flesh. Jews for centuries made this distinction with no problem, so there is no reason to assume that Jews and Christians shared any similar genealogy of belief, but then it stands to reason that such beliefs were taken to be an issue for most early Christians. Such a clear tension in Christian belief systems that is exacerbated today by comparing Christianity to other so called "Abrahamic" traditions is usually glossed over much to the detriment of a more deeper analysis. This fact plays a role in certain eschatological schemes, some of which profess a dual road of salvation for Christians and

Jews and cannot be simply dismissed or brushed aside for these issues are first raised by Paul in Romans 9 and have continually added confusion to the discussion of whether Christians are Jews. It is important to our current analysis to discuss the changing views on the roles of the Jews throughout Christian history as reinterpretations of the Pauline doctrine deal rather crudely with questions of Jewish law and the salvation of the Jews mentioned in the Old Testament.

28. In fact in the Bible as it is presented to us, Jesus is adamant about others not knowing that he is the Messiah, and quite secretive about some of the healings he performs, and when pressed on the matter discloses his wishes and goals to only a select few men. It also brings us to another issue: was the Bible revealed through Jesus, or gathered together and altered by later followers who took considerable part in controlling the narrative, and even sharing in some of the scripture? If second and third hand sources can claim divine authority simply by the mere mention of the name of Jesus, then we must ask on what basis or authority does anyone have to take the name and claim Divine Revelation from Jesus. Luke was a disciple of Paul and was purported to have written Acts. Mark travelled with Paul, but at a certain point parted way with him. Peter and James were quite ambivalent to Paul's teachings in a few instances. Mark was a student of Peter and may have sided with Peter and James instead of Paul just as Luke may have sided with Paul. This could be the reason why Peter is made to look foolish in some Gospel narratives, even though he was directly chosen by Jesus to lead the Church. This leads us to a final point of tension: Since Peter and James were seen as early Church leaders, then why was Paul given such a pivotal role in the establishment of Christian doctrine? Why are Peter and James continually seen as the leaders of "Jewish Christians" and Paul and Simon Magus seen as the teacher of the Gnostics and Neopagan mystery cults that combined Zoroastrian and Christian myths with an Orphic cosmology? The views of Peter and James are dwarfed by those of Paul. Finally, if John was an eyewitness account, then why does his account not show up earlier, and why is his Gospel so dissimilar to the other three Gospels?

29. Although there are a number of sources of manuscript evidence, there is still a problem of varying accounts. Just picking and choosing when expert opinion and scientific consensus applies is as arbitrary as choosing and applying only certain aspects of the religious doctrine that is meant to be accepted as a whole. Surely the number of manuscripts cannot suggest much, because we can safely say that repetition does not imply relevance, or impact, or historical importance. Dr. Skrbina argues in the "Jesus Hoax" that the fact that miracles occurred leaves more to be desired in terms of evidence. While miracles are traditionally regarded as a violation of the Laws of Nature and direct intervention from God, they would have to be taken notice by more people. If these miracles actually occurred, they should've left behind mountains of evidence because of their astonishing and incredible nature. Then again, we have no

way of assuring what really happened. There seems to be not much evidence that if Jesus could do anything that he could have opened up a hospital or homeless shelter, but this clearly seemed to be out of his range of influence. Rather Jesus seemed to be in a struggle against Jewish priests and Roman officials. Jesus talks about war as much as he does about peace. In Jesus, there is more of a feeling of fighting back, than in Paul, where we see more of a message of peace and love. After all, causing division and deception is more effective than war. Besides, since historical analysis is based on only facts that can be derived through scientific means, only what can be confirmed by those scientific means can be proven and science seldom goes outside of the bounds of the "laws of nature" for its analysis.

30. Finally, the view of the Pauline epistles that can be contrasted with the Gospels is the doctrine of easy belief, or salvation by faith alone. This presents us with a dialectic of purity and grace that is not explained. In Paul there is no doctrine of purity, but a doctrine of grace. There is no fasting and works, and struggles, but the struggle is manifest in the works of the flesh. So one must abstain from taking sides with the ways of the world. Man must be adopted by God because God cannot abide in us. Evil is a part of humanity. Man's lot in life is predestined. How does this square with another belief that we are made in the image of God? It seems that this doctrine attributes immorality to God. This becomes a problem for thinkers like St Augustine who have to borrow from Platonism to believe that this world is a devolution. But Paul had already accomplished this. Paul had already made the claim that he could commit any sin, and it was not his choice, but the Sin in him that caused him to commit those sins (Romans 7:17). This is why St. Augustine said, "hate the sin, and not the sinner". This rather slick doctrine is what most rigidly separates Christian belief systems from other similar views. Indeed, no other doctrine makes such a rare claim. The view fails to describe how the goodness and creativity of God could have engineered such fundamental errors to emerge from human programming. Rather, if we are the blueprints of the divine, how can God not abide in us? This is not a subtle point nor should it be taken as one moving forward.

31. Still we must ask ourselves the most important question which is rarely addressed: How much can Christianity be said to contribute to the lapse of Roman power? As Christianity maintains an influence in Rome, Rome begins to decline, and the Church moves westward, where it gains new adherents, and organizes a vast cultural influence of disparate tribes of Northern Europe, which were once opposed by Rome. All this coincides with the Golden era of Christian learning and reign of the Christian Church. Christianity united the cults, and Rome came to worship three Jews (Paul, Jesus, and Mary). Such a monumental shift in power can hardly be imagined to a once persecuted Jewish sect, which was rejected by most Jews, and used by the Roman rabble to aid in the destruction of Rome itself.

32. In Romans 9 Paul is adamant about a dual road of salvation for both Jews and Gentiles. What is unclear is how this salvation is to come about. Either this salvation occurs by a free choice of faithfulness in Christ on the part of the believer, through pre-determination of God's grace, or by being chosen by birth. However, if God has left the believer out of the deal of faith, and since there is no salvation by works, one is forced to wonder what precisely is the road to salvation that is prescribed by Paul. If this means that man is born sinful and that man's fall from grace is an act of God, then God is simply responsible for all the immorality in the world. If there is no salvation by works of the flesh and salvation occurs by faith alone, then one is free to commit any sin as long as one's intention to do good by works of faith outweighs his fleshly undertakings. This dualism between flesh and spirit has some dangerous and contentious undercurrents, and we must note that the road to hell is paved with good intentions. It is furthermore the number one criticism against Christianity: that it allows all things to remain as they are, as long as one accepts Jesus as God. Everything is allowed, as long as one repents. This is because Christ has died for our sins, so we simply do not have to worry any longer about that hard road to redemption through good works of righteousness and justice. What about serving the poor and fighting against oppression? The poor are the blessed, so one must service those in power who are tarnished by their high status and must be purified by poverty. When God puts you in a low status in this world, he raises you up in the world to come. Similarly, those who are raised up here are the lowly ones of the hereafter.

33. While I do not agree that all these criticisms are a complete representation of the Pauline line, we simply mention there are critical take home messages that have been employed by various teachers throughout history, that have taken these views to support an easy road to belief, and a libertine view on one end, but also a dispensationalist creed of dual road to salvation on the other. Sandwiched in the middle of these two extremes is a moderate Paul, with a simple binitarian formula of God's rule in heaven and Jesus' rule to come on Earth, which combines the two rules of God and Man in the world to come. It is still important to remember that Paul does not mention the Gospels but refers to the Old Testament many times. This could be because Paul was trying to convince the Jews to follow his version of Judaism, or it could simply mean that he never read the Gospels, and that they had not been written as of yet. Indeed, one is written by his disciple Luke, which would have to occur after his joining of Paul's ministry. Also, it is important to note that the mention of the trinity, and more specifically the "Holy Spirit" is not expounded on, mentioned, or discussed, and seems to be gaining steam rather late in Christian thought.

34. Here we must make a note of what a Hoax actually is. We are not simply claiming that the facts present themselves to us in a ready-made package, but we are claiming that the facts are used to accomplish hidden ends,

while the purpose of how the facts are laid out is carefully and conveniently obfuscated. A hoax is characteristically different from a myth, or a historical fact, or even a religious figure. One needs all of these to accomplish a hoax. Any good lie is sandwiched between two truths. The parasitic nature of deception, and conspiratorial acts is that they must work with the system and is often why they are unnoticed. Jesus attended the synagogue (Lk 4:10). Jesus came to fulfill the Jewish Law (Mt 5:17), but Paul came to tear down the law (Gal 3:18). If the law of God was not already on the books, then indeed there would be nothing to fulfill. This passage indicates that the Jews were negligent of their own laws and were even making new laws which they did not follow as well as tying up heavy burdens for others to wear. Jesus accuses the elite class of Jews who were known as the Pharisees as the culprits. Paul is a proud Pharisee, and Roman citizen. Where Jesus saw Herod as his enemy, Paul sees him as his kinsman (Romans 16:11). Christ tells us to beware of the yeast of the Pharisees (Mt 16:6). Christians ignore this as well as Paul's friendly relations with those in power, and how he continually escapes persecution. All this and more will be discussed in the course of our exploration.

35. Paul preached the abrogation of the law and was a Jewish nationalist. He knew he could not establish an overt resistance against Rome, so he chose a covert subversion on a religio-political scale. Whereas Christ was sent to the lost sheep of the House of Israel to reform the religion of Judaism with an ethico-religious teaching, Paul sought to convert the world to his own religion. Early Christians preached a downright hatred of the State, and especially of Rome, as well as a hatred of Judaism. There are two ways to stage a resistance: the obvious way is in an overt and armed struggle, and the other is covertly by guile and sabotage and lies. Some people are under the subconscious delusion that ideas are not as powerful as weapons. Although these cannot be helped, we plead to the fair minded to see that we are only presented with the arrangement of facts, but we are not readily made aware to what end certain actions are carried out, or what the goals and purpose of certain historical movements represent. We can only discover as much as we can connect the sequence of events back to their relevance in our day and age. It is clear that Gentiles rather than Jews would have been more likely to believe the Jesus story as told to us by Paul, but we must also remember that Christianity is originating from Jews. Many might claim that because we say there is a lie we believe it was a hoax, which is circular reasoning. We must point out that where the truth is twisted there must be some ulterior motive and where the question "who benefits" must be asked, all questions of practicality go out of the window. Yes, of course, we cannot presume that anything Paul says was a lie, but we cannot similarly claim that just because Paul says something then it came from Paul and it must be true. More rigors must be taken in analyzing the facts.

36. Finally, all claims that our views are based on Antisemitism, or a bias against the West, must be squarely dismissed. None of those critical of Jews in

the early centuries can be said to have a marked racial bias against Jews. Many Jews, and Christians, and Europeans have done more than us to criticize from within these very same doctrines. We are critical of what we see as a perversion of Christian and Islamic faith. The ideology of Racism is based on Biological Determinism, which is a modern invention. Indeed, in the past Jews were said to originate from many ancestral tribes and ethnic groups that became conglomerated around the time of Moses. To refer to someone as being Jewish could either refer to their choice of religion, their ethnic or cultural identity, and even their racial makeup. Today Jewish groups, and Christian European groups comprise many ethnic designations, and cannot be said to be of any one Nation or Race. Our criticism of people within these groups should not be taken as a sweeping criticism of anybody who professes to be of origin from groups of Semitic people, European people, or European Jews and Christians, who are indeed racially dissimilar to people of Semitic origin. We will conversely point out how some of these doctrines have been used to commit religious genocide and claim racial superiority. It is important to point out that most of what is presented is from Jew's and Christian's own sources and work. We do not take sides with history, or assign blame, but can only take what we know and move forward.

37. Modern scholarship has not presented adequate answers. Paul constantly victimizes himself and employs a false humility. He consistently accuses those who accuse him of pigeonholing. The whole Pauline system of Christianity bears the mark of a false accusation. But Paul is never accused by either Mythicists or Historical Realists as constructing a lie. Both views contend that the original Christian religious sects are segments of both earlier Jewish and later Mystical traditions, whose social and mystical aspects draw from various religious movements and groups already in full swing around the 1st and 2nd century. But none readily make the claim that Paul invented Christianity as we know it today. What is interesting, is that they are both willing to claim that Paul made up some of the Christian narratives or at least took some interpretive license that was not granted to him by others and provided a truly alternative scope for the establishment of certain Christian institutions, yet they never claim that his goals were subversive in nature or provide any context as to why Paul would invent such beliefs. All we ever hear regarding the mysterious deeds and life of Paul from such scholars is that such a figure presents an unorthodox and paradoxical view. If what St. Paul says is true then he is by far the most interesting puzzle history has proposed, or if Paul was a turning point from within the Christian ministry in its early stages, or if Paul had either manufactured his own version of Christian teaching to turn the Gentile world against Rome as we are now claiming, Paul serves to be one of the most influential figures in history on a scale unimagined. Paul's teachings differed from possibly earlier forms of Christianity, and the Church chose the Pauline line of theology over and against a more Jewish conception favored by some early Christians who were more in line with traditional aspects of God the Father

being somewhat exalted from creation. Many claim that the Jesus of the Gospels is different from the Jesus represented by Paul, and still different from the Jesus mentioned by the early Church. However, while Mythicists claim that Christianity somehow devolved from syncretistic and Gnostic Jewish sects, the Rumor or Realist school often says Christianity was a reification of some earlier Jewish teachings, while colluding with less powerful sects and combining certain Roman elements, which gave Christianity a distinct view apart from the Jewish world view. This latter group often sees Christianity as a Jewish and Roman synthesis.

38. It is not hard to see that these views differ from our own in certain respects but we will have to nonetheless zoom in on them here to carefully examine the claims. Another interesting distinction between these two groups is the claim of Mythicists, that all religious tales are about esoteric and hidden or sometimes metaphorical lessons. These teachings, for them outline a mystery religion, and the crucifixion and resurrection of Jesus is seen as a recipe for alchemical transformation, or a manual for transcendence. This process is the transformation of the Spirit, which is outlined by allegorical symbols. The Rumor or Realist angle treats such tales as simply developed by those who held primitive beliefs on the forces of nature. These groups were simply transcribing ancient philosophies and tales of the mythical world and mixing them with Jewish teachings, whose oppositional narrative was driven by political strife. According to some Mythicists, the metropolitan aspect of Jewish society within Alexandria readily absorbed these more syncretistic and pan-religious frameworks, which included notable views of the Greeks and Persians and Indians. For many of these types of scholars the Hellenization of the Jews and introduction of secret and heterodox religious orders with antinomian and revolutionary tendencies is seen as a main line of influence. These groups preached one way or another about a hidden power available to Man that came through rejection, renunciation, and destruction of the material order. They focused on a reversal of power. For Scholar Robert M. Price certain stray beliefs from a variety of religious traditions found their way into Judaism. For Scholar Bart D. Ehrman however, Christianity is a wholly Jewish phenomenon, and the story was accidentally altered by copies of copies of manuscripts that could not have been kept track of in ancient times due to a lack of modern methods of printing and record keeping. The apparent contradiction in views between those who claim to have a purely objective basis for looking at the facts does not seem promising. We can assure ourselves that there are as many differing views on what Christianity seems to represent outside of Christianity than there are inside Christianity. Certain Alexandrian Jews like Philo had reduced Biblical miracles to metaphors and allegories, parables and myths. Others like the Herod family and Flavius Josephus who became a Roman slave mixed freely with Roman power and did not feel a spirit of separatism.

39. The fact that these views are both from an atheistic perspective, and springing from academic circles and secular viewpoints is an essential distinction to be had with our earlier models of either the conventional narrative or the Hoax thesis. Many think that Secular Humanism, Scientific Atheism, and Historical Realism are the same set of beliefs, when in reality there are key distinctions to be had from the variety of these forms of argumentation. However, it can mostly be said that within a naturalistic and materialistic framework, where one heavily relies on the tools and advancements of modern scientific progress, one is almost certainly relying on a view centered on historical progress. This would preclude the belief that earlier forms of information gathering are less reliable than the tools we have today. The progress centered view is like the one of Scholars like Bart D. Ehrman, who holds a popular secular humanist viewpoint on the issue assuming that progress has culminated in modern advancements that make the job of those relaying historical facts more fine-tuned than the claims of ancient spectators. The fact remains that there is no reason to believe that so-called modernists are not operating with a similar level of cultural bias as ancient actors. He points out that most Christians are not aware that there are 27 books in the New Testament, or anything about the historical era in which the events take place. Much less are people aware that the New Testament is not originally written in Hebrew, but in Greek. Jesus did not speak Greek but spoke Aramaic, as is the general scholarly consensus. In "How Jesus Became God", Ehrman seems to argue that the development of the Christ narrative over time led to Jesus becoming deified and attaining more and more of the characteristics of the God of the Old Testament. He suggests that unlike what is written in Paul, Jesus never told people to worship him. Indeed, he points out that such a belief is even hard to find in the letters of Paul, but doesn't appear until the Gospel of John, written before the close of the century. Other than the fact that we have already mentioned that this view seems to assign no motive, it relies too much on the myth of progress, in which the development of history, and the methods used to analyze history, take precedence over treating the material on its own terms. This insistence, that to shift from non-God to Son of God, and hence a God, or equal to God, and then finally to God incarnate, cannot have been so seamless as to evade the grasp of the Jews. Something else must truly be at work, but Ehrman gives us no clues. How could such a drastic change take place so rapidly and among an already developed Jewish system of theology?

40. Ehrman argues that the Gospel of John clearly represents a departure from the other three Gospels as we will come to see. The content of the Gospel of John is over 90 percent different from the text of the other three synoptic gospel. In chapter 15 of the Gospel of John it is not entirely clear that Jesus anoints himself as God. The verse appears to read that the followers of Jesus, Jesus himself, and God are connected in the same root system in a life-giving tree. This may sound a little bit mystical and even pantheistic, as does the plainly Platonic sentiment expressed in the opening line of the Logos appear-

ing with God at the beginning of creation, but we can also attribute such poetic passages to Philo. Philo combined Jewish teaching with Plato, who borrowed from Heraclitus the term "the Logos". Philo was an Alexandrian Jew living around the same time as Jesus who was a notable philosopher and had an influence on Christian teaching. While Heraclitus regarded it as a sort of cosmic mind and an ethereal substance, Philo used the term Logos to refer to the "creative reason" which he regarded as the first-born Son of God.

41. Anyways, Ehrman[17] seems to support the view of Albert Schweitzer of Jesus being an apocalyptic Jewish prophet, who ended up being a mere mortal and got himself killed, even though he disregards John as not providing much evidence of what Jesus actually said. What is truly laughable are Schweizer's views of Paul's mysticism which verge on the perennial, describing the so-called mystical aspects in Paul the same strain that is found in the teaching of Brahmins, Plato, Buddhists, Stoics, Spinoza, and Hegel[18]. One does not have to try hard to see that none of these kinds of mystical forms share any similarity, although it does reflect a dangerous trend in German Protestantism and Idealism, that reflects certain occult elements in regard to its views on the mystical. A mysterious term that appears in the Gospels is "Son of Man". This term appears in the Book of Enoch as well, where Enoch uses it to refer to himself. In the Bible, Adam is also referred to as the Son of God (Luke 3:38), as he is a product of a divine act of creation and not a biological offspring. Many Christians in the second century subordinated the Son of God to God the Father, ending in an early Church schism. Jesus says in the Gospel of John that he did not come of his own accord, but it was the Father who sent him. The terms of a Prophet can be misconstrued with those of a King, and a King with those of a Lord, and a Lord with those of a god, and all these were interchangeable in ancient times and had similar meanings in Jewish apocalyptic literature. Other Scholars like Robert Eisenman claim the opposite. Enoch for example was seen as a man who attained heavenly heights, and was given knowledge, and the ability to judge the angels. Enoch was said to have walked

---

[17] Ehrman, B. D. (2016, March 30). *How Jesus Became God - UCC Part 1 of 3.* YouTube. Retrieved April 8, 2022, from https://www.youtube.com/watch?v=7IPAKsGbqcg. Paragraphs 41-47 are drawn heavily from presentations made by Bart D. Ehrman on his book "How Jesus Became God" delivered on January 29-31 2016 at Coral Gables Congregational Church. The lectures can be accesses both through his website and official youtube page.

[18] *Schweitzer, Albert (1931). The Mysticism of Paul the Apostle. Johns Hopkins University Press.* In the book Schweitzer makes the following statements, "Whenever thought makes the ultimate effort to conceive the relation of the personality to the universal, this mysticism comes into existence. It is found among the Brahmans and in Buddha, in Platonism, in Stoicism, in Spinoza, Schopenhauer, and Hegel', and, "Paul cuts across the Early Christian world-negation in the same way as Buddha does with that of Brahmanism". These views portray a Hegelian and almost Perennial view of religion which can be seen to have a clear bias against orthodox views.

with God and seen the heavenly throne. He was purported to be an ancestor of the prophet Noah. His transformation into the archangel Metatron, as the scribe of the Tetragrammaton or God, was as a supreme cosmic judge that would return to Earth to signal the coming of a New Age. This Jewish apocalyptic fervor was seemingly on the rise in 1st century Palestine.

42. But the claim that Christianity was a Jewish apocalyptic sect seems especially dubious when lined up with the claim that the Gospels were made up and altered and cannot be trusted. According to Ehrman, Jesus thought of himself as a prophet, and said he was the Messiah. The terms Son of God, Divine being, Messenger, Angel, Messiah, and King all had similar connotations. In Genesis Chapter 6 the daughters of Men mate with the children of God and beget giants who bring God's wrath and judgement upon the world. In Ancient times there were humans who were divinely ordained, divine humans, humans chosen by gods, half human-half gods, demigods and daimons, local divinities, and nature spirits that were angelic or transcendental beings similar to the avatar of the Hindu. God and angels were said to take on the forms of men, and descend even temporarily, or send others to delineate certain tasks. Exaltation Christology anoints Christ from a human to a Divine Being describing his transformation. Many believed that this had occurred during Christ's baptism. While Incarnation Christology, that Ehrman says later appeared in Paul's binitarian formulas, has Christ go from a Divine Being to a normal human. Christ was either going from a Divine Being to a human, a being that was human but was adopted by God at the time of his baptism, or a being that was exalted to share the status of God at the time of his resurrection after his crucifixion when he ascended into heaven.

43. The Pauline conception of Christ was partially owing to the dual view of Christ as Son of God by his resurrection, and son of David by his flesh and blood birth, where he was formed by the word of God (Romans 1:1). Paul felt that Christ was an Angelic Being, who became human according to the view by Ehrman presented here. We must remember that the Logos, although used in several contexts to refer to the Word, which is a Jewish conception, is not exactly the same thing. The Logos as previously mentioned was a universal principle of Reason and Will ascribed by Heraclitus to the Cosmos ("kosmos" was a term invented by Pythagoreans, who incidentally thought of Pythagoras as the son of Hermes), but "The Word" was the breath of God, which meant that God called things into existence ("Jehovah" taken from Yahweh meaning "be and then it was"), sometimes used by mystical and Gnostic Jewish sects to refer to the Spirit of God around the 2nd century, such as those of Marcus the Magician. If the Logos existed alongside God from the very beginning, then this means that God existed alongside his own creation, as many of the Ancients felt that the world was eternal which was a belief that was derived from Parmenides who argued that "from nothing, nothing comes". Does the passage in John 1:1 have to mean that God and Jesus existed before the creation of the

world? Ehrman, as we will come to see, also attributes Paul's binitarian formula to a pre-Pauline statement of faith without providing any proof.

44. However, he does feel that this is a drastic change from earlier conceptions of Jesus as the Messiah and Savior, but not necessarily equal to God. Some may even take the passage in the higher philosophical sense of God being equal to the world, or equal to his own creation. Indeed, some philosophers had set up emanations and intermediary forces between humanity and the divine realm, such as the demiurge of Plato. A strange view of Ehrman that bears mentioning is that Christianity was rejected by the Jews, even though there were Hellenized Jews that supported Rome, and even sects that he and other authors describe as "Jewish Christians". He believes that Jesus was killed by Rome, even though he says there is no way to know how Jesus died based on the biblical accounts. This clears Jews from either inventing or derailing early Christianity, even though they were themselves at the centerpiece of the movement. It also treats Christianity as an organic phenomenon bubbling up in an estranged environment of conflicting cultural, political, and religious tensions.

45. Christianity was either made up or rose up naturally, but it cannot be both. Those who hold this view must decide which they support, but often seem to imply both conflicting positions at once. Pushing back against Mythicists, Ehrman says he cannot trace Christianity from other myths like Sumerian, Egyptian, Hindu, and Gnostic influences, and holds these as quite a separate range of influence, but admits he is not an expert on these other religious subjects. He alleges, as do many scholars, that Timothy 1 and 2, Titus, Ephesians, Galatians, and Thessalonians, may have been forged by someone pretending to be Paul. He discusses the topics in his book "Forged". He claims that while several works of authors were used to signify the teachings of so and so and were not penned by the name attributed to them, another common practice of pretending to be an author and forging a document written by him was still a possibility in ancient times. Indeed, we find Pseudepigraphic works attributed to Plato and other famous writers of ancient times. We find it odd that the Bible is written with four different and varying accounts. This is unlike other works contained in the Old Testament and is a marked difference that is not clearly discussed by many, other than authors like Crossan (founder of the Jesus Seminar), which Ehrman happens to disagree with.

46. According to Ehrman, the Christian story went through the following stages. In the beginning God had three different modes of existence. This was known as Modalism and was held by many early Christians. The other extreme would be that the three aspects of God were truly unique in a sort of "Tritheism". The view of Patripassianism, or "The father suffers" (implying that God the Father suffered with his son on the cross), was vigorously opposed by Tertullian as a form of Sabellianism, and heresy. Sabellianism was a view that attempted to combine the various Platonic elements within Christian thought,

and was influenced by the teachings of Plotinus, as well as the Jewish Neoplatonists. The influence of the Alexandrian Jewish community (both Tertullian
and Plotinus were of Northern African origin), was beginning to spread to
Rome by the third century. Tertullian was an early subordinationist, who argued that Modalists believed that God had begotten himself. Tertullian separated God into three separate but equal parts, to avoid further confusion. He
maintained that though these three parts were separate and had distinct status,
they were essentially unified. In the third century Arius argued that Christ was
merely a tool used by God to create the world, and that the Father was in every
way superior to the Son. A man cannot have two masters and a house divided
cannot stand! The argument was that if God is perfect that there should be no
change in him. But alas this view was slovenly and sneakily shoved aside to
reaffirm the Pauline doctrine by the founders of the Christian Church in Rome
in 325 A.D. This took place under the guise of Constantine and the opposition
of Arius to St. Athanasius. The Nicene Creed, which was the first of seven
councils called to reformulate Church doctrine, settled on a creed drawn up by
Athanasius which affirmed the Trinity by using the platonic notion of "homo-
ousia", meaning "of the same essence".

47. Ehrman admits the solution does not seem logical. The view led to the
daring conclusion that Jesus is one hundred percent God and one hundred percent Man. Since the Roman emperor was "Pontificus Maximus" or the chief
leader of the religion of the Roman empire, such changes were easily brought
about in the era of Constantine's conversion. The Roman emperor was the
Chief deity of the Roman cult. Even by calling himself King of the Jews,
Christ would have committed treason. What is intriguing about the Roman
system is that it is similar to the Egyptian priestly order or the Hindu Brahmin,
where rites and sacrifices are left to the upper crust of society who controlled
rank and order by assigning lesser gods to rule over the general public. However, the Roman cult held local deities to still function among some of the
people they conquered and allowed them into the Roman pantheon[19]. In Ancient times there was no division of Church and State, as recommended by the
Pauline epistles. The orders of Heaven and the orders of the State were closely
linked. It should figure that Paul had to beat Romans at their own game by
inventing his own chief deity, and making the people worship him instead of
the lesser gods offered for Rome for their salvation, which precluded the destruction of both Rome and the Jewish temple. To do this he had to create an
ideological divide between the power of this world and the power of the divine
realm. Those who deal with the view of a historical Christ have maintained
that Christians were among the Pagans, among the Jews, persecuted by Rome,

---

[19] Historians and scholars of Theology have labeled this form of belief Henotheism,
which is the view that one could subsume the gods of those adjoining nations or the
ones of the conquered into one's own pantheon. Some anthropologists posit this practice to be the origins of all pagan religions

promoted by Rome, and held Jews responsible for murdering God. This conflicting bag of squirming circumstances is laid before us as a general narrative, but it is hard to believe that there were no other motives at play. It is more than likely that Christianity was a branching off from Judaism that mostly opposed the Paganism of the Roman Cult, but was more directly opposed by Jews than Romans. Romans would have no reason to promote a small scale Jewish heresy, which is how Christianity was viewed at first. Furthermore, Greek and Persian thought was already spread to Jews before their dispersion in Rome.

48. Ehrman wholly rejects the Mythicism position or the view that Christianity was stemming from Jewish Heresy and Roman Myth. Although it is important to remember Gnostic texts were at their height of influence around the second century, where in the The Enneads of Plotinus we see vigorous attacks on Gnostic sects. It appears that almost 1 out of 10 parts of the Enneads deals squarely with the issue of Gnostic misinterpretation of Neoplatonic thought. Early church heresies, and second century sectarianism of Jewish communities give us works like the Gospel of Judas, mentioned by Iranaeus in 180 C.E[20]. This showed the belief systems of groups like Cainites, who believed the world was a cosmic accident and plague on humanity. This world to them was an accursed blunder, so they chose to follow Cain who was the first victim of a malicious God. God wished to keep humans bound in their mortal chains. This God must be vigorously opposed by breaking the Sabbath, breaking dietary regulation, and engaging in sexual profligacy which scorns life and its affectations. Sects like these revered ancient mystery cults of Ancient Greece and Babylon, and encouraged the lifestyles of Sodom and Gamorrah, and openly cursed God.

49. According to Ehrman, most of these texts are written in Coptic, but it is not a stretch to imagine that such texts had links with Alexandrian Jews. There are fragments of Plato's Republic contained in the Nag Hammadi Gnostic Library, which includes a passage from book 10 describing the tripartite soul. In short, Gnosticism was distinguished from a faith-based belief system, and a belief in religious actions and works of the flesh, where the focus was more on heavenly and divine knowledge that could liberate oneself. This is the belief that either divine knowledge or fortuitous circumstance that creates a confluence of events, could transcend one from his or her material casing in order to realize the object of one's speculation and thought or insight, by becoming

---

[20] Ehrman, B. D. (2013, December 25). *Lost Gospel of Judas Discussed at RSE Part 1*. YouTube. Retrieved April 9, 2022, from https://www.youtube.com/watch?v=qIXwSjyxe88. From paragraphs 49-54 we rely on this video presentation by Bart D. Ehrman found on his website and official youtube channel of a presentation he gave concerning the Gnostic Gospels at Ramtha School of Enlightenment located in Yelm, Washington on November 6, 2013. We compare his views on early Christian heresies with those of Price who considers them proto-orthodox.

identical to the vehicle of all thought and insight. We certainly find echoes of this chain of beliefs in Paul, but not in the ordinary message of the four Gospels. Essentially that this world could be transcended by divine insight that brings one into the grace of realization of the coming salvation. This is what author Eric Voegelin described as the "immanentizing of the eschaton" found in Gnostic beliefs, which stemmed from a profound sense of alienation with the world. In certain mystery cults the supreme knowledge was only available for adepts who understood the esoteric meaning of certain versions of texts, while the general public would receive only the exoteric or surface meaning. This notion of two truths or double truth and dualistic thinking has been a destructive force in human culture, which causes men to elude reality by the use of symbols and hide their true ends by inane categorizations of separating truth and reality. Such is the function of the belief which views Earth as a cosmic jail and God as a bad lieutenant.

50. In the view of the Gnostics, Man was created by an exiled deity who summoned humans back to their spiritual home by enlivening the spark of divinity within them that causes them to see this world as a deception and a curse. Hence, similar to Zoroastrianism, Gnostics believed in a good God and an evil God. Spirit gave rise to a transcendent God being wholly separate from the world of debased matter, which is corruptible and corrupts our awareness through gross materialism. Unlike Plato's philosophy, which Gnostics heavily borrowed from, Gnostics believed the world was evil, and the creation of an evil entity. Plato felt that the creator was wholly good and inseparable from the Cosmos, but also that the creative force in the world was an immaterial entity separate from the world of becoming. Gnostics on the other hand felt this world was an Emanation, and that gods live in the fullness of the Pleroma, but an evil "demiurge", which was incidentally the God of the Old Testament, had encased spirit in matter. This partial adoption and partial reversal of the Platonic view is probably what had Plotinus gnashing his teeth, for the Neoplatonists had to surmise that the world was wholly intelligent and wholly good, and that it had not been brought into existence by anything previous to itself. We will discuss the influence of Plato in another chapter but find it helpful to distinguish some of these beliefs, so we won't fall into the Gnostic trap of confusing these terms and amending them to our own ends. But the Gnostic belief that one man's heterodoxy is another man's orthodoxy is accepted by most Bible scholars today of an atheistic bend. The tale of the Gnostics uses Sophia, which is a female god from the realm of the Pleroma. When Sophia begins to create without a male consort, her creations become unbalanced Archons, or lesser gods, that begin to create an alternative reality or dimension. Sophia put a spark of divinity in man that could be awakened by the redeemer of the divine realm to make a spirit eligible for liberation. Sophia was the last of the Aeons. Her wisdom wished to understand and encompass all of the cosmos but overextended its grasp. The resulting imbalance led to an evil entity named Yaldabaoth or "Child of Chaos". This evil male entity claims to be God him-

self. He entraps Sophia in matter, and only those who attain secret knowledge can free the divine spark within themselves. Interestingly enough, Sophia or Wisdom appears as a female in Plato's republic. The spirit of God or the "ruah" in Hebrew is also a term that has a feminine connotation, and certain Jewish mystics had made use of it as atheistic scholars like Elaine Pagels author of Gnostic Gospels is quick to point out. Here we have the divine Logos of the Creator, and the divine spark within man placed by Sophia, which combine to form a cosmic rebirth to free man from the profound alienation and the captivity of this world. So grace or goodness does not exist within the world! It's just as simple as that. You must go outside of yourself for salvation. Sin and Evil are a natural part of you. In order to be saved one must literally pull oneself out from the inside. If one were to seek divine proof of all things all one had to do was then cite the teachings of Paul.

51. In the Gospel of Judas, Jesus gives a secret revelation to Judas that would free him from the illusion of death. In the story told by the Gospel, the disciples are blessing food and Jesus laughs at them. He assures them that THEIR God will receive the due praise. This fit of jealousy makes the disciples proclaim Jesus as God, but he tells them that they do not know him. He says whoever knows him will show him the perfect man. This is when Judas stands up and declares Jesus is from the Aeon of Barbelo, and not from this world, but from the mother of all the Aeons. Jesus shows a vision of twelve priests sacrificing women and children, and fornicating with men. Horrified by the sight, the disciples ask Jesus who they are. He tells them that it is none other than the twelve apostles. Judas, on the other hand, is shown a great house but cannot enter it. The house is not for mortals. This pretty much sacrilegious and grotesquely misanthropic view may disturb some. That is not our purpose. Our purpose is merely to show by what frames of mind the message of Jesus can be corrupted and altered to fit in line with the view of redemption by faith alone. By knowing just how far off the mark from the original message one can tread by maintaining its essential components, one is left with an entire revaluation of the facts in question. Suffice it to say such a revaluation is as possible then as it is now.

52. Continuing this tall tale, we see the luminary cloud of self-originate Aeons that propel the angels, luminaries, and firmaments (forces of nature), but also the realm of Chaos or Earth. Sacklas and Samael are the second and third emanations, whose names mean fool and blind god. Yaldabaoth means "Child of Chaos", also known as the true ruler of the world is one of their most sinister emanations. These entities create Adam and Eve. We are told that the disciples praised only the human shell, invented by these dark entities. Only Jesus and Judas knew that his body had to be shed so he can return to the pleroma. He tells Judas, who is mentioned in the Gospels as the betrayer of Christ, as surpassing all the disciples in knowledge. He thanks Judas for sacrificing the man that bears him and entraps the body of the God. Here there is no

mention of resurrection and nor can one be conceived in this particular sense. Gnostics borrowed the view of the transmigration of the soul from Plato who borrowed it from Orphic-Pythagoreanism which seems to have influenced his work "Timaeus".

53. The Gospel of Thomas is another interesting text from this Gnostic line of work. It seems, interestingly enough, to contain some sayings of Jesus that are found in the Gospels and are accepted by ordinary Christians today. If anything, this shows that there is cross referencing and that these communities did not exist within a vacuum but were clearly influenced by the other views around at the time. Sometimes Thomas is mentioned as the twin of Jesus, as James is mentioned as his brother. Thomas or Bartholomew was seen by some of the Gnostics to take the Gospel to India and far off lands. Most notably, India is a place where occultism draws much influence by often subverting Hindu teachings. Quite conveniently for its Indian affiliations, The Gospel of Thomas and Acts of Thomas seemingly preaches a sort of ascetic teaching which also melds well with the more Platonic and Gnostic elements that are concerned with denial of the flesh as a house of suffering and sin. Some of the beliefs of self-denial, celibacy, and implementation of the ideals of the Kingdom of God in this life can be seen in the Pauline message. In the Gospel of Philip, Jesus apparently kisses Mary Magdalene, who is an enigmatic figure in Christian history, but especially important to Gnostic groups, who often viewed her as a reflection of the teaching of Jesus in its most perfect form. Even in the popular movie entitled the Da Vinci code, Mary Magdalene is seen as a central figure for cults, traced to the Merovingian dynasty, and worshipped by Tom Hanks, who at the end of the movie bows down to the mummified remains of an ancient Jewish woman. As we will later see the doctrine of Freemasonry, that is readily promoted in these films are loosely based on such legends of ancient bloodlines which have transmitted a divine blood whose sacred incarnation remains at work in the world today shaping world events as a promise for things to come. Views of Sacred bloodlines exist among White and Black Nationalism movements, Ismaili Muslims, Messianic Jews and those within the Christian Identity movement which follows the theories of British Israelism. Such views have been conveniently used to support or legitimize the ideals of an eschatology of national restoration that combines blood and soil.

54. In the Gospel of Mary Magdalene there are many missing pages and lines in what remains, but in it Jesus purportedly gives a secret revelation to Mary on the ascension of the soul to heaven. This gives Mary a new outlook through which she reassures and comforts the other disciples who await the death of Jesus. She tells the disciples not to worry, because although ignorance rules on earth and wicked powers do not wish for the soul to ascend, there are many possible realms or different levels for the soul to ascend to. The hypostatic union of the soul with the divine is seen as a constant theme in Gnostic

literature. What about death and resurrection and judgement? These have taken a backseat to the doctrine of eternal life and ascension. A hierarchical cosmology is seen, much in line with Platonic thought as is the turning of the world as all things are exchanged for an ultimate good.

55. This conglomeration of second century views provides a scope for the indelible variation within Christian belief systems in the first few hundred years before the development of the official doctrine, but it also exposes an undeniable capacity for heretical views within Christian teaching today. But perhaps we speak too soon. We must consider these texts and views on their own terms. What worldview do they suggest to us, and what would the world look like if their views were indeed the original views of Christianity? One author who has written several books on how Christianity is nothing more than a constructed myth of an Ancient superman is Robert Price. Price believes that the Christ tales present a mythical tale of a perfect human being. We can already see how such a belief would be antithetical to the belief of Bart Ehrman, who believes that the texts share historical facts that were tailored for religious dictates. While both believe that nothing supernatural probably occurred, Price believes more fervently that they made the whole thing up. His recent adoption of the view that Christianity was developed by the Romans as a psychological operation to control militant sects of Judaism[21] that we will later discuss, is attesting to the fact that Price doesn't know what to make of these tales, and certainly believes that it is whatever you make it out to be, and so is self-entitled to go wherever the facts lead him. We certainly admire his openness. The Christ Myth for him is a sort of crystal ball that shows you whatever you want to see, granted you have enough faith to make the excursion.

56. Price sees the type of sects that produced works like the Gospel of Thomas and Gospel of Judas to be berating the disciples of Christ, which is interestingly something that Paul also did to bolster his own apostleship (Gallatians 2:11). Granting that the whole episode could be a literary construction, Price knows he can stretch the tale as much as he wants knowing that precise definition is not the goal of the mystical and metaphorical[22]. This leads us to

---

[21] Price, R. M. (2019). Robert M Price review of Creating Christ. https://www.creatingchrist.com/post/robert-m-price-review-of-creating-christ. The following link contains a review/endorsement by Robert M. Price of the view that Romans created Christianity in a review of a book written by James S. Valliant.
[22] For Price's view on the Gnostic Gospels we turn to his appearances on Aeon Byte Gnostic radio found on youtube which include the following episode titles: The Gospel of Thomas, Marcion and the First Bible, Simon Magus: the Father of all Heresy, the Gnostic Paul, The Christ-Myth Theory (and its problems), Who was Moses?, The Reality of the Archons, and Finding the Demiurge in the Bible. In paragraphs 56-66 we use Price's interviews on this radio show found on thegodabovegod.com to expound on his views on Gnosticism which we explore in depth through his book "The Colossal Apostle".

the sects we were discussing like the Cainites, Ophites, Manichaeans, and later Albigensians and Cathars, who were fond of neo-Platonism, and the metaphorical Logos theology of Philo of Alexandra. These groups believed in a sort of heavenly atom or "prima materia" from which all things were made. This heavenly substance was necessary from alchemical union and transubstantiation of matter into its actual spiritual light essence and form. This alchemical unity was a process culminating in making all contradictions one, which required practices of asceticism and ritual purification. Price declares that Marcionites and other sects were "soft anarchists" much like we affirm about the Pauline message. According to Price, there are four types of early Christians. These include Jewish, Hellenistic, Gnostic, and Encratite. Whoever wrote the Gospel of Thomas seems to be from the Encratite persuasion, with some of the Gnostic coloring of esoteric symbolism in notions like pointing to the man who existed before he was born having true understanding.

57. This is true generally of the Nag Hammadi texts that are a mix of Jewish mysticism, Neoplatonism, and a "Christianized" Zoroastrianism. In one text the disciples are asked to describe Christ. One says he is like a wise philosopher, another like an angel, but Thomas who possesses real understanding says Christ is beyond description. Jesus offers a cup for Thomas to drink and proclaims that whoever drinks of the cup is most like Christ. This is a familiar theme in Gnostic and Hermetic views and attempts to echo the view of the last supper. But here like is only understood by like. To understand God one must become like God himself. Another common formula is when Christ discloses to Thomas a secret teaching.

58. Once again Christ berates his disciples, and says that if he told the others his secret they would probably stone him out of ignorance. The Gospel also makes mention of James as the brother of Jesus, who Jesus puts in command after his death. These facts are rarely mentioned or debated by Christians, although they appear several times in various texts. If Peter and James are the leaders of the Church, then why is Paul given so much credence and James and Peter continually defamed? There is clearly some sort of split within the early Church that makes it hard for us now to discern the facts, because whoever won the schism has edited what has appeared in our Bible. To make matters even more strange is the curious fact that the brother of Jesus (supposedly James the Just) is wholly left out of the narrative of the four synoptic texts and Peter is continually berated in the Gospels and in other places seen in writings now disputed to be by him to be praising Paul. This is of course more proof that history is written by the victors. The Jordan river is used as a metaphor for the world beyond the next life, and to prepare one should "replace a hand with a hand" or change one's habits. This is like the saying in Mark, where Jesus says, "if your right eye offends thee, then pluck it out and caste it from thee" (also repeated in other synoptic texts). The greatest sin is a contradiction against yourself. Tammuz and Ishtar take turns governing the underworld, but

we should stay far away from hatred and lying to ourselves. We should abstain from wrath, and not dwell on saving or sacrificing ourselves, but on an everlasting life which is to come. The only savior necessary for the Gnostic equation is already within yourself. Christ is within, and inwardness is the solution. In saying 7 of the Gospel of Thomas, Christ says, "Blessed is the lion which becomes man when consumed by man; and cursed is the man whom the lion consumes, and the lion becomes man". In other words, you are what you eat and what eats you.

59. Recall earlier that the excerpt from book 10 of Plato's Republic describes man's tripartite soul with a lion representing his passion or will. After all, as Feuerbach so eloquently put it, one is what one eats. What you consume you become. It tells us not to become like a fish or a lamb or be consumed by ourselves. Lambs and fish follow others, until they are consumed. Another reference is to snakes and vipers and serpents which represent the debasement of human nature by consuming others like themselves. These represent greed, rapine, and general licentiousness, as well as cowardice. One who is of this kind hides in their den and prey on any and all who disturb it, and will even devour one's own eggs. We are reminded of the classic image of the snake eating its tail, or a snake without a head, or a snake with three heads. The dragon and the classical Leviathan that encircles the throne of God is a dark celestial order, which maintains an ever elusive grasp. This dealt with the slaying of the chaos dragons.

60. The foremost Christian heretic is perhaps a man named Marcion. He was an ardent Paulinist from Sinope. He would eventually travel to Rome to express a belief that an alien God had sent his only begotten son for the salvation of the world, while the Jewish God was a malevolent entity that dominated the world. As no one knows the Father but the Son, believers are adopted by God, as in the preaching of Paul. Some of the Dutch radical Bible scholars Price adheres to have theorized that Marcion may have written Galatians, and even if he did not, his views probably influenced the Paulinist creed to a great extent. We don't know what to make of this line of thinking, except to point out that many of the Dutch radicals were Hegelians who had a tinge of Gnosticism in their own worldview, but we address this in our later developments of historical thought and Christian teaching. Whatever the case may be, several scholars hold the view that Marcion and Gnostics wrote some of the Pauline epistles. Price says books like 2 Timothy may have been written by Polycarp, as even Schleiermacher and others see Polycarp as an early disciple of John (of course Schleiermacher was influenced by the Moravian Brethren who were connected to occultist Jan Comenius who was a foremost religious heretic). Marcion champions faith over reason, and did not believe in the divine spark of reason of the Gnostics. He preached that man can only reach his salvation through grace, like Paul.

61. Marcionites lived and preached an ascetic lifestyle in preparation for the Kingdom of God which they said was set to arrive very soon. Marcion included 10 of the epistles of Paul in his version of the Bible. Price connects Marcion to the Magi like figures appearing at the time. Simon Magus, also known as Simon the Magician, as well as Marcus the Magician, are seen as figures that have similarity with the life of Paul and Marcion, in the opinion of Robert Price. Both Paul and Simon have similar run-ins with the Jerusalem council, where they claim to be especially chosen for the role of apostleship. They attempt to gain access to the powers and knowledge that the Disciples have by buying their way in to achieving apostolic gifts. Price points out that Simon Magus was known by early Christians as "the father of all heresy". Simon claimed the curse of Moses was put on people by God and one was only saved through grace alone. Simon lived in Samaria, where an alternative temple was built for worship rejected by Judea. Like Paul, Simon claimed to have seen Christ in a vision. Peter explains to Paul that if you communicate to God by visions and dreams, this may not be true because senses lie. But Simon is also adamant that the Son was revealed to him by the Father. Simon had a consort named Helen which he said represented Sophia, while he himself embodied the Logos. Price says that Simon mixed the Torah with Heraclitus, linked to emanation cosmology, and is not unlike the Lurianic Kabbalah. In Gnostic circles Simon Magus is seen as a supreme Magi, and a sort of Faustian character. Price says figures like Simon Magus and Paul were trying to proclaim themselves as the new Jesus. Price talks extensively about these connections in his book "The Colossal Apostle", that we will examine.

62. Gnostics and Lutherans both use Paul as a major authority, and at the time of the reformation in opposing the Church such groups become strange bedfellows as we will later discuss. Price argues that 1 Corinthians, Letter to Galatians, and Philippians, all contain references to Gnostic style beliefs like the Godhead, fallen souls, a redeeming man of light, the collective consciousness or redemption of the world soul, and mentions of Archons and Aeons as the dark powers in control of the world, thereby ending in either the accursed cycle of reincarnation, or culminating in the path of eternal life. Price argues that if you rely on Judaism alone like Ehrman does there is less there to construct a myth, so early Christians had to have borrowed some of their beliefs from somewhere to supplant this new emphasis on "the coming of a new age" in the Kingdom of God. We find here that Price sometimes mysteriously borrows from New Age and Gnostic belief systems to support his own view of Christian origins and to make his own case, and even shows a favoritism towards these particular set of beliefs, much like Ehrman does. Ehrman explains the selection of Christianity over small Gnostic sects by saying one man's orthodoxy is another man's heresy. This view clearly does not take religious subversion into account, putting all beliefs on a level ground by assuming that methods of popular science give the last word. Still, we must admit it does seem odd then that Ehrman dismisses Jewish scrolls like the Toledo Yeshu,

which as Price says, mysteriously mention Paul as Simon Magus, saying he was a magician, and taught that the law is not binding on Gentile converts. Price claims that everyone in Samaria was a Simonian. There is a type of asceticism and withdrawing from the world in Paul in Corinthians 1:7 in Paul's seemingly unique views on marriage. We see that he is very critical of the Jewish law in certain instances, claiming to have torn it down, and that it has been renewed, or abolished in certain cases. Paul talks of salvation for all nations, and not just the Jews, but talks of a New Covenant (which as we point out possesses the double meaning of uniting all nations under the rule of Judaism). Price feels that the Jesus of the Gospels is not the same as the Jesus of Paul's epistles which seems to be an unmistakable fact.

63. However, if this story is simply a mythical construction in the style of Homer only retaining some base historical elements, and represents a mythic hero archetype, then it is about a man of light who comes to collect the photons of divine spark within Man that exist only in certain select human beings. This stance would almost seem to affirm that the Gnostics possessed a correct understanding of religious scripture. Groups like Sethians, Melchizedekian, and Jewish mystics are Astro-theologists, according to Price. These views were reaffirmed by people like Martin Luther, who said in the dispute between the Epistle of James and the conflicting views found in Paul, that the epistle should be burned and that the epistle of James was "made of straw". Price says that, reflecting on the language of myth the Christ tale represents a movement from a warlike God to an agricultural deity which promoted work and livelihood. The same claim is made by Astro-theologists and experts of Myth like Joseph Campbell, as wee will come to see.

64. Price is clear that he believes that none of the titles or people who show up in old or New Testament literature point to any historical figures, or historical epoch, or historical facts. As such, his view affirms nothing about the historical or cultural context of the 1st century. Price goes on to mythologize and reduce to allegory all the information contained within the Old Testament as well based on what he sees in the character of myth in general and not based on strict historical analysis or terms. He believes that Moses represents the title "to draw out" and is a title similar to Ramses which means "drawn out of the sun". Similarly, Samson had long hair which represented the rays of the sun. He uses this as further evidence that Jews had to keep reclaiming land, and pagans kept coming back in and mixing up with the Jews. Soon God would punish the Jews for mixing up with the Pagans. This mixes with the Sethian view of the Hypostasis of the Archons, and a new view of Judaism was born and or manufactured, according to Price. The theory is not dissimilar from Jung and his disciple Hans Jonas, who saw the Christian project as a mediation between paganism, Judaism, apocalypticism, and Gnosticism. Apparently, God has a very wide reach in their view and quite multicultural in his various and contradictory forms of expression but that goes more to the point that they

believe these are cultural and not theological manifestations. We rather view this as a metropolitan mix, derived from certain segments of Alexandrian Jews who took their own spin through trial and error at Pauline styles of theology in a method of copy and pasting old and new sources. But this again does not answer the main question: if Paul and Peter are made up figures than who made them up? If we cannot trace these ideas to any other source or name, then we are forced to use such figures and constructions to find out the motive for who constructed the lie. It is clear to us that whoever constructed new myths should have done so for the process of cultural and religious subversion which has been a primary cause in history and especially throughout the history of development of Western learning derived from Greek influence, which has come to influence both Jewish and Christian theology.

65. Yet and still the mythical view seems to suggest that Dionysus, Osiris, and Tammuz were representatives of cycles of time and ages and cultural expressions of man as spiritual tokens, instead of signs pointing to real instances of scientific, historical, and religious value. Look how the Dönmeh or Turkish apostates were central in secularizing Turkey and were originating from a Frankist cult. One can often see that the Gods of mankind have been invented by cultural schism and for political expediency. Surely, they can at least be used to this end. This can be seen in a deliberate attempt to liberalize the Old Testament by presenting Christ as the correction. The God of the Old Testament is likened to an oriental despot or totempole god, and not the God of the Philosophers. But if God is all love, all pure, and all good then he cannot act, and is reduced to mere potential. This is why "the demiurge" fails by mixing itself up in the chores of creation. Or is Christ created or uncreated, and does he come before, after, or through the Logos? No one can explain. If one has to become well versed in Platonic philosophy to find an explanation, one has already seemingly lost the debate.

66. Ehrman is clear, as Bible believers claim, that Nazareth was real, Bethlehem was real, and Jesus was the most attested to Palestinian Jew of the 1st century[23]. According to Ehrman, Jesus is more attested to than Josephus, who is used to prove the existence of Jesus. Just because someone was called the "Son of God", which Ehrman feels could represent a number of characteristics that don't automatically ascribe divinity to that particular person, it certainly does not mean that the story was fabricated, as Price seems to believe. After all, Caesar Augustus was known as the "Son of God" and no one doubts his existence. Ehrman feels however that Matthew, Mark, Luke, and John were

---

[23] Ehrman, B. D. (2017, March 24). *Bart Ehrman & Robert Price Debate - Did Jesus Exist*. YouTube. Retrieved April 9, 2022, from https://www.youtube.com/watch?v=GzjYmpwbHEA. Paragraphs 66-70 contain arguments and views presented by Bart D. Ehrman and Robert M. Price in a public debate held in 2017 by Mythicist Milwaukee

based on different sources. While Matthew and Luke seem to draw from a mysterious "Q" source, Mark draws from different sources. This does not count John, who apparently draws from a totally different source from all three of the other Gospels. This is ever more confused by the fact of Paul writing before the Gospels appear on the scene. Paul was a Jew and so was Jesus, and Paul seemingly knew Peter and James, who were the early leaders of the Church. Jesus started out as Messiah, was transformed into "Son of God", and was killed on the cross for treason against Rome. It is important to note that Ehrman presents Paul's view of Jesus dying on the cross as an incontrovertible fact, so he does not differ with what Paul says about Jesus' death. Paul makes the emphatic claim that Jesus has to die, and that the suffering of God is necessary for human sin.

67. Price is not convinced. Did the historical "superman" really have powers beyond those of an ordinary man? Whatever you may think, it certainly does not stand to reason that this means that there was a historical Clark Kent about whom tales were fabricated to make it seem that he was more than an ordinary human. Why would anyone want to fabricate such a tale? Price can see no reason to make up a story that has consequences for billions of people and is clearly not like any comic book written. Ehrman seems to think that somehow Christianity can just grow on its own out of Judaism, even though it is a doctrine that is vigorously opposed by Jewish monotheism. Both want to treat the phenomenon as some sort of organic growth, but this somehow does not square with their interpretations of Christianity being a momentous growth, culminating in centuries of stray religious doctrine. If these were ordinary occurrences like Ehrman believes then Price is right, and there would be no reason to make anything up. This however does not address the reasons why Paul wanted people to believe it was real. If Paul created his own superman, then how did people come to believe in him as a historical figure? Even worship him? If you simply remove the miracles from the story and take the bare historical facts, hardly anything of substance is left. We also see that Price is right about the number of attestations to Jesus that being well attested proves only that many believed it and not that it happened. Roman writers of the 1st century certainly accused many Christians of inventing gods for themselves. We find that Price is right about this but we certainly don't see the parallel cases with the writings of Homer, or anything on that scale of myth.

68. Ehrman is not convinced that Romans 13:3, "For rulers hold no terror for those who do right, but for those who do wrong. Do you want to be free from fear of the one in authority? Then do what is right and you will be commended", is about non-earthly powers as Price and the Gnostics believe. Ehrman says that Paul is saying to obey authority because Jesus was killed by authority but this is a laughable understanding. The passage clearly states that one must obey authority, but only insofar as one wants to become free from the fear of that authority. The passage is an ingenious line that is the classic

Paul doublethink. At once it tells us that a good way to avoid authority is doing what is right so one is not questioned by the rulers, but this is only a useful trick to evade the attention of those very same authorities. On Price's view, such a Gnostic interpretation may have clearly influenced later writers, but that doesn't tell us much about Paul's letters, because the appearance of the Gnostics is such a late phenomenon according to most historians, appearing in the 2nd Century, where Paul's letters and at least one or two Gospels seem to be circulating in the early part of the 1st Century yet well after the supposed death of Jesus. Indeed, it seems almost the other way around, that Paul influenced the Gospels and Gnostics which came later. Price however does not claim that Paul was simply a Gnostic but that he founded Gnosticism. Just as Simon Magus was seen as the fountainhead of all heresies.

69. Price feels that the story of the resurrection and the empty tomb are antithetical to death and crucifixion, and the only way to make sense of it is to compare it to a Kabbalistic theophany of the "Angel of Yahweh, and predeuteronomic hebraic polytheism", which is also mentioned in the Bible, and by Roman writers. In Philo, two Cherubim stand for the dual nature of God. Today Christ has been portrayed as a liberal pharisee, a conservative zealot, a vegan feminist, a socialist, an eastern mystic, and a Hasidic revolutionary. I think it was Marshall McLuhan who said the discovery of electricity was the arrival of the Holy Spirit in the world. All this is doubtable as hell. However, we are forced to think that with the enormity of claims something profound seeks to be understood. Indeed, the greatest stories are ones that create a template for other stories, and become models for countless other tales.

Chapter 4
"Paul converted the Pagan to believe in the God of the Jews" / a far cry from home or a far cry from a far cry?

70. In the Ancient world there are many examples of humans becoming gods[24]. Ultimately the Roman Pantheon differs from the Jewish in the hiddenness and distance between God and humanity, which caused the Pagans to view the Jews as atheists and misanthropes. Roman and Greek gods existed on a distant part of the Earth but were not hidden or separate from humanity. Men like Apollonius of Tyana and Caesar Augustus became representations of god. Jesus and the emperor were both seen as God-man. The following is a breakdown of the book "How Jesus became God" by Bart Ehrman that explains the view based on the use of the Bible for historical evidence which excludes the Biblical or supernatural point of view as an explanation of the events. In the second chapter he discusses angelic beings which are depicted as falling from a heavenly to an earthly realm and Enoch who is raised above the angels and referred to as the "Son of Man". There is also the female character of Wisdom which appears in the Book of Enoch as well as Gnostic texts, the Wisdom of Solomon, and Proverbs. The Hellenistic Jewish philosopher Philo of Alexandria saw the Logos as a "go between" of spirit and matter. Thus, one could transcend matter by the exchange of wisdom for divine logos. Here were established various scales of divinity as it was even said that Moses appeared to other men as a God. In chapter three Ehrman declares that all the things that Paul said Jesus did can be written on a three by five card. Not only does Paul cover none of the significant events of Jesus' life beyond his tale of death and resurrection hidden in plain sight as both historical motif and formula for self-transformation, but the Greek tone of Paul's letters and the Gospels do not match their origins from the class of semitic or Jewish people from northern Palestine who spoke Aramaic and lived on the Sea of Galilee, also known as Lake Tiberius.

71. Conversely, scholars suggest that a criterion of independent attestation be met for the various fabricated sources of the separate texts known as the Gospels. They theorize, for example, that Matthew's sayings originated in the "M source" and Luke from an "L source", and even allege that a majority of

---

[24] Ehrman, B. D. (2014). *How Jesus Became God: The Exaltation of a Jewish Preacher from Galilee*. HarperCollins. In Paragraphs 70-75 we offer a very brief summary of the views presented in Ehrman's book entitled "How Jesus Became God".

sayings issue from an unknown "Q source". Finally, there is a message of apocalypticism, not seen in the Gospel of John or the Gospel of Thomas, where the promise is instead one of everlasting life. Furthermore, Jesus claimed to be the Messiah but not God, as it was customary for Jews to expect a King and restoration of their Ancient Kingdom. Jesus was certainly claimed to be the future King of Israel, according to Ehrman, but such a king was traditionally in Jewish sources never seen as divine. Because Jesus was crucified, he was not seen as divine by some but certainly seen to have lost his position of becoming the future King of Israel. Ehrman admits that these changes were reconciled by Pauline theology which saw the resurrection as a bridge to the coming salvation of the future Kingdom.

72. In Chapter four he discusses the resurrection Christology of Paul, mainly related to the claim that Jesus died and was resurrected on the third day to bring about salvation to both Jew and Gentile and wipe out the sins of Adam. But if Paul himself indicates that his view of Christ was based on older traditions, Ehrman refuses to ask key questions. If these traditions were borrowed from older traditions, then whose? Is it possible that Paul made these sayings up as he himself relates that he was taught by no other mortal but by Jesus himself in a vision? Why does this view seemingly first appear in no other sources than the writings of Paul? Ehrman provides key differences in resurrection Christology during the second century that may help. One view of Paul suggests that Jesus was a "spirit-body", but quite another view can be seen in writings such as the Apocalypse of Peter that suggests Jesus was pure spirit. A third option can be seen in books such as the Gospel of Luke and Gospel of John where Christ is resurrected in a new resurrected body that is perfect (although this view can also be found in some letters of Paul that suggest that Christ resurrection describes the resurrection of all who inhabit the Kingdom of God and receive a new body that is immortal). As one will come to discover, we view the term "spirit-body" as paradoxical and oxymoronic in the context of Pauline thinking but also within the greater context of the Christian view of what the Spirit represents.

73. At the beginning of chapter six, Ehrman recounts a personal tale of having to cause a rift in his dating a Jewish girl because of his fundamentalist Christian beliefs he previously held. We are not sure whether these tales are meant to provide the framing of historical views or shed light on questions of faith or merely to prime his audience into accepting his view by suggesting that to do otherwise would be to pay lip service to antisemitism, but we must admit the tactic or aim is not immediately clear. I guess the take home message is that how one personally views salvation determines several aspects of their personal interactions. Ehrman takes care to point out how each Gospel begins differently. He finds that Paul focuses on the transformation of Christ, Mark on the exaltation or raising up of Christ, Luke on his divine incarnation, and Matthew on Christ as a fulfilment of the law of the Jewish prophets. John saw

Christ as a pre-existent being that existed alongside the Creator-God.

74. In chapter seven Ehrman comes to the conclusion that John's Gospel is different from the other Gospels but certain aspects of it are seen as issuing from a mysterious pre-Pauline hymn while certain other aspects are blamed on an evolution of viewpoints, but we have to ask ourselves, to what end is portraying God as Logos best served? It is obviously to conflate the Jewish God with religious world view of the Gentiles. There is also no discussion about Paul's doctrine of Christ as "Second Adam" and salvation for all mankind, or Paul's view of original sin. Paul's views took the conflict between Law and Gospel to the extreme and brought forward a New Covenant theology. This view is quite easily paired with the views of Marcionites and Gnostic teachers like Valentinus, as Marcion rejected the Jewish scripture in favor of the Gospels and the Gnostics reverted to Pagan and Greek style beliefs of Logos theology and a sort of stoic pantheism that mixed in transcendental themes of Platonic philosophy and complex relations between a plethora of divine figures. Origen had said God made souls before we came into existence. Justin Martyr argued that Socrates was a "pre-Christian" Christian. Sabellianism and Modalism made extensive use of Platonic themes. Ultimately Ehrman admits that the problem of heterodox views and paradoxes within orthodox views have only been clumsily resolved by the views of Eusebius. One instance of St Ambrose writing to Emperor Theodosius about not repairing a synagogue is repeated here to reinforce claims of Christianity in its more orthodox variation being used for antisemitism. Finally, the lack of originality of the Christian message both in its Jewish origin and Greek expression is not critically discussed and we hope we have provided a fair outline.

75. In Ehrman's other work entitled "Peter, Paul, and Mary Magdalene" he devotes a section to each of these figures in the Church that were all seen as the chief disciple of Christ by various groups of early Christians[25]. Interestingly enough, there is much crossover between the section on Peter and the section on Paul. This is due to the fact that various groups of Christians saw either that the ministries of Peter and Paul paralleled one another but also that they were in grave conflict and presented differing views on a number of topics within early Christianity.

76. We will now analyze a more recent work by Ehrman on Paul in more detail. Ehrman admits in the introduction that there is no such thing as a disinterested study of historical fact and that history is as much art as it is science (pg. 9). We believe this to be true. This is made especially clear when the early

---

[25] Ehrman, B. D. (2006). *Peter, Paul, and Mary Magdalene: The Followers of Jesus in History and Legend*. OUP USA. In paragraphs 76-89 I offer a detailed analysis of Ehrman's work entitled, "Peter, Paul, and Mary Magdalane" with page numbers included.

Christian writers use first century figures for theological disputes occurring in the second century, like the use of Peter in the Acts of Peter where he can be seen preaching in Rome (pg. 3). Why is Peter shown as the leader in the church in Rome when Paul's letter to Romans suggests otherwise, and also there is no clear proof that Peter ever traveled to Rome. Mark did not know Jesus either but was known as Peter's secretary just as Luke was seen as Paul's secretary (and who is also reported to have never met Jesus) (pg. 7-9). This would make most early sources other than the mysterious Gospel of Matthew (purportedly written by a disciple of Jesus) and the early mission of Peter to be the earliest sources for information about the early Christian movement. Both sources show a heavy influence from previous Jewish traditions not seen in the Gospel of John (whose text is strongly anti-Jewish), Gospel of Luke, and Acts (also purportedly written by Luke). Early Christian thinkers like Justin Martyr and Origin draw heavily from Neoplatonism as well as the Gnostics who often merged their views with Pagan philosophy. The mystery of these orthodox thinkers sharing their Neoplatonism with the Gnostics is quite puzzling unless they share some sort of progenitor that encompasses both. While the most likely candidate is Paul, Ehrman provides us no clues.

77. This points to the heart of the conflict in the early Church where James and Peter (leaders of the Jerusalem Council and heads of the Church in Jerusalem) are seen as "Judaizers" and force men to become Jews but act like Gentiles as claimed by Paul in Galatians but seen as wholly endorsing Paul in his role as apostle to the Gentiles in Acts. While Ehrman points out that in the Gospel narrative Peter is seen as "fickle and vacillating" (pg. 17), Christ says about him, "upon this rock I build my Church" in Matthew 16:12. While the start of Christianity was among Jews like Peter, the spread of Christianity was attributed to its spread among the Gentiles which was a mission undertaken by Paul (pg. 12-15). Paul is not seen as the leader of the early Church as are Peter and James and the mysterious John the Apostle (pg. 19). Despite the official narrative, Paul's role seems to eclipse Peter's. According to Ehrman, Christianity is the largest religion in the world with Catholicism being the largest denomination (pg 24). Of that Church, Peter is considered to be the first Pope. Ehrman believes in Schweitzer's view that Jesus was an "apocalyptic prophet" and a sort of rebel leader among the Jews who preached a radical ethic.

78. In the book of 2 Clement, purported to have been written forty years after the Gospel of Matthew, it has Jesus tell Peter to "not fear those who kill you" (pg. 36). This illustrates that the writer felt that the promise of the afterlife is assured for the believer. In the Apocalypse of Peter, mentioned earlier, Christ is seen hovering above his mortal frame laughing at his own crucifixion (pg. 37). In an Ethiopic version of the text, it takes one on a tour of Hell. These demonstrations go contrary to the view of John's Gospel with its extended narrative on the Passion of Christ and the portrayal of Jesus bodily resurrection (pg. 39-40). Teachers like Basilides who was seen as a disciple of Glaukia (pg.

48) (seen as a student of Peter) taught that Christ did not suffer on the cross, as Peter says in the Apocalypse of Peter, "they are putting to shame that which is in his likeness". Basilides felt that Jesus had switched places with Simon of Cyrene who carried the cross for Jesus as he was led to his execution (pg. 42-47). This view however states that Christ did not die by crucifixion in direct contradiction to the view of Christ's death and resurrection.

79. Another key issue is the debate of whether Christians had to accept Jewish customs like the ones followed by Peter and Christ in order to become members of the Church (pg. 59). One of the most confounding aspects of Paul's letters is the road to salvation that has been made open to both Jew and Gentile alike in Romans 9. Suffice it to say, Christians disagree over what exactly is prescribed by Paul in terms of the soteriological view concerning Christians and Jews but we offer a full-length discussion of Paul's letters at the end of this book and there is no need to repeat it here. We feel that Ehrman does not do justice to the real scale of contradictions when looking at the text on its own terms. It is important to realize, however, that Paul feels his mission to Gentiles parallels Peter's mission to the circumcised as stated by Paul in his letters (pg. 62). Peter is also shown to be in a conflict with Simon Magus whose claims on visions as well as drawing a dialectic between law and grace makes him to seem like a thinly veiled Paul. Paul is seen by Gnostics sects as their main source of inspiration, while Irenaeus says Simon Magus and not Paul is the fountainhead of all heresies. The Acts of Peter mentions Peter's battle with Simon Magus (pg.63-67). This parallels the battle of Philip and Simon Magus placed in Acts which curiously has Philip presenting a challenge to Simon Magus in the same way. In Paul's letter to Galatians, he is seen in a conflict with Peter, who is seen in a conflict with Simon Magus in second century sources, but the figure mysteriously never shows up in Pauline accounts.

80. Besides the fact that the tales of Peter like those mentioned by Clement and Acts of Peter show up in the second century, they seem closer to Gnostic sources and orthodox views of the Catholic Church that started to formulate around the late second century than to the actual crucifixion of Jesus which supposedly took place in the year 33 A.D. Another reason Ehrman dismisses that these works were authored by Peter is that Peter cannot read or write being a fisherman from Galilee. It should strike one as odd to make this generalization or assertion. For one, it cannot be generalized if one can read or write, simply based on one's place of origin or time period. Furthermore, one must point out that people can learn in one lifetime to read or write or even be able to dictate to someone reliable who can read or write as was the case with many poets and historians of ancient times. Another reason these letters are rejected is because of their style of writing or their theological stances. They must be internally inconsistent for their praise of Paul who everywhere seems in conflict with the ascetic and law-abiding ways of Christ's chief apostle in terms of marriage, dietary restrictions, circumcision, and other issues. In 2 Peter 3:16

Peter is seen warning about those who twist the teaching of Paul and create confusion (pg. 77). It concludes, as does Irenaeus, that the letters of Paul are a main source of heresy.

81. Peter is seen to have travelled with Clement. In the "Homilies", the preface contains a supposed letter from Peter to James. The statements in the letter from 2:3-5 attack an apostle to Gentiles who teaches the dissolution of the law. Here it seems clear that Peter is attacking Paul. Ehrman comes to the conclusion, as does Robert Price, that here Paul is thinly veiled as Simon Magus. In Homilies 17:19 it states,

"If, then, our Jesus appeared to you in a vision, made Himself known to you, and spoke to you, it was as one who is enraged with an adversary; and this is the reason why it was through visions and dreams, or through revelations that were from without, that He spoke to you. But can anyone be rendered fit for instruction through apparitions? And if you will say, 'It is possible,' then I ask, 'Why did our teacher abide and discourse a whole year to those who were awake?' And how are we to believe your word, when you tell us that He appeared to you? And how did He appear to you, when you entertain opinions contrary to His teaching? But if you were seen and taught by Him, and became His apostle for a single hour, proclaim His utterances, interpret His sayings, love His apostles, contend not with me who companied with Him. For in direct opposition to me, who am a firm rock, the foundation of the Church, you now stand. If you were not opposed to me, you would not accuse me, and revile the truth proclaimed by me, in order that I may not be believed when I state what I myself have heard with my own ears from the Lord, as if I were evidently a person that was condemned and in bad repute. But if you say that I am condemned, you bring an accusation against God, who revealed the Christ to me, and you inveigh against Him who pronounced me blessed on account of the revelation. But if, indeed, you really wish to work in the cause of truth, learn first of all from us what we have learned from Him, and, becoming a disciple of the truth, become a fellow-worker with us." (pg. 80)

Peter attacks Simon Magus on attaining to Christ through visions, which is something that Paul claims as well. According to Ehrman, Paul is the most controversial figure in the early Church, but this does not match up with the overwhelming emphasis on Pauline view which comprise over half of the New Testament Canon. The letter that is attributed to Paul by the majority of scholarship is Romans. Paul seems to have some connections to the Jewish elite that serve the Roman empire that the other disciples of Jesus did not have. These are not discussed by Ehrman in any great detail. According to Eusebius, the three main centers of the early Church were in Jerusalem, Antioch, and Corinth. In its beginning stages Peter and James were seen as the leaders of the Church in Jerusalem (pg. 81).

82. The Epistle of James seems to contradict Paul's message that salvation comes from grace and not through works according to the Law, as James declares in Epistle of James that faith without works is dead (pg. 90). Ehrman seems to blow past the various accounts of Paul's vision on his road to Damascus that all seem contradictory and gives no explanations to why Paul would manipulate his audience, or why his secretary Luke would. Ehrman sees a contradiction but cannot call it a lie even while taking such claims at face value (pg. 96). In Acts 9:23 Paul meets with the apostles even though he does not meet the criteria for one who is to be a disciple or apostle for not having stayed with Jesus in the time of his ministry (Acts 1:21). There is no critical discussion whether Paul is converting from one religion to another as he himself declares he is not through his unique blend of New Covenant theology. After all, Paul declares in his letter to Philippi that he was circumcised on the eighth day and of the Nation of Israel, from the Tribe of Benjamin, and a Pharisee. Jesus however tells us to beware of the yeast of the Pharisees (Matthew 16:6) and declares them false teachers. Moreover, Paul was raised in a pagan environment unlike Peter (comparing Galilee to Tarsus) (pg.102).

83. The Jews felt they had a special covenant with God and had it written throughout their holy book in countless places that they were in a special covenant with God that had changed shape throughout the history of Israel. It was also written in Exodus 19:6 that the people of God (Israel) shall be a nation of priests (cohen) (pg. 106). This meant more than the keeping of certain rituals but also meant that one should perform works of righteousness and that in a just nation the religious expert and ruler are the same. Both in solemnity and through the divine grace of God one was to keep a life of piety, blamelessness, purity, and continual praise of God. Israel did not keep this promise and reverted to temple worship and formed unique interpretation of scriptures seen in a complex range of oral tradition culminating in midrash and Talmud texts of the fifth century and beyond. The problem is that what it means to be a Jew has changed since the Christian traditions were codified and we seldom know what the traditions of 1st century Rabbis represents any more than what the early Christian sources seem to suggest to us. Hence the use of the term Jewish to describe Jews during the time of Jesus is quite dubious yet it is constantly repeated by atheistic scholars like Ehrman and others. Paul still declares however that salvations is reserved for the Jew first but also for the Gentile. Ehrman does not tell us why Paul says salvation comes to the Jew first but also to the Gentile.

84. Luke also tells us about the high-status Paul shared among the Jews. Paul was purportedly taught by Gamaliel who was a chief rabbi at the time (Acts 22:3), but sometimes apparently went by his Jewish name Saul despite his claims that he is a proud Jew. According to Ehrman, "most scholars put the population of the Roman Empire at this time around sixty million people, with something like 7 percent of them Jews. Judaism, in other words, was a small

minority religion in the empire as a whole" (pg. 103). Furthermore, before becoming a Christian, Paul was supposedly given an order by the high priest of the temple to persecute Christians, although one has to wonder why Roman leaders or Jewish elite would punish other Jews for a breakaway sect (pg. 106-109). It was however Paul himself who boldly declared salvation to be not from "having my own righteousness that come through the law, but the righteousness that come through having faith in Christ" (Phil 3:8). This outlines a strange unique aspect of the Pauline synthesis concerning salvation by faith alone and not by the works of the law in contradistinction to his strict and proud Jewish upbringing, which culminates in a "new spirit" that gives new life everlasting a resurrected body that cannot perish. But for those who follow the old law Paul warns, "law was given on account of transgressions" (Gal 3:19) (pg. 114-116). Finally, Paul argues that since Abraham came to faith without the law before the Torah, the struggle of faith is primary to the law itself (as Kierkegaard argued as well in his famous "Fear and Trembling" which founded existential philosophy). Paul further paints Christ as a "second Adam" and the first fruit of the resurrection (1 Cor 15:20). Contrary to the Gospels, Paul does not speak of future judgement or tribulation but in 1 Thessalonians 4:14 talks to Christ descending on Earth wiping away sin, and a future physical resurrection in our perfected bodies (1 Cor 15:50). In Gal 1:15 Paul declares he was set apart from his mother's womb to preach this message and was directly chosen by God and by implication does not preach on any authority given to him by other men which he says in a number of places (pg. 123). At this point this certainly would exclude the disciples of Jesus and even Jesus himself as being Paul's teacher, as well as the leaders of the Jewish community. Yet and still, Ehrman does not think Paul's message is unique enough to be caste into the mold of first and second century Jewish thought. It is clear to us however that Paul preached a totally unique message of salvation never before seen or heard by his own admission.

85. In Romans 15:19 we read how Paul traveled to new lands to preach "his" gospel, careful not to build upon a foundation laid by someone else. When Paul went to a city, he was the first "Christian" on the scene and took special care to define what it meant to be a Christian. This contradicts with the story that Paul went to Jews first and then to Greeks as he reports in Romans and Ehrman uses to describe as his literal itinerary. Would Paul have any need to go to Jews first as apostle to the Gentiles? It is clear that this message is talking about how salvation is brought into this world through the Jews and spreading to the Gentiles. Now there is a story that even a Jew would believe. If one analyzes Paul's travels in the Mediterranean, he did not go to cities like Athens because he was concerned to make an impression on Jews, or at the very least such a course seems untenable. Paul worked with leather so he could travel with ease as a tent maker and had money, but also was no stranger to dealing with animals, as we also see that he does not oppose eating of meat sacrificed to idols and has no aversion to any meat due to dietary restrictions of

any kind. Ehrman paints a cartoonish picture of Paul owning a leather goods shop as a travelling merchant preaching his message on the go. Finally, Ehrman makes a more critical statement on pg. 133 of his book where he says, "Paul converted the Pagan to believe in the God of the Jews". We do not understand however how Ehrman can claim that in Paul's message of blood sacrifice and resurrection "the body matters". This is a puzzling statement when Paul says again and again that flesh is a curse and connected with sin but Man is only made right through the spirit. We are forced to conclude that Ehrman does not properly understand the dialectic of flesh and spirit presented in Paul.

86. Also, if Paul taught Gospel apart from Law, then how could he claim that his message is a fulfillment of the law of these very same prophets? Furthermore, if Christ's power surpassed worldly power and the power of sin, why must he descend into the world to save others in a physical reign? Ehrman rightly considers how Paul's speech in Athens in Acts contradicts his condemnation of Gentiles in Romans. Ehrman doesn't know who started the Church in Rome but suggests that it was probably not Paul or Peter. This is an example of different views held side by side in the Pauline letters. Another example are his views on Women. Paul seems to put some women in leadership positions in some of his letters (Romans and Corinthians) but seems to demote them to a secondary position within the Church and within society in general in other places (Timothy and Ephesians). Paul has some interesting views on Marriage and Women in his letters that Christians supposedly accept apparently in conjunction with the dominant secular and liberal dogmas of today which render them unfavorable and impossible. The first would be a view that it is better to be abstinent than marry. Another unique view is that divorce is forbidden, so if one is to marry one should choose wisely (this teaching is supported by the Gospels in the sayings of Jesus as well). As Christ is ruled by God, Men are ruled by Christ, and women are ruled by men. This puts women at the bottom of the totem pole of existence. In quite a dark twist, women still bear the curse of the law by childbearing (pg. 147).

87. Ehrman does well to point out more contradictions in Acts and the Letters of Paul. In Acts Paul has Timothy circumcised but in Letters refuses to have Titus circumcised and argues against enforcement of the law of circumcision on Gentile converts (pg. 155). Paul argues in 1 and 2 Corinthians that future resurrection will take place when Christ returns, and that the resurrection in the spiritual sense has already taken place in Ephesians (pg. 157). The Pastoral Epistles argue that Churches are highly organized but in Romans and Corinthians basic views have not yet been settled. The writer of the pastorals seems to attack Gnostics, but those Gnostics paradoxically saw Paul as their teacher (for example Valentinus was a disciple of Theudas, who was a disciple of Paul as Ehrman claims) (pg. 160). Other thinkers like Marcion, who travelled to Rome felt Paul's God was different than the God of the Old Testament (pg. 161). Of course, we must point out that Ehrman, Robert Price, and Elaine

Pagels make the claim most fervently that one man's heterodoxy is another man's orthodoxy. While this is a touchy feely sort of democratizing tone, it also obfuscates any claims of originality in doctrine (pg 163).

88. In Galatians 2:16 Paul states, "A person is satisfied by faith in Christ...not by works of the law", but in the Epistle of James 2:24 it states, "a person is justified by works, not by faith alone". This stark contradiction in doctrine, terminology, and rhetoric, when paired with the endorsement of Peter and James of Paul in Acts, which is further complicated by the conflict between Peter and Paul in Galatians who he refers to as "the circumcision party" (pg. 165-166), is the central theme in both the heretical acceptance of the Pauline doctrine, and the groups like Ebionites who seemed to challenge the Pauline conception of Christianity (pg. 168), Arians, Mandaeans, and Christian Arabs who saw Paul as a false teacher and fake apostle. Teachers like Martin Luther all the way in the sixteenth century still felt such contradictions cannot be reconciled and pleaded that the Epistle of James was falsely constructed along with other writings like Jude. Early Christian thinkers like Tertullian however claimed that groups like heretics and Marcionites had "discovered" Paul's letter to Galatians and were actively using it as a way to derail the true Christian message. A third option presents itself in Paul's own words which suggest that Paul made different standards for different people and so was a Jew with the Jew, a Roman with the Roman, and in short did whatever he would have to in order to get the person in front of him to believe what he wanted, including circumcising his friend and eating food sacrificed to idols. With all the points where information presented by Ehrman lends to the fact of Paul being a deceiver or subverter, he never questions the basic narrative that Paul believed everything he taught or that any of the themes in his writing had any greater end or purpose. The only reason we can give for this is that the obvious way to sell more books is to pander to Christians by ultimately remaining neutral, but then we can also ask if the writer is truly sincere about helping Christians configure their beliefs and sorting out their delusions or simply trying to play both sides of the issue. We can only speculate on the authors intentions but only point out that in certain cases much more can be done to bring certain views to their logical conclusion.

89. Price's views on the matter are more drawn out but a little more honest in terms of his citing of various scholars, but also his identification of where the early Christian message originated and the matter of who the early supporters of Paulinism were who stood to gain considerably from the Pauline line of teaching that had several distinctive tones and features. Price realizes that Protestants long ago chose Paul over Jesus and that Schweitzer's view that Jesus did not come to end the world but end Jewish dispensation was influential to the modern world (introduction pg. viii). While Price seems to support more Gnostic views, his admitting of his own particular taste makes him more down to earth than the pretentiously styled so called objective views of Ehr-

man. Price is clear on the fact that the earliest Pauline Christians we know are the Marcionites and the Gnostics. Price does not see these groups as arising in the second century but much earlier. This organization of events backs our main contention that Paul's letters spawned the Gnosticism and Hermeticism of the late second century propelled by Neoplatonism of Hellenized Jews and Syncretistic religious sects which later morphed into Kabbalism, Albigensian Heresy, Manichaean dualism, Rosicrucianism, and Freemasonic influences that took us from an age of religious rule to one of secular learning.

90. Price agrees with Ehrman that second century sources tell us that Paul and Peters mission closely paralleled one another and that so called "Jewish Christian" like the Ebionites used Simon Magus to slander Paul while championing Peter (introduction pg. xiv). We read Price's "The Colossal Apostle"[26] to narrow in on some facts about the second century debates concerning the Apostle Paul. We have concluded that Price does not merely present facts but puts them in line with his own views which seem to support the narrative that both religion and ancient myths are based on some sort of Astro-theology or mystical cosmology. Mythicists and those who believe in the theory of racial memory derived from Jungian archetypes, draw from various religious traditions in order to draw comparisons and hence, are almost perennial or theosophical in their expression and tacitly support a syncretistic or occult viewpoint in the process. Such is true not only for Robert Price, but also for Elaine Pagels who writes about the Gnostic Gospels. Here one can see a comparison between Paul and Buddha which existed earlier among German and Dutch radical thinkers who were influenced by Hegelian views (pg. 5). There is also the grave task of trying to prove the ahistorical or mythical through the historical and even justify events in ancient times by psychologizing them into hallucinations. Before we whip out the DSM V we should be aware that the probabilistic methods of historians must ultimately rely on cold hard physical evidence and not hearsay or the ultra-subjective visions and hallucinations experienced in the past (pg. 6). Saying one had a vision or aberration of the mind is mostly used back then as it is today: as an excuse to commit some evil or insane act. Still more unlikely, we see Paul's conversion being compared to the Great Renunciation story of the Buddha when reaching Nirvana on the path of the Boddhisattva (pg. 7). Either way, such episodes cannot be compared. As much as the Buddha was seeking truth, Paul has already found it and there is no need to search within or actively negate the world. Paul is also compared with Joseph Smith who sees Angel Maroni and Luke's narrative with the Bacchic tales of Dionysus (pg. 8-11).

---

[26] Price, R. M. (2012). *The Amazing Colossal Apostle: The Search for the Historical Paul*. Signature Books. In paragraphs 89-102 we give a detailed analysis of Price's work entitled "The Amazing Colossal Apostle" with page numbers included.

91. A myth is elusive and is often mired in metaphor and we conclude a lie is much more likely than any earnest and complete alternate rendition of the facts in question. We must point out that a myth is ahistorical; proving a historical myth is the opposite of finding a historical fact and should be much more difficult (pg. 13). Price shows an interesting passage from the Babylonian Talmud that suggests that those healed by the power of the name of Jesus had a powerful curse put on them and that it is better for them to die. It is quite strange however that Price does not count this as Jews being hateful towards Christianity but counts the narrative that Paul's Jewish zeal led him to persecute Christians as anti-Semitic (pg. 16). As he later states however, according to Gordon Rylands, that the legend of Paul persecuting Christians may have been invented by Peterine Christians as the legend of Peter's denial of the Lord was an invention of Pauline Christians (pg. 17). It is no wonder that in Acts and 2 Peter, Paul is somehow misconstrued as teaching against the Law. There is also the strange case of Pauline authorship being continually questioned even by fellow Christians. Origen said Paul could not have written Hebrews, as Martin Luther argued that the Epistle of James was spurious for contradicting Paul and also relegated Hebrews and Jude to the same status of being part of a canonical appendix and not as main books of canon (pg. 25). Tertullian said Marcion discovered the Pauline epistle to Galatians, Schleiermacher rejected First Epistle of Timothy, and most scholars roundly reject that Peter has written anything that survives today. The Tubingen school dismissed Ephesians and Colossians as "sounding too Gnostic", and also Philippians due to the Valentinian sounding Kenosis Hymn. F.C Baur posited the "Hauptbriefe" or main Pauline letters consisting of the four letters 1 and 2 Corinthians, Galatians, and Romans (pg. 26-30).

92. Tertullian referred to Paul as the apostle of Marcion and the Heretics (pg. 37). The first commentators on the epistles according to Price were the Valentinus, Heraclean, and Basilides who were all seen as forerunners of Gnosticism. Here the references Price prescribes are quite instructive; Price leans on Thomas Kuhn's "The Structure of Scientific Revolutions" (pg. 38). He describes the Enuma Elish where, in Ea being switched for Marduk, shows a game changing paradigm shift which changes the very structure of belief. Price presents four theories on Paul that are more like possibilities: 1. That Paul collected letters himself 2. Pauline writing became a substitute for Paul to canonize the teachings of Paul because Paul was not around 3. The Epistles are constructed from whole cloth as myth 4. Pauline letters are an afterthought of Luke and John, securing a new approach to understanding the Christian message by Churches in Asia Minor (pg. 47-68). W.C Van Manen who Price cites extensively parallels Paul's encounter with the Church in Jerusalem led by Peter and James with Marcion's encounter with the Roman Church. Writers of the Tubingen School equate Paul with Simon Magus.

93. It is quite strange that those who most fervently promulgated the dialectic between Peter and Paul were the anti-Jewish Christians like Marcion who was the first to collect or explain Paul's letters. Marcion's collection included Galatians, 1 and 2 Corinthians, Romans, 1 and 2 Thessalonians, Ephesians, Colossians, Philippians, and Philemon (pg. 71). Price concludes, "there is just enough textual variation to show that there was not a uniform universal archetype" (pg. 79), but then we must ask, why call these letters "Pauline" at all then? Either way, groups like Cainites who most likely produced works like "The Ascension of Paul" and Marcionites championed the Epistles as the greatest example of Christian teaching. Other apocryphal writers like the Prayer of the Apostle Paul and the Apocalypse of Paul show up as late as the third and fourth century. In the "Revelation of Paul", Paul is in the fourth heaven being barred from the eighth heaven by the cosmic demiurge. In the Prayer of the Apostle Paul, Christ is said to be the first born of the pleroma of grace. In the Revelation of Paul Chapter 13, the world is seen as nothing when compared to the wealth of the soul. In the fourth century Apocalypse of Paul, he is hailed and greeted by Enoch, the scribe of the Lord (pg. 92-96).

94. In these worlds Christ reigns on Earth for 1,000 years and there is a heavy emphasis on passages like in 2 Corinthians 3 where Paul is seen bringing a better covenant than Moses (pg. 100). Paul is seen as a mediator of a covenant between Jews and the rest of the world. There are also the views of Paul in marriage that tell us that children in marriage are made Christian by a believing spouse, that those who have wives should live as though they had none (1 Cor 7:12-16, 1 Cor 7:29) (pg. 107). This is of course a view preparing for a life without war or sex but in continual love with all who do the work of the Lord. It is a belief that overwhelmingly lends itself to Gnostic and antinomian teaching, but more on this later. Price expands on Gnostic views in general. He informs us that the concept of an Apostle. Is not Christian or Jewish but is found in Gnosticism where it is meant to portray someone who is initiated or an adept. Gnostic teacher Theudas explains that the unknown God is hidden away in the fullness of the Pleroma in unapproachable light and did not create the world. God instead emanated a pair of divine beings, at the end of which process emerged Sophia (pg. 131). Alienated from the Godhead, she was banished to the outskirts of the Pleroma and had no partner. Her emanations grow out of sync and, in an inversion of Plato's "God of the Philosophers", create an entity called the Demiurge which believes itself to be all powerful. This was borrowed from Plato by Hellenistic Jews and especially is seen in the philosophy of Philo of Alexandria. The Demiurge in Gnosticism was an overwhelmingly negative force however unlike Plato who called him "Worker of the People", this was a tyrannical deity who imitated the Godhead in creating a "mudpie substitute" for the reality of the Pleroma (pg. 132). This created a chaotic world made from broken shards of light stolen from the divine realm, and the dismembering of a primal man of light (possibly taken from the Zoroastrians). The Archons or fallen sons of God used sparks of alien

light that Price says were something like DNA that program a self-replicating order into the other-wise stillborn substance of matter (pg. 133).

95. Sethians believed Christ was a second coming of Seth who was born of light unlike Cain. The Ophite believes Jesus was a resurrected Attis. Also known as "Melchizedek", Jesus possessed self-knowledge and a mystical formula, and was the redeeming man of light. Naassenes used the image of the serpent as the symbol of rebirth (pg. 134-135). Christ was seen as a promethean bringer of light. Price praised Elaine Pagels who wrote extensively on Gnostic writing and views and is the most mainstream scholar dealing with the subject. We will analyze her works just shortly. Pagels repeats the claim that Price explores that Gnosticism was in part spread by celibate charismatic women who were self-styled and makeshift apostles. But neither these or even Paul make the cut of apostleship as it is defined in Acts 1:21-22 as "one who accompanied us at the time of the Lord Jesus", starting at John's Baptism until the day he was taken up. In other words, only those who observed Christ's ministry and were present at his resurrection need qualify. How Paul's view came to dominate while Gnostics were left behind is now unclear. It may be though the goals of the Gnostics were similar to Pauline views, such views are ultimately more syncretistic, even though they were quite early subsumed into the rhetoric of Paul who teaches of not only salvation apart from the law but also a stark duality between flesh and spirit.

96. Much in line with the basic emphasis and drive for this book is Price's statement found in his chapter "The Original Gnostic Apostles" (in the book "The Colossal Apostle" that we are now analyzing), which state, "The first deception of deity is to conceal his divinity, the second is to pretend to be human" (pg. 153). Truth has successfully been communicated here by two mutually negating lies. The formula was inverted by the Gnostics into a method of reaching divine immanence or transcendence, in which the enlightened soul became united with its heavenly twin. Another main system of thought is explored in relation with the origins of Paulinism and that is the views of Simon Magus who is everywhere portrayed as an enemy of the Disciples of Christ.

97. Simon Magus, analogous to the Gnostic demiurge, is mistaken for divinity, but unlike the other Disciples who reserve such a place for Christ in heaven, Simon accepts the charge that he is a divinity equal to Christ and God. Simon Magus is depicted as Samaritan and as part of the Northern Tribes, like Ephesus and Tarsus and other parts of Asia. In 1 Kings 12 we read that these tribes succeeded from a Davidic federation. According to Price, the Hasmoneans were most likely the group responsible for bulldozing the Samaritan temple for setting up a system of worship outside of the Temple. The Samaritans connected the Messiahship not with a continuation of the Davidic Kingdom but with a "restorer" figure like the prophets of old (pg. 185-187). The Samaritans, according to Price had a different canon than other Jews. Matthew 10:5

says stay away from Samaria, but Luke tells us the famous tale of the good Samaritan. Perhaps the conflict in the early Church had to do with a pre-existing divide among Jewish people. Justin Martyr had complained that all of Samaria had fell into Simonian heresy. Simon himself appears to us to be a master shapeshifter but a shapeshifter is hard to prove.

98. Another story has to do with the syncretistic flavor of Jewish religion on the outskirts of Judea (namely in Egypt or Turkey). This fact is paired with the incorporation of foreign elements like Lady Wisdom in Proverbs 8, Sirach 1, and Wisdom of Solomon 7. The view of gods and their female consorts is compared with the cults of Shiva and Kali (pg. 154). Similarly, the motif of the Holy Spirit in the occult is taken to mean the feminine aspect of God whose male aspect is pure energy and gives birth to a divine son which is the savior of creation. The Divine Sparks were reminiscent of Qliphot of Isaac Luria who devised in his Kabbalistic system an inversion of the Sephirot or "Tree of Life", whose thirty-three emanations consist of the anatomy of God. George Mead, the famous theosophist, apparently wrote a book on Simon Magus. Simonian Magic was also somehow related to the baptism ceremony.

99. In Mark 3:33, Jesus' adversaries accuse him of healing with the power of demons. Jesus is also depicted as a magical trickster by Jews in the Toledot Jeshu (a Jewish writing that appears centuries after the time when Jesus lived) (pg. 191). Marcion of Pontus, who was from Northern Turkey, also believed Jesus was the son of a higher God, sharing the belief of the Gnostics that lesser gods had created the world to imprison spirit in flesh. Marcion declared that the Gospel of Luke and the Letters of Paul be used as the New Testament which for him would exclude the writings of the Old Testament (pg. 192-193). Marcion's teachings were technically older than Valentinus and Basilides. Nazoreans, Ebionites, and Elchasites dismissed Paul's teaching as heir to the teachings of Jesus (pg. 194). In Acts, Simon Magus tries to buy apostleship, just as Paul is seen as raising funds for the early Church. According to Price, Marcion was the first Paulinist. As we already saw Ehrman say, the attacks on Simon Magus in the Clementine Recognitions 17:19 is reminiscent of attacks on Paul. Hermann Detering came to the radical conclusion that Paul is none other than Simon Magus (pg. 199). Josephus tells of a Simon who was a pretend sorcerer from Cyprus, but apparently never mentions Paul, just as Justin Martyr never mentions Paul. The silence about Paul by some members of the early Church speaks quite loudly at times.

100. In the Qumran Scrolls appears the "Man of the Lie" who rejects the Torah and founded a rival sect comprised of "the simple ones of Ephraim" (referring to the people of the Northern Tribes) and naïve Gentiles (pg. 210). Price thinks the conflict of Peter versus Paul is just a conflict of Ebionite versus Marcionite doctrine. The conflict culminates in the catholicizing document known as Acts. According to Irenaeus, Simon Magus said men are saved by

grace and not works. Self-styled prophets like Mani (who also referred to himself as an apostle) believed in the fourth century and beyond that Christ was a
reincarnation of Zoroaster and Buddha (pg. 216). The rules of abstinence and
the doing away of traditional marriage relations in exchange for celibacy broke
down views on marriage and led to either complete celibacy or extreme libertinism. The Gospel of John most elegantly portrays the views of Marcionites
because it is precisely in the Gospel of John that Moses and the Jews know
nothing about God and the Kingdom of God is not of this world. The soteriological view of ascetics and Gnostics is linked with the relation between inner
potential and primordial chaos which can be linked with teleological view of
Aristotelian cosmology. The view of inner transformation is paired by Price
with the Vajrayana sect of Buddhism whose teachings and practices are heavily driven toward personal enlightenment. Ultimately the mystical doctrine of
grace through suffering and eternal rebirth is seen as influencing Advaita Vedanta, The Blackstone Valley Immoralist Sect, Mashiach ben Joseph of the
Messianic Jews, Maitreya Buddha, and even Phibionites (Borborites) and
Frankists who preach the holiness of sin in pantheistic union with the divine
(pg. 227-237).

101. We must ask if Price's general thesis is correct and all of these figures
were mythical parables for a religious conflict occurring around the second
century when the various books that comprise the New Testament were really
composed, than the mystery is not solved but has now been added an extra
dimension of mystery as to who or what entity (state or religious group) composed these texts in order to invent these historical sounding myths. In other
words, if Paul did not write the Epistles than who did? In Ehrman's case we
think that it would be enough not to use unreliable material with holes and
contradictions in order to fill in the gaps of historical information and using the
unreliable to measure the unknown. On an internet show with Muhammad
Hijab, Ehrman stated that reading the Gospels is like asking a friend for directions while driving but ten percent of the information you receive from that
friend is unreliable. He claims that you must read the Gospels to discover what
kind of historical information one can actually get from them. But what if one
is being taken for a proverbial ride. The goal of someone deliberately mislead-
ing someone on the road is to delude, distract, and obfuscate the real truth.
Again we must ask who would invent such things and to what end?

102. There are of course many methodological presuppositions within the
Atheistic worldview. We reject the notion that Faith is defined as evidence of
things unseen. Everything can be seen as a symbol for something else. One
cannot use the truth for falsehood but one can make a representation of truth
and override meaning with contextualization so as to communicate many different messages at the same time. We must remember also that knowledge is
infinite. To isolate anything is to make it unknowable in relation to the totality
of events. Since no one has complete knowledge, and such a state is not possi-

ble at any rate one must "go with what one knows" and use what one knows in order to discern the unknown. Such a stance or posture is one of faith. Faith is not belief that comes before knowledge in order to test an opinion one has through experience but faith is what happens when one gains incomplete knowledge and tries to apply to the complete relation of events in the world. Faith is not beyond belief but what comes after knowledge. Instead, we read in Paul in 2 Corinthians 5:7, "we walk by faith, not by sight". While we agree that the purely empirical cannot suffice for the truth, we find it paradoxical for those who preach through visions to have made such claims. Conversely, if faith is what comes after knowledge than all of what we see is a sign for the bigger picture to emerge. One must see with sight and act with faith.

Chapter 5
"God became human so that humankind may become divine"

103. Perhaps the most confused and disjointed rendition of Christian beliefs can be seen in Elaine Pagels work "Beyond Belief"[27]. Pagels claims that the tradition of Western Christianity has both limited and expanded our views on the progress of knowledge through the centuries (pg. 4). While Pagels tries to redefine what it means to be a Christian most fundamentally, she also attends Church services which she describes as a "celebration of progress". We find it problematic that Pagels both claims that Orthodox Christianity suppressed the true message of Christianity for centuries but somehow led to the collective progress of humanity. Pagels claims that men like Tertullian and Irenaeus limited their view of faith to exclude those who had reached independent verification for their beliefs through their own mystical doctrine and what Christ represented to them (pg. 7). These thinkers who were not accepted by the orthodox teachers found proof of their beliefs beyond the mere written word. She begins her book with a praise of the Christian message in Tertullian's practice of gift giving, and the non-proselytizing aspects of their beliefs on conversion. Galen, who was the physician of Marcus Aurelius spoke in praise of Christians (pg. 8). We must not however forget that all of these practices can have a dark side. Gift giving is often a product of nepotism, and Christian have historically persecuted those of other faiths. Marcus Aurelius sure did not have a problem with killing a Christian or two himself. Pagels advances the view that Christianity could have been or is in part defined by the view that God requires love and not material sacrifice. But can this view really be reconstructed or reconciled with the Christian message today?

104. What Pagels does not understand despite having access to Greek manuscripts and being able to read them is how to explain the Christian so called mysteries in a concise way and we will go ahead and present them to you here so you will not need to read a thousand cryptic messages that point to the "beyond". Christians understand that Man is born three times. First, he is born in the Earth as a primordial brother to all men and part of the human family. Secondly, he is birthed through the water of the womb, which is the Baptism of rebirth through the Spirit of God. Thirdly, he is forged in flames by his own will, effort, and work which are all a testament to his final destination either becoming rarefied or tarnished in the process. Christianity caused some

---

[27] Pagels, E. H. (2004). *Beyond Belief: The Secret Gospel of Thomas*. Vintage Books. From paragraph 103-127 I give a detailed analysis of Pagels work Beyond Belief and the various views and arguments made therein with page numbers included.

to lead lives that were based on promiscuity, greed, magic, and racial hatred but as we see this is only part of the story as related by Justin Martyr. Pagels mentions how, strangely enough, Justin Martyr referred to the Baptism ceremony as an "illumination" (pg. 14). This language is clearly indicative of the type of initiation seen in mystery cults. Certain mystical interpretations and forms of the Christian message felt that one was not separate from Christ and that one could seek unity with the divine. Certain Gnostic texts and apocryphal texts like the Didache quote the Gospel of Matthew and other gospels (pg. 16). Other sources that are favored by orthodox thinkers like John differ widely from the other gospels. For example, the Gospel of John does not have Jesus eating a Passover meal with his disciples but instead being crucified on Passover by the Jews (pg. 24). This suggests to Pagels that there were a variety of views in early Christianity, but Pagels says she "cannot love" the monolithic definition of Christianity and opts for a more democratizing perennialism (pg. 29).

105. In the Acts of John we see Christ engaged in a circle dance and prayer with his disciples, celebrating his death and proclaiming his love for them instead of the somber instance of the Passover meal. Pagels styles conflicts in the early Church as the battle between the Gospel of Thomas and the Gospel of John in securing canonical status. While the Gospel of John mentions Christ as a pre-existent being on par with the divine, the Gospel of Thomas mentions the power of transformation incurred by Christ's spirit when embodying the human element. As it states in the Gospel of Thomas, "If you bring forth what is within you, what you bring forth will save you". What you do not bring forth will destroy you. This is a view of developing inner potential (seen by us as part of an Aristotelian framework) and not one of adopting faith which is precluded by complete sacrifice. The Neoplatonists Origen was one of the Gospel of Johns earliest defenders (pg. 36). Origen noted that no other Gospel directly speaks of Jesus divinity as John does. The Gospel of Thomas offers a more "mystical" view. In the Apocryphal Acts of Thomas, we read that Thomas went to India, being sold into slavery by none other than Jesus himself to spread the message to faraway lands.

106. It is here that Pagels seems to suggest some cross-pollination between the Vedic and the Apostolic. Thomas identifies Jesus with the "image of God" within each of us, as Jesus is God's own light in human form, and much like in the Gospel of John and the Gnostic writings, connects Jesus to the universe through a primordial light formed in heaven (pg. 41). In Greek, "Christos" is the translation of the word "Mashiach" or Messiah and means "the anointed one" (pg. 42). In 1 Corinthians 12:3, Paul gives the view that those who come to believe in Jesus are inspired by the Holy Spirit (pg. 45). Pagels brings in witnesses like Leo Tolstoy and Thomas Merton who took more syncretistic views, but we have to ask what relevance these sort of occult views have on early Christianity other than to make a point in favor of syncretism using the symptoms of the pan-religious fervor of the modern age (pg. 51). God is how-

ever timeless and not concerned with human progress: in the Gospel of Thomas we read, "for whoever takes his place at the beginning will know the end". Pagels haphazardly compares Jesus' teaching with a Buddhist Koan once again connecting the mystical teachings of the West to Eastern religion (pg. 53). This is an odd comparison as well because there should be comparable examples in Jewish tradition and later Pagels admits this so the smuggling in of Buddhist doctrine is wholly unnecessary other than to win points with those who are of a more theosophical persuasion. Of the notion that it will be in the end as it was in the beginning, detailing the cyclical notion of time, there exists many comparable examples in Western philosophy and among the pre-Socratics.

107. Pagels says, "What Irenaeus here dismisses as heretical later became a central theme of Jewish mystical tradition" (pg. 58). The view that the image of God within links God to humanity and fate in general, connects the teleological and eschatological function of humanity attaining its highest potential and connects the Pauline to the Jewish whose heretical form is akin to Gnosticism, as admitted here by Pagels. The real issue is how Pagels can claim this while also knowing that the Gnostic view sometimes suggests that the God of the Old Testament is an evil entity and inverts Judaism. Also, it seems that various works like the Gospel of John and Gospel of Thomas are having an inner dialogue, where we see an anti-Thomas narrative at the end of the Gospel of John, in which a skeptical Thomas not believing in the resurrected body of Jesus asks to inspect the wounds of Christ (pg. 58). Finally, we must ask along with Pagels, who is the mysterious John? If we know the Gospel of Thomas and the writings concerning Thomas are mentioning Thomas who is mentioned in the other Gospels as a disciple of Christ, then how come we have no clue who John is? What does that fact say about the viability of the Gospel of Thomas versus the Gospel of John? It seems like very little is known about the John or Thomas who supposedly wrote these works. John is hypothesized to be several figures that played a role in the early Church (pg. 63). Is John the secret disciple whom Christ loved above all others mentioned in the Gospel of John 13:23, or John the Son of Zebedee? The Gospel of Thomas opens just as the Gospel of John does with a rewriting of Genesis but then diverges and states, "what came into being in him was life, and life was the light of all people". Christ declares, "I am the way, the truth, the life". Conversely in the Gospel of John, Jesus is "monogenes" or the only begotten son of God (pg. 66-67).

108. Pagels discusses perennial philosophy with David Steindl-Rast and Roshi Richard Baker who are also connected to the Lindisfarne Center (a "thinktank" group seeking to merge science and religion through the perennial philosophy of Teilhard de Chardin and Alfred North Whitehead), one of whom tell her if they read the Gospel of Thomas they wouldn't have converted to Buddhism (pg. 74). That doesn't answer the question of why this person is still a Buddhist today or how they can claim to be one after believing in the Gospel

of Thomas. Looking for God within does not have to be equated with seeing yourself as God but pantheism can be a slippery slope, and sometimes inflation of the ego causes those who view mystical visions of sudden epiphany with their own grace and power. Such can be said about Martin Buber's "I and Thou" relationship (really first discovered by Kierkegaard) and the tat-thvam-asi or "thou art that" of Hindu tradition mentioned by Pagels (pg. 75). Before asking how Hinduism and Buddhism which repudiate each other's doctrines can even be compared, we must point out that to supplement what is not found in western religion with eastern tradition has long been the foundation of occult theology but has continually been employed by Price and Pagels, as we have seen.

109. According to Pagels, it was Polycarp who taught Irenaeus who wrote the definitive statements against what he considered heretical factions within the early Church. Polycarp supposedly called Marcion "the son of the devil" to his face (pg. 80). He sent his associate Pothinus to Gaul in the western hinterlands (it is interesting to note that Rome had also attempted to subdue the region of Gaul under Titus Flavius) (pg. 82). The spread of Christianity to Europe as the Roman Empire collapsed is a major part of our story because it is in Europe where the major swath of Gentile converts to Paul's message were found. In Asia minor, there were self-styled prophets like Montanus, Maximilla, and Priscilla. Priscilla for example had said that Christ appeared to her in female form (pg. 84), and the followers of Montanus were known to be overtaken by charismatic visions and taken over by the Holy Spirit. A Christian leader denounced the influence of the Gospel of John and Revelations and charged that they were composed by Cerinthus, who was a man that John had denounced as a heretic (pg. 85-86). Even Tertullian apparently sided with the "spirit filled" Christians and denounced the early Church (who now sees him as being part of the Montanist heresy). Irenaeus was surprised to found out that some of the other students of Polycarp had fallen into the Valentinian heresy.

110. The mysterious "John of Patmos", and Paul of Tarsus and Luke's writings all revere divine insight from visions, but Paul himself complains in Corinthians that too many are claiming to have supernatural insight (pg. 89). Of course, we must point out that the claim that one has received direct guidance by supernatural forces or by visions has been made by many to lie to others and claimed by many more. What is stranger is that we do not observe the ritualistic methods like sleep deprivation, sex magic (the extreme use of pain and pleasure to incur altered states), psychedelic substances, fasting, or breathwork and chanting or meditation normally used to incur visions and altered states.

111. Pagels seems to focus more on feminism and antisemitism than do Price and Ehrman but all of them dwell on these themes for an uncomfortable amount of time. On the surface it would seem that such authors are inundated

with liberal bias, but this may also be a way to reach a wider audience. The way Pagels speaks however sometimes makes one feel that all the suffering in the world was incurred only by Jews and women. She derides Irenaeus as a misogynist for ridiculing a "foolish woman" for receiving visions (pg. 92). Pagels claims that the followers of Marcus the Magician are thus "indignantly" criticized by Irenaeus but we quite sympathize with his attempt to clarity and respond to the extraordinary claims made by Marcus the Magician and question Pagels taking sides with history in this way. Other obviously heretical beliefs of Marcus like that he had believed and told his followers that a goddess appeared to him with a naked body covered in Greek letters and spoke the name of Christ are particularly offensive (pg. 94). Such "visions" would certainly make it hard to conduct a Church or civil society.

112. We must object also to the use of Gnosticism or Gnostic theology as a liberalizing doctrine because of some of its main tenets. For one, the doctrines of sacred initiation can be just as strenuous as orthodox doctrine and have just as much of a capacity for abuse. Gnostics claim to have secret knowledge and often create a hierarchy of adepts or enlightened ones who know the part of sacred initiation and control these rites quite rigidly for their devotees and neophytes who wish to walk the path. Furthermore, Gnostic and Hermetic cosmology as well as the Kabbalistic are often based on a cosmic syzygy or universal dualism between male and female energies. This is seen as the "Shekinah" of the Kabbalistic Jews, or female aspect of God which is also an indwelling spirit. The focus is ever more about female and male spiritual energy and how to combine the two in one spirit or vessel. We must point out that this view accentuates the vast gulf between the two poles of male and female, which represent energy in terms of their male expression and spirit in terms of their female expression, also seen as the two poles of reality. The potential for abuse in all these various viewpoints is quite telling and can in no way be seen to support some democratizing or liberalizing notion. The inter-polarity of male and female causes one to transcend sex either by radical asceticism or extreme libertinism or a combination of both. Hence tantric sects have relied on various types of sex magic. Since male and female energies brought one into existence one would have to combine the two inside one vessel in order to transcend life and death and seek continual rebirth. Some of these rites require extremely rigid methods of preparation and not all of them are so friendly to women as we would expect. This was less an attitude of free love and rather one of stern religious semblance in order to transcend the material.

113. Pagels cites expert on Kabbalah Gershom Scholem. He recounts how such mystical sects rely on not dogmatic theology as claimed by Pagels as well, but "living experience". One can yet and still imagine how the rules for such ceremonies were highly structured. Another aspect of a cosmic dualism occurring in these mystical traditions is a focus on human speech becoming a form of the mystical or divine as seen in the vision of Marcus the Magician.

This is the dualistic doctrine of Logos equated with human speech. The basic view of magic is presented here: human speech can become a form of mystical and divine truth by encoding each letter or symbol or number with its own character or meaning devising an incantation altering human apperception and hence altering the basis for reality with the use of words. To explain, Pagels quotes Marcus the Magician who talks of how each separate letter realizes neither its own nature nor that of others and "while everyone of them is part of the whole, each one imagines its own sound to be the whole name" (pg. 95).

114. St. Irenaeus complained about the followers of Marcus the Magician and says, "while they say such things as these about creation, every one of them generates something new every day, according to his ability; for no one is considered 'mature' (or 'initiated') among them who does not develop some enormous lies" (pg. 96). Irenaeus attributes the Secret Book of John and the Gospel of Truth to Valentinus, the teacher of Marcus the Magician. He attributes the Gospel of Judas to Valentinus as well. Athanasius issued a decree that all such books be burned. In the Secret Book, Peter and James travel to heaven. In the Prayer of the Apostle Paul, another apocryphal text, Paul is taken up into the third heaven (pg. 97). In quite a puzzling passage on page 100 of her book, Pagels states, "Paul must have known about techniques that certain Jewish groups used to induce a state of ecstasy and invoke visions" without any other information. This culminates in the discussions around second to sixth century Hekhalot texts (pg. 101) that interpret such biblical mysteries as the vision of Ezekiel and address the various stages in the hierarchy of being (including the flaming chariot or wheel called the Merkabah which is a vessel of the spirit, the lesser Yahweh or Metatron seen as the perfection of Man, and the Tetragrammaton or holy throne surrounded by Seraphim and Cherubim representative of the highest angelic states). All such mysteries were used by Christian teachers like Irenaeus to represent mysteries about Christ.

115. The Secret Book of James talks about visions received by the disciples as does The Gospel of Mary Magdalene, where Peter declares that Christ loved Mary Magdalene above all women. In it, as we saw earlier, Jesus gives a secret revelation to his chief apostle seen here as Mary Magdalene (pg. 103). The secret revelation apparently concerns the ascension of the soul into heaven. It reveals that visions are seen in the mind that is between the soul and the spirit. These various aspects of human consciousness were extrapolations of divine cosmology which molded human capacity and understanding. Most notably, Peter and Andrew respond negatively to the teaching. In Jeremiah 23:25-32 we read, "I am against prophets, says the Lord, who use their own tongues and say 'says the Lord'. See I am against the prophets, says the Lord, who use their own tongues and prophesy lying dreams" (pg. 106).

116. The theology gets more complex as time progresses and progressive revelation is after all a hallmark of mysticism. This innovation is perhaps

achieved by use of foreign resources such as Greek philosophy or Persian Zoroastrianism. Justin Martyr was, for example, influenced by the peripatetic, the
Pythagorean, and the Neoplatonic (pg. 108). Most notably, when Irenaeus and
Justin Martyr refer to "the scripture" they are most probably referring to the
Old Testament because the books of the Gospels were still being contested at
the time and the canonization process for what books were to be included in
the New Testament had not yet begun (pg. 110). Irenaeus had his own interpretation of the stories in the Old Testament like the angel appearing with four
heads (one of a lion, one of a hawk, one of a bull, and one of a man I believe)
in the vision of Ezekiel: that it was a sign that the four Gospels would come to
reveal the revelation of Christ (pg. 111). St. Irenaeus was one of the first to
implant Christ's role in stories of the Old Testament that required mystical
interpretation. St. Irenaeus rejected but helpfully described the teaching of the
Gnostic sects who suggested a Primal Father in their myth about the creation
of the world. This Primal Father was also known as the divine silence and "the
source". This divine nature poured forth streams of divine energies (Emanations or Effluences).

117. These energies divided into masculine and feminine, and their syzygy
brought forth time and the elements in a cosmic void. These were the teachings
of Valentinians and his student Ptolemy. To quote Valentinus in his interpretation or rewriting of Genesis, he tells us, "All things I see suspended through
spirit; All things born along through spirit; flesh depending on soul, soul bound
to air, Air depending on ether" (pg. 116). This cosmology however strange is
not however unprecedented. Such views can be found in the pre-Socratic philosophers such as Empedocles. Pagels and apparently St. Irenaeus are to claim
that these are on the contrary somehow novel doctrine based on a false rendering of the original message given to the Church. It would seem that the original
message was not so original after all and is based on heretical Jewish practice
merging with Greek and Persian mystery cults. It is even more strange that
students of Valentinus like Heracleon wrote the first commentaries on the
Gospel of John, which was also championed by St. Irenaeus. The same way
Stoics used Zeus and Hera to represent metaphors for Natural Law, and Plato's
followers used Homeric tales to describe the transmigration of the soul, the
Gnostics used religious texts and reduced them to allegory and parable (pg.
117). St. Irenaeus complained that such mystics read widely on mysteries and
delved deep into aspects of religion that were hard to interpret and did not
acknowledge what was communicated directly and plainly. They ascribed allegory to Jesus turning over tables of the money changers for example to mean
that one should cleanse out one's heart and destroy idols.

118. Other strange instances can be had when the author of the Gospel of
Truth speaks of God as the Mother all of the sudden. The "Round Dance of the
Cross" refers to Jesus directly as the Logos or grace itself (pg. 124). Pagels
compares it to the Buddhist doctrine that those who realize suffering somehow

find release from it but the comparison is unwise because the Buddhist narrative nowhere suggests that to be an act of grace but only an act of self-realization, and besides Buddhists are atheists (pg. 125). Pagels use of the term "cosmic dance' is sweeter than diabetes. Finally in the Secret Gospel of John, Jesus declares, "I am the Father, I am the Mother, I am the Son". God appears as the "divine feminine" and Pagels suggests that this is suggested by "ruah" which is the Hebrew term for the soul and has a feminine character (pg. 126). In the Secret Book of John it explains "the primary ogdoad" which consists of the first emanations of divine energy (pg. 128). The various emanations or dimensions of divine energy are akin to the tree of sephiroth of the Kabbalistic texts.

119. The terminology of being "born again" has the primary features of being born through the woman's womb and rebirth by waters of baptism. The use of a second birth suggests again the ritual aspect of the use of the feminine form or mother archetype (pg. 130). Here we see references to the heavenly father and mother as in the Gospel of Philip as well as Paul's teaching that "flesh and blood shall not inherit the Kingdom of God" in 1 Corinthians 15:50. Paradoxically, however, physical traits are used to mean non-physical essence (pg. 132). For example, flesh is taken to mean the "divine word" and blood is taken to mean "the Holy Spirit", which is also defined as being filled by the "fullness of God". There was no one way to reach "apolutrosis" or "sacred or spiritual marriage" as claimed by Pagels (pg. 136).

120. Although these were teachings that competed among early circles in Rome and more Hellenized circles of Jews and the Catholic, other regions of the Church like Greek, Russian, Ethiopic, Serbian, and Coptic Christians differ widely on interpretation and practices and even on Holy days like Easter (pg. 134). It however, suggests that cultural differences did play a role in early Church and not just inter-religious debates and also suggest that these various churches and forms of Christians differed in their historical development as well. Although Pagels admits she cannot decide upon which message seems to represent Orthodox Christian thought, she feels at the beginning of chapter five that there is "something special" that occurs in the presence of a Buddhist monk or at a Bar-mitzvah or to her daughter as she performs in a Protestant choir to uplift her heart (pg. 143). While we are not surprised by her choices of what she describes as the most benign forms of religious worship, we have to seriously ask what the point is reducing centuries of theological, philosophical, and political disputes to this "do what thou wilt" democratizing and liberalizing view.

121. Still Pagels is insistent that Gnostics like Valentinus draw their inspiration from the same place as the orthodox thinkers and used books like Paul's letters, Genesis, and the Gospel of John. Ptolemy (a student of Valentinus) also held that God emanates "the Word" which emanates the still more material frame of the human body, but Irenaeus charged that Jesus was the Word incar-

nate (pg. 150). Irenaeus also charged that, unlike the belief of the Gnostics, Jesus was Lord and God on Earth as well as equal to God in heaven. The formula for God equals "The Word" equals Christ was put forth by him and others against the Gnostics on the one end and Arians on the other. Irenaeus also implants Jesus into the Old Testament where the words "Lord God" or "Word of God" or "Spirit of the Lord" appear. Irenaeus even claims that Mankind is made in the image of Jesus who created humanity and is the image of the lord as his physical representation of God in human form (in other words humanity was created by Jesus). He condemns Jews to hell for being disinherited by the Lord (pg. 153). He says that Jews worship God in vain but a close reading of Romans nine suggests otherwise. I wonder if St. Paul would agree with his statements about Jews when Paul claimed that salvation is for the Jew first but eventually also for the Gentile. Irenaeus compared followers of Valentinus with Jews for attempting to subvert religious doctrine.

122. Pagels is triggered by Tertullian's attacks on women. Pagels insists that those who held to a softer interpretation could not think that that God could harden Pharoah's heart and then crush him for it (pg. 159). This view shows almost no sophistication with the words of St. Paul in Romans that states that God makes one vessel for his grace and one vessel for his wrath. Paul's view of predestination presents another puzzle piece which unlocks the true meaning of the Christian message. Time is already set for Paul rendered by the fact of God's entrance into history.

123. In the Gospel of Matthew, Jesus refers to a Gentile woman as a dog (Matthew 15:26) but in the Gospel of John he preaches to a woman at Jacob's well in Samaria which signifies going beyond old traditions and cultural norms. Pagels compares the teaching of Heracleon (a student of Valentinus) of the experience of grace to the teachings of St. Augustine who evoked others to practice 'faith seeking understanding" (pg. 160-161) almost three hundred years later. St. Augustine himself, we must point out, was formerly a Manichean and blamed by the Pelagians for inventing the doctrine of original sin. He seems to have retained some of the influence of his previously held beliefs, just as St. Thomas retained some influence from the Aristotelian philosophers who he did battle with. Pagels says that the Secret Book of John sets forth the via negativa approach, which she posits as a way of recognizing what cannot be known about God (pg. 163). Most interestingly, via negativa is popularly derived from the theology of Maimonides who combined the views of Aristotelian thinkers into Medieval Jewish thought. Even today Maimonides is renowned for his interpretations of the Torah. Via negativa suggests that the only way to know anything about God is to say what God is not and arrive at an abstract vision through contemplation and the process of elimination, similar to how Aquinas settled these matters. Yet, Maimonides affirms many things about God in his almost deistic conception (such as that God is a simple substance, acts through necessity, and is immaterial).

124. Gnostic and mystical texts deal with a sort of spiritual psychology as well as divine hierarchy (pg. 164-166). It describes the woman as the Epinoia "creative spirit" of man brought out of him to unveil his heart and complete him. Noein means to perceive which can be seen as the guiding principle for "creative speech". Among these states of psycho-spiritual capacity in Man are pronoia or anticipatory awareness, ennoia or internal reflection, and prognosis or foreknowledge. All of these are then personified by female figures or presences which strikes us much akin to the Muses in Greek thought. It comes also with the belief that the God of Genesis is only an anthropomorphic "image of God" and not akin to the divine source which is unknowable. This image prevented Man from knowing the divine source, created the world to entrap mankind, and made woman subservient to men through the eating of the forbidden fruit which forever castrated him from the spiritual.

125. Irenaeus charged the Gnostic with inventing another God above the Father. By the time St. Eusebius wrote about the conversion of Constantine which supposedly occurred in 313 A.D, the Christians were able to recover Church property, and were even granted an adjustment of the imperial grain supply for church services to "supply people in need" (pg. 167-169). We must ask if Christians were now vassals of Rome like Jews in Judea (whom they criticized for fulfilling that role) or did Christianity finally conquer Rome whose decline would begin shortly as Christianity would spread to Europe? Either way does not square well with the Christian and Pauline tales of the future Kingdom of God, as pointed out by the Protestants for centuries that declared the alliance of the Church with Rome to be the beginning of its decline as a stalworth moral force keeping its hands free of power and awaiting the return of Christ. Pagels now refers to the "antisemitism" of Constantine (pg. 170), but we must ask, did not these views issue from mainstream Christian views and would they have been better among the heterodox who wholly rejected the Torah? Constantine refused to allow Jews to enter Jerusalem and said that a Jew attempting to stop the conversion of Christians from Judaism to Christianity should be burned alive.

126. In 325 A.D, Constantine convened the Council of Nicea where the four books known as the Gospels and Paul's letters were canonized (pg. 171). Athanasius who argued for the trinity argued against the followers of Arius, who preached that the word of God was not divine on a level equal to God. Constantine, who claimed to see "in hoc signa vinces" (in this sign we conquer) in a dream vision with a cross, drew up the holy symbol of the cross that would become associated with the Christian teaching to this day (pg. 172). After unification of the Church, Marcionites, Valentinians, Montanists, and Arius were stamped out but Constantine would soon turn against Athanasius as well proving himself to have accepted the Christian religion based on political maneuvering. Most notably, Constantine is not seen as taking sides in the de-

bate between Athanasius and Arius but took a number of measures to purge Christianity of its Jewish origins and align it with the religion of Rome. God was made synonymous with Emperor, and the people were made synonymous with the Holy Spirit. Constantine's later support of Athanasius' opponents the Arians ended with his death in 337 A.D (pg. 174). Pagels conclusion is that one can find truth in a number of ways if one goes beyond belief but this discounts self-deception and inflation of the ego in the mystical enterprise which arrives through the constant strain of false humility. No one can be sure if things would have been different if Gnostics had won these debates. Julian the Apostate most famously rejected Christianity in favor of Hellenistic Paganism and championed Gnosticism. His attempt to rebuild the Jewish temple to disprove the prophecy of the destruction of the temple of the Jews in the Gospel is quite interesting as the pendulum of power in Rome now shifted between Jews and Christians.

127. Athanasius is responsible for the statement that inspired one half of the title of this book when he states, "God had become human so that humankind may become divine". This view culminates in the humanism of Protagoras that states, "Man is the measure of all things" and transhumanism which suggests that Man must die while still alive in order to become reborn and become immortal (like a God). The view is both misanthropic and highly hopeful that it almost erases any notion that Man was first made in the image of God. A key step toward Man not conflating himself with God was here removed by both the Gnostic and Orthodox, which was born up in the notion of Man being the fundamental project of the divine. Human salvation was the most important feature of God's work.

128. So somehow Buddha and Greek legends have made it into the competing narratives around the early Church period that consolidated those mainline teachings like those of Paul and not main issues. One such issue is Paul's view of progressive revelation where the salvation of the Gentiles is brought about by the New Covenant which has come to the world through the Jews. The view that Man is made in the image of God and that he is born in Original Sin are in complete opposition but seem to be front and center within the description of what the Christian message seeks to represent but neither Ehrman, Price, or Pagels explores this. Paul's view of Original Sin seems to be completely original, but he is not seen as the progenitor of such a view curiously enough. Finally, the question of whether Paul was a Jew who followed the Old Testament and to what extent he considered his message a continuation of Judaism is not clearly discussed. Some of the Gospels seem increasingly anti-Jewish but Paul's letters promise salvation to the Gentiles through what is promised to Israel and has them grafted into a new message of salvation that is wholly his own creation. This true basis for Church teaching is not seen as the coinage of Paul as we have explored much of the work on Paul and others by many notable scholars. There are four possible views of salvation mentioned in

Paul: 1. Only those who are considered Jews are saved and a Christian is now part of Israel 2. Christians are in a separate class apart from Jews and Jews need to understand that all those who claim they are of Israel are not of Israel and become Christian 3. Jewish salvation also has now been made available to all those who are outside of Israel and both Jews and Gentiles are able to be saved in a world salvation 4. Only a remnant of Israel will be saved but not all of the Jews and it is up to Christians to bring those who are left outside of the message of salvation into the New Covenant. Furthermore, Paul's views on Sin culminate in a stark duality between flesh and spirit and past and future. In the spatial duality of flesh and spirit, one can readily see the progression of a detached and contemplative mood of science that focuses on the immaterial. In a temporal duality between past and future we have the past law and the future salvation through faith in the coming Kingdom of God which belies a message of evolution and progressive revelation. Here we have a built-in message of God changing through time, suffering along with humanity or feeling joy through humanity and being personally invested in human salvation, but also that salvation is of the Jews. The concatenation of these various themes is what has either been carefully obfuscated or strategically ignored by most scholars. Lastly, there is no real discussion on the Lost Books of the Bible and why they are left out.

Chapter 6
When in Rome...

129.The mythicist and realist position or Pagels view which uniquely combines the two, while presenting similar evidence are in fact in complete disagreement and going forward represent two views of atheistic interpretation of biblical literature, where the rumor view treats the story as borrowing from elements of truth to construct a fiction, while the mythicist view counts the Bible among the great literature of history and treats it as a useful fiction. Yet and still, in other places Christianity is an intersection between Eastern mysticism and Western philosophy. We must remember that around the time before the development of the canon of scripture used today, varying interpretations of sects now considered heretical were reinventing the Christian narrative. There were Marcionites who proclaimed to be followers of a new God, who said Paul was their teacher. Ebionites, who were Christian Monotheists, believed in one God, kept the Jewish law, and proclaimed Paul to be an archheretic. Some Gospel literature, like the letter of Barnabas reflects a considerably anti-Jewish tone, while certain other books like the Gospel of Matthew have a pro-Jewish tone. Both Price and Ehrman believe that Paul only wrote seven of thirteen letters that appear in the New Testament today. According to Price, Papias and other sources mention Marcionite influence in the early Church, as he was an early popularizer of Paul and a compiler of Pauline letters. Marcion also claimed like Paul, to be an apostle of God. Historians like Ehrman feel that Price is putting too much emphasis on smaller sects, while biblical scholars like F.C Bauer have pointed to similarities of Paul and Simon Magus. Certain tendencies among the Jews, and surrounding Paul, certainly point to him as a source of division in the early Church, both with his supposed confrontation with Peter, and with the acceptance of the Pauline view of Jesus only by certain groups of Christians. Paul's apostleship is about getting funding for the early Church, while Origen (who himself was proclaimed heretical) mentions groups like Valentinians and Ophites. Tertullian makes the claim that Marcion "discovered" some of the epistles of Paul. Ironically, today Tertullian's views would also be considered heretical. Another Scholar who presents a clash between the Pauline line of Christianity, and a more Jewish view of what transpired is Robert Eisenman who has written a considerable amount on the development of early Christianity surrounding the period of the Roman-Jewish war, including a lengthy work on James the Just.

130. Like other pro-Jewish scholars Eisenman claims that there was a serious conflict between Paul and the early Church[28], that is personified by James

---

[28] Lambert, D. (2019, April 26). *Robert H Eisenman | Paul The Liar & The Dead Sea Scrolls (James The Brother of Jesus)*. YouTube. Retrieved April 9, 2022, from

the Just, who was known as Zedek or Saadiq ("the righteous one"). In the Book of Acts James is seen as a leader of the early Church. In the view of Eisenman, a convergence of interest forms between the Zealot revolutionary political and militant style Judaism, and the mystical "out in the wilderness" focus on the purity of religious practice of the Essenes, led to the formation of the Christian sect. In the Bible the Essenes of John the Baptist style Christianity are challenged by a pro-Roman and pro-Pharisee style Judaism which are portrayed in the Gospels in the guise of the family of Herod. This latter view is represented by Paul, in the view of Eisenman. In the Book of Acts, Paul is rescued by Romans in a Temple when Jews try to force him out, but this is only one of Paul's great escapes (in another story he escaped out of the window in a basket) (Acts 21:31). Paul certainly has a knack for representing himself to those in power as someone who deserves a share of authority. Paul tells Roman soldiers to protect him because he is a Roman citizen, and he is allowed to preach. He is given armed escort by Roman soldiers.

131. This is similar to Josephus, who as a traitor to the Jews, like Herodias, took refuge in Rome in the house of Flavian during the Roman-Jewish war. In Romans 16:11 Paul pronounces Herod, the enemy of Christ and John the Baptist, as his "Kinsman". The word in the text is meant to refer to literal kinsman. In the narrative of the Gospels Jesus is most famously seen in his various conflicts with both Pharisees and the House of Herod. Jesus says beware of the yeast of the Pharisees and pronounces the Pharisees a den of vipers for murdering John his teacher and cousin by plotting with Herod. It may be important to realize that around this time Paul was murdering Christians at the appointment of the high priest. Paul has a famous conflict with James who was attacked in the temple by the Pharisees. The publisher of Josephus was Epaphroditus, who also funded the first Church of Paul in Ephesians. Paul reversed the ideological landscape of the Essene community as an attack on the doctrine of books like the Dead Sea Scrolls, according to Eisenman. Eisenman reports to us that the community of Qumran was the most anti-Roman and anti-Pharisee sect when the scrolls were taken to Masada. Eisenman tells us that the God mentioned in the Qumran scrolls is a lot like the God in the Quran and Old Testament, as a God that is without compromise. For centuries Jews and Muslims have claimed that the depiction of God in Christianity matches the worship of pagan idols, but Christians have recanted that the Jewish temple and Muslim Holy Shrine represent the same sort of idolatry. The Romans characteristically referred to the belief in the Monotheistic, unseen, and personal God as Atheism.

---

https://www.youtube.com/watch?v=eWFTGKBd6J8. On this episode of Mythvision podcast hosted by Derek Lambert they interview Robert Eisenman to discuss his views of why he finds many historical sources that suggest that Paul is a liar or false teacher.

132. Paul had to formulate a new covenant theology to persuade the Gentile masses. In an article entitled, "Paul as Herodian"[29], Eisenman discusses Paul's connections to those in power. His seeming love of sinners, touting forgiveness for all, shows his Gentile sensitivity, and low standards for dietary restrictions, including the portrayal of the Messiah as a wine bibber. James on the other hand kept the law, remained with the Jews, ate no meat, drank no alcohol, was married, and forbade divorce as Jesus had. James had a dispute with the temple authorities brought on by the fact that the high priest was controlled by Herod. The "seekers of smooth things" or House of Ephraim, represented the threat that would betray the Jews, and these were represented by people who first opposed Rome but then abandoned the struggle, and instead preached hostility towards the practice of circumcision of the Jews to join with Greeks. Paul even alludes to the vegetarianism of James being weak. Jews like Tiberius Alexander, Josephus, Bernice, and Agrippa II were all seen as pro-Roman and connected with the Herod family that was riddled by divorce and remarriage. These were seen to be in the inner circle of Titus Flavius, who led the destruction of the second temple. Tiberius Alexander was a Jew from the family of Philo, who was his grandfather. Tiberius ended up serving in a Roman battalion, and helped Flavius destroy the temple, fighting on the side of Rome. This paints a radically different picture than the classic narrative of Jews being oppressed by Romans. Make no mistake the Jewish struggle was real, but certain of the Jews took the easy road, as did the complainers in the days of Moses who had rejected the law to build an idol for themselves.

133. The problem with Eisenman is that he readily connects the Zealots to Jewish Nationalism of today. There were two types of Jews, the militant nationalists, and collaborators. Eisenman is a Zionist who connects the land to the Jewish people and says the Jews should be hard with the Arabs because Jewish nationalism has roots in history. We cannot honestly endorse the oppression of Israel of the Arab people, but Eisenman has no problem supporting it. Eisenman, however, correctly points out that no one calls anyone Lord or God in Jewish literature, but only in the Greco-Roman world, and has shown some of the divisions among early Jews that make the Christian message plausible in light of the Pauline diversion. The practice was certainly not common. Moreover, Eisenman agrees that Paul was a subverter.

134. Of course we find quite a simpler view in the powerfully inept reflections of Reza Aslan[30], heavily drawn from S.G.F Brandon. This is a popular tale of the Christ of Paul being some sort of social liberator. Aslan is a Muslim

[29] Eisenman, R. (1996). Paul as Herodian. *Journal of Higher Criticism*. https://depts.drew.edu/jhc/eisenman.html. This website and journal is apparently ran by famed Bible scholar Darrell Doughty

[30] Aslan, R. (2013). *Zealot: The Life and Times of Jesus of Nazareth*. Random House Publishing Group. We explore the various themes raised in the pop history book by Aslan in paragraphs 134-137.

who grew up in a secular style home and "found Jesus" at a religious camp. The experience was short lived besides sounding totally made up. He soon converted back to Islam leaving not a trace of his previous Christian beliefs. We find it odd that Reza saw the value of mentioning this, and we feel it was done because it certainly does not deter Christian readers to say you gave their faith an honest chance and were powerfully drawn into the Pauline message. We find a similar tactic being used by Bart Ehrman. Just because you were a former Christian or Muslim and now have come to recant your faith does not add credence to your views. Aslan states in the book that he did this because he felt at the time that Jesus was an "American". This repulsive sentiment makes us think of why anyone would make a drastic change in world-view simply to appease mass opinion. Indeed it sounds like the subversive acts which we are now taking care to point out, but we digress.

135. Aslan takes his sort of democratic ideal and forces it into the Gospel narrative. The result is a few clever sermons. We will take what he offers to fill in some of the historical context. It seems that at the time of Jesus, the Zealots like Simon bar Kochba and Simon Son of Giora proclaimed themselves Messiah, as there were many apocalyptic prophets. Like many others, Aslan uses Josephus to prove the existence of a historical Jesus, but this seems strange to us as Josephus was basically the Jewish spokesperson for the Roman empire. Also Josephus' writing came too late to prove anything, as Dr. Skrbina has shown. Luke's talk of a census being held in Rome cannot be verified, nor can the story of Herod's murder of firstborns. His claim that Jesus was a politically conscious Jewish revolutionary is nonsensical and reflects a democratic social-ist ideal of Jews as liberators. In Aslan's book Paul's words are treated as fact, even though they present to us nothing about the life of Jesus. He relays the myth that ancient books bearing names of writers represent a school of thought of that particular author instead of a forgery. This view was dismissed by Ehr-man in the book "forged", and also his book on Peter, Paul, and Mary Magda-lene. Forged works were certainly around in ancient times. A quite striking claim is made that is repeated by a number of scholars. The claim is that the Pauline style Christianity simply wanted independence and recognition, while the evil bloodthirsty Romans tried to murder them all. If many other Messianic movements arrived after Jesus was supposedly murdered by Rome, then how can we reconcile the fact that Jesus' own movement against Rome had failed even though it was one of the most successful historical examples of such a movement? This presents an internal contradiction in the view that Jesus was a Jewish revolutionary because many of these movements carried on well after he was gone so either Jesus was not an example of a revolutionary supposedly held in high treason against Rome or not significantly tied to these types of Messianic movements that required a militaristic style rule.

136. Nor was Rome as nonviolent as we think, nor Jews as peaceful and oppressed as we like to paint them. However, there is a popular notion that

always mentions that Flavius preserved the scrolls of the Torah upon the destruction of the Jews, because he felt that the true source of authority among
the Jews could only be found in the books that they protected, and it may have
played a role in their staunch resistance. Still, Reza would like to believe the
message of the Bible is about a "New World Order" or promises of democratic
socialism, where both women and Gentiles, poor and rich, would worship together. Jesus in the Bible was critical of his own Jewish leadership, hung out in
small towns away from the Romans, and did not compete for any earthly stations or power, so this is quite antithetical to this illustration of Jesus as a social
liberator, or Jewish revolutionary in the style of today. Aslan correctly points
out that the role of John the Baptist is obfuscated in later Gospels. Jesus goes
from being a follower of John, to John following him. As Christianity spread
to Rome, Antioch, Damascus, and Ephesus, it turned against the Jews. Aslan
just like other scholars provides no reasoning as to why this sudden change
happens, and why in all the places it ended up happening where Paul spread
his teachings to the Gentiles. It stretches credulity to think such a novel message caught on because of mass appeal but rather the ability to shapeshift into
various modes of religious practice.

137. Aslan's main arguments are already found in works by Hermann
Reimarus and S.G.F Brandon. Perhaps the theory that finds Rome most
blameworthy is a theory now gaining popularity among a small group, which
is often labeled the Roman Providence Thesis of Christian origin. This set of
views sets out to illustrate that Christianity was manufactured by Rome, and
that Christianity itself was an experiment for mass subversion. The Roman
Providence thesis was popularized by Joe Atwill. He claims that Christianity
was invented out of whole cloth by the Romans during the Roman Jewish War
and finds parallels to the war in the story of the Gospel[31]. According to Atwill
the Bible was written in Greek in a Pro-Roman perspective in order to suit
those in power. What Atwill fails to mention is how the same Christianity
could have been used against Rome by pretty much signaling its collapse and
developing an anti-authoritarian attitude among Christians to match the oppositional attitudes of some of the Jews that lived in the Roman run province of
Judea. Instead, we see Josephus tells us a tale of the coming of the Jewish
Messiah, which he apparently believed was none other than Titus Flavius.
While we may not agree with Atwill's major premise, we at least like that
someone is asking the question of why Christianity was manufactured, if the
claim is that it was totally made up. If it was made up or based on a rumor then
what impetus was there to spread such a colossal lie? Indeed, many within
Bible scholarship with their peer reviewed journals, and those from religious

---

[31] Heade, F. (Director). (2012). *Ceasar's Messiah* [Film]. Nlightning workZ.
https://www.youtube.com/watch?v=zmEScIUcvz0. This documentary on the book
Ceasar's Messiah by Joe Atwill features a summary of his arguments presented by
Joe Atwill himself. We explore some of Atwill's main points in paragraphs 137-142

institutions do not find it useful to even begin to pose the question.

138. This view also holds that the view of the Dead Sea Scrolls is antithetical to that of the Gospels similar to what Eisenman and Price claim. Christianity had to have been manufactured by a group who had decided to use a tactic other than direct military force and came to rely on a method of religious and political subversion. Up to this point at least we may have some nominal form of agreement because the focus is on assigning motive. For Atwill however, the story begins in the Julio-Claudian dynasty. In this era Rome was transformed from a Republic to an Empire.

139. During the reign of Caesar, Augustus, Tiberius, Caligula, and finally, Nero in 54 CE, Roman Emperors enjoyed a godlike status. Judea was revolting against Rome until the rule of Herod, which cancelled out the rule of the Maccabees and Hasmonean Dynasty, and when Jews complained of graven images in the temple, the Romans took note that power and authority for the Jews rested on their holy books. Jews knew that you could defeat Rome with the power of God, and Rome knew that in order to subdue the Jewish rule one would have to summon such a power in order to make Jews feel the wrath of God had been visited on them and that divine justice had been reached. What Jewish belief required as confirmation of their beliefs was a massive show of force and one of almost Biblical proportions so to speak. Vespasian who had just fought the Druids and Gauls in Europe now arrived to defend Rome in Judea and was now focused on the Jewish revolt. He captured Josephus as a slave in one of his campaigns, and Josephus, being the sycophant and traitor that he is, earned the title of Flavius Josephus, becoming so attached to the family of Flavius and Vespasian and most notably becoming a traitor to his own people and working against his people. Granted all this it is surprising that many people take the writing of Josephus seriously. It is not a stretch to think that Josephus was used by those in power. But that this proves that the Bible was invented by the Romans is clearly a stretch.

140. It is, however, not a stretch to believe that as the Roman Jewish War progressed, that some of the messianic literature of the Jews was destroyed, but other of their books were seized for interpretation and development of scholarly, religious, and historical relevance by the Romans. This could help us fill in the blanks of why Paul was from a wealthy and educated class of Jews, and how he formed connections with those in power in order to propagate his message. The trick, according to Atwill, was for the Romans to understand that destroying or wiping out the Jewish religion was not an option, because you cannot simply destroy a belief, but to create a more benign form with a less militant outlook, as Jewish sects were many at the time, seemed like a convenient solution. Atwill says very little about Paul. There is, of course, a third option between Jews manufacturing a plot against Gentiles to convert them to peace loving Christians and Romans inventing Christianity to

subvert the Jews: That an elite group of Jews created a fifth column within the Roman elite which Cicero eluded to. Josephus claims that Titus Flavius gave him copies of Jewish scripture. Josephus purports to have fulfilled biblical prophecies by identifying the movements of Vespasian with the birth of the Jewish Messiah. The Roman imperial cult of "emperor-god" rises at the same time. Titus Flavius became the son of his father, and therefore became the "son of god". The matter of who became deity was even voted on in the Roman Senate. The granddaughter of Herod, Bernice, became the mistress of Titus Flavius. Some Jews of Alexandria, as already discussed, were tight with circles of Roman power. Cicero points to this fact. Certain Jews were willing to sell out their own people for an advance of Roman power and wealth. Yet Atwill says very little about the Jews. He and these other scholars put all the blame on Rome.

141. Flavians were the heroes of Rome and even built the amphitheater. The Gospels were backdated to fit the Julio-Claudian period Atwill claims, and worshipping Christ is worshipping Caesar in disguise. A Jew today who praises Roman power is a Flavian slave. It is an odd fact pointed out by Nietzsche and others that Christianity seems to support the status quo, and tends to defend those already in power. This is the classic notion of "slave morality", which we find no reason to develop here, but save for our discussions on philosophy. Notably King David was also called Christ or "anointed one", and "evangelion" means not just good news, but news of good victory. According to Atwill, the Romans borrowed from Astro-theology, and the philosophy of the Stoics, and tales of Elijah and Isaiah taken by the Old Testament via Josephus, to construct a new religion. This sect would be friendlier to pagan belief systems, just as the belief in Jupiter was used in one instance to defend Christianity by Justin Martyr.

142. Recently, both Eisenman and Price have endorsed variations of the theory. Other mythicists with an atheistic tendency, like Richard Carrier, argue that while Christianity is made to divert Jewish hostility, it is unlikely that it was done by the Romans themselves, but probably instead by Roman friendly Jews like Paul. But Carrier never blames Paul, instead psychologizing his views as schizophrenic hallucination. It is interesting that Atwill does not really mention Paul that much, who is the second most important figure in Christianity other than Jesus himself. Mainstream Bible historians like Ehrman have squarely rejected the thesis, saying that sophomores in college could dismantle the thesis. This seems like a variety of options and opinions. While it is the only theory discussed so far that addresses the question of motive, it presents a paradoxical view of history. To the extent that the Jewish uprising reached into the inner circles of Rome, can we say that it was truly suppressed? Many like Nietzsche claim that Christianity helped destroy Rome by weakening it on the inside. Could Romans have failed so miserably to form a dastardly plot that would blow up in their own faces in an almost cartoonish manner? We have

the odd fact of the pairing of the rise of Christianity and the decline of Rome after the conversion of Emperor Constantine. Did Rome conquer Jews through Christianity, or did Jews conquer Rome by Christianity? As one begins to analyze the facts, the latter seems much more plausible. The Fall of Rome, the rise of the Church, and continued survival of the Jews, shows that it was Rome who perished instead of Christians and Jews in the end. Was Rome so blind-sighted and culturally inept as to not recognize the political threat of the views of the Gospels which were antithetical to power? Were the general public who couldn't read aware of typology of hidden texts or what was even meant by them? Flavius must be rolling over in his grave if that is the case. We are still glad that Atwill had the range to challenge the mainstream view and assess some kind of motive, but it says not much about the role of Paul, which is the subject of our current inquiry. We anticipate the role of scholarship moving towards the Roman Providence Thesis versus our own Antagonism Thesis, while Rumor and Mythicist views should be readily discarded for failing to mention why anyone would invent such a tale which ended up as a determining factor for world events unlike other social movements and mythical representations which are squarely left in the past. The last view concerning the various competing views of what Christ represents draws on the range of Ancient Astrology and Mythical symbols that were much older than Christianity and is more akin to the Mythicist views than a historical viewpoint.

Chapter 7
We saw his star, and came to worship him...

143. A line of theories that deal with the birth of Christ as an astrological event of significance connecting it to zodiac cycles and dating of old events will be collectively referred to as Astrotheology by us. A theory that makes practical use of astrological and astronomical dating of world events in relation to Biblical stories is the "New Chronology" of Russian Mathematician Anatoly Fomenko. His general thesis alleges that it is not only true that certain historical documents are fabricated to match old timelines but whole timelines are fabricated. This includes the invention of nations and peoples, the addition of centuries of events, and stories usually taken from other timelines. This is similar to what is described by Orwell in "1984", when he writes of a "Ministry of Truth" employed by those in power used to edit history to reach a more favorable conclusion for the victors. Reworking historical narratives is a process of creating and fabricating a history that justifies our present status, but also creates a false hope by predictive programming of what is to come. Our expectations match our experiences of the past. History is colored by methodology, ideology, anthropology, cultural bias, and approached by both the dogmatic and superstitious, with as much prowess and energy as those seekers of truth who are willing to critically analyze all views in hopes of attaining a closeness to God and Truth, instead of settling for the shallow goal of reaching a personal salvation, attaining to scholarly heights, or obtaining mass sums of wealth.

144. Fomenko argues that the currently adopted paradigm of historical dating was established by Joseph Scaliger, who applied an outdated astrological map to old timelines. He collected copies of copies of historical material. He wrote histories of Persians, Jews, Egyptians, and Romans. Scaliger does not appear to have been well regarded in his own time, was known for bad memory, and attempted to use analysis of history to prove he was heir to a royal fortune. Fomenko suggests such haphazard methods have created a variety of material drawn from historical timelines, where the same events in history are given different dates by translators and seen as separate events. This has created phantom copies of historical events, where archeological dating and carbon dating is fed back into the system of phantom dates. Most of these "historical documents" were compiled by Humanists, scientists, and clergy members, around the time of the Renaissance and Enlightenment. Through advanced studies in topological and astrological data sequences, Fomenko reconstructs the historical timeline to theorize that over a thousand years were mysteriously added into the historical timeline during the period known as the "Dark Ages".

145. If you're looking for more persuasion than that, then I guess we can refer you to the New Chronology, which is volumes long. Good luck reading through it. We have not the time or the space (or even the expertise) to consider such monumental claims. The theory has not caught on but is gaining a little steam. Isaac Newton in his "The Chronology of Ancient Kingdoms" had set out on a similar quest. Newton found the work was more important than his work on physics and included a theoretical model of the Temple of Solomon. Newton's attempt apparently contradicted the accepted dating of Ancient Greece and Ancient Egypt by several centuries. Later critics, like Jean Hardouin, had claimed that many historical documents had false dates. There are certain claims that works that are supposedly written by Greeks and Romans were forged by Benedictine Monks. He said that the New Testament was originally written in Latin by finding contradictions in earlier texts. His later follower Edwin Johnson had said the character of Paul was invented in the 1500's, and so were the antiquities of early church fathers. He offered a radical criticism of Christian historiography. Hermann Detering and Arthur Drews provided similar suggestions. In fact, over seven hundred scholars have made claims that certain historical periods appear to be fabricated. Take for example the visit of Marco Polo to China. The account was taken as a fact by Christopher Columbus but contained many false facts about Chinese culture and geography. Modern scholars suspect that Marco Polo never even took a visit to China. Columbus thought he was in India and reported as much. Columbus had set off for the discovery of the tip of the pear-shaped world that would lead him to heaven, or at least the "New Jerusalem". Both historians and historical figures made up false claims about history. There is evidence of histories being forged and historical hoaxes.

146. John V Armagnac who married his own sister, forged a papal bull. The Monks of Crowland Abbey fabricated their own history. There is the infamous case of the Donation of Constantine that justified the rule of the Catholic Church but ended up being a hoax. Historical hoaxes are a possibility. Perhaps a more shocking illustration is the city of Pompeii, supposedly destroyed in 79 AD by the eruption of Mt. Vesuvius, and rediscovered in 1748, where it was identified by an old inscription. From 79-1748 Pompeii supposedly was "lost to history". However, in many curious cases it shows up on old world maps depicting the Bay of Naples where the city was originally built. It is even mentioned in a 1631 memorial. Pompeii was bombed by allied forces in 1943 in "operation avalanche" for fear of it being used for Nazi weapon storage facilities. The city was leveled and destroyed, which resulted in the destruction of many historical sights. The British and Americans then funded a project to refurbish old monuments to recreate the supposed historical accuracy of the original sight, however this was simply just a modern rendition of the closest view of what it most likely may have looked like. It is indeed nothing more

than a historical theme park, like most so called historical sights of today[32].

147. Since the theory ignores written sources, and relies on matching old timelines with astrological dating, there is no reason to assume this version of history is better than the good faith of historical revisionism, when it relies on mainly the same material presented in varied contexts. In addition to this, mathematical models usually allow for more than one set of explanations. Fomenko's radical view of New Testament events occurring in Russia in the 1100's is based on the same historical tales passed down to us. Fomenko further makes the claim that Carbon dating is unreliable, as others have claimed, showing different dates on the same piece of material measured at different times. In other words, there is no methodology of gathering historical facts that is beyond controversy and criticism. Were these stories fabricated or given wrong dates? If the narrative is false, it leaves much to be desired of whether or not it can even be found out to be falsified from another event in history. There is also the strange fact that Fomenko worked for the Russian government and claims that Jerusalem was located in Russia. Russian historiography goes back to the time of Turkic and Proto-Slavic people, and Russian culture before the industrialized Czar was closed off and xenophobic. This means their history would have to be fabricated apart from the European history, which seems improbable. Historical documents are not like articles of today and were not copied over and over with exceptions in certain cases. Ancient historians worked relatively independently and made only single copies of their work.

148. A similar view is found in the Heinsohnian Hypothesis put forward by Gunnar Heinsohn. The view is represented here by the white nationalists. It states that the first millennium C.E is an arbitrary construct, considered too long because of 700 phantom years from an accumulation of errors that mistake geographical movement for phantom timelines. Sixteenth to seventeenth century scholars such as the aforementioned Joseph Scaliger but also Denys Petau created the modern timelines mainly by the supposed dating of certain historical works. Three main periods have been traditionally assumed for the first millennium C.E: Imperial Antiquity (1-230 C.E), Late Antiquity (300-640 C.E), Early Middle Ages (700-930 C.E). For Imperial Antiquity the bulk of evidence comes from the Roman Southwest, for Late Antiquity the focus is on the Byzantine, and for the early Middle Ages the focus is on Europe. Hence, a geographical sequence was turned into a chronological or historical sequence.

---

[32] *HISTORYGATE: FOMENKO, NEWTON, and COUNTERFEIT POMPEII.* (2019, May 3). YouTube. Retrieved April 9, 2022, from https://www.youtube.com/watch?v=Sdw9s-_mY20. This quite brilliant program from the show "Observation Deck" is heavily sourced in paragraphs 143-147. Many of the historical hoaxes including a link to Newton's New Chronology, which is available for free in the public domain is there via project Gutenberg.

149. We cite for example an article on Unz review entitled "Revision in Islamic Chronology and Geography" by someone named "First Millennium Revisionist"[33]. He argues that the contemporaneity of Imperial Antiquity with the Early Middle Ages period due to the historical misappropriation of scholars takes no account of the peoples of Eurasia that were proto-European tribes like the Saxons who could not have so late emerged from their forest and cave dwelling state to stand up to the Roman empire in Imperial Antiquity. It is clear from the tone and presentation of terms like "Germanic-Slavic" that the author would like to assume some unified origin for the white race in the distant past. The author cites Walter Baur who proposed that "contrary to the story propagated by the victorious Church, orthodoxy was preceded not followed by giant heresies". This would mean that even in the very invention of the Church it had to fabricate its history and continued doing so. The author also cites Joe Atwil and Francesco Carotta for stating that Christianity is a perversion of the cult of Caesar. Therefore, he presents a world view tailored together from the various sources we have so far presented. The author's use of morphology and anachronisms and terms such as Al-Gabal (God of the Mountain) of the priests of Elagabal being substituted for Allah, because one of the legends contains mentions of a black stone that is being worshipped is akin to arguments put forward by some mythicists and Astro-theologists which conflate certain terms and etymological sequences. Here the author states that Muslims worship the Black Stone which is not technically true. The stone and the Kaaba are objects that were used for Pagan worship in pre-existing centuries that were admittedly re-appropriated by Muslims. Yet the story of Islam does not seem to hide this detail, so the authors point has not been made well to say the least.

150. According to Heinsohnian chronology the rise of the Church in the first three centuries and the growth of Islam from the seventh to the tenth century are contemporaneous events. But how exactly does making Christianity and Islam rising in the same period provide obstacles for Islamic theology? Why would, in addition to that, Arab historians correspond with timelines of the Europeans when they have no shared history of written records? There is also the important fact that the Islamic calendar starts after the Prophet and his companions made the migration from Mecca to Medina so the Islamic dates use A.H or "after Hijra" to signify the start of the calendar which started independent of the Western calendar. The author here moves to suggest that the conflation of time periods and their taking for a geographical sequence and

---

[33] First Millennium Revisionist. (2021, October 1). Revision in Islamic Chronology and Geography. *Unz Review*. https://www.unz.com/article/revision-in-islamic-chronology-and-geography/. We source this article and analyze some of its key arguments in paragraphs 148-155. What is the point you may ask? It is sticking with our current theme of historical hoaxes and the bad contributions of well-known scholars whose views are taken quite seriously abroad and have made several unprovable claims about history and religion.

applying it to a historical or chronological one seems to implicate another group with the rise of Islam: The Nabateans.

151. The Nabateans dominated long distance trade from their capital city Petra, and controlled caravan routes that linked China, India, Arabia, Egypt, Syria, Greece, and Rome. Hadrian visited Petra around 130 A.D. Petra reached its development in the late second and third centuries. In contrast, the eighth century Arabs had just learned the coin making skill that the Nabateans possessed in the second century. The author also claims that Muslim coins that appear later have Jewish and Roman markings, but this suggests nothing other than that they were possibly found and appropriated by later Arabs who then would not have a need to make new coins being merchants and tradesman themselves. The same can be said about the Umayyad architecture that was simply built on top of the existing structure and hence copied some of the techniques of earlier methods. This does not constitute a relearning of the previous techniques and methods but only a reappropriation. Another tribe of Christian Arabs that for the author seems to be synonymous with the rise of early Islam as suggested by Heinsohn is the Ghassanid, who were known by Diodoris Siculus as Gassandoi, 'Casani" by Pliny the Elder, and Kassanitai by Claudius Ptolemy.

152. Here, however, the author claims that the Ghassanid were, "Christian allies of the Byzantine", and that they had, "the same reputation for anti-trinitarian monotheism as the Abbasid Caliphate". This does not square well with the history of Christian Arabs in general as we shall later see. Suffice it to say, not only did Christian Arabs have their own historical development apart from the Pagan tribes who came to accept Islam, there was a considerable amount of writing that exists from Christian Arabs about the Muslim Arabs who they seemingly colluded with militarily against the Byzantine Greeks who they never accepted as rulers. The quite meticulous and complex separation of tribes among the Arabs seem to be another roadblock for this view. From the Umayyad to the Abbasid the focus of Islamic activities shifted from Damascus in Syria to Baghdad in Iraq. Islam is made to seem "Jewish" because of the shared lineage of Jews and Arabs, as Abraham is mentioned one hundred and thirty-five times in the Quran. This however does not square well with the fact that Islam mentions Abraham as a proof against the Jews as do the letters of Paul, both of which state that since Abraham had not received the Torah which was received by Moses he could not be technically considered a Jew or held accountable to the law of the Torah. Islam and the Bible also mention that Abraham himself was from Babylon and gave birth to two Nations. These two nations, today known as the Semitic Jews and Semitic Arabs are known as Semites for being the children of Shem who was the son of Noah mentioned in the Bible.

153. The author haphazardly refers to believers in Christ who remained faithful to laws of the Torah as Jewish-Christians, but such a term is chimeri-

cal. We know that Christians such as Arians existed in the first three centuries, and were probably not accepted by other Jews, whose religion has itself evolved through the ages through various sects and reforms. The author makes the almost ludicrous supposition drawn from a book by Patricia Crone and Michael Cook entitled, "Hagarism: The Making of the Islamic World" which claims Islam was created by Jewish exiles to recapture Jerusalem. This makes no sense simply due to the histories of the Muslims which show them fighting a bloody battle with the Jews of Yathrib (Medina) and also the many verses in the Quran that state that Christianity and Judaism are false religions born from the altering of God's original message that was sent to every Nation.

154. The author states that, "The Quran emerged in a region linguistically Syro-Aramaic rather than Arabic", but his point is spurious mainly due to the fact that, as we shall learn later, Syriac and Aramaic are themselves proto-Arabian languages and the alphabet was supposedly even brought to Arabia from the Nabateans in the fourth century. As the author has pointed out, the geographical revisionism of moving of Mecca to the Nabatean capital city of Petra is seen in the works of Dan Gibson who has attempted to subject Islamic historiography to the same methodology that Mythicists commonly employ on Christianity. His claim is that when Abbasids supplanted the Umayyad rule they merged the historiography of Petra and Mecca. The city of Petra contains more Jews. Such authors attempt to connect Christianity and Islam with so called Jewish roots. The prospect of Jews creating their own mortal foe which they genocide today, claims their Messiah is the anti-Christ, critically harms the notion of western progress and the existence of Israel as a western friendly state, and fought Jews in the Prophet Muhammad's own time, is quite unlikely.

155. Apparently, the Nabateans had been allies of the Maccabees, however as admitted by the author, Petra itself became a Hellenized Roman city. Other facts have been questioned by historians like the Temple Mount having the standard dimensions of a Roman Fort, and was labeled incorrectly as the Jewish Temple by Crusaders. The author states that the Umayyads kept the name Aelia Capotolina that Hadrian had given the city, calling it "illiya". We must note that this is also close to the Hebrew name Aliya which means ascension or return to the Holy Land. It is suggested by historians and the history of Muslims that Nabateans sent Christian knights to the Battle of Yarmuk to fight Romans. This is seen in response to a Roman attempt at conquest of the Christian Arabs in earlier centuries. The Bible mentions Arab tribes like Moabites, Edomites, Midianites, Amalekites, and Ishmaelites. All were descendants of Abraham. Arabs and Jews are ethnically homogenous as a result. In Exodus 2-3 the Hebrew conquest of Canaan originates from Midian and Moses was a son in law of a Midianite priest. The area of Midian corresponds to the native home of the Nabateans. Quite paradoxically, Arians and other Christian groups who vary in beliefs also occupy the same denomination as other Gnostics like Docetists, while they reject Paulinism and the Trinity. The Sabeans mentioned

in the Quran as the "People of the Book" along with Christians and Jews have writings in Aramaic and are also referred to as Gnostics but reject Paulinism. Their religion seemingly derives from Christian views and Zoroastrian views that are much more Ancient. Islamic thinkers did not accept that the Catholic Church was the foremost representative of the Christian faith and their being in close proximity to Christian Arabs is all that can really be confirmed.

156. Anybody who has come across theosophical or New Age belief systems will encounter the Jungian/Bastian belief system that is supported by the more mainstream proponents like Joseph Cambell, but there is also the more extreme views of Astro-theology and theosophical literature supported by those like Joseph Maxwell.[34] Plainly speaking, this view derives from a hodgepodge of ancient astrology of zodiac cults, pagan mysticism, and occult theology that promulgates a bogus metaphysics, and Gnostic as well as pan-syncretistic views and practices, that allege that religion developed downstream of Ancient historical myths and archetypal motifs. Yet instead of saying it is a Homeric style tale, they claim that all stories, including the story of Jesus are represented by one great story repeated throughout time. This group claims that Judaism and Christianity were born in Egypt, and modeled after the Egyptian cult of the Gods, and the Egyptian priestly class. Yet and still, there is another group of theosophical leaning, which claims that these views and customs and traditions originate in India. All in all, some believe that a singular worldwide civilization, derived from the popular Atlantis myth taken from Plato, ruled the planet and gave us the collective series of sacred symbols which comprise the various belief systems throughout the world, as well as the modern advancements of civilization, agriculture, and technological progress.

157. In Egypt the lunar and cosmic cycles brought the monsoon rains which flooded the Nile delta, bringing forth a period of chaos, but ultimately a gushing forth of life and abundance. This is seen to represent baptism and rebirth, as signified by the water of life in the mother's womb. This moon or nature of female energy was balanced by creative male ingenuity represented by the Sun God, who was named Amen Ra. In an Ancient Egyptian proverb it states, "if your light be single, then there is light in you", and this is seen to represent the inner light of Reason. This is the eye on the pyramid, or the missing capstone known as the eye on the back of the dollar. This is also known as the eye of Horus. It is next to an Eagle with outstretched wings that was used in Egypt to represent the Goddess Isis. The Pharaoh was often seen as the incarnation of God, just as the Roman emperor was. He was depicted with both a rod and a staff. This represented a dual nature. One aspect was the rod used for

---

[34] Maxwell, J. (Director). (2008). *The Naked Truth* [Film]. https://www.youtube.com/watch?v=ZRGEts3PxDA. This documentary is cited throughout paragraphs 156-160. There is an interesting refutation of the main points raised in the documentary made by a gentleman named Benjamin Stanhope that can be viewed here: https://www.youtube.com/watch?v=sNQXK1My_5o.

protection. The other was a staff that was used to lead. Just as Jesus had the adversary of Satan, Horus had the adversary of Set. This was a classic tale of light versus darkness, most popularly depicted in the Lion King, as Walt Disney was a freemason. Horus was from the house of bread or "Bethlehem". Horus was depicted on a boat and carried a cross like object. The theme of water, blood, and spirit is constantly repeated, with wine representing blood or carnal nature, in juxtaposition with the theme of eternal life and rebirth of water. The twelve disciples, or twelve tribes of Israel, are exchanged for the twelve houses of the Zodiac. In the story of Buddha and Krishna, there are spiritual medians and holy spirits. Their births were noted by the wisemen of the times. Krishna, who was a shepherd, was born in a village, and ascended to heaven after his death, and is said to return at the end of days on a white horse. Similarities also exist between Jesus and the Babylonian god Tammuz, or in the Persian Mithra. In Job 38:33 it reads, "knowest thou the ordinances of Heaven", and implores man to set up God's domain.

158. That ties in to another key part of this belief system. This would be a reversal of the meaning of the coming judgement on man, quite paradoxically changed into a coming of a "New Age" of fantastic abundance and scientific advancement. It often fits within the framework of the coming of the Kingdom of God or Kingdom of Heaven as an earthly rule or kingdom. This is the view that the fish in the Gospel narrative represent the age of Pisces or rule of the Church. The age of Aquarius is represented by the coming of the water bearer, symbolized by Christ who walked on water. The end of the age scenario is recounted in Luke 22:10, Matthew 28:20 ("I am with you until the end of the age"), Mark 10:29-30 ("in the age to come eternal life"), and Luke 18:30 ("Kingdom of God"). The Son of God died on the cross, that is the sun dies on the cross of the zodiac for the winter solstice. Before he dies, he dons a crown of thorns, represented by the rays of light. As the sun enters a new house of the zodiac it enters on the 30th degree and ends up in the 33rd degree. This is why the sphinx head begins with a human and ends with a lion. The start is the reason, and the end is passion. It depicts a completion of the celestial sphere that repeats in cycles. The cycle described thus constitutes one full cycle of rebirth.

159. The Great Mother or Goddess motif is employed a lot by those in the astrotheological business. This seems like a win-win situation since it helps them oppose the patriarchy and provincialism of the Old Testament religion, which seems fashionable. Isis is used most frequently, as seen in Helena Blavatsky's book Isis Unveiled, which is a virtual Bible of astrotheology. It is highly endorsed by Joseph Maxwell, whose views are shared here above. Most of the views of Jordan Maxwell that are supposedly well-known ancient beliefs cannot be found anywhere other than in the work of Madame Blavatsky or the works of occultist Gerald Massey. Isis is seen as the Prkrti of Hinduism, or the divine receptacle. This is a pagan twist which treats nature as divine, but only insofar as it is the receptacle of divine reason. The worship of Ra or the

sun, and the worship of El or Saturn, was brought through Isis (Is-Ra-El). According to Maxwell the temple of Solomon was the temple of the sun or "Sol". When the Israelites prayed to a golden bull they worshipped the Taurus, which is followed by Aries the Goat, which symbolizes an exchange of war symbolized by a bull for sacrifice and prayer represented by a goat. This is also accounted for by the change of symbols from the bull head to the ramshorn. This is followed by Pisces, which represents a period of grace and atonement of life in the Kingdom, which is followed by a redemption and abundance signified by Aquarius. Symbols like the Passover lamb, and other symbols, were skillfully employed to maintain the old structure of symbolic significance.

160. As one could surmise the symbolism of devouring the flesh and blood of God to gain eternal life was seen as impregnated with allegorical inventiveness. The bread-like substance called Mana brought down by God covered in dew, used as a provision for the Hebrew travelers made reference to in the Bible is purported to be symbolic of a sacred initiation, where certain psychoactive mushrooms (that characteristically rise up overnight covered in dew) were used. This points to pagan rituals, where mushrooms were consumed by a priest and then the priest's urine was drunk by the initiates. The view was first brought forward by John Marco Allegro in his "Sacred Mushroom and The Cross" and may also be related to the work of Gordon Wasson who was connected to the C.I.A. Almost no one has taken the work seriously, even though Allegro did notable research on the Dead Sea Scrolls. His view of Christianity as a fertility cult, which practiced sacred marriage rites through rituals involving the consumption of psychoactive drugs is highly dubious. The claim is often made that because this symbol or tradition vaguely resembles another, then they must have come from the same source. This is a favorite among psychonauts and drug enthusiasts and promoted in works by other notable "New Age" thinkers like Andrija Puharich, Timothy Leary, and others.

161. In Joseph Campbell's book "The Inner Reaches of Outer Space"[35] he espouses similar views, connecting the themes of ancient mythological tales after denigrating the view of the Bible. Campbell does not just reduce religion to myth, but also reduces the views of popular science to a similar status. He views the tales of the Bible as tribal and warlike and suggests that the Jewish God was a God of War, depicted as a male despot. The old gods he claimed were like Indra, Zeus, or Ares that ruled by strength. He believes the Judeo-Christian (and by extension Islamic, however it is interesting that Islam is not mentioned along with this strange Judeo-Christian synthesis employed by Jungian types) worldview has been tragically exchanged for the Goddess worship of past ages.

---

[35] Campbell, J. (2012). *The Inner Reaches of Outer Space: Metaphor as Myth and as Religion.* New World Library. From paragraph 161-166 we continuously make references to the print version of this book.

162. There is the strange fact of the ancient pantheons of gods all representing astronomical figures. The figures represent similar numerological sequences, which do not appear to be a coincidence. For example, there are 540 doors in Woden's hall, where 800 warriors pass through. This gives us a figure of 432,000, which appears again and again in ancient myths. 432,000 is said in Hinduism to be the span of the Kali Yuga, which is part of another 4-billion-year cycle. Scientists today estimate that the universe must be about 4 billion years old. The Puranas and Nordic myth contain similar measurements, but so do Asian and Mayan figures. In these myths, Zoroastrian, and Babylonian myths, there is described a great flood, known by almost all the nations of the world in their ancient mythical tales. The Mayans, and even the Dogon tribes of Africa, as well as the Ancient Egyptians seemed to know precise astrological configurations, including the procession of the equinox, which would take quite a feat of precise math to measure even close to a precise date. The Ancient cultures of the world seemed to have been aware, not only that the Earth was orbiting the sun, but that a cycle of 230-million-year rotation signified the completion of the rotation of the sun around the center of the Milky Way Galaxy. This was represented by the sun's passage through the twelve houses of the zodiac and by the blackhole at the center of the Milky Way galaxy that was shown in Mayan cosmology.

163. How, at the beginning of so-called recorded history humans had knowledge of such huge cosmic patterns boggles the mind. The Giza Plateau for example could be taken as a giant astronomical clock, with the Sphinx pointing to a constellation in the sky which lets us know of the location of the sun in space. The first city of Babylon, Kish, had a span of 432,000 years, where ten kings reigned in the Antediluvian times (legends derived from the era before the flood). In the Bible, 1,656 years occur before the flood, equaling a period of 86,400 weeks which is divisible by 43,200. In Gematria, which is a system of numerology used for Kabbalism, the number four, three, and two add up to nine. For example, the degrees of a circle, a square, and a triangle all add up to 9. The number nine, for Campbell, has divine significance, and represents the Goddess, whose number is eighteen (1+8=9). A healthy human heart at rest apparently beats 86,400 beats per day. Dividing the platonic year 25,920 (although alternative measurements have been given) by 60, seems to give us a quotient of 432.

164. Indeed one sees these references in many places, but also the ideas are so abstract that they seem to have import almost anywhere. For example, in the Book of Revelation, a number is mentioned that suggests to us that at the end of the world 144,000 people will play some sort of a pivotal role. The book contains other instances of numerological sequences like the number 666, which adds up to 18. The number 144,000 is related to sacred geometry derived by the Platonic/Pythagorean forms. The number is one third of the number 432,000 mentioned in the Nordic, Sumerian, and Indian myths. Zoroastri-

anism, which is the source of the Magi of ancient times, became the religion of King Darius in 521 BC, and also contained a description of the great flood. Indeed, even the Philosopher Xenophanes, who was the teacher of Parmenides, mentions the great flood. In the religion of Zoroastrianism, Gayomard, the first man, was corrupted by an evil deity Angra Mainyu, and Zarathustra, a noble prophet, comes to affirm the restoration of Ahura Mazda, the God of light, against the reign of darkness propagated through Angra Mainyu. The reincarnation of Zarathustra, Saoshyant, and the incarnation of evil, Arihman, are to engage in a final battle. In the battle good will finally triumph over evil. It was Nietzsche's idea that the dialectic created a spectrum of integration that reached beyond itself and pointed to something beyond the duality of good and evil. This he chose to represent through the Prophet Zarathustra, who when he returned would end dualism, and teach man to be life affirmative rather than life denying.

165. Somehow, the Egyptian myth of Osirus, the god of the underworld, being resurrected by his wife Isis who combines the fragments of his penis and uses the magical sperm to create and elixir of immortality, is also seen by proponents of astrotheology to play a pivotal role in the development of the Christ narrative. How these cultures and slogans and times are linked is a mystery, but astrotheologists are convinced that these similar instances point to a "golden bough" of transmission. There is a growing tendency to treat all religious traditions, and even those of mystery cults and secret sects, as on the same level as these Abrahamic traditions that have literally shaped nations. There seems to be a tendency to use other people's culture for secret knowledge to enhance one's own syncretistic agenda. The reappropriation of Indian culture into European, or Asian culture into Northern European culture, into a Eurasian blend by occultists is laughable. Instead of understanding each tradition on its own terms, and letting the various tradition's elders speak for themselves, this pan-religious and perennial fervor employs the tactic of leveling and reappropriating, while there is a subtle hatred of one's own traditions. One has to ask what is wrong with one's own mystical tradition or in uplifting the heritage of European Christianity? Especially when this tradition shares a so-called common narrative with the other traditions as they claim. These folks consider it beneath them. They promiscuously reach out to explore anything other than their own prudential roads, in a hatred of themselves and a sort of crude escapism. Even still they explore these subjects having been trained in the hermeneutics and esoteric schools of the West.

166. We do not support a kind of cultural celibacy either, but think it does some good to understand each tradition on its own terms without taking full interpretive license. A suspicion we have is that, while this view is lashing out against dogmas of today, it is often in a stale attempt to be different, or be a rebel without a cause. This matches their championing of Gnostic, heretical, and antinomian phrases and notions. They promote a push towards an international religion or system of understanding, which is quite dangerous. They

openly promote a kind of process theology, that seeks to reform or improve on religious designs from their academic posts, while themselves believing in nothing. What we feel applies by and large to mythicists, astrotheologists, secular humanists, and perennial philosophers, is their insistence on the progress of historical myth. They believe we are living in an age that is the heir of such wondrous insight that comprises the whole development of human history.

167. The most visible issue with this myth of progress and faith in the future (most compellingly seen in New Age mysticism), is that it reaffirms Pauline teaching, that all one has to do is have faith and wait for collective salvation. Another issue is that it treats all hitherto religious and cultural development as the sub-evolutionary stepping stones of history. Without even flinching the same group claims that these ancient beliefs are foundational and necessary for the amalgamation and final result of their eventual merger. The paradoxical view that our salvation and emancipation for our religious misgivings will arrive in the future, but that the development of these views lies in the distant past, is quite amazing. If the progress of history maintains a cycle of improvement and evolution then the beliefs of those of Biblical times were the appropriate ones for their time and place, and the best there was at the time of their development. Yet the same group says they are now outdated. Either they are outdated and provincial and barbaric forms or they are part of a greater story. At any rate, we can dismiss our current achievements as awaiting the progress and change that the future will bring so they are already inadequate. The paradoxical view of progress has little to offer.

168. Their devised appropriation of cross-cultural synergy that is crystallized by man's religious traditions is one that claims a convergence of religious beliefs and traditions. Since this convergence is assumed, there would be almost no need to treat the three main western religions as unduly morbid or violent. They can only mean to be just one representation of man's violent tendencies and thirst for vengeance, and it can no longer be improved on if it is archetypal, especially now that the whole edifice of human morality can itself be questioned since this is part of a great system of convergence and an archetypal motif of a spiritual dance and a historical play. If indeed the progress narrative has to be believed then monotheistic religion was an improvement on pagan systems, which had two sets of divinities (one for the average man and one for the rulers). But this would mean disowning their own view of Goddess worship being superior to the belief in a personal and monotheistic God beyond description, as described by Abraham.

169. Surely if all religions are part of the same evolutionary drive, then the Bible cannot be discounted as part of this great chain, but these groups disparage the Bible. Most of Campbell's book looks at Bible verses, and does a side-by-side comparison to Pagan texts, often to show their inadequacy. Both Campbell and Maxwell fully support Gnostic views on religion and theosophi-

cal teachings. This shows an inherent bias in their work. There is a fascination with the rebuilding of civilization before the flood, which was modeled on scientific and technological advancement. We take note, that in the same ancient myths such a civilization was condemned as being unworthy of service to God and out of sync with natural limitations, but these groups openly promote a return or "archaic revival" to a great civilization of the past, which they say ruled the world. This focus on the emergence of a world faith is especially troubling and sneakily totalitarian. There is an unsettling vibe of forced agreement found in this implicit semblance and tacit compromise. This threatens the diversity found in the religions of the world, which is the very thing perennial philosophy seeks to honor. Even according to this same myth of progress, all of our successes and failures are waiting to be reworked in some future time. Either religion played an important role or its accomplishments are collectively eschewed by the march of progress. This is the snake eating its tail and the repetition of discarded images of history haunting us in the future. I for one would not mind if such an ineffectual specter were to altogether vanish and decompose. But then again it repeats, much like its "ouroboros" snake mascot.

170. In order for us to establish the real origin and cultural context of certain aspects of the various adaptations in the Christ narrative throughout history let us turn to the historical development and founding of certain Christian themes. This will help us fine tune our current understanding of how the Christian message changed throughout history. If we do not discover the import of certain Christian ideas, then we cannot test whether what happened 2000 years ago has any relevance today. We cannot simply pretend that the first 300 years says all there is about what Christianity represents. If we are to take Christ's own words then we are to try to sniff out the claim that a culmination of world events has been fulfilled with the birth of the son of Mary. Does the past reach into the future? The light of the future casts the shadows of tomorrow as the musician Sun Ra once wrote. So we use our present to speak about our past for our future, and what is to come. Christ told us to be wary of the coming changes, while Paul taught us to accept our own nature and fate. The development of the concepts of new covenant theology, as well as the coming Kingdom of Heaven, stood opposed to the coming judgement and apocalyptic beckoning. While the end of this world was coming soon, the beginning of a new world lay in the distant future. This tension created the struggle to define the Christian narrative. The changes help us see how the views of Paul were chosen over those of Christ. It is important for us to explore how the assimilation of Christianity by Europeans and the formulation of Christian Zionism or British Israelism as the direct consequence of Pauline teachings, which were largely directed to non-Jewish followers. We now direct our attention to the fall of Rome, the spread of Christianity to Europe, as well as the fate of the Jews in the balance as we dwell on the political and historical development of Christianity in its spread to Europe.

PART II

PAUL AND THE SPIRIT OF "WORLD HISTORY"

/ "ISRAEL-MAN" AND THE POLITICAL ANIMAL

Chapter 8
Historical Lies and the Myths of the Future
/ Historical Progressions
/ Days of Future Past

171. Lewis Mumford once wrote that Man is the symbol making animal[1]. Religious imagination has been seen as an ultimate line between Animal and Man. Our rituals bring the past into the future, while our rites of passage keep our traditions fresh by renewing the promise. By definition a myth is something ahistorical. A myth is a sort of mediator between a metaphor and the real thing. A metaphor is too fleeting and reality is too tactile, but a myth is something that outlives time and stretches across cultural peculiarities. By contrast, a religious symbol is what adds a supernatural or transcendental element to the structure of legendary and mythical instances. I feel what religion does that is so interesting, is that it has a unique ability to place the symbols of man's construction back in relation with the historical movement that those various shapes embody, while bringing the individual directives of faith, inner wealth, and cosmic security into the frame. If religion were an inescapable aspect of human behavior, then it's wealth would be untold. If religion were something added to the human experience by sheer contrivance it stands to reason that it is man's crowning artistic achievement, and one that can never be surpassed if only by its sheer volume of achievements. Man was more religious than political to begin with. Mankind was more artistic than scientific at the outstart. Whether this primordial thrust is a complete reflection on what Man is capable of, or is built for, is beyond our present means of analysis.

172. Religious imagination, historical narrative, and philosophical outlook provide the basis for most of our political and cultural experience. Religion itself is perhaps a mediation and deliberation between practical mysticism and historical legend. This dialectical suspension rests in its indelible quality and capacity to provide us with the height of Man's potential, but also the spiritual anguish of the most depraved and tortured psyche but also a distinct political character. But out of the travails of so called subconscious delusionment[2] we have the crystallization of man's thoughts in religion, culture, philosophy, politics, and history. These are the "architectonic" arts or the arts that give rise to all other arts. Labeled thus largely because they provide to us the basis for our

---

[1] This is the general thesis of the work "Technics and the Nature of Man" by Lewis Mumford

[2] This is a technically not a word but I use it to delineate a state of delusion and did not feel like finding another word to explain myself

other arts and sciences. They provide not only the background, but also the foreground in terms of what is possible for man to achieve in the future.

173. In order to study the question with clarity one must simply get rid of one's scientific and religious dogma. One is neither to rely on the cold sterile and detached philosophical eunuch of science with its insipid material reductionism, or the fatalistic tinge of accepted first principles that are too abstract, so we leave it to God. If faith can mean anything, then it must mean the acceptance of a challenge. The challenge is to question and refine one's own set of beliefs, trusting in God to bring one back to the center. Faith is not a tandem hopefulness and radical openness, or a bitter calculation of fatalism. Faith comes after the game of knowledge is played, and not before it begins. While the skeptic is always waiting for all the facts to come in, the man of faith must go with what he knows. He says to himself, "If I can only be me, then I must test myself". Faith is an understanding of what one has been given the opportunity to create. Faith can be associated with the end of deliberation when one chooses to act.

174. Faith is an inference to the best explanation after all the data comes in. Faith takes time to bring in all the data. Patience is a virtue and knowledge is a commercial[3]. Knowledge is a mere advertisement for what should be done. Religion curses the intemperate who don't let God judge the final outcome, and who go with either side on occasion, and choose neither infamy or fame. We find these in the entrance to hell in Dante's inferno. One cannot remain neutral on a moving train as we reiterate, but one must also remember that a hypocrite is worse than a non-believer.

175. The accomplishments of religion cannot be understated. Indeed between the ocean of credulity and the abyss of skepticism is the road of faith. To paraphrase Pascal, Reason confutes dogmatists, and Nature confutes skeptics[4]. The righteous path is always seen as a middle path between two extremes. All things in moderation, even moderation. God helps those who help themselves. We are all familiar with these proverbs like sayings, and indeed those of us who learn to master and apply them are often the most successful. Instead of religious moderation we now have modernized tools and professional experts of specialized tendencies. The compartmentalization of truth has created a swamp of lowered expectations on the one end, and overspecialized versions of experts that do not agree. History is much more honest. Time does not lie. All time does is read the ledger. Instead, what we have today is the corporatization of knowledge and truth, and the commodification of religion.

---

[3] Vinnie Paz says this in the song "I who have nothing" by Jedi Mind Tricks from their debut album

[4] In "Pensees" or "thoughts" by Pascal in section vii on Morality and Doctrine the quote "Nature confutes the sceptics, and reason confutes the dogmatists" can be found.

176. The notion of double truths, and even triple truths, or the notion that truth has as many aspects as there are eyes has once again become in fashion. Only sophistry remains. What is considered truth in one instance, is subsumed as the truth of one particular area where it is limited and confined, and one can only then say that a philosophical truth is not a religious truth, or that a religious truth is not a scientific truth. We reject such a methodology. Without the notion of one truth and the consistency of truth, truth itself becomes disjunctive and irregular. At the outset of human history, and as far back as humans begin, religion and medicine and art were linked. This was a personalized quest for spirituality, science, and cultural refinement, based on natural simplicity. Just as philosophy came out of religion, it seems that out of philosophy, science emerged. Those who blame metaphysics and religion for seizing on science to promulgate lost truths, must remember that their quest for knowledge is the fruit of the philosophical and mystical endeavor. After all, what we call science today was properly termed "natural philosophy" at its outset, and Aristotle had used the term "metaphysics" to imply the book that comes after the book on physics and nothing more[5]. One can no longer call these different subjects, as Aristotle clumsily approached them, as one can separate truth from any greater notion of truth. The truth is beyond compartmentalization. Truth can only agree with truth. As such, the truth is all one and interconnected. The compartmentalization of knowledge is based on the categories of Aristotelian philosophy and we find no reason to accept them at face value.

177. Those who believe in the myth of progress generally suggest a justification for the present status of things and do little more than to support the status quo. Knowledge has been taken out of the hands of the personalized endeavor and handed over to specialists. Not only does religion and faith reject this, but so should any seeker of the fundamental truths. The study of so-called "theology" is an interdisciplinary study, just as the so-called rigorous truths of science are often colored with religious and spiritual implication (and of which they make no apology). Furthermore, we reject the notion that knowledge is purely for the sake of knowledge, and that it is to be divorced from the sacred. The assumption that truth must be secularized is no longer useful, as is the belief that what is sacred to someone is simply a manifestation of some evolutionary drive, unaffected by objective knowledge. As J.S Mill once said, the understanding that the difference between two viewpoints can produce is often "a nugget of truth".

---

[5] Magee, B. (Writer). (1987). Martha Nussbaum on Aristotle (Season 1, Episode 2) [TV series episode]. In *The Great Philosophers*. https://www.youtube.com/watch?v=DbTUAqlLlHg. Martha Nussbaum makes the claim in this show that Aristotle never intended to "invent metaphysics" but chose the title "metaphysics" for his work that came after his work entitled "physics".

178. Meanwhile, theology has been hijacked by prodigiously self-righteous clergymen, who pray in order to be seen, and history is crafted to suit the current political narrative. While some may protest that this is not true across the board, the impact is significant enough to produce an unfavorable outcome. For example, the meaning and interpretation of religion on its own terms, the study of manuscript data and archeological finds, and the study of history are commonly separated, making it hard to see the bigger picture. This jigsaw framework of overspecialization prevents mutual discussion. One cannot rely on this piecing together in terms of justification of one's faith, but one cannot advance in knowledge either without questioning what one knows. Suffice it to say, those who take this approach will struggle to understand the import of certain religious ideas and continue to hold a false dichotomy between the ancient systems of faith and the modern secular world. We endeavor to show that history has been centralized and corporatized by the myth of western civilization as it related to Paul's New Covenant theology. One must listen to everyone and believe nothing until one can prove it for oneself as the astute William Cooper once so eloquently spoke. To put matters to rest, we give our definition of faith.

179. Faith is not merely a structure of belief, but a harmonization of one's own range of influence in relation to the world. Faith means relying on one's own intuitive grasp of the situation, rather than hear-say evidence, and continually asking the question, "who benefits?". When one has to continually ask the question, "who benefits?", then the questions of normal practicality are tossed out of a window. One can lead one to a lie with the truth, and lead one to a truth with the lie. This is why Nietzsche points out, "Buddha said: Do not flatter your benefactor". He said this saying should be repeated in a Christian Church[6]. When one has shown the proper deference, one can give to God what is God's, and to Caesar what is Caesar's. But when all roads lead to Rome, one is left with few options. One is left to question. The belief that one simply has to trust the information as it is being presented is a naive realism. Belief is a dead thing, whereas faith must be continually tested and renewed. Many have started to doubt the Platonic definition of truth as something that exists outside of yourself, or the Aristotelian notion of truth being potential. We do not downplay the role of knowledge, but we elevate faith as something that comes after knowledge, and precisely in the applications derived from an incomplete set of rules. We hold to Kierkegaard's definition: "An objective uncertainty, held fast through appropriation with the most passionate inwardness, is the

---

[6] Hollingdale, R. J., & Nietzsche, F. W. (1989). *On the genealogy of morals* (W. Kaufmann, Ed.; W. Kaufmann & R. J. Hollingdale, Trans.). Vintage Books., pg 192. Section 142 of Nietzsche's Gay Science reads, "*Frankincense.* Buddha says: "Do not flatter thy benefactor!" Let one repeat this saying in a Christian church: - it immediately purifies the air of all Christianity"

truth"[7]. We follow William James who was influenced by C.S Pierce, who states in his "Will to Believe" against the skeptic who says, "Better risk loss of truth than chance of error". One cannot wait for all the facts to come in and sit on one's hands. After someone has figured something out, there is a life to go and live in application of that truth. One cannot abandon hope for truth for risk of error. Such an exchange will leave one in the abyss of skepticism. We hope one can appreciate our redefining of faith that makes faith more robust and active.

180. We also hope one can appreciate the fact that there is a history of philosophy, a philosophy of religion, a science of religion, a history of science, and a science of philosophy, and so on and so forth. Art, history, science, and philosophy are enmeshed with the development of religious ideology and their political expressions. What does Paul's view suggest in terms of historical, cultural, and political expression of: 1. Christianity's spread to Europe. 2. The morphing of Judaism and Christianity during periods of reform before the start of secular learning in the form of religious reform movements. We hope to paint a clearer picture of this in light of what we feel the three main so-called western faiths have achieved, and how they have altered the development of history culminating in the victory of the Pauline message. Some key historical developments can help us frame the issues with a little more clarity.

---

[7] Baird, F. E. (2002). *Philosophic Classics, Volume IV: Nineteenth-Century Philosophy* (F. E. Baird & W. A. Kaufmann, Eds.). Prentice Hall, pg. 292

Chapter 9
Those Who Know Not Where They Come From, Know Not Where They Go

181. One finds much convergence in the religions of the world. Both on meta-phorical, philosophical, and ethical and moral teachings of various faiths there are seen almost identical truths. While some claim that this weakens the fact that religions are stemming from their own unique sources, it also strengthens the claim made by those very same religions, that these are universal truths inscribed in the heart of man from the very outset. This tension has only been clarified by a few. Another related but altogether different view is that reli-gions of man were a steppingstone for the progress of certain historical memes and even today's scientific advancement. This tension can clearly be explored within the context of the development of Christian beliefs that take Paul for granted assuming him as a source for early Christian thought, as well as their spread of Christianity to European society where it developed separate from Coptic and Eastern Orthodox factions.

182. If the view of "evolutionary development" of religious teaching means anything then it seems to suggest that religion played a quite pivotal role. This is the perhaps paradoxical view of the myth of progress or faith in the future. If religion was accepted around the world, it seems to suggest it is the best that man had in that stage of development, and that whatever we have now is equally inadequate to the development of what is to come. One cannot expect a post religious world out of this, but simply a carrying along of religious truths in new formats and vehicles of expression. This is what Nietzsche saw: that the new liberal values were adopted as a kind of slave morality left over from the Roman-Jewish elite that lay decimated in the face of Pauline theology. Meld-ing of old religious forms into new ones and the progress of history is even affirmed in Paul's own new covenant theology.

183. We cannot simply window shop through history for transcendental truths, and we can't take at face value the plain and objective truths about history that are contained in historical documents or what those who purport to do histori-cal analysis suggest to us about them but must first see what habits these truths have already engendered on the development of the psyche of the Western European. No group on earth has a privileged right to this information. No visible organization takes precedence when discussing such matters. Science holds to methodological materialism, and religion holds to the authority of scripture. Don't ask why if you know what is wrong. It is always better to start a well-intentioned fight. Do not tempt God and force God to play his hand

when we are given the opportunity to learn and question. To do this is to reject grace and fall into temptation. Whether we obtain grace or salvation lies in whether we take our privileges of faith and forsake them for the temptation of settling for the easy road of passivity. Realizing grace means putting our faith to the test and not in tempting God and putting God to the test to save us. When privileges are mistaken by pride to be entitlements, then our grace is not transformed into a man-made structure of belief, and our faith is not tested.

184. In the Bible, it is continually mentioned that God's people were a loose knit group of people from various nations, and if we are all children of Adam, who was a child of God, then it can be said that mankind in general was chosen to express the mission of God. It would seem that every man or woman speaks through God. If it is by God that every man or woman speaks, then truly nothing is said outside of the jurisdiction of God, for it is God that gave us the tongue to speak, and it stands to reason that it is God who told us to use the tongue together with the heart in service of the truth. Not every person, but only some speak with God. Not every individual is chosen to speak with God. Even those who speak with God know not by what they speak to, nor do they have the capacity to discern the full range of experience of such an event. Humans have not the faculties to understand the power of God and his ability to speak directly to whomever he wants, because humans themselves cannot possess this power. They are simply too limited. No one speaks for God. God has the power to speak for himself. If we are to believe in the power of scripture, then we must believe that God speaks. His message is always heard and always clear. It seems however, that no one has a special power and discernment to understand the speech of God. Even the prophets, who have carried out God's message are often baffled by the directives of God's command but carry them out because they are sure it is God who has commanded them. One can only reach God through the heart. Grace is better than love. Mercy is better than kindness. Those who study oftentimes profess that there are others who understand the directives better than themselves.

185. The prophet is a witness to God's truth and teaches it in the best way he can. The disciple dictates it to the scribe. The scribe uses the language of his own time and place to remember and transmit the clarity of the message in its original purity. The meaning of the language is varied through the context of time as it is applied to the development of speech, until it reaches us in our own language and tongue, and this naturally assumes no one corrupted the message along the way. What we receive is a translation of the language and message in the guise of our own language and cultural setting, that is admittedly limited in describing the scope of previously assumed, and even ancient frames of reference. The words are interpreted to us in our time by teachers and scholars and pass through the hands of priests and judges. The priests who are the teachers and preservers, and promoters, and interpreters of the message, are to be distinguished with the judges who are yet a higher set that interpret

and apply the teachings in an institutional format. Finally, it reaches us. All these steps remove us from a direct experience with the text and affiliation of the original law, but they are also the reason we should take a closer look if we can find the messages contained therein to be of great consequences to humanity. Whether or not you believe the message, you must understand that many do believe it, and as such you are not removed from finding the importance of thinking and challenging the meaning that is presented to us on a daily basis. If you are concerned about its untruth then you must prove it to the section of humanity that you feel has been led astray, and if you believe the message then it is your task to find how the text originates in order to discern for yourself.

186. The Sumerian list of Kings, the Hindu cycles of time, and the Biblical list of prophets, and even the Chinese legacy of the sage-kings, as well as the Egyptian pantheon, start at the beginning of mankind. They all attribute the forces of mankind, and life in general, to have been influenced by supernatural forces. While today's science leaves much to be desired in terms of a concrete explanation of the origins of life and of the universe, the agreement of so-called "primitive man" on these matters arrives with surprising clarity at the same conclusion. What scientific tools or methods did they use to come to their conclusions we will never really know, because again we only can reach a probabilistic view of their lives which are arrived at by us through our own incomplete tools of modern science. The Hebrew story of the origins of man is not a significant improvement from the polytheistic framework, but it does deal with the polytheistic framework and is the one that we are currently involved with. Although its abstract nature of an imageless God allows itself to be hijacked by pantheistic and monistic sentiments, as well as neo-platonic frameworks, it provides a rather advanced model for the organization of nomadic tribes for the purposes of establishing a bond that is beyond any ethnic predicament.

187. In a study of the saga of Moses, one sees the law established, that is supposed to be clarified by Christ, and abolished by Paul. One sees that in a Jewish context, the blessed status of the nation of Israel, and for Christians the coming return of Jesus as an aid to all mankind, represent a sort of replacement for strict adherence to the law. But Paul still states, and assures us, that he is a Jew, and that salvation is of the Jews. We have to learn more about the origins of this group, and for most of the work on the history of Jews and Christians we will borrow from their own scholars. We have chosen Martin Buber's work on Moses[8] to represent a benign source when dealing with such issues (indeed one can expect no more benign source than a liberal Jewish scholar!). The story of Moses represents to us the foreground for all mishaps pertaining to "the Law" and the "Old Covenant", as labeled by some Christians.

[8] Buber, M. (1958). *Moses: The Revelation and The Covenant*. Harper and Row. We cite this work with page numbers included over the next ten paragraphs.

188. Jews in the Old Testament found themselves continually held captive by foreign rulers. Eventually they would be absorbed into the State. Is this a story of God's people being liberated and brought back to the Holy land, or a story of the Jews using the position as God's own people as a mantle to commit genocide, and extort powerful rulers for wealth and land which causes them to lose favor with God? The Bible clearly mentions both. We cannot as a result simply assume that God has given unconditional status to any group on Earth. God saved the seed of Adam through Noah. The flood story is mentioned in every ancient culture known to man, including by Plato. According to the Biblical tale, Noah was apparently the last seed of Man that was saved on Earth. Once again man divided into various tribes and nations. The cities became polluted. They became centers of idol worship, usury, sexual degeneracy, and decadence. Finally, a man was led out of Babylon into the wilderness. His name was Abraham, and he was apparently not a genetically distinct individual. He was a Chaldean from modern day Iraq. Two nations would come from his seed. One was the Jews, and the other was the Arabs. One represented by Isaac and another by Ishmael. One of the nations was that of the Jews who found themselves enslaved in Egypt. Moses led the Jews out of Egypt, and into the desert and or wilderness. In the wilderness the Jews were instructed how to build a nation for themselves. The theme of returning to the wilderness and leaving the city is a critical theme. Although some Jews found a way to serve those in power, and Moses being part of the priestly class of Egypt is proof of this, he rejected wealth and power. He even rejected the mantle of leadership for the most part among his own people as well.

189. But the Jews wanted a clear definition of leadership, and even pleaded for a divine ruler. In Ancient times the order between heaven and earth was sustained by the divine ruler. But as Buber points out, there was a distinction to be had between the magic of spontaneity that was centered around the use of chaos, and the magic of formula, which uses the already existing order to obtain a deeper insight (pg. 23). The "Elohim", by contrast, was "having no fixed place", and everywhere at once. The House of the God of Moses was a traveling house. It could not be localized by magic (pg. 27). The Throne of the God of Israel wrapped around the whole of the Universe while remaining still. The Jews were a nomadic people drawn out of the city into the wilderness to build a nation for themselves according to the decree of God. The characteristics are described in Numbers 23:9, where it states, "Behold a people that dwell alone among the nations" (pg. 32). The first precondition of serving God is a drawing out from the many and a loneliness in the crowd. Of this nation of various tribes and elders there was a God that would only speak to one man through the use of signs. God did not even speak directly to Moses himself. God is "the one", and "the unnamable". The God of Moses is beyond description and beyond definition. God is "I am that I am", or "Ehyeh asher ehyeh" (pg. 51). God is "half interjection, half pronoun". According to Buber, this type of speech is

what distinguishes religious doctrine from mere literature. The speech sounds like something from the Upanishads, instead of out of Homeric tales. What is even more distinct about the God of Moses, is that he rules over the Angels as well as the Demons. Yahweh "absorbed everything demonic" (pg. 57). God takes over the whole of a person when he directs them to complete a certain task. Each man has a direct relationship to God by fulfilment of the Covenant. A Covenant is a relationship with God, established by obedience to the will of God. An idol, conversely, is a mediator between oneself and God that is purely obsolete.

190. God says in the Bible, "Who makes peace and creates evil, I Yahweh do all these things" (Genesis 32:29) (pg. 58). God says in the Book of Job, that he sends rain to the desert where nothing ever grows out of pleasure. God orders the heavens, and man is just a clay pot. Man is no mediator between the divine and corporeal. Man meets the divine on its own terms. God gives those he chooses four stages to fulfill his will (pg. 60). The first step is a flight to the wilderness. The second step is the continued service of God, and purification of one's soul through practice of divine ritual. The third step is the vision, which results in a quest or a trial in the fortification of one's faith. The final step is an encounter with the divine and a state of peace and justice and harmony, in the establishment of the rule of God. God summons a prophet or "nabi", which is to be distinguished from a king, to prepare the people, and to draw them out for the preparation of service to the cause of God (pg. 62). A sign of God is an incarnation of the Word. As God says in Exodus 4:22, "My first-born son is Israel" (pg. 65). God shows the nation of the Jews the futility of magic of the Pharaoh. Moses comes to prescribe not a manmade law, but a universal creed. When Moses takes the Jews out of Egypt, however, they complain to him that enslavement under the Pharaoh is preferable to death in the desert. Immediately, the Jews wished to be established as an independent nation. But Gideon had already warned them as we read in Judges 8:23, "I should not rule over you nor shall my son rule over you. The Lord will rule over you" (pg. 88). God tells the Jews "ye are a stiff necked people" (Exodus 34:9). Buber takes this to mean a permanent passion for success and a rebellious mind. Indeed, the obstinacy it takes to follow one's own truth is equal in proportion to one's doubting of one's own knowledge. Such are the prerequisites to become a truth seeker. But when this formula is out of balance, much is left to be desired, as many have noticed. Once the message is reached then one has to hang up the phone.

191. Moses organizes his people to fight. Many tribes and clans are hence absorbed into the Jewish people, such as Amalekites and Midianites, and others (pg. 90-93). As in Ancient Africa, Arabia, Persia, India, China, the key formula for the State was God, King, and People (pg. 176). Moses was a representative of a theo-political ideal (pg. 101). This was the Covenant or "Berith" (pg. 102), which was expressed in one of four ways. The first way it was expressed

was between two peoples who share power on an equal footing. The second way it could be expressed was in a way where one power was subsumed and protected by another power. The third way was the covenant that God made with all living creatures in Genesis. The fourth way, expressed here, is a covenant between God and a people or nation, brought about by a theo-political arrangement, and a strict adherence to God's law. God does not give up authority but brings those he protects into his own jurisdiction (pg. 103-104). As it says in Deuteronomy, God wished to make Israel a kingdom of priests. The "Mamlaketh Kohanim", or "rule of the lord" (pg. 106), is where God becomes Melek or ruler, only after the whole organization submits to following God's command. The spirit or "ruah", is what is brought forth through the law, and by the power that radiates through the law (pg. 164). Dietary regulations, sexual ordinances, and laws concerning property were maintained. The establishment of the covenant is followed by the Decalogue. They are not argued for by ethical or philosophical means, but are religious and political (pg. 119-124).

192. The only parallel in history that can be found is the religious and ethical teachings of Jesus that are not aimed at society or a nation, but rather the individual. Jesus, however, did not focus on theo-political rules, having seen them already established in Moses. Jesus applies the law of Moses in terms of the individual. This is the meaning of his coming to fulfill the law. What else could it mean? The law that all the other laws hang on is not worshipping other gods in the form of idols. According to Buber, the soul of the decalogue is to be found in the word "thou". This symbolizes the divine voice (pg. 130). There is the exclusion of worship of all other gods. This combines with a dedication of his invisible but manifesting presence, and the removal of external sensory representations. The community protects "life, marriage, property and social honor". This all sounds good. But then Buber wrongfully extrapolates that the covenant is not like a contract and cannot be broken because it is a divine bond. If this were true, why would this not be explicitly mentioned in the Bible? If God does not care for the soul of a man, as Buber alleges, and merely wishes to establish his nation (pg. 104), then why is the Covenant connected with the words on the tablet at all? The situation seems troubling. According to one view, God makes laws, renews laws, makes covenants, breaks covenants, and exacts penalties and offers blessings. All this is within God's jurisdiction. Divine rule should not be limited by earthly rule.

193. If you disobey, "Ordaining the sins of the father upon the children unto the third and fourth generations" says God, is what will be exacted (pg. 142). Say not to yourselves that we are the children of Abraham, but out of these stones God can raise up new children of Abraham. God has no need for a Nation that fears him, period. No nation should be established in God's name if all nations are to serve God. The rule of God is destiny. No earthly institution whether religious or stately can have jurisdiction over the rule of God. We cannot assist the rule of God. It is for the rule of God to give assistance to us.

Oppression of widows and orphans is forbidden. The unjust community is visited by war. Those who turn away orphans and widows, God will make their wives widows and their sons orphaned. God orders those who follow him to release slaves every seventh year and allow the usufruct land to lay fallow.

194. Israel begins to worship a golden bull instead of Yahweh. Moses seeing this, breaks the tablets. The smashing of the tablets signifies a breaking of the covenant. The Jews are no longer protected. Moses establishes the tent of meeting, where he convenes with God alone. He establishes the priestly class of Levites to assist him in purging the savage whims of the people (pg. 147-153). Moses pleads to his own people that whoever is with Yahweh should go with him, meaning that certain of them had rejected his teaching. Moses teaches a free relation to the soil, to free the slaves every seventh year, and to protect the poor. He shows how the land is a "berakah", or blessing power (pg. 177). Moses is not a professional priest like the Levites, but it is the Levites who band together to rebel against his special relationship with God (pg. 181). In every religion the first heretics are the most learned scholars. It is often they, who by learning the laws, learn to manipulate them. A "Baalization" process occurs as Yahweh is transformed by them into Baal.

195. Baalization is identical to the claims made by Paul. As articulated by Buber, the claim is that "the whole people are holy, for YHVH is in their midst". On this basis they attacked Moses, for if all are holy then nobody has priority over anyone else. As a result, there is no need for one human to exercise power over another person, and the authority of Moses is illegitimated (pg. 184). These people wanted to "possess God". As Moses himself notes, that he has no office or any special authority, but is merely a messenger. Some of the Jews took advantage of this. Moses not differentiating between the realms of religion and politics, as Paul clearly does, is an important point. If all the people are holy then no man can give orders. The attempt was to cut off the leaders' power by establishing a column within the society, but external to its normal functions. Buber notes that this has been the motivation for many secret societies and cults of the past. The secret society often regards itself as a protector of the essence of the tribe, and as its spine, or the "true tribe" within the greater tribe (pg. 185-188). This is the history of antinomian sects. Buber correctly notes, "The true argument of the rebellion is that in the world of the law that has been inspired always becomes emptied of the spirit, but that in this state it continues to maintain its claim of full inspiration; or, in other words, that the living element dies off". This is coupled with the belief that the law must renew itself in the purifying fires of the spirit. This combines with an "eschatological expectation", that the rule of God will bring an end to the law, as in the presence of God the law is no longer required.

196. This all sounds all too familiar. It sounds just like Paul. There are no special laws for either Jew or Gentile. The commands are made for all mankind.

But both Talmudic Jews and Paul have constructed new laws to deal with humanity that override some of the laws of Moses. They have taken full interpretative license to corrode the true meaning of the law. This is what Jesus emphatically rejected. He came to affirm the law of Moses and to reject the oral tradition of the Pharisees. He merely told the Jews that they should identify with his message as their saving grace, for he had come to fulfill the prophecy of the Jewish messiah. Neither Talmudic doctrine of another person coming instead of Jesus as Messiah, or Paul's prophecy that God will come and rule on earth, matches the simple decree of these laws which forbid oppression and deal with corruption of wealth, food, and sexual relations, which are quite easily deterred by an adherance to the law. Since these practices are detrimental to the health of any society and exacerbated by the use of idols for worshipping God, it is quite optimal to eradicate such practices in favor of God's decree. The major stumbling block is the priestly class inventing new models to purify the law through remembrance of the spiritual essence. These reforms are often dangerous innovations. We find that Christians and Jews do not take these doctrines and warnings seriously in regard to their own teaching and doctrines that have become transformed by the process or world history or western history.

197. There even grew, among some of the Israelites, a worship of the Phoenician rain-god Baal. This was an agrarian god that was worshipped through fertility rites and an elemental ritual expression based on the tilling of the soil. Buber writes, "Human sexuality becomes bound up with a divine sexuality; the divinity is drawn down into the duality of corporeal nature; and the relation of man and wife" (pg. 193). This driving force of libido represented the unity of organic life and the moisture of soil. While Baal represents a contradiction from without, the contradiction from within, between Moses and the priestly class characterizes the true test of the Jews. One is Baalization of Yahweh seen in all sorts of Kabbalistic rites. The other is a feeling of entitlement that every Jew is born holy and therefore contains the Spirit. These are all brought out by a sense of anthropomorphism, which in the case of Baalization takes place in the form of trying to invent your own God, and in the second sense it is making God conform to your own human schedule, through the self-fulfilling prophecy of setting up an eternal rule on earth (pg. 194). However, there is plenty of evidence as well that before this promise was fulfilled all of this idolatry would have to be purged from the hearts of the people of Israel. At his death, Moses could see the promised land as he climbed a mountain alone. There as he laid his eyes on the land of promise he died alone. Moses led his people to the promised land, but died before he could enter, and died alone, and the people did not make it into the land with Moses. This is a telling sign because even after entering the Holy land, God raised up an army of non-believers, the Babylonians, to destroy their temple and put the Jews into captivity.

198. The curious segment of history that occurs in Judea when it is later located within the Roman Empire[9] was a pivotal period in Jewish history during the
time of Roman-Jewish war. After this period both the Talmud or Jewish oral
tradition and the Gospels, as well as the canonical books now included within
the New Testament, were being formulated. These first three hundred years
provide an interesting relationship between Jews and Pagans. Jewish scholars
argue that the lack of development of a codified structure of law led to the rise
of heresies like the Christian faith. As Christianity rose up it became a major
persecutor of Jews. The glory of the Church was depicted as an elegantly
dressed noble woman, while her sister, the Synagogue, was shown in tattered
clothes looking down at herself. Jews viewed Jesus as a follower of Hillel.
Because of Jesus' opposition to the Sadducees, he was killed by Rome. They
are not willing to take any credit for the murder of Jesus that they were blamed
for by the early Church. At its very worst expression, Paulinists blamed Jews
for the murder of God. According to Jews, it was Paul who falsely told Christians that old rituals were replaced by a new covenant. It was also Paul who
first espoused the credo that God had sent his son as a sacrifice for the salvation of all of mankind. Jews have made the claim that it was a Christian and
Roman alliance that opposed Judea. According to certain Rabbi, it was a Roman friendly Jewish sect that created early Christianity to appease Roman rule.
Hatred from both parties led to the destruction of the Second Temple. As we
have seen, the Jews represented a diverse group within Rome and some assimilated Jews like Philo rejected circumcision and biblical miracles, claiming
that these were allegories for an ontologically transcendent basis for methods
to the attainment of knowledge and truth. They felt that true spirituality could
only be achieved through the inner light of Reason, and not by externalized
practice of ritual.

199. Still, there were those who believed the law was all powerful and had to
be instituted at all costs. Yet there was another group that believed that what
was sought through the performance of ritual and enactment of laws was the
inner peace, which was the meaning or essence of the law, that was unveiled
through the Spirit of God. There were Jews who supposed that a claim to the
land and the nation of Israel bore the most significance. These Sadducees were
the temple authorities, and generally did not believe in the life to come but
believed that laws had to be instituted in this life for the security of a nation.
Then there was a priestly class who felt that guarding the oral tradition and
religious practice was the most salient concern. The combination of these two

---

[9] Over the next six paragraphs we rely heavily on material presented by Dr. Henry
Abramson https://henryabramson.com/about/. He features on his youtube channel a
series of videos on Jewish history which include the following 8 titles: 1. Judaism and
Early Christianity 2. Jews and Judaism in the Year Zero 3. Who Was Philo Judaeus of
Alexandria? 4. Who was Paul of Tarsus? 5. Who Was Josephus? 6. Who Was King
Bulan Of Khazaria? 7. Sephardic Jewry and the Islamic Conquest of 711 8. Was Chris-
topher Columbus Jewish?.

were the zealots, who felt that defense of the temple and of oral tradition meant a fight against Rome and a struggle for independence. Still there was another group that rejected the oral law and the temple authorities and found political solutions untenable. They raved against the corruption of the temple authorities and the hypocrisy of the Pharisees. They charged them with supporting Rome and charged the Pharisees with engaging in a self-fulfilling prophecy. They retreated to the wilderness to engage in rituals of purification until the angels of God would come down and destroy Rome and Judea on their behalf, purging the world of filth of idolatry and the hypocrisy of the priestly class. They felt that some of the Jews would not be able to escape the wrath of God at such a time because of their own hypocrisy. These were the Essenes.

200. The thoughts of Philo were used by early Christian church fathers in development of the trinity, which drew on the Heraclitian conception of the Logos, that was a primordial and transcendental reflection of the divine. He knew more about Greek texts than Hebrew scripture. There is evidence that Philo did not speak Hebrew. Philo was an apologist for Roman rule and believed that stories in the scripture like the flood were not real historical events. He felt this was merely a metaphor for the purging of lower and base elements. He felt circumcision was a metaphor for abstinence from sex. He stated that rulers like Caligula were only part of God's plan. There was no reason to oppose those in power because God had put them there. Similarly, Paul made the claim that those who profess a new covenant with Christ are saved, and that the law of the Torah is not binding on those who have faith, mainly because of his view of justification and atonement by faith alone. Torah means guidance and not law. However, in the Gospels we see that Jesus and Mary followed the "old law" contained in the Torah. Jesus is mentioned over twenty times in the Talmud, and it is claimed that he never existed. Paul makes over two hundred references to the Old Testament but does not mention the Gospels. Paul seems to have some mixed feelings towards the Torah. In Paul's letters we read of disputes with early church officials, and we read of the famous dispute Paul has with Peter, who he attempts to defame in front of some peers. Paul apparently had disputes with many Church officials over the Law of Moses, and taking interpretative license in where it applies to Gentiles. Paul specifically seems to take such metaphorical lessons from the prohibitions against circumcision and the treatment of animals that relates to certain dietary restrictions. Paul also seems to play up the role of abstinence as opposed to marriage, often touting his freedom of not having a wife. At age fifty seven Paul is put under protective custody by Romans, it can be supposed. Soon after, he disappears, leaving a legacy of his message of salvation for the Gentiles. Both Philo and Paul used Greek views to romanize Jews and judaize Pagans.

201. Next we have Josephus. He is told to us by both historians and Christians alike to provide undeniable proof for historical facts. He is hailed as a historian but what this title means for a second century slave, if anything, is quite con-

cerning. Suffice it to say there were no professional historians back then. Furthermore, the views of Josephus seem to be compromised based on the unique position he was placed in as a slave of Flavian during the Roman Jewish war. Not only was Josephus a traitor to the Jews but he did not have a firm grasp on Jewish tradition as he seems to have pretended to. This includes his plagiarism of portions of the life of Yohannan Ben Zakkai to add to his own life story. Josephus mistakenly combined Jewish prophecy with the Roman cult of the gods and said Flavian was the Jewish Messiah. This means that Josephus had no understanding of the Jewish law or pretended to have such knowledge in order to use such a law against his own people. There were many religious subverters. Sadly however, this tells us little concerning the history of the Jews. The writings of Josephus are some of the only works to have survived from the era because they had the support of those in power. To make matters worse, the mention of Christ we see in Josephus could have been added by later Christians. So we not only have the possibility of religious subverters of the past, but those who in a later stage of history put their own opinions into works of the distant past making it seem they were original sources. To make matters worse, some Jews carried this out both on behalf of and over and against their own people.

Chapter 10
The Denial of the People of the Lord
/ Not All Who are Called Israel are Israel

202. We can read that Moses' wife, for example, was an Ethiopian woman. Moses married the daughter of a Midianite priest, just as Solomon was conceived of David and the wife of Uriah who was not Jewish. It seems that the early Jews were not just Semitic people. They were a blend of Arab, Persian, and African peoples. It seems in the Torah that there were various nations who were led by God to come together into one group. Accepting Judaism is not a racial designation arrived through predestination, as we find in the writings of Paul (Romans 9), or what would be the point of military campaigns or a system of laws? Various ethnic groups have accepted Judaism throughout history, plain and simple. If you hate Jewish people thinking that they are a race, then you are a racist. If you despise Judaism without considering the various cultural and historical settings that have informed Judaism as we see it today, you are not aware of what you attack or even who. Finally, if you do not know Jewish history you cannot know Christian history. It is for this very reason that the New Testament has the Old Testament still attached to it. Yet and still, it is often left unsaid as to what extent the Jews are linked to Christianity. There are still Arab Christians living in Syria and Palestine and the various parts of the Middle East belonging to Orthodox factions. Many of these Churches are ignored by the West and by Western travelers to the Holy Land until quite recently. What is even more interesting is that they are largely ignored in our present analysis because of their development being so culturally estranged from the European development of Christianity. When the term Christianity is employed by us it is used to refer to the Western European brand, which includes the fall of Rome, spread of Christianity to Europe, the protestant reformation and the secular age.

203. Today we see that the number of Jewish people from European descent vastly outnumber the populations of Semitic and Arabized Jews that once populated the world. You have instances in history like the conversion of King Bulan to Judaism, which converted large swaths of the Khazarian Empire. Around Georgia, this Turkic people about whom little is known about intermingled with both the Islamic empire and European civilization for almost five hundred years, and mysteriously disappeared. These were the Khazars. A very small percentage of European Jews, like the Ashkenazi, still have a tiny and miniscule genetic connection to these people. Khazars maintained the use of pagan symbols like the star of Remphan, which is mistaken for the "Star of David". Certain ethnic influences like those Europeans have found their way

into the practice of so-called "Orthodox" Judaism, not unlike the common misappropriation of Arab culture and Islamic beliefs. In the 9th century, Rabbinic reform was taking place, and in the 11th century the Khazar empire was absorbed into areas of surrounding Hungary and Ukraine. Around the same time some Jews were living comfortably under Islamic rule. According to many Jewish historians, the Jews have fared better under Muslim control than under Christian civilization. This may come as a shock to many who suppose that Christians and Jews who live under western secular rule have been constantly opposed by Islam. This fact alone causes many to believe that Jews and Christians have always faced a hostile threat from Islam, which is foreign to the development of western thought. History paints a different picture. The pact of Umar was set up to defend Syrian Christians during Islamic conquests. Islam also defended Christian and Jewish religious sites. Christians, Jews and Sabaeans were mentioned in the Quran as people who professed a Monotheistic belief system and were therefore protected by Islamic law that was founded on the law of Moses and given Holy Scripture. Since most observant Jews found many similarities between Islamic law and the Jewish law, from which it was derived, they lived among the Muslims. Many prominent Jewish scholars, including Maimonides, enjoyed such protection, gaining high status and wealth. During most of recorded history, Arabs have lived in the Holy land and allowed Jews to live there in peace. In stark contrast is todays Israel, supported by Christian fundamentalists in a crusade against Islam, and run by European Jews, who treat Semitic Jews and Arab Christians like second class citizens, while borrowing their language and cultural traditions, and stealing the land that has belonged to Palestinians for centuries.

204. What is little discussed is the extraordinary position of the Arab Christians. They are perhaps most interesting for their being of a Semitic background, Arab cultural framework and ethnicity and language, but overall coming to adopt western traditions because of their unique heritage of Christian teaching constantly being courted by westerners who turn out to regret their Arab roots, and seen by Muslims as colluders with the western empires. They were also despised by Jews and not recognized by European Christians as legitimate heirs to the Church. In a book entitled "Narrow Gate Churches" by Atallah Mansour[10], it explains the often-ignored views of those Christians who are natives of the area where Jesus lived and preached. In Israel, attacks on Egypt backed by the French and British had such Christians succumb to Israeli rule in 1956 (pg. 2). Some supported a secular Pan-Arab movement against Israel which saw Israel dividing the Middle East between Africa and Asia.

---

[10] Mansour, A. (2004). *Narrow Gate Churches: The Christian Presence in the Holy Land Under Muslim and Jewish Rule.* Hope Publishing House. We sight this book continuously for the next 12 paragraphs with page numbers included. Sadly, the role of Christian Arabs who play a foundational role in the origins of Christianity are mostly ignored by most scholars. Among the tribes of Christian Arabs languages like Aramaic and Coptic are preserved.

Since eighty percent of the Arab world is what can be nominally considered Muslim, the term Arab is often synonymous in the west with Islam, which is another reason why the legacy of Christian Arabs is largely ignored (pg. 3-4).

205. The figure head of the Pan Arab movement was Gamal Abdul Nasser that faced a stern defeat by Israel in the Six Day War and met an early demise in 1970. The victory of his successor Anwar Sadat in 1973 enabled Egypt to regain the Sanai Peninsula which led to the Camp David Accords in 1978. Soon Anwar Sadat was assassinated by the Muslim Brotherhood, but Mansour does not mention their collusion with the west here which is otherwise well known through their ties to oil rich Arabs who controlled Lebanese Media outlets. Israel backed Lebanese Christians in a civil war against their Muslim compatriots. Since then, religious tensions in the area have heightened.

206. Still the region contains many archeological sites and holy sites which Mansour says comprise a "fifth Gospel" (pg. 5). Among these are the humble town of Nazareth. According to Mansour the congregation of the faithful (now quite a fractured union) comprises the "sixth Gospel". Christian Arabs like Mansour support the Ecumenical unification of the Church, but I wonder how much of that is Mansour's own personal perspective.

207. The Eastern Churches of Nicosia state, "we all believe Christ is God and Man" taking the message of the Gospels and St. Paul for granted (pg. 6). Most notably, Arab Christians (like Al-Kindi) played a crucial role in the translation of books in medicine, philosophy, and science from Greek to Persian to Arabic. The Native Christian Arabs have absorbed a variety of traditions including Byzantine Greek rites, Roman Catholic rituals, preachers of the Church of England, Southern Baptist teachings, and some retaining separate and unique traditions with a number of them having some Coptic and Ethiopic influence in the past (pg. 9). Both the historical value of Judaism and Christianity, as well as the fifty nations that practice Islam in the region with billions of adherents, makes religious life in this geographical area extremely significant as a political factor (pg. 10).

208. After the advent of Islam many groups like Egyptian Copts, Lebanese Marionites, Syrian Arab and Iraqi Assyrians, and Chaldeans survived according to Mansour, while others did not (pg. 11). While Muslims share some important religious commands and laws with Jews (such as dietary restrictions and laws against adultery and interest), Christians share the Old Testament scriptures with Jews (pg. 12). Mansour points out that Christian Fundamentalists from America who support Zionist backed causes look down on Palestinian Christians for attempting to inherit the Holy Land promised to the Jews, even against their own Christian brothers apparently (pg. 13). Mansour points out that David's grandmother Ruth was a Moabite and Solomon was the son of Bathsheba, the widow of Uriah the Hittite. Moabites and Hittites were not

Jews. Besides, the Bible does not insist on racial purity and if it did semitic people would have preference over non-Semitic people, but we see history tells us otherwise (pg. 14). Jews from Yemen and Ethiopia as well as Christians from those regions have little similarity with ones from Russia, Germany, and Poland. Palestinian Arabs are genetically more similar to Jews of that area, while Ashkenazi are more similar to Greeks and Turks in terms of genetics.

209. In the Bible, Solomon gifts twenty cities to Hiram the Phoenician (pg. 25). Apparently, the cities were in Galilee and in such poor condition that he wanted a refund. The city was also known as Galilee of the Gentiles and as a port city and was known to be frequented by foreigners. St. Eusebius even claimed that Peter preached in Israel and that 'all of the bishops were of the circumcision" (pg. 28). Towns like Al-Jish, Moalula, Petra, Advat and Shivta all testify to an Ancient Christian culture (pg. 29). The Sassanid and Lakimid were of the larger Christian Arab tribes (pg. 30). Many stories exist about these Arab Christians backing Arab Muslims against the Byzantines who tried to subsume them under their own rule, like one story of a Ghassan horseman who famously slaid the chief of a Byzantine army. The Nestorians sent thirteen thousand Christian knights to Yarmuk to help Muslim armies (Muhammad p.b.u.h also employed help from Ethiopian Christians in migration from Mecca to Medina) (pg. 30).

210. The Greeks referred to Arabs as the slaves of Sara or "Saracens" (pg. 31). The Syrian Monophysite historian Abu al Faraj Ibn al Ibri (also known as Ben Hebraus wrote, "God the Almighty and vengeful lord sent us the Arabs to rid us from the Greeks" (pg. 32). The Muslims helped maintain Church property. Armenians also sided with Muslims against the Byzantine Church. Mansour states, "no reason to doubt it was more than religious beliefs that brought division to church ranks since these happened along national/cultural lines". Both Nestor and Arius were not powerful enough to challenge the grasp of the Byzantine (pg. 38). Mansour states that the good relations with Muslims depended on the internal stability within the Muslim rule itself and not due to a pronounced hatred of Christians. Mansour provides some facts about Islam that are quite useful. Islam does not consider itself to be an independent revelation from Judaism and Christianity. What Mansour fails to mention is that the Quran also plainly states that Christianity and Judaism are considered to be perversions of an original message. Yet and still, Islam demands the faithful to revere Jesus Christ (both as a Messiah rejected by the Jews and a sign of the end of days) (pg. 36-39). Muslims believe that Jesus was born of the Spirit of God through immaculate conception in order to be a sign for the Jews (mainly because the pious nature of the Mother Mary).

211. However, we cannot accept that Islam is Judeo-Christian as Mansour states. Firstly, because such a term is chimerical. According to the Gospels, Jews are seen as the murderers of the Lord Jesus Christ, and as such Judaism

and Christianity cannot be easily combined, but also because at the time of their origin such terms as Judaism and Christianity did not exist. Secondly, Islam rejects Judaism and Christianity as false religions as previously stated in the previous paragraph. Thirdly, the so called "western" development of both Jews and Christians in Europe and its culmination in the secular humanist worldview often excludes Islam. On the other hand, there are key differences between Islam and Christianity that are rarely discussed: 1. Islam does not believe in the death of Jesus 2. Islam does not believe in the Sin of Adam and Original Sin 3. Islam believes that the Prophet Muhammad is the seal of the prophets and not the final prophet as Christians believe the final message of the Torah points to Paul's message of Gentiles which brings salvation to the world. According to Michael Shermer, a futurist and promoter of science and liberalism, Islam is the last culture on Earth to never reach "the enlightenment" seen in Europe emerging in the seventeenth century as the harbinger of western values like individualism and democracy as well as women's liberation. These views were held by thinkers like John Locke and John Stuart Mill but also Kant and Voltaire. For all these reasons the term Judeo-Christian has little meaning as does "western" or "oriental"..

212. However there is in Islam a mention of a Nestorian or Arian Monk who predicted the prophethood of Muhammad p.b.u.h. According to Mansour, the first Muslim governors were "quite prudent and liberal with non-Muslims and invited them to either embrace Islam on equal terms or maintain their ancestral traditions for a price. Among the Arabs in general, men who were traders, fighters, merchants, and nomads were prized but farming was seen as humiliating. Muhammad p.b.u.h stoned three men for riding on one donkey that struggled to carry them. A commander in Homs in Syria paid Christians back their Jizya (taxes) when he failed to defend them by military might. Syrian and Arabic are both daughters of the Aramaic language (pg. 41).

213. According to one Christian writer named Michel le Syrian, "(God)...brought the children of Ishmael to liberate us from the Greek heavy yoke" (pg. 41). Christians such as John of Damascene (and even Jewish scholar Maimonides later) had high connections with the Caliph (pg. 43). Arabs are descendants of the Copts, Assyrians, Nobi, Aramaic, and Phoenicians nations. The Nabateans for example are linguistically Arab, Aramaic writing, and Greco-Roman in their art and architecture (pg. 49). It was this group that in 321 introduced alphabet to the Arabs. Christian Arabs have been known to touch base with certain western influence due to their Christian past. Levantine Arabs, or Palestinian, Lebanese, and Syrian Arabs who speak English and French are such a group (pg. 50). These groups fared pretty well until the reign of the Ottomans who maintained an anti-Arab and Anti-Christian attitude due to their ethnic conflicts which reached way back into the past. Most notably, the Arab League includes many non-Arab African states like Somalia and Mauritania who traditionally practice Islam (pg. 51).

214. During the Crusades, Native Christian Arabs were either ignored or not recognized by European invaders (pg. 53). These groups wishing to take Jerusalem back for the Church never accepted Native Christianity as equals and wished to subsume them under the rule of the Church. While Muslim rulers did not force local Christianity to convert, the crusaders treated local Christians as if they were of inferior status. During the crusades they were also sometimes seen by Muslims as colluding with the enemy. Native Christians fared worse as a result of the Crusades says Mansour, because of these various factors. Territories inhabited by Native Christians of the time were Bet Horon, Tira, Beit Lehem (Galilee), Manot, Safad, and Beit Jubren (pg. 54-55). This means that Christians were heavily concentrated in rural areas. While crusading armies saw local Christians mostly as heretics, some groups like the Marionites allied themselves with the Catholic Church. The Marionite Church asked French King Louis IX for protection. Marionite legends suggest them aligning with the Greek Byzantine church against the Umayyad (pg. 57).

215. The indiscriminate killing of the Fourth crusade had even the Greek adopt the slogan, "Rather the sultan's turban than the pope's tiara" (pg. 58). The non-Arab mercenaries named Mamelukes took over Egypt in 1261. Abbasid rule had come to an end with Caliphs using mercenaries and corrupt officials and eventually fell by Mongol invasion. In 1453 the Ottoman rule began. Lord Robert Cursor (British), Rene Chateaubriand (French), and Mark Twain (American) all traveled to the Holy Land but wrote quite unfavorably toward Native Christians, concluding that they were mostly hostile to westerners (pg. 62-63). One writer Felix Fabri exclaimed that the Ishmaelite or Jew is favorable to the Native Christians and two Scottish protestant missionaries found local Christians 'anti-Jewish and anti-Christ". Mark Twain wrote that local Christians in Holy Land are miserable and hostile (pg. 64-65).

216. In 1835 Ibrahim Pasha took over Syria. In 1917 General Edmond Allenby led a "last crusade" that was in the words of the diary of British Senior Intelligence Officer Richard Meinertzhagen shown to be filled with praise for Zionist plans (pg. 69). According to Arab tribal law, if someone dies on your land even in the desert you are held responsible. Hospitality has to be kept as a rule in the desert where there are harsh conditions (pg. 70). Such a rule no longer remains. The Sea of Galilee is rapidly drying up since the British Invasion (pg. 73). The rise of Arab Nationalism (Nasser) and Islamic Modernism (Jamal Al Din Afghani) have not been sufficient to meet the challenges faced by oppressed people (pg. 78). To make matters worse, Christian Arabs are caught between their Arab heritage and western progress, caught between two worlds essentially. Even Napoleon lived in Egypt and Palestine for less than two years and attempted a feigned conversion to Islam (pg. 82). At the beginning of the nineteenth century, Christian Arabs make up less than ten percent of the population of Palestine (pg. 89).

217. The Prophet Muhammad used the law of Moses to unite the Arab tribes, as Moses used the law to unite the several tribes that comprised the nation of Jews in the wilderness of Sanai. Islam maintains dietary restrictions, laws against usury, promotion of charity, laws concerning marriage, and many other similar statutes to Jewish law. There were also laws against adultery and laws protecting property. The son of Maimonides was influenced by Sufi Islam. Muslim scholars like Al-Kindi led movements to translate and preserve texts of classical Greek civilization. Muslim and Jewish scholars ushered in an age of learning that rivals and predates the European enlightenment. This period was pivotal for the development of later western thought since it led to the rediscovery of the previous ages of Greek learning. A low-tech world civilization was set up without large governments, pseudo-governmental corporations, massive trade bureaucracy, and the centralized industrialized state.

218. This is quite a different picture from what we hear today, that either a Judeo-Christian alliance, or a Secular Humanist view of the world has united civilization. On the contrary, the strict adherence to ritual seen in Confucianism that united China, the tough laws of the Republic of Rome, and swift organization of Islamic civilization, show us a height of cultural unity and productivity that is unmatched in history, and still revered for its honest and elegant expressions of human nature. Especially in the West, the occult has roots in the Jewish Kabbalah. This was based on the belief that it was possible to transcribe the throne of God and summarize the whole body of possible knowledge within the range of human experience, that was a microcosm of the macrocosm. This was because Kabbalists believed to have mapped the cosmos according to the anatomy of God. They derived this knowledge from sacred language that was hidden within daily events. Each number and letter had a spiritual disposition and could encode sacred figures, that were known as transcendental objects. Hence, one could reverse engineer God. Some Gnostic sects even wished to kill God and reinvent him. Mainstream Christian historians have pointed out that many early heresies and heretics helped expound and influence mainstream Christian teachings. One does not have to look far to see that Jewish heretics have seduced Christian teachings, and that Christian Gnostics and Hermeticists have, not only influenced Jewish traditions, but also originate from those very same traditions. Even the Ismaili sect of Islam has been noted to have influence on certain Christian heretics. Early Christians, according to Christian scholars[11], faced various threats. They faced a political threat

---

[11] Gore, Dr. Bruce. (n.d.). *Church History*. Youtube. https://www.youtube.com/watch?v=kHtCDU-v-BU&list=PLYFBLkHop2alLjioK9sr37uazi_TG7hRD. For the next 9 paragraphs we present a church history from the perspective of a mainstream "American" view for which we have borrowed from the lectures of Dr. Bruce Gore who teaches Christian history from a Presbyterian perspective. We find the flow of his presentations and the perspectives presented therein to match those we have found most readily expressed by

from Rome, a theological attack from Judaism, and a philosophical threat of Pagan philosophy. How many concessions did early Christians make in order to adapt? By taking Paul's advice of being a Jew with the Jews, and a Roman with the Romans, they seem to have adapted rather quickly. In Antioch, where Peter preached the Gospels, a group called the Alogoi rejected the notion of God and Logos being the same. A group called Ebionites believed that Jesus was not born the Son of God, but was merely adopted upon baptism through his union with the Holy spirit. Other groups like the Marcionites seemingly disparaged the Old Testament and elevated the teachings of Paul in espousing a new covenant theology. Early Church fathers like Tertullian who fell into the Montanist heresy, Justin Martyr (an Aristotelian thinker), Origen (a Neoplatonist), Paul of Samosata (an Ebionite), and many others, would be considered heretics today. Paul of Samosata who taught Arius, rejected the Trinity, while thinkers like Sabellius used Neoplatonic views of emanation to describe how The Father, the Son, and Holy Ghost were all of one substance, or one Divine Essence. This was the notion of "hypostatic union" derived from the teachings of Plotinus. Another view was Docetism, that held that Christ was formulated by divine substance, and was neither flesh nor phantasm.

219. These schools carried well into the time of the conversion of Constantine. To believe that the conversion of Constantine was preordained to send Christian teachings across the world and all the seven seas is not very convincing, since no unified statement existed on what his beliefs actually entailed. We see that the conversion of Constantine mirrors the conversion of Paul, who was greeted by a vision of Christ which appeared to him in a dream and enlisted him in the establishment of some sort of institution. This institution bore the mark of the crucifix. Like Paul, he took this vision to suggest the building up of religious institutions. Christian legend suggests that it was this that caused Constantine to hold the Council of Nicea, where Christian doctrine would be firmly established for all time. Constantine had summoned the two opposing parties of Arius and Athanasius to finalize Christian teachings. Christianity and Rome were now one and the same thing. No more give to Caesar what is Caesar and to God what is God's. Giving to Caesar was giving to God. Constantine spread Christianity to Britain, Iberia, Gaul, as well as parts of North Africa. Was this move based on Christ's teachings? It was Christ who taught that whenever two or more gather in his name, to praise God, then they are an institution unto themselves. All that was needed was two or more people. Christ also noted that large displays of public ritual were antithetical to a real connection with God that is found most likely when praying alone in the desert, fasting for forty nights and forty days. Do Christians pray like this? It was Constantine that purged certain Jewish holy days from Christian practices. What Christians practice as Christmas is actually "Saturnalia", which was a gift giv-

---

mainstream protestants and evangelicals that one may encounter in the U.S who have all agreed on the importance of certain thinkers and events in Christian history.

ing festival in Rome to celebrate the Winter Solstice. Since Saturn was a homosexual god who devoured his own children, the day was known as a celebration of licentiousness and dark passion, whereby the laws were reversed or relaxed.

220. The most important Christian thinker after Constantine was St. Augustine. He was born around the fourth century and educated in Carthage to be a teacher of rhetoric. He admits that in his youth he was given over to Sin. He would soon join a Gnostic sect started by the Persian teacher Mani. This dualistic sect known as the Manichaeans believed in a strict duality between good and evil, which was brought on by their Gnostic and Zoroastrian influence. In a meeting with St. Ambrose, the young St. Augustine apparently rejected his former ways after reading Paul. However, much of the influence of his early days can be said to be influential in his later teachings which included "hate the sin and not the sinner". It would seem this notion of Sin as an inexorable element of human experience seemed thoroughly convincing to him, as did the notion put forward by Plotinus, that evil is a privation of the Good. Both the Gnostic view of a strict dualism between good and evil, and the Platonic view of Evil having no existence on its own being a privation on the good gave Sin a distinct existence apart from the individual. It is quite a wonder that the belief of Plotinus of evil having no inherent existence could assist Pauline theology, especially in that Paul believes the world to be naturally evil, and that a lack of evil is a sign of the entrance of good into the world. In Plato the world was a devolution of the forms which were also considered to be divine in his Pythagorean synthesis. The dualism between spirit and flesh seen in Paul was seen as a natural aid to Greek conceptions. Good had to come into the world from outside. God entered into history. During the fifth century, Rome was having a problem with the Germanic tribes. The Piks, Gauls, and other proto-European tribes were also being approached by missionaries like St. Patrick. These would provide a basis for the unification of the various Northern European tribes that had for the most part been seen as barbarians by Rome. This was one of the primary ways that Christianity was to outlast Rome. Paul was right. The spread of Christianity to non-Jewish people helped to preserve what was left of Christian teachings. What was left was more in line with Paul than with Christ and more suited to the Gentile and Pagan than the Jewish, African, or Arab.

221. However, the decline of Rome coinciding with the rise of the Roman Church could not be more clear. Just as Jewish tribes had outlasted the nations of Egypt and Babylonia, Christianity had outlasted Rome. Were nations rising out of the ashes of religious zeal, or were nations the test tubes of man's spiritual reminiscence that propelled religion? Constantine fractured the Roman empire but preserved the Church of Paul. Once Christianity spread to Huns, Burgundians, Visigoths, Vandals, Lombards, and eventually culminated in the Merovingian dynasty, the stage was set for Europe to be a central hub of Christian learning. European Christians would organize crusades to liberate the Ho-

ly land. They once again engaged in the self-fulfilling prophecy of the Jews, that God's kingdom would reign on Earth, thereby uniting the various kingdoms and races of the world and purging the infidel. During the seventh and eight centuries it was Christian warriors like Charles Martel that stopped the spread of Islam to Europe. He led a decisive victory in the Battle of Tours. Christians were not merely preachers that were not spreading their empire by the sword as they claim Muslims have. If this were true, then no Christian nations would have remained. It was precisely the unified military force that led European society to preserve the Western Church against external threats like Islam. Christians are quick to note that an Arian priest named Bahira predicted the rise of Muhammad. Many Coptic Christians and Jews were aware of Islamic teaching. This suggests to them that Muhammad used heretical elements within Christianity to unify a military force in Mecca, to attack Medina, a central hub of Jewish trade, and unify the Arab tribes for a military and economic advantage. Islam claims that it was sent as a correction for Jews and Christians. Islam made the claim that a great nation will be raised against Jews who rejected Jesus, and against Christians who claim that God appeared in the form of a man. Islam, like Judaism, combines theological and political elements to form a theocratic state.

222. The Carolingian and Merovingian Kings protected the church from Northern European tribes and Slavic people, as well as Berbers and Moorish warriors of the south, and had a divine right of kings that was supported by the Church. They built schools that would house great Christian thinkers like St. Anselm and St. Thomas Aquinas. While Anselm's Ontological proof of God is still used today, Aquinas' expounding of Christian philosophy in terms of Aristotelianism is part of mainstream Christian views in the West, as well as his suggestion that the Church and the State both function in their own spheres separately. These thinkers were the basis of both the contemplative religious and secular learning traditions as most of Western thought is a reaction to this period of scholasticism. Aquinas would go further and separate faith and reason and paint a notion of double truth, whereby religious and philosophical truths were held to be different categories of human knowledge. Aquinas had undoubtedly borrowed this from the Muslim heretic Averroes in his disputes with Averroeism, that had a strong influence on Christian philosophy. Once again goes to show that one man's heresy is another's justification of faith, and that the three main so-called western faiths freely interacted in the period that was known as the "Dark Ages" in Europe. While religious learning was at its peak and philosophy and mystical poetry at their heights, Europe was in the dark ages. This narrative has been undoubtedly framed by secular humanists and liberal scholars who fail to see the trajectory of Pauline views in their own set of values. The separation of faith and reason has relegated religion to an affair of secondary importance, but faith and reason had to first be separated as a natural first step. This is seen more in the Catholic Church and not so much in the Eastern Church, which rejected the statement "filioque" or "and the son"

when praying to God, which presents a conflict between the needs of heaven and needs of establishing the Kingdom of God for all mankind in the corporeal realm. The split was between how one prays to the Father, and how one could serve the Son is accentuated in the Western church because of the unique relationship between Western Christianity and Platonic philosophy.

223. Not surprisingly, a conflict of authority soon arose. Popes would shift allegiances and make political arrangements which included the rejection of certain rulers. Kings would reject popes and even set up new appointments. The old formula of God, King and People was reduced to a complete separation between heavenly and earthly duties. These changes were clearly political, and not religious, but were brought through the guise of religious doctrine. Although several institutional changes may have taken place, the essential message of Paul was still a central part of Christian theology. During bouts like the Great Papal Schism, many Popes would claim authority. To make matters worse, the office of Pope had availed itself of some pretty unsavory characters. John XII, Boniface VIII, Julius II, Benedict IX, were all said to have committed acts of sexual immorality, including sodomy and pedophilia. Pope Alexander the VI ceremony entitled "Joust of the Whores" contains details too gruesome to mention for our present purposes. Suffice it to say, it included sex slaves. The Medici family had won the papacy. Lorenzo's son, Leo X would use the Church's selling of indulgences as a veritable money laundering operation. The Medici were more interested in the Hermetic Corpus than the works of classical Greece and Rome that influenced the writings of the early Church. They commissioned Botticelli and Da Vinci to make works praising Hermetic concepts. The Hermetic teachings would influence thinkers like Giordano Bruno, which caused the rise of secular humanism and the waning of the authority of the Church.

224. Writers like John Wycliffe, in his "On Civil Dominion", called for divestment of all property of the Church by the State, and pleaded for serious reforms. He saw the papacy as being imperialized by the State and rejected it, and also wanted to translate the Bible to get it into the hands of everyday people who could use it to challenge the authority of the Church. It is not hard to see that such actions won the support of religious heretics and Jews because they opposed the Church. The minute the writings of Paul made it into the hands of the ordinary people a new era of religious subversion was born. To oppose the cultural and spiritual debasement of the Church, Pope Savonarola would give passionate sermons called the "Bonfire of Vanities", where he set ablaze the signs of cultural decadence in the age. A champion of his stance was Niccolò Machiavelli who gave a revolutionary new vision of politics that would unhinge the idea of political power from the idealized state. Machiavelli was an admirer of the Roman Republic. His view that history, ideology, war, economics, philosophical disposition, and cultural and religious manifestation all being linked in a science of social organization, had an influence on many

thinkers throughout history, but most notably can be seen in the work of Friedrich Nietzsche, who considered himself a student. Like Nietzsche, Machiavelli viewed the history of the world through the lens of using religious morality and political organization for a tactical advantage. Machiavelli felt that religious morality and scientific advancement was only secondary to political and military expertise, which were the true engines of history and true formulators of the laws of mankind.

225. In Germany and in Geneva, similar waning of Church power was at hand. In 1492 the war of Roses was fought. The kings of France and Britain were constantly at each other's throats. New religious pundits were on the rise in the form of a reformation of the Church. In the sixteenth century, Martin Luther offered opposition to the Church. Attending a wealthy school where he read texts of Greek philosophy in Wittenberg Germany, it is a notable fact Luther was an ardent Paulinist who often employed the Epistles to argue against his competition. He made the bold proclamation that the Epistle of James should be burned and removed from the Canonical scriptures. This was because the Epistle contained the teaching that was antithetical to Paul in the notion that one could be saved by one's works. Luther felt that God does not save fictitious sinners. He said sin was a daily part of life and one should sin boldly. Salvation was only by grace. In his "Bondage of the Will", Luther took a strong stance on predestination. Luther declared Reason a whore and broke his monk vows to marry a widow.

226. Another thinker was John Calvin who took a strong stance on the separation of Church and State. He defended the use of interest and usury. His writings on religion, politics, and economics were quite influential. He condemned a heretic named Michael Servetus to death. What was the great sin that Servetus had committed? It was a dispute he staged with Calvin over his denial of the Christian trinity. Servetus believed that his Christian beliefs precluded belief in the Trinity. He wrote letters to Calvin explaining the belief in the Trinity as illogical. Servetus was a polymath. Calvin also wrote tracts against libertines who used the thoughts of Martin Luther to promote sinful behavior using the doctrine of salvation by grace. Apparently, Luther's doctrines had a variety of effects, and one of them was antinomian heresy. A third character who played an equally pivotal role in the scope of reform was the British William Tyndale. Many of the phrases used in his English translation of the Bible are popular terms today and have had a lasting effect on the development of the European ethos, as well as the Christian psyche. Christ spoke Aramaic. The people who wrote the Gospels spoke Greek. The Church translated the works into Latin. From Latin they were translated to English as we read them today. Today what we read is as much Tyndale as it is Jesus. This is to say, not the ideas, but the way they are presented to us, if that has any relevance to us. And should it not?

Chapter 11
The Blood of the Covenant and the
Road to Zion

227. The Doctrine of the Church has become increasingly Westernized, and even Anglicized. The Divine Right of Kings, and the rule of the Church or Kingdom of God has led to a belief that Western Civilization, and especially European Whites, have been chosen to offer God's decree to the rest of mankind. The problem is that this doctrine does not utilize the theo-political model mentioned earlier, nor does it divorce itself from political aims. It is thus this paradoxical realizing of an all-embracing eschaton of universal peace that is at odds with the understanding of a coming judgement upon man. Either explicitly or implicitly, many scholars have suggested that both Christianity and Classical Liberalism present a unique capacity of thought that could have only been formulated in the West. Indeed, we do find it a strange coincidence that scientific enlightenment started in Europe and that the impetus for vast technological achievement started in Western Civilization, by which we mean European and so-called White civilization. What is rarely discussed is how these views are clearly derived by the unique message of salvation in the teaching of Paul which was brought to Europe in his unique capacity as a self-described apostle to the gentiles, bringing salvation for all mankind.

228. What gave European Christians the capacity for scientific enterprise that culminated in secular learning first championed in the West? This ideology first of all assumes that Greek and Roman learning are European or Western forms of learning, but this claim is not historically substantiated. This is due to the fact that Europeans were considered the barbarians of Rome. Europeans covered themselves in mud and rushed into battle, lived in caves, and engaged in nature worship. It is quite ironic that today, in order for modern civilization to thrive such people have to be wiped clean off the face of the earth, even though they more clearly represent the origins of our current civilization more than any other people, because according to their own science and legend such was the origin of mankind. The promotion of Modern Western civilization as we see it today is the support of a New World Order, which wishes to improve and take control of all the natural systems of the world to create an artificial environment. The view in the West of an "end of history", that is suggested by a pseudo eschatology of world peace, is based on the assumption that modern western man will usher in the Kingdom of God or the rule of Heaven on earth. This was early on the belief of the Archetypal Man of the Gnostics and Kabbalists, and that Man was a microcosm of the macrocosm of the Universe. Only through Man could one reach the splendor of God. Whether in Kabbalism

where man is a microcosm of the macrocosm, Hermeticism where God creates Man in order to know himself, Gnosticism where Man is born with the divine spark of God within him that resembles the divine, or the Judeo-Christian synthesis where God has to become like Man in order to prepare mankind for eternal salvation sacrificing himself in the process, Man is seen as the collective measure and meaning of everything in existence. In all of these traditions Man's relationship to God is seen to be on more equal terms. The only other place where Man was both seen as an ideal form, but also the lowest level of creation was in the Pagan cosmology. However, in Pagan cosmology there was no treatment of mankind in general as the focal point of all of existence.

229. An important aspect of historical saga is that it often involves a tale of a great nation or people. Over time this has been misconstrued to mean a blood oath passed down through the generations, where the purified blood of a sacred race of people contains the signature of having faced or retained some god-like qualities. These are the tales of the original man, not unlike the tale of the archetypal man, who is the man of light that has come to redeem the light in man. This tale, however, puts more emphasis on the divine rite passed down through a sacred oath known only to a select few. It had come to fruition in the tales of British Israelism[12] or the "New Jerusalem", that had shown up now and again in western folklore and has permeated various segments of Christian thought throughout the ages. One aspect of the story is that the Sons of Seth differ from the sons of Cain. One half of humanity's blood was cursed as a result of the union of Eve and Satan. Other Kabbalistic myths of demons like Lilith, were about a disobedient wife of Adam that was created by God, who cursed God until God created a new wife for Adam. The demon apparently appears in any ejaculation of sperm that is outside of the union and sanctity of marriage to bring the soul of a person to heights of depravity and accursedness. The demon was said to prey on infants and nursing mothers and to be a curse of fertility. Such demonology regularly appears in pseudepigraphal works that bear the name of Solomon.

230. Either way, it seems that some believed that a sacred lineage of man was passed down and preserved through the ages, especially in the white races. As Darwin believed that the civilized races would conquer over the barbarians, it was recently discovered that there is a disproportionate amount of data from white males in the human genome project. Whites are generally used as the standard for western medicine, which assumes there is not much variation in Man, since man is a machine, whose functions are essentialized. The claim of

---

[12] Cooper, W. (n.d.). *Hour of the Time* [episodes 864-865, 1289-1290]. http://hourofthetime.com/milton-william-bill-cooper-mp3-collection/. We rely on the legendary series Hour of the Time hosted by William Milton Cooper that explores the concept of British Israelism or Christian Identity that has come to influence certain Evangelical factions, which are prominent in the United States. We refer to the episodes mentioned above for the information mentioned in the remainder of this chapter.

the equality of Man comes from the idea of collective one size fits all salvation, just as the idea of noble races comes from stories of sacred lineage. Quite unsurprisingly, all derive from the literature of the Jews. Are we to believe in modern science that has cast the various segments of genes to determine the differences in people? Science has a way of changing its story. We are often told that civilization was formed in the west, and that most of the advances occurred in Europe. At the time of Greece there were already comparable Empires in India, Persia, and Egypt. Yet and still, some theosophists like Helena Blavatsky and Gerald Massey have constructed a myth that Aryans began civilization in India or Africa. Being from the Indian subcontinent, it seems like most of the claims of people who possess European features from such a region is greatly overestimated. People look Persian, and even Arab, but not White. The myth of Aryans has not been substantiated. To make matters worse, South Indians seem to possess genes similar to people from the Ivory coast of Africa. No one single development of race or heritage can be seen to provide a basis for language or civilization. The oldest languages are Polynesian and indigenous. There are, however, groups that claim, not only that Western Civilization began the most important advances for the human race, but also that Whites are the descendants of Ancient Israelites and are the "thirteenth tribe of Israel". Some of these groups have made the claim that Adam means "blood in the cheeks", when it is actually derived from "adamat" or clay. This comes from a story as ancient as Babylon that says that the gods constructed humans from clay. They also believed that the dark spring tides under the moon combined with menstrual blood and represented a curse on women. In Paul's writings we see that men were freed from the law because they did not have to circumcise, but women were still cursed with the law by child-bearing. Hence a curse on Women and the ignoble races was established by occultists who espoused the religious and historical view of British Israelism. The perverse and demented sounding ideology of British Israelism is some of what spawns the racist ideology of groups like Hitler and the KKK, but it is also mentioned in the writings of William Blake and Lord Byron, where they can be seen referring to the concept of the "New Jerusalem" taken from the Neopaganism of Swedenborg. The concept of British Israelism and Christian Identity has been whitewashed and called "Philo-Semitism" by some.

231. What is most illogical in these types of groups is not the insistence on a local or national type of identity based on a humble origin of a unique and heroic type, but that this creed is to be realized on the basis of universal values for all time and for all mankind. If the creed is so unique that it is the sole right of a single nation or people, then would it not defeat its own purpose by becoming universalized? If their root ideology were to take shape around the world in their quest for world domination that they claim is guaranteed to them by destiny they would quickly then lose what makes them unique, which is their own local heritage based on their superiority and rarity among the rest of mankind. Precisely what makes a cultural heritage unique is paid dues after

centuries of rites and rituals that are passed down by traditions of a select group of elders that the rest of people cannot appreciate. What would be the point of such rites if anyone could participate? What would be the value of instituting such cultural rites on a worldwide scale and hence diminishing their value and importance and uniqueness?

232. The belief in a sacred cultural rite that will usher in a "New World" different from the old world, is in this way quite confusing both to the old traditions and the order of the world in its proclaimed origins and its visible goals. One of the beliefs that is mentioned often among such groups is the establishment of the "third temple" and the "ancient state" of Israel to signal the return of Jesus, or at least hasten the coming of the Jewish Messiah. This is the agreement between Christian Zionists and Messianic Jews. Not only does this rely on a false religious eschatology, but it often dupes certain Christian sects into believing that the aid and establishment of the Jews in the "holy land" will help Jesus convert them when he returns. Many American churches preach the doctrine and ideology of British Israelism or Christian Zionism. Hand in hand with this belief system is a dual road of salvation for Christians and Jews derived from the teachings of Paul. In the founding of the British secret intelligence of Elizabethan England, such beliefs were commonplace. Especially among men like Elias Ashmole and John Dee who were regular patrons of the British Royal Society, and some of its founding members. These men practiced Alchemy and spread ideas during the European Enlightenment that were to the purposes and ends of religious and political subversion. They would develop groups like the Rosicrucians and Freemasons and were very notable proto-enlightenment thinkers that promoted the key tenets of science and liberalism.

233. It was men like Ashmole and Paolo Sarpi, that were not only the champions of scientific humanism, but also founders of the occult. One of the views of such occult origins was the story of Jacob of Arimathea, most popularly seen in Gospel narrative as a family member of Jesus, or someone connected to Jesus, who apparently assumed the responsibility for the burial of Jesus. This is important for many reasons. The main significance of this little tale is the mysterious disappearance of the body of Jesus that is mentioned in the Gospels, along with his resurrection as a flesh and bone human, where he appeared to his disciples. Both Christians and Muslims believe that Jesus never died like a normal man, although they seem to slightly differ on how this all took place. Christians are not sure in what state Jesus existed after he was resurrected from the dead, or in what state his supposed essence was preserved in the three days after he supposedly left the world. Muslims, on the other hand, believe that Jesus must have escaped his death. Either way, the people who believe that the literal blood of Christ was passed down through the generations to continue the blood of the covenant are not referring to the Passover ritual referred to as the last supper, or the sacrificing of animals on Yom Kippur, but instead a tale of Joseph of Arimathea taking the bones of Christ's dead

body to England along with the supposed wife of Jesus Mary Magdalene and the children of Jesus, to continue the bloodline of King David. This group believes that not only did Jesus die a normal death but was married and had children to preserve his legacy. Some claim this legacy was preserved through the bloodline of the Merovingian kings. Although there are many other accounts that differ with this one employed by such groups, it is important to note that most of the tales are seen as allegorical at best as they wish to replace the tales of revelation and covenant with God with a story of a nation or people that is representative of all mankind, and whose sacred lineage holds the essence of what is divine in Man. The tales of the disciples of Jesus traveling to far off places like Mary Magdalene taking a boat to France or England were undoubtedly used to justify the Divine Right of certain British and French Kings.

234. The writings of Paolo Sarpi, and men like Nicolas of Cusa, who were the founders of Humanism, actively sought to subvert religious ideology for political ends. Nicolas of Cusa was especially influential in developing the narrative of progress of Man being sought in scientific discovery and invented the idea of the "Coincidentia Oppositorum" or "coincidence of opposites" that states that every idea presupposes its opposite and was the basis for the Hegelian Dialectic, while Sarpi was a promoter of liberalism in general, whose books were a veritable Bible for the occult. While it may seem strange and unheard of to many, such beliefs were so widespread that even Martin Luther seemed to have signed his correspondence with a Rosicrucian seal. Coupled with the fact are his Gnostic beliefs of a dismissal of Reason, and denial of the free will with salvation by grace alone, reflected an "absolute depravity" of man in his psycho-spiritual state. Where it becomes controversial is when it is seen that Luther was not a person trying to reform religion from the inside, but a religious subverter like Paul who had come into the religious game from the outside in order to change the rules, but this very same claim has been made by many intelligent researchers who are not willing to settle for what is merely observed on the surface of things. We have already shown that the beliefs of Gnosticism varied slightly from mainstream Christian beliefs and were certainly rejected by some Christian thinkers in the first part of this book. These groups drew from certain Christian and Jewish elements and made clear attempts to subvert Christian doctrine since its conception. At this time Europe was rife with religious sectarianism. The separation of Church and State had made it easy to hide one's subversive tactics from the State, since religion was no longer tied to dealings with the State. Here, secret sects and occult groups not only operated under the radar of official rulers, but also mingled with the political and scholarly elite.

235. The belief system of Gnostics seemingly accepts a view that matter is a degeneration of spirit and form as an unstated premise, just as Paul believed that this age was cursed by its attachment to law and flesh instead of faith and spirit which will be fulfilled in the age to come. It should be noted that Paul

and the Platonists via their Orphic and Pythagorean underpinning accepted the same thing. They added to this a vertical hierarchy of being, and also provided a horizontal and an eschatological or teleological framework. Through the use of his reason Man could transform matter and become like God. The mysterious split of King Henry VIII in his establishment of the Church of England was supposedly not grounded in religious doctrine. Later, the strange instance of King Edward VII and the Palestine Expeditionary Force by the British Military, which was funded by prominent Jews like Rothschild, is a regular reflection of Christian Zionism founded on the tenets of Gnosticism, Rosicrucianism, and Freemasonry, that were founded by those groups like the Templars, Albigensian, and Islamic Apostate sects like the Ismailis. Jewish Nationalism, that was founded by those groups claiming that Jews have an unconditional bond with the land of Israel, and based on Classical Liberalism share the belief in a coming of a new age with Paulinists, Messianic Jews, and Secular Humanists, which suggests a pseudo eschatology of world peace and universal brotherhood in the prophecy of the healing of the world, also known in Messianic Judaism as "Tikun Olam". This is the belief in an inherent progress and final stage of events that one should devote one's life toward. Why has the European and Christian heritage been indelibly linked to the establishment of Modern Israel? These reconfigurations of religious values can be traced to thinkers like Robert Fludd, who gained initiation by men like Johannes Valentin Andreae, pushing a utopian worldview based on Protestant teachings. Highlighted by the fact that Lincoln had made a pact with Russia in the American Civil War, the Confederacy would as a result choose to side with the British. Certain elements of British Israelism would become clearly engrained even in the American experience, which was itself a product of centuries of religious sectarianism.

236. Protestants, Jews, and Occultists all sought to subvert religious institutions and supported secular aims because it allowed them to openly challenge religious institutions that were the most prevalent. Most are unaware that the British had taken sides in the American Civil War, meanwhile British agents like Karl Marx were being funded by British Secret Intelligence and paid by terrorists like Lord Palmerston. The American Civil War and the French Revolution were full of groups that were practicing religious subversion and Freemasonry. Robespierre was a Freemason. Richard Brothers and Arthur Scofield, who would interpret and import dispensationalism and millenarianism into biblical teachings, borrowed from the teachings of John Nelson Darby, who referred to God as "the Architect", which was a masonic phrase. Both men served on the side of the Confederacy. The father-in-law of President Theodore Roosevelt was William Bellinger Bulloch, who was a statesman in the American South, as well as an owner of several slaves. His family too supported Freemasonry. Albert Pike, who participated in the Civil War on the side of the Confederacy, wrote a book called "Morals and Dogma", where he explains a World War that will be instigated through a final war between Christians and Muslims, that would summon the coming of a "New Age". He felt

that the goal of eliminating the doctrines of both Islam and Christianity would play a pivotal role. Jewish Messianism has a similar goal. Some Rabbis have gone so far as to claim that Islam is the broom of Judaism, preparing the Middle East and Western Nations for the rule of Israel by spreading a false Islamic and anti-Christian doctrine. Other thinkers like Helena Blavatsky who invented the "Aryan" myth and wrote "The Secret Doctrine", and founded the Theosophical Society, as well as Guiseppe Mazzini, who wrote "Alta Vendita", and founded Young Italy, espoused similar themes about destroying or subverting religion. These works were known as the Bibles of freemasonry and occultism.

237. There are many religious symbols, relics, treasures, and themes of death and rebirth used by these groups. The underlying theme is a sacred clan or group that functions as the inheritors of a sacred rite. Even though the claim is of a unified and unique heritage, none can be found among the various tribes of Gauls and Druids and Celts, who were all distinct peoples. It was Darby who claimed that Russians were a force known as Gog, and that the British were the thirteenth tribe of Israel which would summon its destruction. The writer Richard Brothers had changed this to mean all White Europeans were the thirteenth tribe. Helena Blavatsky expanded the term to "Aryans", which according to her included all the light skin people of the world. Her main argument was concerning a unique "anthropogenesis" or sacred lineage of the ascended masters that was, according to her older than Egypt, beginning in India. Obviously, no historical trace exists to back up their claims. The Twelve Tribes of Israel were Rueben, Simron, Levi, Judah, Issachar, Zebulon, Asher, Gad, Dan, Aaphtali, Joseph, and Benjamin. In the Bible the sons of Joseph, Ephraim and Manasseh, are declared to be inheritors of a vast worldly expanse. Ephraim is declared to be a multitude of Nations. Manasseh is declared to be the progenitor of a "great people". The claim is made by the followers of these groups that Manasseh is made to be the "thirteenth tribe" of Israel. The view taught that this particular prophecy foretold how Israel and Britain would become strong Maritime powers, and signal the return of the Messiah.

238. This is a highly interpretative and imaginative scale of events based on our recent quibbles with history. Events are cast to the Danube and Black Sea in Crimea, at the foothills of the Caucasus mountains, where the tribes of Scandinavia originate. Some claim that the Babylonian king Nebuchadnezzar sent a Jewess to marry an Irish King to continue the bloodline of King David. They arrived in Scotland, and eventually to England in Glastonbury, where a rock called Jacob's Pillar is said to be. Paul describes a rock that followed the Nation of Israel and the early Church. He said it was on this rock that the Church was built. This was taken to mean a physical piece of land. The rock represents an ancient foundation of earthly and eternal rule. There is also the Philosopher's Stone or the alchemical base material that represents the dark and negative, material, and divine feminine essence within matter. This was a rock that was said to have brought forward the ancient teachings of every lan-

guage, civilization, and religion on earth, and was said to represent the Prisca Theologica of Ibn Rushd, or underlying wisdom that unites various traditions and religious sects which influenced perennial philosophy. However, there is no proof of any divine relics hidden underneath the Great Pyramid or Masjid Al Aqsa, which is said to have Solomon's temple buried underneath it. Countless expeditions in history have claimed to search for such relics. To think that God, who sent his son to the world, would base power on such trinkets is beyond bizarre, but then these groups don't really believe that either. How could they when they rely on such claims of worldly power and hide their true intentions? A common belief among such groups is that the throne of the King of Great Britain is a continuation of the throne of King David, even though such kings are not taken seriously in the Bible and Old Testament which shows their rule as purely transitory and are expressly condemned.

239. In the "Secret Destiny of America" by Manly P Hall, it is argued that the discovery of America was predicted by Plato in his stories of Atlantis, and championed by Francis Bacon, who writes in his book "The New Atlantis" that a world domination will be brought about by a scientific elite. This lost civilization or secret origin, through which a "New Age" is set to come about as the Kingdom of God of the Lost Tribes has once again gained a foothold through the Eurasian theosophy of men like G.I Gurdjieff, Julius Evola, and Savitri Devi. Some of these authors claim that civilization began in Eurasia among the proto-Europeans "Aryans" of Germanic and Slavic origin, even though the Germanic and Slavic people are distinct and are unlike the Bohemian which combine cultural traits from the French, German, Swiss, and Slavic people. This theory really stretches credulity when names like Saxon are changed to "Isaac-son", and British to "Brith-ish", signifying a special covenant between White people and the Ancient State of Israel in history. Historically no links can be found between the English and Hebrew languages. None of the reasons provided for their unique religious teachings can be met with anything mentioned in the Bible as we have stated earlier.

240. The link between science and magic, knowledge and power, was being promulgated through the various forms of incantation, preparation, synthesis, interpretation, and admixture of various elements and concepts. The practice of Magic, which is also known as alchemy, hermeticism, and recently theosophy, was a second century phenomenon like the modern version of Pauline line Christianity, Gnosticism, heretical Jewish sectarianism, and the formulation of Jewish oral tradition. Early Rosicrucian documents stress their links to the Knights Templars, who trace their origin to the Cathari and Albigensian heretics of the European dark ages. As the Spanish Inquisition allied the French to the Church, the British subterranean vengefulness came to fruition in an attack on the French Aristocracy, as well as the Pope. This meant the fortification and reformulation of religious doctrine through the grafting of British Israelism. Many like Erik Prince, CEO of Blackwater, are believers in a crusade that

must be fought. Any militia that claims to be a Christian militia is really a religious army.

241. Oliver Cromwell sponsored the return of Jews to England. John Milton engaged in an intense study of the Kabbalah which is the basis for Freemasonry. Newton studied alchemy and corresponded with John Locke on the subject. His interests included finding the measurements for Solomon's temple and finding when the third temple would finally be built, which he based on astrological charts. Newton's mechanistic view of the Cosmos, along with Descartes view that the body was just a machine, was promoted over the philosophy of Leibniz by the Royal Society of Great Britain. The Royal Society used its influence to popularize Darwin's work instead of Alfred Russell Wallace, who made significant discoveries on Natural Selection, which were then formulated into Darwin's own theory. There were attempts to prove that English Common Law was the same as Jewish Oral Tradition. Jews were involved in the funding of both the Crusades and the Atlantic slave trade, as noted by many historians. There were many myths like the Curse of Ham which was used to justify slavery, and attempts to show that the House of Judah was racially inferior. The Bible clearly states that King David and the House of Judah conquered over the Land of Israel. This means that many tribes existed in Israel, but at the time of David they were conquered and unified. Some groups even claim that Aryans are none other than the Assyrians, who were the ancient enemies of the Jews, reversing the previous doctrines that attempt to prove a link between Whites and Israel. Lord Palmerston and Lord Shelburne had committed the British Empire to Zionism. Benjamin Disraeli was a Zionist Prime Minister of Great Britain around the era of World War I. The opposition of Palmerston was John Russell, the father of philosopher Bertrand Russell. Bertrand Russell is hardly noted for being a Fabian Socialist and Eugenicist, but regularly helped to promote such views. He felt that eventually a technocratic society would rule the world, similar to the views of Bacon.

242. The British Empire had made attempts to weaken the Turkish Caliphate, and succeeded in the funding of Jewish radicals, and Muslim heretics, that were used to create the Jewish state and the Saudi Arabian Kingdom. The house of Saud was aligned with British Power, and Israel was created as its sister state. It is no wonder that today such Nations enjoy such a cozy relationship with Western powers even though they do not possess secular government and are properly theocratic institutions propped up by an alliance with the West. They now falsely pretend to be the guardians of these ancient belief systems. British spies also were used in the French revolution and to overthrow the Czars of Russia. The Earl of Shaftesbury, who was a patron of John Locke and founder of the Whig party, supported an anti-conformist faction within Protestantism that supported the State over the Church. From this period roughly to the period of 1912, where General Allanbee claimed to have liberated Palestine by means of a Crusade, so called Western Civilization has had

an obsession with obtaining the rights of the Holy Land in Jerusalem. Despite all of the pretense towards Secularism, this secret hope remained fervent for over nine hundred years and culminated in the mysterious return after two thousand years of the Jews to their Holy Land. If anyone seriously believes at this point that what is written in those so-called ancient books does not play a role in the affairs of the world, then they are sadly mistaken. The Jonathan Edward style revivalism and Franklin style Hellfire club were expressions of such Protestant heterodoxy, and though varying in style, were two heads of the same snake.

243. Franklin would fabricate his own piety and use religion as a means to spread political propaganda masquerading as Puritanism. He would help popularize the phrase "God helps those who help themselves". In Thessalonians 4:11 we read, "And aspire to live quietly and to mind your own affairs, and to work with your hands, as we instructed you". Paul instructed his followers to be day laborers and to be dependent on no one (next verse). He, however, did not instruct his followers to live wholly separate from a life of service to the State, or spending time away from the temple. He preferred a quiet sober life in public view and in public service. Still the so-called believers of Paul are adamant that their views led to a calm inventive spirit, even when science that was propagated early on by Alchemists threatened to destroy religion and subvert religious teachings. Why did the Western Enlightenment only arise among White Europeans? Clearly the problem is much deeper than the "spirit of work" and the "puritan work ethic" and has much deeper roots than present day Western States. The so-called West has always had a fascination with the future and the coming age.

244. What has also been made abundantly clear is how mainstream such an ideology has become with new adherents claiming a special role of western civilization in establishing a world system. Mainstream Christian organizations like those of Jerry Falwell and Pat Robertson regularly include Christian Zionist interpretations, like those found in the Scofield Bible. Today Zionism is mainly a Christian phenomenon and not a Jewish one. In the Book of Ezra, it states that the so-called lost tribes were never lost. Even Paul mentions the twelve tribes, as we recall earlier, mentioning his own origins from the Tribe of Benjamin. Jesus mentions the Twelve Tribes. When were these tribes lost? The Bible does not make reference to tribes being "lost". What we have instead is a libertine socialist style faction of French Freemasonry that wishes to make a utopian new world order, and a British Israelism that is derived from the Jewish style Nationalism of the previous ages. It is a struggle between religious sects and occult expressions. Europe gave rise to the rebirth of Israel founded by European Jews. This would be a mark of great significance for any theological worldview involving Jesus. Jesus clearly warned of such clear usurpation of power in order to achieve a divine status.

245. There is yet to be proof that Jesus would have accepted any organization or building that now calls itself a Church. Jesus accepted all and rejected no one. Jesus made acquaintances with fishermen, prostitutes, tax collectors, social outcasts, criminals, sinners, and the poor. Jesus was not about starting a business or being a professional. Jesus taught that the only way to have self-respect is to practice humility. He never sought anyone out, and never emerged from his own people where he preached in a small town in gatherings of only a few. Jesus did not preach to the crowds but taught parables to his close companions. He never desired to know the world of the learned or the soldiers and statesmen. Jesus had no weapons, no money, and no political support and taught that no one needed any of these things to be a good person. Jesus openly confessed that any man who teaches this will be persecuted by the many. Jesus kept to himself and kept the company of a small group of friends and family.

246. He taught not a political or philosophical treatise or doctrine. His teaching was purely religious and ethical maxims. What was evil for the world was transformed by Jesus into a good. No one understood Jesus and Jesus constantly claimed that he was misunderstood and constantly misinterpreted by his own disciples and followers. He declared wealth and honor and power and dominion to be corrupting forces in the world. He declared that the common man only sees the visible surface and not the unseen, and that in the constant battle of good and evil, good will triumph. The love of man and the love of God battle each other. Love works on either side. Jesus taught that to give is to acquire, and that hatred is proof of avarice, and propriety of sin. He claimed that when true love takes effect, it will manifest through everyone.

247. Jesus did not claim that his message was for the Gentiles, or that he had come to abolish the law of Moses or to alter it in any way. Jesus taught that God was the father of the entire human family, and that one does not have to work for bread. Man does not live on bread alone. Love for God and love for man is the same. However, love for man and denial of God is hatred of mankind. Fear of man is the cause of all hatred. Fear of man causeth snares. He surpassed the Pharisees in fasting, praying, and knowledge of scripture. He exceeded the commandments of chastity and fellowship. Jesus used expressions that took on the tone of Oriental proverbs, and not of Platonic ideals. He warned people not to do good deeds to gain the approval and honor of other men. He called men who pray to be seen hypocrites. Jesus told his disciples to pray in seclusion offering prostration to God. This is how Jesus prayed. He taught that violence begets violence, and that in order to be forgiven by others, one must himself forgive others. Where your treasure is there your heart will be also. What you resist persists, and what you desire attracts you. Those who are bound by desire see only the outward shell and container. Such people focus on appearances. Do not pray in order to be seen by other people. One must go inside the heart to find the light of truth. No man can serve two masters. One must be fearless. Do not even pagans love their brothers? Love everyone

instead. Quite a contrast from the political machinations and games we have just witnessed. Christ predicted that false teachers would appear in his name and that the majority of mankind would be led astray in the process. Christ said very little about earthly rule. He came at a time that matched the Messianic expectations of the Jews. None of these simple sermons that are found in the Gospels can equate themselves with what has purportedly been imagined to be about Jesus by the founders of various heretical forms mentioned above. None of the tales of blood and magic can abide the teaching of Jesus.

Chapter 12
Out of the Many, One
/ E Pluribus Unum

248. The Pauline message is inherently democratic, which is another form of articulation which it seems to share with the Greek. Some Christians even refer to the doctrine of inclusivity that is a one for all message of salvation. The Pauline view is an all-inclusive message that assures a soteriological progression of all for one and one for all. It is important to note that such historical movements that clearly are subversive in nature are highlighted by the political tension in Europe exploited by the Church. Such rare historical shifts after clear patterns of stability do not just rise up like a fungus or mold. They are rather brought about by a confluence of man-made efforts which are usually overestimated for being "organic" or "spontaneous" eruptions of moral strife or cultural evolution. Nothing can be farther from the truth. After the expulsion of Jews in 1492 during the Spanish Inquisition, Jewish Kabbalists became Christian Kabbalists, and Christian Kabbalists became Jewish Kabbalists[13]. The Rosicrucian supported Sabbatean and Frankist forms of Judaism, just as certain Rabbis welcomed the Protestant Reformation, which would make a move towards religious toleration. In 1666 both British Empiricism in the philosophy of John Locke, and religious subversion of figures like Sabbatai Zevi "the false messiah", were making their rounds. Locke twisted the words of the Bible to support the notion of private property, which he said God gave to Adam rather than "private dominion" through the will of the creator, and had reduced man to a blank slate determined by society. Locke was supported by the Earl of Shaftesbury, who was a proponent of the Protestant Reformation. The "prophet" Sabbatai Zevi led many Jews into apostasy with false claims that he was the Messiah, including Queen Christina of Sweden who was the patron of the philosopher Descartes, also a major enlightenment thinker. When Zevi converted to Islam to escape persecution many of his followers would secretly convert with him, while retaining their previous beliefs and practices in secret. These were known as the Donmeh, or Jewish Muslim apostates. Similar to Ismaili and Druze, they would act as a curious faction within Islamic civilization that was familiar with Western mysticism and western philosophy. It is

---

[13] Livingstone, D. (2013). *Black Terror White Soldiers: Islam, Fascism & the New Age.* Sabilillah Publication. The information in the next 14 paragraphs are from the work by Livingstone from information contained in his book on pages 115-159 in the chapters entitled "Renaissance and Reformation" and "The year 1666". For the rest of the chapter, we rely on pg. 257-269 of the same text from a chapter entitled "The Protocols of the Elders of Zion".

not hard to see how such a group could come to play a pivotal role in the destruction of the Caliphate that was necessary to establish a Jewish state.

249. As pointed out by researcher David Livingstone in his book "Black Terror, White Soldiers", centuries of religious subversion lay at the root of key political changes in Europe. One of the more prominent followers of Sabbatai Zevi was Jacob Frank. In 1757 a group of Kabbalistic Jews that were protected by the Christian community of Poland used the Zohar, a book of Jewish mysticism, to attack traditional Jewish practices. His followers would break the Sabbath and perform orgiastic rituals to spite the orthodox practice of Judaism. Followers of these groups had no problem proclaiming that they were Christians or Muslims to evade capture. Jews were expelled from England in 1290, in France in 1306, in Saxony in 1348, in Hungary in 1360, in Belgium in 1370, in Slovakia in 1380, in Austria in 1420, and in the Netherlands in 1444. This coincided with religious factions. Some Jews known as conversos or the derogatory term "Marranos", meaning swine, suggested that they were secret Jews. The history of this has been acknowledged by Jewish historians. Other trends like the Baal Shem Tov (literally meaning "amulet maker") rose up at the time, who was declared to be a direct descendent from the line of King David, was the founder of Hasidic Judaism in the 18th century. The Hasidic movement relies on the teachings of Maimonides and the Lurianic Kabbalah. These are not then properly termed Orthodox movements but are essentially modern reforms akin to Protestantism. There is also a connection between Protestant reformers who studied the Kabbalah and Jewish texts, as well as the Hebrew language, to gain a deeper understanding of Biblical texts and unlock the secrets of the Bible, mainly so they could pretend to be the real Christian movement and spite the Church. Secret Jews, Gnostic sects, and Merkabah mysticism were on the rise. One monk named Lucas of Tuy complained that Jews buy off powerful leaders with gold, and propose blasphemies to the Christians. But I contend that the Christians already had their own hands full with their own heresies, and one could make a similar case from a Jewish standpoint.

250. In either case, conversos joined orders like Franciscans, Dominicans, and the Discalced Carmelites. Dionysian mystical sects influenced Western Mysticism in figures like Meister Eckhart. Another key influence were the Ismailis who derived a heretical derivation of Zoroastrian, Islamic, and Pagan beliefs. Such factions preached a demonology that affected power in the world through control of demonic forces or Djinn. Islamic, Christian, and Jewish apostasy lay at the root of modern "Orthodox" factions. In Islam we find the Ismaili, in Christianity we have the Hermeticists, and in Judaism the Kabballah. Look no further than the priests of every faith for the main source of religious heresy, as was previously stated. The house of Borgia, Ignatius of Loyola, and Christopher Columbus are argued to be conversos by some historians. Ignatius of Loyola who founded the Jesuits, was previously a member of a heretical sect

known as the Alumbardos, which means "the illuminated ones". Author Robert Maryks in "The Jesuit Order as a Synagogue of Jews" further explores the connections. In Cecil Roth's "History of the Marranos", he says that the discovery of America and its connection with Jews is not merely a "fortuitous coincidence".

251. Columbus in his correspondences cites his journey in discovery of new land to be a mission intended to find a safe haven for persecuted Jews. He addressed certain themes with Hebrew words and took note of Jewish high holidays. He apparently planned his journeys according to Jewish holy days. His triangular signature is seen by some to resemble the symbol seen on Jewish gravestones. He writes in his journals of obtaining gold from Asia taken from the made-up accounts by Marco Polo in order to finance a crusade and rebuild the "New Jerusalem". He took slaves and punished natives who would not offer to tell him the source of their gold. Other explorers like Vasco de Gama and Prince Henry the Navigator were members of the Military Order of Christ, that was a reformulation of the Knights Templar in 1312 by Pope Clement IV. Columbus sailed using the Red Cross of the Templars. Columbus' voyage to "the new world" was funded by Conversos Louis Santangel, and Gabriel Sanchez and Kabbalist Don Isaac Abrabanel. Hernan Cortes and Miguel de Cervantes, as well as Francesco Pizarro (Cortes' cousin) had secret Jewish converts among their men as they were engaged in conquest. These were the first foundations of what would become the Atlantic Slave trade, Western expansion, and Colonialism in general. Ed Kritlers best seller "Jewish Pirates of the Caribbean" recounts the tales of these cases. Scholars like Abraham Farrissol have claimed that even Martin Luther was a Marrano. Luther's disciple Phillip Melanchthon, whose uncle was a well renowned Kabbalist, wrote about the rule of Israel in the last days. Another figure connected to Martin Luther who practiced and espoused teachings of mysticism was Johannes Ruechlin, who wrote "De Arte Cabalistica" explaining the Kabbalistic sciences. Since ardent Paulinists like Luther believed that salvation was of the Jews they extolled the knowledge of Kabbalists to undo the earthly institutions which were needed to come apart to establish New Jerusalem.

252. He said that the Kabbalah was the greatest aid to Christians who sought to meld the mysteries of faith with those of scientific inquiry. Luther supported Ruechlin, who was most notably a Greek and Hebrew scholar, in a controversy known as the "battle of the books". This was an attempt to convert Jews to Protestantism. While in Wittenberg, Luther convened with many Rabbis to know the secrets behind certain Bible passages. Jewish converts to Protestantism would spread the new church by attacking their former faith. Paul of Burgos and Luther in his "On the Jews and their Lies" made similar attempts, according to some scholars. According to the research of David Livingstone, some regarded Luther as a crypto-jew who would educate Christians away from the bad elements of their faith, and hence reformulate Christian doctrine

to move it closer to Jewish law. Abraham Ben Eliezar, who was a Kabbalistic scholar, considered Luther to be a prophet who signaled the rebuilding of Jerusalem. The link between Europeans and Jews was explored in the last segment on British Israelism, but here a collaboration can be seen in Christian and Jewish sects within a pivotal period in European society.

253. In England, the philosophy of the Enlightenment was tied into the Reformation for the simple fact that both opposed the Church. This is what made it necessary to establish the Church of England. Sir Edward Spencer's poem Faerie Queen contained Neoplatonic elements, as did Luther's hymns. The prophecy of Merlin, which proclaimed that Saxons would rule over Britons until freed by King Arthur was related by Geoffrey of Monmouth, who used Pagan tales like the Aenead to construct his legend that was also mixed in with Biblical tales. John Dee, the Royal Astrologer of Queen Elizabeth, used numerical configurations derived from texts of the Kabbalah to channel spirits. He openly practiced magic and alchemy. John Dee coined the term "British Empire". He firmly believed in colonial expansion. It was rumored that Sir Francis Drake's defeat of the Spanish Armada was aided by the sorcery of John Dee. There is an odd connection between this and the later connection of Winston Churchill summoning Aleister Crowley to help use magic to defeat the Nazis, who incidentally practiced similar teachings through the Thule society, where the teachings of Dietrich Eckhart and Lanz Von Lebenfels influenced Hitler. Dee was said to have been the inspiration behind the Shakespearean character Prospero, and Marlowe's Dr. Faustus. He was a close friend of Sir Walter Raleigh. Walter Raleigh is well known for having helped the English to colonize America. In his "History of the World" he apparently believed that a secret order of Magi controlled world events from ancient times, and also espoused a belief in magic.

254. John Dee was said to have made prophetic predictions concerning the end of the world, including the fall of Rome and Constantinople that would signal the coming of a New Age. He composed a sacred alphabet known as Enochian and was a British spy. He believed that the Book of Revelation of St. John pointed to a New World Order just around the corner through the formulation of a "universal religion". Dee attempted to influence Rudolph II, the King of Bohemia, to support his imperialist agenda by convincing him he was possessed by demons. Dee followed the Fama Fratenatatis of Johann Valentin Andraea. He helped secure the marriage of Elizabeth Stuart, the daughter of King James, to King Fredrick, securing a dynastic alliance. The Rosicrucian tract called "The Chemical Wedding of Christian Rosenkreutz" is a symbol of their union supposedly. The belief of Menassah Ben Israel in his letter to Oliver Cromwell was that the readmission of Jews to England would help bring about an end times scenario, and should be hastened. Cromwell was instrumental in England's move towards becoming secularized. Menassah believed his wife was a descendant of King David.

255. Radical preachers like John Dury and Samuel Hartlib, who formed the Hartlib Circle, advocated alchemical and Rosicrucian themes. This group would also become connected to groups like the Invisible College, and the British Royal Society. Hartlib reported that the French philosopher Rene Descartes spent time in the house of Elizabeth Stuart, and developed a close relationship with her daughter as well. As we will later see, most of the patrons of the modern philosophical movement like Descartes, Spinoza, Leibniz, Kant, and Hegel, all belonged to religious offshoots of Rosicrucians secret societies. This brings us to the conclusion, once again, that changes in religious subversion, political tumult, mystical exploration, and philosophical angst are not that far divided, and are much rather inextricably linked with the changes and developments of certain historical patterns.

256. John Amos Comenius, who was the Bishop of the Bohemian Brethren was a heir to the Hussite faction supported by Protestant reformers, and was a member of the Hartlib Circle. The Waldensians and John Huss were condemned by the Church for bringing a Jewish influence into Christian teachings. Comenius wrote a book called "The Didactica Magna" which championed universal education. Later people like Thomas Jefferson would propose the idea of public education to educate the citizenry through Republicanism. John Milton, who was a key influence on men like Thomas Paine and quotes his version of Satan in "Common Sense", was also connected to the Hartlib Circle, and fervently studied the Kabbalah. His quote that it is better to reign in Hell than to serve in Heaven is a favorite saying among such groups. Milton's Satan can be seen as a noble rebel who challenges an illegitimate power. This is a perfect Gnostic representation. Menassah Ben Israel was also reported to have met with an occultist known as La Peyrere. Some regard La Peyrere as the father of modern Zionism in his attempts to align the Jewish power with the King of France. La Peyrere as the others we have mentioned were not apparently without influence to those in power, while pushing for antinomian religious views. This was clearly a tactic employed by Paul in his meetings with those in power. Paul sought out those with positions of influence that would help him establish his version of Christian teachings.

257. Meanwhile, all the talk of the New World Order and beginning the world anew, as well the talk of the Kingdom of God and New Jerusalem was instilling the myth of progress, and the planning of a theological world state. At the time, this involved an overthrow of the Catholic King of France. Menasseh Ben Israel wrote about the "lost tribes" of Israel and the "Hope of Israel". Cromwell had dissolved the Parliament and appointed himself "Lord Protector". Samuel Butler in a satire on the Restoration called the "Characters", tells of Rosicrucian who attempted a misguided Reformation of the Church. Being a critical analyst of thought and culture, he was clearly not convinced of the type of knowledge these groups pretended to, and compared them to the An-

cient Gnostics in the work "Hudibras". According to researcher Richard Christopher Hill and others, the Jews would take sides in the Anglo-Spanish War, to create an Anglo-Dutch alliance which culminates in the British-Dutch East India Company.

258. In a 1609 Charter, Francis Bacon, also known as the writer of the Rosicrucian influenced "New Atlantis", is mentioned as a shareholder of the Virginia Company of London. Charles II officially established the British Royal Society, which would become a premiere promoter of the arts and sciences in lieu of humanism and occultism active among British intellectuals. This was most clearly the afterthought of over two centuries of religious subversion during the Protestant Reformation. So-called "Natural Philosophers" like Robert Boyle and Isaac Newton and Charles Darwin were funded and popularized by the Royal Society. In his book "Millenarianism and Messianism in English thought", Christopher Hill explains that members of the Royal Society used mathematical speculations, and numerological Gematria style magic to explain Biblical dates, the movements of the heavens, and the date of the end of the world. Some had predicted that 1666 would signal the coming of the age of prophecy.

259. Some of the readers of Manasseh Ben Israel were followers of the false messiah Sabbatai Zevi, who had convinced a huge swath of the Amsterdam Jewish population to follow him. In the "New Atlantis" of Francis Bacon, who most famously coined the term "Knowledge is power", conceived of a civilization run by Philosopher-Scientists. He was an avid Statesman, a Chancellor of England, and supervised the translation of the King James Bible. Scholars throughout history have suggested that the writings of Shakespeare were actually written by Bacon. Shakespeare's fascination with occult themes like fairies, witches, and ghosts would be known also to Bacon, whose cover of New Atlantis was adorned with Rosicrucian symbolism, including the "all seeing eye" and masonic compass. Bacon argued that the discovery of America was the discovery of "the New Atlantis", where a technocratic elite would control the resources of the world by machines that travel through the sky and underwater. He said that man should dominate and control nature and subdue all life, as is found in the King James Bible. The man that can manipulate and change nature into whatever form he desires was like unto God. This was clearly the Gnostic view that "Reason" governs and rules over matter, and by discovering the inner light of Reason, also known as Logos, one could master the forces of Nature. Here Nature is equated with the dark, negative, material, feminine, impulse within matter which is a malleable stasis, and Reason is compared to the male of ingenuity and strength and inventiveness that should dominate and control the female in every respect.

260. Some of those who first arrived in America on the Mayflower were Rosicrucian. What theorists like Max Weber have neglected to point out is that

such communities clearly diverged from traditional Christian doctrine. Others like Christians who are sympathetic to the cause of Classical Liberalism wish to equate these doctrines with the New Covenant theology of Paul. Classical Liberalism was piggybacked on Rosicrucian and Protestant theology to weaken the influence of the Church. The influence of the religious offshoots that have clear political motives are not clearly mentioned or discussed in any depth. Nicolas Hagger in "The Secret founding of America" points out the closeness between the doctrines of Puritan and Rosicrucian philosophy. Dutch Puritanism was especially linked to Rosicrucianism. Another founding member of the Royal Society was John Wilkins. He was the Chaplain of Frederick V. Pierre Degua De Mons was a founder of French settlements in Quebec and was a member of the "School of Night", which was an official school of atheism centered around Sir Walter Raleigh. Raleigh was a popularizer of tobacco. Christopher Marlow, who wrote Dr. Faustus, mentioned earlier, was a member of the sect. Not surprisingly, his tale "Dr. Faustus" which is considered a renowned classical text is about a scientific genius, who upon being dissatisfied with life strikes a deal with the devil. It is not clear that everyone who came to America simply did so to escape religious persecution or for Holy reasons suggested to them by God whispering in their ears. Many of these quests centered around a vision to erect a wholly new community forged through the ideals of some of these occult sects.

261. America may have been destiny, but those who have controlled and pioneered what America stands for don't have to speak for us. We have to allow ourselves to take the good with the bad without taking sides with history. It may come as a surprise to some that men like John Locke, who penned the famous dictums of Life, Liberty, and Property that are the basis for modern industrialized civilization, regularly convened with men like Benjamin Furly, leader of the group "the Lantern". Henry More, Lady Conway, Locke, and Benjamin Furly regularly met with students of Jacob Bohme. Hegel would regard Jacob Bohme as the first German philosopher, and his philosophy would play a key role in the work of both Hegel and Schelling. Furly along with van Helmont associated with Petrus Serranius. He was a proponent of Millenarianism and a friend of philosopher Baruch Spinoza.

262. Spinoza developed the model of Nature's God. This is the type of God that Jefferson refers to in the Declaration of Independence. It is a God of the Deists and the Philosophers that Jefferson refers to as "Nature's God". This is perhaps not what Spinoza himself had envisioned, but it is nonetheless how it has been used. Spinoza claimed that his God was an attempt to prove the monotheism of the Old Testament but was rejected by the Amsterdam Jewish community. A school of thought led by Johann Jacob Zimmerman also exercised a key influence. William Penn, who created Pennsylvania and founded Philadelphia, where the founding fathers drew up the Constitution, was associated with the same clubs. His naming of Pennsylvania may be an ode to Tran-

sylvania, where some of these clubs and organizations had supposedly originated under secret religious rites drawn up during the time of Vlad the Impaler.
John Winthrop was a member of the Hartlib Circle and cited John Dee's personal work "The Monas Hieroglyphica" in his personal correspondence. He
would establish the Massachusetts Bay Colony and draw a compelling argument in justification of the Puritan community, where he justified slavery and
poverty through the doctrine of predestination by citing the letters of Paul. He,
along with Reverend George Phillips and Exeter Academy, helped to spread
the doctrine.

263. The other side of this fundamentalist style religious deception, which has
been clearly shown to be a bastardization of certain elements of Christian
thought, are the theosophical sects. This includes those who wish to combine
several elements of the various faiths into one faith, reflecting the creeds of the
various systems of faith and perennial philosophy. Yet, we find there is too
much forced agreement in these sects who call for the worship of a God called
"Pan" in a pantheistic and pan religious framework. Various blends of theosophical teachings, perennial philosophy, and interfaith movements have attempted to reform Christian teaching. The Italian Carbonari, led by Giuseppe
Mazzini, which took part in the Italian unification influenced the sects of
Memphis-Misraim freemasonry. Freemasonry was said to have traced its origins from Ancient Egypt. This introduced the sect of Count Cagliostro into
Memphis Misraim. Sergei Nilius was apparently the first in these groups to be
given a copy of the controversial work "The Protocols of the Elders of Zion".
The work is used as a justification for the overthrow of the Russian Czar but its
origins are still not clearly understood. It was an early source for fears of Anti-
Semitism and in many ways had put such ideas on the map. It was brought to
the attention of Sergei Nilius through a woman named Yuliana Glinka, who
was a student of the Mystic and charlatan Helena Blavatsky. Blavatsky had
been one of the original proponents of the Aryan Myth that suggested the false
notion that Europeans had traveled to India from Russia to start the Caste System and originate Hindu teaching, which were the foundations, she claimed,
for all of the various faith traditions around the world. Blavatsky would regularly use Egyptian and Buddhist Indian themes to preach about Christianity
and its connection to her own so-called path of spiritual awakening. Blavatsky
founded the Theosophical Society, but was also a member of the Italian Carbonari.

264. According to Peter Grose, a biographer of Allen Dulles, Dulles was former President of the CFR and most infamous head of the CIA. He not only
cultivated ties with the Nazi movement but was in Constantinople during a
post Ottoman reign. There he discovered the "Protocols of the Elders of Zion", which he procured and gave to a British newspaper. Even though the
work is said to be a justification of the pogroms against Jews led by the Czar,
the work is heavily plagiarized from works of occult literature. Large portions

of the work seem to be taken from Maurice Joly's 1864 work "A Dialogue in hell between Machiavelli and Montesquieu". On the face of it, it is the attempt to show how a ruthless reign can be attained by a separation of powers. What is most interesting about the work is its focus on mass psychology, economics and finance, as well as the control of the media to keep a docile population. The work hardly mentions at all the duties of those in power and is used to show how democracy itself can be used as a tool to tyrannize a population, while the democratic citizen allows themselves to be engineered into a slave via the "herd mentality". With the ruthlessness of Machiavelli's Prince, and the various channels of power that are used to obfuscate responsibility in a "separation of powers", outlined by Montesquieu in his curiously named "Spirit of the Laws", the manufacturing of consent is an easy task. This is all too easily mentioned by Madison in the Federalist Papers or Book 8 of Plato's Republic (which was originally termed "The Regime" by Plato and was renamed by Cicero to appease Roman readers). Joly was himself a member of the Paris Commune and a Masonic Lodge, as many were during the rise of the French Revolution, including the figurehead of French Revolution Maximilien Robespierre. Marx as well was kicked out of France during the French Revolution and was a member of the faction "The League of the Just", which was a secret organization promoting Millenarianism. Marx and the Young Hegelians would play a pivotal role in French and German politics at the time. Marx wrote Satanic and Apocalyptic verses in his youth.

265. There was a concerted effort between Christian and Jewish heretical teachings. Mikhail Bakunin, an Anarchist political theorist, and Satanist was like Marx, another political antagonist at the time. He said that the opposing views of nationalism and liberalism, between Rothschild and Marx, was to determine the future of world events. Bakunin despised Marx for being too centralist. He complained that, although on the surface Marx seemed not to be supporting large banking institutions, he was involved with the very same groups that speculated on the labor of the people. At an early age Marx's family would have him baptized to hide his Ashkenazi Jewish heritage. At the time hatred of the Jews was reaching a new boiling point, just as it had during the times of the Inquisition and Reformation. Giuseppe Mazzini even wrote in his "Alta Vendita" about the Jewish leadership of groups like the International Workingmen's Association. The logo of the group appears to resemble the Masonic square and compass. The symbol also appears to resemble an upward turned triangle which looks like an all-seeing eye, and one half of the Star of the David (which is actually an ancient pagan symbol possibly adapted from the Hindu symbol of the heart). The symbol is supposed to represent an upward turned triangle for Reason, and a downward turned triangle for Emotion and Desire (representing the union of the male and the female energies). In Hinduism it is referred to as Shatkona, and in Japan as the Kagome for the Shinto religion. Especially in Hinduism, the symbol is used to refer to Shiva who is the embodiment of transcendental passion. Besides the use of Pagan

mythology, Marx used the five-pointed star of Satanism on his Communist logo and wrote praises for a demonic force named "Oulanem" in his poetry. The stated goal of the League of the Just, of which Marx was a member, was the "establishment of the Kingdom of God on Earth". This was to come about through the ideals of equality and justice, which stem from utopian socialist principles. One is likely to point to Locke as a Christian thinker, but one could just as easily say Marxism is a bastardization of the notion of Christian charity mixed with the pseudo-eschatology of material progress. The amorphous ideals of Pauline eschatology have been custom fitted to many strains of heresy.

266. The "universal rites" of Freemasonry were created by Albert Pike during the American Civil War. Palmerston and Pike were members of the "Palladium Rite". Palmerston was Marx's employer. The Order of Zion or B'nai Brith is a Messianic and Masonic offshoot. It is also known as the Constitutional Grand Lodge of the Order of the Sons of the Covenant. This group started many reform movements like the American Jewish Congress, and the World Jewish Congress. These are offshoots of Freemasonry designed for American Jews. Zionism, properly understood, is only nominally Jewish. Zionism is a movement pretending to Jewish orthodoxy but is a secular nationalist movement which conversely threatens to empty Judaism of its religious and moral and even historical context. Groups like the Frankists, who were followers of Jacob Frank, would sometimes practice a "double Marronoism". This entails the false conversion to Christianity while retaining one's Jewish faith with one's Jewish community, but also secretly rejecting the major tenets of Judaism just like Marx's father. This most clearly shows how secret and sacred oaths can be weaponized. Rabbis Antelman and Samson Raphael Hirsch have claimed that the secular and heretical scope provided a basis for reform.

267. An early leader and supporter of B'nai Brith was Judah P. Benjamin. He has been linked in several cases to the assassination of Abraham Lincoln while he was serving as Governor of Louisiana. The founding of B'nai Brith came from the Paris banking houses of Rothschilds, where the trafficking of drugs, targeted assassination, and political subversion were all tactics employed. In the book entitled "Dope Inc" by Jeffrey Steinberg, he shows connections between involvements of groups of European and Jewish influence in the development of organized crime. This reflected a connection between Great Britain and Zionism. Moses Hess, a Talmudic Rabbi who wrote "Rome and Jerusalem", taught Marx and Engels the theory of Communism before they stole the theory and booted him from their organization. His other book "The Holy Family" was a theory of economic development which strove for a religious utopia. Marx's own theory would reject the religious underpinnings for a Hegelian framework. However, this was no escape from Christian teachings, as the dialectic of Hegel was itself based on the Christian trinity. Hegel drew heavily from Hermetic and Kabbalistic teaching. Marx's organization and his own view of the progress of history through the world spirit was borrowed

from Christian mysticism and especially in line with Paul and was comprised of members who were students of Hegel known as "the young Hegelians", whose list suspiciously includes some of those radical Bible theorists like Bruno Bauer whose work inspires much of those who propagate Theosophy and Mythicism today. Marx's "First International" organization was supported by Giuseppe Mazzini. Benjamin Disraeli, who reflected Zionist views, became a Prime Minister of England. He founded the Alliance Israellite Universelle.

268. Adolph Cremieux, a friend of writer Victor Hugo, made Maurice Joly his pupil. Joly faced prison time for the publishing of his controversial book "The Dialogue in Hell Between Machiavelli and Montesquieu". Joly's real name was Moses Joel. Just like Marx he had changed his name from a Jewish name. Marx was born Moses Mordechai Levi. The most famous advocate of Zionism was Theodore Herzl, who envisioned it as a secular movement. He foresaw the breakup of the Turkish Caliphate, the British establishment of Palestinian Mandate, and the Great War. Herzl wrote in his journal, "indeed Antisemitism, a powerful and deep-rooted strength of mass sub consciousness will not harm the Jews". He writes, "an excellent idea enters my mind, to attract antisemites and make them destroyers of Jewish wealth". This was necessary to bring about a sense that assimilation could not be sought among Jews but also help to bring about a group edification. He said that the assimilation of Jews was necessary to bring about the next step. Herzl was championed as a liberal of great stature and significance and his ideas led to the Hashkala or Jewish Enlightenment in Europe. There was a powerful national element spurred on by the Zionist and British faction. There was also a mystical element of Synarchist teaching of Helena Blavatsky, whose associate would bring our attention to the Protocols. This was reflected in an Eurasian style mysticism, combining elements of the Order of the Dragon with Eastern Mysticism, using Master Rakoczy as a prophet. According to legends told by Blavatsky to her followers, Master Rakoczy was said to be the legendary St. Germain. His thought was connected with Francis Bacon, a reincarnation of a priest of Atlantis, and Merlin the Magician. The strange legends about the Bathory Sisters bathing in the blood of their slave women, as well as the stories of Vlad Dracul, were originated by members of the Order of the Dragon.

269. Today no visible element of traditional religious practice remains in Israel, where citizenship and ancestry are determined solely on the basis of genetic makeup. Another strong pull around the 19th century was the development of Darwinism and Eugenics. Nothing more clearly resembles a pseudo-religious scheme than Darwinism itself. Already floating around was the belief that the movement of history had mankind at its pinnacle developed by Hegel. Lamarck's theory of Evolution today seems more correct for taking into consideration the role of environmental factors. Alfred Russell Wallace improved the theory by addressing the problem of teleology. Darwin's course to explain events was in genes passed down from human to human in a long chain, while

relying on Naturalism to explain the changes. Darwin made the claim that black and brown races were closer to apes and intermediate forms of life between apes and humans. He said the progress of time would make the gap even larger, with white races on the one side and the baboons on the other, eliminating all other races other than the white race. This sort of prophesying in terms of science would later play into the development of biological determinism, and Eugenics. Darwin and Charles Lyell, who delivered Darwin's paper before Wallace's theory made it seem that Darwin had come up with his first, and both were members of the British Royal Society. Thomas Huxley, who was an early promoter of Darwin's theory was in support of population control and exclaimed that the theory of evolution helped dissuade sexual mores and was useful in terms of social engineering, sought to convince others of Agnostic attitudes in regard to religion, connecting such claims to a sort of ethical stratagem in testing one's own faith. Ideas of equality before the law of God, the separation of Church and State into distinct roles of influence, an emphasis on marriage and divorce which seems to challenge the notion of marriage, the predestination of God, and the coming of the Kingdom of God in the realization of man's true potential, are all ideas that are nominally related to the birth of Darwinism but are also connected to Christianity in the West. Darwinists today promote a kind of overarching faith in science and human reason in the realization of progress. They generally by faith view humanity as a steppingstone for something greater to emerge, and that our past was just incidental to our own mistakes and limitations. The ideas of Malthus also influenced Darwin.

270. The idea is most clearly a development of the hatred of man, through which man has to be transcended. It is later misconstrued and confused with Classical Liberalism of Locke and Bacon which sought a transformative power within man that would help him conquer and subdue nature. Although the belief that man was born a blank slate and was ascribed by Nature's law to a particular course of actions was prevalent, the idea of man's seeking of transcendence through, and by, his own depraved material nature, and thereby recasting himself in the fires of the Spirit to be reborn, was a Heraclitean view first developed by Anaximander. Anaximander was a pre-Socratic philosopher who felt the nature of all things was a single principle which he called "The indefinite" and was the first to put forward a notion similar to evolution. Pythagoras and the Hindu mythology most notably felt that all life was a sort of recycling of spirit by the forms of nature. The belief of an equality driven, freedom reducing ethos that blames humanity itself, and seeks to reclaim its bitter resentment for the world through salvation and grace that is tempered by time and energy, is a Pauline offshoot as noticed by Nietzsche, who said that all liberal tendencies were an outgrowth of the progress of Christian Ethics, which was weaponized by Paul into a "slave morality". It began the subtle notion that humanity can be collectively redeemed. Out of many types of men there would be one type of man that was to emerge. This was to be the definitive stage of man. The "Archetypal Man" or higher type of man that rejected the will of

collective conformity or "herd mentality" was raised against the ordinary man. Thus, he seemingly rejected the Hegelian notion of mediation between slave and master morality.

271. Nietzsche criticized Utilitarian and Christian views for lacking considerations of artfulness and aesthetic sensibility, and critiqued Darwinism for its rigid outlook. He damned democratic ideals for creating the herd instinct in man. Nietzsche felt that the pressure of Nature was to create something unique and bold, and not to fashion collectively. Nietzsche viewed the world in terms of Epicurus and Heraclitus, which is to say, in terms of passion and overcoming. He felt that intense beauty, momentary bliss, irreconcilable strife, and the indelible quality of will and mind were imbued in all things. He felt that these modes of life brought spiritual value. The thought of Nietzsche has often been seen as the pinnacle of western thought, and had a profound influence on art, spirituality and philosophy.

Chapter 13
The Birth of a God called "PAN"
/ The Myth of Progress and the
Religion of Progress

272. Modernism has developed through a pseudo-religious ethos, and a coun-
terfeited Christian ethics. This has not been readily accepted by those who
claim to be Christian purists, and those who claim to invent new systems of
morality supposedly that do not have to borrow from Christians, such as liberals. In "Beyond Good and Evil"[14], Nietzsche explains that the herd instinct is
centered around the notion of "preservation of the community", love of thy
neighbor, fear of thy neighbor, and a leveling effect of the extremes of human
behavior. He writes in the preface of the same book that Christianity is "Platonism for the people". He equated the modernist drive to a Christian and Buddhist ascetic instinct. In Section 61 he states, "nothing in Christianity and Buddhism is as venerable as their art of teaching the lowest how to place themselves through piety into an illusory higher order". He felt utilitarianism, the
democratic spirit, collective morality, the drive for collective progress, and the
species leveling of Darwinism, to be of the herd instinct. In Section 201 he explains, "the imperative of the herd timidity: we want that someday there should
be nothing any more to be afraid of". The will for this day, he said, was "progress", which was only tempered and put in place through the herd mentality.

273. He felt that the democratic movement is the heir of the Christian movement and proclaims it in the following section. He ridiculed the "dotish
philosophasters and brotherhood enthusiasts who call themselves socialists and
want a free society, but in fact are one with the lot, in their thorough and in-
stinctive hostility to every form of society, except that of the autonomous
herd". He warned that this is who "Socialist dolts and flatheads" will anoint as
the "man of the future". He called such a man "the perfect herd animal". He
also noticed that "the time for petty politics is over; the very next century will
bring fight for the dominion of the Earth-the compulsion to large scale poli-

---

[14] Nietzsche, F. W. (1989). *Beyond good and evil* (W. A. Kaufmann, Ed.; W. A.
Kaufmann & H. Zimmern, Trans.). Vintage Books. In the next four paragraphs we
summarize Nietzsche's view on how liberalism is the heir of Christian worldview. We
do this to emphasize how Nietzsche used his philosophical training to outline the view
of progress inherent in the secular worldview that it has borrowed from Christian eschatology. We attempt to make the case in parts of this book that the pseudo-eschatology is
nothing more than secularized extrapolation of the Christian view of the end of history
in the coming of the Kingdom of God.

tics" (Section 208). Nietzsche realized that the myth of progress and faith in the future was promulgated by the utterly faithless. He writes in Section 212, "a man of tomorrow and the day after tomorrow, has always found himself, and had to find himself, in contradiction to his today: his enemy was ever the ideal of today". Nietzsche did not see history as a linear progression away from the previous order, but saw ebbs and flows of a singular moment, which was bound to repeat itself. His notion of cyclical change was much more akin to the Hindu repeating cycles of time than the Greek or Pauline view of history.

274. He also complained that philosophers, artists, and historians should try to distinguish themselves from the skeptical and patient truths of the scientists that are too often detached and caretakers of faith that rely on pity, but they all too often join in. He said that pity was the basest instinct to move mankind to action. He writes, "slave morality is essentially a morality of utility" (Section 260) and saw the "slowly arising democratic order of things". This subtlety was in contradistinction to the ethos of the noble warrior of the past. He disliked the fact of Paul focusing on, not only man's depravity in a sort of boastful humility, but his assertion that suffering and pain, and even death, could be redemptive. Nietzsche felt that if there was any such person as Christ, he was an affirmer of life, but was ripped off by Paul, just as Socrates was ripped off by Plato. He said that Plato's version of Socrates was really a Plato in front, and Plato in back, with a Socrates shoved in the middle. He said the Socrates of Plato was a chimerical construction just like the Jesus of Paul. The works of Plato and Paul that look at the world as a devolution have caused the hatred of man.

275. Nietzsche said that God is dead, and it is we who have killed him. He found the fact that God had to come to humanity to sacrifice himself to be a laughable fiction. He promoted a more pagan ethos, in which the power of God could no longer exercise human restraint and would not need to express itself in human terms. Nietzsche saw the God of the Old Testament as a more realistic description of an all-powerful deity. His views on the matter are often misrepresented and equated with either agnosticism on the one hand, or outright nihilism. Nearly everything that Nietzsche is blamed for is something that he blamed on Paul. After all, Nietzsche claimed that Paul had accomplished a task of a most stupendous undertaking which is also the most fundamental talk that a human could accomplish in one lifetime and this he termed the "revaluation of values". His own attempt to undermine the system of morality propagated by Paul meant that he had to perform a task of a similar magnitude. He found Animism to be especially appealing. His views had a clear influence on people like Jung and Rudolph Steiner, but he would have opposed their attempts to conglomerate or merge together ideas of various faiths. Nietzsche rejected the idea of eventual gradual change or inevitable progress, which was a major tenet of both liberal and "New Age" types of spiritual concoctions, as seen in the techno-Buddhism and transhumanism of today. There is little proof

that he would have approved of the Theosophical society using his teaching of the will to power as a religious ideal.

276. Nietzsche seemed to criticize the major tenets of Darwinian Naturalism[15]. He said the idea of an organ developing through vestigial organs was absurd. He says, "the ability of an organ does not explain its origin" and questioned how something partly formed could ever develop or improve through use in external circumstances. He also said, "Darwin forgot the mind". Darwin offers no discussion on the intricacies of animal psychology, and the propensity of Man in this case, which is different from his animal counterparts on several fronts. He noticed that the weak often rule over the strong because the majority becomes cleverer than the strong. This democratic impulse itself was the greatest argument against Darwinism. Men do not strive for freedom but beg for change and progress in some sort of inane impulse of collective morality that comes to settle in with the subtlety of vengefulness. What is more, is that sexual selection does not occur in humans the same way as it does in animals. In humans at least, such a process of selection is deeply irregular and has many historical shifts and cultural anomalies. Nietzsche did not believe in the existence of transitional forms. He felt change happened suddenly and most violently and on the spur of the moment. He saw the "will to power" to drive the changes in Nature instead of the steady progress of Darwinian evolution. He found the notion of Darwinism to be inextricably linked to liberal idealism. History has instead shown us that the weaker overtakes the stronger by continual compromise and childish effacement. This points to a concerted devolution and stultifying of progress. He said, "I am inclined to the prejudice that the school of Darwin has been deluded everywhere". He posited the herd instinct as a stultifier of the will to power, whose development was irregular and unpredictable. In a quote from "Nachlass" he writes, "The progress of the species. The very opposite is quite palpably the case".

277. The Darwin family and the Huxley family were the foremost promoters of the theory of Evolution as we see it today. The families would marry into one another with the belief that preserving the genetics of white males that had an aptitude for science was of primary importance. Aldous Huxley, who was the most notable heir of the Darwin and Huxley families was a promoter of population control. This may come as a surprise to many who view him only as a cultural critic. Charles Galton Darwin, who was also an heir to Darwin

---

[15] Additional sources for this paragraph can be found here:1. Pence, C. H. (2011). Nietzsche's Aesthetic Critique of Darwin. *Louisiana State University Faculty Publications*. 2. Grigg, R. (2012, May 30). *Nietzsche anti-God anti-Darwin - creation.com*. Creation Ministries International. Retrieved April 14, 2022, from https://creation.com/nietzsche-anti-god-anti-darwin 3. Daniel, P. (2013, August 2). *Nietzsche's Rejection of Darwinian Evolution | With All I Am*. With All I Am. Retrieved April 14, 2022, from https://withalliamgod.wordpress.com/2013/08/02/nietzsches-rejection-of-darwinian-evolution/

wrote a book called "The Next Million Years", where he espoused the practice of Eugenics as a means of population control. Aldous Huxley and Jean Coutrot founded the "Center for the Study of Human Problems", largely to promote population control genetics, and a synarchistic blend of Fabian Socialism. Other members of the Fabian Society of Great Britain were influenced by occultist John Ruskin. Perhaps the most famous Fabian Socialist was Eleanor Roosevelt. Her and Philosopher John Dewey helped promote the cause of Fabian Socialism in America. Other famous members of the Fabian Society were Bertrand Russell, H.G Wells, George Bernard Shaw, and Julian Huxley, who would become the first director of UNESCO. There we find attempts to bring women in to the workplace and abortion clinics like Planned Parenthood, that were used an early means of population control. The theory was that once the family was done away with there would be no more reasons to police sexual behavior. Increasingly, propaganda was used to make the goal of sex to be satisfying an innate urge for pleasure, and not for the purpose of family. The institution of marriage was turned into an archaic religious rite that had no place in modern society. This was of course said to empower the woman, but women are no safer today than in the past as noted by many gender rights activists.

278. Indeed one must ask oneself if women are any safer in the workplace where today they are regularly exploited as sexual objects. Women are put on display as commercial items in TV commercials and young women are made to feel less significant if they do not resemble the airbrushed images of the magazine. Natural beauty is not appreciated. There are single mothers and pregnant teens. There is human trafficking and prostitution. The ease of copying and distributing digital images has made violent and illegal child pornography more rampant. Many have noted that the drive in feminism to emulate male power has supported patriarchy by turning women into men, instead of helping them to be women on their own terms. We must realize that we all came from a family and that family is the true cornerstone of civilization and economic success. This does not mean that we should hate others who do not practice or support marriage as a religious sacrament, but we should see the basic benefits in society in raising children from happy families. This simple truth has eluded us.

279. Today usury and sodomy are the major destructive elements in a society and have become weaponized. The destruction of the family and the destruction of wealth are symptoms of a greater disease. Those who are in debt and those who come from bad families are the number one reasons for crime. If we had more people from good families that were not in debt, we could repair the ills of society. Instead of these moral prohibitions that are all too simple, we employ cumbersome methods of social engineering seen today. Not only have such methods made women less safe, but they have contributed to a growing crisis of manhood. There is a growing concern in society that there is no set definition on what a man is, and what the role of men in society should be.

Due to this, many men are experiencing an extended adolescence, as women are finding alternative lifestyles apart from men. There is a trend of feminization of males and masculinization of females through biochemical, genetic, and social pressures that has had further repercussions for the family. Again, we are not in judgement of those who practice alternative lifestyles, but seek to promote an understanding of the need for preservation of marriage for the basic health of the society. The rise in divorce is another symptom of the problem.

280. In the 20th century Eugenics was popularly supported by Winston Churchill, Theodore Roosevelt, Herbert Hoover, John Maynard Keynes, and Sydney Webb[16]. Sexologists like Marie Stopes, and Margaret Sanger supported Planned Parenthood. Nazi style Eugenics was first begun in the United States by Rockefeller funding. The disciplines of Psychology and Anthropology were weaponized to these ends. Notable Frankist and Sabbatean Jews like Paul Warburgh and Jacob Schiff helped fund the rise of Nazi Eugenics, but also large-scale measures of population control, and central banking.

281. Alfred Richard Orage who edited the magazine "The New Age" was a friend and supporter of Satanist and Mystic Aliester Crowley, Alfred North Whitehead, and George Gurdjieff. Whitehead's process theology, and Gurdjieff's notion of Man as a "spiritual machine", was an essential component to the development of a "New World" religion. Annie Besant, the successor of Helena Blavatsky, was a regular speaker at the Fabian Society. Nicholas Roerich was the disciple of Gurdjieff, and another key Theosophical teacher. He was funded by Russian Intelligence and attempted to create a pan-Buddhist state from Tibet to Siberia. This was prophesied by Blavatsky, including a figure that would represent Lucifer as a "world teacher" or Matraeiya. Her allusions to a Messiah type figure made references to Jesus and the Holy Spirit. She had supposedly learned the above-mentioned prophecy in one of her fake channelings to "Master Morya", who was an "Ascended Master" she communicated with. The most shocking connection is the connection of Roerich to Vice president Henry Wallace. Wallace and F.D.R were avid supporters of secret societies as well as Fabian socialism. They had put the symbol of the "All Seeing Eye" on the back of the dollar bill. Wallace was a member of the Theosophical society and referred to Roerich as "dear guru" in his correspondence. The so-called Christian symbol of the "eye of providence" is actually a representation of the Deistic God of Jefferson and Franklin. Wallace had provided the essential support, among others, for the work of parapsychologist

---

[16] Livingstone, D. (2015). *Transhumanism: The History of a Dangerous Idea*. Sabilillah Publications. Most of the information in the next 15 sections or paragraphs can be found in the book by Livingstone in a chapter entitled Brave New World and the book has greatly influenced both the direction and scope of our research into how the idea of the transcendental of the mystics and the humanism of the European Enlightened merged to form "Transhumanism" which was a word coined by Julian Huxley, the founder of UNESCO.

Andrija Puharich. His founding of the Round Table Foundation conducted the infamous experiments known as MK Ultra.

282. These experiments had included Seances with discarnate entities which were borrowed from the practice of Madame Blavatsky. Among the associates of Puharich were Warren S. McCullough, who was an early advocate of brain implants, and pioneered the creation of cybernetics. The student and successor of Annie Besant, the student of Blavatsky, was Alice Bailey. Bailey, who started the Lucis Trust, named after Lucifer the fallen angel, talked often of a coming of a "new convergence", which would bring about the "Omega Mind" or "Christ Consciousness". The idea is identical to one put forward by Pierre Teilhard de Chardin, who was also a member of the Fabian Society along with Maria Montessori, who created the Montessori program, and Alfred Sauvy who coined the term "third world".

283. Trustees and financiers of the Lucis Trust have included leading members of the Council on Foreign Relations like John D. Rockefeller, Robert Mcnamara, Norman Cousins, and Henry Kissinger. The Lucis Trust operated a so-called "religious chapel" in the U.N. dubbed the "meditation room". Such groups are often operating under the belief of the progress of man, but it is hardly noted that they are the number one proponents and most visible promoters of such views as well. Yet this underlying belief that Man must overcome himself and his own barbarous nature amounts to a sort of self-hatred. The hatred of Man, and division of Man into subcastes, presents a logical goal of technological order and world unification, which on the one end promotes the evil within Man as the natural order, whose solution is evolution of technological means. The controlled opposition is set as Man being the problem of nature, and technology being a natural solution to the problem. The technology that Man creates is supposed to be both the problem and the solution to the problem of Man's own self-inflicted suffering, as paradoxical as that may sound. Man does not even have to become godlike, but the God simply comes down and becomes all of mankind. This is the drive of humanity to surpass itself in a hatred of self. The drive has been most eloquently termed Transhumanism. In this sort of worldview, the human itself is a transitory phase.

284. The interfacing between the limbic and the motor cortex of the brain is seen as reductionism, but in this view, nature is also reduced to thoughts. It was Gregory Bateson who applied cybernetics to the entirety of nature, claiming that Nature is a cybernetic mind. This anthropomorphism is not unlike the Gnostic and Kabbalistic view of Man being a microcosm of the macrocosm. Such beliefs have been popularly espoused in all sorts of international and world forums. One conglomeration of such efforts was seen in the Rockefeller and Ford Foundation funded Club of Rome. The project was seemingly sponsored by a CIA front organization called the "Congress for Cultural Freedom", founded in 1968. Aurelio Peccei and Alexander King headed the organization,

whose members included NATO officials. Non-governmental organizations and non-profit groups were set up like the World Wildlife Fund, and the Friends of the Earth, to further the agenda of bringing about a planned economy on a world scale under the pretense of environmentalism. According to Livingstone, the group was very influential, determining both platforms for the 1960 presidential election in the U.S in their report "Prospect for America". In a report entitled "Limits of Growth", a Malthusian scenario is laid out for the purposes of population control. It used cybernetic models to explain the limited resources of the world that would bring about a radical restructuring of society, including world planning.

285. Peace groups, human rights organizations, and groups fighting world hunger and climate change all seek global solutions. Peccei calls such groups "the yeast of change". He says that such people are like antibodies in a sick organism. The motif of the world being as a single organism, reducing all of Nature to the biological sort of evolution, is a favored concept for those who advance the Pauline view that all are united within a Universal bond through the Church in Christ. That this culminates in a utopian style Kingdom of God only fits the teleological framework of both Whitehead and Chardin, as reinforced by the correspondence theory of truth and teleological metaphysics of Aristotle, and the Hegelian view of the apotheosis of the State. The sense of the universe as an organism is one put forward by Plato and promoted by Whitehead. This is the mystical and religious side of Darwin. The concept of the "Noosphere" used by Teilhard de Chardin is a kind of reimagining of the universal mind or collective consciousness of the Gnostics. Also endemic in these groups is the worship of the "mother goddess", idealized by Earth itself. In the occult view, this is the worship of change itself. The male form is creative and the female form is malleable in Hermeticism. The female form is prized for its ability to transform into almost anything. The womb of Nature can even give birth to God. This was because Nature became imbued with a divine creativity through the mythos of Gaia or "Mother Earth" to balance Saturn with his sickle who represented "Father Time" or El in Neopaganism.

286. William Harman founded the Institute of Noetic Sciences. Parapsychology and Noetics is a scientific rebranding of paranormal research and occultism. The CIA funded Operation Stargate, and used Harman and the Stanford Research Institute to conduct the M.K Ultra studies. Another study entitled "Changing Images of Man" included Margaret Mead, B.F Skinner, Erwin Lazslo, Carl Rogers, James Fadiman, Ralph Metzger and Joseph Campbell. The aim of this study was to transform the prevailing world-view from one of Industrialism to one of Spiritualism. Investors of the Institute of Noetic Sciences also created Christian groups like "The Fellowship". Nathaniel Temple Jr. was one such character. The Fellowship and the Three Swallows Foundation have worked to preserve the Christian right in America.

287. The group included Henry Ford, and Norman Vincent Peale, who was current President Trump's mentor. Most famously the group had instituted the National Prayer Breakfast. Groups like "The Fellowship" claim to serve the rich and powerful in a game of spiritual warfare using the idea of Paul's Christ. It is an extreme view of Calvinism that comes together in the philosophy of Norman Vincent Peale that drives this organization. Hilary Clinton considered Douglas Coe, the founder of the Christian Fellowship, a "spiritual mentor". One may find it a little odd that in our day and age members of two opposite political parties could be part of the same Christian religious organization. But one then also has to wonder how much of the U.S Foreign Policy is driven by wars to protect the State of Israel. Indeed, the documents like the "Project for a New American Century" suggest to us that Neoconservatism has been driven by religious, and even Zionist goals.

288. These groups regularly promote such concepts as a "conspiracy of love" in noble lie type maneuvering to achieve their goals. This idea was quoted by Pierre Trudeau in a speech that influenced writer Marylin Ferguson, who used the ideas of Teilhard de Chardin and Theosophy to write "The Aquarian Conspiracy". She gives quite a useful survey on the leaders of the New Age movement whose premier figures include thinkers like Carl Jung, Aldous Huxley, Abraham Maslow, Jiddu Krishnamurti (who much to his credit left the Theosophical society and rejected its teachings), as well as Chardin. Other famous names and popular writers were Herman Hesse, Alfred North Whitehead, Margaret Mead, Gregory Bateson, Alan Watts, D.T Suzuki, Thomas Merton, William Harmon, John C. Lilley, Sri Aurobindo, Buckminster Fuller, Alfred Korzybski, and Marshall McLuhan. McLuhan was an avid futurist who had declared that the invention of electricity was the descent of the holy ghost into the movement of history. A most famous line by McLuhan declares that humans are the mere sex organs of the machine world. Humanity is part and parcel to the total experience of the machine encapsulated by Nature and Time. Every individual is a part of humanity's collective salvation. This was the inevitability of change and faith in the future, that one should come to oppose more vigorously with religious sentiment knowing that it truly represents . Such a view is an idol parading Man's misfortune. Man cannot be the problem and solution. The thirst for an archaic revival birthed through a sort of anthrofuturism is the impetus for technocratic pseudo-spiritual malaise.

289. Furgeson and Maslow developed the Association for Humanistic Psychology. Futurist Barbara Marx Hubbard, a follower of Chardin, became president. Science fiction writer and developer of the idea for the Satellite Arthur C. Clarke was a supporter of "Chardinian" philosophy. He had stated that any sufficiently developed technology is indistinguishable from magic. One can compare this with the statement by prominent Sociologist Jacque Ellul that all forms of magic represent a primitive attempt at technology by trying to "hack" Nature. Many like Jack Parsons, who invented rocket fuel, were Satanists

linked to the cult of Ordo Templis Orientis. When Oppenheimer had helped to create the atomic bomb, he did not have Jesus to thank. Instead, he quoted from the Pagan scripture of the Bhagavad Gita, announcing that Shiva the destroyer of worlds had come to pay a visit. It should be plain to anyone that Oppenheimer was probably not a follower of Krishna or Shiva either. Rather it is the occult fascination with magic and the misappropriation of pagan myth that is lurking behind the technocratic impulse. David Bohm, who worked on the project until he was kicked out for moral objections, was a follower of Jiddu Krishnamurti, and immersed in New Age teachings. The Esalen Institute founded by Michael Murphy was also a key proponent of such views as were those authors and writers that belonged to the Human Potential Movement. Chardin was known as "the patron saint of the Internet".

290. His book "Phenomenon of Man" contains an introduction by Julian Huxley. Maslow aided the research of sexologist Alfred Kinsey. Kinsey was a devoted member of Aliester Crowley's organization Thelema, and even attended some of his orgiastic parties. Crowley talks about offering blood sacrifices of young blond hair blue eyes virgin boys in his writing. Only the sacrifice of a pure infant or child would suffice. Jean Houston worked with Crowley, Barbara Marx Hubbard (a self-proclaimed Jewish agnostic), and supported Timothy Leary, a key proponent of the psychedelic movements of the 60's and 70's, but also was a spiritual guide for Hilary Clinton. This is just like Vice President Henry A. Wallace and his relationship with Nicolas Roerich who he referred to as "Dear Guru". It seems that over 100 years worth of presidential nominees have been mentored by these so called mystics and the details are matters of public record. Such ideas were regularly worked out in workshops like "The Mystery School for Renaissance of the Spirit", and programs at the Esalen Institute. In a book by Bob Woodward, it tells of the close relationship between Jean Houston and Hilary Clinton, who apparently helped the former first lady commune with the spirits of Gandhi and Eleanor Roosevelt. The former U.N Secretary General described Ferguson's book as "remarkable". He recently received a reward from the Teilhard Foundation.

291. The Temple of Understanding is another New Age cult. They are engaged in a celebration of St. John two times a year through a "pagan" style festival. St. John is often referred to as the "patron saint" of the Freemasons, who use the Revelations of St. John as a guide and stem from the Maryamiyyah cult. Perennial Philosophers like Seyyed Hossein Nasr purportedly are followers of the philosophy of Rene Guenon. The Traditionalism of Guenon was a response to Perennial Philosophy but ultimately only a reaction insofar as it gave the religions of the world credence and formulated a "type" for them, but told adherents to embed themselves within a religious practice to achieve the most benefit for the religious mindset instead of combining the various faiths. The Lindisfarne Association is a premier association based on the process theology of Whitehead. The integral philosophy of the "organism" as Whitehead es-

poused, and the drive towards "planetization" of Chardin, were used as a roadmap. The work of the organization was highly influential in the development of the New Age style theology, which sought to link spiritual practice with the scientific method. Maurice Strong was a significant proponent of the push for globalization at the time. He was also the finance director of the Lindisfarne Center, which was said to have been a monastery in the 7th century which housed the Lindisfarne Gospels. Today the Lindisfarne Center is a proponent of practices of Yoga, Chinese medicine, Hermeticism, Celtic Animism, Gnosticism, Kabbalah, Pythagorean philosophy which influenced Plato, and ancient mystery religions.

292. Elaine Pagels who was discussed earlier for connecting the Gnostic Gospels with Buddhist texts is a member of the Lindisfarne Group. This should preclude anyone's ability to take her seriously as a unbiased researcher. The group is a critic of science and technology, but also seeks globalization and alternative methods for living which promote "spiritual evolution". The Eli Lilly Company was contracted by the CIA to produce the psychedelic drug L.S.D in 1953 under subproject 18 of MK Ultra. The project was supported through Lindisfarne. James Lovelock, who developed the Gaia Theory, was also a member of the Lindisfarne Group. While being critics of the goals of science and technology and seeing a divine mission of mankind to protect the Earth we do readily identify how some of these trends are instead pushed by elites for the basis of promoting alternative religion and cultural subversion. It is not hard to see how such ideas of transcendental nature of things which would lead to a collective and inevitable change were used to promote a religious ideal that was antithetical to any orthodox practice of religion. We are not opposed to people exploring their spirituality or what makes them comfortable but are opposed when these so-called changes are not coming from the person themselves but by social engineering and religious subversion. Certain of these ideas might even make sense, but we have to see how they fit into the bigger narrative.

293. What we are most vigorously opposed to is the grandiloquent schemes and megalomaniacal dreams that seek to bring about changes on a world stage. As noted by artist Hiroyuki Hamada, "What's infuriating about manipulations by the Nonprofit Industrial Complex is that they harvest the goodwill of the people, especially young people". This is the false slogan of humanity to prop up a hierarchy of the most learned and wealthy. Radical and Liberal talk shows like Pacifica station were funded by Rockefellers and Ford Foundation. This is a staged rebellion and continued push for a collective morality and collective brotherhood for change, but also bad trend that seeks to capitalize on certain religious misdirection and misplaced angst over religious fears. It is also not a secular trend as many suppose, but one of a pronounced spiritual change. This is not freedom of religion, or open religion, as some suppose. Instead, it is a concerted effort to bring about the birth of a one world religion, as Christ warns.

294. The Wallace Global Fund (founded by Henry A. Wallace), Rockefeller Family Fund, and Winstron Foundation helped fund environmental rights organizations like the Sierra Club, Occupy Wall Street and Green New Deal. Club of Rome founder Alexander King explains their basic philosophy. He states simply "the common enemy of humanity is man". In searching for a new enemy to unite the world, the human centered cause of pollution and climate change was chosen as an ideal. The clear solution presented to deal with the problem was globalization enacted by the very same actors who created industrial and technological change, and also are its main benefactors, while blaming the common man and treating the average person as an enemy. This is a clear controlled opposition or revaluation of values seen in Paul when he used the symbol the Romans used to spread terror as a sign of salvation.

295. Groups like the CFR, Trilateral Commission, and Rockefeller Foundation that work to combine British and American interests, come out of the Royal Institute of International affairs[17]. These groups spread wars and rumors of wars to enhance their agenda. The CFR was originally thought of by men like Walter Lippman, who had borrowed the term "Manufacturing of Consent" from Edward Bernays work on propaganda. Bernays suggested a mix of Freudian tactics of mind control to govern mass psychology much like the tactics suggested in the Protocols of the Elders of Zion. Bernays was the nephew of Sigmund Frued, who had famously created the feminist revolution by getting women to smoke, meanwhile increasing the sale of cigarettes. His tactic was based on a suggestion by a practitioner of psychoanalysis to convince women that smoking a cigarette would make them seem more sophisticated and manly, and would allow women to have their own penises. In quite a perverse twist, the cigarette was used as a symbol for the male genitalia to convince women that such an act could liberate them. Hence, the symbol used to oppress them was now used as an icon of personal liberation and salvation.

296. "Modernists" versus "Fundamentalism" was created as a false dichotomy, and essentially a controlled opposition. In reality both are just rebranded forms of occult ideology. While the moderns rely on New Age Theosophy, the fundamentalist and millennialist factions rely on Christian Zionism. In response to the supposedly "orthodox" view of Zionist factions, the secularizing of Christians was used to enhance it. The Modernists view religion as little more than a useful metaphor, just as the fundamentalists based their ideals on a sort of Eu-

---

[17] Arnold, D. (2016, September 27). *The true Israel—Wrong views of prophecies on the Jews - Interview with James Perloff.* YouTube. Retrieved April 15, 2022, from https://www.youtube.com/watch?v=1wCs1chCfLM. James Perloff is a writer who is the author of many books including a book on the Council on Foreign Relations and is a Christian of Russian Jewish descent. The next four paragraphs or sections are derived from information in this interview of James Perloff conducted by Dean Arnold who is a Christian radio host.

ropean nationalism not found or supported in the Bible. The Ecumenical Council and First Council of Churches is such an attempt of power consolidation and religious subversion. Author and Scholar James Perloff explains the connections between the Modernist movement and hardline Zionism quite clearly. He explains how the First Council of Churches and the National Council of Churches was funded by groups like the Rockefellers. John Foster Dulles, whose wife was a first cousin of the Rockefeller family, was instrumental in the creation of the CFR, as well as the CIA. One may also want to ask themselves why a private think tank would have connections to a Secret Intelligence operation supposedly run by the U.S Government but it is a regular affair for private firms to draft legislation handed over to their political benefactors. Abraham Kuhn of Kuhn Loeb and Co, as well as Jacob Schiff, met with Trotsky and funded the Bolshevik Revolution. During the same time similar groups were funding another project that would influence Evangelical Christianity: The Scofield Bible. The Scofield Reference Bible, widely used today, made very interesting changes to the direction of Christian Zionism and Christian fundamentalism.

297. Arthur Scofield was a member of the Confederate Army and a proponent of John Nelson Darby, who began the Plymouth Brethren. He used the Bible to support views of a physical thousand year reign of Christ, and view that God wants Christians to help return Jews back to Palestine to hasten the return of Christ. The Lotus Club, which was attended by Mark Twain and the Carnegies, as well Margaret Mead, funded the release of the Scofield Reference Bible, through Oxford University Press. They were linked to Samuel Untermeyer (the founder of the Federal Reserve Bank) and Jacob Schiff. In 1904 Theodore Herzl would go to Pope Pius X for the offer of conversion of Jews to Catholicism for Catholic support of the Jewish State. When the Pope refused, other ways had to be constructed to elicit the support of European Christians to the cause of the Jewish State.

298. The Zionists found that instead they could rely on the good old liberal Protestant ministers which taught a dual path of salvation for Jews and Christians, similar to Paul. Not since Martin Luther had such a powerful shift occurred in the relation between Jews and Christians who at the time weakened the Church enough for Jews to gain prominence in Britain and Amsterdam. So certain Presbyterian ministers were hijacked or piggybacked on Zionist Scofield version of Christianity, which was published some four odd years after the Pope denied Herzl's request. The Scofield Bible charges Christians with the "sin of antisemitism". It also mentions the so-called "Greater Israel" from the Euphrates to the Nile River in Genesis 15:18, with a contrived and unconditional blessing of God on Jewish control of the Holy Land. Jesus never preached about returning the Jews to the Holy Land or the rebuilding of the Third Temple. Jesus proclaimed that he, The Messiah, was the Temple. John Foster Dulles proposed the League of the Nations in 1919. This was around the

time of the fall of the Ottomans, the rise of the Bolsheviks, and the Balfour Declaration, which was issued by British Government to Lord Rothschild in the establishment of the Jewish State. The fall of the Czar, the end of the Ottoman Caliphate, and the British and Zionist takeover of Palestine could not have been a random coincidence or fortuitous circumstance. As a chairman of trustees of the Rockefeller Foundation, and as Secretary of State under Eisenhower, John Foster Dulles travelled to Amsterdam, and worked on the World Council of Churches. One of its offshoots is the Tony Blair Faith Foundation. Christian Zionism was set up as a controlled opposition for the Modernist movement. This was the dual path of salvation mentioned earlier. "Salvation is of the Jews". One path for Christians and one for Jews. But both are saved.

299. Before moving to Switzerland, Scofield was a known con artist. He worked with the East India Tea Company for a while and faked his theological certifications. He fought for the Confederacy in the Civil War. In the Bible, Jews were not able to enter into the Holy Land because of a lack of faith, even in the time of Moses. The promise to Jews is not unconditional. However, since Jews are a small nation, they required help from Christians to establish the State of Israel, which is an invention of Modern Secular European Jews like Herzl. In the Book of Enoch, the story of Genesis is explained as punishment for the rule of a Satanic World Organization. This World Order had usurped the rights of God, and the forces of nature, using genetic experiments and scientific technology to create an artificial environment and "heaven on earth" through bioengineering. Using this knowledge, they created a race of giants that used up the resources of the Earth. They created a racial utopia but were cursed by God. This story shows us the roadmap for world domination. The first step is the consolidation of power. The second step is the establishment of a technological world order. The third step is the arrival of the antichrist and his reign.

300. A further goal is to create a schism between Christianity and Islam. Posing Islam as a threat to "Judeo-Christian" civilization has been a tactic employed by the New World Order. When examined these claims are spurious. Throughout history, Islam has shared much with the moral principles described in Jewish and Christian systems. Islam further prevented the proliferation of secular learning but paradoxically protected Christian and Jewish institutions of learning. Not only this, but Jewish and Christian scholars have had to rely on the expertise of Muslim Scholars throughout the ages to rectify their own beliefs. It seems almost paradoxical to play into the wholesale rejection of the so called three main Western faiths, because such a rejection would clearly uproot most of Western history and lay one prey to the hosts of religious subversion that hope to do away with religious ideals[18]. In the book "Jewish

---

[18] The next 11 paragraphs or sections are based on interviews conducted of E. Michael Jones based on the information in his books. Here are some additional sources for

Revolutionary Spirit" Catholic Scholar E. Michael Jones explains that the Jewish rejection of Logos is tied into a revolutionary, international, antinomian, and oppositional attitude towards the rest of the nations. Whether or not you believe his viewpoint, he offers some historical insight into major historical changes in the life of American Christians. The traditional values of nations have been continually threatened by the view of an international struggle for human rights and socialism, which is often framed as liberalism and secularism, and even recently as an environmental movement. What actually has transpired instead is a push for world government couched in religious subversion.

301. There has been an alternative brand of less conciliatory rhetoric seen in some groups of Christians. These groups see the Jewish rejection of Logos to be a direct consequence in their selection of Barabbas, a political revolutionary, over Christ. We call this "Logos theology" which suggests that western progress is mainly built upon the Christian ethos. The arrival of Christ was a warning to those claiming an unconditional promise and racial superiority. The word Jew is used in the Gospel of John over 20 times, not to refer to a racial grouping, but a religious order or affiliation. Judaism is a category of belief and not a race. Similarly, Logos is not used to refer to Christ only, but also the universal order of things. On his mission, Jesus had to distinguish himself from mainstream Judaism of the time. Jews have in history opposed the Church, just as much as the Church has opposed Jews, through the founding of revolutionary and reform movements, as claimed by scholars like Israel Newman. What strikes us as odd concerning these views is then the considerable collusion between Jewish and Christian reform movements. Jews wanted a King and carnal Kingdom of this world. They yearned for political rule. Some interpret Paul's message to be pointing towards a physical reign of Christ. Baptism was invented to end the Jewish chain of genetic superiority. According to Dr. E. Michael Jones, Antisemitism was created by Wilhelm Mahr as a biological determinism. Anyone talking about Jews as a religious category would obviously reject Darwinism and biological determinism. While we may not agree

where the content was derived: 1. *Roman Catholic Report: E. Michael Jones Interview* (September 3, 2008). YouTube. Retrieved April 15, 2022, https://www.youtube.com/watch?v=jB8RVzGqJil. This interview discusses E. Michael Jones book "The Jewish Revolutionary Spirit" 2. Unknown (2015, May 9). *Libido Dominandi: Lust, Power, & Control*. YouTube. Retrieved April 15, 2022, from https://www.youtube.com/watch?v=qQeRu7BUEr8. An interview on the book "Libido Dominandi". 3. Jones, E. M. (2012, October 13). *"Why Are We Here, Because We're Not There"*. YouTube. Retrieved April 15, 2022, from https://www.youtube.com/watch?v=eGkb8Kuy9SI. This is a recording of a public talk given by E. Michael Jones on his book "The Slaughter of Cities". 4. Kelley, T. (2019, August 28). *E Michael Jones - OIT Radio - The Rise And Fall Of The New ...* Internet Archive. Retrieved April 15, 2022, from https://archive.org/details/emichaeljonesoitradiotheriseandfallofthenewatheism_201908. This interview of E. Michael Jones is conducted by Tim Kelley for the radio show Our Interesting Times and is entitled, "The Rise and Fall of New Atheism".

that Logos poses a reflection singularly on the development of western thought, it does signal to the fundamental conflict between Christians and Jews, which is often overlooked to over-accentuate the similarities of the two faiths. Many have overstated the origins of Christianity within Judaism, they hardly notice that the Jewish minority has often attempted to gain control of Christian views by the use of religious innovations, while large scale movements to either purge or assimilate Jews have often had bad consequences and left a considerable moral strain on the Christian conscience that seeks to both express and suppress its entanglement with its Jewish roots, which it has treated with a certain amount of ambivalence. The pairing of Jewish and Roman themes has hence become quite ingrained in the European ethos.

302. At the time of Jesus, the synagogue was reduced to a debating society. Several Rabbi's have often remarked that whatever is forbidden in the Torah is permitted by the Talmud. Julian the Apostate worked to punish Christians, and went to Persia for Jewish support. When the Church clamped down on Jews funding wars for Christians to die in, and Christianity gained a foothold in Europe, it turned against the Jews. As a result, the Jewish people migrated East to places like Poland and Lithuania. In places like Germany and Russia, hatred of the Jews was spurred on by allegations of usury. In Prague, where the Protestant Reformation began, the city was a former trading post for slaves. Luther and Henry VIII offered no doctrinal differences, but rather broke with the Church to fulfill their own lusts. With a lack of protection from the Church, Europe and America became increasingly swayed by Jewish intellectuals.

303. His claim that Jews innovated to create liberal movements in the U.S culminates in figures like Franz Boas, Milton Friedman, Margaret Mead, Woody Allen, and Wilhelm Reich, who have all created a faux and quasi-religious collusion of Freudo-Marxian synthesis. The goal of figures like Louis Wirth in the promotion of consumer culture consisted in the breakdown of the traditions of family, that was crystalized in Hollywood, which represented the gravest attack on American and Christian values. Many like Cardinal Dougherty proposed a boycott on the theatres for spreading licentiousness and inviting people to sin. The Black-Jewish alliance goes back to the creation of the terms Black and White by Jewish Sociologists. Joel Spingarn, who founded the NAACP, used it to spy on black people. Now gender issues are used instead of racial issues for the same agenda. Once blacks learned that they were being used as pawns in someone else's political game, gender issues were highlighted instead. The proponents of such views create divisions between black and white, young and old, and male and female. This is a purpose of breaking down social mores in order to accelerate social change. The breakdown of the family as a Christian institution is the stated goal of thought farms like the Frankfurt School who were further proponents of a Fruedo-Marxian Thesis. Thus, both Muslims and Christians have surrendered their values to a

"techno-liberalism" or liberal elites and have in turn became puppets of Jews and occultists.

304. This was seen by Plato, Confucius, Sun Tzu, and St. Augustine to be the cause of a breakdown of society. The formula for tyranny is the same everywhere, and is even told to us in the Bible. Three steps are used to break down a civilization. The first step is the rule of the passions. The second step is licentiousness in the form of sodomy and lavish lifestyles. The third step is to steamroll over the society with usury to fulfill the exorbitant lifestyles of the people. Finally, with people being ruled by their passions and enslaved to their whims they are easy to tyrannize. "A man has as many masters as vices" or to paraphrase Plato: an excess of freedom ends up an excess of slavery.

305. St. Augustine termed the rule of the passions "libido dominandi". This is the subject of another work by E. Michael Jones. The rule of the passions is linked to the lust for power. Sexual liberation can be used as a means of social control. Sin masquerading as passion and blind love in our culture has made sexual deviancy and obscenity equivalent to "freedom", but it can equally correspond to a lack of agency and control, as demonstrated by various sexual diseases, sexual addiction, mental disorders, substance abuse, and health issues related to overconsumption. He describes a case during the Palestinian Intifada, where the Israelis broadcasted pornography to the television sets of the citizens in Ramallah. Snipers were then placed on the rooftops of the houses so no one could leave. It should be clear to anyone that the Israeli's don't seek to liberate the Palestinians by giving them the freedom to watch porn. This is the cost of having the many channels that can be used to communicate important information turned into the vehicles of cultural disintegration. This cultural defacement is seen in the story of Samson and Delilah. It points to the tactical advantage of controlling the cultural setting. Political manipulators, industrial enslavers, and academic assimilationists require a morally stultified and culturally deranged population in order to accomplish their goals. The irony is that, unless a man has a refined sense of duty and honor, and is indebted to principles and beliefs that have been engrained through practice and sacrifice, he will easily submit to anything.

306. Techniques of social control are designed to allow you to abandon your sense of morality and practical reason by the leveling employed by the notion of equality. In the French Revolution, Libertines like Marquis De Sade gave recommendations for political action like displaying naked women in the theatres. In the Macy's Conference it is said that younger children that are more sexually active are more democratic because of their diverse sexual experiences. Promoting same sex marriage and multiple sexual partners can be seen as an alternative way to destroy the notion of family. Wilhelm Reich made the claim that women can be changed if introduced to mass situations, so technology was employed for far reaching cultural change. What does obscenity have

to do with cultural freedom? Yet obscenity like the Vagina Monologues was first promoted at St. Mary's College. The entrance of women into the workplace and urban lifestyle was promoted by feminists.

307. In the view of E. Michael Jones, in his book "Barren Metal", the conflict is most clearly outlined in the battle between British Empiricism and German Idealism. Although we do not regard German Idealism to be a solution because of its origin in Classical Liberalism which is based on religious subversion as we shall later see, we acknowledge the hegemony of British views. According to E. Michael Jones, the Reformation was used as a basis to steal Church property and summon the economic decline of Europe. The ideals of the Church had brought Europe on a world stage, and not the antics of John Dee or Newton. As the Medici's brought the Hermetic traditions to Europe, soon men like Robert Fludd would form the Royal Society, and the Whig party would be taken over by Masonic Lodges. Newton, who said "I frame no hypothesis", used such beliefs as a cover up for his pagan cosmology that was derived from Empedocles. The theory of love and strife, circular motion, and finality of natural law was applied to the so-called "laws of economy" by Adam Smith. The economics of supply and demand and the "invisible hand" is based on notions of physical laws beyond man's control. This invisible hand or blind watchmaker, or basic duality in the world between business and finance, which was akin to material and force functioning off of the basis of randomized change, is seen as a replacement for God. This moved economics from a moral driven philosophy to one of pseudoscience. This led to the false belief that self-interest and competition govern the Cosmos, similar to the views of Darwinian Evolution. The opposite of the maritime, international, colonial, trade establishment based on banking schemes and laws of finance, is the landed power dependent on labor, infrastructure, and external tariff. This concept of land power versus sea power or international trading and corporate finance was put into an extraordinary use by Adolph Hitler, who invaded Ukraine, the breadbasket of Eurasia, and concentrated the labor force. If Christians want to gain back power, then the plan must be twofold: first re-establish Christian values that strengthen family ties, and secondly break free of the system of international trade that keeps one on the hook of maritime power relations. What E. Michael Jones and other do not see is that, this will be especially hard if secularized Christian values are adopted by the liberal elite where a historical case has been made that such values are the natural progression of the delegitimization of Law seen in the Christian ethics. Finally, the adoption of a Hegelian view that posits Christianity as a synthesis between Greek and Jewish values cannot be allowed without letting in those very same elements that tried to subvert Church doctrine through Logos theology, as we read about in the first part of this work.

308. Either way, while Hitler was shutting down international banking institutions to set up labor and industry, the English ruling class was losing their

property to the Jews because of compound interest. The Jews convinced the British that they were a lost tribe of Israel, and the theories of a collective white race developed. As a result, British people lost their ethnic heritage believing their legacy was tied to Israel. But studies of old geneticists like Madison Grant reveal that proponents of racial creeds did not view the "white people" as a race. He identified the Alpine, the Mediterranean, and the Anglo Saxon as three distinct varieties of so-called European people. These groups are actually quite ethnically and genetically distinct. However, since internationalist sentiments rising from liberal groups, such oligarchs who control these international movements have engendered both a hatred of national identity, but also a hatred of ethnic groupings. If you want to fight international consolidation of power you have to attack its roots. The roots of these movements as previously discussed was liberalism.

309. Especially liberalism that is based on sexual liberation. This is true for the simple fact that the children are the future. No children, no future. If liberalism was seeking to control the population through dysgenic measures, then it must be squarely rejected, even if on the very basis of sexual freedom. If you believe in sexual freedom, then you believe that no club or group should be able to influence those decisions from the outside by social engineering. It is then quite paradoxical that these same groups base their views on findings from scientific experts. Anyways, when labor becomes the villain, usury becomes the hero, says E. Michael Jones. The people succumb to Keynesian manipulation, and the ideal becomes "poor and sexy". People are told to go to the gay disco and forget about their problems. Jones complains that America is one big gay disco. The oligarchs introduced birth control to baby boomers, and planned parenthood to the youth to double the workforce. Central was the socialism employed by thinkers like Louis Wirth. A class versus nation ideology was used to help Jewish immigrants cope with life in American cities. Wirth felt that Catholicism and Fascism were identical, and that an ethnic shift corresponds with a religious shift. Certain groups were just not viable for Democracy until they became ethnically unified. Groups like Poles and Irish, who were always viewed as racially inferior to the British were thrown into urban centers, following Wirth's strategies of "sensible adjustments in housing". This led to ethnic, religious, and racial tensions, which in this case were manufactured from the outside. The Detroit Race Riot of 1943 is a direct result. Blacks and women were the last resort for oligarchs who required cheap labor. This was how the American city was born as the last crown jewel in the project of liberalism which began in Britain and finally imploded through the exploitation of feminism and multiculturalism whose goals lead to the drive of "planetization" of world culture and the disintegration of the traditional family.

310. When Martin Luther King went to the Lithuanians and Poles in Chicago to tell them that the so-called "White people" had enslaved his ancestors, they had no idea what he was talking about. In fact, they probably did not have any

conception of "White people" being from ethnically distinct communities. The ideology, that was created by sociologists who, used black migration into ethnic neighborhoods to cause social disruption, while at the same time pioneering the race issue. This can be seen in Gloria Steinhem who was then employed by the CIA and used the publication of "miss magazine" to attack the black male, spreading feminism to the black community. This was a multipronged approach that broke down families while instituting ethnic barriers. Feminism and racial politics were being weaponized against Christian communities. On the racial front the plan was twofold: first to wipe out those questionable European whites who were ethnically distinct and assimilate them into American society, and the second was to start black migration to the city and extract cheap labor from poor blacks. They used race to supplant ethnicity. Race is an artificial construction, but ethnicity can be derived from cultural traditions and especially from a common language. Ethnicity had to be replaced by class ideology and family had to be replaced with a more feminist outlook. This was the invention of the American dream. As one filmmaker put it "The American dream was a dream dreamed by Jews" as most of the image of what the American Dream stood for was supplied by European Jews who controlled Hollywood like Louis B. Mayer. Indeed, it is not a myth but a reality, that most of the media companies during the start of Hollywood like Warner Brothers and other studios, and the top six media corporations concurrently known as "Big Media", have Jewish ownership.

311. As previously discussed this long-term view of planning came out of Darwinism. The applied science of Darwinism is none other than the practice of Eugenics. The theory seeks a material cause to the beginning of the world. The New Atheism movement posited by those like Sam Harris, Daniel Dennett, Richard Dawkins, and the late Christopher Hitchens, promote evolution and materialist science as the guiding factors of innovation and societal change. Their world view can be seen in Dennett's statement that the Universe came from nothing, or a very small "something". If the Universe created itself from nothing then there are two options: Either the Universe created itself from nothing, or the Universe had to have been there before it existed. Dennett is the only trained philosopher in the entire group and even he stumbles to articulate any positive view that atheists actually claim to hold. The group attempts to do metaphysics with biology. Darwin's book "Origin of Species" was subtitled as "the preservation of the favored races in the struggle for life". He clearly did not support liberal goals of amalgamating cultures and races. In his memoir, Christopher Hitchens declares his revolutionary blood passed down by his Jewish ancestry. He was schooled by his Zionist mentor Israel Shahak and admits this in a debate with Rabbi Boteach. The main question that E. Michael Jones doesn't answer: why Christianity was not able to defend itself against the attacks by Liberals and Jews? This would be because Christianity was already undermined and weakened by its link to Western philosophy. However, enticing it is to bring up this subject now we leave these sub-

jects for the next part of this book. We suffice it to say now that some sensible version of Christian values must be adopted because Christian values crystalized in liberalism have become hardened in the European psyche and Jews, Secularists, and occultists all seem to benefit on the attack on Christian and Islamic values.

Chapter 14
The Radical Response to the
Internationalist Agenda

312. Another more mainstream view that is based on Christian and Jewish teachings but has not thrived in the context of European and Western thought systems is Islam. While Jews and Atheists have found a common enemy in Islam, many Christian thinkers like E. Michael Jones find it necessary to open up a dialogue with the Muslim world. For better or worse, Islam has been challenged for never reaching the Enlightenment by Atheists like Michael Shermer and is attacked by the "New Atheism" movement far more than Christianity. Islam rejected Western learning and the push for Modernism and is heavily criticized as a result. It is seen as an intransigent and unchanging view that molds the minds of adherents to repel modern thought, as claimed by critics. All these criticisms of Islam are seen by a Muslim (myself being one) as rather impertinent. Islam has been given an ultimatum by the West to assimilate or perish.

313. As Moses had come to unify the Jewish tribes that were the descendants of Abraham[19], so Muhammad (p.b.u.h) had come to unify the Arab tribes that were the descendants of Abraham. The Jews were the sons of Isaac. The Arabs were the sons of Ishmael. Both were told by God that their seed would become many Nations that span the Earth. Muhammad (p.b.u.h) employed a religious and political strategy. This was the forecasting of certain events based on Biblical prophecy and projecting historical realizations into a strategy for the future, combining the teachings of the prophets of old. Islam made the claim that the religion of God existed before Moses, and that the prophets of every nation

---

[19] The ideas in the following section are to summarize the views of Shaykh Imran Hossein in two of his books which we feel apply the views of the Islamic world to their recent political struggles and turmoil. In addition to being a student of Islamic learning the Shaykh has studied and corresponded with others in the field of International Relations. While we do not agree with everything the Shaykh has said and especially in his recent stance on Russia and the Crucifixion of Jesus, we find that some of his views are greatly beneficial when applying the unique stances of the Quran and Islam to the struggles of the modern world. The information we present for the next 24 sections or paragraphs can be found in these sources: 1. Hossein, Shaykh. Imran. (2011, January 27). *Gog & Magog in the Modern Age By Sheikh Imran Hosein 1 of 14*. YouTube. Retrieved April 15, 2022, from https://www.youtube.com/watch?v=SwTzlnc2wYQ. A public talk given by Shaykh Imran Hossein on the mention of Gog and Magog in the Quran 2. Hossein, Shaykh Imran. (2012, January 4). *Jerusalem in the Quran Part One (1/3) - Imran Hosein*. YouTube. Retrieved April 15, 2022, from https://www.youtube.com/watch?v=5l57LCDOQb0

were originally sent to preserve the one true message. The belief of Islam is that Christ would someday return as a warrior-King to slay those who claimed to be God in the flesh. Here it is quite interesting that both Jewish prophecy that suggests that the King of Israel will rule on Earth and the Christian view that God would return to rule on Earth are precluded in the Islamic view of Antichrist or Dajjal. Islam contradicted the notion of Homo-ousia, namely, that God could exist besides himself from all of creation, but somehow give birth to his own essence. The famous rejection of it occurs in Surah Ikhlas, where it states that God is without beginning or end, not begotten, nor begetting. Muhammad (p.b.u.h) also taught that an alliance of Christians and Jews would assume the false messiah as their God, and set him on a throne in Jerusalem. This ruler would cause deception and oppression that will make people believe they are living in a paradise and cause them to reject God's message. Because of this they will be visited by plagues and eventually God will raise up an army to defeat them, just as he did in the past with the Babylonians and Romans. Shaykh Imran Hossein is an interpreter of Islamic end times prophecy and has attained degrees in western learning as well. As he tells us, and according to ancient traditions mentioned in the Bible, there were two nations who reigned in ancient times that were extremely powerful. In Jewish, and by extension Christian and Islamic eschatology, these are known as the nations of Gog and Magog.

314. To maintain order in the land, Allah sent a great warrior named Zulqarnayn in order to protect these people who were quite barbaric in their ways. He returned peace in the land by building an Iron Curtain to contain the two nations. The nations of Gog and Magog awaited the coming of the last prophet to be released. When Muhammad (p.b.u.h) was sent as the seal of the prophets, he tells us that the release of and eventual domination of these nations would coincide with a genocide on the Arab people. "Woe to the Arabs" he says as he wakes from sleep in a cold sweat. He then declared that a hole in the barrier built by Zulqarnayn had been made. Zulqarnayn is probably King Cyrus mentioned in the Bible. Apparently, the Nations of Gog and Magog were not able to be defeated by methods of conventional warfare upon release. Both their language and intelligence in constructing weapons would outmatch all competitors. Soon, Gog and Magog would create a secular world order. This would culminate in the return of the Jews to the Holy Land after 2,000 years, mysteriously in the wake of a secular movement, as well as an Arab genocide visited on them by people who originate from the Caucasus, which was an area between the Black Sea and Caspian Sea now known as the Dorian Gorge, where Zulqarnayn imprisoned Gog and Magog. Today the Jews and Christians and Muslims who await the coming of trials and tribulations of the last days are comfortably seated in the chairs of western progress, and are too busy to notice the signs all around them. Then there are the Messianic groups that hasten such development and are caught in the bind of self-fulfilling prophecy asking: Have we been summoned because he is to come, or have we

come because he is to be summoned? They await the coming of their Messiah. When it arrives will it be Jesus?

315. The fake Messiah will claim to be God uniquely positioning certain groups of Christian Zionists. According to the Islamic tradition, ten signs signify the end of the time. The first is the birth of the Antichrist, followed by the nations of Gog and Magog, and then finally the return of Jesus. Other signs include a pillar of smoke, the beast of the Earth, the Sun rising from the West, the Earth sinking down in three places, and a fire in Yemen. In the traditions of Gog and Magog, the nations invent weapons and aim them towards the sky to declare that they have slain Heaven. Gog and Magog are also said to deplete the water resources of the world. Finally, they are to cause an unprecedented increase in population and spread out across the Earth, causing the corruption of food, wealth, and sexual relations. This is brought about by the financial collapse of the monetary system through interest, with all the wealth in the world being controlled by interest. This is based not only on prophetic tradition but also lines from the Quran, which similar to the Bible, forbid taking money on interest. Also connected is the reversal of the sexual roles. The corruption of food is to be brought about by the desertification and overuse of land, as well as the use of pesticides which causes an overuse of water resources. Combined with practices of animal agriculture that exploit the land and enslave the animals the corruption of the land has become rampant.

316. The story of a meeting with the Antichrist is narrated by Tamim Ud-Dari, a Christian convert to Islam, about how he was lost on an Island and encountered a pillar of black smoke that resembled a shadowy beast. Being lost at sea he could not determine his whereabouts. When he asks the strange creature its name, the creature refers to himself as "Jasasa". Jasasa is an Arabic term meaning organization or spy. The creature led him to a Monastery where a man was chained up. The man asked him several questions about the state of things in the world. The man was apparently unaffected by time and had a strong build. This Jewish man was apparently the Antichrist in the vision of Tamim Ud-Dari. No one is sure if the events came as a vision or an actual event, but the story was immediately confirmed by the Prophet in an Islamic tradition, who said, not only that this man had spoken the truth but immediately asked him to repeat the story to a crowd of his followers.

317. Most interestingly, the questions asked by the chained-up figure were about the food and water resources. The first question was about date palms growing in Jordan. This indicates the desertification of Jordan, as seen today. A day would come when date palms no longer grow in Jordan. The date trees in traditions usually are allegory for the Arab Nations, just as the fig trees are allegories for the seed of Israel. The use of pesticides and aluminum sheds has caused severe desertification in Jordan. The second question was about the water level in the sea of Galilee.

318. The water level in the sea of Galilee is seen to represent growing tensions in the place where Jesus preached. This is culminating in the environmental man-made changes that seem to decrease the water level in the sea of Galilee. Today the water in the sea is decreasing due to man made changes. The Hadith or Traditions say that such a change will come about by Gog and Magog drinking the water. The chained-up man finally declares himself to be the Antichrist that will oppose the religion of God, and says that he will rule in all the cities of the world upon being released. The city is seen as the center of moral corruption. The growth of population will be a cause for the majority of mankind to become arrogant and sinful and misuse one another. In the final days, ninety nine out of a hundred will be prepared for the hell fire. The success in the last days is not in numbers. Nor is it in the technological world system which seeks to dominate and oppress the poor by taking control of the world resources. Shaykh Imran Hossein asks what Island could it be that launched a secular quest for world domination, and seems to have had a fascination and obsession with Jerusalem? This can be none other than the Isle of Great Britain, where the Antichrist was chained up and set to be released. When the Prophet told the Arabs that Dajjal is a Christ-like figure that stands between two ages and is an entity that could not be killed or maimed, the pagan Arabs did not understand him. When he told Jews that God would realize two nations, Gog and Magog, as a punishment on fake Jews and fake Christians in their rejection of the message of the real Christ, and association of God with idols, their punishment will be brought about by their own patterns of unbelief and by a collision with one another. Thus a promulgation of a movement against Islam was born in a Jewish and Christian alliance.

319. In Surah Al-Kahf of the Quran we see a story of a great warrior who had an effect on two ages known as Zulqarnayn or Dhul Qarnayn. He was the epitome of a just ruler who had placed power on the foundations of trust and faith. He used equity and honor to fight oppression. As he traveled, he followed the sun across the world, and spread out east to west. He then went in a third direction, most probably to the North. He arrived in a land sandwiched between two seas and two mountains. This place is geographically similar to the Darian Gorge, between the Black Sea and Caspian Sea. Oddly enough the location is near the Caucasus mountains, which are said to be the Eurasian origins of European races. When Zulqarnayn encountered people living a primitive way of life, although he had the power to defeat them, he built a barrier to protect them until their appointed time. Now we have no impetus to protect the primitive who live in harmony with nature. Whoever does not accord with our modern progress is gently swept aside or assimilated. These were not people inundated with technology. These were people who had no protection from the sun and no protection from the elements, according to Surah Al-Kahf. The Shaykh asks us to compare this simple life with those globalists who are dumping sewage in an open stream or disrupting natural patterns for the use of cell

phones and other devices. He says the plane is nothing more than a "flying donkey". One that is ridden by the Antichrist with its ears stretched towards the sky. "You are not a human being if you do not respect the Earth" the Shaykh warns. It has been seen that the people from Georgia (near Russia) speak a language that is distinct from all the family of languages. There is also the mysterious rising up of the Khazars seen in the time of the Prophet. The story could indeed signify many different things. Another point of tension is the strange competitiveness between Russia and the West.

320. When the power rests on the foundations of faith, your responsibility is more to the people than to the economic resources that their land provides. Zulqarnayn was not a mercenary or a conqueror. Not only is Antichrist not a figure like a normal human, but like Christ appears across time, so was Gog and Magog released in the lifetime of Prophet Muhammad (p.b.u.h). As a result, the time of the coming of the end of the world is already at hand and most of history is behind us. This is what both the Prophet Isa or Christ, and the Prophet Muhammad (p.b.u.h) came to confirm. Two powers will appear, both set on world domination. These powers will do battle until one overtakes the other.

321. As this change takes place, the primitive people of the world will start to decrease as the secular rule spreads across the world. The nations of Gog and Magog will comprise the population of most of the world. Their population will increase rapidly. This will be a godless age of secular rule. While the world order is established, most of humanity will be led astray. In Arnold Toynbee's "Civilization on Trial", he says that Modern Western civilization is in a race to seize control of the sky, the birds, the sea, the fishes, the animals, and the land. This level of hubris is literally unforeseen. The corruption of the wealth, corruption of family relations, and corruption of food sources are all taking place by means of exploitation of the natural world, and a knowledge and learning that is divorced from the sacred, used to invent strange and new technologies and unneeded innovation. Methods of taking the salt out of the Sea with desalination and making food grow in the desert by use of chemicals and aluminum sheds by draining water resources, is seen as progress. Chemical pesticides harmful to natural ecosystems threaten the use of the land and water. In "Greening the Desert" by Allan Savory, he demonstrates that old methods of permaculture are far more successful in adapting to terrains than a chemical sweep. We don't always do well to reject the traditions of the past. Farming methods developed by those who were before us seem to be much more "advanced" and beneficial to obtaining food sources and preserving those food sources than the ones used today. He demonstrates the greening of a Jordan desert by creating swales and contours, while harvesting waste from pigeons to use as fertilizer. Yet and still, we are led by the worst of us. It is not merely that we are what we eat, but as one gardener said, "we are what we eat, eats". We must be weary of those who give us easy fixes. Israel boasts of their

technological superiority over the Arabs, but it is clear that in the future the wars will not be over oil, but over water. Scientific hubris used to exploit the land has been a disaster. We hardly have to mention the nefarious and cancerous practice of industrial farming.

322. As we see the disruption of the traditional family, we see more evidence of people not relying on close relations, but on mass information provided by corporate or governmental modes. This is called the rule of experts. With the formation of mass culture, we see people rely on the opportunities provided by cities rather than their local environment. The car brought about the destruction of the nuclear family for the simple fact that it was a mobile bed. The plane was said to rid the world of borders and the extended family by letting people go anywhere in the world. Finally, the idea of space travel tells us to look upon this world as if it were expendable and another steppingstone for another world where we repeat the same process. All this is supposed to be called progress, but we see the goal of science and progress is the transformation of the natural world and Man himself into the unguided and blind hands of the blind watchmaker of creative evolution. It was a convenience and a choice and luxury to own a cell phone at one point, but now these things are no longer choices. It is mandatory to own a car or cell phone to get around and be a normal person. If it is not a choice then what is it? Technology is imposed on us but we must ask ourselves: how much technology is necessary to live a good life? The answer is very little. Liberals are engaged in a sort of self-hatred that views humanity as a stepping stone to something better, while Conservatives want to gain success in their nation and religious creeds while not understanding that it is the very technological system they impose to promulgate those beliefs that is what is inevitably responsible for the deterioration of values and social mores. Trends like the rise in depression, suicide, divorce, mental illness, pornography, mass killings and serial killing and raping, erectile dysfunction, same sex relationships, multiple sexual partners, reversal of sexual roles, rise of birth control and abortion, addiction to drugs, spread of sexual diseases, and public displays of obscenity and nudity, point to a general trend. The trends suggest that we are living a life that is not in tune with our deepest needs, and that the exploitation of the resources of the earth has reflected poorly on ourselves.

323. It cannot be said that Jews and Christians and White Europeans across the board are in a plot to spread these evils. One must be more discerning as we have attempted to be in the course of this presentation. It only points to a general trend that can be seen coming from only one direction. That direction is Modern Western Secular civilization under the Judeo-Christian synthesis born of Europeans. Many Jews and Christians and Muslims are beginning to notice that the lifestyles promoted to us today in the movies and TV shows are antithetical to religion in general, and many White European Christians and Jews have done more than ourselves to alert people to these various changes. We will not stand for the wholesale condemnation of any race or people.

324. However, we must be honest and tell the truth as long as we have the ability to do so, and alert people to deception to correct their views out of concern. If they do not listen then we must learn to love them anyways, but we must also be aware of our own ignorance first. It is easy to criticize, but what do you have to offer that is positive instead of what they preach? Christ says that false prophets will come and preach in his name directly after he is gone. We examine the historical trends connected with the rise of secular learning which have come to dominate on a world stage, and we find, quite paradoxically, the crafting of the nation of Israel in a false attempt to bring about the coming of a New Age. This was brought about when the Pax Romana was replaced with the Pax Europa, and the Pax Europa with Pax Britannica. In the view of the Shaykh, this represents the three periods of rule of the Antichrist. As the Pax Europa grew out of the Pax Romana unified by the Pauline doctrine, it crystallized into the British Crown. This Kingdom which rose up and fought back the Islamic Caliphate for 1,000 years became the ruling power in the world through colonialism. It culminated in the rule of finance and trade through which was funded the establishment of the State of Israel. As certain religious eschatological trends suggest to us, the Pax Britannica will be replaced by a Pax Judea. This will be the rule of the world through the State of Israel, until God raises up an army to destroy and dispel the Nation causing corruption in the land. The other option is for the State of Israel to succumb to the law and not try to dominate and oppress, but instead follow the commandments that were originally laid out for them to try to re-establish the covenant. This possibility has not been ruled out by us. What strikes us as odd is that the Shaykh never asks the question of what fundamental change brought about the unification of the disparate European tribes just as Islam was sent down? This is Pauline Christianity which the Shaykh never notices in his support of the Orthodox Church in Russia rather than the Catholic Church controlled by the West. The Byzantine and Catholic split did not occur until well into the Medieval period.

325. To summarize our findings thus far, a dual alliance between Christians and Jews that emerged in Europe is what we are concerned with, but we are not concerned with sweeping generalizations. We wish to narrow in and fine-tune our arguments based on the information thus provided. We have seen strange trends like how, near the Caucuses, a Eurasian state of non-Semitic people came to embrace Judaism. Combined with this is the fact that certain Jews chose to hide their Jewish heritage to get along with European society which harshly discriminated against Jews. Finally, we see the predominance of European Jews to the population of other Jews around the world. According to scientific genetic research, this group has had a disproportionate amount of achievement and success in the realms of scientific discovery and scientific invention, and generally possess a higher I.Q than the rest of humanity. The Ashkenazi or European Jew consists of over 90 percent of the world's Jewish population. While the Church cracked down on those it considered religious

heretics, Jews helped influence the rise of religious toleration in Europe and sponsored the Protestant Reformation. Finally, the Zionist movement that began around 1895 was a secular European style nationalist movement driven by Philo-Semitism, drawing its roots in modern day Europe, and especially supported by Great Britain.

326. The spread of Islam never reached Europe. What started during the French Revolution and Bolshevik Revolution and Industrial revolution, is what we refer to as Modern Europe. Some Jewish scholars and Rabbi have made the claim that the Holocaust was justified because it helped establish the State of Israel. Many Jews believe that Israel was a "gift of the Holocaust". We obviously cannot get behind such statements, as well as statements like those of Ehud Barak after the September 11 attack, that the attack would bring about a good turnout for Israel that were made on the BBC. There are two centers of power in the world today that do not include China or Africa or Arabia. These two powers are N.A.T.O and Russia. A mutual conflict between these two powers of equal strength must bring about a necessary dominating force. This conflict will most likely bring about the end of the technological age, leading to a primitive future and a return to the means of conventional warfare. In the Quran, Jerusalem is the only town linked with the rule of Gog and Magog. If the Jews were led back to the Holy Land by Gog and Magog under the false pretense of the establishment of a Messianic State, and continue to spread corruption and oppression in the land, then Allah's army will be raised up to destroy them. But this cannot occur until the final stage of conflict between Gog and Magog. One side must overtake the other.

327. In the Bible there is no notion of "Eretz Israel", or Greater Israel, stretching from the Nile to Euphrates. But there is also evidence that the Holy Land refers to the city of Jerusalem, and not any greater swath of land. Many like Scholar Richard Elliot Friedman, have shown errors in the Biblical texts. If the Bible is written by Moses, then how can Moses describe his own burial site? When Moses was in Sanai, how come Sanai was not referred to as part of the Holy Land? In the Bible it clearly states that Moses was not able to make it to the Promised Land, but stood atop a mountain where he could see it in the distance. Later the Jews are found exiled in Babylon, supported by Rome, and even occupying the city of Yathrib or Medina before the spread of Islam, where many of them converted to Islam. In Jewish history, they never really had a preference to govern or rule over the area now referred to as Greater Israel. This is a recent development. The timing of such events could not be stranger as it is supposedly the culmination of a secular movement.

328. Shaykh Imran Hossein warns that these changes have come about because there was once a man so stricken by his faith that he smashed the idols named Abraham, but now the idols are sitting in the Security Council of the U.N. Because Babylon was a wicked city there was a blessing placed in the

land of the wilderness for Abraham and his followers. The Modern Secular State makes religion conform with reason, but reason cannot judge the faithful. The Devil, named Shaytan (Satan) or Iblis in Islam, Satan or Lucifer in Christianity, is perhaps the greatest Logician. Though he had risen to the level of Angels, he used his intellect to override the obedience to Allah, and neglected the fact that, only by sacrifice for the good can one attain faith and only by sacrifice for truth can one attain wisdom. Such a being assumed knowledge to be a possession and birthright of the righteous. It can only be through this very same process that our knowledge is affirmed, because knowledge cannot simply be for the sake of knowledge. Knowledge alone cannot suffice. Knowledge requires actions to back it up. Belief is a dead thing. Faith is renewed and is alive. "Thoughts determine what you want, and actions determine what you get". Since Abraham was tested, he was made the proponent of the religion of all mankind. Abraham used his knowledge to make a sacrifice and act in the world through faith and received wisdom from the most high. Abraham is the Imam of all mankind, including George Bush and Donald Trump, says Shaykh Hossein. The children of Abraham, the Arabs and Jews, have played a significant role in shaping world events. God led Israel out of Egypt and into wilderness where he gave them laws to follow, and a covenant based on the following of those laws and ordinances. Certain Jews rejected these laws and fell out of favor with God, but others have remained faithful to the true message of faith, and not relied on the fear of man and idols of man. Fear not of man for fear of man causeth snares. Fear of man is the opposite of the love of God.

329. When Moses told the Jews of the laws and told them that he was there to lead them, the Jews rejected his authority with the claim that an all-powerful God does not need anyone to defend him or speak on his behalf. When Moses commanded the Jews to fight for their own dignity and freedom for they are God's people, the Jews told Moses to take his God and use his power to fight. When Moses made the priestly community of Levites, the head priests decided that all were capable of deciding and interpreting the law and that no one was chosen above anyone else. Hence, there were two types of rejection. One type of rejection was a sense of entitlement, and the second was an antinomian protest. In the Bible, God sends prophets to correct the Jews who find themselves continually imperiled because of a lack of faith. The Bible says Jews were chosen by God, but it also uses the Jewish people as an example of the obstinacy of all mankind in perceiving what is good for them. The Jews continually mix with the heathen, defame the Holy Land, and invent their own laws. They amended the books of God to make it seem they had an unconditional right to the Holy Land. But the Bible today refutes this. To be chosen by God, and to become the friend of God like Abraham, has been described as a complete destruction of the egoic mind. It can hardly be described as a calm Sunday afternoon, after prayer breakfast.

330. To this end, the Jews can hardly be blamed. They were given a perhaps impossible task. Have the Jews succeeded in this task? What is clear is that history suggests that the Jews have failed several times to live up to the status of the chosen people of God. This does not discount that in some future state they could establish a benevolent rule. We welcome the setting in order of Jewish affairs and seeking peace with all mankind. The Bible however is clear. King David established the first and only legitimate rule in the history of Israel. Solomon was his heir. Solomon himself had many heirs and so placed his Kingdom in the protection of the Queen of Sheba. This was so the Kingdom would not fall into the hands of the "Jassad", or body without a soul he saw sitting on his throne. He prayed to God to not let his Kingdom succumb to evil forces at work in the world. This is according to the Bible and Quran, if one is to view them as a continuous narrative as Islam suggests. King Solomon taught us many valuable lessons. One of his primary teachings is that those who oppose truth would try to divide the truth into two parts. Those who loved the truth would keep it whole, even at the expense of losing it, while those who were truly deranged would split the truth in half leaving it to be ineffectual and in ruin, cleaving truth from truth to save their pride. The Bible mentions requirements for control of the Holy Land. One is to follow God, and the other is to follow the rule of righteousness. If this is not fulfilled, then Allah raised up an army to dispel the people from the land. If God used Egyptians and Babylonians and Romans and Muslims to remove Jews from the Holy Land and remove Christians from the Holy Land, then the conclusion must be clear that certain of the Pagans and Non-Jews were following God. At the time these people surpassed the Jews in knowledge and righteousness, and so God used them to punish Israel. One can hardly deny the role and influence of the Bible. God chooses people at the time he chooses them.

331. According to Islam, when God sent the Messiah to the Jews, they declared him a bastard and boasted of killing him. Before the arrival of Jesus, the Chief Rabbi of the Holy Temple was a man named Zechariah. His wife was Elizabeth, and his son was John the Baptist. The relative of Elizabeth was Mary who sat in the Holy of Holies, protected with the Sacred Relics. Zechariah was the guardian of Mary. When Zechariah saw Mary sitting in the temple alone where no one could enter or leave, she was surrounded with gifts and food and jewels, he was amazed. He asked who had given her these things, and she declared that the Angel had brought them for her because she had asked God. She was the most pure and most learned of all girls in Israel at the time. God had chosen her to lead the women in Heaven. She said she had asked God and he had answered her, and that she was to ask for a baby boy, and that God would send her the angel to give her a boy as well. It was promised to be hers by God. God chose Mary to fulfill his promise to the Jews.

332. Everyone knew who Mary was, but no one knew how she got pregnant. God sent his servant Joseph to protect Mary, and they fled before anyone knew

that she was pregnant. Mary didn't knock on someone's door and leave the child, or throw the baby in a dumpster, as is done in some American cities, but instead had faith and declared that the baby was from God. The baby stood up and declared himself to be Messiah on the day of his birth and the Jews called it sorcery and magic. Jesus declared the Temple to be a "den of thieves" run on the interest and usury generated by the money changers, who were probably using the money changing system for thievery of the people. They did not follow the law of Moses but followed their desires by acquiescing to those in power. This was neither beneficial to their own degraded spirit, nor was it good for the people who they claim to serve. This line of thought infuriated the Jewish leaders. What disparaged them more was that Jesus accused them of inventing new laws in their oral traditions. The Jews considered this a preaching against their Temple, which they considered a sacred object which they used as an idol. They wanted to curse Jesus with the Roman crucifixion, but Allah only made it appear that he had died. This means either Jesus escaped the crucifixion or is being preserved in a supernatural state. Jesus will return. The Shaykh says you can tell Francis Fukuyama that history will not end until Jesus comes back. When he comes back every Jew will have to finally accept him as ruler and those who don't will end up like Pharoah, at the bottom of the sea drowning by their own ignorance.

333. The chain of events according to Islamic eschatology in regard to Jesus is this: First the release of Gog and Magog, then secular world rule is established, and finally Israel takes center stage in the affairs of the world. After this Jerusalem is set up under false pretenses of an accursed rule, and Jesus is returned to settle the score and kill the Antichrist. An army is raised up from Khorasan (modern day Iran, Afghanistan, and Northwestern Pakistan) to attack the oppressive rule in Jerusalem and replace it with the Just State. Until then, Muslims are instructed to offer prayers, fast and keep strict dietary regulations, give testimony of faith, forgive debts, feed and clothe the poor, help the orphans, treat well prisoners, free slaves or treat them the same as themselves, teach the ways of the prophets and messengers, fight racism and nepotism, stay clear of money systems based on interest and usury, stay clear of alcohol and drugs that incur sleepiness, live a simple life with only a few possessions, practice reason and justice, stay away from spiritual materialism and sectarianism, and make the focal point of marriage and the raising of children who are taught to fight against greed and oppression. The greatest Jihad is to speak truth in the face of an oppressor, and the ink of a scholar is worth a thousand times more than the blood of a martyr, said the Prophet p.b.u.h (the first tradition is authentic and the second one is found in a source around the 16th century). What is important is to fight in the way of Truth and condemn falsehood. In the Quran it says that God is the truth manifest.

334. Muhammd (p.b.u.h) fashioned the political and legal system from the theological laws and ordinances which were identical to that of the Jewish

laws. Many of the Jews of Medina chose to leave Judaism and accept Islam. Others of the Jews and Christians either helped the spread of Islam or were protected by the cause of Islam. These included the King of Ethiopia. What Nation will be raised up to oppose the false propaganda of the Messianic and Zionist State of Israel? Will it be the Africans, Russians, Europeans, or Chinese? There are over a billion Muslims in the world. Islam is readily seen by Samuel P. Huntington, and those Neoconservatives at the CFR as the bane of modern civilization. In 1919, a secular rule was established in the Muslim world, and the twin states of Saudi Arabia and Israel were formed by the British Government. The House of Saud has not historically represented the goals and aspirations of the Muslim people or of the Arab tribes native to the region. The Wahhabi sect is one of many sects that rise up during the last days in order to confuse and obfuscate the truth. The Wahhabi interpretation of Islam is a Protestant style reform movement that says when people die in a Hajj stampede it is choice of Allah. Interestingly enough, in the Quran it states that religion should be made of no compulsion other than the sincerity of those who profess faith and practice accordingly. The Government of Saudi Arabia gains a handsome revenue in exploiting religious services. Rather than using Islam to fight oppression, they use it to control and justify their own power and corruption. Yet and still, if there were any nation willing to oppose the injustice of the State of Israel, which will now be set up by America to be the ruling state in the world, it will most likely arrive from the Muslim world. This is why there is a growing fear that Islamic thinking and Islamic traditions pose a threat to Western learning.

335. This follows the legacy of British Israelism. In a tradition it says that Dajjal will rule the world in a day like a week, a day like a month, and a day like a year. This points to three distinct periods of rule. As we moved from Rome to Europe to Great Britain, we now move from the rule of Britain passing to the rule of America, which finally sets up Israel as the ruling state in the world. This is the Antichrist deception and the beast of the land now being ridden by Benjamin Netanyahu who predicted the 9/11 attacks in his book on the war on terror. Those who speak of this and glorify the present rule, as well as deify the progress of the modern age, don't know how to read the signs. The Afghans threw out the Russians and will throw out the U.S. The Quran and Traditions of the Prophet (p.b.u.h) explain many changes in the world. First they explain the rise of Islam itself, its opposition by Western Europeans reflected in the Crusades, the legacy of British rule, the Balfour declaration and the destruction of the Islamic Caliphate, the modern world of technological rule through the predominance of secular knowledge, the rise of the international monetary system, the reversal of sexual roles, the destruction of the land and water resources, the rise of Kabbalism and Freemasonry, and genocide of the Arab people. Indeed, something must explain the mysterious return of the Jewish people to the land of Israel or Canaan after 2,000 years.

336. The Sea of Galilee to the North and the Jordan River to the south encompass the entire Holy Land. The city of Jerusalem is the heart of the Holy Land in its direct center. Some of the Jewish scholars erroneously equated the Holy Land with wherever Jews were exiled. They expanded it to include Egypt where the Jews were enslaved stretching it to the Nile, and to Babylon where the Jews were exiled, as far as the Euphrates. Where else will it include? Rome? America? The World? In a speech made by Israeli Prime Minister David Ben Gurion in Look Magazine (1962):

"Western and Eastern Europe will become a federation of autonomous states having a Socialist and democratic regime. With the exception of the USSR as a federated Eurasian state all other continents will become united in a world alliance, at whose disposal will be an international police force. All armies will be abolished, and there will be no more wars. In Jerusalem, the United Nations (a truly United Nations) will build a Shrine to the Prophets to serve the federated union of all continents; this will be the seat of the Supreme Court of Mankind, to settle all controversies among the federated continents, as prophesied by Isaiah. Higher education will be the right of every person in the world."

337. This is a truly shocking prediction. It is also made at the behest of those Jewish intellectuals like Illan Pappe and Norman Finkelstein, who criticize the so-called Jewish State as anything but a purveyor of justice and human rights. Jesus was sent to the Jews to match their expectations of the coming of a Messiah. The time is at hand. With both the desertification of the land, and the destruction of the water sources, Jesus is set to arrive. Jews and Christians who demonize truth and let falsehood reign, as well as the Muslim hypocrites, will be held accountable according to the Law of Moses. "Those who live as Pharaoh lived, will die as Pharaoh died", warns the Shaykh.

338. When the Prophet Muhammad was sent to declare himself Prophet (p.b.u.h), he exemplified the Jewish Law to make it be known that he was sent by God. He came to warn the Jews that if they return to the Holy Land with their corruption and tyrannize over the people, then they will be expelled. Jesus and all other prophets came with the same message, not just for the Jews, but for all mankind. The false Messiah will rule the world from Jerusalem and this will be the single most fantastic deception ever devised. The word Dajjal used for Antichrist in Islam means "deception". Modern Israel and the U.N have declared that righteousness is not a condition for the use of the Holy Land. Today in Israel, citizenship is determined by genetic descent and not religious practice, as was mentioned before. The deception spans ages, but began on a small monastery, on a small island. Which island is it? Dajjal is seen as the one with "one eye". He is represented by the spiritually blind. Where is the island of spies? We know that at one time there was not a place in the so-called world that the British Empire did not reach. Britain helped bring about a new age of secular learning. This would culminate in the Industrial Revolution.

Finally the American system of currency was no longer backed by gold and silver but ensured by private institutions that lent them money on interest. This will lead to the eventual collapse of the dollar and the instituting of a digital currency through a world bank. The system of digital currency will be like a body with no soul that will be seated on the throne of King Solomon.

339. In section 205 of "Daybreak" by Friedrich Nietzsche we read the following conclusion:

> *"Of the people of Israel.* Among the spectacles to which the coming century invites us is the decision as to the destiny of the Jews of Europe. That their die is cast, that they have crossed their Rubicon, is now palpably obvious: all that is left for them is either to become the masters of Europe or to lose Europe as they once a long time ago lost Egypt, where they had placed themselves before a similar either-or. In Europe, however, they have gone through an eighteen-century schooling such as no other nation of this continent can boast of and what they have experienced in this terrible time of schooling has benefited the individual to a greater degree than it has the community as a whole. As a consequence of this, the psychological and spiritual resources of the Jews today are extraordinary; of all those who live in Europe they are least liable to resort to drink or suicide in order to escape from some profound dilemma something the less gifted are often apt to do. Every Jew possesses in the history of his fathers and grandfathers a great fund of examples of the coldest self-possession and endurance in fearful situations, of the subtlest outwitting and exploitation of chance and misfortune; their courage beneath the cloak of miserable submission, their heroism in *spernere se sperni*, surpasses the virtues of all the saints. For two millennia an attempt was made to render them contemptible by treating them with contempt, and by barring to them the way to all honours and all that was honourable, and in exchange thrusting them all the deeper into the dirtier trades and it is true that they did not grow cleaner in the process. But contemptible? They themselves have never ceased to believe themselves called to the highest things, and the virtues which pertain to all who suffer have likewise never ceased to adorn them. The way in which they honour their fathers and their children, the rationality of their marriages and marriage customs, distinguish them among all Europeans. In addition to all this, they have known how to create for themselves a feeling of power and of eternal revenge out of the very occupations left to them (or to which they were left); one has to say in extenuation even of their usury that without this occasional pleasant and

useful torturing of those who despised them it would have been difficult for them to have preserved their own self-respect for so long. For our respect for ourselves is tied to our being able to practice requital, in good things and bad. At the same time, however, their revenge does not easily go too far: for they all possess the liberality, including liberality of soul, to which frequent changes of residence, of climate, of the customs of one's neighbours and oppressors educates men; they possess by far the greatest experience of human society, and even in their passions they practise the caution taught by this experience. They are so sure in their intellectual suppleness and shrewdness that they never, even in the worst straits, need to earn their bread by physical labour, as common workmen, porters, agricultural slaves. Their demeanor still reveals that their souls have never known chivalrous noble sentiments nor their bodies handsome armour: a certain importunity mingles with an often charming but almost always painful submissiveness. But now, since they are unavoidably going to ally themselves with the best aristocracy of Europe more and more with every year that passes, they will soon have created for themselves a goodly inheritance of spiritual and bodily demeanor: so that a century hence they will appear sufficiently noble not to make those they dominate *ashamed* to have them as masters. And that is what matters!"

340. The claims of Islam have had a strong effect on the population of Americans that are most harshly considered by the history of those laws and ordinances that began with British rule. These would be the so-called African Americans, whose history has taught them that they are not from America but that neither are the Whites, and that the religion that was given to them upon arrival to this continent was given to them to make them adhere to the standards of White European society. The idea of a society of powerful landowners that would control indentured servants, who would in turn, govern the slave plantation, was originally conceived by John Locke. It is perhaps then no surprise to us that the total blend of Masonic themes oriented with race would find their most critical reversal in the thought of Noble Drew Ali[20], who used Rosicrucian and Islamic thought to repudiate Western religion and Western philosophy. He felt that this would be a most critical step in improving the psychology of black people that had been systematically oppressed by Western society. He saw the culture of the Moors, Islamic Society, and Eastern and

---

[20] Bowen, Patrick Denis, "The African-American Islamic Renaissance and the Rise of the Nation of Islam" (2013). Electronic Theses and Dissertations. 963. We rely on this dissertation to present information regarding both the origins of the Moorish Science Temple and Nation of Islam. It is an excellent resource on how the rejection of white domination meant the adoption of Islamic principles which were henceforth seen as the antithesis of Western Christian values.

Occult ideas to be a useful roadmap to organizing a defense against the patterns of belief that have caused Blacks and Asians to love their oppressors.

341. He may have even been keenly aware of the racial myths propagated by the Western Occult and claimed to be of African and Cherokee descent. In light of his views, he founded an organization called the Moorish Science Temple that has had more success than its Black Hebrew counterparts. Blacks have shared a heritage in both development of Jewish and Christian customs. Moses' wife was an Ethiopian, and for years the Coptic Church has survived in Ethiopia, sharing books that were used by the Ancient Hebrews. But for Noble Drew Ali, nowhere was the legacy of Africa more clearly seen than in its affiliation with the Islamic Moors. It could be that he used these people, either because they were the enemy of the Catholic Church and European rule during the Crusades, or because he equated the Moorish kingdom with the practice of Islam that was predominant on the west coast of Africa during the Atlantic slave trade. Noble Drew Ali taught that all non-Europeans were part of a unified Asian race called "Asiatic" or 'Moorish". He also taught that Europeans had usurped the rights of blacks who were the original discoverers of America under the Spanish Kingdom of the Moors and that America was actually "Al-Morocco". His message was anti-State, anti-Christian, and anti-European. This was a powerful version of an entire brand of movements of 'black Muslims" or "black Hebrews". The movement is a response to the propaganda used by European Whites to enslave Blacks, who at the time of Noble Drew Ali were facing oppressive laws of segregation imposed on them by European whites.

342. He was drawing on the centuries of oppression by the British who enslaved the Blacks and the Irish. Leonard P Howell who developed the Rastafarian Faith, used the tale of the transfer of power from King Solomon to the Queen of Ethiopia to suggest that the Covenant of the Kingdom of God was in Ethiopia. Indians, Irish and Africans were all enslaved by the British and Dutch Pirates, many of whom were of Jewish descent. Leonard P. Howell is better known as G.G. Maragh, which is a name he adopted from Hindus. He took on some Hindu customs like abstaining from meat in constructing some of the tenets of Rastafarianism. A lesser-known fact is that the Gaelic accent of Jamaicans comes from being enslaved alongside Irish. This is mainly because those who subscribe to the theories collectively known as British Israelism routinely considers groups like the Irish and Italians to be born from a form of Black albinism and considered them lower than Blacks and Indians in their racial teleology. It was clear that the history, culture, and religion of African people was lost during this time, as well as the ability to govern and control their own communities and education. Many tribes of West Africa like the Yoruba had accepted Islam sometimes for political expedience and were converted to Christianity by force at the time of their enslavement. Noble Drew Ali saw this as a strategic replacement of their African, Arab, Persian, and Asian origin, and replacing it with European Christianity to take away their

birthright. The slavery practiced in America by European settlers was not like the one practiced in North Africa at the time mainly because it was practiced by Africans on other African tribes and as a result reflected intertribal conflicts and was not externally imposed by a colonial or military force. Ancient slavery included a variety of practices that are in some cases similar, and in other cases totally unlike the kind practiced during the Atlantic Slave Trade. The racial teleology and ideology and technology of the Europeans made slavery during the Atlantic Slave Trade several shades harsher.

343. In many cases it can be said that prisons today are barbaric institutions used to house the poorest of society. A disproportionate amount of the American prison population today contains African Americans who are serving time for non-violent drug offences. A few years back this number was as much as over half of the entire prison population of America. Add to this the checkered past, but also the irrational hatred of Islam seen in the media as well as in Hollywood movies (seen by people like Jack Shaheen in "Reel Bad Arabs"), and you have a situation where Blacks who equate Islam as a rival to the West seek to weaponize it against the West. There is also the fact that many Jewish financiers like Aaron Lopez controlled the companies which bought and sold many slaves, while the black rights movement in the form of the N.A.A.C.P created by Jews like Joel Spingarn convince blacks that historical oppression has been perpetrated by Whites. We obviously, as noted before, do not go for the wholesale repudiation or condoning of acts carried out by any group in history, but it is important to see how certain movements to blame all Jews and Whites take away from the greater issues at play which have historical relevance. The strategy of Noble Drew Ali was instead to empower Blacks to look upon the intellectual achievements of Europe as secondary to their own historical contributions, thereby empowering them to create a new positive image instead of blaming other people. Many Blacks would have considered that poverty in America and harsh treatment of slavery during the Atlantic slave trade was much worse than the time in Africa where at least the rulers were Black, and one had the ability to attain and maintain honor in the love of one's own. Noble Drew Ali also drew from other sources. His Circle 7 Quran, which is used in the Moorish Science Temple for their doctrinal beliefs, includes parts of Rosicrucian texts and Theosophical writings. This includes parts of the Rosicrucian text "To Thee I Grant", but also opens with the Theosophical writing of Levi Dowling called the "Aquarian Gospel of Jesus Christ".

344. The idea that either Christianity, Judaism, or Islam were drawn from Asian origins and Vedic teaching was an idea of Theosophists, who merged Buddhist and Hindu beliefs with Christianity. This was the source of the Aryan Myth created by Helena Blavatsky. However, as we have previously discussed, South Indians have genes from the Ivory Coast of Africa and seem to be genetically distinct from Europeans and from the Indians from areas of Northern Pakistan. Furthermore, Indians of the Northern regions seem to be

genetically distinct from those of the Southern regions, and many of the over 36 ethnic divisions that exist within the Indian subcontinent are invariably mixed and very diverse. The claim is that Christianity reflects truths that are Eastern and hidden to the West, because of their mysterious origins and alien history. This was reversed by Noble Drew Ali, who posited that these secret teachings were Afro-Asian. Some of the teaching is similar to those of the Ahmadiyya Sect of Islam, which was started by Ahmed Qadiani who declared himself the Mahdi or Imam of Islam and said that the people of Kashmir are a "lost tribe of Israel". The appearance of a sacred grave site called Roza Bal where a great priest was said to have been buried was purported by followers of Qadiani to be the burial site of Jesus. Most notably, a belief that Jesus had a natural death is antithetical to some claims made in the Quran as claimed by some, because Islamic teaching seems to make no record of Jesus' death, but also claims that Jesus was made to appear as if he was crucified, when in reality God had placed someone or something in his place. Ahmadiyya Muslims say it was the grave of Jesus who escaped his death and went to India. There is obviously no historical basis for these claims, but it is interesting to find their reappearance in the Western Occult, which has practically gained a sole subsistence from Jewish, Christian, and Islamic heretics.

345. The Circle 7 Quran[21] begins with Jesus explaining the meaning of the Vedic law to the Vedic priests. "There was never a time when man was not" he declares, as they are astounded by his knowledge. Already we see a deeply humanistic tone. This is the "Archetypal Man" of primordial origin that existed before creation. Man's soul is subject to movement, and his body is subject to change and degeneration, but his essence is "pure spirit". Wisdom originates from the highest plane of spirit moved by the thought of Allah, and is not bound by time. Man holds within him the perfection of the creator summed up in the phrase, loved by Gnostics everywhere, that Man is made in the image of God, and the one by Protagoras, that "Man is the measure of all things". Gnostics take this to mean the inner light of Man, which is Reason, reflects God. The plane of the Soul is a "plane of the Ether", or a vibrating space between spirit and matter. A belief is held that no man lies in himself and that everything is connected, but there is a strict duality between spirit and matter, and the higher and the lower self. The demonic world is full of the idols of man. A

---

[21] Ali, Noble. Drew. (1926). *The Circle 7 Quran.*
https://www.youtube.com/watch?v=72qYMJHJvfI
The Circle 7 Quran is a work used by Noble Drew Ali in order to educate his followers and contains sections from other works such as the Rosicrucian text "To Thee I Grant" and "The Aquarian Gospel of Jesus' by Theosophist Levi Dowling. One can only imagine that such a work would have a powerful effect on his followers and begins with the suggestion that Jesus lived beyond his crucifixion and traveled to the East and preached in India. In doing so he reversed the Egyptian and European origins of the occult into a Afro-Indian or Afro-Asian cultural and religious matrix which he termed "Asiatic". In doing so, he reversed the claims of British Israelism.

man named Ravana who is a Vedic priest takes his followers to go and meet Jesus. When he arrives, Jesus begins expounding on the nature of Man and Truth.

346. "What is Truth", asks the Vedic priest in a quite similar fashion to Pontius Pilate in the Gospel of John. He responds that the truth changes not, but ultimately two things exist. Namely, both truth and falsehood exist, but cannot co-exist. The light shineth in the dark and the darkness knoweth it not. But this is a dualistic formulation. Truth is ought he says, and has no cause. Falsehood, on the other hand, is not, but is manifest. That which begins must end, and all things are reflexes of the ethereal substance lodged in matter. This begins to sound like Heraclitus or Empedocles. "What is Man?", asks the Vedic priest. Christ responds that Man is truth and falsehood mixed. This is another clear Gnostic depiction. The Holy Breath of Truth mixed with Falsehood and bore Mankind. Power in the world is not force, but illusion, because force changes by what is willed. Understanding is the Gnosis of "Ought". This reflects truth and wisdom, which is unified with God, who Noble Drew Ali refers to as "The Triune Allah". He taught his followers that Heaven and Earth do not exist externally, but only exist within Man, and are expressed as the reality he creates for himself and others. The cycle of truth relies on beliefs that are kept alive by faith. Faith must come to fruition by righteous acts. There is no way to Allah by Temples and men's mouths, but only if Man wastes nothing and lives in the purity of heart can he find God. Noble Drew Ali was clearly impressed by the fact that the previously culturally distinct people of Europe, who fought and killed each other for years were unified into a single cultural front, and a singular political force that polices and dominates the affairs of the world. He felt that the so-called progress of this civilization was based on the foundation of "Asiatic" principles laid down by the colored people of the world, who were generally part of an alliance of trade that included Indigenous, African, Asian, Indian, Persian , and Middle Eastern heritage. The Asiatic race represented the true world culture that is kept in cultural stasis by European hegemony. He used a mix of Indigenous or Shamanic, African Yoruba, Sufi Mysticism, Rosicrucianism, and Zoroastrian and Asian views to challenge Western culture, and especially the view that the Europeans started civilization put forward by British Israelists mentioned earlier.

347. Today the debt to the teaching of Noble Drew Ali has been acknowledged by high-ranking Black Muslims and Egyptologists, such as Louis Farrakhan. A later disciple would orchestrate a faction of the Moorish Science Temple. He was to begin the largest "Black Muslim" movement in the country, and one that challenged the views of Christian Ministers like Martin Luther King Jr. This was none other than the notorious Master Fard Muhammad. Fard went by several aliases and mixed the teachings of Jehovah's Witness literature of Joseph Rutherford, UFO-ology, and views of Race and Religion that spawn from heretical factions, with the teaching of Noble Drew Ali, as a former member of

the Moorish Science Temple. Fard taught that Caucasians were the Gentiles, and that the black race was his "uncle", and also the true founders of civilization. He also taught that he himself was sent as appointed ruler and "Mahdi", and liberator as "God appointed ruler" to teach the Black Man that he was heir to the "New World". "The Teaching for the Lost Found Nation of Islam in a Mathematical Way" was a book distributed to his followers that includes the various "wisdom traditions" he told to his followers, some of which included facts about astrology and geometry. Master Fard himself was most probably a man of North Pakistani descent, but told his follower, his top disciple being Elijah Muhammad, that he was God in the form of a black man. He used the Islamic statement of faith There is no God but Allah and Muhammad is his Messenger to refer to himself claiming that he was God and that his student Elijah Muhammad was the Muhammad that was foretold to be the final apostle of Allah. He posed as a light skinned black man and called himself the "Asiatic" God or Prince of Islam.

348. Fard taught his followers that black people or Africans were gods of this world, and that an advanced aircraft built by our Japanese "Asiatic" brothers was in orbit around the world. He said this device called "The Mothership" would eventually destroy America and lead to a peaceful and civilized rule of Blacks. This "Original Man" was the Black Race of the "Tribe of Shabazz", that ruled the world from the Holy City of Mecca. They practiced Islam and performed miraculous experiments which gave birth to plants and wildlife we see today through a sort of "green alchemy". Soon however, an apostate named Yaqub, who became an evil scientist would perform genetic experiments that led to the birth of a demonic race. The White Skin Race of Devils were rounded up. Blacks at the time were synonymous with Islam, and banished to wastelands of Europe were the Whites. While in Europe, "The White Race" invented the treacherous and deceitful religions of Judaism and Christianity to delude the people and reverse the message of Islam. They used this tactic to blaspheme God, and to enslave the Black Race.

349. Moses and Jesus were even sent to convert the White Devils back to Islam, but they were heedless. Due to the corruption of White Devils, Blacks lived in Hell for 400 years but liberation is near. After Fard's disappearance, Elijah Muhammad taught followers that he was the "Messenger of Allah", and servant of Master Fard, the Supreme Ruler of the Universe. Later, Malcolm X would be assassinated after exposing a pact between the KKK and the Nation of Islam and embracing Orthodox Islam. Today Minister Farrakhan still teaches followers that Master Fard and Elijah Muhammad are alive aboard a Mothership and await the destruction of America. Many splinter groups of this organization were formed. These include the Five Percent Nation and the Nuwaubians. It was not dissimilar to the message of men like Marcus Garvey (the father of Pan-Africanism), and William Sanders Crowdy and Frank Cherry (founders of the Black Hebrew Israelites), but had a decidedly more militant

view, and broader theological application which included a restructuring of the worldviews of Western European history and applying new cultural settings. They seemed to have borrowed the view of sacred bloodlines.

350. Dr. Jame Small is a lecturer on this alternative view of history, and admits of its relations to the teachings of the Occult, including groups like the Knights Templars, who supposedly traveled to Ethiopia in search of the Ark of the Covenant, according to a legend. Thinkers like John H. Clarke, and Michael Bradley talk about "The Iceman Inheritance, after the title of Bradley's book. This is a view that says that African and Olmec Civilization was far before European Civilization, which even at the time of Greece and Rome was uncivilized. It further states that Nubian, Egyptian, and other civilizations, that were from Africa, spread the ideas that made Greece and Rome possible. This is argued in a work entitled "Black Athena" as well. During this time Europeans were cavemen, and even according to Aristotle, Greeks combined the intelligence and organization of the Chinese, who he said were too focused on laws, and the freedom of the Europeans, who he said were the stupidest and most free of all races (Politics Book 7). Due to the inhospitable climate of the Northern European weather, the people of Europe had to resort to cannibalism and became barbaric and hostile to their fellow men as a result. They also had to rely more on technological means to survive. Dr. James Small[22] makes the claim that civilization in Africa is not 5,000 years old but actually over 800,000 years old. The Vedic timelines proposed following works like "Forbidden Archaeology" by Michael Cremo dismiss Darwinian Evolution, saying that there is evidence for human beings going back much further than the slow and gradual evolution proposed by scientists today. The Ancients believed that imitation of the Natural Law would allow man to create a social ecology that mirrored the function of the Heavens. They also made references to civilizations much older than themselves that had discovered such advancements. Researchers, like Dr. James Small, believe that this information is encoded in messages that are older than Christianity, and provide the basis for the major three so-called western religions. He draws the religions of man from Ancient Egyptian myths. In Egypt, the basis for religion was the Man, Woman, and Child. These three archetypal representations were the primordial basis for religious practice according to Egyptologists and promoters of ancestral magic (where one could obtain knowledge through the dreams of their ancestors).

351. This Man, Woman, and Child trinity exists in almost every mythology, but is best represented by Egyptian legend. In the Egyptian creation myth, the

---

[22] Sa Neter (2020, February 6). *Prof. James Small: Christianity Comes Out Of Kemet, What Happen To You, This Is Basic Knowledge.* YouTube. Retrieved April 15, 2022, from https://www.youtube.com/watch?v=Aco-f583W30. Professor Jame Small is a leading Egyptologist and discusses history from the point of view of Neopagan elements of the African Diaspora. He describes the origin of many views such as the view that Jesus was black. We rely on the above presentation for the following 5 sections.

Chief Deity was Ammon, who "created himself out of himself". He produced an emanation named Ra, which was a symbol for cosmic energy or force, and Ptah, who was the architect of Matter. Out of the primordial blackness of an ethereal substance of space arose Nun, or "black water", and Shu or "air", as well as Tepnut or "moisture". Geb and Nut, or Earth and Sky, spread out over everything. Nature was put in place and fashioned by the divine. Dr. James Small does not believe that Osirus existed, and that people had animal heads, but rather that these represent symbols and stages of the Universal development of Man. In the Book of Coming Forth by Day, it shows a depiction that seems familiar to the philosopher and pagan and priest.

352. In this depiction there are twelve judges that weigh the heart of each person on a scale against a feather. If the heart creates weight in the world of an amount more than it takes out, it sinks. In other words, if what you produce in this world is less than what you take out you are squarely condemned. The scale represents Justice, and the feather represents Truth. The scale of justice is represented by the Goddess Ma'at, who as Dr. James Small complains, was changed into the blind lady of Justice by the Europeans, who took her headband and put it over her eyes in rebellion. The Jackal that sits beside the scale represents discernment and judgement, as a jackal hides its meat to allow it to ferment. The heart is weighed instead of the brain, because the heart is seen as the seat of the "spirit-body". Our spirit must be in balance with the truth, and with the good we create in this world. Kut, or the boundless essence within nature, is darkness with no beginning and no end. The disciples of God are represented in terms of the relations of the family. Aset or Mother, Ansar or Father, and Heru or Child, which represented a cosmic trinity that was the basis for all religion according to James Small and others.

353. This trinity was a metaphor for infinite rebirth, where death was seen only as a transition. 12 deities (Horus, Set, Thoth, Khnum, Hathor, Sobek, Ra, Amon, Ptah, Anubis, Aset, and perhaps Osiris) comprise the major deities of the Neteru, or Egyptian Pantheon. Symbols like the cross, the halo, the staff, the rod, the all-seeing eye, as well as mother and child, came from Egyptian religion. Many of the deities can be seen holding a cross like figure called the Ankh. Also many of the early Church fathers seem to be of African origin. Just as many would suspect, such origins are hidden in Ethiopia and Cairo.

354. Until establishing autonomy under Hailie Selassie, the Ethiopian Church was under the authority of the Coptic Church. In the Coptic Museum in Cairo, there is a depiction of Christ and his 12 disciples as Africans. It could be that the Christ story was an earlier story of African origin, but was later made a composite religion by Jewish mystics in order to obfuscate the true origins of the Church. There are certainly attempts, like those of Pope Alexander V, to paint the image of Christ as a "white male", resembling his son Cesare Borgia. Quite a shameful fact ignored by most Christian historians is the painting of

the image of Christ as a blond hair blue eyed white male. It is clear that Africa and Syria, instead of Rome and Judea, played a substantial role in the development of the early Church. St. George Church in Lalabella, and St. Mary's Cathedral are places that are said to have been visited by Knights Templar and contain markings of the cross of the Templars. The rumors of a secret order of priests that guarded the Ark of the Covenant were widespread. Despite all the theories about digging and evacuation under the Masjid Al-Aqsa to discover lost relics, all claims that these relics give any power or ordinance have not been substantiated. Jewish Messianic cults have not been able to produce or reproduce such objects despite their claims. The history of the Church in Africa and Asia were de-emphasized to promote Europe as a natural heir of the Christian Church. What has made Christianity a uniquely "Western" experience? Many of the claims of Western learning have to be re-examined. The underpinning of Western thought has to be examined in the peculiarity of it's philosophical traditions. The Hellenization of the Jews and subsequent decline in Greek classical systems came to fruition in Rome. The Christian message was raised during this time.

355. Some of our views can be more carefully elaborated, or at least given the credence of Western scholarship if we respond to "The Historical Roots of Our Ecological Crisis" by Lynn White Jr[23]. The piece begins with Lynn White having a conversation with famed Eugenicist, Perennial philosopher, fabian socialist, and liberal scholar Aldous Huxley. The concern was the control of the population of rabbits by introducing myxomatosis by local farmers. When Huxley shared the concern that whole populations of rabbits had to suffer because of human intervention, Lynn White informed him that the Rabbit itself was introduced to help the diet of local peasant farmers. It was Man's meddling with Nature that had produced such unfavorable results.

356. Lynn White claims that this problem is not a new one but has been around since Rome, when whole forests were cut down to build ships for expansion of the Roman Empire. He notes, "Western Europe and North America arranged a marriage between science and technology, a union of theoretical and empirical approaches, to our natural environment. The emergence in widespread practice of the Baconian creed that scientific knowledge means technological power over nature can scarcely be dated before about 1850". He says the shift toward the industrial age marks, "the greatest event in human history since the invention of agriculture, and perhaps non-human terrestrial history as well". He makes the unusual claim (at least in Western scholarship) that "modern technology and modern science are Occidental", and even that, "all significant science is western".

---

[23] Skrbina, D. (Ed.). (2015). *Earth Alive: Readings in Environmental Ethics* (First ed.). Creative Fire Press. On pages 33-42 of this book, Skrbina reprints Lynn White Jr.'s 1967 essay entitled, "The Historical Roots of Our Ecologic Crisis"

357. 11th century methods for milling grain, and 12th century harnessing of wind power developed in the West. In 1444 Bessarion, a Greek ecclesiastical traveled to the West. He was quite surprised and overtaken by the unprecedented level of automation applied to ships, arms, textiles, and in the manufacturing of glass. Here, Lynn White is quick to dismiss any foundation for the technological world view of pure empiricism other than in the worldview of a Christian cosmology, which he quite paradoxically claims are heavily borrowed from the scientific and philosophical achievements of Greek and Islamic thought. At this juncture we find it appropriate to pose a few questions. The first of which would be to ask what it was about Christian thinking that made it either able to subvert or meld with Greek philosophy and Islamic Science? To what extent can Greek and Islamic systems escape blame when they are a main line of influence? Finally, why is the tension between Jewish and Christian thought ignored in a chimerical Judeo-Christian synthesis and the patterns of belief of first Paul and later the Western Occult driven by New Covenant theology not brought into play? The only reason that Greek and Roman thought has survived for so long has been because one of its main historical tasks has been to act as a proof for Christian theology, as many Christian thinkers during the patristic period were not only Neoplatonists but felt that Pagan philosophy was a preparation in the world for Christian theology. Indeed, only if one takes a deeper look, they find those traditions are the philosophical underpinning, and inextricably linked to the development of the Christian doctrine, as originally expounded by Paul, can the various changes in the expression of Christian thought be seen in the development of Philosophical, Historical, Theological and Political, as well as Cultural changes in Europe. While we are convinced that changes in the religious worldview played a major role in our current stage of ecological crisis and our separateness from nature, we feel that Lynn White only scratches the surface.

358. We also have a sort of nominal agreement with the fact that so-called post-religious or post-Christian views that are supposedly resolved by secular, liberal, or humanist thinking, that presupposes that it transcends certain Christian views, ultimately succumbs to these views because the alternatives provided by such thinkers are often a recourse to those same Christian belief systems. This especially can be seen in the pretense that liberalism transcends the dualism of Man and Nature that exploits nature for its own ends. Lynn White suggests that the Ancient Western Philosophers always denied that the world had a beginning, and that the view of a hierarchy of being that supplied the Christian view of Man's separation from nature is exclusively derived from Christian theology. It is clear that this is either a deliberate overstatement or shows no sophistication with Greek and Roman mythology. Prometheus, one of the race of Titans which fathered Zeus, taught humans the use of tools and metallurgy as he competed with Zeus to win the favor of humans. He was seen as the god who brought fire to humans. Hesiod declares, "gods and mortals

sprang from the same source" (Works and Days 108). Many scholars have suggested that the motif of gods becoming human among the Greeks and Romans was seen as a sort of predictive programming for the Christian ideal. There is the praise of the inventive spirit seen in the Aeneid. In the Roman legend, Virgil placed among "the blessed dead" those who discovered ideas or invented ways to improve the life of humanity. The portrayal of Greek and Roman gods as human forms suggests a period of cultural decadence. This was seen by some, like Plato, to be a sign of decline, and Plato made a stark dualism between the abstract and perfect world of the forms, and the impermanent and depreciated world of becoming. Christianity at one end seems to resemble Stoic thought in the view of resignation of life and a sort of fatalistic tone. Paul constantly talks about sacrificing and suffering being a kind of sign that one is chosen by God. Paul also made a dualism between spirit and matter. Lynn White never mentions the view of Christ being a second Adam, coming to atone for the sins of all mankind, is readily found in Paul, but one has to strain oneself with verbal gymnastics to prove it exists anywhere in the Gospels or the sayings of Jesus.

359. Christianity is not exclusively the place where a view of Man as mediator between the divine and material realms can be found. The view that ancient pagans viewed nature as a sanctuary is derived from modern New Age thought and indeed many Pagans viewed manipulation of the natural elements and mastery of the material world as a sort of "gift of the gods". One could transcend nature. Magic, as the writer Jacques Ellul pointed out, was a sort of primitive technology or technique. Not only was Alchemy and Science indistinguishable for some, but it has also been pointed out by Arthur C. Clarke that any sufficiently developed technology is indistinguishable from magic, which is another word for Hermeticism and the Kabbalistic sciences. There is plenty of demonism in pagan magic as well as in heretical offshoots.

360. He haphazardly mentions Zoroastrian thought that is heavily dualistic and partially retracts his sweeping accusations that the Christian message bears a unique responsibility in the view of Man being separate from nature. He says that the Western Catholic Saint acts, whereas the Greek Orthodox Saint contemplates, so there are varied views within Christianity. However, the Greek view of the natural world being merely symbolic or emblematic, and simply pointing towards the existence of something beyond also misses the mark. Such a tradition usually equates God with Reason, which is again an anthropocentric viewpoint.

361. Lastly, Lynn White presents us with an alternative view in the thoughts of St. Francis and proposes a Christian Saint as a patron saint of the environmental movement, finding a suspicion that the Zen tradition will not be easily received in the West for its cultural peculiarity. But this is awkwardly stated. If the foundations of Christian thought are so unshakeable and responsible for the

hierarchy of being we must ask why Lynn White recommends St. Francis of Assisi as an alternative? How could teachings both critical and understanding of western tradition have been single handedly both surpassed and defined by St. Francis' teaching who was simply overlooked by all theorists thus far? Another awkward point is to explain how the theology of Judaism, which rejects Christ but not the Messianic expectation of a coming of a divine rule, and the Christian message, which views the world as playing secondary role in the salvation of Man who is fully the product of original Sin, can be arranged in to the singular and quite chimerical term "Judeo-Christian", and that this worldview can be termed as uniquely Western. As we shall explore, such changes are neither Eastern nor Western, but do culminate in a strange religious synthesis, which can only be mended by the philosophical roots of so-called Western thought.

362. Strangely enough, it was also previously observed that certain eschatological and soteriological expectations did not develop in exclusively Western currents but were first developed and seen in the Messianic expectations of the Jews, which occurred after the time when Jesus had ascended to heaven. This can be seen in the various instances in the Talmud and Zohar that refer to the coming Kingdom of God and salvation of the entire world through the fulfilment of the Messianic expectation of the Jews, which culminates in the promise of a return to the Holy Land. All roads lead back to Rome. But in Rome, it was not the Roman system that would set stage for the movements of history, but instead it was the often-overlooked Jewish Citizenry within Rome that would set the precedence for events on the world stage. So, as we began with a look at what the law of Moses represents and who the Jewish people are, we now turn to a work by Martin Buber entitled "On Zion"[24] mainly to take a look at those traditions of the Jews which came after Jesus had ascended. Since we started this part of the book on the historical and political schemes and the Theo-political vision of the Jews in the past we end where we once began to their eschatological schemes for the future. Here, we come to understand how Zionism, Nationalism, The Kingdom of God, World-Rule, the Kabbalistic view of the emanations of God, the feminine aspect of God, and the soteriological value of suffering through grace and purification by punishment are found.

363. According to Buber, "the association between man and earth is expressed differently but even more forcibly when it is a matter not of the earth in general but of the land of Canaan in particular". He goes on to describe the association of sin and land when sin is committed in the land and the people of the land neglect the practice of righteousness (pg. 12). The land can only be purified by offering to God the first fruits. When the people become estranged from the land it manifests a state of inner decay. The inexhaustible relation of

---

[24] Buber, M. (1986). *On Zion: The History of an Idea*. Schocken Books. We rely on this work by Buber for the remainder of this part of the chapter.

God, people, and land is described. "The promise means that within history an absolute relationship between a people and a land has been taken into the covenant between God and people" (pg. 18).

364. In the formula of God, people, and land, the land is given a special significance as earth or "Eretz" (Ard in Arabic). The land is a land of affliction and a land of promise. In the Talmud, a similar and familiar view to the Pauline doctrine is explained. This is the view of Jerusalem as the center or navel of the inhabited world, and Zion as the "eschatological center of the world" (pg. 31). The prophecies are found outside of the Bible, and not given to any prophets, but formulated as oral tradition, which can be likened to the letters of Paul. This is a false sense of security of a self-fulfilling prophecy which gives unconditional gift of the land to the Jewish people, who are seen as the true essence and representatives of the entire human race. This is the view of Zion as the centralizing factor in a moment of world historical importance, where it is seen as playing a pivotal role in the meaning of the creation of the world.

365. Buber speaks of the merging of Halakha and Haggadah into one as the merger of Biblical past and Messianic future (pg. 39). This he explains is found in the Talmudic notion of "chastisements of love". He explains that God's gifts come only by suffering (pg. 44-45). This sounds like an all too easy and unsettling link between the Pauline and Messianic notion of a faith in the future and the salvation of the world. The notion of beginning the world anew links the salvation by faith alone soteriology, to the Messianic and eschatological expectation of a future coming of the Kingdom of God. We must point out that all too often such a world view sees the evil and injustice in the world as justified to make room for the coming rule of peace that will involve all of mankind. Just like the role of Christ in Christianity, "Israel is the medium through which God preserves humanity as a whole" (pg. 45). Hence, the land of Israel is seen as a microcosm and a model for the entire world.

366. Election of the people during the time of creation represents love. God is perfecting his creation through Israel, just as in Christianity, Jesus represents the perfection of Man, "The union of the people and land is intended to contribute to the perfection of the world in order to become the Kingdom of God" (pg. 48), writes Buber, and "no other people has ever heard and accepted the command from heaven as did the people of Israel" (pg. 49). Buber seems to say this without flinching, even though the continual invasion and expulsions of the people from Israel, the estrangement of people from the land, and falling away from rule of God are also part of the history. The curious separation of the historical from the purely religious sphere proposes a faith in the future all too familiar to us at this point. The smuggling in, of the doctrine of emanation in "The Shekinah", or indwelling feminine aspect or hypostasis of God, is not surprising (pg. 51). The attribution of sexual and human characteristics to God is synonymous with idolatry, which we hope need not be pointed out in re-

maining a quite obvious fact. It is this almost Gnostic and Hermetic element that views punishment and grace as dwelling together in the exile of Israel from its land. As Buber and other Rabbi claim, the dwelling in the land outweighs all the commandments of the Torah (pg. 53). In a very Pauline passage Buber states, "Creation strives to approach God but the Revelation strives to become embodied, it prepares for itself within the realm of Nature the vessel most suited to receive it". Seven principles prepare one for entrance into the land according to Jehuda Halevi (pg. 65). First is inspiration from God in prophetic form. The second is an understanding that religious activities can only reach perfection in the Holy Land. The third is the journey of the heart to the Holy Land. The fourth is a physical journey to the Holy Land. The fifth is a sort of renunciation of worldly connections that do not take precedence over the affairs of upkeep of the land. The sixth principle is to act on one's faith and to bring faith to fruition in action. The final principle is the unity of the indwelling spirit or Shekinah in the heart of the pure, which almost sounds suspiciously like the Hermetic principle of a unity with the divine (pg. 69-71).

367. Buber discusses the exemplary mention of Jerusalem in the "Cabbala's Book of Radiance" (pg. 72). He writes, "just as 'the Assembly of Israel', is blended with the Shekinah, so too Zion is taken up into the emanations of divine substance". This is to eradicate the "demonic force" that forms a shell around the "world-brain" (pg. 73). Here we see a creeping in of the doctrine that the world is an accursed place if it were not for God's chosen people restoring faith and salvation in the heart and center of the world. Buber writes, "Human sin acts on the earth of Zion and on all worlds. Israel is destined to atone in Zion for man's sin" (pg. 74), and, "The disaster that has come upon the world derives from the fact that his people and his land are separated from one another" (pg. 77).

368. In short, the world can only be redeemed by the redemption of Israel in the Zion-centered view of the Rabbis who follow the Talmudic and Kabbalistic strains of Messianic Judaism. This sect or version of Judaism is one that gave birth to what is commonly termed "Orthodox Judaism" and Hasidism that was also formulated in Europe during the time of the Protestant Reformation, and has devolved into many occult, Sabbatean, and Frankist factions (pg. 90). Using Rabbi Liva's work "Eternity in Israel", Buber discusses the familiarity of 16th century Europe with the concept readily found among the Jews: this being the doctrine that regards the people and their state as a unity. This, he points out, is to be readily observed in both Machiavelli and Calvin (pg. 78). In a quite alchemical passage, Buber explains, "when the earth reaches up to heaven and makes the latter will its own, the divine penetrates into the human'. But for all his liberal grandstanding, Buber still compares other nations to animals and writes, "just as man was the last of the creatures to be created, so Israel was the last of the nations, and just as human nature cannot be deduced from that of other creatures, so the nature of Israel cannot be deduced from that

of other nations", and, "so it is the Israelites who more than all other nations are the children of God (pg. 82). Until then, the world will have to undergo "punishment as purification" (pg. 83-84).

369. Darkness comes to the universe before light is brought into being. "After this, the Israel will be born that is called "Israel-Man" (pg. 84). This will be the salvation, not just of Israel, but the salvation of all mankind through the Kingdom of Israel, reversing what is curiously termed "Israel's original sin" (pg. 86). This quite Christian sounding language, and magical subtext is readily employed by Rabbi Liva, including the eschatological ascent into the Kingdom of God, also promised by the Pauline new covenant theology, but also a part and parcel to the Utopian transhumanist and New Age movement, where the doctrine of grace through suffering, and faith in the future are staunchly defended. There is also the doctrine of resurrection or rebirth, sometimes styled in evolutionary and even revolutionary terms. In our present context these themes do nothing more than to drive home the expectation of collective salvation of all mankind. "Everyone who comes to the sanctuary must be born again, in his mother's womb, be suckled again, be a little child again and so on, until he looks directly into the face of the land and his soul is bound up in its soul" (pg. 96), Buber announces with pride. Both Rabbi Nahman of Brazlav and Rabbi Mendel of Vitebsk are some of the many examples of Hasidim who took on an early interest in the resettlement of land by their own migration to the Holy Land. The resurrection of the dead will have its center in Jerusalem, according to Jewish legend (pg. 108). Here we find the ways of Heaven and Earth are both carefully distinguished and curiously mixed in quite a paradoxical fashion that leaves more questions than it provides answers. As Buber writes, in a quite illuminating passage (no pun intended), "it is right that man should withdraw from learning the Torah from time to time and concern himself with the way of the earth, as wise men say" (pg. 107). This can only be said with somewhat of a shit eating grin. This view has crystallized in the West since the French Revolution made its call for Universal brotherhood under a secular and democratic age. Hence, collective salvation can have many meanings and is not bound by the terms that we select for it in order to box it in. We now narrow in on the revaluation of values presented to us through Pauline synthesis and its relation to Western Philosophy, as we move from the historical and political aspects of religion to the philosophical and metaphysical implications.

PART III

LOGOS DETHRONED

Chapter 15
Ethnos / Theos / Logos

370. Cultural and lexical progression or Ethnos, the realm of divine symbols and artifacts of Theos, and the organizational or symbol making power of man or Logos, correspond to our artistic, technological, spiritual, and philosophical development. These devices we use to construct our worldview cannot be divorced from their historical representations. The Logos is what mediates reality, but now the Logos is mediated reality. The Logos has become ontologically transcendent and content neutral. Logos has been taken out of reality and sidelined but has also shifted the currents of Western Philosophy by becoming engrained through the deification of Truth. The truth itself is made transcendent and separate from reality. Truth enters into the world, but curiously enough, the world it enters into is not true. The revaluation of values is the dethronement of Logos in the development of Western philosophy and in the psycho-spiritual matrix of religious thought. The full effect of the Pauline message is not clearly discussed within philosophical speculations. Furthermore, the role and importance of the Pauline message on Western philosophy has not been clearly noted, as Paul is often taken for granted as an exclusively religious thinker. However, very little distinction can be made in the realms of philosophy and religion as they pertain to one another.

371. Christianity has gained much exuberance in the West through the discipline of Philosophy that has gained a unique importance in Western thought. Ancient man used artistic expression blended with religious catharsis to express the deepest truths. Soon Philosophers rose up to challenge these Animistic views and attempted to find an underlying substance or principle to define all matter. Both Philosophers and Monotheists had come to the conclusion in a Monistic quality to the happening of the world directed by a single will. The conclusions they reached over how this needed to be articulated greatly differed. One felt the path was by Reason and Understanding, and another by Devotion and Faith. But a third form rose up out of Philosophy to challenge both Religion and Philosophy. This was Science, which began as Natural Philosophy. Before Science divorced itself from Religion first and then Philosophy (and some believe it still hasn't)[1], everyone believed that the Original Man

---

[1] In his "Introduction to Positive Philosophy" by August Comte, he declares three phases of human knowledge to be the "theological" then the "metaphysical" and finally the "positive". By theological he means religious, by metaphysical he means abstract and by positive he indubitably refers to the scientific method and provides no transitional arguments for how these phases correspond to one another or at least as much as we have read. Our forebearers such as Skolimowski have outlined three phases of human knowledge with clear transition as the "Mythos" or pagan, "Theos" or religious, and

was a created being. He was formulated by an intelligent being that either existed within, or outside the observable Universe. According to the oldest evidence, Man began in the Polynesians or some other tropical place, found himself in Africa, and then India. From there Man spread from Africa to Arabia and India to Persia, and eventually to Europe. In Persia, India, Africa, Mycenae, and China major mega-civilizations rose up. For as long as Man has been noted there has been an inextricable link between his artistic and spiritual modes of experience.

372. Civilization would usually develop up to a point of religious legalism and cultural refinement, where the lack of principles of the laws, and cultural decadence led to a decline in social mores in the form of ritual and rites that became devoid of meaning. Hence, too much success was seen as a curse to the early Man. Man was not to create his own Heaven, because Earth was nurtured by Heaven. The Truth did not exist outside of Man, nor was it ontologically transcendent, because Truth was manifest. History had peaks and valleys. Man was progressing. Man had declined. Culture ebbs and flows. It does not progress. It does not become isolated. It does not accelerate. If things only change and not progress, then nothing moves forward. There does not have to be progress. There certainly is no future. We have histories. History shows us that when two forms of life collide, they either clash or merge. There is never a clean break, or a wide enough absorption of one into another. This is not a hierarchical progression. It would rather seem that the realms of culture, religion, philosophy are not different categories, but are interrelated developments. One can see this in the progression of the concept of Logos in Western history. These are the symbols and concepts one uses to contextualize their experiences and interface with the world.

373. No one can show beyond a shadow of a doubt where Man originated, or how he came about. Yet we are pushed to define ourselves. The oldest religions found the world as a world peopled by divinities, and supernatural forces. This was a divine entity that imbued a complex mind beyond human comprehension. Their arguments for believing this are as good as our own. In Nature, Man saw his Essence reflected. The oldest myths say Man was fashioned through Nature by a Chief Deity. Man was created out of the Earth. Soon this intelligence that fashioned Man was taken out of the World and made wholly transcendent. The Divine aspects were pulled out of Nature and pushed into

---

"Mekanos" or the mechanical age. We have repealed his vision by noticing that the religious is not be conflated with "primitive" and that the so-called metaphysical phase is vacuous and actually corresponds to the attack of philosophy on religion moving from the God of the theist to the Deistic God of the philosophers. Furthermore, we point out that philosophy and science are closely related unlike the modern positivist trend in philosophy and law have attempted to make compartmentalized. We do this by pointing to the simple fact that all early philosophers were considered sages and poets and all early scientists participated in philosophical debates of their time.

the ascended realms. So, Man took God out of Nature, and put him into the Temples. The divine aspect of nature was exchanged for a Polytheistic hierarchy of lesser and greater gods, and the divisions of time in which they rule. Man was both spatially, and temporally dislodged. Man was turned into the bottom rung of a spatial hierarchy and the final product of a teleological system. He was also made into a historical progression and a subset of a teleology hidden in Nature. The separation of Mind from Matter was based on a separation of God from Nature. This was the ancient belief that Matter and Nature were a devolution of Mind. These ideas were already expressed in Hindu and Persian myths centuries before Plato, in ideas like the resurrection of the body, the dualism between spirit and matter, an evil force of a subterranean and subtle energy in the world, an emphasis of free will and choice fashioning nature in the image of the divine, and the coming of a New Age. Within these contexts they were hotly debated and even criticized. Chinese and Indians have long had arguments for all topics of Western philosophy, despite the claim by the West that social stratification in these societies made this improbable.

374. Such concepts can be readily traced to Zoroastrian and Hindu origins. A battle against good and evil, the idea of guardian Angels and primeval forces, the existence of spirit forms, were attributed chiefly to the teachings of Vedic and Zoroastrian religions. The focus was on a supernatural light which melded the entire Universe. This was the light of Truth. Imitation of the Prophet Zoroaster was prescribed to followers. Certain virtues of honesty, sincerity in work, compassion for fellow men, loyalty to one's family, and a general sense of charity are prescribed. In the Menog-I-Khrad, and Yasnas, which are Zoroastrian religious texts, it mentions the flood myth, and displays a morality very similar to Judaism. Many blends of Zoroastrianism and Judaism were found in the era of the formative period of Christianity. The Magi famously appear in the Bible. These were the priests of Zoroaster. We also find blends of Zoroastrianism and Judaism, previously mentioned as appearing in the Nag Hammadi Gnostic Library. The appearance of these, as well as Christian sects, like the Mandaeans and later Manichaeans, cannot be coincidental. There was a considerable influence of Zoroastrian teaching on those of Judaism.

375. Neither can the fact be denied that King Cyrus, mentioned in the Bible, was a well-known historical figure at the time. This contemporary of Ancient Greece is mentioned by Xenophon, a disciple of Socrates, as the example of a just ruler. He is the most likely candidate for Zoroaster, being a contemporary of Zoroaster, as well as Zulqarnayn, mentioned in the Quran. These figures obviously played a pivotal role in the development of not only religious thought, but contemporary roles of statesmanship. The writings of Xenophon were avidly read by the founders of America. King Cyrus was an exemplary ruler by all accounts, and a man of exceptional piety, both filial and spiritual. He was seen as the great ruler who may have built the Iron Curtain for Gog and Magog. He was also viewed as a Jewish Messiah, or Savior of the Jewish

people. We see in the "Cyropaedia" of Xenophon[2], that the connection between the thought of the Bible, and those that were seen as playing a pivotal
role in Greek and Roman thought is clearly unveiled. It does, however, leave
one to think why these earlier connections are not elucidated upon. It should
not come as a surprise that the role of secular scholarship has been to cleverly
obfuscate any connections between the ancient religions and so-called Classical Western Civilization. This presents an over-estimated view of the accomplishments of the Greeks as well as presents a clean break from Pagan thought
during the rise of Christianity, when the divisions are not that obvious. This is
just one connection between Religion and Philosophy. Greek thought was influenced by Persian thought. Plato was certainly not unaware of the Jewish
system of morality, and this can hardly be assumed. The semblance of views in
Platonic, Stoic, Jewish, and Zoroastrian thought cannot be ignored. Their proximity in development cannot be overstated. The dualistic philosophy of Plato,
where the mind was essentially opposed to Matter and Form, and the world a
deception or devolution, was not only expressed in Vedic and Zoroastrian systems, but was also a bastardization of Jewish thought. In this dualistic view,
the Divine Realm only regulated its own affairs, while the world down here
was a subtle imitation of the ethereal forms. What we have down here is a
mere residue of the perception and play of the Divine Realm. The world is an
illusory projection. In Babylonian, Hindu, and Egyptian mythologies there also
exists a hierarchy of Being. The Earth is seen as a stage of trials.

376. The inhabitants of the earthly realm in Hinduism were a devolution of
primordial beings on a transcendental stage, where the pangs of gross materialism were the punishment and torture of the cosmic jail cell, whereby matter
was contaminated by impermanence and change. Matter was therefore seen as
a lesser stage of Being in Hindu Metaphysics. The views of Pythagoras, and
subsequently Plato, reflect this divine cosmology. Sacred knowledge could be
used for the promulgation of Life, or for Demonic terror and spiteful deception. This was a result of a battle between god-like creatures, whose technological capabilities and physical constitution was beyond belief. These beings
were reincarnated and resurrected through time, because the soul did not perish
along with the body. The Pythagoreans possessed a similar set of beliefs. Plato
was said to have travelled to Egypt and participated in Ancient Mystery religions like the Eleusinian Mysteries, as he puts in the mouth of Socrates in Meno. Another belief that Plato had in common with the Hindu and Zoroastrian
Myths, that he shared with Hebrews, was a belief in the Great Flood. Many
great cultural traditions in ancient times makes mention of the Great Flood[3].

---

[2] Cyrus Cylinder: How a Persian monarch inspired Jefferson. (2013, March 11). *BBC*.
https://www.bbc.com/news/world-us-canada-21747567

[3] Stories of the Great Flood exist among African tribes and in Egyptian legend where
the Egyptian God Ra sends Sekhmet to destroy a portion of humanity. Tales of the
Great Flood are also found among Native American tribes and in Babylonian legends. It

377. Nietzsche wrote that the Socrates of Plato was Plato in front, and Plato behind. Many have acknowledged that Xenophon is a more reliable source on the life of Socrates. Plato's chimerical conception of Socrates was forged with his own Pythagorean and Heraclitan beliefs. Many have made the claim that Plato is the most original thinker who ever lived. Nothing can be further from the truth. It is important to understand that Polytheism soon devolved into a pantheistic and monistic framework which was its predecessor, but this was brought about through rather laborious philosophical enterprise. Thales was said to have claimed that "all is full of gods". Later, a supposed student of his changed his pantheism to be a single principle or archetypal form. This was the prime matter or substance that formulated all things. This was what he called "the indefinite", or covalent energy between substances. This negative shape of matter that was organized from the outside through an ontologically trans-cendent principle within matter was first espoused by Anaximander and was developed by Heraclitus. Heraclitus was born in Ephesus, most notable for being one of the places where the early Church was spread by Paul. Heraclitus deserves to be given a more central place in Christian theology, because it was he, and not Philo, that originated the concept of Logos. Heraclitus and the Sophists regularly made use of the concept of Logos. It was rather Philo who connected this concept with the Jewish conception of "the Word". Philo called the Logos the first-born son of God. Logos and "The Word" are not the same and cannot be easily reconciled and are hard to equivocate. The Logos is the very Essence of matter itself and propagates change on the material level. The Logos was within matter, synonymous with Reason, deeply impersonal, but superior to matter itself in a sort of panentheism. As Heraclitus writes, 'the Thunderbolt steers all things". This was similar to the "Divine Fire" of Zoroas-trianism. The view had a great influence on thinkers from Plato to Nietzsche. The concept also has a clear influence on Christians of the Greek and Turkish persuasion, who adopted it as a central theme in their patterns of belief[4].

---

is mentioned by both Confucius and Plato, as well as in Zoroastrian and Hindu tradi-tions. It has also been theorized to appear in Norse myth in the story of Bergelmir in which story a race of giants is eliminated. The collective strength of all these independ-ent cultures and civilizations alluding to the same world-historical event is probably quite rare and one has to wonder why such legends are relegated to the category of myth. While science has a way of changing its story, the unanimous cry of the ancients seeks to challenge the conventional narrative at several turns including in the origins of humanity where it was almost universally agreed by ancient people that mankind was a creation by some sort of superior being and was originally conceived to function within the confines of the earthly realm as a piece of technology but had otherworldly origins. Similarly, the flood is seen as a sort of secondary origin point for the various nations of the world.

[4] Miller, P. L., & Reeve, C. D. C. (Eds.). (2006). *Introductory Readings in Ancient Greek and Roman Philosophy*. Hackett Publishing Company. We rely on this work for the information on the pre-Socratics presented in the next four sections. The work pre-sents the views of pre-Socratic philosophers from remaining fragments of their writing.

378. Any view that claims that this concept of Logos has guided Western History does not wrestle with the fact that these concepts had a much earlier origin in African, Arabian, Persian, and Vedic thought forms. The Logos was something outside of Nature, that imbued Nature with properties of Mind and Change. This force was ontologically transcendent, unlike the Qi of Chinese thought, or the Chakra of Vedic literature. Heraclitus fell into ill repute for challenging the gods, who he said were far removed from human thought and toil. Heraclitus felt that war and strife governed all things. He had a general negative view of humanity. As he declared that Homer should be flogged, he gave Mind a central place in his cosmology. Like Anaximander, Heraclitus had assigned Change or Becoming to be the essential quality of Nature or Mind. Mind and Nature were at odds. Nature is the opponent of Mind. There was a merging of contradictions. This was the paradigm of Natural Law. Nature's Law and Nature's God were not Animistic or Polytheistic, but the God of the Philosophers and Mathematicians. This was the God of Necessity. This God was bound to create. Pythagoras had claimed that Nature was ordered by the Divine. Nature was harmonized like a musical scale with precise numerical sequences. The Divine ratios were put forward by Pythagoras to be part of a cult like adherence. His followers considered him to be the Son of Hermes. In his cult, they worshipped the Platonic solids and taught, as did Heraclitus, that Energy is neither created nor destroyed. Anaximander, Pythagoras, and Heraclitus believed in a sort of passage of souls through matter that was later maintained by Plato in the Timaeus.

379. All of the thinkers mentioned so far were not even born in Greece but were either from Italy or Asia Minor. They lived closer to Persia or Turkey, around the same area where Paul originated. The origins of Socratic philosophy, as well as Christian theology, were not originating in Greece and Rome, but in Persia and Turkey. This Anatolian influence has been derided in the West for the most obvious reasons. The myth of a Greco-Roman Nexus should be replaced with an African-Turkish one. It is perhaps no surprise that this Western myth was devised by Europeans. Because the origins of society, democracy, and major philosophical and cultural achievements, as well as the so called three Western faiths are sought for in light skinned people of the world, they were deliberately limited to the achievements of Hellenistic Civilization, as well as, the maintenance of a Judeo-Christian perspective, which tends to conveniently exclude Islam. The Milesian teacher Xenophanes complained that the Ethiopians said their gods were flat-nosed and dark, while Thracians said they were red-haired and have blue eyes. Each race had mistakenly believed that the gods were painted in their image like Michelangelo. I once heard in a verse by Killah Priest, that the white image of Christ was really

Cesare Borgia, the son of Pope Alexander[5]. The fact that this was told to me in a rap song instead of a scholarly article is quite fascinating. The resemblance is uncanny. The idols that humanity has formed always resemble humans. Xenophanes said that the gods of Homer perform deeds that are in ill repute among humans. To him God was one, and all of him thinks and hears and sees. His vision of God was closer to the God of Moses, which was ineffable and indescribable, and beyond human comprehension. This God brought all things into existence and was changeless and boundless. This is the simplest and most concise definition that reflects God. This was an all-permeating force that created nothingness and the stage of existence, and did not exist separate from matter, but was an ever-living source of all matter and existence. For some Philosophers and Saints, this being fashioned existence, through nothing (a virtual space), and created harmony and form (a Hindu conception). For Plato this very same harmony and form reflected the Essence of the Divine.

380. While Xenophanes and Parmenides saw Nature as one changeless boundless entity, Anaximander and Heraclitus ascribed a principle that existed apart from matter and was primary to matter itself. Both agreed that reality was essentially one but disagreed over whether matter held separate from this underlying principle or force. Anaximander and Heraclitus felt that matter itself had no ultimate nature being subject to change, while Xenophanes and Parmenides held that there was no separateness between the various aspects of the world, and therefore no change. Heraclitus felt that all was fire and change. This was a tension and strain that was ordered by a principle existing outside of the material world, but responsible for its organization. Parmenides felt that all was one, and that if "all was fire" as Heraclitus had claimed, then nothing changed. Surely it did not "change" from being "fire". To say all is change is to make an absolute statement. If there is no separation, then there can be no strife or conflict. This was the debate between the One and the Many. Parmenides asserted Being. Heraclitus asserted Becoming. It was Leucippus and Democritus who would come to assert that all was mere convention and appearance. All was mere form with no abiding essence. As Aristotle writes, "Leucippus and his associate Democritus declare the full and the empty (void) to be the elements, cling the former 'what-is' and the other 'what is not'. Of these the one, 'what is" is full and solid, the other, 'what is not', is empty (void) and rare". This meant that reality was mere representation based on certain convention or Natural Law, whose origins were largely ignored, as Aristotle continues on to say, "Concerning the origin and manner of motion in existing things, these men too, like the rest, lazily neglected to give an account". The view that reality is mere perception neglects to give an account, at least, for how such a summation could be attended to while in a state of perpetual delusion or appearance. Nothing guarantees the accuracy of our perceptions. As noted, "Democritus

---

[5] Song B.I.B.L.E By Gza and Killah Priest on the debut Gza album entitled Liquid Swords released 1995

leaves aside purpose, but refers all things which nature employs to necessity". Instead of the spontaneity and uniqueness of "The One", pluralists like Democritus and Plato employed themes of Necessity and Change that relied on a hidden order or rhythm to the cycles and layers of reality.

381. The marvel of Platonic philosophy, in all of its triumphs and all of its failure, is a casual melding of these two staunch opponents. This was the melding of Being and Becoming, although some might say he affirmed both and adhered to neither. In Plato's Parmenides, a young Socrates presents a theory of an atomistic and dualistic view of the world, including the forms, which is in-turn slapped down by the impenetrable logic of Parmenides. He is seen walking out of the School of Athens with a group of followers, including Zeno, following behind. Parmenides was seen as dropping out of the debates of the philosophers. How do the forms trickle down into the minute instances of everyday experience? What makes these forms coalesce and condensate through time? For Parmenides, thinking and being are the same. Plato was from the school of Heraclitus and had a Heraclitian teacher named Cratylus. So not only did Plato put the argument against Parmenides in the mouth of a young and unseasoned approach of a confused Socrates, but he also then ascribes to Heraclitian philosophy in the Cratylus. Plato was born in Athens in 429 BCE[6], and was the son of Ariston, who traced his ancestry to a former King of Athens. His mother Perictione was related to Solon, who was the architect of the Greek constitution. When his father died, his mother married Pyrilampes who was a friend of the Statesman Pericles. Contrary to popular opinion, Plato was not the social rebel that his teacher was and had much status within the higher rungs of Athenian society. Plato was also influenced by the teaching of Pythagoras who said all was number.

382. The Platonic system came down on the side of Necessity and Change, instead of Oneness and Being. This dualistic notion of Being and Becoming, taken alongside the separation of thinking and being, is the real hallmark of Platonic and Western Philosophy. Plato devised a system where being and becoming were themselves mediated by a transpersonal reality, on an already existing fractal web. This was the Soul of the Cosmos. This tripartite soul had "Being" and "Existence " on the very bottom rung, while placing Becoming and Change as the mediator of reality through forms and divine archetypes, which were seemingly promulgated by a "Demiurge" or "Cosmic Mind" on top of it all. This Demiurge was the mirror image of God and the overarching world-mind that placed order in the world. This Demiurge represented goodness and necessity and was a perfect reflection of the Cosmos. Time and

---

[6] Miller, P. L., & Reeve, C. D. C. (Eds.). (2006). *Introductory Readings in Ancient Greek and Roman Philosophy*. Hackett Publishing Company, pg. 44. We rely on this source for the biographical information about Plato's background history his coming from a well-known family.

Thought could not be separated from Natural Law and Reason. Hence, every-thing was bound by Necessity. Man was made a mediation between Knowledge and Belief, Being and Becoming. Pluralists like Anaxagoras, Em-pedocles, Leucippus and Democritus, tried to force a criticism of Parmenides. As told by Pliny the Elder in the 1st Century,

> "In the East, doubtless, (magic) was invented, in Persia and by Zoroaster. All the authorities agree with this... I have noticed that in ancient times, and indeed almost always, one finds men seeking in this science the climax of literary glory, at least Py-thagoras, Empedocles, Democritus, and Plato crossed the seas, exiles, in truth, rather than travelers, to instruct themselves in this. Returning to the native land, they vaunted the claims of magic and maintained its secret doctrine"[7]

383. Like the Jewish God, Plato's God was a participant in the world, shaping and molding experience, but unlike the Jewish God, the God of Plato was syn-onymous with Reason itself, whose actions did not directly influence the world. For Plato, this being only governed the higher aspects of man, and did not reflect the entirety of the Cosmic experience. These higher principles were the "few and the wise", while the lower impulses were "the many" who had no traction to reality. Similar to the Pagans, and unlike the Jewish God, this God belonged to a Hierarchy of Being that was not outside of human intelligence. In Judaism there is most notably no hierarchy of Being. There is God, and then there is the rest of creation, and this God does not delineate power, but is the source of all power. God is furthermore melded into every aspect of his crea-tion. In Hinduism and in Plato, God was not identical to his creation but was transcendent. However, there are key differences between the personal nature of God in Hinduism and the impersonal nature of the Demiurge. God could, for example, enter the world rather than make himself seen. Rather in Plato, The few and the wise which consisted of Honor and Reason, led the rabble of the senses and the jealous impulses. Plato believed in the transmigration of souls like his teacher Pythagoras. Society had to be ordered just like the Natu-ral Laws. Just as the masses correspond to conflicting desires, the several cor-respond to opinion and knowledge, while the few and the good are ruled by Reason. This was a tripartite hierarchy of being, and the three compartments of the Soul of the Divine. In Hinduism, Platonism, and Paulinism, there is a stoic or ascetic sensibility, which is reflected in the idea that the corporeal existence is a lower stage, and a cosmic accident. This notion had to be opposed or pushed back against by later Advaita mystics, Neoplatonists, and Christian mystics. This was the Christian and Buddhist opposition to the will to life, which Nietzsche vigorously opposed, because it gave man an externalized

---

[7] Livingstone, D. (2015). *Transhumanism: The History of a Dangerous Idea*. Sabilillah Publications, pg. 11

conscience, which seems to judge and critique one's every move. The view of the Indian philosophers became crystalized in Buddhist thought, while the Jewish dualism was explored by Paul, who was championed by Gnostic thinkers like Valentinus and Neoplatonist thinkers. Paul spoke of the "mirror image of God", which he regarded as the God that was worshipped by the ignorant as God the father, but this was not the true God, which was only known by Paul. It should be no surprise that the view that this world is a passing phase contributes to a loss of sincerity, and the beginning of nihilistic and resentful revenge against the world.

384. However, the very notion that something outside of reality can be wholly good seems to imprison man's conscience and seeks to bring down what is outside of oneself through the use of complicated doctrines and soteriological schemes. While the world contains the finer points of the Divine, it is a degraded form of material contamination for Buddhists and Plato. In Plato, God was separate from the world but bound by necessity to have an effect the world from the outside, by engendering beauty and goodness in an already forlorned world. This was through his crafting of the archetypal forms, which were the tools he used to shape the world in his image. This Blacksmith God that crafts what is temporal from the eternal essences was utterly limited and bound by necessity and could only have an effect on the world through forms. His goodness and form emanated movement and ratio. As Mind governs Matter, so does Goodness and Reason govern the Mind of God in Plato's definition. The subordination of God to human reason, and binding of God by the necessity and eternality of matter itself was not only anthropomorphic, but it also seemed to give God a separate reality. Reality was something that existed alongside God. The boundless limitless God of Xenophanes, that was beyond human comprehension, was exchanged for a Monad bound by necessity and change. Was this just a Noble Lie? Was it, not the God that the people wanted, but the one they needed? Most notably, this system of God was not accepted among the Greeks even though it is seen as a thought of primary importance.

385. Plato's Socrates constantly demeaned the Greek Gods and the system of Democracy that was in place in Athens during its cultural peak. Plato however, saw the decadence of Athens as leading to a cultural decline and applauded the Lacedaemonians for being on the right side of history. He had a disdain for democracy, and saw the minds of the many as erratic, needing to be molded by the few and the wise. The masses should not philosophize and should be kept to daily chores for the aid of the State. In the Apology, Plato puts in the mouth of Socrates a vicious declaration, that those who destroy Athens and condemn it will see it as a city that killed Socrates. Socrates was a critic of Greek decadence. He was charged with supporting the rule of the few. Just like Paul, who used the idea of a divinely inspired man who was murdered by the State to undermine the values of a rather prosperous civilization, so was Plato a propagandist. His State was devised for outward force and inward compliance,

where the culture and arts, through the methods and propagandistic means recommended by him, were strictly regulated. He used the caste system, and the laws of Solon to devise his framework.

386. Most notably, Plato's student Aristotle joined forces with Philip of Macedon, and taught his son Alexander to conquer Athens. Macedonia was most notably one of the first places which Paul visited in "Europe" to begin his ministry. The thoughts and lessons of Plato were directly responsible for the undermining of Greece when Aristotle turned against his own people. Aristotle was a traitor, just like Josephus. Socrates apparently would rather die by his own people's hands than forsake their honest graces that led to him becoming educated. Aristotle apparently did not share this sentiment. The Hellenization or spread of Greek philosophy was directly linked to the work of Plato and Aristotle, whose thoughts were quite ironically too high-minded to be tethered to the confines of Greek learning. The offshoots of Stoicism and Epicureanism were seen as a sign of decadence during the period of Hellenization, along with the Gnosticism of the Jews devolving into Paganism. As mentioned by Plotinus, the degradation of Greek thought after the period of Hellenization brought the perversions of religious cults. Greece was a small polis regulated by democracy, but Rome however, was a large Republic with both central leadership and a Senate. The style of governance from Greece to Rome is vastly dissimilar. Plato was not a Greek thinker any more than Paul was a Roman thinker. Both opposed the society from the inside through political propaganda.

387. Plato used a heroic figure to detail the ideological basis for the destruction of those who destroyed him. He understood that the idea was more powerful than even the man. Many view some of Plato's works as a calculated revenge against Athens. Plato's beliefs are held in so much importance and high regard, because they have piggybacked on Christian beliefs and have been used to defend the Trinity. While some see his views as the highest achievement of Greek civilization, it is apparent that the Greeks themselves did not see him this way. It was those very same beliefs, after all, that would lead to destruction and enslavement of the Greek people. Plato, in the Timaeus, writes of "noble races" which once ruled the world before the Great Deluge or Flood. Plato placed an emphasis on the inner life of an individual. Intelligence was placed in the Soul, and the Soul was placed in the Body. The Soul was a metaphor for the human imagination itself and the Essence of the material world. Essence was therefore mixed with Existence but was ultimately separate from it and superior to it. Until it's resurgence through Christian heresies and German Idealism that was heavily influenced by Martin Luther's emphasis on Will over Reason and the Occult, which drew heavily on Gnostic and Hermetic views, this transcendental idealism was the Absolute Mind as a replacement for the gods. Hence, the philosophy of the West has grown out of a rejection of theological truths, which were later piggybacked on Christian beliefs.

388. The Man represented Intelligence, while the formless substance of matter was seen as a receptacle of Form and viewed as Wisdom or Woman. Matter and harmony, formulated by the interrelation of Intelligence and Wisdom brought forth the Beauty of Form. This is a Platonistic and Pagan conception, rather than a Jewish or Christian one. Specialists of myth like Joseph Campbell have pointed out that pagan conceptions of the Sun, being a source of eternal energy and rational will represented the Male Ego, while the cycle of rebirth and regeneration of Nature through its own shadow, was seen as the Moon, or the Divine Female. In Ephesus, where Paul went to build a Church, a temple of the Divine Mother was built, which was to be exchanged for Mary in an attempt by Bishop Nestorius of Constantinople. It is clear that to the Ancients certain of these pagan metaphors held considerable sway.

389. As the fall of Man relates to the devolution of the forms into matter, certain Christians saw it as an apt metaphor to describe the patterns of belief seen in verses like Romans 7:17, where Paul declares that Sin in man is responsible for evil. This was the idea of evil as separation from God, and privation on the good. As Paul debated the Philosophers in the Agora, and in Corinth, and visited the places of the former philosophers, he seemed to readily incorporate several of their belief systems. He pointed to one of the gods in the temple that was labeled "the unknown god" and claimed it to be the God of Israel, both able to come in the world, and go beyond it. For Paul and Plato, abstract order was better than solid disorder. Both Essence and Being were made Divine in a sort of divine duality. Law and Morality were like numbers and figures, and of an invisible order. For Plato, similarity was indivisible, so the repulsion and division of forms was dissimilar to the Essence of the eternal and uncreated. Reality as we perceive it was a devolution of Matter from Form, and Nature was an imitation of the Forms. Matter possessed no reality apart from Form and Number. Nature abhors a vacuum, and all things find their balance in the same array of light. He said this light was akin to light gathering in a unified vision. This was the equating of reality "out there" with perception. The intricate balance of the harmonic scales, which reflected the nature of becoming and the cycles of change were thus put in motion in a cosmic unity. While the Platonic systems were attuned with Orphic and Pythagorean cosmology, they later contributed to Gnosticism and Hermeticism views that came into view around the 2nd and 3rd century, similar to the doctrine of the trinity and Paul's conception of a dying and rising god. Three philosophical/religious systems that developed in the first three centuries of 33-300 A.D were Gnosticism, Hermeticism, and Neoplatonism. Each melded with the Pauline line of Christianity because of its cosmological framework. In Gnosticism, this world was a mistake and a prison for the spirit, and each spirit wished to return to its original home through the divine spark that existed within. In Hermeticism, knowledge of self was akin to knowledge of the divine which was it's reflection and as above so below. In Neoplatonism, this world was a derivative or diminution of the essence or true form. Finally, in the Pauline view flesh and

spirit are made whole within the Spirit of God, and the drive toward salvation assures us that this world is in a fallen state. Each correspondingly gives birth to a view of how one can come to know God. In Gnosticism, one was to know God through a secret gnosis, freeing one from material imprisonment and making one a true individual in realizing one's own essence. In Hermeticism, God created the world in order to know himself, so the process of the world is simply an act of self-discovery. In Neoplatonism, this world was an emanation of the mind of God, where the transcendental and immanent aspects of the divine were interlinked. In the Pauline view, the Word of God became flesh in order to enter the world and the world-historical sphere, for the salvation of all mankind. Each system assigned to Man a special role on how to gain knowledge of the divine that reflected back on his own essence in circumference to the divine.

390. The cooperative causes that formed the Universe as devolution of the forms were rejected by Aristotle, who envisioned an "inward potential", and an outward Telos to be the cause of Nature. Plato also expressed a belief that Women and Animals were fashioned from Man. Aristotle would maintain a hierarchy of being in terms of humans, animals, and then plants, but also had a cosmology based on a Prime Mover. This was a godlike force which guided Matter to its particular end by fashioning an already existing Nature through the Void of space. According to Plato, "all things which have lesser parts, retain the greater", as he says in Timaeus, but for Aristotle, each aspect of reality functioned in its own domain of understanding and potency. Aristotle compartmentalized knowledge and experience. He turned the quest for knowledge into different subjects and began the rule by experts. He coined the term technology and was known as the father of "logic". In his "Rhetoric", he calls for Rhetoric to be reintroduced as a counterpart to the Dialectic. Aristotle argued that the Truth that can be proven true by necessity is different from Truth that has to be subjected to "technologousin" or "rules of art", which was similar to a forensic method of a courtroom. He formed a notion of double truth that has reverberated through Western learning. He found that Truth had to correspond to the facts which could only be derived through a method of art used to bring forth what is real in an idea through rigorous tests. Thus experience needed a methodology supplied through reason and a statement about what is real is not necessarily a statement about what is true. Hence the truth of method is an objective truth that, so being detached from experience, can provide a true measure of phenomenon. He thus formed the correspondence theory of truth that was important for the development of logic, which argued that notions of truth be reduced to the scientific method or "epistemologos". The crafting of symbols or "techne-logos" was related to the art or method of speech. Hence the blacksmith God that would bring about the true potential from within by crafting symbols that resonate through time which he added to the Platonic notion. Plato's God was instead only concerned with the divine realm and all the symbols that existed here were mere imitations of the divine nature. Art

was thus an imitation of an imitation. Everything in reality was mere imitation but not for Aristotle who rejected the ascended realm. He insisted the divine existed in the potential of each thing which was to complete itself through time and effort and contemplation on the divine aspect within. These views are important for Paul, who by all accounts, most probably received a regular Hellenistic education but even if Paul was not influenced by these views, they certainly had an influence on his key audience which was composed of Gentiles and Greeks and certainly these views factor in heavily in those who were considered founders of the early Church, such as Tertullian, Origen, Eusebius and others.

391. By compartmentalizing knowledge, Aristotle divorced knowledge from Sacred Truth. He separated Physical truths from Metaphysical truths and created the syllogism. The syllogism separated the existential from the predicative. This was the beginning of the subject and object distinction that would plague Western philosophy. While Plato had a cosmological dualism of spirit and matter that was affirmed by some basic religious reaching at the time, Aristotle would inevitably be the philosophy that had come to dominate in the West by creating a temporal dualism using the Telos in Nature. He was an early espouser of a Utilitarian principle in Ethics which reflected his cosmological view of everything being for its particular end. Aristotle also had a heretical effect on Christian teachings. Aristotle's viewpoints promoted the contradictory notion of an eternal chain of cause and effect only limited by a Prime Mover, itself unmoved. This Prime Mover was only engaged in thought, and did not engage in creation, but only expression. This Prime Mover only molded the already existing material that was used to shape the cosmic realm, and indeed is known and experienced only by himself. Aristotle rejected the spatial duality of a "blacksmith God" crafting the forms in a higher realm, and settled for a Divine Architect. This was still a Deistic conception. Instead of the spatial duality of Plato, Aristotle introduced a temporal duality, by introducing a Final Cause which pulled the future into the past towards its true potential. This was a sort of Cosmic Utilitarianism based on a hidden potential. The future moved backwards through the past, as the Prime Mover pushes reality towards its Final Cause.

392. For Aristotle, one must go backward to go forward. But only first if one is able to get out of one's metaphysical straitjacket. He confined God to both thought and necessity, while promoting the delusion that everything moves towards its proper end. He created the notion of built-in progress which leads to the separation of identity from entity. He rudely exclaimed that all pre-Socratic thinkers, other than Anaxagoras, had spoken nonsense. He is also, unfortunately, the only source for these views in some cases. He exchanged the Ontological chains and puppet strings of Plato for an intricate teleological web. Yet both Plato and Aristotle held to the belief that Mind was superior to Matter, and Form or Essence to Existence. While Plato had removed the Form from Matter, Aristotle removed Thought and Potential from Existence. The

Philosophers have always placed thought and imagination and reason in a higher realm than experience and feeling and trust, but I cannot think of a vainer and more arrogant task than thinking up how thought itself is its own highest task. It does not seem like a coincidence that the very same people who exploit thinking would place it in the highest realm of their ontological scope. "Noesis Noeseos Noesis", or a thinking that is a thinking on thinking, is apparently the highest task of the intellect, according to Aristotle. This redundant and inane, self-contained, and masturbatory function is all that the Cosmic Mind has for itself. Finally, Aristotle arrived at the transcendental. Thought is its own limitation. But once having decided this, why relegate thought to such a high order of things? Apparently thought can never get beyond itself. How do the Prime Mover and Final Cause interact?

393. Plato felt that philosophical speculation is akin to Geometry and had a sign on his Academy that said to let no one enter who is ignorant of the art of geometrical forms. Aristotle felt that Logic was the highest realm of philosophy and is known as the father of Logic. When Logic and Math combined in the 20th century in the form of philosophical speculation, the result was the Symbolic Logic of Bertrand Russell and A.N Whitehead. This would later lead to the discoveries of language and math used for research in cybernetics. One can say that Plato's math and Aristotle's Logic is a two-headed bird that represents Western thought. The teaching of Socrates that was purported to have been most fervently rejected was essentially the limiting of truth to the expression of certain words and terms taught by the Sophists. Sophists viewed the meaning of statements and the contextualization of facts during argumentation to be of the utmost importance. They stressed the properties of language and grammar like the Analytic Philosophers of today. A protege of Russell was Wittgenstein, who reduced the discovery of truth to what he called "language games". The Sophists of old would agree. In his "On Nothing", the Sophist Gorgias, renowned in Athens, attacked the Eleatic Philosophers like Xenophanes, Parmenides, and Melissus. He writes, "For that by which we communicate is Logos, but Logos is not the objects, the things-that-are". This was a clear separation of language and reality, which seemed to use the distinction to undermine reality, rather than just plainly pointing to the limitation of words.

394. A.N Whitehead made the claim that all of Western philosophy was a footnote to Plato. We cannot help find this statement rather presumptuous, and find it to be expressed with a grave ineptitude of knowledge which reflects the foundations of thought that were available before Plato picked up a pen. The rather miniscule thoughts of Plato have been bolstered because of their use in justifying Church Doctrine. While comparable views in Chinese, Indian, Persian, Arabian, and African heritage have been pushed aside, they seem foundational in defining the views that led to Plato himself. Also, the great debt paid to the pre-Socratic thinkers is curiously ignored. The Milesian Monists (of Asia Minor) like Thales and Anaximander, as well as the Eleatic Monism

(from modern day Italy) of those like Parmenides and Zeno played a pivotal role in the development of philosophic thought in Athens. Indeed, most of the thoughts of the Atomists were a reaction to these previous views. Perhaps a question can be posed why such views of Plato and Aristotle led to a period of decadence through Hellenization and eventual decline? There is also the fact that these views do not reflect Western learning in the least bit.

395. What can perhaps be said, is that the rejection of transcendental knowledge for the experience of purposeful observation, and the shift from cosmology and metaphysics to the brute facts of scientific inquiry were most importantly reflected in the teaching of Aristotle. In his "Science and the Modern World", Whitehead extolled the virtues of Aristotle and dubbed him "the greatest Metaphysician". Martha Nussbaum has pointed out that Aristotle never meant to classify Metaphysics as a subject apart from physics, but only invented the term to connote his writing that came after the book called "Physics" as we pointed out earlier. Whitehead makes the determined claim about the so-called "dispassionate" stance of Aristotle, although one cannot be readily assumed. Aristotle openly attacked his predecessors in order to advance his own opinions. One cannot seriously make a claim either way about Aristotle's psychological disposition. Finally, Whitehead calls Aristotle a "European Metaphysician". This illuminates the facts that in the early 1900's, even the most educated of the British citizens wrongfully equated Ancient Athens with Modern Europe possibly due to the view that Mediterraneans and Europeans share a similar cultural heritage. Nothing can be farther from the truth, as found in the words of Aristotle himself, who readily dismissed Europeans as stupid barbarians, fit for slavery in Greece in Book 7 of his Politics as we mentioned earlier. Aristotle was clearly not a "European". Whitehead made such claims possibly for the shallow fact that Aristotle may have had a similar skin tone.

396. Aristotle was not exactly a patron of Greece either. While Plato ventured far to bring foreign concepts to the aid of the Greek people, Aristotle betrayed the Greeks and went to work for its conquerors. Money lenders from the Middle East funded Macedonia under Philip II, and Greece as well, mainly in order to destroy Persia. Aristotle was always allied with the victors. Like Plato, Aristotle believed in Eugenics. He recommended the promotion of pederasty (Politics 2: 1272a 22-24), as a measure to reduce the population. This practice was seen as immoral by Plato in his "Laws". Both had a pretense that human Reason could encompass the knowledge of all things. In a way, they reflected the sentiment of Protagoras that "Man is a measure of all things", while rejecting personal truth. What followed the schools of Plato and Aristotle were various factions and divisions that were collectively referred to as Hellenization. This included various thought schisms like the Cynics, Ascetics, Epicurean hedonists, Stoic fatalists, and the return of the Sophists. Neoplatonism grew out of this web of chaos and Hellenization following the period of Aristotle. A few centuries later, the main center of Hellenization were places like Alexandria.

397. Jews like Philo would have been all too familiar with conceptions of the Logos, which he said was the creative reason of Man, and the first-born Son of God. He exchanged Reason for the Covenant made by God mentioned earlier which declares Israel the first-born Son of God. He also looked at the notion of circumcision, as a metaphorical command, imploring one to practice temperance. This mirrors the thoughts of Paul about a "circumcision of the heart". He did not see any of the commands of God as not being subject to interpretation. He saw many of the stories mentioned in the Biblical texts as allegorical, and pointing to "deeper truths". Philo was a Neoplatonist, and Jew, who would have been all too familiar with the Pauline notions of "circumcision of the heart", employed in his letter to Romans (2:25). He made a distinction between inwardly and outwardly forms of adherence to the Law of Scripture. Paul draws a firm dialectic between flesh and spirit as we will come to see.

398. By the turn of the Second Century Neoplatonists like Plotinus and Proclus had their work cut out for them. They had to defend their doctrines against the cult of Rome, which they attempted to supersede and offered their philosophy as a remedy to the problems of the Roman State, but also waged an attack against the doctrines of the Gnostics, Stoics, Epicureans and others, which seek to offer their own interpretations of God and Reality. Perhaps the foremost Platonist after Plato himself was Plotinus. He was a metaphysician of the highest caliber. His idea of Hypostatic Union serves to be one of the most influential philosophical concepts ever devised. He expanded the tripartite soul of Plato to a cosmological and metaphysical framework. He thus single handedly brought back Metaphysics, and since we saw the science both invented and derided by Aristotle, we might even credit this man from modern day Ethiopia to be the inventor of Metaphysics properly understood. His Three Hypostases consisted of the One (a primordial and unique summation of Being), the Intellect (the divine will or "Nous"), and the World Soul (or psychic mind and unified mind of the Cosmos). His Soul was an emanation of the Intellect, or Divine Will that ordered the World Soul into the higher (Universal), or lower (material) divisions. The Soul or Mind that governs Matter is an emanation which is eternal. The world as a result never ceases to exist. The idea of the emanations of God, or "Homo-ousia" seen in the united Essences of three parts of God, is clearly similar to the idea of the Three Hypostases of Plotinus, which appears over two centuries earlier.

399. Plotinus was evidently not a fan of the Gnostics, who he felt were playing fast and loose with Platonic Philosophy. He dedicates over a tenth of his acclaimed work "Enneads" to challenging their views. He saw in their decadent mysticism quite a shallow appropriation of concepts like the Demiurge. Other than this, no clear link can be found in the statement of Athanasius against Arius, which championed the Trinity, even when a large part of the Christian Church rejected it as a heresy. Though the Hypostatic Union of Plotinus is

impersonal and immaterial, nothing of the sort can be discovered in Jewish Monotheism without the interpretive lenses one would use to interpret modern art works. The complexity of assimilation necessary to find the Trinity in the Old Testament is a laborious task, let alone the task of discovering how the Holy Spirit plays into the Pauline theology with the use of just the Pauline letters, which make little to no inclusion of the Holy Spirit within the formula for divinity mentioned in 1 Corinthians 15. Modern day Christianity, as well as past Christian thinkers during the Patristic Period, neither claim to assimilate or deny the philosophy of Plato, and their relationship with it reflects an often complex and open relationship that we shall come to explore.

400. Another role that Plotinus played in the development of Christian theology was in his conception of Evil. In Plato's "Symposium", the connection between the good and the beautiful is explained by an allusion to the cycle of rebirth. The beautiful is an offspring of the Good, but only in proportion to its likening to the father, and its reproduction of beauty by the act of love. Evil on the other hand is a bastardization and a privation of the good, into which it is subsumed. Matter is evil. Matter is subservient to the balance of the One. The Many are ruled by the One. Hence, Unity requires supreme balance, in the view of Plotinus. Some Neoplatonists like Proclus made the claim that Evil had no "being" or character whatsoever. Proclus writes, in a treatise on the existence of Evil that all things have their being from the good and are preserved by the good. Non-being and corruption occur on account of the nature of evil. Thus, it is necessary that evil exists or that nothing is corruptive of anything. These views led to the view of St. Augustine who famously pleaded us to hate the sin and not the sinner. The view that evil is just part of our makeup has clearly continued to hold considerable sway over man's psychology. Evil was seen as a privation on the Good, having no existence on its own. The Good was bound by necessity, and evil was nonexistent. How this became the basis for Christian teaching is quite amazing, but it is right there in Paul. The view was expanded on by Luther in the view of total human depravity and irreconcilable presence of Sin, that can only be redeemed through the grace of the Divine.

401. It was hard to justify evil or suffering, let alone acknowledge its mere existence within Neoplatonic systems. Evil was relegated to the realm of impermanence and non-existence, while The Good was made pervasive and given wholeness or completion. The denial and or assimilation of the existence of evil has Paul and Plato written all over it. The pervasiveness and utter ubiquitous nature of sin and degeneration on the physical plane is the perfect cover up for all immoral acts. The notion of a struggle for faith and sacrifice in the form of good works was replaced with the dichotomy of sin and grace, as well as flesh and spirit, which ultimately puts faith against law. Yet and still, Neoplatonic thought represented an inflexible love of the human spirit, but the same cannot be said for the disposition of Paul. An argument can and has been

made that Paul believed in predestination and did not believe salvation was up to human efforts as clearly reflected in many of his letters. Plotinus seems to rather have defended the Soul against the attacks on free will posed by some of its opponents.

Chapter 16
Christianity is "Platonism for the People"

402. It is still somewhat depressing that during the early Patristic Period[8] many Christian thinkers fell into the allure of Neoplatonism, rather than choosing to explain Christianity on its own terms, but then again this would have to have been coupled with a rejection of Paul since so many Greek elements are present in Pauline theology. Platonic thought was essentially a doorway into many heresies which used such thought as a foundation, including those of the Orphic, Hermetic, and Gnostic varieties. For example, the 2nd Century Nag Hammadi Library contains sections of Plato's Republic, Hermetic texts, Zoroastrian texts, and was apparently compiled by a Gnostic and syncretistic sect. The section of Plato's Republic explains the tripartite soul[9]. Clement of Alexandria regarded Pagan philosophy as a preparation made by God to pave the way for Christian teachings. Justin Martyr was an early Christian thinker who readily employed Pagan concepts to defend Christian beliefs, and was said to have referred to God as the Demiurge. According to St. Irenaeus, the student of Justin Martyr, Tatian, fell into Valentinian Gnosticism, founding a sect called the Encratite. Gnosticism existed in Judaism before bleeding into Christian teaching. Jewish Angelology and Demonology was a mix of Divine Emanations and Spiritual terror. Cerinthus, Maricon, Valentinus, and Basilides all offered various spins on Christian teachings with a Gnostic bend. They were considered heretics by the early Church fathers and can help us determine the underlying views which began to formulate the Christian doctrine.

---

[8] Copleston, F. J. (1962). *A History of Philosophy Volume 2 Medieval Philosophy Part 1: Augustine to Bonaventure*. Image Books. We rely on this old edition to provide us with key information about the philosophy of early Church fathers during the patristic period and the influence they gained through Neoplatonism in sections 402-405. The views of writers during the Patristic period are cited here from Copleston's book pg. 27-55. It should surprise anyone that the lack of consideration that early Christianity had any influence in terms of Greek philosophy that was used against the Gentile masses was obfuscated by the fact of its Jewish origins which has recently been promulgated in order to make it the antithesis to the Roman values where it is seen as supplanting a "moral science" to aid in the natural philosophy of the Greeks. We believe that the influence on Jewish, Christian, and Muslim thinkers of Greek thought represents a unified pull into the genesis of secular learning.
[9] The part of the Republic existing as a fragment from Book 10 explains the tripartite soul as a Man guided by a lion or beast which represents passion and followed by a many tentacled beast representing conflicting desires. The man in the middle represents the Reason which is at one end being guided by Passion or Thumos and being followed by Desire or Eros.

403. Tertullian apparently did not have the same view of Jesus as modern Christians. Though he believed in the Trinity, this was not the triune God that we see today. He subordinated Jesus and the Holy Spirit to God the Father, who he claimed were linked through hypostatic union. His focus on Stoicism, and on Ascetic practices drew him into the Montanist heresy. Some of Tertullian's other statements taken from Stoic thought, reflected a belief in a "corpus sui generis" or spiritual substance. This was similar to the primordial essence of all matter that was discussed by the pre-Socratics. In 303, a writer named Arnobius wrote the "Adversus Gentis", which made the deity of creation subordinated to God, and asserts that the experiential origin of ideas exists as an idea of God. This belief in the idea of God or mind of God as a creative medium was clearly derived from Neoplatonism. Both Tertullian, and St. Augustine, were from Northern Africa. One of the most well-known Christian thinkers from the early period is Origen. He presents us the most direct link to the ideas of Plotinus and was even taught by his teacher Ammonius Saccas. If Plotinus and Origen were virtually classmates, then it presents clear links between Neoplatonism and early Christian teachers.

404. For Origen, God was immaterial. This God created the world from eternity, by the necessity of his own nature. Origen and Eusebius were both from modern day Palestine. Origen, Justin Martyr, and Eusebius all made the claim that the philosophy of the pagans was to prepare the world for Christian thought. Eusebius makes the ridiculous statement that Plato and Moses were in agreement, and even on the same level. The Laws of Moses have contributed to the rise and fall of nation-states throughout history. Plato was a talented author, a skilled philosopher, and a clever poet, but by no means can be said to have attained legendary status. Eusebius however goes on. He compared the Phaedrus to the writings of St. Paul. Some of the early Church fathers would haphazardly make God identical to Reason. Others would place Reason in the conception of the Universal Man of World Soul. One can hardly reconcile this with the notion that God creates the world freely, not by necessity, but out of pure goodness and a free will. The God of the philosophers is bound to create. Even creation could not come about directly but had to be mediated by the spiritual world.

405. Other than the clearly derived instance of a God taken from Plato's cosmology there is the notion of Original Sin, also known as the problem of evil or suffering previously discussed. This problem was pushed aside by a voluminous writer and ardent Paulinist. We are speaking of none other than St. Augustine, who was a foremost mentioned supporter of the Christian doctrine as espoused by Paul. He not only wrote attacks on Arianism, but converted upon reading a passage in Paul, and at the exhortation of St. Ambrose, according to legend, who stopped Augustine in his tracks and brought him out of a life of sin by having him contemplate a line from Romans. St. Augustine is renowned for his confessions, in which he explains his inward struggle to

maintain faith. Caught between a life of licentiousness at the baths with his father and a pious Christian mother, Augustine apparently came to faith after finding himself overtaken with sin. He was originally a teacher of rhetoric, and soon joined the heretical sect known as the Manichaeans. This sect was a Christianized version of Zoroastrian teachings. It first began with a teacher named Mani, who referred to himself as an Apostle of Jesus similar to Paul. In Zoroastrianism, there was a good principle of Ormuzd, and Arihman, the incarnation of evil, which were engaged in a struggle on the basis of fundamental materialism. The influence of Persian sects and Gnostic teaching may have remained an influence on the views of St. Augustine throughout his life. Augustine admits that the appeal of this sect was that he could place the sin he saw as so clearly a part of his human nature outside of himself. He had not yet come to the conception of an immaterial reality offered by Church doctrine and in the teachings of Paul.

406. Augustine had clearly derived the doctrine of evil as a privation on the good from his knowledge of the Neoplatonism of Plotinus and Manichaean dualism. While converting in the year 386, Augustine founded a monastic community in 391. While gaining prominence in Hippo, Augustine was accused by Julian of Eclanum for having invented the doctrine of Original Sin, Julian pleaded with Oriental bishops to stand against "the profanity of Manichaeans". He was a respected member of the Christian community but was ultimately considered a heretic along with the sect of Pelagians of the 5th century[10]. The sect was most notably considered a heresy for having rejected the notion of Original Sin which can be found nowhere in the sayings of Jesus. Julian noted that this was due to an influence that came from outside of Christianity. He found them to arise from the Manichaean doctrine. In 430, European Vandals sacked Hippo and St. Augustine perished in the attacks leaving behind a legacy of Christian teachings that were widely influential, especially among Franciscan thinkers. Augustine had divided knowledge between Divine Authority and Human Reason. This was perhaps a leftover of his previous dualist conceptions. The authority of human reason became a constant dispute within Christianity.

407. This is perhaps most clearly described in his view that the material world arises from the "soul", and so corporeal objects were not proper objects of knowledge. As Wisdom pertains to contemplation, Knowledge pertains to action and experience. Knowledge arrives in a person's soul through the light of God, but only in the realm of the eternal truth which is the ascent of divine reflection. The split between contemplation and action is a hallmark of Western thinking. Truth is not equal to mind, but superior to it in a quite paradoxical fashion. How could such a truth even be conceived? Later St. Thomas

---

[10] Pelagianism refers to a heresy around the 5th century of Christians who rejected the notion of Original Sin.

Aquinas would reject the doctrine of Illumination or Christianized version of Plato's theory of Anamnesis, first seen in the dialogue Meno. It was not until the Philosopher Leibniz that this doctrine made a reappearance, but on quite different terms, as we shall later see.

408. There has been a struggle to see how creation "ex-nihilo", or creation out of nothing, as seen in the Bible can be squared with a Platonic epistemology. Augustine bridged these doctrines with the notion of "seminal reasons" placed in the world by God through the unfolding of time. For Plotinus, the creation of the world by God was not a free act. Man was however placed at the top of creation, and the soul of man was a divine substance. The present state of man's suffering was as a punishment for faults in an older and more orderly state of affairs. This was quite similar to the Platonic view of devolution. For Plato this was the time before the great deluge, and for Augustine it was the time before the fall from grace, but the concept is nearly the same, and the principle attained is also quite similar. The notion was that man had to arrive at the State of Grace through the suffering of this world, to emerge into the light of the Divine. The Divine was to be attained by Man. Whether this was to be done through ascension as in Plato, or with God coming down to partake in human affairs like in the Pauline view, it had to be done to justify the hierarchy of being.

409. This led to an ethic primarily centered around the passivity of love, as seen in St. Paul's writings. Love binds God and orders creation by the grace of God. The bridge between Faith and Reason can only come about by the Grace of God. This is a trinitarian conception of how love comes to manifest which has been quite influential in the West. He writes, "the law was therefore given that grace might be sought; grace was given that the law might be fulfilled". In this view, the cause of evil was not God, but the created will. God is, however, responsible for the created will. This paradoxical view is what made the Philosopher Friedrich Nietzsche attracted to the Christian view of God, which he said was upon a realization that God was the creator of evil. Augustine also wrote scathing attacks on the Roman Republic in his City of God. He makes a separation between the role of Church and State that continues in Western Political theory. He declared the Church superior to the State, which must permeate the whole of the State. During this time Rome was nearing collapse. As the only thing left standing of Rome was the Christian Church, this doctrine of separation of Church and State allowed the Church to do its bidding apart from the official decrees of the State, while being able to hide their goals and objectives from those in power, often getting the better of them. It is not hard to see how the separation of Church and State opens the doors for religious subversion by pseudo-religious political hacks. The Church would engage in political activity and pretend that it was the business of the Church, just as the Kings would claim the backing of this or that Bishop or Pope to attain justification for their crimes. This political dualism was made more sinister by the fact that

Augustine extolled human free will but deprived the State of its aura of divinity. This was the beginning of secular rule.

410. Under the Ostrogoths (an early Germanic rule around the 5th century) rose up a prominent Christian philosopher and Neoplatonist named Boethius[11]. This was a Christian thinker who used an Aristotelian conception of Nature instead of Platonic cosmology. He studied at Athens and produced philosophical prose that had a poetic quality. He held high magisterial office until being executed for high treason. Boethius transmitted Aristotelian logic to the early Medieval period, translating into Latin the Organon of Aristotle. He also wrote several influential original works while imprisoned, including the "Consolation of Philosophy". For Boethius, God was the perfection of all Form, and Matter was a derivative quality of Form. Matter was just a correlative principle extracted from Form. Form and Matter are terms frequently employed by Aristotle. Boethius marks the beginning of scholastic theology. The Neopythagoreanism and Neoplatonism of his student Isidore is evident in the construction the Blue Mosque. Like Aristotle, Boethius held that simplicity, oneness (indivisibility), and self-sufficiency were the essence of happiness and perfection. These were the characteristics of the Divine. This was the doctrine of "divine simplicity", where God's essence was reduced to Goodness or Truth, instead of the Platonic view of emanations, or the Jewish view of God working through the entirety of creation. He held the notion that, through reaching perfection, Man could participate in divinity.

411. His student Cassiodorus would create the seven liberal arts (Grammar, Dialectic, Rhetoric, Arithmetic, Geometry, Music, and Astronomy). The Science of the Trivium and Quadrivium were used to construct the Blue Mosque. This was the same compartmentalization of knowledge, dividing up of truth, and divorcing of knowledge from the sacred that led to secular learning. Since this was also around the time of the fall of Rome, it would lead into the Carolingian Renaissance, and the spread of Aristotelianism to Europe. The Carolingian and Merovingian Kings continued the seven liberal arts and built large centers of learning. This was a notable period, not only for the collapse of Rome, but the twin rise of the Christian and Islamic Kingdom. Hellenization had an impact on Jewish learning which quite naturally lead to Paul, who was well trained in both Jewish and Roman systems of learning.

412. Rome had a problem with two things: one was the invasions from the outside by European invaders, and the other was an internal struggle of decadence, corruption, and cultural schism. The spread of Christianity to the Gen-

---

[11] Copleston, F. J. (1962). *A History of Philosophy Volume 2 Medieval Philosophy Part 1: Augustine to Bonaventure*. Image Books. Most of the information here about the teachings of Boethius and Cassiodorus can be found in this edition of Copleston's work on pg. 116-123.

tile population, which was a project undertaken by Paul would provide a critical tipping point for Roman power in this critical stage. Rome's conversion to Christianity not only marked the spread of Christianity to Europe but signaled its collapse. The European Christianity which outlived Rome came to dominate in the world. Paul knew what any good spy and soldier knows: the best way to win a war is by deception, and the clearest way to overtake an enemy is by ideas, and not by guns. Thus Christianity became a phenomenon for the Gentile masses which attracted them away from Roman rule, in which case it became a pro-European and anti-Roman formulation. In short, it strengthened Rome's enemies, while weakening Rome itself. Furthermore, the systems of Greek and Roman learning, the collusion of pagan practices, the philosophical underpinnings of the West, and spiritual materialism of the Gnostics, can be seen in the development of European thought. This also signaled the rise of the Catholic Church. Yet another civilization would rise up to challenge, not only the basis for Christian society, but also presented a unique political challenge to Christian society that had gone along by separating the theological and political sphere, and the philosophical truth from religious truth. This was the Empire of Islam. Arabia, which was known as the wilderness of the Bible, had once again produced a challenge to the claimants of divine rule. The Golden Age of Islamic civilization is seen as both an influence on the West and something that threatened to overtake European Christian civilization by spreading rapidly through indiscriminate force. The view that Islamic Science had just as much influence on Christian Europeans, as did Classical Greek Philosophy, is not widely noted.

413. Nietzsche was a student of Greek and Roman culture, but to him nothing was more stultifying and stupefyingly monumental, as the collapse of Rome itself. He studied the Roman Republic and was a philologist that is known by some to be the pinnacle of Western ideas. He described the takeover of Rome by Christians to be a rise of anarchism and hatred for the world, which replaced the Epicurean and Aristocratic life affirming virtues of Roman civilization, whose cultural achievements were transformed into a debased slave morality. He blamed Paul, the "chandala of Rome"[12], as a hidden influencer, with a sectarian movement that "stood apart from Judaism". He describes the subterranean "unio mystica" of drinking blood to be a vampirism, which drew on the pan-syncretistic fervor of the cults of the Great Mother in Mary, the dying and rising god of Osiris, and the Persian Mithra, to have been melded into Jewish concepts. Christianity after all, taught that "salvation is of the Jews". The Christians were most extreme in their denial of the world. (Antichrist 58)

414. "Everything wretched, intrinsically ailing, and invaded by bad feelings, the whole ghetto world of the soul, was at once on top. One needs only but to

---

[12] The next 7 sections are composed of arguments from Nietzsche's Antichrist in sections 58, 59, and 60.

read any of the Christian agitators, for example, St. Augustine, in order to realize, in order to smell, what filthy fellows came to the top", he writes. Nietzsche apparently could not come to appreciate the attacks of St. Augustine against Rome, or his promulgation of Man as a sinful being, Nietzsche felt that false humility was itself a sort of pridefulness, but it was only built on a kind of spiteful resentment. He felt that Man's conscience was forever plagued by the "impartial spectator", that cleverly undermined its own potential by bringing down others. He complained that Man is the beast with red cheeks. He put these things in the mouth of the prophet of the Zoroastrian religion in his poem "Thus Spoke Zarathustra".

415. He was apparently convinced that Christianity had deranged the simple virtues found in older religions, which promoted the mentality of a warrior-saint. He thought that before the subtle revolutionary and metaphysically deranged views of Paul, Christ must have been a figure comparable to the warrior-saints of old, or at least the warlike prophets of the Old Testament. He felt the Old Testament God was a much more accurate representation of an all-powerful being. Nietzsche was not a fan of Plato either. He said that Christianity was Platonism for the people as we mentioned before. Certainly, some of the early Church fathers even made comparable statements in saying that pagan philosophy was a preparation in the world for Christian teaching. Nietzsche even despised the so-called German culture, which he said was used as the "Swiss guard" of the Church. He felt that Rome was not wiped out by Teutons, but enveloped and emaciated slowly by the Doctrine of the Church devised by Paul. He preferred Roman and Greek culture to modern European culture, and the culture of Islamic civilization as even more palatable than the rule of the Greeks and Romans. He wrote, "If Islam despises Christianity, it has a thousandfold right to do so: Islam at least assumes men" (Antichrist 59).

416. In a follow up passage he states, "Christianity destroyed for us the whole harvest of ancient civilization and later it also destroyed for us the whole harvest of Mohammadan civilization. The wonderful culture of the Moors, which was fundamentally nearer to us and appealed more to our senses and tastes than that of Rome and Greece". Many may be shocked by these statements, but we are not surprised. This was by a well-known and erudite master of Western learning, who had seen through the scamming of Europeans and Jews and wanted to return to his Polish-Slavic heritage. He saw a slave morality that grew out of Paul's teaching to be a subversive dredging up of a herd mentality and moral psychology, which was most detrimental to a man of high stature that stood apart from the commoner. He felt that this subterranean lust for power had crystallized in the thirst for a new order or new world of collective salvation, which idealized faith in the future through the myth of progress. Nietzsche saw that hollow and grandiloquent dreams of progress to be refuted by the fact that the cultural achievements of Greece and Rome were hardly matched in his own time, especially in terms of social organization, or level of

expertise and talent. He saw the men of that time to be superior to the Modern European. The warrior's mentality had sunken down like a ghost ship of history, and only a pale schematic "every man" of nineteenth century Europe was left to propagate the world. He felt that the West had opposed the spread of Islam to its detriment.

417. He writes, "Because it had to thank noble and manly instincts for its origin, because it said yes to life, even to the refined luxuriousness of Moorish life! The Crusaders later made war on something before which it would have been more fitting for them to have groveled in the dust, a civilization to which even that of our nineteenth century seems very poor and senile." He added that the Crusaders must be seen without the eyes of prejudice: as a band of looters that despised the wealth of the Arabs. He admonishes his own German people, praises the Romans, and even above Rome, praises the culture of the Moors. He noted that, "Christianity and Alcohol, the two great means of corruption" had laid to scourge the great men of Europe. He states, "Intrinsically there should be no more choice between Islam and Christianity than there is between an Arab and a Jew. The decision is already reached; nobody remains at liberty to choose here. Either a man is a chandala or he is not. War to the knife with Rome! Peace and friendship with Islam". This scathing retort is at least an honest reflection, and we find it to be a mostly ignored chapter of Nietzsche's philosophy. Of those Neoconservatives that defend Nietzsche's views it should awaken them from their slumber, and of those who feel that Christian virtues go hand in hand with progress it should give some pause.

418. What is most telling is where Nietzsche exposes Christianity as a Jewish hoax devised by Paul, a point first clarified by Dr. Skrbina in "The Jesus Hoax", he also uses it to extol the virtues of another civilization which has been noted by some intellectuals in the West to oppose Western values. Since we do not find the coupling of these two critiques to be accidental, we explore Islamic civilization in our philosophical context to arrive at what was appealing to some. The philosophy of Islam, which combines Jewish and Christian learning, presented a unique challenge to the West in terms of its political and philosophical views and aspirations. It also inadvertently empowered certain Jewish and Christian sects in an attempt to expand wealth, knowledge, and power and incorporated the learning of the Chinese, Persians, Hindus, and Greeks. Around the 7th century, the rise of Islamic civilization created a far-reaching shift in Western learning.

Chapter 17
Smashing of the Idols /
The Rise of Islamic Civilization

419. The political tides have placed Islamic civilization as clashing against Western progress. It has become obvious that most of the people that claim this can't see past their own thick foreheads, including fatheaded Americans and delirious Arabs who have come to regard the so-called progress of the west as a world historical movement. Contrary to popular opinion, Islam has not been in opposition to the West and even helped, albeit indirectly, to change the scope of Western learning. Today Wahabis, referred to by Shaykh Imran Hossein as "Protestant Islam" is well in support of the West, in terms of secular rule, and in terms of support for Western trade. Christian Zionists and Jewish Messianics have found in Islam a sacred terror. These groups have even worked hard to stage false flag terror to convince the world of the false narrative of Islam opposing the West. We find it rather strange however, that only in the last half a century has this appeared to us, and most of history seems to serve as an example of precisely the opposite fact. This is namely, that most of the political advances and scientific advances of the modern age began with Islamic learning. Islamic learning would never divorce knowledge from the sacred.

420. Islam made the claim that one day most of the known world would embrace one of three religions of Islam, Christianity or Judaism but that Jews and Christians would join to destroy Islam. However, it also spoke of a secret alliance between the false Jews and false Christians, that would bring about a convergence of interests in secrecy and rebellion, to set up a rule of corruption against God. While Jews had denied the arrival of the Messiah, and Christians await a God-like figure to establish a rule on Earth, both look to the throne in Jerusalem to find God seated on the throne. This God is nothing more than a "Jassad", or a body without a soul. Christ himself seems to have warned that if anyone says, look there, he is in the inner rooms of the Temple, referring to the Messiah, they should not be believed. Islam was in line with some of the Coptic sects and the Arians who claimed the Church had accepted a false doctrine and had associated the person of Jesus with God who brought all things into existence including Jesus Christ, whom he made the Messiah. Among the Oriental sects of Jews and Christians, Islam emerged, unifying the Arab tribes into one Nation. Since the Prophet (p.b.u.h) had claimed that no Arab was superior to a non-Arab, and no non-Arab superior to an Arab, he presented Islam as a universal message, primarily addressed to Jews and Christians, but also other Monotheists as well. Islam made the claim that Jesus was born of a miraculous

birth and sent by the Archangel Gabriel as a corrective measure. Jesus came to warn the Jews that if they take their Messiah as a God, and hold the Laws of God in contempt, then he will send Christ to slay the Messiah which they wrongfully accept as God, instead of the God of Israel. The symbol of this false God was the Jewish Temple, while Jesus declared that his body was the temple and that the Kingdom of God lies within. This oppositional stance of Islam is, however, counterbalanced with a call to Jews and Christians to end their apostasy, and seek reconciliations under the cloak of Divine Law in the name of Justice and Truth. Islam makes the claim that the religion of God has been on Earth since the beginning of Mankind, and that every Nation was given the message of Truth. This was a simple message to leave behind the ways of idolatry, and moral corruption. Arrogant pride, and heedless innovation was to be the cause of mankind's failures. Man must use reason to see the signs of nature that pointed towards the orchestration of the divine influence, and the unity of all creation. Following the line of prophetic teachings from Jesus himself, the Holy Quran states, "And those who are Jews, and those who pervert the words from their places, and say, we hear but we rebel, and do thou listen without hearing?" (4:46). It says that Jews distort words on purpose, twisting the meaning with their tongues to find a suitable interpretation. "Do ye crave that they should believe you when already a sect of them have heard the word of God and then perverted it after they had understood it, though they knew" (2:75). The claim is pretty simple: whoever made up the false claims about the Jewish Messiah being the God of Mankind had created a diabolical and accursed lie, but such an act is not surprising because it would not be the first instance that scripture was corrupted. Such a scripture was first corrupted by the very first instance and people that received it on behalf of Mankind.

421. The Quran confirms the opinion of Nietzsche, that a revolutionary and anarchistic fervor was sublimated by religious sects, and of Jewish origin. "But woe to those who write out the Book with their own hands and say this is from God, to buy therewith a little price! And woe to them for what their hands have written, and woe to them for what they gain!" (2:79) it says. Here both the goal and the purpose is clear. The Quran admonishes both the Jewish sects that change and adapt religion to their own ends, as well as the Christians who claim that God had taken a son for himself. In Surah Ikhlas it states that God is without beginning or end, neither begetting nor begotten. It also states that real Jews and Christians exist who understand and oppose the false message of these derelict sects of hypocrites and non-believers. However, a general trend is that those who practice these faiths will be led astray by corruption of wealth, control of the world's resources by cities, and reversal of the sexual roles. These signs of the last days, known even to the Christian are opposed by Islam, which makes the claim that all these acts are a direct product of religious subversion. Many of these claims can now be verified thanks to the information presented in part two of this book. We invite those who read to independently verify our claims.

422. Since it does not suit us to dwell on the various achievements of Islamic world in terms of scientific and mathematical learning by men like Omar Khayyam, Al Khwarizmi, Ibn Haythum, Al Battani, among others; we will instead focus on a few developments of Islamic philosophy that had a profound effect and reverberation through Western systems of learning. A notable fact is that Islam made no distinction between knowledge and the sacred, or between faith and reason, but also made little distinction between the theological and political domain. There is still a considerable amount of cross-pollination of ideas. Copleston and others have concluded that, "the influence, positive and negative, of Islamic philosophy on Christendom is now a matter of common knowledge among historians"[13], and also notes that Aristotle's work would not have spread among Christian thinkers if it had not been for translations and commentaries of Muslim Scholars. Since Aristotle was previously noted as being one of the most influential Western thinkers, we find this a rather startling fact. Christian Syrians first translated the work of Aristotle and other philosophers into Arabic. They also translated Greek works into Syriac, and then from Syriac to Arabic. The University of Baghdad as well as the translation movement of the scientist and philosopher Al-Kindi, were pivotal in ushering in a new period of Western learning when classical texts were revived for the first time and not just for use by religious officials.

423. Many Muslim thinkers developed a love for the ideas of philosophers during the period of classical Greek learning. One of the first of these was Al-Farabi. He divided the Sciences into Physics (which included psychology), Metaphysics (comprising of Philosophical Speculation and Natural Philosophy) and Ethics (which he referred to as "practical philosophy"). He adopted Aristotle's argument of the Prime Mover. The world lacked necessity and was made contingent on the will of God. Later Islamic theologians would take issue with philosophers for separating Essence and Existence, claiming this was an innovation of Platonic philosophy. In time the influence of these views was purged, but not before they spread to the West. French Rationalism and German Idealism would take the idea that Essence precedes Existence to imply a total split between the two. Descartes, Leibniz, and Spinoza would speak along the very same terms. Many Christian philosophers, like Aquinas, came to rely

---

[13] Copleston, F. J. (1962). *A History of Philosophy Volume 2 Medieval Philosophy Part 1: Augustine to Bonaventure*. Image Books. In the next six sections on Natural Philosophers derived from Islamic or Arab lands is used to show the influence they exercise on the enlightenment thinkers and secular thinkers of the European Scientific Enlightenment such as Descartes, Spinoza, and Leibniz. Such thinkers used ideas of Neoplatonism similar to Christian and Jewish philosophers like Aquinas and Maimonides. We rely on this editions of Copleston on pg. 211 to 227 on his section entitled Islamic Philosophy for the next six sections, but we take note on how Islamic traditions differ from these views which never were developed in Islamic theology the same way they were in Jewish and Christian theology during the 15th through 18th centuries.

on Islamic Philosophy to clarify the views of Aristotle. These thoughts were more fully developed by Ibn Sina, a Persian philosopher, and inventor of the Cartesian style dualism. He held the theory of emanation of the World Soul being the cause of illumination of the human intellect. The general process of the Universe was flowing out from God, whose oneness was always held as a main principle.

424. Ibn Sina, along with Averroes (the Westernized name of the Almohad Philosopher and Jurist Ibn Rushd), are especially known for having a profound influence on the Christian schools but were known as heretical within Islamic circles. Still their influences are largely overlooked when compared with the thinkers of the European Enlightenment, who often stole ideas from well-known texts of these philosophers that were largely based on Neoplatonic apostasy and melding of the views of Plato and Aristotle with those views brought forward by Islamic Theology. Their thoughts would've been in circulation among the underground circles of the European Literati and would funnel in unique concepts used to fuel heretical factions in some cases. In other cases, they were all too readily used to defend the existing Paulinist versions of the Christian Church Doctrine. Ibn Sina, known as Avicenna in the West, developed the Metaphysics of Aristotle. His thoughts are overlooked in the West and ignored in Islam.

425. At the age of 16, Avicenna had reportedly mastered Islamic Jurisprudence, Astronomy, Physics, Mathematics, and Medicine. Ibn Sina founded the idea that the mind necessarily apprehends the idea of being itself, which is only mediated by experience, and provides an illustration of a man hanging in space frozen in darkness. This man would not know where he is, or even be able to check if he exists, but will only know his own thoughts, and as a result be able to affirm his existence. One may doubt one's own existing, but indeed one cannot doubt that one is doubting. This was hijacked by Descartes, who presented a similar argument for his famous Cogito Ergo Sum or "I think, therefore I am". Descartes' dualism was based on the Aristotelianism of Avicenna. The skepticism of Descartes gave birth to the notion of Empiricism, along with the views of Locke in his "Essay Concerning Human Understanding" which argued that the mind was a sort of clean slate borrowed by the founder of German Idealism Immanuel Kant in his "Critique of Pure Reason". Ibn Sina also taught that the world was not necessary on its own, but is contingent. His Modal Ontology relegated the realm of cause and effect, which includes the material world, to a pure possibility, hence the world's essence did not involve existence. The only thing that had a reality was the "Necessary being", which Ibn Sina equated to the oneness of God.

426. Ibn Sina argued that the chain of causes is not infinite but must be caused by an uncaused cause. This shows a clear influence from Aristotle. The "Cosmological Argument" or argument from contingency, is a standard proof of

God's existence. If God was the" Necessary Being" or uncaused cause, then he could not receive his essence from another, being a truly first and unique being. Since God cannot have parts, since this would imply depending on the causality and contingency of the movement of parts, God must be a simple substance and truly Whole and One. This God created the world by a Pure Act, and imbued potentiality in matter. God being identical with the Absolute meant that God was pure love, pure goodness, and that his creation was Eternal. This view stands in contradiction to the views of the Bible, Quran, and Modern Science, which is admittedly an odd pairing, because of its claim of the Universe existing before time. However, it is also important to note that it was the standard view up until Einstein's theorems and the professed belief of Einstein himself, who believed in Nature's God, which was identical to the God of Avicenna and Aristotle. This is also the Nature's God mentioned in the American Declaration of Independence. Simply put, it is not the God of theists that serves as a foundation for these beliefs. For Avicenna's Deistic style God there was no free choice of creation, but his creation was instead a Necessary Act. God only governs over the realm of intelligence, and hence sees and governs all. All intellect proceeded from this one source. God governs over Universals and not Particulars.

427. Similar to Plotinus (and the Gnostics who piggybacked their views on Platonist cosmology), Avicenna and Al Farabi relied on emanation cosmology. This process of emanation represented various forms of intelligence active in the world, similar to Persian mysticism, although Avicenna relied more on a process of individuation than the total emanation of his predecessor Al Farabi. They ascribed to Man the ability to be illuminated by intelligence or intellectual abstraction conferred by a Universal Mind. This doctrine of Illumination was followed by Plato and defended by St. Augustine. The claim that God had knowledge of Universals only and not Particulars pitted him against Islamic Theologians, the most notable of which was Al Ghazali, who engaged in a long debate against Aristotelianism. Thinkers like William of Auvergne and Richard St. Victor made extensive use of Avicennian Modal Ontology in attempting to prove the doctrine of the Trinity. The distinction made between Essence and Existence in Avicenna's Modal Ontology became a major staple of philosophical discourse for the next 900 years.

428. We find the historical debate between Copleston and Russell[14] on the existence of God can present us with several unique questions on the nature of the inquiry, but we also find it to be quite lacking in reaching the heart of the matter. The empirical observation of contingency can yield us many interpreta-

---

[14] *A Debate on the Existence of God The Cosmological Argument F C Copleston vs Bertrand Russell.* (2019, October 8). YouTube. Retrieved April 21, 2022, from https://www.youtube.com/watch?v=K3SqQNquG8A. This 1948 debate on the existence of God first appeared on BBC radio and is available on youtube. We comment on this debate in the next seven sections.

tions in modes of seeing how this relation can come about. The claims of Paul present to us a radical shift to empirical mode of proof. Paul wanted to prove that God existed based on what he claimed was an empirical fact. All he needed, as he claimed, was the Christ crucified. It is both through the Modal Ontology of shifting forms of existence, but also the chain of contingency of "cause and effect" that is linked to the empirical nature of determining events in the world that has fascinated Christian philosophers. This is because Christians had to especially wrestle with the occurrence of the entrance of God into human history and with their faith being proved as it was to the doubting Thomas by empirical proof. The fact of a chain of contingency that cannot cause itself is an anathema for a scientific mind, who must concede that a particular thing must be isolated in order to be defined, but is this a reality that is available to the observer? A "thing" must first be isolated and determined in order to be successfully observed, and in this one has to separate it from the rest of existence. All the observer has is the chain of contingency, in which nothing is coming to be, but simply is, and nothing exists by itself, but through another. Perception requires duality because one first has to clearly separate himself from what he observes. This would seem to be a purposeless exercise in a slippery world that defies observation, and in it nothing can be isolated, but also nothing is proceeding from its own particular nature. The fungibility of this world is a fluid and dynamic web of interconnectivity that should in all cases defy observation.

429. While something may exist in possibility, it exists only "essentially", and by means of universal truths which are in turn necessary and eternal. Russell objects to this, in that Essence itself entails Reason, and not possibility or contingency. Besides one cannot know what the terms contingency or necessary signify, and that existence only refers to a thing described, and not a subject named. Here is a total split between the empirical and the existential, or to put it more boldly, a split between reality and truth. He finds that the world cannot be assumed to have a cause, and whether this cause can be described as God is an entirely different question. Copleston quickly justifies his view with the point that one can only describe what is truly essential through experience with existence itself. Russell maintains that we can never regard the Essence of a thing, and Copleston that Essence and Existence are identical, if not intimately related, but concedes that one may have an explanation without an intimate knowledge of what caused the chain of contingency in the world.

430. This is where Russell makes a radical departure in light of scientific knowledge and claims that explanation does not match intelligibility or the scope of understanding, because intelligibility examines a "thing in itself" and not its relation to others, for the very demand of explanation is too high, for an explanation can never be partial but must be total. Furthermore, a thing named is not a thing described. A disgruntled Copleston quickly finds himself unable to discuss a proposition that for the other side has no meaning. Fortunately for

us it has plenty meaning, although not in the way either Russell or Copleston can suggest in their polite impasse. For his version of the argument from contingency Copleston turns to Leibniz, for whom, especially in the "Monadology", we see reality has nothing to be worked out. Instead, reality is full to the brim, for he says that from God's perfection there is "nothing but the magnitude of positive reality". For Leibniz, God is the only being whose existence is both possible and actual, and whose essence involves existence.

431. For Ibn Sina, who is the creator of the argument from contingency as a cosmological proof of God, none of these versions or rejections are worrisome. But the unique simple incorporeal monad of infinite attributes could just be the universe in itself. If someone were to say that there is not a contingent explanation for the existence of the Universe then they have affirmed a Necessary Being as the Universe itself, having met Avicenna's requirements. As such, this argument establishes a Necessary Being whether that is a creator God or the Universe itself which some Platonists and Aristotelians saw as Eternal. As for Russell, if you cannot establish the contingency or relation of all objects and reject that the universe can be found to have a cause outside of itself, then the Necessary Existent is the universe itself, and does not necessarily entail a being or God. Granted as such Russel's rejection of the argument is only a capitulation and not a refutation of the Necessary Existent Being. Although Ibn Sina also insists that the Necessary Existent Being has uniqueness and simplicity, so as a result must be incorporeal, this does not follow from the argument he presents as the attributes of God, since the Necessary existent could be the Universe itself, or an intelligent machine that projects the universe as a simulation, since no change or sentience or free will can be derived or detected in this Necessary Existent. Any feedback loop is simple enough to create infinite variation. Indeed, the Necessary Existent or incorporeal substance, which is the principle and cause of all things is bound by its own necessity, and transfixed throughout time, so it doesn't have to be met with the constraints placed on it by human rationality.

432. But if, for God, there are no unrealized possibilities, then how can there be said to be possibility and contingency at all? In the way of Leibniz and Spinoza if "nature abhors a vacuum" then all that can be is being exhausted for the project of Existence, and nothing is left out. But if nothing is left out then if one thing is removed from the chain of contingency the whole of it should cease to exist. To say that something can replace a particular part of the chain of contingency is to emit the fact that the chain of contingency itself is bound by Necessity. Here it seems that the concept of "Oneness" is more important than the concept of "Necessity". So then how can anything exist as a possibility? If all is taken together then nothing can be seen as contingent, but as one big "happening" in the totality of existence, and as such, it is one, it is unique, and nothing is separate in it. This Monistic view rejects the separation of Essence and Existence, as well as the possible and actual. Nor can the breakdown

of the physical or cause of the totality of the physical be said to be incorporeal, nor can it be said to change in relation to itself, for the totality of what is can neither add or subtract, contract or expand, change or diminish, but can only shift itself and move itself in relation to what is, which has to contain the totality of substance without internal contingency or division, or outward exclusivity or eternality.

433. This brings us to a very interesting question: Could God create something outside of himself? It seems for Ibn Sina the answer is no, since God is wrapped up in his own internal consistency, and the outward manifestation of the world necessarily emanates from God. If this is true, then in what sense is God truly transcendent from the world of phenomenal events? It can only be true if God manifests creation, then creation has to exist outside of God, and that this contingent and relative and malleable reality that supposedly exists through the free will of God will have no reality on its own. For what creates the binding of necessary events according to how they express at each moment, for it is as if all of reality gathers itself and decides what it wants to be next through the will of God, for each will of God is necessary and unique and immutable, not interchangeable and possible or contingent to every other will. The truth is that if God has free will then there can be no future and no binding by cause and effect. As T.S Elliot once wrote, "what may have been is an abstraction, remaining a perpetual possibility, existing only in a world of speculation"[15]. What is salvageable in the argument, and what I find as Ibn Sina's great contribution is that the chain of contingency yields necessity, for it is within this very chain that nothing can be removed, for a subject implies a relation and a relation cannot be separated and implies unity through mutual dependence. This, however, does not tell us much about God as it does about Natural Philosophy that had a profound effect on many Christian teachers like Richard of St. Victor.

434. The issue is the so called "objects of the intellect" and how they exist, and in what realm and what state, because before God we may question these, for in the case of Ibn Sina they seem to be above God in a sense. If there is a such thing as an object that exists outside of imagination, and senses that can mediate reality itself but itself exists only in a realm of universal knowledge, then it seems that one does not have to believe in these to believe in a Necessary Being, but they are required for belief in the Necessary Existent, which is not clearly defined. As Ghazali objects, the knowing, the knower, and the thing known must be the same in order for there to be any intelligibility whatsoever. The designer of a game is different from the one who masters it. For one of them it is a matter of practicing and gaining skill, but for the one who designs the game every possible move has already been played. So various instances in different matches may give us various results among different skill sets, but

---

[15] Poem "Burnt Norton" by T.S Elliot

there can only be a set number of players; possible moves, and who will win is to a large part determined by the design of the game. In this way although the set number of events is not decided, the course has been plotted. This may remove the possibility of things existing that "could have been" in many respects.

435. It seems that the game of necessity exists on a playing field of narrow possibility, and even narrower frame of causality, and that although we may be able to make many possible moves, we still have to do it within the constraints of range that is provided to us by the chain link fence of necessity. If we decide that the arrangement of "all that is" could not have been possibly different then we accept that this is the best of all possible worlds, and we agree to play the game and explore the range of experience, or we can deny causality and move into a world of uncertainty and skepticism and moral and epistemic detachment, as Russell has, in search for an objective viewpoint, or we accept Ibn Sina's argument and everything has to be the way it is proceeding from its God's necessity. The chain of contingency leaves little room for us to choose: It damns us to the fate of causal necessity. Further still, we can go for Russell and claim that causeless and naturalistic miasma has no cause or explanation, but only the consistency of its own natural composition. However, this solipsistic and detached state of mind that denies that the Truth is all that can ever be had is what he professes to in his work entitled "Appearance and reality". The rule of contingency is a rule of fatalism[16].

436. For now, none of these will suffice for it seems to me and I take the view that it is all one, so it does not change, but it is not Necessary, and although the future is open ended, everything is controlled by God who sets everything on its appropriate course. The Universe may have its own way of course correcting. This so-called epic debate is just two sides of the same coin, presented to us over and over in the history of Western philosophy under different pretenses, is just the debate of the one and the many, between the choices of Monism and Pluralism which is also known as Atomism or Materialism. Radical Monism rejects attempts at trying to understand reality as inventing endless categories and subdivisions, and in Atomism one has to posit inert matter existing within a limitless void and laws to organize them without understanding their genesis. It is clear that Western civilization is a reaction to Atomism rather than the radical sort of Monism normally associated with the pre-Socratic Eleatic school.

437. In 1126 an influential Philosopher and Jurist was born in Cordoba[17]. This was Ibn Rushd, who had engaged in a most wide-ranging promotion of Aristo-

---

[16] This line is a paraphrase of a line from Paul Tillich's "Courage to Be".

[17] Copleston, F. J. (1962). *A History of Philosophy Volume 2 Medieval Philosophy Part 1: Augustine to Bonaventure*. Image Books. Pg. 222-224.

telian concepts. He was known in the West as the commentator of Aristotle, and the foremost authority on Aristotelian views after Aristotle himself. He gained notoriety by being the physician for the Caliph. He rejected the views that were heavily centered on emanation and was rather of the view that potency and act existed in all things and moved through a Universal Mind. In terms of potency and act he created the distinctions Natura Naturata (Nature natured: Nature already in existence), and Natura Naturans (Nature naturing: Nature doing what it does). These distinctions were later thought to be coined by Spinoza, but he had apparently only reintroduced the concepts that were already well known in medieval times. He saw the "prima materia" or prime matter as pure potentiality, which was not subject to the creative will, hence he saw it as co-eternal with God. This was the old Aristotelian cosmology of a Pure Act forming matter through the aid of potentiality and change, imbuing matter with form. Averroes also made Reason an overarching judge of theological matters. He made theology subordinate to philosophy, and made a critical split between faith and reason, which became a problem for several thinkers, like St. Thomas Aquinas, who in attempting to defeat Averroes notion of double truth was forced to put faith and reason in separate spheres. Ibn Rushd is also known for his Prisca Theologica which was an early attempt at perennial philosophy.

439. Within Islamic thought, one of the most fundamental questions is if one can really even begin to start a search for truth for the sake of closeness to God, and if there is any council on correct methodology or proper authority on this subject. While many agree that God is unknowable or ineffable, Islam is not divorced from the use of logic and reason to discover new facts about the world. Furthermore, there is the issue if the dictates of revelation and prophetic injunction (which often includes Christian and Jewish sources) are so clear as to be understood completely by the adherents. There is also the use of several non-Islamic sources that were made use of in this period, which included works of Alchemy like those of Zozimos. The question remains if there is any right method of inquiry that may perhaps allow us to rid ourselves from relying on authority alone to solve such religious problems. In Islamic Epistemology, such a question has always been of primary importance. Although in the West many philosophers have tried to marry reason and faith as the basis of all truth, Muslim philosophers have often highlighted the tension between reason and faith and considered them strange bedfellows when faced with the mountain of truth which is beyond all reach and the valley of doubt from which there is no escape, and where both are scant observers of the compendium of signs that are timeless. Knowledge is infinite. What is available to Mankind is knowledge of the world of the Seen, but remove the veil put over the eyes of Mankind and there is a world of the Unseen that is beyond the shadow of our imagination and the elucidation of our truth. Instead of material and non-material reality, Islam focuses on the seen and unseen where no mental or physical qualities exist outside the realm of what can be known or outside of what exists here now. There is infinity in the plenitude of signs, yet everything

is unified and tied together on a single thread. Thus, there is infinity in plenitude, but oneness in relation.

440. Fraught with fear of innovation, a fear scarcely known or felt in the West
who thrived on the notion of things to come and the myth of progress, these
various thinkers seek to guard the fervor of their own rendition of religious
beliefs within a method of inquiry, by claiming that neither a strict adherent or
irredeemable skeptics possessed an adequate way to substantiate knowledge.
While strict adherents followed the conformity of tradition or "taqlid" based on
chains of transmission and the views of their previous teachers, the skeptics
deferred to reason and argued that the books of religion were the sum of all
true inquiry, but also that rationality is the correct end of faith. Faith was a
steppingstone, but on the other hand, logic can only refer to itself. Science can
only rely on technique and soon becomes trapped in its own intersubjective
framework. Logic seems extremely limited and rigid when defining the ex-
tremities of faith. One could just as easily take a leap of logic, as one could
have a calculated faith. Attempts to reconcile the immutability of faith with
irreconcilability of human reason through a method of inquiry, neither trusting
either pure tradition, nor the standard force of our own reason, can be seen in
the debate between Ibn Rushd, the jurist and commentator of Aristotle, and Al
Ghazali, the great theologian.

441. The view that cognition in the form of observation and reflection is made
obligatory by the law of God is a rather weighty assumption, as Ibn Rush
claims in his "Decisive Treatise"[18]. In this view he states that the Quran tells
us to reflect upon the existent things and draw up true syllogistic reasoning
based on what already exists. This ought to seem truer, that by delving into
comparison of the world around us we may build up incrementally to a more
total understanding of the way God created the world, however it seems that
the more knowledge we acquire of the world around us the stranger it seems
and more complexities we avail. The bonfire of enlightenment only unveils the
surface area of ignorance, so we continue to tread along the path we've already
established. But here, Ibn Rushd makes an honorable statement, that we should
also examine the statements of those outside of religion to see the innate ability
of religious reasoning to contend or conform to views and beliefs that are foreign to our own understanding. We should reach beyond the limits of those
who simply profess a similar creed, for it is as Imam Ali said, "an intelligent
adversary is better than an ignorant friend", and we must remember that the

---

[18] In the "Decisive Treatise" by Ibn Rushd where we mainly employed the Charles E.
Butterworth translation, he argues that philosophical truth precedes truth of revelation
and that to reach God by observable facts is recommended by scripture. Furthermore,
Ibn Rushd seems to say that control of knowledge and esoteric elements of religion
should be left to adepts who can interpret both based on knowledge of revelation and
reason and who exemplify the relations between esoteric and exoteric aspects of understanding.

claim of the Bible or Quran is a truth inherent in all things and presented to all people alike. Only when innate intelligence is met with justice and virtue can one truly attain the nature of true inquiry necessary for correct judgement. Here is a good place to start one's philosophical inquiry.

442. This view further expounds on the forms of knowledge that are properly understood as secular, as well as religious views, to come to a pinnacle of rational understanding for the purpose of practical law. "It is not obligatory to renounce something useful in its nature and essence because of something harmful existing in it by accident", says Ibn Rushd, and we must be weary of those who are quick to dismiss an entire system of belief because of one or two critical errors which can be amended or curtailed. For there are lessons even in the mistakes of others, and we must be thankful for their failed attempts for there was once a time when we ourselves were ignorant. Although Ibn Rushd is confident that demonstrative reflection will always agree with the truth, and that those "grounded in science" will discern what is true, both Ghazali and Ibn Rushd agree that mere consensus on what is available to the apparent sense of the masses, and a view haphazardly pieced together and based on the interpretation of scholars, is not a successful method of inquiry in discerning truth from falsehood.

443. However, the strange view of Ibn Rushd that verses are somehow sent down to discern those who are true adepts of science and interpretation seems to be a problematic assertion for many, not because it is anti-democratic, but because it creates "philosopher-kings" instead of righteous men with the humility to seek truth and to expound on the methods of faith. This distinction between esoteric and exoteric meaning and the use of double meaning in constructing verses can also be seen in the works of the Gnostics. Although it is tempting to rely on such procedure to adjudicate the dull masses into a lurid compliance, constantly standing over them and shepherding them as philosophical adepts (for it is often claimed exclusively by philosophers that the realm of philosophy and its practice are far away from most people) the notion that philosophical inquiry alone can settle the matter of interpretation seems a bit hasty to assume, for philosophers themselves are often in disagreement about such matters in more of an extreme way than the laymen, because the tools of the philosopher practically span the breadth of human knowledge. The startling fact is that the views of philosophers differ more greatly than the disagreements between most average folk. The wide gulfs of misunderstanding are directly linked to their "paralysis by analysis", and miasmic ability to think instead of act. And who will select such adepts besides the very same philosophers who we began with to settle such inane disputes as the ones now raised between philosophers, or perhaps some greater authority than them will have to select these philosophers among the many? The system seems rather unworkable, and for good reasons has never been overtly constructed but used as a blueprint for secret societies and shadow governments that groom leaders for

the people. As we have pointed out, this is the true drive of perennial philosophy that has spuriously been named "Universalism", as we will come to see.

444. Our attempts at knowledge may block us from seeing an ultimate truth
that lay before our feet. It may also be remarked to Ibn Rushd about such verses as in Surah Al-Talaq that talk about seven heavens and the seven earths.
When they asked Ibn Abbas of the meaning of such a verse, he told the companions of the Prophet that the discovery of the meaning of such a verse would
lead one to unbelief and so it was purposefully hidden. Naturally, it can be
supposed that if those who are meant to guard the meaning of such verses refuse to disclose the meaning, or are somehow lost to us, then we are out of
luck. This brings about a tension that truth by direct experience may shatter our
rational methods or material goals in discerning what is useful to us. The limitation of knowledge to elucidate what we know based on our prior assumption
for the purpose of expediency may prevent us from seeing that truth which is
tethered to habitual experience as much as it is to demonstrative proof.

445. For our human frailties are ever so apparent when distinguishing who is
the correct judge, for only those who understand more understand those who
understand less. If we cannot readily identify an adept, a scholar, or a judge,
are we neither to discern truth or to contend with falsehood? Or are we simply
to wait for all the facts to come in and patiently wait in indecision? We cannot
wait. We have to go with what we know. It seems that our ability to discern
who is the authority on such matters is given to others by our own tacit consent, and often based on the limit of our own understanding that we ascribe to
others who we say know a little more, but this is all guesswork. Must we have
the solace that at the end of the day even the jurist who errs is awarded for the
attempt? Such scholasticism, elitism, and statism cannot be a solution for problems of personal faith and personal truth, which are based on the sincerity of
the adherent and not the stature of belief or even the limit of one's knowledge.
Although it is true what Plato says that, "the masses will never philosophize",
true faith in the sense of Abraham presents a radical rejection of all convention
in search for the truth, where even established doctrine and one's own beliefs
can be set limitations that may fog our lenses and skew our sense of measure-
ment. We must remember that belief is a dead thing, while knowledge and
symbols are inert, and only the truth we use will give us understanding in the
world. Opinions, emotions, and beliefs can fall short and the necessary criteria
to meet the standard of truth, but a man of true faith can never settle for what
others have set forth, and the insatiable quality that exists to pursue truth wherever it may lead will still have an effect on him or her who seeks it out at all
costs. In his introduction to the "Book of knowledge", Ghazali explains that
many have "duped the people into believing that there was no knowledge except such ordinances of government as the judges used to settle disputes when
the mob riots". We must consider setting up the thirst for knowledge as a personal affair to be kept out of the hands of those who are only concerned with

social engineering or personal status. Not to be wrapped up in immediate fortune, and to pursue truth beyond the characterization of beliefs and opinions of others must be the true task presented to the men of faith, for the very act of faith is to exclude all belief and settle only for the highest proof, for the ultimate acceptance comes about when one has exhausted his sense of choice. Just as one can choose to believe, one cannot choose to have faith, but rather faith approaches us only when we've already made the sacrifice towards truth, and quite often our own dogmas and beliefs are what must be offered up to God in search of a real experience of unmediated and unmitigated truth.

446. In his "Confessions", Ghazali mentions how reason often convicts the senses of equating distance with size, or darkness with stillness, or fear with sudden movement, but our reason and rationality is a judge with more lucidity and poise then our senses. However, just as thoughts are hidden from sight, may there not be another judge that would convict reason of falsehood, just as reason convicted sight of falsehood? Ghazali makes a good point here, that sometimes our search for knowledge is simply an attempt to gain power, recognition, or material benefit, and is not an honest attempt to reconcile truth with the error of our ways. Just as in our dreams we are shown a world with consistent facts and representations, our reason and rationality do not always accord with truth. Although the Prophet warned of seeking useless knowledge saying, "The most severely punished of all men on the day of resurrection will be a learned man whom Allah has not blessed with his knowledge", and it seems that those who do not possess correct judgement and a compassionate nature will use knowledge in order to dominate, manipulate, and control others or to destroy themselves, that there is knowledge that leads to dangerous innovation in the form of destructive technology or idealistic and divisive rhetoric is no small danger. But the prophet also said, "the ink of a scholar is worth more than the blood of a martyr", and that a man who speaks truth in the face of an oppressor understands the struggle of the faithful and makes the greatest Jihad. The greatest Jihad or Jihad Al-Akbar is a struggle to gain knowledge of self of one's true nature. Here we see that knowledge is neither elevated to the highest status but is kept in check by a sort of external and internal struggle that exists between those who would use knowledge in order to oppress, and those who would choose physical strength over mental faculty, instead of those who simply use knowledge of self to gain closeness to God, and to challenge the oppressor who uses deception and collusion to rule.

447. This brings us to the Quran itself which is the main article of faith for Muslim adherents, and which itself expounds on the various aspects of knowledge in many ways. In Surah Lukman, it addresses a slave named Lukman, who through his character and piety is given the choice between prophethood and wisdom. The distinction made between prophethood, and wisdom is interesting. Here it makes a distinction between the state of prophethood in which one receives either revelation or guide from God him-

self in order to have earthly status and to be a leader for the people contrasted with the state of wisdom, which is described in the story of Lukman as a knowledge of the inner workings of nature, and a sort of harmonizing intelligence. Strangest of all is that this state is chosen above prophethood by the slave Lukman. Not only does Lukman choose wisdom over prophethood, but he also shows that the verses on God guiding whomever he wills are not meant to elevate certain people beyond the rank of others, but to show that even a slave or a person of low status that is continually humiliated based on his or her assertion of the truth may possess what we seek, and humility is the mark of the truth seeker in understanding such a person. Again, in the story of Khizr in Surah Al-Kahf, we see that once the lawgiver Moses was told that a man possessed more knowledge than himself, he did not care to know how it is possible for a man to have higher standing than a prophet of God, but rather immediately made haste to find him out and to gain the benefit of his wisdom. Moses was already a man who was given knowledge directly from God, a cunning and fierce warrior, and the fearless leader of a nation, but when given an opportunity to gain the true wealth of wisdom he naturally made no hesitation. It matters not the status of the teacher or the nature of the inquirer, for then the Law of Moses is put to the test as being deficient by the standards of reason to provide the best circumstances for the victory of God. We must give the rational mind its due place, but as William James said, the rational mind only displays one level of consciousness, and "parted from it by the filmiest of screens, there lie potential forms of consciousness entirely different". For this we must look beyond Reason, for imagination is greater than knowledge, and truth is greater than imagination. Perception is better than sight, and participation clearer than observation. All in all, reality is stranger than fiction. However, since there is no authority on the matter the task is for each one of us to look for ourselves, and though one may be led to the truth, often one cannot be forced to look with the eyes of discernment. To align knowledge and truth with reason which seeks justice and understanding, and faith with action that seeks nearness to God is the true measure of understanding. Anything that falls short of this, at least in terms of religion, has been as harmful as it is helpful. Reason and logic are just tools to construct justice and faith.

448. Imam Abu Hamid Al Ghazali was a Persian philosopher who challenged the Neoplatonic views of Ibn Sina and Ibn Rushd. Even today some of his ideas are considered dangerous in Wahabi circles. He fully deprived so-called western philosophy of its theological scope in the Islamic world by alleging that the belief in the God of the philosophers was equivalent to believing in idols, or that saying that God has partners. Ghazali argued that cause and effect could not explain the changes in the world. We equate causes with their necessary effects, but we only do this by correlating certain features of the causes with their so called effects. Ghazali asked, what if an intermediary happening or an event occurred in between the instances of our own observation that we could not notice? This argument was used later by Hume to defend a view that

science could never attain to complete certainty. Ghazali wrote a book called "The Incoherence of the Philosophers" as an attack on Aristotelianism. Ghazali had said that the notion of Natural Law put God in chains. He said that the Universe was Necessary and not Contingent, as according to God's will. Ghazali said that God controlled every minute aspect of the entirety of Existence. He rejected the notion that God did not have knowledge of particulars. He put an emphasis on having a direct connection with God without need for authority. His view was one of Divine Immanence and Divine Free Will, as opposed to the "action at a distance" Emanationism. He affirmed this in regard to the creation of the world, almost treading on a sort of pantheism seen in later Sufi writers like Ibn Arabi. Ghazali claimed that all that we know is God, but that we can never attain full knowledge of what God is, being infinitely limited in our capacity to do so. He affirmed the personal nature of God. Ghazali's mystical reflection caused him to abandon a life of fame as a theologian, and he became a custodian in a Mosque in Damascus, Syria. He held that all forms of anthropomorphism must be scrubbed out from religious practices. He charged the Philosophers with having committed "Shirk", or association with God. This itself was a powerful remedy against dualistic notions of Truth and God.

449. The Almohad Caliphate produced an Islamic isolationist bend[19] in Islamic kingdoms of Spain. It was during this time that Maimonides fled east, no longer being able to appreciate Dhimmi status. Several notable thinkers appeared during this time, including the previously mentioned Jurist Ibn Rushd. But another often overlooked thinker is Abu Bakr Ibn Tufail (known as Abubacer in the West). He was not only holding high political office, but also was a distinguished scholar that was said to have discovered Ibn Rushd. His work Hayy Ibn Yaqzan is a synthesis of Islamic philosophy, art, spirituality, science, and view of world history, contained within the poetic prose of a fictional tale. It was one of the first works to explore a State of Nature style argument on the basis of human psychology, and influenced Robinson Crusoe. The tale is of a man who comes to learn of God while growing up alone on an Island, was designed to show how Man could attain the knowledge of God both without the use of religious training, and outside the help of experts and so-called civilized people, and through an innate moral sensibility and reason that comprehends Nature as a single and infinite whole. The ethical treatment of nature and animals and a high regard for the oneness of all life is shown to be of a high importance for the author. The kind of arguments made in the book which prefer a natural simplicity to be closer in following God, than the life of cities and scholars normally equated with education of the youth would influence

---

[19] Tufail, Abu Bakr. *Hayy Ibn Yaqzan*. Frederick A. Stokes Company. The Simon Ockley translation of the text and A.S Fulton revised introduction on the Almoahad Caliphate is what we reference for the following 2 sections where we discuss the work of Ibn Tufail.

thinkers like Rousseau, who later argued that children should be raised in the countryside.

450. In Hayy Ibn Yaqzan or "Alive son of Awake", we are shown the development of a "solitary man". He begins by fashioning his virtues through the imitation of Nature, and in seeing the vastness and plenitude of Nature as a reflection of the Divine. He sees infinity in plenitude, and oneness in relation immediately perceived through the aid of the divine without effort on part of the individual. This view of Nature as a Divine Harmony reflected in the Oneness of the Eternal Spirit Being, seen in the light of material substance as energy and unified consciousness is quite a refreshing take, but is also in the spirit of the Islamic worldview, which incidentally did not see nature as a curse on mankind. This view showed respect for all life, but scoffed at man made traditions. Innate Reason and a drive for goodness was to deliver us to divine reflection through contemplation of the signs of Nature. We must use our innate goodness to set things in order and become an aid to all life, reflecting the Oneness of Spirit. What is prescribed is getting lost in the wilderness of one's inner reflections, while submerging into the harmony of nature through serenity and solitude and ascetic practice. This takes one away from those worlds built on shifting sands, and the opinions of men. The virtues of simplicity, sincerity, and honorific treatment of Philosophy and Science, shows us that it was possible to achieve a high cultural refinement apart from Greek and Roman civilization, and also one not obsessed with conquering Nature by technological innovation. A departure from this was seen in the heavy focus on utility and the spirit of law in the West.

Chapter 18
Nomos / Telos / Logos

451. The main tension, as I have come to understand it, lies in the link between Platonic, Stoic or Hellenistic, and Christian moral systems, which has been extrapolated rather promiscuously into the metaphysical domain by Gnostics and religious apostates. Legends of Gnostics like Mary the Jewess, who was known as the inventor of hydrochloric acid, the "daughter of Plato", teacher of Democritus, and inventor of Alchemy, show a fascination in ancient times for the wisdom of the Persian and Jewish wisemen (later phrased as Orientals)[20] who were seen as possessing supernatural abilities. The Samaritan Simon Magus mentioned in the New Testament, was seen as a topic of preoccupation by early Christian thinkers. Simon Magus, who was given the title Magi, used a Platonic system of hierarchical stages of existence in his Aeonology, where the Universal Principle was seen as equivalent to a perfect intellect, and where the image of the incorruptible Form alone ordered all things, and reflection, name, and thought, were the inverse of mind, voice, and reason, that curiously enough, was represented by the six-pointed star. These legends and other similarities between Plato and Paganism make it clear why the synthesis of Plato's moral philosophy has been an anathema to Western arts and science ever since its birth. The emphasis on human and ethical concerns that parallel a metaphysical cosmology of creative order, and an ultimate sustenance based on a force of goodness, beauty, and power, has also been catalogued in many forms of eastern spirituality and western mysticism, that seem to underline an archaic fusion that provided the basis for all sorts of religious heterodoxy, that parasitized and cannibalized the philosophy of Plato into various forms of the arcane and pseudo-spiritual practices, and helped to propel religious heresy in several respects. If we are proceeding in a chronological fashion to take into account the developments of historical cultures and religions, this points to an intermingling influence of these very same ideals that can be traced from the spiritual teachings of so-called sagacious reformers, that have a haunting similarity to the spiritual and moral doctrine of Plato, as well as to other Pagan and hetero-religious sects.

452. Plato is according to himself farther removed from the distant masters he draws his resources from in time than we are from Plato himself. The same goes for Confucius. It seems that the further back one goes, one finds the learned men of the time referring to resources that exist further and further and deeper into the past, comparing the knowledge that they held as the scraps of

---

[20] Mary the Jewess was mentioned in the annals of Zosimus as a founder of the study of Alchemy.

what is left over from the great men of old. Because Pagan religions are more Ancient than the views of Plato, and they have been constantly misconstrued in terms of Christian and Buddhist teaching, it behooves us to at least understand the basic version of Hindu, Zoroastrian, and other Pagan teaching. Any claim that these teachings can have influence or import into Western ways of thinking, or that European influence has led to these beliefs, cannot be clearly established. Largely since, these views were firmly grounded in a complex civilization that existed before so-called Western and European dominance, but another constantly overlooked reason is because these views were single-handedly derailed by the Aristotelianism of the Pauline message, which sought to disrupt Pagan philosophy. Since this has been mentioned as the stated purpose of preaching and letters of St. Paul, we can at least take this claim quite seriously. It also is useful to point out that Plato's philosophy was not a mainstream philosophy at the time, and as such drew on a wide range of influence outside of Greek systems of learning. What we are struck with is the similarity between the moral teaching of Plato and Ancient religious thinkers of the various Pagan religions, and the radical departure of these views found within the teaching of Aristotle. Suffice it to say this framing has had a complex range of influence on Christian teaching, as espoused by the Hellenized Jew St. Paul. St. Paul's primary task was to make his version of Christianity palatable to a wide range of Gentile and Pagan followers, so it should not be a stretch to believe that through his training in rhetoric and receiving a classic "Hellenistic" education these views were "circumfused" and grafted into the way he delivered his message. It is however, quite a stretch of credulity to assume the secular tendency in the modern world owes any shred of similarity to the views and opinions of Platonic philosophy, that was both influenced by Pagan religion, and parasitized by the Pauline message so as to become tied into the Christian message. This was the genius of Paul's reconstruction of Jewish teachings.

453. With the advent of Aristotle's compartmentalized forms of knowledge, the basis for spirit reaching through its ephemeral nature to a return back to its Essence which was pulled by Spirit as its charioteer, Man and Nature became forlorned for a more mechanistic view of the cosmos that was pulled forward by innate potential into a future state. Most regrettably, this was a world in which cosmic entities and the vitality of Nature and Spirit were no longer part of the greater soul or "Supreme Personality". This "Supreme Personality" was often seen as the basis for pure thought and creation. However, soon God's entrance into the world had critical consequences for ancient thought. Aristotelian rejection of the Forms, and Paul's insistence on the physical nature of God created a cosmic schizophrenia and a metaphysical dualism between matter and spirit. In Paul's view Christ was the Word of God made flesh, which he equated with the Nomos, and Logos. In all respects, Law and Reason were synonymous for the Pauline view. Paul used arguments based on what he saw to interpret the Law to his own ends. Matter and Form had to be joined by Spirit to form a trinitarian and Aristotelian cosmology. Thus, the realms of

nature were no longer peopled with spirits and living entities beyond matter and order, and a being once free of all time and personal agency. Nature had been replaced for the divine substance and its incessant conflagration that melds it with the material world. This was often seen as the divine fire or pure light that was subjected to collusion with matter and substance. These categories had replaced the unity of Time and Being seen in the Platonic cosmology that we argue was borrowed from Eastern religion. All was brought forward with a detached cosmic world and a cosmic utilitarianism molded by the planning of divine influence. Logos was brought down to the earthly plane, as the material and immaterial were superseded by the entrance of God into history,

454. The pre-Socratic philosophers whose metaphysical doctrine was not divorced from their ethical outlook on life, serve as important hallmarks for unpacking the import of certain religious ideals, as these remarkable men were not only philosophers, but sometimes also mathematicians, religious figures, and luminary poets, warriors, and statesman. For them the manifestation of the cosmic entity was on the basis of an all-permeating spiritual principle. However, they were not among the first to debate the doctrine that whatever can be first perceived in the rational mind must be first conjured in the soul. This doctrine of open communication between the heavens and the earth through love and sanctity for life provided a type of pantheistic outlook. This was seen especially among the Milesian Monists like Thales. Thales was known as one of "the great seven sages", who said, "all things are full of gods", especially in the nurturing and sustaining element of water. This was an all-embracing property of moistness, or alteration through a sort of fluidity or natural flow. God was matter, whose quality and essence were everywhere the same. Matter was alive but possessed an indefinite nature that was often subservient to the will of the Divine Essence.

455. This indefinite nature was further described as deathless, and indestructible, and to steer all things by Anaximander, and in a state of boundless oneness by Anaximenes, who compared it to air. This eternal breath of life, or all permeating soul force, was seen as infinite, and always in motion with the sort of fluidity that Thales described. As in relation to infinity, it forces a polycentric design on nature where nodes of connectivity and influence of the divine are syncopated by gravity and energy, or a sort of bringing together and pulling apart in Empedocles. In Vedic systems this was known as the "net of Indra". Vedic philosophers also believed in the basic unity of knowledge or existence, consciousness or Universal Mind, and a sort of supreme joy or bliss that was the supreme essence of Beauty. As these orders of love and strife were explained by Empedocles, they ensouled all elements in an inherent propensity towards a creative and immaterial impulse.

456. The most influential to Plato himself was Pythagoras, who espoused his own religious order based on the principle of harmony of the "kosmos"[21] in composing a dualistic realm of limited and unlimited, where the material compositions of strings was seen as limited, but their order, structure, harmony, and form that could only be perceived by mind. Pythagoras believed in reincarnation, as did Plato. His followers claimed that he was the son of the gods. He was known as the "son of Hermes". Their belief in reincarnation, as well as their apparent belief in the cosmic unity of Universal Mind, is often overlooked by scholars on the subject. This" divine mind" cannot be understood by pure reason alone, but by a sort of divine dispensation, as Pythagoras himself had received his gift from Hermes in being able to witness the transmigration of souls. However, knowledge of the symbolic nature of the divine by means of the study of the kosmos provided a map for Man to study his own divine nature, and attain closeness to God, "for all things are always equal", as Anaxagoras declares, and if Man is to be the measure of all things, as the Sophist Protagoras once told, then down on earth so shall it be as it is up in heaven. It was within the capacity of Man to chart the orders of the heaven and emulate their design here on Earth. The Hermetic saying, "as above, so below" purported an internal harmony and order through a self-creative mind. This Mind existed in the nature of all things and in the Essence of all creation. Nature was modeled on and existed within the circumference of the eternal reflection. Plato had also made his view of Becoming, which was juxtaposed to Being, borrowed from the Heraclitean view that "all is flux" as is seen in his work entitled "Cratylus".

457. This was a subjection of the state of Being to the Essence of Being, narrowing in on the idea of ontological transcendence. Nature was caught up in an eternal "becoming". As Jehovah itself means "be and then it was", the creative manifestation of thought, will, and creation, was seen as the source of ultimate endurance, and not subject to change. The creative principle also was seen as indivisible, continuous, interconnected, through even the smallest and indivisible forms, as it was the basis of oneness and wholeness without which nothing could exist, for nothing is equal to nothing, so Being was made eternal. During the "dark ages" of Greece, before Hesiod and Homer, there existed many spiritual systems who explored this as the basis for all goodness and truth. The oldest of which was Hinduism, which is seen by some as the mother of all religions, and most of its scriptures or Vedas are recorded in Sanskrit , one of the oldest known languages. In the Rig Veda, an ethereal desire from the one cosmic entity imbued Nature with the germ of mind, connecting all entities with identity and form, which is similar to the concept of Nomos and Logos. Pride and passion through virility and blame cause man dishonesty and strife. Disillusionment with the divine is a natural result, as is a sort of spiritual blindness.

---

[21] Miller, P. L., & Reeve, C. D. C. (Eds.). (2006). *Introductory Readings in Ancient Greek and Roman Philosophy*. Hackett Publishing Company. Pg.4-5

However, to give everything in faith, and to speak eternal truth, and to treat all beings as gods, never straying from the duty of service, can open man's heart to contemplation of the divine. One did not have to look far to arrive at the Divine Nature.

458. The indwelling Spirit of the divine presence or the Soul, was first being expounded on in Vedic philosophy. In the Vedic philosophy the impersonal spirit or Brahma bestows Prakrti or Nature with Laws, but maintains an all-encompassing Mind or Buddhi (intelligence)[22]. This divine order in between the womb of nature gives birth to an intelligent and divine entity known as the universe itself, for the intelligence of God and the creation of God are both part of same entity, and constitute the male and female aspects of God, as the personalized gods had female consorts, which usually contained a natural and material aspect of the Divine Nature, such as energy or time. The doctrine that all is God, and that Man can only grasp the transcendental truth by rendering it in its full significance, and therefore be reunited with the spiritual energy of all things by personal devotion often expressed in terms of a moral code was not the invention of Plato. But this also meant that the Hindu faith was primarily non-proselytizing, relying on a doctrine of the Eternal Soul, which corrects the Buddhi or Intelligence, mainly by reincarnation of souls into various castes, mentioned in the Rig Veda. These castes are not dissimilar with Plato's parts of the Soul, and the social castes established in "The Republic". By "non-fruititive" works of karmic resonance, as one is entitled to his action and not the fruit of them, all are eligible for attainment of the divine through the higher castes, and eventually are able to free themselves from the cycle of rebirth, sharing in the nature or Essence of the Divine realms, thereby becoming like unto gods themselves. The idea of a personalized god or "daimon", as a median between the limited ego and unlimited personality of the Godhead, was seen as the gateway for true liberation of the self from the material. An aspiration to the station of the divine is what is meant by the world Eu-daimon-ia. This word coined by Aristotle is "Happiness", which is quite erroneously offered as an explanation of the goals of religious practice. The realization of the self was the main goal of Hindu philosophy. This came from a belief that the world was simply a hologram, or a sort of illusory drama, much like Plato's "moving image of eternity", or the simulation theory put forward by the physicists of the day like Sylvester Gates.

459. Compassion for all living beings without incurring anger or enmity by conquering one's own lust, greed, envy and pride, thereby freeing oneself from the material attachment of the desire to attain worldly pleasures, whose

---

[22] A. C. Bhaktivedanta Swami Prabhupāda. (1983). *Bhagavad-gītā as it is* (A. C. Bhaktivedanta Swami Prabhupāda, Ed.; A. C. Bhaktivedanta Swami Prabhupāda, Trans.). Bhaktivedanta Book Trust. Pg. 1-32

maintenance can cause one to engage in forms of trickery and deceit, was part of the common duty bestowed on all mankind in their relation to the all. In it, we see the philosophy that an honest street-sweeper is better than a dishonest king, for only the former maintains his true duty and purpose, for true happiness consists in making others happy through the grace of correspondence with the divine. God is seen as the light of lights and an imperishable truth, and "the instructor, the learner, the hearer, and the enemy are always within the heart". This was a call to look at the problems of the world as a reflection of one's own disharmony. A doctrine of self-reliance is also put forward for the sake of mutual fidelity as one of the scriptures states, "Let him carefully avoid all undertakings the success of which depends on others". In this doctrine, truth is the purity of the soul and virtue is spotlessness of mind or the courage to guide one's will with the light of truth[23].

460. One must also protect oneself from the irreligious and impious, who forsake the traditions of the pious family to create unwanted progeny for the welfare activities in society. One cannot allow sin to proceed, just as one cannot have compassion for the dress of a drowning man, so one is not taught to disengage from the world, but to actively fight against the wicked and the corrupt, as one of the most important books of Hindu Philosophy the "Bhagavad Gita" or "Lord's Song" explains. This is not a go to the temple and make your sacrifice and go back home type of invocation but outlines the mentality of a spiritual warrior who does not have "material compassion" and "spiritual materialism" in order to barter with death, but is a true devotee of the Lord who is without pride, fear, or desire, and lives solely for compassion and truth. Intelligence begets intelligence, and no one can steal away knowledge or skill or devotion. Anyone can steal your property, but while a thief steals one's property, a liar steals one's reality. Which is worse? The eternal personality of the Godhead that possesses all wealth, strength, power, beauty, and knowledge can provide isolation from pain far greater than the comforts and confines of material compassion, and those methods that search for absolute truth for the sake of power. Krishna tells Arjuna who is a student of truth, "Those who are wise lament neither for the living nor for the dead. Never was there a time when I did not exist nor you nor all these kings; nor in the future shall any of us cease to be", as he explains of the soul passing from body to body as a man passes from youth to old age. He continues to explain, "the person who is not disturbed by happiness and distress and is steady in both is certainly eligible for liberation. Those who are seers of the truth have concluded that of the nonexistent (the material body) there is no endurance and of the eternal (the soul) there is no change. This they have concluded by studying the nature of both". But no one is able to destroy the soul, so he convinces his student to fight in a war against his own teachers and family members on a sacred battlefield to

---

[23] Champion, S. G., & Champion, D. S. (1951). *Readings From World Religions*. Fawcett World Library. Pg 13-42.

reclaim the stance of the righteous. "Neither he who thinks the living entity the slayer nor he who thinks it slain is in knowledge, for the self slays not nor is slain"[24]. The Hindu flood myth includes seven sages who are saved by God as he turns into a giant fish and sweeps them across a flood, after which they are responsible for the regeneration of humanity. Manu or the new man is the term of "genesis" in reference to the flood myth, which appears in the Hindu epic known as the Mahabharata.

461. Another doctrine emerging during the "dark ages" of Greece were the teachings of Zarathustra, a prominent reformer of the Zoroastrian faith. His teachings known as the Avestas and the "Gatha" told of his metaphysical doctrine, which was a sort of dual-aspect monism that doubled as a moral philosophy, much like Platonic thought. With discussions of guardian angels that controlled natural forces and muses, the animation of reality by the spirit forms, and a monotheistic dualism that preached honesty and self-reliance through good deeds (much like later Christian teachings), a lot of Zarathustra's teachings mirror those of the Platonic synthesis. "That nature is only good when it shall not do unto another whatever is not good for its own self- Do not unto others all that which is not well for oneself" proclaims the Shayastna scripture, in a passage similar to Christ and Confucius. Do not do unto others what you would not have done to yourself, also known as the negative golden mean, is seen reflected in both Confucianism and Zoroastrianism. "Thou shouldst be diligent and moderate" it says in one passage and promotes "regular industry" as the doctrine of self-reliance and self-subsistence. This is perhaps the most striking feature for this Persian religion, which was a stately religion during the same time Plato wrote and parallels his teachings in several respects. The emphasis on righteousness, honesty and moderation, in dedication with those who bring one into a state of perpetual paradise is the focus of the teaching. And in the soul no greater joy exists than knowledge and light of Wisdom, which is the blessing of the "divine fire". The Sacred fire or Divine Flame was a literal symbol used at their altars. This Sacred light conquered the demon of "the Lie" known as Angra Mainyu. The only task of the demons was deception and corruption. The use of a "divine fire" echoes the teaching of Heraclitus, who conceived of the "pyr-aizoon" or ever-changing fire that melds all things.

462. In a striking passage from the Menog i Khrag it says, "It is knowledge, of which no one knows a superfluity. It is learning and skill which no one is able to deprive one of. It is understanding and intellect, which it is not possible to buy at a price. It is wisdom, with which everyone and one's own self are untroubled and satisfied". Zarathustra says in Gathas, "see ye the bright flames

---

[24] A. C. Bhaktivedanta Swami Prabhupāda. (1983). *Bhagavad-gītā as it is* (A. C. Bhaktivedanta Swami Prabhupāda, Ed.; A. C. Bhaktivedanta Swami Prabhupāda, Trans.). Bhaktivedanta Book Trust. Pg. 77-87

with the eyes of the Better Mind. It is for a decision as to religions, man and man, each individually for himself". In the Zoroastrian deluge story, a deadly frost hit the mountains and three types of beasts all perished, but when the snows melt and the waters subside the land will be happy, so the righteous are instructed to build an enclosure and take certain types of animals along, but most importantly they are also to take a thousand righteous men and women. This makes the flood story seem more interestingly like a plan for eugenics, as only the best plants and animals and women are selected, not only "God's elect". The concept of the chosen one as the chosen one simply because he is chosen, and for no clearer reason quite obviously reflects the teaching of Paul and his predestination. Beings have real god-like qualities which prepare them for initiation in the divine order, as being in a state of a Magi, or "wise man"[25].

463. This strong sentencing of the righteous apart from the unholy and wicked who dwell in hell and are cursed can be seen in Plato's Myth of Err, in which the transmigration of souls after death can bring you to a higher or lower stage based on your resilience, whereby you abstain from the water of forgetfulness, and diligent good works and virtuous acts during one's lifetime save you from an accursed fate. Strangely enough, these myths are only similar to Christian teaching as they are related to Plato. Years after his teacher Socrates death, as one of his transitional works, Plato wrote a dialogue entitled the "Meno" to explain the dimensions of the immortal soul, which arrives at Wisdom through "recollection" of the soul by virtuous acts, and a courage to inquire about the truth. Plato's character Socrates is always focused on the questions of moral reform in regards to wholeness or truth unlike the metaphysical and Pythagorean concerns of Plato as they relate to "kosmos". Inquiring whether virtue can be taught, he first observes where justice and temperance exist within the great men of the city, and if they are capable of teaching it. Mentioning the "effluences" of Empedocles, and the pores through which flow the laws of perception, Socrates says Meno deprived himself from seeing the deeper truth when he fled from a sacred initiation. He tells Meno that he would understand him better if he had participated in a ceremony of a mystery cult near Athens where townsfolk imbibed "the kykeon", purported to be a psychedelic brew, as they communed with the muses on the road to Eluysus. This Orphic ceremony, which Plato interestingly enough puts in the mouth of Socrates, could be related to rites of Bacchus or Dionysus, which were squarely condemned by Heraclitus. Heraclitus alleges that the rites were similar to the ceremonies of the Magi, where he said followers apparently praised the god of the underworld and worshipped a phallus. Similar religious rites are mentioned in the Hindu Soma rituals, and Zoroastrian Haoma which were seen as plants of divinity. These cult derivations of major religions were not uncommon even in ancient

---

[25] Champion, S. G., & Champion, D. S. (1951). *Readings From World Religions*. Fawcett World Library. Pg. 80-101. We rely on the readings from the Zoroastrian scriptures in this book for sections 461-462.

times, but it is hard to say whether these were mainstream practices or as most probably reflect heterodox views. Occultists today readily confuse and conflate such traditions as the true meaning behind the various wisdom found in these ancient traditions. Such rituals with visionary plants somehow clarified the point when Socrates asks Meno, "do you think someone knows what a part of virtue is, when he does not know what virtue itself is?". Granted the context, it seems like quite an odd outburst for which not much is said or found in the annals of philosophy.

464. Anyways, he further states, "it is not possible for a person to inquire about what he knows, or about what he does not know", not needing to inquire about what he already knows, and not knowing what to inquire about what he does not know. Philosophers commonly refer to this as the paradox of knowledge. But, "the soul is immortal" says Socrates, and can grasp all only by divine dispensation and courage to recollect knowledge through diligent revealing of careful scrutiny. By true beliefs or the courage of faith to reveal in oneself knowledge by careful questioning of oneself, he or she ties down these invocations to rational boundaries to analyze the shape and color of virtue, which exists within the soul, by extension of wisdom. Hence Virtue is to wisdom, what truth is to belief, and all are equally significant when recognizing the infinite knowledge contained within the Soul. The thing called virtue is the currency of the soul, for the thing called wisdom hangs on the soul and is benefited by virtue.

465. Socrates asks in the Republic about the youth, that if someone were to explain to them, "that he has no intelligence in him although he needs it, and that it's not to be acquired except by slaving for its acquisition-do you think it will be easy for him to hear through a wall of so many evils"? What are these evils? None other than the mindless pretension and empty conceit in the false honors of wealth and praise. "So these men, for whom philosophy is most suitable, go thus into exile and leave abandoned and unconsummated. They themselves live a life that isn't suitable for truth; while after them, other unworthy men come to her-like orphan bereft of relatives and disgrace her". For the philosopher must be bold enough to approach what is indeed most valuable, but wisdom offers many reproaches. Wisdom is portrayed as a woman, similar to in apocryphal Jewish writing. This erotic passion for philosophy flows from divine inspiration into the souls of men (494a-499b). In a very elegant passage starting at line 588a, that can be found in the Nag Hammadi Gnostic library[26] discovered in Egypt, dated back to the time 100 years after the death of Christ when the Christian church and Bible were first being formulated, it speaks of

---

[26] Plato. *The Republic*. http://www.gnosis.org/naghamm/plato.html. The Gnostic Society Library provides an archive of the codex versions of the Nag Hammadi Gnostic Library discovered in Egypt quite recently. Codex 6 contains a section from Book 10 of Plato's Republic 588A-589B.

Man's passions as being like a lion which a man must hide but learn to use for the proper timing of letting the beast out of the cage, for man has the potential of being like a many headed beast, not unfamiliar with the beasts described in the Bible who encircle the throne of God.

466. Banned from the Bible but having place in many of the oldest versions of the text is the Book of Enoch, which holds a view of the origins of man not too unfamiliar from Timaeus, purports that Man was the product of genetic engineering and a concerted devolution from a supreme primordial state. This devolution of Man can be seen in every flood myth and many secret societies wish to embody a return to the sacred bloodline of the lost civilization in a sort of archaic revival, to a time when a sacred race of people ruled the world. In the Book of Enoch rebel angels descend on earth and impregnate mortal women and these women gave birth to genetically engineered giants, but also teach them sciences of root cutting, metallurgy, cosmetics, astrology, and other sacred enchantments forbidden to men, just as taking wives was forbidden on the Elohim, or the "children of God". Finally, God and the Earth seeing that their children, who were giants called Nephilim, used up the resources of the Earth and formed a tyrannical religion of apostasy through the Earth itself finally cried out for the righteous ones for God to restore the Earth to its original sanctity. The Earth was seen as having a direct connection to God and being an alive spirit or entity all on its own (Book 9). Now it was a place where such demons and giants that dwelled on the surface of Earth were to be purged by the flood, but their spirits remain underground locked in a triple stage darkness causing havoc among men with corruption, greed, and ignorance through their telepathic energy.

467. Finally, God sent the archangel Uriel to Noah to reveal to him that "the Watchers" or rebel angels have corrupted mankind and spread plagues through the use of their secret knowledge, but Gabriel was to turn them against each other so they may destroy each other. Noah was thus instructed to take refuge in the Lord of Spirits. The Earth is planted with the "plant of righteousness", and every sort of desirable tree and vine grows in abundance after the deluge as the righteous escape. (Book of Enoch, Chapter 10). Enoch, who was an ancestor of Noah, was raised up to heaven to be the "scribe of God" and is known in Hekhalot mysticism as Metatron or the "the lesser God". Here, Enoch refers to himself as the "Son of Man". Here is a picture quite different from modern Christianity as Angels intercede on behalf of Angels, Angels intercede on behalf of men, but Man also intercedes on behalf of the angels of heaven which descend to Earth in a primal rage and rebellion against God. Enoch carries the command of God to deny the petition of the Watchers for lusting after blood and flesh when they had the chance to live all the days of the Earth plus many more in the sight of God. This also makes the covenant between men and women, one of the eternal blessings of mankind, as it is the envy of angels.

468. To afflict, oppress, destroy, cause trouble is the work of these Watchers, who are demoted to the status of demons. God Says in Isaiah 45:7, "I form the light, and create darkness: I make peace, and create evil: I the LORD do all these things", so as to say that good and evil was created for mankind to prove that the righteous and holy attain victory, for all the evil spirits that dwell on the earth are eternally cursed and curse any man who associates with them and their evil works. Here is the dark side of divine justice, which is often sidelined for the doctrine of universal peace! In the book of Enoch is a picture of Wisdom being hidden in plants, and the angels controlling natural forces. In Chapter 33, it explains the orbits of the stars which proceed according to laws in their due courses and spheres that bring rain, clouds, and winds. Everything is measured in advance to propagate a divine harmony. The works of righteousness of the elect hang upon the lord of spirits, who will send one to correct the intelligence of men. This happens when the righteous ones of heaven descend to earth and mix their seed with the righteous. The sun is counted as a male spirit and the moon as a female, which upon further examination could point to the sun's being pure light and energy, and the moon being made out of static elements and being more like solid rock, much like the earth. "The light of the moon is light to the righteous and darkness for the sinners". In chapter 42 Enoch speaks of the heavenly abode of Wisdom, who has a female character of its own, much like in the passages from The Republic of Plato mentioned earlier. Enoch proclaims, "Wisdom found no place where she might dwell, then a dwelling place was assigned to her in the heavens. Wisdom went forth to make her dwelling among the children of men and found no dwelling place. Wisdom returned to her place and took her seat among the angels". This angelic presence is only available through divine dispensation. Unrighteousness, settled like rain in a desert land among those she sought not, because even unrighteousness seeks only the good. All things in heaven and earth, and in the stars of the material universe and the ethereal substance that permeates all with intelligence is measured.

469. Another work of "metaphysical psychology", that was composed by a figure that lived around the same time as Plato but in a far distant land, is the Chinese Tao Te Ching, that was written by the mysterious Laozi. It speaks of fundamental forces in the cosmos that are part of the inner structure of man as a sort of spiritual psychology. Laozi says in chapter 25 of the Tao Te Ching, "Tao (the happening or the way) is great; heaven is great; Earth is great; the human being is also great. These are the four great powers, and the human being is one of them. The human being follows the Earth. The Earth follows Heaven. Heaven follows the Tao. Tao follows what is natural." Jacob Needleman writes in an introduction to a modern translation, "In Christian and Jewish mysticism, in the Philosophy of Plato and the Hermetic tradition, in Islamic mysticism, we find this idea pouring forth in an endless symphony of symbolic forms", which is now known as the doctrine of Emanationism. His funkateer-

ing of these various forms of religious practice notwithstanding, such methods have been employed by the occult to reach a semblance of knowledge that encapsulates the transcendence of the Divine. Needleman may have missed the mark, mainly because the Tao of Chinese, and the spirit or "ruah" of Jewish mysticism may not be similar at all to "emanationism" of Plato and the Hermetic tradition due to the lack of ontological transcendence found in those older Eastern traditions, for this all-permeating divine principle is not separate from matter in Eastern cosmology. Still, there is a concerted emphasis on knowing one's true nature that crops up in each of these various spiritual manifestations both in the east and west. "Knowing one's ignorance is strength, but ignoring knowledge is a sickness" says Laozi in another passage (Chapter 71 of Tao Te Ching). For those versed in Platonic philosophy such thoughts might seem very similar. Knowledge of one's own ignorance is a prerequisite to both Platonic philosophy and many forms of religious mysticism[27].

470. Centuries after Plato, his teachings and doctrine of the Soul was being kept alive by the Hermetic tradition[28] appearing close to the 2nd century. Hermes was also known as Mercury, or the trickster god. Hermes Trismegistus, also known as the Thrice great Hermes, was purported to be the first philosopher and teacher of antiquity who was supposedly older than Moses, sometimes identified with the Egyptian God Thoth, or the Greek God Hermes, who were worshipped side by side in an Egyptian temple known as the Hermopolis, alongside the Egyptian Imhotep. All these "gods of knowledge" were equivalent to archangel Metatron, the biblical Enoch, acknowledged in Islam as the prophet Idris, who brought science and philosophy to man, but the corrupt used it for oppression. Hence, all forms of magic and innovation were hidden from men who would use it for evil. Still, there were some who had transgressed by seeking out this forbidden knowledge which was made available only to show its deficiency.

471. These various traditions are remarkable, if not only for their ambiguity and historical significance and for various metaphysical sciences, but also for the influence they exercised on the heretics and apostates of the main three Western religious traditions occurring during the same time as the popularizing of Pauline theology. Classicism during the Renaissance brought back the exist-

[27] Laozi. (1989). *Tao te ching* (J. English & G. Feng, Eds.; J. English & G. Feng, Trans.). Vintage Books. This section at the very end talks about the introduction to the text which is written by author and scholar Jacob Needleman.
[28] McKenna, T. (2017, March 16). *Terence McKenna ~ Alchemy & The Hermetic Corpus ~ May 1991 ~ Workshop*. YouTube. Retrieved April 25, 2022, from https://www.youtube.com/watch?v=rzjrl24aHiQ. For the next three sections we rely on the views of prominent writer and popularizer of psychedelic culture and occult religion Terrence Mckenna in a talk he gave probably at the Esalen Institute on a workshop on Hermeticism.

ing Hermetic Corpus that was supposedly hidden in a Syrian Monastery during the Middle Ages. The reason why these texts were freely circulated among non-European people was that the European versions and fragments had been destroyed by Christians. Under the rule of the Medici, who were not particularly known for their piety, the Florentine council commissioned to retrieve the Hermetic Corpus, which was prized by men like Pico Del Mirandola, Giordano Bruno, and Leonardo Da Vinci, who also prized the works of Plato, both of which would open up a legacy of revolutionary mystical heterodoxy and religious heresy. From Book 9 of the Corpus Hermeticum, it talks about the imagination,

> "if then you do not make yourself equal to God, you cannot apprehend God. For like is known by like. Leap clear of all that is corporeal and make yourself to a like expanse with that greatness which is beyond all measure. Rise above all time and become eternal then you will apprehend God. Think for you too nothing is impossible. Deem that you too are immortal and that you are able to grasp all things in your thought. To know every craft and every science. Find your home in the haunts of every living creature. Make yourself higher than all heights and lower than all depths. Bring together in yourself all opposites"

472. To be everywhere at once is the goal of a Hermeticist, whose goal is to become like God. By shutting up the soul in the body one cannot know God. "For thought alone can see that which is hidden, inasmuch as thought alone is hidden from sight", but, "if you have power to see with the eyes of the mind he will manifest himself to you". This last passage strikes us as rather similar to the Pauline message of divine visions and the inner working of Spirit. For Hermeticists, God is seen as the creative impulse within matter. Among these doctrines is the use of plants, colors, and music for use in alchemical rituals for the conjuring of angels. Giordano Bruno, who purported the universe to be infinite and beyond all motion and time was known to be a Hermeticist. A lot of the heterodoxy and sacred rights were concealed to protect from persecution by the Church. Later on, Hermeticists were directly linked to the spread of secularism and the reformation.

473. Such practices could be seen as arriving from the contact of the Crusaders with the sects of Ismailis who believed in the conjuring of demons known as the Djinn. One such group was known as "the brethren of Sincerity" stemming from an Ismaili sect. Crusaders were not only upset about Islamic influence into Christian society, but also attacked their Orthodox Christian brothers with equal ferocity, as well as the secret orders of the day otherwise known as competing sects. They also laid waste to many Jewish communities. Among the most prominent teachings of the Sufi orders was the status of being a "salik" or a wayfarer, to be a stranger to the world or a wanderer, and to believe without

seeing. The importance of not being attached to any custom or a place for the sake of knowledge, and of holding correct beliefs on the way to discovering truth, can be seen as a summing up of Plato's philosophy as well. Plato gives an example of a man who asks directions to a road and makes up an answer, but gives correct directions. Can such a man be said to be offering up what he knows? Shah Ni'matullah, a prominent Sufi poet writes, "The point appeared in the circle, yet wasn't. Rather, it was the circle, traversed by the point. To one who has completed the circle, the point exists on the circumference. The whole world I said is His imagination, then I saw: His imagination is Himself". Here is an image of infinity with no beginning and no end. Here is an image of unity without completion.

474. In Plato's late work the Timaeus, a wise figure instructs Socrates on the origins of Man and the cosmos with a sort of phenomenological science. He tells Socrates, what is becoming in the world of matter is merely grasped by opinion, but the unchanging now that "is" can only be grasped by a reasoned account. Even though this is a wildly dualistic account, it can be said that at the very least this philosophy focuses on the cause of things and their purpose, instead of their activity and their production. As for the world, "it has come to be", mainly as a reflection of the "divine will". But the Divine Architect or craftsman of otherworldly forms, being eternally good, made the world as an image of himself, in beauty and excellence that can only be comprehended by true wisdom. What being is to becoming, truth is to convincingness he re-counts, so God is not jealous, and wants others to ascend to pure understanding and creativity equal to himself (we hope this all sounds a bit familiar). The foundation of existence is the reproduction of the beautiful and divine. But the universe being supremely good possesses intelligence as a whole, as the craftsman puts intelligence into the soul, and makes all souls part of his/her own. The view of God as an architect or watchmaker is tied into the creative element that drives Man. This has been a favorite conception of God in occult theology. The tying and tethering of God to the procreative and seminal instincts within Man is not by accident. The world then is made with love for the sake of friendship and unity, as Christ says in a Gnostic text, "When you make the two into one, and when you make the inner as the outer, and the upper as the lower, and when you make male and female into a single one, so that the male shall not be male, and the female shall not be female...then you will enter [the kingdom]". Here we see again, the mixing of contradictions is what inseminates the totality of existence with change through strife and creativity. In the Hermetic tradition, this was known as coincidentia oppositorum or "the coincidence of opposites"[29]. The merger of contradictions to produce a state of resolution was the basic structure of the dialectic used in the dialogues of Plato.

---

[29] This term "coincidentia oppositorum" was originally coined by Nicolas of Cusa.

475. Plato tells of a great civilization who was far advanced but did battle with the proto-Athenians who were a just nation in the Critias. The great civilization of Atlantis was wiped out in a flood that may have occurred around 11,000 B.C. However, a further detour into the compartmentalization of knowledge of the divine, a divorcing from first principle in the doctrine of emanation with the advent of science and logic wiped out these ancient traditions as well as the departure from ancient traditions into abstract sciences. This was due to the singular fact of Aristotelian philosophy and the spread of Hellenization. In such a philosophy nothing is created for the sake of pleasure, but mediated by reason towards some end, in a metaphysical outlook of approaching a singular-ity, which was an attack on the view of a dynamic cosmic dance that was a celebration of life, complexity, and beauty. This cosmic utilitarianism wiped clean the remembrance of sacred origins, automatically driven towards its end point or Telos. The communicative wrath of Telos smothered all change, and impregnated being. In his De Anima, he begins with mere coincidental proper-ties in a departure from the pure Essence of Being, obsessed with the so-called affections of the soul which are properly in the body. Motion or emotion seems to be a driving factor for Aristotle's soul which is dependent upon the con-straints of bodily function and mediated by "this agency for an end". But this confusing motion sometimes reaches as far as the soul and sometimes begins from the soul itself, as in the science of perception of external objects coming into the soul. What reaches to its end begins exactly where it left off, really gets nowhere. By the very fact of its existence, it is in a stage of ripening. If the future continually pokes and prods into the past then there can be no motion forward, but only a perpetual feeling of being left behind for the sake of a new beginning. But appearance can overpower the truth, and every real philosopher knows that seeing is merely believing, while becoming is more like under-standing. Discounting the view of his predecessors, he moves on to the two substances, which are matter and form. "Matter is potentiality, and form is actuality" says Aristotle, and also says "substance is actuality". It would seem that, potential form trapped in the actuality of substance wouldn't seem to have any permanent existence, but only function as a sort of hologram. "I think therefore I am" (The Cogito Ergo Sum of Descartes) here would really be I see therefore I become. Quite problematically, the natural body is only potentially alive, and as such cannot be counted as actuality or form. The form and actual-ity is the potentiality and motion within the body moving toward it's particular end. While attempting to give credence to the physical world, this view treats Nature as a secondary device and the body as a depreciating mediation toward something better.

476. For touch and feeling is a sort of communicative property, Aristotle takes it away from plants, who we have now discovered exhibit communication with both each other, and the outside world in considerable and remarkable ways. Taking the Soul out of Nature and alleging that "the soul is not a body, but requires a body", he moves beyond the unity of spirit of the archaic philoso-

phy, and moves into a type of physiology or psychology of mind, divorced from the realm of Spirit. Most notably, Aristotle attacked both Plato and the pre-Socratic philosophers, while clearly being indebted to their views. Now if matter is brought out of the future state into the past by the actuality of form, then neither matter or time can truly exist, but they appear as a cyclical process, perpetually recycled toward a greater end. If every aspect of the Universe is part of a greater end, then the finality of change in the Universe can never appear to us a finished product. Such creative novelty points to the flux of material in a constant rotation, much like Anaxagoras and Plato imagined. If God is an understanding of understanding, then there is simply no time to think, but thought and will manifest creatively at every second with the complete lack of agency or control. If one is continually propelled, then one is forced to accelerate change. Time is not only motion towards an end, but a sort of rhythm and harmony derived by the creative impulse.

477. The organizing principle seen by pre-Socratic philosophers, and in the Platonic synthesis and even in some versions of the Eastern traditions, as Mind, woven into the substance of the cosmos, as pure mind or understanding, with the ability to manifest thought and will into creative novelty, that is corresponding to this cosmic push or original celestial Essence, was abandoned for the doctrine of self-transcendence, which not only have had a profound importance for religious mystics and occultists, but also which perfectly fit the designs for the pursuits of technological advancement or statecraft in their teleological, eschatological, and soteriological schemes. Humans no longer yearned to climb holy mountains or create a resonance with the divine, but to master one another. This is endemic to any philosophy that views Man as a passing phase, while claiming to uplift him. Using duality to proceed and using the self to get beyond the self is the view of self-transcendence. Infinite complexity which reinvents itself in every moment for the sake of pleasure, and not for some teleological end, was taken out of the picture almost permanently for some. These themes and views, however, had a lasting effect on the views and opinions of Western thinkers throughout the ages. Many of these ideas have lent themselves to Pauline theology because of their focus on the material contamination of the body seen in a dialectic between flesh and spirit, and the continual push of history toward a future state of affairs seen as an indelible faith in the future. The ability of the Pauline message to reach across time with its anthropomorphic take on divinity, an "anthro-futuristic" view of time encapsulated by its new covenant theology and future arrival of a Kingdom of God and a New Earth that could function without law or strife, and its transcendental view of matter as a vessel prepared for the renewal of all mankind, is quite astonishing. Many other philosophies have come and gone, but the Pauline message remains. This gives the message of St. Paul the ingenious capacity to circumvent and preclude any truth in service of it's own theological ends. Once again, this is a fact barely recognized by most scholars, yet this is not a

surprise, because no other doctrine perfectly exemplifies the motives for one that is hiding in plain sight.

478. This survey or scanning of the various religious views that had gained prominence in the Medieval world helps us to understand the various influences around at the time of the rise of the Church and unification of Europe, which most apparently set the stage for the later rise of Secular State during the period known as the European Enlightenment. One bridge between Islam and the West was the Jewish and Christian sects and philosophers that gained prominence within Islamic ruled territories. Jewish philosophers like Maimonides[30] were benefiting from Muslim rule and the tolerance of Muslim rule that even let in strange sects like the Ismaili's. The general terms of acceptance in Muslim society and the practice of religion were often much too broad and encompassed too wide a range of legal relations. This allowed many to continue in various paths of apostasy, because unlike what is now assumed, Islam did not bring with it a totalitarian scope. Similar to Christianity and Hinduism, Islam presents itself as a non-proselytizing faith whose adherent must evaluate the commitments of faith on their own personal terms, as recommended by the scriptures. But once the decision was made to follow in the path of Islam, adherents were told to swiftly dedicate themselves with sincerity to the cause of Islam which was a political, legal, and social endeavor. This disperse legal tendency caused them to assimilate many sects and cultures, but also similar to Rome it was too open of a policy to maintain local cultural traditions. The Jewish Kabbalah, which consisted of works like The Jezirah (Book of Creation) and the Zohar, rose to prominence in this time, as did the Mishneh Torah interpretations of Maimonides. This was a doctrine of mystical transcendence, which even had an effect on the son of Maimonides and other Jewish thinkers. However, instead of the mysticism of the omnipresence of God found in Sufism, the mysticism of the Kabbalah relied more on Emanationism and the transcendental scope. It presented a hierarchical framework as seen in the tree of Sephirot. The Emanationist philosophy of thinkers like Salomon Ibn Gabriel, known as Avicebron in the West, was used to formulate texts like the Zohar.

479. Most mystical tenets of the time included substitution of the Logos for a "Divine Will". This corresponded to the will or passion of Man. Ultimately, it would have a major influence on later Western thinkers who made Will superior to Reason, and Freedom (also sometimes referred to as Mind or Spirit especially by Hegelian philosophers) superior to Natural Law. This was perceiving the world through revolutionary shifts and evolutionary changes quite central to the views of Heraclitus, who viewed all things as strife and change. The

---

[30] Copleston, F. J. (1962). *A History of Philosophy Volume 2 Medieval Philosophy Part 1: Augustine to Bonaventure*. Image Books. Pg. 227-232. We rely on the chapter in this book on Islamic and Jewish philosophy for the next four sections to outline the philosophy of Maimonides.

Aristotelian drive of the Telos in Nature, or a hidden potential within things, putting back in place the hylomorphic composition and order of the Universe, became more attractive than the abstract realms of Platonic thought. The idea that contemplation of the lower stages leads to higher states, apprehensible only to those in a state of divine stupor or spiritual ecstasy and intoxication, promoted the notion of an ecstatic Intuition as opposed to Reason. Finally, the concept of Nomos reflected the inclusivity of faith and the tacit agreement of Law. Law encompassed all.

480. In the work of Maimonides we see a decidedly Aristotelian and Avicennian influence that would remain active in Jewish thought. The thoughts of Maimonides, and St. Thomas Aquinas, represent a decidedly Aristotelian turn in religious cosmology that anticipated a religious reformation of both Christianity and Judaism in 16th century Europe. Moshe Ben Maimon or Moses Maimonides was born in Cordoba, Spain. He felt that Aristotle was comparable to the Prophets of Hebrew law. "From Moses to Moses there was nobody like Moses" is a statement parroted by Hebrew scholars but should be seen as a demotion of Moses rather than a promotion of Moses Maimonides who the statement purportedly refers to. The fact that Jews do not view this as a heretical utterance tells us all we need to know about their susceptibility to merge the designs of their religion with Aristotelianism when it was in fashion to do so. This is clearly a slam against Jesus, as is the claim by Atheists that Spinoza was the greatest Jew who ever lived. Most notably, both the views of Spinoza and those of Moses Maimonides were squarely based on Aristotelian and Avicennian views that were widespread at the time and also that both of their views were attempts, albeit within the framework of an Aristotelian system, to prove the God of the Old Testament. However, much in keeping with what is said in Hebrew scripture, Maimonides had to allow God to be able to suspend Natural Law, and argued that God had created the world ex-nihilo, in contradiction to the other Aristotelian features of his philosophy. Some Jews held that his works were too generous to Greek philosophy and tread on heresy, especially with views similar to Ibn Rushd that Truth arrived at by Pure Reason was equivalent to the views of Revelation. He used the old Avicennian and Aristotelian arguments from First Cause to prove the existence of God.

481. Unlike Aquinas, Maimonides refused to attribute positive characteristics to God, but claimed God as a Pure Act, without matter or immaterial, and infinitely removed from Creation. His view, known as "via negativa", is the view that you can only talk about what God is not. This he said was apparent in the various types of intelligences between God and Man. While his works were seen as more accessible to Orthodox Jews than the works of the Kabbalah, they present a common use of Greek and Jewish ideas. He separated Essence and Existence, and held that all things could be described by something outside of their nature. He maintained that God was an immaterial, simple substance

without parts, similar to Avicenna, but in seeming contradiction to the views of the Bible.

482. One of the most notable Christian thinkers to appear at this time was St. Thomas Aquinas who showed a similar debt to the views of Aristotle. At this time, the schools of St. Albert the Great were engaged in the height of the scholastic period, and one of the most premier patrons of Dominican learning was St. Thomas Aquinas. St. Thomas would begin his explanation of the world not as an idea of God, as in the Augustinian view, but from the subjectivity of the created world in relation to God. In other words, he used the old Aristotelian view to argue from causes in the world to the supernatural instead of seeing reality as derived from the ethereal. St. Thomas Aquinas made the most severe distinction between theology and philosophy in a complete compartmentalizing of faith and reason. He said that the distinction cuts very deep and even can be viewed in terms of human psychology[31]. He said that truths of Reason and truths of theology are dissimilar. He further saw two different realms between knowledge and experience. In his attempt to defeat the notion of double truth that plagued the Aristotelian philosophers of his time, Aquinas saw Aristotle as the first human intellect and mind attuned to philosophy and was nothing more than Aristotle dressed in the robes of a Christian Monk. The reform of both Jewish and Christian traditions came from a blind acceptance of Aristotelian views. The most pivotal dualism of Aquinas rests on his acceptance of the Aristotelian distinction between Form and Matter. Form acquires its individuation by Matter. Aristotle's having relegated the forms to a Universal instead of Transcendental category had to make corporeal substance a potentiality in the hands of an Efficient Agent. Hence the changeability of Matter was its privation, similar to the Platonic derivation of Matter as a devolution of the transcendental forms.

483. Aquinas formed a hierarchy of being and intelligence similar to Aristotle. This was primarily based on the false belief that rational inquiry demonstrates scales of consciousness, from vegetation to irrational minds, to rational Man, and finally Angelic beings. This false notion used to justify anthropomorphic and humanistic tendencies was found to support Darwinism, especially in the Darwinian notion of Man's "lowly origin". Quite plainly, it is the use of Man's flawed nature to put down all other life. Like Avicenna and Maimonides, Aquinas made a wide distinction between Essence and Existence. Existence on its own had no essential form but is only activity which gives rise to the individuation of matter. Aristotelian philosophers apparently believe that Existence is a mere accident of Essence, so are dualists at the end of the day. Aquinas felt

---

[31] Copleston, F. J. (1962). *A History of Philosophy Volume 2 Medieval Philosophy Part II: Albert the Great to Duns Scotus.* Image Books. We rely on Copleston's explanations of Aquinas' philosophy for the next four sections.

that everything that did not belong to Essence was extraneous composition. He used Avicennian Philosophy to prove God as a Necessary Being.

484. Similar to Maimonides, Aquinas proposed that we can only know of God that he exists but can say nothing about the Essence of God. He said that God can only be known by comparison. In the Platonic realm, God was banished to the higher orders of things. In the Aristotelian sense, God was far removed from the world through a chain of contingency. If the claim of Aquinas is true, that we can only know God by seeing how God is manifested in the world then Aristotelianism provides a bad road map. Indeed, if we are to follow the conclusions of Avicennian philosophy to their logical end then it is just as the Great Doctor himself alleged; God is far removed from the affairs of the world. This was the crux of a sort of subjective idealism, that ideas are the links between physical objects, that ultimately gives rise to Empiricism. It was a separation of the rational and the sensitive, the body and the soul, theology and philosophy, secular and divine, faith and reason, which ultimately gave rise to desacralization of knowledge, whose ultimate manifestation was the separation between Essence and Existence.

485. This at least led outwardly to the divide between the Church and the State, readily found in Aquinas. Making the State the handmaiden of the Church, the State was the caretaker of Reason, and of the Natural and Civil Laws. The Church however, maintained the lofty status of being caretaker of the Soul, and of the Laws of Eternal Rule. This idea is clearly reflected in several of the Paulinist creeds that declare a collective salvation is to be found in positive affirmation and a general ascetic and agreeable quality, not by actions of faith but by acceptance of grace. The political domain was a mediator for otherworldly goals and aspirations. One was told at once to accept the ways of the world, but also to undervalue one's own relation to the happenings of the world. This engendered a considerable amount of aloofness, but also a broad range of acceptability. After all, Man was Naturally flawed, and for that to be true Nature was itself incomplete. God's entrance into history created a Telos that swallowed up Men's actions in a redemptive movement, while the Laws were removed from human affairs. Man could not seek salvation through the Institutions of Man. The Spirit of the Laws was reflected in Nomos, which was utterly removed from the affairs of Man. Later on, Thomas Paine would declare government to be a Necessary Evil. We see nothing clearer in the notion of Necessary Evil than a perfect representation of the Pauline line of thinking. One could not avoid participating in Evil, because Sin is a part of Man. One could no longer reject Sin, or avoid participation in Evil, than deny one's own Nature. The State is a perfect representation of man-made humiliation, dispensed through man's own misgivings about himself. The Pauline system relies on Equality rather than Egalitarianism, and Ubiquity before Uniqueness. In Christianity, the cross doubles as a symbol of redemption and power.

486. This was taken to the extreme in dualistic sects of the Albigensian and Cathari[32]. Vowing to curse the flesh in a quasi-religious manner, they endeavored to forbid marriage, readily broke worldly oaths, rejected the Laws of both Church and State, and generally regarded Matter as synonymous with Evil, including their own flesh. They considered even their own flesh to be cursed. They ultimately believed that Sin had no real existence, because Man himself, or Woman herself (especially true for Woman), were the extension of the Divine. This Divine quality was ultimately embodied in the combination of all Good and Evil elements in order to reach a spiritual stasis to emulate the Divine. To become like God, was not as good as replacing God altogether, or even killing God and reinventing him. This was possible because each person could access the Divine through their immaterial souls, which was the Nature they shared with the Divine Immaterial Essence. Amalric of Bena reportedly held such views, and the Waldensians devolved into Cathari sects. David of Dinant, is noted by St. Thomas Aquinas, as having come to the heretical conclusion that God is Prime Matter. Thoughts of these pantheistic and Aristotelians blends were a decidedly pre-Spinozistic shape. These thinkers are properly proto-Spinozean.

487. John Scotus Eriugena [33]was the most developed of these types of philosophers that were usually declared heretical. He was quite an original thinker that anticipates the thoughts of Spinoza and Hegel. He saw Nature as consisting of the totality of all things. This refreshing sentiment was not seen since the Monists of pre-Socratic times. In terms of his metaphysical speculation, he included four aspects: a creating uncreated aspect, a creating created aspect, an uncreating created aspect, and an uncreating uncreated aspect. God is one, so is the source of all things, and that which all things return to. All beings were therefore reflections of the Divine, and Man was the actualization of the singular Will of God. Numbers proceed from the Monad, and are undivided from each other, and thus do not form a plurality. Creatures participate in Divine Goodness and God reveals himself in Nature. Vision and operation are one in God. His notion of Reason against Authority put him at odds with the Church. His thoughts would not resurface until the later thinkers of the European Enlightenment.

488. Siger of Brabant[34], who Dante put in Paradise along with some other notable Aristotelian thinkers, were usually considered heretics. Lesser-known Franciscan thinkers, like Bonaventure and William of Auvergne, resisted the influence of Aristotelianism. Thinkers like Bonaventure did not make much of

---

[32] Copleston, F. J. (1962). *A History of Philosophy Volume 2 Medieval Philosophy Part 1: Augustine to Bonaventure*. Image Books Pg. 204-211

[33] Copleston, F. J. (1962). *A History of Philosophy Volume 2 Medieval Philosophy Part 1: Augustine to Bonaventure*. Image Books. Pg. 129-157.

[34] Copleston, F. J. (1962). *A History of Philosophy Volume 2 Medieval Philosophy Part II: Albert the Great to Duns Scotus*. Pg. 156-164.

the split between theology and philosophy. The tension in ideas led to the split between Realism and Nominalism. This early split would be the recast as the split between Rationalism and Empiricism, which would finally be synthesized by German Idealism, and the emphasis on the spiritual beliefs of the Occult. The idea was a tension between the Truth that exists outside of us, and the Truth that has a reality of its own. The Franciscan thinker Duns Scotus was the premier representative of Realism. He devised the phrase "Thisness" or "Haeckaiatas"[35]. The view was attacked by Sir William of Ockham who represented the Nominalist tradition, which rejected the relation of Ideas to the world and affirmed creation in time.

489. Franciscan thinkers made a general favoring of the Freedom of Will above Love, superiority of Will to the Intellect and Reason, but also a superiority of Love and Faith above Knowledge. Duns Scotus had felt that the Thomistic doctrine of the Intellect only awaiting the Essence of things suggested that a mind could no longer grasp "Being as Being". This meant that metaphysics could no longer transcend physics, as Religion needs it to do. Since in Thomistic Philosophy, the intellect can only perceive Universals, he saw this type of view as too reductionist. He anticipates Kant. Scotus felt that the Heraclitian doctrine of change in either object or soul would render the world unintelligible, and that a correspondence between the mind and the reality it perceives was essential to knowledge. He attempted to return Metaphysics to the study of "Being as Being", without change or generation being involved. Nominalists attacked the claim and held that the summation of reality was apparent in its physical concomitants, and no such definition as "Being" could be derived from the whole of it. Still, he made a distinction between the Sensitive Animal Soul, and the Rational Human Soul, similar to John Scotus Eriugena and later Spinoza, but also held that these Souls operated in unison. Duns Scotus' views are more Neoplatonic than Aristotelian. Anselm's Ontological Proof that since a greatest conceivable being is available to us in possibility, and such a being would be greater if it existed in Reality, was a popularly used proof in Franciscan views. One of the most sensible declarations in terms of Christian thought seems to be a belief found in Duns Scotus. This is namely the belief repeated earlier, that Love is superior to Knowledge, and resides in the Will. The concept of the Will had a short reign in Christian thought, but was stamped out by Martin Luther and others, who parroted the Pauline belief in predestination.

490. The notion of Sin having its own Reality in the Platonic sense, and man as the happy flaw or "Felix Culpa" of a Necessary Being, was at least an honest interpretation by Aquinas of the Pauline message. Man had no control or choice over his own sinfulness, and the voyeuristic and ascetic mode of contemplative sanctity, and essentially a removal from life was his only recourse.

---

[35] Copleston, F. J. (1962). *A History of Philosophy Volume 2 Medieval Philosophy Part II: Albert the Great to Duns Scotus*. Pg 199-268

Detached from the world and dumb and alone for all of Eternity, he was to imitate God. The emotional reveries of a detached Essence, and a stale contemplative freedom was to remind him only that suffering was salvation. Natural Law gave all Man the necessary powers and determination to seek collective redemption. The notion that a simple confirmation of faith, a yea or nay, could be a salvific aid, and the collective Essence being realized by a single Will, was favored in the West. The notion of equality has battled against the notion of an egalitarian structure which promotes harmony and unanimity.

491. Since the world was separate from Man itself it had to be forever cleansed and dressed in Ritual. Everything possessed an undercurrent of Pagan value systems, and heroic symbolism, not readily associated with Western Christianity but clearly a part of its early development. In "Waning of the Middle Ages" J. Huizinga[36] discusses the effect of these primarily Roman themes on European Culture of the Fifteenth Century. He says that the oscillating mood between the zealotry and cruelty of a fear of hell, but also a "naive joy" that spoke to the childlike simplicity of blind cupidity and sacrificial arms was the natural result of the attitudes of Christian worship known to Europeans at the time, who were apparently much like their pagan forefathers (pg. 27). This was reflected in a hierarchy of symbols expressed in the grandeur of visible signs. In no time was the rule of the symbolic more at play then at the close of the Medieval Age. Furthermore, there was an ascetic quality that mourned happiness as well as misfortune, and a feeling of "ridicule and insipidity" reigned supreme (pg. 35). This all mixed with a lamentation for a return to the grandiloquence of Rome. This was represented in the idolizing of Saints and heroic figures who were thought to transcend humanity and quite often replaced the sacrificial rites of pagan cults.

492. This was the outward asceticism of spiritual materialism; "an asceticism of the blasé, born of disillusion and satiety". It has been suggested as having nothing in common with anything religious (pg. 37). They not only idealized the old but sought the future which represented a promise of escape from the dream of the present (pg. 38). The ideal of the democratic age set loose by mass industrialization and a leveling of cultural myths was suppressed by the aristocratic period of post-medieval Europe. Politeness, manners, and decor were seen as the height of moral virtue (pg. 39). The ethical and aesthetic value of politeness and grandeur has become eponymous with the age. Ceremonies accompanying marriage and funeral gatherings had a pomp and spectacle nowhere matched, and yet Huizinga notes the connections between art and fashion were alive in this age even more than the present (pg. 55). There was a disdain for the smallness of man as art and fashion seemed to be symbolized by what was beyond man (pg. 61). The common man was to till the land, the

---

[36] Huizinga, J. (1949). *The Waning of the Middle Ages* (Anchor Books Edition 1954 ed.). St. Martins Press. We rely on this work for sections 501-508 of this book.

nobles to cultivate virtue and law, and the priests to maintain religious works, each in their own sphere (pg. 59). Both the Hundred Years War, and the Crusades brought forward the ideal of chivalry and martyrdom, where a curious celebration of life brought with it the belief that we all share the same flesh and are equally expendable (pg. 62-63). The link between ascetic and stoic virtues was seized upon. Chivalry and hero worship was said to be of Roman origin.

493. Charles the Bold read stories of Caesar, Hannibal, Alexander, and wanted to emulate them (pg. 71). The grouping of three pagans, three Jews, and three Christians is found in a work called, "Les Voeux du Paon" by Jacques de Languyon (pg. 72). It shows Hector, Caesar, Alexander, Joshua, David, Judas Maccabees, Arthur, Charlemagne, Godfrey of Bouillon. This is a perfect representation of the Western System, which is properly a Pagan, Jewish, and Christian mixture promoted by White Europeans, and founded on the creed of the Pauline Church. The ideals of Rome and Jerusalem were curiously mixed in Christian Europe. The idea was borrowed from a Greek concept of "Kalos Kiagathos" or the Noble and the Good (pg. 77). The Zealot movement of the Jews had most characteristically borrowed the Universal and Religious ideal to serve the nationalistic and militaristic endeavor. Added to this was the dissolving of one's purpose into the coming Kingdom of God or New Jerusalem, which presented a unified goal and fighting cry. The old motif of defending imperiled virginity against an artless dragon perhaps begins here to proliferate, as well as the King Arthur style myths that combined Homeric legend with Pagan tales of the Germanic tribes with stories from the Bible (pg. 79). This was the tale of adventure mixed with blood and romance, but fused with religious and ethnic infusion. Honor, fidelity, and love were of an utmost seriousness. Still when one compares the passion for life back then with the stale and recursive dry humor of today and repetitive seriousness, one cannot but think we barely understand Romance or Honor. Still, there was still less of a sense of individualism in this age which brought with it the ability to experience a deeper affection. The edges of the mind were a veritable cathedral. At the center of town was a carnival instead of a courthouse.

494. While for the most part, the Church was hostile to the grandeur of tournaments and festivals, the pagan fervent of the day and their allusion to military valor created an enticing spectacle even to modern curiosity. The medieval European was paradoxically "outwardly religious and inwardly betrothed", and yet a detached sentiment of the day is what is often complained of as the "Dark Age", but it was considerably more of a peaceful period than now. This is mainly due to the fact Modern Tech has made the destruction of warfare more total and removed the soldiers from direct participation for the sake of their own honor and country. Most war today is led by proxy and most conflicts back then were relatively small engagements. We suspect that the main reason they refer to this period as the Dark Age is because European culture had not spread around and did not rule and control the World Politics scene.

Yet the rituals of Knighthood had a resemblance to heathen initiation rites and repeated ceremonies from pre-Christian times. The invention of bizarre emblems and devices for ritual ordainment has been replaced by us by a rule of experts, but the idea is the same. The Nationalism and religious angst was always pointed toward Jerusalem. One had to use and oppose Roman rule with the salvation of the Jew (pg. 92).

495. There was a focus on National and even Racial pride (pg. 94). The conquest of Jerusalem was at the centerpiece of the heroic and religious plight. Henry V, Philip the Good, and Richard II, as well as the Duke of Burgundy all laid crusades and plans to achieve the same goal (pg. 95). The conquering aspects of love and pride were all in the name of a detached and sublime expense which culminates in the romanticization of death, beauty, danger, and mystery. This was the search for the ineffable and the profound. An anti-human sentiment was alive in the whole display. Man sought to transcend himself. The sacredness of Love became much like the earlier Jewish-Alexandrian deification of Truth. Added to this was the Mystical and Philosophical foreground that brought with it religious apostasy and apocalyptic fears. The combining of love and piety, romance and sacrifice, mixed with the rude sexual culture of the aristocracy, and marriage feasts were known to be accompanied by licentious pleasantries and gross symbolism. This was the origin of the Christian Gothic impulse toward subdued beauty and the sacrifice in order to achieve progress. A mystical pagan expression known as the Roman De La Rose personalizes Love and Shame and employs an imagery similar to pagan hymns. The poem was compiled by Jean De Meun. His supporters like Pierre Col declared the female genitals to be the Sacred Rose of Romance in a fit of blasphemy, and attempted to prove it from the Gospel of Luke (pg. 108-118). The symbols of the Rose and Red Cross were also employed by the Rosicrucian.

496. Thinkers like Jean Gerson had complained that love and piety were mixed with shamelessness (pg. 117). He attacked the Roman De La Rose, where Nature attacked Chastity for its lack of fruitfulness. Mixed with this were the somber images of death and the "the macabre ", which were also imbued with religious sentiments (pg. 144). The materialistic elements of life were mixed with the harsh reality of impermanence. Bodies of Saints like St. Thomas Aquinas were preserved and venerated (pg. 167). Death was seen as another source for a belief in equality; death was seen as the great leveler (pg. 146). The arousal of these sentiments was personified in the Passion of Jesus Christ or the suffering of Jesus. This was also the central motif of Pauline theology, which had gained a strong pre-eminence in the Pagan style rituals of post medieval Europe. This was also the age of indulgences. The purchasing of relics and idols that were put to religious service is extremely telling. This was simply worldliness in otherworldly guise. There were grand displays of humility and philanthropic gestures, with large displays of heroic sacrifice. It brought an air of indigestible irony. Nicolas de Clamanges and Jean Gerson wrote exten-

sive treatises denouncing the veneration of Saints, multiplication of holy days, ceremonies and festivals (pg. 153). The evils and superfluity of these idols and innovations presented God, Jesus, Holy Spirit, Angels, Mary, Saints, and a hundred others.

497. This was an excessive concatenation of divine symbols verging on depravity and sheer decadence. This drive or impulse can be summed up in the reduction of the infinite to the finite. It was an almost blasphemous boldness coupled with a superficial pagan element. The sanctity of labor was so much idealized that poverty no longer was esteemed as a sign of virtue and grace. The treatment of Saints reflected the Pagan and Roman pantheons. On the one side was the miraculous hidden powers of the sacred poets, and on the other a quiet, commonplace, ascetic, and deformed existence (pg. 165). On the one side was a contemplative and detached life, and on the other the chronicles of passion, lust, and limitless sin. The rituals like the Rosary were devised in this time (pg. 199). The world was made a "cathedral of ideas". This was the legacy of Neoplatonic idealism and Pagan sensibility. Huizinga notes that Realism was readily translated into anthropomorphism, gross symbolism, personification of the divine, spiritual materialism, and hierarchic subordination (pg. 203-205). Symbolic and ritualistic gestures were made mechanical, and all symbols were incarnations of the Word in an often pantheistic and materialist bend. Transubstantiation is magical, if only in its emphasis on transformation from within. There was also the political symbolism and religious iconography in the displays of the coat of arms. The Realism thought bubble did not penetrate and probe into the structure and origins of things by unveiling analysis and information, but rather saw its personification in Heaven, where it caused ordinary material objects to become illuminated by the ethereal Essence. Sin was oftentimes more readily personified than Virtue, because Sin could only manifest on the physical plane, while Virtue was immaterial.

498. For as says St. Paul: *Videmus nunc per speculum in aenigmate, tunc autem facie ad faciem,* or "For now we see through a glass darkly; but then face to face." Vengeance was well understood, as was the notion that "the deed judges the man". St. Augustine and St. Thomas Aquinas held a view that all things in the world could be performed by the aid of demons and magic (the view was repeated by Martin Luther and Descartes). Incessant witch burnings and works like Malleus Malefecarum, or "The Hammer for Witches", was a reaction and response to the heretical mood of the day, but also to the view of a generalized evil set loose in happenings of the world (pg. 241). No art and magic was for its own sake, but to bring to the surface hidden realms of experience. This vast array of symbols shows the interpenetration between Mythos and Logos, and Nomos and Telos. While the artistic and communicative symbol making structures pointed to an ethereal stasis, the movement of Natural Law to its eventual summation in Man was seen in the political and ethical framework.

Chapter 19
Man is Born Free
and Everywhere He is in Chains

499. In the mid twelfth century the competing rule of the English against the French had put Richard I, or Richard the Lionheart, as the leader of a new crusade, after Phillip II of France departed. Richard led campaigns against Saladin and died in 1189, but not before leading a third crusade which was primarily financed by prominent Jewish serfs in the risky but innovative world of credit loan finance inadvertently contributing to the economics of Northern Europe and Eastern London, as commerce was seen as another business for the Church to clean their hands with. The Jews of France were expelled by King Philip II, and French and Avignon Jews found safe haven under the reign of Richard I. Scholar of Crusades Dana Cushing puts Jews of Twelfth Century in England as a significant source of funds[37], but notes that they were under the protectorate of the King and treated as legal chattel. As already mentioned however, slavery in the past was not equivalent to even the modern-day prison sentence or concentration camp, but slaves (some slaves) were allowed to own wealth and property. One estate was that of Aaron of Lincoln, whose estate was so large that it had its own separate branch of the treasury. Jurnet of Norwich also contributed to a significant portion of the King's income. In 1290 Jews were expelled from England, and through the 1300's France, Saxony, Hungary, Belgium, Slovakia, and later Austria and Netherlands expelled Jews. This created a religious tension for several centuries where the Jewish people were caught between Christian Europeans and an Islamic Caliphate that had lived past its Golden Age and grew intensely divided. Europe and Islam were rife with internal divisions and external strife. Collusion between Islamli sects and the Templars was a sure sign of religious division. Once again, the religious and political mood of the day was hijacked for the purposes of religious subversion.

500. While the Ismailis represented a blend of Shia Islam and Occultism, the Templars who had contact with them devolved into a religious heresy. The Templars were a military order founded in 1119 in Jerusalem and placed under direct papal authority in 1139 by Pope Innocent II. They had a headquarters at the site referred to as the Temple of Solomon and were set up to protect those making pilgrimage to the Holy Land. In 1307 however, hundreds of Knights Templars were arrested in France for heresy, sodomy, and other abuses. Before

---

[37] Cushing, D. (2011) Richard I and the Jewish "Servi Camarae" as a Funding Source for the Third Crusade.
https://www.academia.edu/983627/Richard_I_and_the_Jewish_Servi_Camarae_as_a_Funding_Source_for_the_Third_Crusade.

this the Templars were known as wealthy bankers. They rewrote passages of the Bible and later went underground, whereby they reemerged as the Rosicrucian Society. Grand Masters Jacques De Molay and Geoffrey de Charnay were burned at the stake in Paris.

501. It is a quite notable fact that a belief in the Natural depravity of the world, the purifying aspects of suffering and sacrifice that were embodied in the Nature of God, and the coming of the Kingdom of God, made hardened warriors. While others welcomed discipline and sacrifice for victory, these welcomed suffering and even death. Templars set out for relics like the Ark of the Covenant, and the Cup of the Last Supper, motivated by a belief in New Covenant theology. God's Kingdom was no longer an ethereal reality, or an ascended palace beyond the confines of the material world, but a real hope that comes to fruition. While the Realist types encouraged an abstinence from the ways of the world in an Imitation of Christ, the distinct push of Nominalism was conferred as the more Antinomian capacity of Christian beliefs, that victory was assured by the fact of God's entrance into history. These types did not believe that it was necessary to go beyond this world for salvation, because God had come into the world and already acted on behalf of humanity to confer grace through suffering and sacrifice.

502. This idea of faith in the future was the crux of dualistic thinking, and also reflected in the split between Essence and Existence. As St. Paul writes in Romans, "For the invisible things of him from the creation of the world are clearly seen". We were to look at the world for the happenings of God, but that these same things were clearly removed from our view. The puzzle presented here in Romans 1:20 is of no assistance. We may see in it the separation of thought from matter, or form from existence. To surpass the world is to change it, and to change it is to master it, and to understand it is to harness one's own Nature and align it to the harmony of Nature, accomplished by a separation of thought from matter, God from Nature, Man from Spirit, and Science from the Sacred. In its simplest form, this is the belief in our separateness from the world. It focuses on the ability to transcend matter, to create the world in our own image, and bring God down to our own level. This is the God that speaks for Man and God himself is tied into the business of being human.

503. Science became a metaphor for God reincarnating in human flesh. Logos was brought down and God was equated with truth and goodness through pressure and change. Symbols were removed from the Sacred, made sacred on their own account, and then placed back in kinship with the Divine. The Jewish and Pagan influence of Paul was obfuscated. Nomos or Divine Law had shifted to Natural or Universal Law, and Telos or purpose was reverted to a faith in the future through the coming of a New Age. On the one end, only a detached and contemplative mood could bring one to the Essence of the Divine, and on the other end, if a man came to truly know God it did not matter

how many sins were committed. All were fallen. One had to be raised to be lowered. All needed to be redeemed. Redemption only came by the Grace of God and not by the works of Man. As Luther said, "No sin will separate us from the lamb, even though we commit fornication and murder a thousand times a day.". He says earlier in the same letter (Let Your Sins Be Strong: A Letter from Luther to Melanchthon Letter no. 99, 1 August 1521),

"If the mercy is true, you must therefore bear the true, not an imaginary sin. God does not save those who are only imaginary sinners. Be a sinner, and let your sins be strong, but let your trust in Christ be stronger, and rejoice in Christ who is the victor over sin, death, and the world. We will commit sins while we are here, for this life is not a place where justice resides."

504. God does not make salvation for fictitious sinners. Be a sinner and sin boldly! The world is not a place of justice and Luther makes no bones about the fact that this is clearly derived from St. Paul. "St. Paul's voice is the voice of divine majesty", he writes. Luther declared that the Epistle of James should be burned in saying faith without works is dead contrary to St. Paul. Just like Paul's message in the early Church the message of Luther was first seen as heretical, and then later accepted as truth. The Reform was coupled with a tiring with the use of abstractions and symbols, into an age of nominalism and humanism. Salvation by faith alone, and never being able to attain absolute certainty came from one's own innate limitations. The fact of God entering into the world to do physical signs and the coming of a new world encouraged a radical empiricism. This sought to replace the belief that Reason was transcendent with the belief in doing work with one's hands and living a quiet life. Luther was raised studying Aristotelian philosophy and signed his correspondence with a Rosicrucian seal. He most famously declared Reason to be a whore. Matter was seen as something with no inherent Essence, but Man's ability to manipulate matter was because of his rule over it. This rule was not determined by Reason, but by the Natural Order imbued by God. This was also reflected in the literalist interpretation of Scripture, as well as the claim that the Scripture speaks plainly enough for every man to understand it. This was a radical individualism as well. Each man had his own responsibility to draw inward to the Scripture and shun away the rest of existence. It was an outward collectivism doubled by an inward resistance and urge toward sacrifice and redemption. Malachi Martin writes, "As we know, some of the chief architects of the Reformation--Martin Luther, Philip Melanchthon, Johannes Reuchlin, Jon Amos Komensky--belonged to occult societies"[38]. Many of them also studied the Kabbalah to obtain the secrets of the Bible (more of these connec-

---

[38] This quote can be found in a book by Malachi Martin entitled, "The Keys of this Blood", published by Simon and Shuster in 1991. It was obtained by a piece entitled, "The Faustian Face of Modern Science" by author Phillip D. Collins whose writing was greatly helpful

tions are mentioned in part II of this book). What is another interesting trend is the development of British Empiricism, that suggested that the mind is like a blank screen. This coincided with the belief in Science, that actions could be perceived as if they occurred in a vacuum. Reality is a hollow projection. French Rationalists made the claim that perceptions were themselves formulated by the internal cognitive framework of the mind as it corresponds with reality.

505. Whether the mind was like a blank screen that projected reality, or like a filtering device which showed us some median between our own thoughts and only what reality suggests, was essentially the debate between British Empiricism and French Rationalism. A final view of German Idealism seemed to portray the whole of reality as a generation of the mind alone. Quite plainly they had borrowed this from Eastern mysticism and the Western occult. In this view reality was inseparable from the activities of mind. In all three the mind and reality were two distinct realms, and experience was the mediator between them. This led to a rise in the Occult and Scientific element, which felt that one could manipulate one's reality by altering how one interfaces with the world through the activity of mind. These ideas can properly be called pre-Modern. The same way that Faith was the bridge between suffering and grace, the mind was the mediator between experience and reality. The manipulation of Natural Law in order to gain a desired end, with the proper incantation, formula, application, or interpretation, could alter reality. By changing one's inner state, one could change how one interfaced with the world, and by changing how one interfaces with the world one could change reality.

506. The negative, dark, female, material, impulse in matter is not Absolute or Necessary. It was the malleable nature hidden by the divine. This was the "prima materia" or the philosopher's stone. It had fallen from being the Absolute, into the realm of the Universal. By becoming Universal it was brought down to the world and spread out in every direction. It was made value-less and abiding through exactness and equality in everything. This was the view of Isaac Newton[39], who is often seen as the greatest scientist who ever lived. Upon his death in 1727 a box of unusual papers was given to his niece, and were later discovered unread, and sold to a public auction. These letters fell into the hands of some notable people, including John Maynard Keynes, who upon reading through the papers declared that Newton was a Judaic Monotheist of the school of Maimonides. Like Jefferson, who appeared around the same time, Newton was probably a Deist, Naturalist, and Unitarian. Jefferson read the Bible and Quran, commented on the flood myth (questioning that it hap-

---

[39] Gotfryd, A. (n.d.). *The Newton You Never Knew*. Chabad of South Brunswick. Retrieved April 26, 2022, from
http://www.southbrunswickchabad.com/page.asp?pageID=%7BEFCC0F2F-5A38-4247-9ADF-D588BFF0E91C%7D&displayAll=1.

pened as well), and famously presented a version of the Bible without miracles. Newton and Locke studied the Kabbalah through secondary sources and corresponded on the subject. In his correspondence with the political philosopher, and proto-capitalist John Locke, he anticipated the apocalypse, and supported and expounded on many traditions of Jewish Messianism. He meant to uphold the cosmology of Aristotle and Maimonides. These thinkers appeared to have accepted the Seven Noahide Laws, and the Mishnah Torah as the basis of civilization and thought. Newton showed concerns over knowing the exact measurements of the Temple of Solomon and considered the reconstruction of "the third temple". He believed that Egyptians had learned the secrets of the Temple of Solomon, and used it to construct the Giza Plateau, taught to them by Hiram the Phoenician. In his Chronology he states, "The Greek antiquities are full of poetical fictions, because the Greeks wrote nothing in prose before the conquest of Asia by Cyrus the Persian". He also linked the Christian belief in the Trinity to a belief in Emanation. Newton was a practitioner of Alchemy and Magic, just like Martin Luther. He felt that sexual energy had to be preserved for creative ends, and complained that John Locke had embroiled him with women and defiled his spirit. He theorized of Matter as God, as a process of drawing back known as "Tzim Tzum" in Kabbalah. The concept is seen in the Lurianic Kabbalah, whose symbol is an eagle representing Maimonides, and a Lion representing Isaac Luria.

507. Around the same time as the life of Newton, the Cromwell Protectorate in England was making key reforms in a move toward acceptance of Jews[40]. During the height of the Protestant struggle, certain Protestant sects held a doctrinal belief that salvation (conversion) of the Jews was necessary for the return of Christ, who they felt would eventually reign on Earth as God. Manasseh Ben Israel, who was born in Lisbon and settled in Amsterdam, promoted a belief that Jewish spread around the world and operation in every country was necessary for the return of the Jewish Messiah. He established communities of Jews in England by cultivating key relationships with those in power. Cromwell attacked the Cathedrals but petitioned to help the building of Synagogues. He created significant advances in Anglo-Jewish ties, which would interminably foster the beliefs of British Israelism, but also fostered the spirit of religious toleration that was necessary for secular reform that came later. The Protestant Reformation brought both inward and outward divisiveness. Not only had it questioned the absolute authority of the Church, but John Wycliffe and the Hussites had suggested a sort of anti-clericalism, which not only led to the formation of Protestantism, but also created political instability of the pow-

---

[40] *Cromwell and the Jews*. (n.d.). Oliver Cromwell Association. Retrieved April 26, 2022, from https://www.olivercromwell.org/jews.htm. This article from The Cromwell Association discusses the history of the expelling and readmission of the Jews to England orchestrated by Oliver Cromwell and Manasseh Ben Israel when the Cromwell Protectorate made new laws concerning religious toleration and free trade which culminated in a shift toward Protestantism in England around 1655.

276 of the Church. No longer was the Church only to

er sought through an appeal to the Church. No longer was the Church only to manage its own affairs, but faith was set free. Faith was made neither political, or on the basis of Church authority. It was put in the domain of the individual.

508. Calvin's support for the separation of Church and State, as well as his defense of usury[41], was essential in the shift. This came with a belief that each man should be able to determine the cause of his own salvation, and that the course was the same with each man, for each man had but only a positive affirmation to give. This was an inner quest apart from institutions, who were a "necessary evil"[42] that man had to overcome by attaining to "the spirit of the laws"[43], rather than the letter of the law. The concept of what it means to be a citizen was set forth by Paul, who declares himself an exemplary Roman citizen, while opposing the State. He is a vessel of improvement within the State, which embodies the true Essence of the State in being the true servant of God. Paradoxically, the so-called reform added new rituals and themes from heterodox sects and Kabbalistic interpretations, that it was said to have purged from Church practice. The Church had its own list of trials and issues, especially through the Jesuit promotion of the Liberal Arts, but the Protestants cannot be seen as a suitable replacement. Proto-Lutheran doctrines can be found in various medieval Gnostic sects, and Luther himself recommended the Hermetic Science of Alchemy. In his sayings labeled "Table Talk", he proclaims "The science of Alchemy, I like very well, and indeed, 'tis philosophy of the ancients". He says what he likes most about Alchemy is the promotion of eternal life, which it expounds through "secret signification". He sought an explanation of the secrets of the Bible by Ruechlin's work on Kabbalistic Science, and marveled at how the tetragram could be a symbol for the trinity.

509. Nearly all of the philosophers of the European Enlightenment were under the intoxication of Lutheran values. Their personal salvation, and cries for reform, and return to the classical period, had to do with the "see it for yourself" mentality of Paul and Luther. First God became human, then humanity became God, and to kill such a God meant the death of humanity. The rise of liberalism can be connected to the teachings of Paul. Those who look for it in the Scientific Revolution are constantly deluded. Enlightenment thinkers capital-

---

[41] Littlejohn, B. (2010, October 20). *John Calvin–Friend of Usury?* |. Brad Littlejohn. Retrieved April 26, 2022, from https://bradlittlejohn.com/2010/10/20/20101020john-calvin-friend-of-usury-html/
[42] The concept that government was a minimal but necessary evil was first discussed by Thomas Paine in the "Common Sense" as far as we are aware. We think the terminology is synonymous with Paul's view of Sin.
[43] The term "the spirit of the laws" is the title of a work by Montesquieu that argues for the separation of powers and roles in government that had an influence on Jefferson and Madison when they devised the rules for civil government in the U.S. We feel that the terminology of Spirit and Law has a lot to do with Paulinism.

ized on the heretical mood of the day in order to advance thoughts that were used for religious subversion and political propagandizing.

510. The foremost was Thomas Hobbes, who was a Philosopher and Scientist, Naturalist and Hedonist. He devised the commonwealth, and rule by consent for the purpose of commerce. He formulated the concept as a "covenant of every man with every man", as opposed to the "bellum omnium contra omnes" or "the war of all against all". He then writes, "the generation that great Leviathan or rather, to speak more reverently, of that mortal God to which we owe, under the immortal God, our peace and defense". His use of the term Leviathan, "mortal God, and "Artificial Man" shows an almost alchemical and occult understanding. He fashioned as the Final Cause or end for Man the birth of an "Artificial Man"[44] (akin to the Golem of Kabbalistic lore), who was to be likened to an immortal God, represented by the State, the machine that speaks for Man on behalf of God. This was clearly the construction of a perfect idol. He wrote one book on Monarchy called the Leviathan, and another on the parliamentary state called the Behemoth. These were the two beasts, one of the sea, and one of the land, that encircled the throne of God, and would be released at the coming of a New Age. The "Beast of the Land" was the landed military force and organized bureaucratic wing which enforced agriculture and labor. The "Beast of the Sea" was the maritime trade that empowered the wealth of the nation through the control of major sea routes and ports. Hobbes used religious symbology to secular ends, which is a trend employed since the outset of Classical Liberalism, and seen in the liberals of today.

511. Following the same line of British Empiricism was John Locke, who fashioned the Democratic and Parliamentary State on the basis of Natural Law and Civil Rights. Like Hobbes, Locke agreed that Nature hid her gifts, and to avail Nature of her gifts, Man would have to use the concerted effort of his own Labor, which maximizes the barely usable products of Nature. This was the Alchemical and Gnostic belief that Nature was a curse, but could be trans-

---

[44] Hobbes, T. (1982). *Leviathan (Penguin Classics)* (C. B. Macpherson, Ed.). Penguin Books Limited. On Pg. 227 in Chapter 17 labeled "Of the Causes, Generation, and Definition of a Common-Wealth", Hobbes states, "This is more than Consent, or Concord; it is a reall Unitie of them all, in one and the same Person, made by Covenant of every man with every man, in such manner, as if every man should say to every man, I Authorize and give up my Right of Governing myself...This done, the Multitude so united in one Person, is called a Common-Wealth, in latine Civitas. This is the Generation of that great Leviathan, or rather (to speake more reverently) of that Mortall God, to which wee owe under the Immortall God, our peace and defence". The terminology employed here such as united in one as all members of one body, Covenant, Leviathan from the Book of Revalations, and finally the term "Moral God" all seem to show that Hobbes is hiding behind Christian and Paulinist terminology as a wolf in sheep's clothing. We do however believe Hobbes was on the right side of history for opposing the Cromwell regime.

formed by the use of Reason, whereby Man would form an understanding of his Godly duty. Locke writes in the Second Treatise of his "Two Treatises of Government" in Section 42, "And that Prince, who shall be so wise and god-like, as by established laws of liberty to secure protection and encouragement of the honest industry of mankind…"[45]. Once again the notion of becoming god-like is employed. Locke changed the idea that God gave Adam "private dominion" to the notion that God had imbued Adam with the right of "private property", and secured only what is his by his Labor and skill. This was a radical reinterpretation of the Bible that reversed the notion of Patriarchy into a narrative of transforming Nature into profit. Each man had to claim what was his and was ordered by God to do so. Locke gave recommendations for the development of the slave plantations[46], and the modern banking system, despite his objections to slavery often mentioned. Locke's ideas were fundamental in devising the Secular State. Another of the first Enlightenment thinkers, and often regarded as the father of Modern Philosophy, was Descartes.

512. Much is written about the subject of Cartesian philosophy. For our inquiry it is important to note that Descartes gave a thought experiment where he pretended that reality could be a programmed deception of an evil demon. This was the characteristic view of the Gnostics. His view of radical skepticism, and divine inwardness was based on Avicennian dualism. He posited the phrase "I think therefore I am" paralleling Avicenna's hanging man. He put thought and matter into two separate categories. He divorced the Laws of Reason and Nature from that of ordinary experience. Descartes believed that animals had no intelligence, and performed crude experiments on live specimens. In Henri Gaston Gouhier's "The First Thoughts of Descartes", it talks of Descartes connections with members of the Rosicrucian[47]. Dr. Nicolaes Wassenaar's "His-

---

[45] Second Treatise of Government by John Locke , Chapter 5, Paragraph 42, lines 20-30 found in an old edition of the Cambridge Texts version edited by Peter Laslett in the "Student Edition" which dates back to 1988. Citations were difficult to find for this old edition especially in the condition that mine is in.

[46] Proyect, L. (2018, August 24). Slavery and the Origins of Capitalism - Counter-Punch.org. *Counterpunch*. https://www.counterpunch.org/2018/08/24/slavery-and-the-origins-of-capitalism/

[47] The following writings were used for the biographical information relating to Descartes, Leibniz, and Spinoza in relation to their involvement in the Rosicrucian Fraternity seemingly taken from the book "Awakened Attitude" by Gary L. Stewart: 1. Stewart, G. L. (n.d.). *Determining Rosicrucian Affiliation René Des-Cartes (1596 – 1650)*. Confraternity of the Rose Cross. Retrieved April 26, 2022, from https://www.crcsite.org/rosicrucian-library/contemporary-writings/rene-des-cartes/ 2. Stewart, G. L. (n.d.). *Benedict Spinoza - Philosopher, Mystic, Rosicrucian*. Confraternity of the Rose Cross. Retrieved April 26, 2022, from https://www.crcsite.org/rosicrucian-library/contemporary-writings/benedict-spinoza/. These writings are used for the next four sections where biographical information about the three authors mentioned above is found. Since all three are premier philosophers of the European Enlightenment their involvement with the occult and intellectual elite are

torisch Verhaal", claims that Descartes was a Rosicrucian. His son Jacob Wassenaar was a known member of the underground sect which was said to guard alchemical secrets. French Historian Charles Adam seemed to believe that Descartes was a Rosicrucian for his associations with names like Cornelius van Hooghelande who published works on Alchemy, Isaac Beekman, and Johann Faulhaber, who had similar connections. He also made contact with the famous Rosicrucian Jan Batista van Helmont, who tried to reconcile mystical and naturalist views.

513. The Philosopher Leibniz was a friend of Rosicrucian Franciscus Mercurius van Helmont, the son of Jan Batista. Jan Amos Comenius, a Czech theologian and mystic was a well-known friend of Descartes, as were members of the Hartlib Circle that later formed the British Royal Society. Descartes Rosicrucian association is also mentioned in a book by Haldane entitled "Life and Times of Descartes", and a book by Baillet which is an early biography. Queen Christina of Sweden, who was Descartes benefactor, was a supporter of the false Jewish Messiah Sabbatai Zevi and danced in the streets of Amsterdam in support. The memoirs of Pierre Daniel Huet suggest similar connections. There is also a strange claim found there about Descartes faking his own death to continue the study of religious mysteries.

514. One of the greatest philosophers to ever live by several accounts was Benedict Spinoza (born 1632). Born to Portugese Jewish parents, he took on a pantheistic framework which rejected Cartesian philosophy. He made the claim that mind and body were not separate but were co-extensive with different modes of expression. He employed a modal ontology similar to Avicenna. Spinoza's philosophy was based on Euclidean geometry. Spinoza viewed Nature as the clearest expression of God. The concept of a Universal Mind or Godhead was already contained within Jewish Mysticism. The phrase "espinosa" meaning "a rose with sharp thorns" is used to explain away his use of a Rosicrucian seal, which was similar to Martin Luther's. It has been noted that the Ethics of Spinoza are in line with several Hermetic teachings. Spinoza aligned the scientific and rational with the mystical and pantheistic. The belief in God as an impersonal Essence, whose "Essence involves Existence", was a term used from Descartes to Leibniz, Leibniz to Spinoza. The concepts of Universal Mind, and God as a Necessary Being whose "Essence involves Existence", was the language of Islamic Apostates like Avicenna. Descartes writes in his Third Meditation, "if it had got its existence from itself, it is evident from what has been said, that it is itself God, because having the power of existing in and of itself, it unquestionably also has the power of actually possessing all the perfections of which it has in itself an idea". In Proposition 11 of his Ethics, Spinoza makes the claim that God's Essence necessarily involves

---

quite interesting especially when one is made to suppose their genius thoughts rose up in a vacuum of isolation.

Existence. Liebniz repeats the notion in Section 44 of his Monadology. These were not new concepts, but were clearly derived from the views of Jewish and Islamic apostasy, which had found a home in the Western Occult and Pagan philosophy. These were not the champions of secularism smashing the idols of religion, but were the manufacturers of idols themselves, using religious subversion to instill the revaluation of values first achieved by Paul.

515. Heinrich Khunrath, who used a hieroglyphic monad designed by John Dee, is mentioned in Spinoza's Theological and Political Treatise. This work, among his other statements, would place him at odds with the Amsterdam Jewish community, which was protected by Protestants. Spinoza was excommunicated from the Jews, who ironically had claimed that his philosophy was a proof of the God of the Old Testament, similar to Avicenna. A personal acquaintance of Spinoza was Philosopher Wilhelm Gottfried Leibniz, who was a Secretary for a Rosicrucian Lodge. Spinoza commented to Jarig Jellis about the alchemical transformation of a Dr. Heluitius. His friend Jan De Witt was tutored by Isaac Beekman. Their philosophy can be seen as a "personal revelation" attested to by adherents of these sects. Many who belonged to these sects but held high profile positions would take care to hide their own connections.

516. The prominent Philosopher Rousseau who challenged the resignation of those who waited the progress of civilization to unfold[48], and those who used grace as a barrier between themselves and the world, was treated everywhere as a rebel, who would inspire the French revolution. While supporting the Pauline and Masonic notion of "collective will", he did well by challenging the likes of Diderot, Voltaire, and Hume who attacked him in the press and forged political alliances with aristocrats who would attempt to malign Rousseau's work. Rousseau might be known to us as the greatest single critic and challenge to Western thought emerging from within its ranks other than Nietzsche. He seems to be the starting point for what might be called Romanticism and Existentialism. Amidst the Enlightenment fervor, his philosophy was a challenge to civilization itself. Rousseau placed Feeling above Thought in a way which had a potent aftereffect. Rousseau saw Man as once in reverence of Divine personalities in Nature. At the first stage of Man's development, Nature was peopled with divinities. Nature was the playground of the gods, but soon he would reject the freedom of the gods and attempt to confine them to temples. Man put so much care into the management of his temples that he kicked out the gods, and made himself into a god. This was the devolution of Man's spiritual sensibility. Rousseau wished for a return to the pastoral life of small villages, away from the mannerisms and laws of polite society and the busi-

---

[48] Durant, W. (1967). *Rousseau and Revolution* (Book Club Edition ed.). Simon and Schuster. From Sections 516-526 we make constant reference to the material in this part of Will Durant's series entitled "The Story of Civilization".

ness of the cities. He wanted the simple routines and pious life that was the source of the sweetest sentiments of mankind found in hut society.

517. He did not see the modernity of city life and schools and commerce as having given rights to the poor and took on poverty himself. Condemned by Aristocrats, fellow Philosophers, and the Church, Rousseau seemed to challenge the direction of Western thought. According to Will Durant, this was the portrait of a true philosopher, obsessed with Women and Nature, disconnected and uncomfortable from the society of educated men, extolling nature, and defending the poor. Rousseau rejected the Baconian creed of Knowledge as power, and instead chose to praise the utter simplicity of virtue and calm strength of passion that came from military valor. He held the belief that the vanity of civilization could be cured when mixed with the sentiments of pity, and a love of one's own, brought about by reflections on nature. While he did not appeal to the religious orders, he recommended the solemnity of religious practice. He rejected both Original Sin, and the Lockean Blank Slate necessary for Empiricism. He exalted feelings and morality above Reason. He proclaimed that Man was born good, not born free. Man's freedom was natural, but Man had fostered the tools of his own enslavement. While Hobbes felt that Man was born evil because of his propensity to harm others, Rousseau imagined a "solitary man" who relied on no one, as Nature had afforded him to have the capacity to live on his own. Among the values of Enlightenment thought that Rousseau railed against were vanity, licentiousness, mannerisms, anthropomorphism, and a sudden apathy for the plight of the poor. He praised and exalted the noble savage, but disdained the educated fools, and civilized barbarians that were set loose in polite society. Still, Rousseau's only hope was to use this knowledge to improve his own people, never venturing far and honoring his native birth in Geneva. He showed an indelible pride for his native countrymen.

518. He lamented the trend that the use of Scientific Totalitarianism, Rational Absolutism, harsh Empiricism, and anthropomorphic spirituality would produce calculating minds, that disregarded the relevant and inescapable pangs of integrity and faithfulness which he felt were more important than liberty and law. He chose the simple life of the village and hut society at the beginning stages of agricultural civilization to be far superior to the corruption of the cities. However, he felt that a sudden return to nature would cause social and political upheaval. We must remember that this was before the rapid growth of technology seen after the industrial revolution. Undoubtedly, if Rousseau were alive today his critique might be several times more harsh, considering the rule of experts and compartmentalization of knowledge seen in our Modern Age. Still, it is shocking to see a voice so vigorously opposed to the now accepted standards of progress emerging from Enlightenment Europe. He felt that in his own age polite society was filled with malicious gossip and frail vanity. He hated religious vanity as well, and so supported a belief that religion was best

expressed in personal terms. He exalted Geneva above Paris. As Hobbes put forward the first physicalist and proto-Darwinian accounts, Rousseau was like an amateur psychologist and sociologist, and he was undoubtedly the world's first anthropologist. He saw aristocratic society steeped in jealousy, fraud, hypocrisy, envy, suspicions, fear, and urbanity. These countered the simpler notions of friendship, integrity, and esteem among one's fellow countrymen.

519. He noticed that the great civilizations of the past like Egypt and Greece were at their cultural climax, and as a result grew soft. Culture is not a friend of Virtue, Rousseau supposed. Rome conquered only when it was a band of peasants and soldiers and having gained wealth and knowledge it soon fell into the decadent phase of Epicurean indulgence. In the Discourse, in a footnote, he offers praise of the Caliph Umar, who burned the library of Alexandria (what was left of it after it was first torched by Caesar), on grounds that if the library contained anything other than what was in their own traditions and Holy book then it was superfluous, and if it exceeded those than it was unnecessary. He foresaw that cultural relativism, and societal disintegration lay in the wake of the neglect of one's own traditions. Philosophy, Rousseau complained, had a similar disintegrating effect, when it doubts Religion, Country, Virtue, Reality, and even Truth. He saw the Stately systems of Hobbes and Spinoza to have had a pernicious influence. He felt that their aberrations would have been left to burn and would be purified by time and corrected if it were not for the invention of the printing press. He praised the savages of America and saw so-called Modern Man as nothing more than a happy slave.

520. Rousseau felt that Nature dutifully hid her gifts from Man for protection. He saw this as the same instinct as parents have when they hide weapons from their children. He said, "Learning without Virtue is a snare". Are the conveniences delivered to us by technology worth the indignity, and smells, and noises of industrialized life? Progress was a bitter pill, and a lack of feeling and sincerity was a symptom of the philosophical and scientific age. Rousseau's Discourses were continually attacked by the intellectual elites of his day. Rousseau claimed that the antiquity of laws is what gave them security within society, and not people inventing their own laws by use of force to conquer others. Innovation was seen by him as a source of evil. He saw natural and biological equality as nonexistent, but socially derived inequality as rampant. He saw that man was born good, but was made bad by social institutions. There is little regard for any Pauline notion of inherent evil within Man in his philosophy. Rousseau envisioned the replacement of plain reason for bold action. A solitary and simple life away from reflection, which had made man a "depraved animal", and formed the infirmity of modern man, was especially seen when he was compared to the indigenous populations. As Nietzsche once wrote, "Man is the beast with red cheeks". Pre-social man was individually sovereign, as now only States are in relation to each other today. The only "natural" organization is that of the family, or the small community.

521. Property brought with it the destruction of the family, and the beginning of vanity, pride, and enmity. The first man who enclosed a piece of land and said that this is mine was a heedless charlatan. This man was either a trickster or dullard but is regarded as the father of civilization. Had he not understood that the fruits of the Earth belong to no one? Crime, slavery, serfdom have made competition and inequality among men. Science, and the State did no more than to add to this disintegration and masqueraded as progress. Rousseau saw a natural simplicity, sincerity in love and practice, and sympathy for one's fellow man as the only solution. He sought this out to embody the true Christian Ethic. Voltaire attacked the Discourses, claiming it was an attack on the human race, and an intelligent attempt to persuade man to behave like beasts. Apparently, they idealized the handicrafts of the modern age more than an honest rendition of what truly separates a man from the beasts, which as Rousseau keenly observed was not in his power to subdue nature and use it for the progress of his own ends, but in a subtle and strange power to confer meaning and express feelings through love of one's own. But Diderot also attacked Rousseau, both on a personal basis, and on his views on society. Diderot wrote, "the good man lives in society; only the bad man lives alone". Rousseau blamed his former friends for trying to control him. While Voltaire and Diderot teamed up to assault Rousseau, he became a recluse and went into a depression.

522. Voltaire and Diderot painted a picture of an indifferent nature and expressed pessimism about Man's inner nature in their poems and writings. Rousseau accused Voltaire of equating God with the Devil, and claiming God was indifferent to human suffering. Rousseau seems to have rightly equated their beliefs to heretical beliefs mentioned earlier. Rousseau was also attacked by the Church for having attacked the notion of Original Sin and the conception of the Trinity, following a more Unitarian approach. He had changed his religious views several times throughout his life. He said the Clergymen should do more to protest against the filth of the theatres. He argued that the theatres and cities were places of religious deterioration where criminality was romanticized and licentiousness was promoted. Festivals for family gatherings, and wholesome entertainment and venues for public education was what Rousseau recommended instead. He invented the concept of public schools, along with Thomas Jefferson. Rousseau accused Voltaire of attempting to malign his personal relationships and publishing unauthorized material of his. He wrote letters denouncing him and had similar experiences with Diderot and Hume. They labeled him a cynic and a madman, while he accused them of being dishonest.

523. He fashioned the education of a child in "Emile", moving from a happy marriage in an agricultural estate to the tutelage of a moral teacher. He felt that children should be trained in morals before reason, and felt that a healthy and robust disposition should be sought instead of a docile nature. Thinkers like

Kant were avid readers of Rousseau and found his tendency to downplay the scope of Reason to be a natural aid to his own philosophy. He disagreed with the radical empiricism of Hume who rejected the notion of absolute truth. Rousseau kept truth, but put virtue before truth. Rousseau also challenged the view that the Democratic State was Man's ideal configuration and questioned whether true Democracy could exist in anything other than a society of saints. He said that Democracy required the average citizen to be constantly involved in public affairs. It seemed to him that the idea could only be worked out in small groups. His view that luxury leads to inequality, corrupting the rich by possession and the poor by envy, is the belief of the Gospels found in many sayings of Jesus.

524. He complained that Democracy was only free for the members of Parliament, who made the people temporarily free during elections and slaves during their time in office. He believed in a more direct democracy, where the people would have the right at all times to replace elected officials by a general referendum. In Rousseau's political system property was maintained by the State. Although a radical view, considering that neither Islamic nor Christian societies put limitations on wealth (except for the Slaves in European society), it was certainly not a new idea, as the same thing is recommended by Plato in his "Republic". Rousseau's view was based more on the view of Christian charity than a consolidation of power. Shades of Thomas A Kempis "Imitation of Christ", which he was known to read avidly are seen in his work. Still, he rejected organized religion. The spirit of Rousseau's work is seen in the Gospel verse "For what does it profit a man to gain the world, and lose his soul?" (Mark 8:36). Whereas he felt that the Church had sold out to the ways of the world, he supported the development of a Stately religion, akin to Islam in his "Emile". He considered that the dictates of Christian teachings often lean toward becoming internationalistic, pacifistic, other worldly, and without a Nation. His own deliberation was a combination of a Calvinist State and the Republic of Sparta. He felt that even the exile of Anaxagoras and the poisoning of Socrates affirms that a strong Civil Constitution comes with Stately Religion, where the political and divine purpose of a society were not separated. Turning against the Church he affirmed Christian ethics, and also criticized the State. He said that Man was liberal in his youth, and conservative in his old age. He said, "Man is born free and everywhere he is in chains".

525. Sociability, self-control, and Happiness that was only brought through the virtues of friendship and courage, were the true purpose of man, and he found his highest sensibilities and greatest honor in serving his fellow man. Rousseau's work "Emile" found mothers as the highest task of civilization. His summation that motherhood was the cornerstone of sanity, health, and moral order is an indelible and unadulterated truth. The charms of home for Rousseau were the best medicine against vice and dishonor. While cities breed immorality and every kind of vice, they are not as conducive to family as the country-

side. He said that meat eaters are more cruel than other men. A man should not be afraid of the cold, eat only simple foods, and have a stoic constitution. The first impulses of Nature are always right for Rousseau. He rejects Locke's advice to rear children with reason and says that mental education should be delayed as long as possible. Science adds to our pride, but reflection in nature makes a child more just. He recommended the reading of Robinson Crusoe, which was based on the work of Islamic Philosopher Ibn Tufail called "Hayy Ibn Yaqzan" mentioned earlier. While religion and philosophy were to be kept away from the child so he could discover his own innate tendencies, Rousseau felt that atheism was more dangerous than religious fanaticism, as Locke did. He said that the truth of immediate experience is a truth most readily available to our senses, but one that no philosopher has appropriately addressed. He suggested that the truths most readily perceived but beyond understanding should be the one's for philosophical study. He complained that atheistic philosophy was a mechanistic toil ending in eternal darkness and without hope. Rousseau held the belief that all men should return to the religion and traditions of their forefathers and was sort of a proto-traditionalist and seemed to have inspired thinkers like Rene Guenon and others. He distrusted the spiritual prescriptions of the thinkers of the Enlightenment. This was a view of promoting religious tolerance quite different from Locke's. Rousseau's Social Contract led to him being attacked by an angry crowd in his home and having to flee.

526. He blamed the harsh criticisms of Voltaire, who had accused Rousseau of attempting to overthrow the State. Will Durant, during his biographical rendition of Rousseau's work marks the quarrel between Rousseau and Voltaire as a blemish on the Enlightenment and considered some of Voltaire's attacks to be disgraceful. Rousseau apparently told James Boswell that the Anglican Church did not follow the Gospel, and that St. Paul would have been a good Anglican clergyman. The views of men like Voltaire and Diderot were decidedly British, especially in their support for Empiricism and Parliamentary governance. Another Enlightenment thinker that Rousseau butted heads with was Hume. The Philosopher David Hume had invited Rousseau to England to escape from vicious attacks. He felt that while his stay in England Hume had tampered with his mail, and reported tales to the press, whose attacks Rousseau noticed were always perpetrated by Hume's friends and acquaintances. He suspected that Hume was involved in a hoax where a letter addressed to Rousseau written by the King of Prussia was fabricated. He found that attacks in the press included information that only Hume could have known.

527. It was his Social Contract[49] that was both hated and loved for its tenacity, but also its supposed irreverence. What was so dangerous in it that had to be so

---

[49] Rousseau, J. J. (1978). *On the Social Contract: With Geneva Manuscript and Political Economy* (R. D. Masters, Ed.; J. R. Masters, Trans.). Bedford/St. Martin's. Pg. 126-131. For the next two sections we cite the following pages of the translation of Rous-

vigorously opposed? Not surprisingly, therein we find some views to support our own takes on history that are now widely rejected by the scholarly community. Rousseau says, 'The Romans, having spread their cult and their gods along with their Empire, and having themselves adopted the gods of the vanquished by granting legal status in the city to them all, the people of that Empire gradually come to have multitudes of Gods and cults". He writes, "Now since this new idea of an otherworldly kingdom could never be understood by the pagans, they always regarded the Christians as true rebels, who beneath a hypocritical submissiveness, were only awaiting the moment to become independent and the masters, and to usurp adroitly the authority they pretended to respect out of weakness". This was the true cause of their persecutions besides being misunderstood. He ends the statements by saying, "what the pagans fear happened". Even under a visible leader the Christian system became "the most violent despotism in this world". He said that split comes in the form of a divisiveness between master and priest.

528. This puts the sacred cult apart from the sovereign power. He writes, "Muhammad had very sound views; he tied his political system together well, as long as the form of this government subsisted under his successors the caliphs, the government was completely unified, and good for that reason. But when the Arabs became prosperous, lettered, polished, soft, and weak, they were subjugated by barbarians (Mongols). The division between the two powers began again. Although it is less apparent among the Mohammedans than among the Christians". He says that "a State has never been founded without religion serving as a base, and to the latter the Christian law is fundamentally more harmful than useful to the strong constitution of the State". He made it pretty clear that the reason for this was the separation of the worldly and otherworldly duties, and that the concept of natural or divine right of salvation theology presents a grave obstacle to developing an engaged citizen. Christianity however was a "purely internal cult". Both the religion of Buddhists and Christians found its sovereignty in supernatural affairs and looked down on the affairs of the world. "Everything that destroys social unity is worthless" he declares. The divinity of empty ceremonials away from public affairs, must necessarily create an exclusivity and intolerance. Although deeply sympathetic to some of its aims, he pointed out that the Christian teachings left no way of

---

seau's work Social Contract. The passages can be found in Book 4 Chapter 7 in the book Social Contract which had Rousseau incur much infamy rather than fame. The passages are part of a broad discussion within the piece on religion where he is highly critical of Christianity and its effect on the notion of the separation of Church and State through the worldly and otherworldly, but one should also note that we find the deistic conceptions of Rousseau about a religion based on the "collective will" to be a non-starter as a plot for religious reform. Rousseau further makes the connection before Nietzsche that Christianity had a subversive nature that allowed it to usurp Roman power by spreading a sort of anarchistic element which Roman writers of the era all seem to have pointed out that Christians were nominally anarchists for rejecting worldly power.

achieving that end. We can now start to see why some of his views were considered radical, as he clearly started to see and condemn some of the views of Paul. He writes in another passage:

> "There remains a religion of man, or, Christianity-not that of today, but that of the Gospel, which is totally different from it. Through this saintly, sublime, true religion, men-children of the same God-all acknowledge one another as brothers, and the society that unites them is not even dissolved by death. But this religion, having no particular relation to the body politic leaves laws with only their intrinsic force; without adding any other force to them; and because of this, one of the great bonds of particular societies remains without effect. Even worse, far from attaching the citizens' hearts to the State, it detaches them from it as from all worldly things. I know of nothing more contrary to the social spirit.".

529. Some of these lines anticipate the work of Nietzsche. This is echoed in Rousseau's stern proclamation, "a society of the Christians would no longer be a society of men". Furthermore, he complained that Christian teachings could only be spiritual dictates that do little more than to support the status quo. "If the State is flourishing, he barely dares to enjoy the public felicity for fear of becoming proud of his country's glory. If the State declines, he blesses the hand of God that weighs heavily on his people". He seemingly rejects the Christian doctrine in regard to the State for not supporting military valor, and turning into a defense for spiritual materialism and the pomp of ritual, rather than real justice in the world. He deals with the views of Paul rather harshly when he declares, "whoever dares say there is no salvation outside of the Church should be chased out". Farbeit for Christ to not judge harshly the institutions of men, because his ethic was supposed to render these institutions utterly useless by creating an ethic that surpasses all forms of resentment and retribution, or at least this is how it functioned.

Chapter 20
Man is the Measure of All Things /
Man Himself must be Overcome

530. Rousseau's ideas were replaced with the crude anthropocentrism of the Industrial Age. Kant is often regarded as a renewal of the Western Philosophy and was regarded as a student of Rousseau. Many ideas that are considered "Modern" originate from his writings. He drew certain rather narrow conclusions from some of Rousseau's ideas. Kant created a sort of spatial dualism between perceptions and ideas (conceptions) that was mended by the phenomenology of Hegel. Kant and Goethe would take the more mystical interpretations of Rousseau's ideas and create a further split between Reason and Morality. A shift from theoretical reason apart from religion and putting faith only in the domain of the Universal was not a new concept. The starry sky above and the moral law within, left our inner world unable to stretch to the cosmic realm. So, what was it based on? Hegel put the two in a dialectical relationship, attempting to find a middle ground between facts and values, and virtues and morals. Emphasis was placed on Man's perceptions, instead of his thoughts. So, the epistemic mood shifted from reflection and contemplation to observation and analysis, and the sly detachment of the observational mode, which is voyeuristic and objective, had its reign. In the ways of Paul, one had to see it to believe it. All was reduced to convention, and Mind had no substance and was devoid of content. This is the true legacy of empiricism, which was first seen when the Truth was removed from reality and placed in an ethereal realm by Plato, brought back into reality but exclusively in the Christian Neoplatonists, made superior to contingent reality by Islamic Science, made separate from religious truth by scholastic thinkers, and finally made superior to faith in enlightenment thought. Since the Truth became Universal and continually subject to change and evolution, it left no place for either Mind or God. The Truth fell from being Absolute or contained within itself to becoming Universal or Ubiquitous and spread out in every direction.

531. Pascal had already declared that the heart has reasons which even Reason cannot comprehend. When Kant read Emile, he apparently became so involved with the work, and visibly shaken, that he missed his daily walk. He attempted to declare the inner world of morality as differentiated from the world of Reason. This separation of truth from the good was based on the collective hallucination of Universality. Universality was just a placid substitute for the utilitarian and democratic notions, originally derived from Paul's view of inclusivity. Besides placing the Good outside of Reason, which was done in order to purify and sanctify it, it ultimately took morality out of the scope of the aver-

age person, and made it a collective ordeal. The Good was left in the domain of the essential, and foundational.

532. The apparent schizophrenia of this compromise has caused its failure. Modern man is conflicted on whether he should act on behalf of the common or universal goal, or abstain from the general course and consult reason. The split between theory and application, observation and action, reality and truth, goodness and reason is Kant's legacy. His delusions of world peace and of an eventual peace between all Mankind are dangerously misplaced to say the least. While they paid homage to Rousseau, Rousseau claimed that the thinking man was a depraved animal and rejected progress, while Kant and Hegel considered Thought the proper end of Man, and for Hegel further deified progress and reason as the apex of Man and Nature. Hegel saw Man as the antithesis of Nature. Supporters of the French Revolution wanted to change Notre Dame Cathedral into the Temple of Reason. During the French Revolution Reason was represented as a charming "lady of the streets". This was the desacralization of knowledge and the anthropomorphic tendency in Man. Kant and Hegel could be said to support it. Rousseau clearly rejected it. Rousseau's father was a Calvinist preacher, and Kant's mother was a Pietist. As such, both thinkers were influenced by certain Protestant ideals at an early age. Kant was more properly a subtle compromise between Hume and Rousseau. He believed in mechanical laws explaining the motions of the Heavens with Newton and Galileo but affirmed the Neopagan mysticism of Emmanuel Swedenborg. The views of Swedenborg can be most popularly viewed in works by artists like William Blake. Swedenborg writes in "New Jerusalem and its Heavenly Doctrine" remarking on a passage in Revelations about the coming of the Kingdom of God,

> "The man who reads these things, understands them only according to the sense of the letter; namely, that the visible heaven and earth will perish, and a new heaven will exist, and that the holy city Jerusalem, answering to the measures above described, will descend upon the new earth; but the angels understand these things altogether differently; namely, what man understands naturally, they understand spiritually; and as the angels understand, so they signify; and this is the internal or spiritual sense of the Word. In the internal or spiritual sense, "a new heaven and a new earth" means a new church, both in the heavens and on the earth"

533. The inner spiritual sense of the Word was the renewal of all life in the future coming of the Kingdom of God. Kant wrote "Dreams of a Spiritseer" on topics related to themes laid out in the numerous works of Swedenborg. Swedenborg claimed to converse with spirits and apparently Kant was not sure if his visions were divinely inspired. Kant was not the only German philosopher

who had a wide-ranging interest in Occult ideas. He wanted to prove a sort of knowledge apart from experience. A priori knowledge, experience, and the moral world created a sort of trinitarian conception. What experience gives us is disjointed, while spatial organization comes from the mind imposing on reality. The mind of Man was no longer passive wax, but a force of organizing potential. This was the notion of the "transcendental" or the "correspondences" mentioned in occult literature and seen in the writing of Swedenborg. This was a split between the World, the "Word", and the Spirit. The World was the experience, the Word was the organizing potential, and the Spirit was the moral law within. The split between the Word and the World was made by the Pauline doctrine, which successfully fused Greek and Jewish thought. Kant[50] felt that "Mind is the coordination of experience". He created a hierarchy of understanding. Sensation was placed at the bottom similar to the Platonistic notion of Eros mentioned in Phaedrus, then perception, then conception, then knowledge, then science, then wisdom and morality.

534. This was a quite Platonic synthesis. It was the mind that brought order out of chaos. "The mind that knows itself is itself an ordering", he says echoing Aristotle. The paradox of Kant lies in the fact that his moral synthesis being apart from Reason and is somehow discovered through it. This not only put Religion outside of Reason but made Morality equivalent to Natural Laws akin to fixed notions of space and time. These facts were predetermined. He put faith outside of Reason, but restyled Morality as an appropriation of the Universal, while both Moral and Physical Law governed the cosmos. But if these Moral Laws are outside the bound of Reason, how can they be proved? If Morality is beyond Reason then how does it appear in the form of Law? Kant separated a sense of Duty from a sense of Happiness. Duty is not synonymous with Sincerity or Integrity. Duty is often based on a sense of misplaced pride and false humility. Words like Right and Duty do no more for common morality than instill a common and base sense of entitlement. Honor and Love are more useful in this regard, as is trust and hopefulness. Duty is a replacement for Faith. This was quite clearly a Protestant summation. Kant said that by putting Morality above Happiness we cease to become mortals and become gods. This doctrine of ascension is familiar and leaves a bad taste in our mouths. Rather than teaching the clear sense that Morality is its own reward, Kant puts it above Happiness. We must be miserable in order to succumb to Duty, and so grace is brought to us by a forfeiture of Happiness. What a drag. I submit that it is nothing more than jaw gymnastics and clearly lacking a good grasp on basic human psychology, but I digress.

---

[50] Durant, W. (1927). *The Story of Philosophy*. Garden City Publishing. For the remainder of section 533 and for the majority of 534 and 535 we use the analysis of Will Durant to critique the views of Kantian philosophy.

535. On Religion and Reason, he reduced Religion to mere Moral faith and hope. Theologians were not amused. He reduced the beautiful to the symmetrical. He extolled a flaccidly disinterested pleasure, apparent in the structures of art seen today. Kant's utopian dreams of world peace were anarchistic and won him even less favor with Statesmen. Yet his view of the inevitability of progress has been used to bolster power in the industrial and technological age by those who gave hubristic prescriptions for Man's suffering, arrived at by grandiose and untimely visions taken from occult fantasy. This belief in the progress of Universal goals and aspirations was taken over by Hegel, who proposed the movement of history was based on the "world spirit". These are quite plainly Pauline notions of collective salvation and inclusion mixed with the coming of a New Age and New Earth, where the promise of God would be renewed. This was an attempt to switch out the theology of a coming Judgement and Apocalypse into a worldly salvation. It corresponded to the apocalyptic message of Christ being substituted for one of collective salvation that would be brought about by a New Covenant. Quite incredibly, the notion of a period of strife manufactured to the purpose of a world government which puts an end to all conflict, is both utopian fantasy and Pauline theology. This view of the "World Spirit" can also be seen in the Telos of Aristotle and Averroes. Kant apparently did not follow Rousseau's dreams of a small Republic. Peace by mutual contraction was the delusionary vision of Kant, and the banishing of all standing armies. Kant admitted in a letter to Moses Mendelsohn that he held some of his beliefs back from the public for fear of reprisal. The British notion of separation of business and pleasure is linked to the Kantian and German notion of the separation of duty and happiness, and the link between beauty and math or symmetry. The Germans at this time had absorbed Neoplatonism and Occult theology.

536. One writer wrote, quite speciously, that God gave to the French the land (politics), the British the sea (trade), and to the Germans the empire of the air (metaphysics and mysticism). This is quite clearly relying on the belief that European civilization was chosen by God to represent the rest of humanity. In terms of German philosophy, Kant was to Hegel what Plato was to Aristotle. Every morning him and the philosopher Schelling rose to plant a "tree of liberty" in the marketplace. Both men saw the French Revolution as an exciting period, and as the pinnacle of western expression.

537. Hegel saw Napoleon as the "World Spirit" on horseback[51]. He felt that Kantian philosophy was the most important event in the history of German Philosophy. Hegel wrote a book on Jesus as a secular leader but never had the

---

[51] Strathern, P. (1997). *Hegel in 90 minutes*. I.R. Dee. For the next four sections we borrow from the work by Strathern for Hegel's biographical information and his high estimations of his own philosophy. Most of the critiques are centered around our own project.

work published. He had a great appreciation for the philosophy of Spinoza. He felt he could turn the philosophy of Nature into the realm of Mind or Spirit. He viewed contradiction, mediation, and alienation as the engines of the "historical process". Man was completely determined by forces of social and cultural development, and was nothing more than a product of history, in both the Hegelian and Darwinian sense. Progress meant that Man had to be overcome. Man was to improve, but in a dark and comedic turn, all of human nature had to be subsumed in the process, in a virtual coo-coo clock of randomized progress, and the uninitiated change of circumstantial fibers of reality and time. Who knows when the bell tolls, and for whom? The problem with innovation is that it can't be predicted, but they predict its arrival. What this view really promotes is a hatred of Man in his current state.

538. The dichotomy presented by Kant between form and content, thought and reality, was a starting point for Hegelian philosophy. The attempts of Hegel had surmised that Logic was only able to refer to itself and could not emerge from itself until confronted with a contradiction. The problem, conflict, resolution was rendered by him as a metaphysical reality. This was the instantiation of progress, and the inevitability and invariability of change. While Kant created a spatial duality between the world outside and the world inside, Hegel created a temporal duality between tomorrow and today. The belief in progress is the belief that tomorrow will be better than today, and that the present must seek to resolve itself of the past by overcoming itself in the future. This was no doubt the coming of the Kingdom of God, assured by God's entrance into history. It also clearly reflects the earlier Kantian visions of Utopia. Hegel, at least, tried to overcome Kant's vacuous rendering of Truth, which Kant had reduced to an organizing capacity. However, his dialectic resembles the trinity. He framed the Truth as a trinitarian conception consisting of Logic, Rhetoric, and Grammar. While Kant split truth into two parts, Hegel settled for three. Each would go on dividing truth from truth into various categories. The separation of truth from truth leads to a wholesale rejection of Absolute Truth.

539. Hegel correctly believed that thought was not separate from reality, but in our view wrongly made thought synonymous with the limits of Truth and Reality. For him Logic and Mind was the ultimate reality. By Science, Hegel meant Metaphysics, and by Logic, he meant his own dialectical system. His philosophy was an ode to Heraclitus, with a focus on the notion of "becoming". While the Kantian side would develop into the analytic forms of mathematical logic, the Hegelian philosophy would develop into a broader continental tradition of the Marxist and Sociologist type. While Kantians wanted to reduce philosophy to math, the Hegelians were focused on the socio-political dimension. Like all philosophers, their views had a broad range of influence in the development of the methodology of certain schools and found themselves derived from both religious and mystical prescriptions. His triadic formulation was "the Absolute Idea", whose antithesis was "Nature", and whose resolution

was "the World Spirit". In a quite Aristotelian fashion, the highest task of the highest order of existence is to contemplate itself. Hegel makes the claim that his system is more monistic than Kant's, but this remains to be seen. Hegel saw the fall of Man and his eventual redemption as a virtual panning out of his own dialectical process of history. He furthermore views himself as playing a central role in its occurrence.

540. He fashioned himself as the representative philosopher of the Prussian State, and his "Philosophy of Right" demands a subservience to the status quo, as the average man is swept up in the changes of history. His model of the State was decidedly British with its parliamentary form of government, which was no longer defined by Man, an "artificial man", or a machine that speaks for Man, but was what, in its due course, defined Man himself. Man was subsumed under the State, instead of the State being a method or tool employed by Man. He made special rules within his State for toleration of religion, and especially toleration of Jews, as Prussian society was growing increasingly "antisemitic", according to Paul Stathern. In a truly anthropocentric twist, Man was at once the measure of all things, the very goal of the historical process, but was himself to be overcome and subsumed in the game of progress and inevitable change. This view was Hegelian and Darwinian, Christian and Kabbalistic. Self-realization and a morbid compliance was the goal. The belief that Man was an impermanent stepping stone of Existence, whose Nature had to be overcome is both anthropocentric and suicidal, teeming with grotesque levels of irony, and cosmic shame was one that believed that Man had to be overcome in the process of salvation. Man was made imperfect but was a sign of perfection. He felt that the German nation was the guardian of the "sacred fire" of philosophy, just as the world's conscience was codified by the Jewish Nation. Such high praise of Jews, while bringing the whole world under the cloak of salvation, sounds like a good Pauline message. His world historical view at once anoints his own people, but goes past them to an international aim, which culminates in the "end of history". This process cancels out the notion of national sovereignty, and even subsumes it under the patchwork quilt of progress.

541. Hegel wished to be buried next to the Kantian philosopher Fichte. Marx had soon arrived in Germany to study Hegel and create his system of dialectical materialism. The Young Hegelians were known as the most revolutionary faction of French and German thinkers. Marx was kicked out of France during the French Revolution. Marx abandoned the project of trying to understand the world and focused on trying to change it. His scientific attitude of manipulation and experimentation was based on the evolutionary worldview of British economics, French politics, and German metaphysics. The view amounted to a sort of scientific totalitarianism. Yet other parts of Hegelian views were derived squarely from Hermetic concepts of alchemical transformation. For Hegel, time and progress were the highest spiritual forms. Nature was reduced to a

process. Time was existence itself. Man was reduced to a ledger, but Time was alive. Hence, the concept of Being or Essence was reduced to a mere fantasy.

542. Hegel believed that Man could secure a rational existence through the security of the State, and that States have learned nothing from history. This is because the State was the process of history itself unfolding. Man owes his entire existence to the State. For Hegel, the history of the movement of Mind bore Man and the State as its necessary result. Man was further obfuscated by being pre-ordained and pre-determined. But to a shocking degree, whatever Man was at the moment was sacrificed for his future. Socrates deserved to die. It was a necessary result of the movement of history. Christ needed to be sacrificed. What pushes us forward leaves us behind. Where is Man in all of this? Swept up in the change, we suppose. Man is reduced to processes which are outside of him, but only understood through himself. What can be ideal of this process that excludes Man? It is the emphasis on the word "freedom" that is employed in Hegelian terminology that is quite puzzling. Time is a linear process that pushes us to become something other than what we already are. So there is no ground upon which to define reality. The rug is constantly pulled out from under our own feet and we have nowhere to stand. The floor is lava. The Divine fire needs time to cool as it mends reality's past and future. How could this so-called freedom ever be realized? Hegel made Spirit or "Geist" similar to Mind, but should it be? The attempt to reduce Man to a rational animal leaves much to be desired.

543. According to many scholars, Hegel saw his own realization of Mind as the ultimate process of reality[52], and as the very achievement of Mind realizing

---

[52] Magee, B. (Writer). (1987). Peter Singer on Hegel and Marx (Season 1, Episode 9) [TV series episode]. In *The Great Philosophers*. https://www.youtube.com/watch?v=ceM8GITkKxg. According to Peter Singer not only did Hegel see the process of world history being worked out in the death of Socrates which he felt was necessary for the height of individual conscience finally coming to fruition in Protestant Europe. Also according to Peter Singer Hegel felt, "The endpoint of the dialectical process is mind coming to know itself as the ultimate reality, and thus as seeing everything that it took to be foreign and hostile to itself as, in fact, part of itself. And that, for Hegel, is simultaneously a state of absolute knowledge, when mind knows (recognizes), at last, itself as the ultimate reality. And also a state of absolute freedom when mind, instead of being controlled by external forces, is able to order the world in a rational way, because now it sees the world is, in fact, itself. And it only has to implement its own principle of rationality onto the world to organize the world rationally. Now the interesting thing about this culminating process is that because it occurs once mind understands that it is the ultimate reality of everything, if you ask the question, when does this actually happen? Well, it happens when Hegel's mind (Hegel's own mind), in his philosophical writings and thoughts, grasps the idea that mind is everything. And then, he's achieved this. It's not just that Hegel describes the goal, the culmination of all this process, but Hegel's philosophy is the very culmination of the whole process he's describing". Although Hegel's feat of megalomania would seem to

its own true nature as the ultimate reality. This apparent vision of visions is the same megalomaniacal tactic employed by all self-proclaimed prophets. This sums up the hubris of philosophers who: 1. Invent an all-encompassing system of thought, and 2. Redefine everything by one's own self-devised system. The invention of both Postmodernism and German Nationalism have been attributed to the philosophy of Nietzsche but are pretty much inventions of Hegel. One of Hegel's favorite concepts was the profound sense of alienation, undoubtedly stemming from his own self projection. Hegel presented a temporal duality that was manifest through contradiction. Hegel melded together form and content, but in order to do so relegated them to a process of historical development. This miasmic web of interrelated processes were spurred on by alienation and abstraction from God, and a need to rationally order oneself into an organic society, which first culminates in the natural state, and then is realized in the ultimate reflection of human potential, which is the man-made State. Most stupendously, he felt this great historical change had realized itself in Hegelian philosophy.

544. This sort of finality seems rather unphilosophical. Indeed, the assuredness of Hegel seems to suggest a mystical influence and a dogmatic stripe. Only religious people, mystics, buffoons, geniuses, and the insane are ever this sure. In his "Hegel and the Hermetic Tradition" Glenn McGee writes, "Hegel is not a philosopher. He is not a lover or seeker of wisdom-he believes he has found it"[53]. Hegel declared quite boldly in his "Phenomenology of Spirit" that philosophy has to shift from the classical definition of love of knowing to becoming "actual knowledge", which Hegel claims to have arrived at himself. Same was true of Descartes, Spinoza, Leibniz, and Kant, who casually defined knowledge and God in a quite pseudo-religious tone. The God of the philosophers resembles an idol made from crude anthropocentrism and the deification of Rational thought. In quite a striking line Mcgee writes, "we must understand Hegel as a Hermetic thinker if we are to truly understand him at all". Hegel gave the Mystic Jacob Boehme a large amount of space in his "Lectures in the History of Philosophy" and uses the Hermetic notion of Coincidencia Oppositorum or "coincidence of the appearance of opposites". This was the notion that the belief in something precluded belief in its opposite, which was an early trick used by Sophists. It was also based on Kabbalistic inversion or "Qliphoth" (the opposite of the Holy or Sephiroth). His theory of the progress of history is most likely based on Joachamite Millenarianism (of Joachim of Fiore), in which the age of the Father, age of the Son, and age of the Holy Spirit, formed three distinct periods culminating in universal brotherhood.

---

place him in rare company, almost all philosophers and scientists who have attempted to invent a system that categorizes all forms of knowledge such as Aristotle and Kant or Newton and Einstein have shared similar conceits.
[53] From Section 544-548 we rely on the introduction to the following work: Magee, G. A. (2001). *Hegel and the Hermetic Tradition*. Cornell University Press.

545. Hegel also employed Hermetic and Rosicrucian themes in his Philosophy of Nature and Philosophy of Right lectures. Hegel's library consisted of works by Agrippa, Boehme, Bruno, Paracelsus, as well as works concerning dowsing, precognition, and sorcery. He also associated with known occultists like Franz von Baader, and employed the belief, similar to Kant, of correspondences or mediating spirits. The idea of correspondences also fared heavily in the writings of Swedenborg. Wurttemberg, where Hegel supposedly was frequently found, was the spiritual center of the Rosicrucian movement, and was also a center for the theosophical pietist tradition. While working in Frankfurt, his biographer Rosenkranz describes his "theosophical phase". Now it is well known that he studied Meister Eckhart, made references to Boehme. In his "Phenomenology", Logic is freedom from the mundane and sensory nature to an ascent and initiation into the realm of wisdom or Universal Mind. The alienation or othering of the Universal Mind and its emanation into the world of creation makes Nature the antithesis of Mind. Our carnal nature was our foe. This was a Pauline, Lutheran and Gnostic subtext, mirrored in the Platonic. In the Philosophy of Spirit Hegel speaks of a return of Nature to the Divine by means of Man. This is quite similar to the Pauline message of redemption. God enters into the Nature in order to save Mankind.

546. In 1840 Schelling accused Hegel of obtaining most of his philosophical view from Jacob Boehme. Both Schelling and Hegel were proponents of Boehme. One of the proponents of their work was Ferdinand Bauer, mentioned by us earlier for having contributed to the history of the Gospel narratives. His work on Gnosticism helped to distinguish the various sectarian designs of the movement. In Eric Voegelin's study of Gnosticism, he declares that Hegel is a study in sorcery, and that his "Phenomenology" is akin to a magical performance, based on the notion of alchemical synthesis. Writers such as Voegelin, Francis Yates, Richard Popkin, and several others have argued that mainstream thinkers like Bacon, Descartes, Spinoza, Leibniz, and Newton were influenced by Hermetic and Gnostic views, and that the ambitions of modern philosophy and modern science reflect an interest particularly in the project of scientific investigation and technological mastery of nature. This was also the goal of Magic. Humanism is apparently a bastardization of the belief that Man was to achieve total knowledge, and through it, bring the world into a perfect semblance. Spirit or Mind was the driver for the ideal of total progress under a pseudo-eschatology, and disjointed teleology. This is not to be confused with the Darwinism that suggested the movement from simple to complex, but also suggested an inherent progress in things, and in that sense was similar to Aristotle's views.

547. However, it could be seen to entail the scientific and technological progress that was reflected in Marx. Yet no thoughts develop in a vacuum. Our view must be much more comprehensive. Faith in the future, and the myth of progress, is a denial of Man in his current stage. The Darwinian notion of

Man's lowly origins coupled with the belief in the Hegelian march of progress to produce deadly offspring. This was Paul's message of inherent evil, and the Aristotelian chain of being plus teleology. The Spirit used to be an attunement with Nature. Soon the Spirit was no longer in the world but reduced to an indwelling and inert immaterial reflection apart from matter. The Spirit was then collectivized and externalized into the artificial man which was a component of the State and human society. Man was then reduced to a byproduct of environmental forces, and the Spirit was reduced to stimulus and response. The mechanization and externalization of Man's ego is a necessary result. This is the herd man that waits for change, believing that he is already saved. This was the Man of Paul. In Judaism and Islam God creates from sheer abundance and without necessity. But this is not true of Pauline theology where a middle position was drawn between Pagan and Jewish thought. God had to be brought down to Man's level, but in order to do this God had to be first removed from Nature.

548. In the Discourse of Hermes to Tat, the mixing bowl or Monad requires creation. God creates in order to know himself. "For the two are all there is: what comes to be and what makes it" (Corpus Hermeticum 14). Like is only understood by like, so Man must become like God to understand God. Emulation is understanding. Understanding is self-knowledge. As Paul tells his followers that he imitates Christ, so they should emulate him (1 Corinthians 1:11). Both Gnosticism and Hermeticism, not only occupy an intermediate position between Pagan and Judeo-Christian forms, but also believe in the divine spark hidden in Man, and Reason inherent in the world. As Hegel wrote in a preserved fragment of his biographer,

> "Every individual is a blind link in the chain of absolute necessity, along which the world develops. Every individual can raise himself to domination over a great length of this chain only if he realizes the goal of this great necessity and, by virtue of this knowledge, learns to speak the magic words which evoke its shape. The knowledge of how to simultaneously absorb and elevate oneself beyond the total energy of suffering and antithesis that has dominated the world and all forms of its development for thousands of years--this knowledge can be gathered from philosophy alone"

549. Robert P. Kraynak in his "History and Modernity in the thought of Hobbes"[54] explains a foundational link between the creation of everlasting

---

[54] Kraynak, R. P. (1990). *History and Modernity in the Thought of Thomas Hobbes.* Cornell University Press. Pg. 96-102. While Kant and Hobbes are not seen as having identical views on human nature, they both saw the path forward as belonging to the reign of the triumph of secular humanism and empiricism. In the beginning of his "Critique of Pure Reason", Kant even seems to champion the philosophy of the British Em-

peace through the commonwealth that was even shared by Kant. Like Hegel and Hobbes, Kant believed that the scientific enlightenment laid the path for everlasting peace. As Kant states, "new prejudices will serve as old ones to harness the great unthinking masses". The individual was subsumed into the dichotomy, or as Kraynak puts it in, "a fundamental dualism, an opposition of both of historical epochs (the past vs. the future), and of mental habits". Man was caught also between the Man that was defined by environment and society, and the Man that was to free himself from the binds of historical narrative to define himself in a radical liberty and individualism. A culmination of the latter form was sought in the French Revolution, which sought a reversal of the previous orders. As Tocqueville observed in his "Democracy in America", in order to make man more Democratic, he had to be rendered more equal. But Liberty and Equality are sometimes mutually exclusive. Liberty suggests that everyone has a right to freedom, but Equality suggests that everybody gets to voice their freedom in particularly the same way. Equality also led to a decline in Social Mores. Hence the Modern State only pretends to individuality but never clearly defines its terms. Historian Paul Johnson points out in his Modern Times, that both Marx and Frued focused on anatomizing religion by presenting manifest content and hidden meaning that was Gnostic in its sensibility.

550. In Jules Michelet's "History of the French Revolution"[55], he declares that the French Revolution was the declaration of the collective will, or Reason, as God. He writes that this collective will states that, "In other words ye are Gods", and proclaims, "Let us be God! The impossible becomes possible and easy. Then to overthrow a world is a mere trifle, why, one creates a world". The followers of the French Revolution believed in "Eternal Justice" and pleaded with "O Justice my Mother; Right, my Father". The goal was to create a perfection outside of Man, where God was Man. God becoming Man. God's entrance into history. The coming of the Kingdom of God. The utopian vision of world peace. The doctrine of inclusion and justification by faith alone, upon which each would be saved on their own terms. The true religion of the gentile masses, not only to sway them, but to control and delude them. A Man-made idol.

551. In an article by Jeffrey Steinberg entitled "The Bestial British Intelligence of Shelburne and Bentham"[56], he exposes the connections of philosophers like

---

piricists like Locke and Hume who he sees as having already laid down the basic fundamentals knowledge along with scientific discovery.
[55] Michelet, J. (1967). *History of the French Revolution* (G. Wright, Ed.; C. Cocks, Trans.). University of Chicago Press. We use section 6 and 7 from this work to outline the grandiose and hubristic sentiments of the French Revolution.
[56] Steinberg, J. (1994, April 15). The Bestial Intelligence of Shelburne and Bentham. *Executive Intelligence Review, 21*(16), 24-27. https://larouchepub.com/eiw/public/1994/eirv21n16-19940415/eirv21n16-19940415_024-the_bestial_british_intelligence.pdf. We refer to this article continuously over the next few sections 551-554.

Hume and Bentham to British Intelligence during the French Revolution. Bentham wrote, "Nature has placed mankind under the governance of two sovereign masters; pain and pleasure". He argued that the principle in utility of social systems is the highest goal. Lord Shelburne was "so taken with Bentham" and referred to him as "the Sir Isaac Newton of Moral Science". Shelburne led the East India Tea Company, made infamous for its involvement in the Slave trade and the international drug trade. His faction, "the Venetian Party", had gained prominence. Wealthy families of Genoa and Venice had bankrolled international trade. The practice of finance through the use of interest and usury was on the rise. In 1787, Bentham published "In Defense of Usury". British Intelligence was intending to use "free trade" as a weapon. Shelburne declared "Let every market be open". He ushered in the era of international trade that was a warning sign of Alexander Hamilton in Federalist Paper No 11. Some of the founders had declared banks more dangerous than standing armies (a quote by Jefferson). Yet and still, the Federalist Papers constantly boast of Enterprise and Empire even though the constant expansion and trade required for these are the very things in which lay the causes of faction and cultural disintegration.

552. The Jacobin terror was funded and orchestrated by British Intelligence, and Shelburne as well as Bentham started salons and radical writers workshops, which welcomed leaders Jean Paul Marat, Georges Jacques Danton, and Maximilien Robespierre. Bentham apparently drew up a slave labor scheme called "the Panopticon". A central view allowed a jailer to watch and mediate all the slaves for the purposes of harvesting electrical power and optimizing work. He said, "Allow me to construct a prison on this model. I will be the jailer". He wished to move to Paris and take charge of the penal system. This grotesque proclamation and fascistic urge is not a new thing among philosophers. He said that human labor was more effective than steam power, and his design included architectural drawings, and called for criminals, the indigent, the mentally handicapped and deranged to be locked away in a slave labor camp along with their children, where children games like merry go round would be used to harness energy. The goal was to create happy slaves, mediate their every mood, and make them unaware of their captivity all for the sake of extracting Labor and Wealth.

553. Faithlessness, and castration of truth, for the void of naive realism is the legacy of works that were a shallow attack on religious customs. He wrote a paper entitled "A Defense of Pederasty", where he defends along with pederasty, homosexuality, lesbianism, masturbation, and bestiality, and said the practice of sexual freedoms was solely forbidden on the basis of religious affairs. The practice of so-called "family planning" was also recommended by Plato and Aristotle, who felt that the values of State were best reflected in family relations, and one could properly govern others only by controlling the family relations which are the basis for the socializing aspects of human beings. The hedonism of thinkers like Hume had even assumed that there was no unifying

self, but just a band of conflicting desires which were seemingly brought together only by the force of Reason. This belief cancelled free will. The belief
of hedonists that there is no underlying essence or soul in a person that indi-
viduates their consciousness, is shared not only by Buddhists, but also Christians, who both believe that human nature is tarnished, and must ultimately
find its way out of depravity and impermanence made possible by both human
caused misery, and the flaws of their own inherent constitution.

554. The philosophy of Bentham ultimately led to the Utilitarianism of John
Stuart Mill, whose protege was the Eugenicist and Fabian Socialist Bertrand
Russell. Social utilitarianism was one of the streams of thought that brought
forward the ideas of International Socialism. Another British Lord, Lord Palmerston, funded Karl Marx and collaborated with the infamous occultist
Giuseppe Mezzini. Disciples like John Bowring and David Urquhart were responsible for seditious acts. They were foreign diplomats who went far and
wide to set up trade relations. In the halls of London University, the preserved
and stuffed corpse of Jeremy Bentham haunts the halls. Perhaps mention of
this ghoulish figure and caterpillar of a man should have been uprooted, but
the dangerous thoughts and views of such thinkers have been vigorously preserved by the British. This is perhaps a testament to their true beliefs. They
believe that one can live forever as long as one's memory is preserved. Both
Epicureans and Idealists seek to escape from nature and the ills of human im-
perfection. For this purpose and to this end a New Man has to be engineered.

555. The life of Karl Marx is a mystery to most. He joined the Young Hegelians in France at a young age. Marx was born to Heinrich Levy as Moses Mordechai Levy, but later had his name changed to hide his Jewish identity. As
noted earlier, the practice of secret conversion was a known practice of some
European Jews during the time of oppression by the Church. At the time in
Prussia, Jews were not allowed to hold high rank and office. However, Marx
was also known to practice occultism. Marx practiced Freemasonry and wrote
satanic and apocalyptic poetry. He was educated at home by his father who
was well versed in the thoughts of the Enlightenment. Marx was employed by
Lord Palmerston, who paid him very little, and probably worked as a spy.

556. Marx moved to London to author Das Kapital, while his cousin Lionel de
Rothschild was MP for the city of London. One of his intellectual rivals, Mikhail Bakunin, claimed that Marx had sold out to rich interests like the Rothschilds in order to promote his work. He writes, "The world is now at least for
the most part, at the disposal of Marx on the one hand, and of Rothschild on
the other. This may seem strange. What can be in common between Socialism
and a leading bank? The point is that authoritarian socialism, Marxist Communism, demands a strong centralization of the state. And where there is centralization of the State there must necessarily be a central bank". He concluded
saying that central banks were in turn parasitized by wealthy Jews and secret

organizations who funded characters like Marx and speculated with the labor of the people[57]. The same problem about Communism was noticed by writer Eric Blair, better known as George Orwell, in his "Road to Wigan Pier". He says the ideal of Capitalism would lead to monopolization and ownership by a few and powerful owners, which is paradoxically the centralization required for a mass industrialized state to perform in a Communist style rule. Large industrial enterprises need centralized power and are the very basis of the "scientific socialism" suggested by Marx and Engels which relies on heavy urbanization and collective change rather than agrarian reform. Efficiency becomes the main end, and as we overproduce the system, we underproduce humanity. This leads to a shallow mechanization and commodification of the human being for the purpose of the development of technology and scientific endeavor, which proceeds at the expense of all mankind. Mass production and industrialization led to "massification of means" and a centralized style of governance in regard to the planned economy. This was also noted by Ellul.

557. But we must also remember, the drive to free Man from himself is what has led to this incessant drive for progress and change. It is a sort of escapism whereby Man is to dissolve himself in future dreams. As long as Man continues to recreate himself without discovering who he is, he changes him or herself into an almost unrecognizable form. He continues to seek a world outside of himself though the tyranny of the hedonistic utilitarian, epicurean fascistic, and disinterested idealist impulses that have forged his misery and complacency. But there was also an antinomian flavor adopted from the mystery religions and from Pauline doctrine. This was the attitude of religious subversion which was the process of using religious ideals to attack religious tradition, while settling for a new interpretation that was not only salvific, but deeply personal. This was mirrored in the process of the Hegelian dialectic, which has been used by some to refer to another tactic known as "controlled opposition" or "divide and conquer". This is the tactic that suggests creating the problem and solution all in one move. It entails setting up your opponent beforehand to let yourself win by dividing the opponent into two sides, in order to weaken them. It is most clearly seen in the tale of Solomon, where he suggests two mothers cut their baby in half and each take a piece. He knew beforehand that forcing such an ultimatum would lead to desirable results.

558. In the excommunication of Spinoza[58] he is cursed by the leaders of a Synagogue for attacking the primarily Christian view of God as immaterial. The Amsterdam Jewish community at the time was supported by Protestant Christians. All the while, Spinoza felt his version of God was true to the God

---

[57] Bakunin apparently wrote this in 1869 in a work called "Profession de foi d'un democrate socialiste russe precede d'une etude sur les juifs allemands". It is also a matter of public record that Marx was related to the Rothschild family and that he identified as an occultist and wrote Satanic poetry.
[58] Durant, W. (1927). *The Story of Philosophy*. Garden City Publishing. Pg. 161-215

of the Torah. He may have been right, for certain of the Jews relied more on the interpretations of Aristotelians like Maimonides than what is written in the Torah. Certain Jews probably felt it was unwise to attack the Christian community that had built their synagogue. Another German Jew, Marx, wrote sacred hymns praising Christ, wrote Satanic poetry, was raised by a liberal father, wrote apocalyptic verses, joined Millennialist factions like the "League of the Just" (who radical Bible scholars like Bruno Bauer were also a part of), while writing attacks on both Christianity and Judaism. One could view Marx in any light one chooses. Similarly, Paul criticized Judaism, claimed to be Jewish, set up a dual road of salvation for Christians and Jews, Jews and Gentiles, while having a brand-new interpretation of Judaism, even starting his own religion which was divinely inspired, all while challenging Cephas (Peter) and other members of the Church and Synagogue.

559. There is not the consistency and stubbornness of the Philosopher seen in Spinoza, or the inhospitable and intransigent, bold, and spiteful nature of the Sage seen in a Socrates or even a much more pronounced and prophetic Jesus type of figure. This is the switching up of a statesman or diplomat. Not someone who is seeking to find the truth or convince others, but to make a name for themselves. As proto-socialist Henri de Saint Simon wrote, the key to diagnosing the ills of humanity lies in "the physiological realities behind thinking and feeling". The rule of experts and the combination of doctor and priest were around the corner. After all, this was the stated goal of all secular humanists. Thinkers like Saint Simon founded the notion of a psychology of the social classes and the views of utopian socialism adopted by thinkers like John Stuart Mill. Engels described Marx's theory as "scientific socialism". Materialistic doctrines of Marx were reflected in views of Bertrand Russell which emphasized the blind forces of nature. In his "Appearance and Reality" Russell comes to the unfortunate conclusion that one can no longer affirm anything beyond the scope of one's own mind. This extreme solipsism was the calcification of the skeptic challenge. Him and other Fabian Socialists like John Dewey, Karl Popper, Elanor Roosevelt, H.G Wells, George Bernard Shaw advocated a sort of technocratic socialism, and scientific totalitarianism, brought forward in a rule by experts. The symbol of the Fabian Society was a wolf in sheep's clothing. Russell took the extreme view that society should be managed by the needle. In 1953 in the "Impact of Science on Society" Bertrand Russell writes,

> "I think the subject which will be of most importance politically is mass psychology. ... Various results will soon be arrived at: that the influence of home is obstructive... although this science will be diligently studied, it will be rigidly confined to the governing class. The populace will not be allowed to know how Its convictions were generated. When the technique has been perfected, every government that has been in charge of education

for a generation will be able to control its subjects securely without the need of armies or policemen ... Educational propaganda, with government help, could achieve this result in a generation. There are, however, two powerful forces opposed to such a policy: one is religion; the other is nationalism. ... A scientific world society cannot be stable unless there is a world government."

He also made the dastardly proclamation,

"I do not pretend that birth control is the only way in which population can be kept from increasing. There are others, which, one must suppose, opponents of birth control would prefer. War, as I remarked a moment ago, has hitherto been disappointing in this respect, but perhaps bacteriological war may prove more effective. If a Black Death could be spread throughout the world once in every generation, survivors could procreate freely without making the world too full. There would be nothing in this to offend the consciences of the devout or to restrain the ambitions of nationalists. The state of affairs might be somewhat unpleasant, but what of that? Really high-minded people are indifferent to happiness, especially other people's".

560. These explain to us the Scientific world view which included dysgenic medical procedures, and the use of pharmacological and pharmacogenomic means to create an obedient mass. It quite plainly employs a hatred of Man in which Man must be overcome. Many of these prescriptions amount to nothing more than population control. After all, the power to control who lives and who dies was for a long time thought to be the ultimate god-like power, in which, the means of science cease to be a "mental mirror" for the universe, and become a practical tool for the manipulation of matter to ends of the purposes of Man. Nature was no longer a sign of God. God had first entered into the world in order to save it and then left the world. Now the Spirit was to be reborn through Man himself.

Chapter 21
Raised to be Lowered /
Pride Cometh Before the Fall

561. The manipulation of matter by a supreme immaterial intellect is a familiar portrait of a Platonic, Gnostic, and Christian assemblage, in which the hidden qualities of matter are divine. In Aristotle's Rhetoric, he coined the word tech-ne-logos or entechnos as the process of art or skill. One could unleash the inner form of something by aesthesis or techne, which were a process of bringing forth and enframing. The mastery of matter and form was the highest goal of the alchemical tradition. Hermes was seen as a Mercurian hidden god, or god that hides himself, pregnant with change, and carrying the wind in his bosom. Hermes or Mercury was seen as a planet hidden by the Sun, and a trickster. Hidden powers gave one a resemblance to the Divine. In Jacque Ellul's "Technological Society", he points out that technology brings a demonic presence into the world, and that primitive technique was widely regarded as the practice of magic[59]. Both have a focus on mastery of the natural elements in order to achieve desired results. Joseph Campbell has pointed out that science fulfills the mythical typology of our modern age.

562. Lucifer was the symbol of the cognitive powers of Man, as in (Genesis 3:5) the serpent promises "ye shall be as gods"[60]. A picture of Satan adorned Diderot's "Encyclopedie". Prominent revolutionaries such as Marx and Lenin loved the story of Prometheus, who stole knowledge from the gods and used it to lead Man to a New Age of promise. This was the promise of the age of scientific salvation. The new scientific age became the Eschaton. In the Pauline Creed, God is forced to come to the level of Man, in order to save Man from himself. In short Man is Man's own problem and the solution has to come from Man himself. Since this cannot be achieved the solution comes from the outside, in the imitation of God and the manipulation of matter. In order for God to be lowered, he had to be made more like a Man. In order for Man to imitate God he had to raise his natural capacity to that of a God. In Chronicles 28:9 we read that God knows the "imagination of the thoughts". We can enslave ourselves with the tools we make to manipulate reality by creating outside of ourselves. When we do this our dangerous mis-inventions can create an alternate reality that we can have no control of, but that was based on our hid-

---

[59] Ellul, J. (1967). *The Technological Society* (J. Wilkinson, Trans.). Knopf. Pg. 25
[60] From section 572-577 we heavily cite the following text: Collins, P. D. (2009, June 11). *The Faustian Face of Modern Science*. https://www.conspiracyarchive.com/. Retrieved April 28, 2022, from
https://www.bibliotecapleyades.net/sociopolitica/sociopol_modernscience.htm.

den intentions and motives that we often are not clear of when we first begin our process of inquiry.

563. In a Gnostic text entitled "Hypostasis of the Archons", the serpent of the Garden of Eden is portrayed as a good guy just as in the Gospel of Judas an inversion of the role of bad and good takes place. Furthermore, the ancient mystery religions promised to free man from his material encasement and offer continued rebirth by the erasing of the curse of mortality in "undergoing an apotheosis, a transfiguration of human into divine". This was most clearly represented in the iconography of the phoenix. The Phoenix, transcends sexual duality of birth and death by giving birth to itself. When the Phoenix dies it lays an egg containing a perfect replica of itself, and is therefore continually reborn. The mythical beast was a symbol of divine wrath and power, or the dark side of spirituality. Essentially the same concept can be seen in ouroboros or snake eating it's own tail. Marx's early satanic and apocalyptic verses used some of the same formula. They reflected on leading humanity astray to forsake God, and entering into a pact with Satan. In a poem aptly entitled "Human pride" he talks about dethroning God and says, "Then will I wander god-like and victorious through the ruins of the world. And giving my words an active force, I will feel equal to the Creator". In a poem entitled "The Fiddler" he writes, "That art God neither wants nor wists, it leaps from the brain from hell's black mists. Till hearts bewitched, till senses reel, with Satan I have struck my deal".

564. Writer Phillip Collins in his "Faustian Face of Modern Science" reasons "In all likelihood Marx probably denied the existence of Satan as a literal metaphysical entity. Yet, it is important to remember that the Luciferian conception is premised upon the same existential contention". While the existence of Evil is generally accepted by anyone who seeks to do good (of course whether they believe this Evil created by God or inherent in the world is another question), its existence is generally denied by some wayward Mystics and nihilistic atheists. Perhaps the most clear similarity between Hobbes, Hume, and Marx, is a general view of the lack of any intrinsic nature in Man. Collins writes, "Marx devalued humanity. Again, it is extremely ironic that such a devaluation stemmed from an anthropocentric belief system". This was the crux of all liberal protest, and antinomian heresy: wearing one's suffering as a badge of contention. Ironically, as G.K Chesterton observed, "All denunciation implies a moral doctrine of some kind, and the modern skeptic doubts not only the institution, he denounces, but the doctrine by which he denounces it". He further states, "In short, the modern revolutionist, being an infinite skeptic, is forever engaged in undermining his own mines". This is because modern revolutionaries view Man as materially determined and morally quantifiable.

565. The rule of experts was already suggested by Plato, and Francis Bacon. However, it needed the appearance of the technological age to make its intru-

sion into political and economic systems by the use of technical experts and mass psychology that were to "systematize the motivations" of the herd. Plato suggested that even the musical tastes of the population should be developed, starting from a young age where the brightest are taken from their parents and put into a system of public education. Bacon suggested that Philosopher-Scientists manage the population. Since Man was seen as a tabula rasa ready to be imprinted, he was essentially malleable as part of the world of becoming.

566. In a most accurate assessment G.K Chesterton writes,

> "The thing that really is trying to tyrannize through government is science. The thing that really does use the secular arm is science. And the creed that really is levying tithes and capturing schools, the creed that really is enforced by fine and imprisonment, the creed that really is proclaimed not in sermons but in statues, and spread not by pilgrims but by policeman-that creed is the great but disputed system of thought which began with evolution and has ended in Eugenics."

567. He goes on to say "Materialism is really our established church", and in that Church, vaccines are the new baptism. While many notable thinkers within the West have offered criticism of the mechanization of the world by Modern Man, there is little talk of the origins of the ideology, and why it was to be found only among European societies. The answer does not come about in studies of the "Protestant work ethic", which fails to account how Christianity was altered through Pauline, Gnostic, and Neoplatonic assemblages, and clearly do not discuss how the message of Paul, and not Christ, was the major influence. We see in Thessalonians 4:11 and other such passages, the quiet conformity necessary to be a Paulist. Those who view Protestantism as laying a foundation for classical liberalism, do not appropriately address the level of religious subversion that was necessary in order to derive classical liberal views from traditional religious ones. The real answer lay in the Pauline message. God singles us out in order to save us. Each must carry their cross alone. From each according to his ability, to each according to his need. Jew first, and then the Gentile as well. Just as Man fell from Grace, Christ was raised to be lowered. Martin Luther was a foremost promoter of the Pauline Epistles as the force behind the organization of the Church, who wholly rejected on the very basis of Pauline doctrine and saw Paul's voice as the voice of majesty and divine revelation.

568. The goal is not reached by introspection and reason, or by good deeds and righteous works. These cannot guide Man to faith, so Man must toil as grace was taken to mean, not that God had given one a favorable disposition, but that Man could not be saved by his own volition. This casting off, especially of the role of introspection and reason, and a favorable disposition bestowed on Man

for the attainment of faith, was a project shared by Radical Empiricists, Religious Mystics, and eventually Puritans and Protestants. It had trickled down to them instead of being invented by them. The ascetic value of work is just a necessary consequence of this worldview, which already seeks a general conformity under Natural Law. To be justified, vindicated, and included are main themes. "Acceptance" is the bridge between suffering and grace. Practical actions and disciplined labor led to meaningful work. That God makes some productive and rich and others mean and in subjection as wretched vessels prepared for destruction was the right interpretation of Paul but such a harsh creed needed time to implement itself. Idleness is just as sinful as covetousness. One was not to make a show of one's wealth, but to store away for the Kingdom of God was just simple good preparation. The maximization of one's task, in doing a lot with a little, was a new type of prosperity and diligence in line with God's grace. This was a utilitarian ethic that was matched with the cosmic utilitarianism of Paul and Aristotle. The search for duty and the dignity of work are just offshoots seen in both Locke and Marx.

569. Even Benjamin Franklin and Lincoln espoused ideas of the spirit of labor and work being an element that can free a man, but their terms were used to draw religious support and use it for certain secular ends, like enlisting Puritans for the sake of collective enterprise in terms of Franklin through his works like Poor Richards Almanac, and the growth of industry in terms of Lincoln who used the Transcontinental Railroad to usher in a new era of trade. Locke challenged the notion of Patriarchy by suggesting that by the time a youth was prepared to own property he could leave the tutelage of his father behind. This essentially made fathers no more than sperm donors within social organization. Perhaps the most influential thinker to expand on Locke's treatments of religion, where he argued that God gave Adam private property instead of private dominion in his First Treatise on Government. Franklin was seen in 1778 by the French Statesmen Turgot as "The New Prometheus"[61] who had snatched lightning from the sky (a direct quote). The philosopher Immanuel Kant agreed with the statement and also called Franklin "New Prometheus". Franklin writes in his autobiography in a letter to his mother in 1738 about his warm sentiments and good opinions of the Freemasons and also writes in the autobiography about attending a meeting at the Moravian Church. Essentially the ideology and iconography of collective salvation, transcendental enlightenment, and liberation from work, are all the same. Bentham had recommended the abolition of poverty by the criminalization of the poor and forced labor. The poor were to be given a culture to extract their profit and resources. During the time of the American Revolution some of the revolutionary militias

---

[61] Franklin, B. (2014). *The Autobiography and Other Writings* (L. J. Lemisch, Ed.). Penguin Publishing Group. The following notes were derived from the autobiography of Benjamin Franklin: 1. Mention of Franklin as "The New Prometheus by Turgot (Pg. 194) 2. Mention of Franklin as "The New Prometheus" by Immanuel Kant (Pg.212) 3. Franklin's letter to his parents about his involvement with the Freemasons (Pg. 292)

consisted on English indentured servants, some of whom joined with the slaves to rebel against the upper classes. A racially based system of slavery was instituted to keep poor whites reliant on the system. Such a racial ideology was crafted by British and Dutch Jewish financiers of the slave trade. The end of slavery was not a coming to terms with the brutality of the slave system, but simply finding a cheap alternative in industrial technology. Blacks and poor whites were moved North to work for corporations to produce machines for the upper crust of society. Essentially, no awakening of conscience can really be seen in terms of the farcical notions of an elevation or evolution of human consciousness touted by liberal and "New Age" thinkers.

570. The father of Zionism Theodore Herzl was a promoter of liberalism. Herzl wanted a Jewish Nation State modeled on Western European Nations. He believed in the myth of progress. He writes in his work entitled "The Jewish State"[62], "the technical progress achieved in our own era enable even the dullest of minds with the dimmest of vision to note the appearance of new commodities all around him", reflecting on the view of the material progress of the western world. He further states, "the spirit of enterprise has created them. Without enterprise labor remains static, unaltering; typical to it is the labor of the farmer; who stands now precisely where his forebearers stood a thousand years ago". He wished to reject these old ways and says, "we are not dependent upon the circulation of old values; we produce new ones. We now possess slave labor of unexampled productivity whose appearance in civilization has proved fatal competition to handicrafts; these slaves are our machines". A year after he formed the World Jewish Congress which helped European Jews create the Jewish State after 2000 years of diaspora. The State of Israel can be said to be an invention of modern Europeans and paradoxically can also be seen as in line with the goals of a secular world order, while also being an aspect of religious prophecy.

571. When Fascists and Nationalists propose garbs of liberalism under the guise of Universal Law, it is no doubt a totalitarian endeavor. All attempts to be anti-fascist and anti-totalitarian devolve into all-encompassing plans that end in the same type of totalitarianism. It is similar with anti-cult groups, where the paranoia and uncertainty leads to extreme secretive behavior.

572. Surely Christ did not seek political solutions for this reason. Especially not in the irreligious, subversive, and secular tone of the preeminent lot of philosophers just mentioned. The plight of the Christian is a personal goal and cannot be mediated by the Universal. One of the greatest Christian thinkers to ever breathe, Soren Kierkegaard, sought to portray this. We propose that a true

---

[62] Theodore Herzl's book Der Judenstaat or "The Jewish State" was first published in 1896 and was originally titled "Address to the Rothschilds" but the plan was rejected by the prominent banking family.

reformation of Christian values should be sought in the philosophy of Kierke-gaard rather than the decrepit and worn-out views of Martin Luther. Kierke-gaard turned his philosophical guns towards both the clergymen and the Hege-lian philosophers. He posed an attack on Hegel and the Reformation at the same time that Marx and Engels wrote. His Existentialism, however, was much different from their Materialism. Like Rousseau, Kierkegaard found that a lifelong dread and melancholy were the true consequences of a philosophi-cal, pious, and even artful existence. He endeavored to tease out the paradoxes of normal human experience that allow for our deepest means of expression. Seeking out too much from authority or social conformity is prejudicial to a spiritually fulfilling life. Outward conformity must be abandoned for inward sincerity, and externalized ritual for infinite resignation. He attacked philo-sophical systemization and categorizations and wrote, "Most systematizers stand in the same relations to their systems as a man who builds a great castle and lives in an adjoining barn; they do not live in their great systemic structure. But in spiritual matters this will always be a crucial objection"[63]. He felt that systems of Universal Law were too impersonal and detached from personal experience. He says, "Metaphorically speaking, a man's ideas must be the building he lives in-otherwise there is something wrong". He explains, "If after writing his whole Logic, Hegel had said in the preface it was only an intellec-tual exercise (and that at many parts he had even shirked things) he might have been the greatest thinker who ever lived. Now he is comic". Instead of synthe-sis or mediation, Kierkegaard dwelled in the realm of the paradox.

573. He says that ideas of scorn and contempt have ethical and aesthetic value but can in no way find themselves in a logic system. In such a system pure beginning is like pure being, by which it is either chimerical or no longer dealt with. He writes that "reflection has the notable quality of being infinite", and that, "the absolute beginning itself breaks forth through the endlessly perpetu-ated reflection". This infinite gulf between the immediate and absolute begin-ning means that "logic" of Hegelian philosophy caves in on itself and undoes itself. When the existence of a thing exists in the past it is already finished, but when it exists in the future it must begin and make a clear break. This system-atic view is a paradox.

574. He saw the ability of truth to permeate as a mark of indifference. He writes, "so called pantheistic systems have frequently been cited and attacked by saying that they cancel freedom and the distinction between good and evil. This is perhaps expressed just as definitely by saying that every such system

[63] Baird, F. E. (2002). *Philosophic Classics, Volume IV: Nineteenth-Century Philosophy* (F. E. Baird & W. A. Kaufmann, Eds.). Prentice Hall. Pg. 275-299. We rely on the re-printing of "Concluding Unscientific Postscript" in this book on nineteenth century philosophy to clarify some unique lines of though within Kierkegaard in response to his rejection of Hegelian philosophy. We rely on the material for the next three paragraphs or sections (572-574) and sections 581 and 582

fantastically volatizes the concept of existence. But this should be said not only of pantheistic systems, for it would have been better to show that every system must be pantheistic simply because of the conclusiveness". He objects that, "objective thinking has no relation to subjectivity" and that, "Truth itself is transformed into a desideratum (something wanting) and everything is placed in the process of becoming, because the empirical object is not finished, and the existing knowing itself is in the process of becoming. The truth is an approximating whose beginning cannot be established absolutely". He notes that no apparent conclusion has any force or power in such a system. "The truth is a redoubling".

575. He was settled on the belief on faith as a dialectical suspension, instead of a mediation and middle ground of synthesis. As Fredrick Sontag comments[64], for Kierkegaard, "Possibility is a state of non-being that is changed by coming into existence, so its actualization can never be called necessary". Things move from uncertainty to actualization without mediation, and what is done cannot be undone. The past is simply immutable. Philosophers and men of faith must live backwards and not forwards. They cannot afford to be incessantly propelled by the Necessary and Universal in constant mediation, but in a tension with the finite self against the demands of the infinite, in a dialectical suspension. This is a clear tension between the certainty of will and the freedom of change. To elaborate, choice and freedom are not the same, and change is inherently uncertain.

576. Kierkegaard thought the incarnation of Christ especially represented this paradox in the form of an anthropomorphic statement. Man stood directly before God without the benefit of mediation or compromise. He believed that Christ chose to sacrifice himself without previous planning by God. Kierkegaard seems to feel that the lowly position of Christ and his insignificance is the single most important statement for those who seek to emulate him. Christ did not establish a Church or theological doctrine, but instead he acted on his faith. Kierkegaard says Christianity should hence be unlike platonic reflection, but instead immersed in the subjective experience. To love God involves being badly treated by men. Preaching is against Christ but living a simple life which is often scandalized by others was more Christ-like. His Existentialism was represented by man's inability to plan one's life out in advance, and he felt comedy and tragedy said more about life than reason and artistry, whose unfurlment was contrived to suit man's ideal of himself. This "ideal" was merely a mask one wore to amuse one's friends.

---

[64] Sontag, F. (1979). *A Kierkegaard Handbook*. John Knox Press. We continuously refer to this work from sections 575-580. Since the chapter headings are mislabeled, we could not be more precise with page numbers for the quotes but the quotes are from the work by Sontag.

577. He exhausted the concept of spiritual love as opposed to romantic love. He saw love as the ultimate form of adventure or daring, and the ultimate commitment and sacrifice. The life of love is a life of secretive and inner struggle. Christ spoke of the love of Man as opposed to love for God. The best defense against hypocrisy and the vanity of social ritual is the sincerity of love. Paradoxically in love, one is no more bound by the ethical than in the ebb and flow of emotion or passion. He sought to expound on this by the example of marriage which he gave lengthy consideration. He saw God as unconditional love and a willing sacrifice, and ties love towards a push for self-denial and transcendence, which mixes in the sublime. This could only be sought in wagering one's highest external prizes. Love is not about your own suffering. He chose to accentuate the more stoic sensibilities of Christian teaching. He felt love itself was a tension between a public and private situation. Only passion could free the modern man, whose will had become too collectivized. The true story of Christ was exemplified by the story of self-inflicted isolation. He saw the disparity between the real and the possible to be a source of melancholy for Man. Such was the lot of any man with a vigorous imagination. The faithful man was a witness to the truth, and not an instructor or preacher. Martyrdom was the only way a man of faith could gain access to the crowd.

578. This was a tragic ideal. As was the comic based on contradiction and juxtaposition, irony seeks a high role in the philosophy of Kierkegaard. He used the Socratic notion of "living truth" and personal or subjective truth to break away from the philosophy of Hegel. The role of the philosopher was as Socrates pointed out, to be a midwife for the truth, helping certain ideas come to the surface. He believed Man to be a synthesis of freedom and necessity. He wrote, "Nothing comes into existence with necessity", and said the "actual is no more necessary than the possible". He saw belief and doubt as more or less psychological tools, and passion as based on one's disposition more than on intellectual effort. Only the knowledge of self represents the true philosophical task. Only great thinkers expose themselves to paradoxes. Sontag writes, "If Hegel says: thesis, antithesis, synthesis; S.K says: thesis, antithesis, no synthesis". Faith for Kierkegaard is very close to the imagination and possibility and becoming of Hegelian philosophy. He writes, "personality is a synthesis of possibility and necessity". Necessity for him is simply the tension between possibility and actuality, in which future and past stand on the same ground. He emphasized the instantaneous nature that gives way to decision, which is not a long drawn-out process, but often is a single and abrupt moment. He compared the aesthetic to the ethical and rational, and acknowledged that each had its own pull on human actions. He felt that people were afraid to be honest with themselves, and that this had caused the primary struggle with defining our own humanity.

579. He criticizes logical and rational thinking as describing a process that is only viewed objectively and abstractly. This process can only refer to its own

uses and can only do this through its own employed methods. He objects that "knowledge cannot explain movement". He writes furthermore that, "the infinite advantage that the logical, by being objective possesses over all other thinking is in turn, subjectively viewed, restricted by its being a hypothesis, simply because it is indifferent to the existence understood as actuality. This duplexity distinguishes the logical from the mathematical". He asks and questions if it can be said, and precisely in what sense, that a category is an appropriate abbreviation of existence. He says that, in this case, something of which a beginning cannot be found cannot progress. Sontag explains, "His discovery was the denial of progress and evolution, so dear to the hearts of many 19th century thinkers. S.K was concerned that the conditions of existence are everywhere the same for all men. Time and place in historical sequence do not change this". He continues to say Sartre had borrowed the point from him. One can not only activate one's faith through sacrifice, but the attempt to remain neutral grants us nothing. He firmly reflected the view that man's extremity is God's opportunity. We do not simply accumulate by history and analysis but thrive in experience and exertion.

580. He gives a profound importance to the "moment" or "existence". To dwell there, a leap of faith and a leap of logic are necessary. He believed in the tension of body and mind, which are not parallel or separate, but in a dialectical suspension, which is the cause of restlessness. In Kierkegaard's philosophy the individual or the protagonist or hero was the ideal starting point. This held true most famously for the philosophical and religious disposition. He was intently focused on the spiritual value of alienation. To this end, he believed the social practice of ritual and religion to be a superficial practice. God too dwells in solitude and stands alone. He draws one out. Sontag proclaims, "S.K's extreme individualism speaks more of a traditional mystic spiritual athlete of monastic life than it does, say, of St. Paul's preaching about the opening of divine grace for all". He hoped to dismantle the obsession with universality and purge it of its religious or spiritual status. He devised the "I-Thou" relationship and that was misunderstood by the writings of Martin Buber, and Paul Tillich who then placed these thoughts in a less than honest historical framework based on an all-encompassing system which was the very thing Kierkegaard wished to avoid. He felt paradox represented the life of Socrates and Jesus.

581. This is because nowhere else except in figures like Socrates and Jesus do we see a conflict between the private individual and the public sphere, and to this problem faith was their resolution. But he also rebelled against the path of objective reflection, that cancelled out the subjective individual as something accidental and altogether spurious. The mediation of truth is either a mirage, or it is the individual himself that is screened out of the equation of either an all-encompassing idealism, or a radical empiricism and skepticism. A purely subjective view of truth is conversely indistinguishable from madness. He remarks

that, "the highest inwardness in an existing subject is passion; truth as a para-dox corresponds to passion, and that truth becomes a paradox is grounded pre-cisely in its relations to an existing subject". In a most brilliant passage, he highlights the difficulty for religious practices and writes,

> "If someone who lives in the midst of Christianity enters, with knowledge of the true idea of God, the house of God, the house of the true God, and prays, but prays in untruth, and if someone lives in an idolatrous land but prays with all the passion of the infinity, although his eyes are resting upon the image of an idol-where, then is there more truth? The one prays in truth to God although he is worshipping an idol; the other prays in untruth to the true God and is therefore in truth worshipping an idol"

582. Thus he concludes, "expression will at the same time indicate the resili-ence of the inwardness. Here is such a definition of truth: an objective uncer-tainty, held fast through appropriation with the most passionate inwardness is the truth", while objective knowledge is continually suspended and does not make contact with the world without being misunderstood. The truth that ex-ists outside of you might as well be a high paradox once existing in a subject, hence he had sympathy for the Platonic notion of recollection, but still warns, "This thesis is an intimation of the beginning of speculative thought, but for that very reason Socrates did not pursue it; essentially it became Platonic. This is where the road swings off, and Socrates essentially emphasizes existing, whereas Plato, forgetting this, loses himself in speculative thought". He em-phasized the truth as it relates to subjectivity. It is a real shame that his thoughts are not taken more seriously among Christians. You almost never hear of Kierkegaard outside of the achievements of philosophy. He is given practically no theological significance. We suspect this is because his philosophy is only for the bold. He protested against the herd mentality and collectivism.

583. To summarize our views we employ the often-brilliant perspectives of Henryk Skolimowski[65]. He rejected the views of Cartesian dualism and Aristo-telian compartmentalizing of knowledge. He sees the unity of truth, beauty, and goodness in the spirit of the Upanishads, and in Plato. He writes, "Plato was an inspired poet who talked with angels and the spirit of trees. Aristotle in contrast was a sober analyst". The ultimate mistake of Aristotle's systematiz-ing and vain categorizations was that it had separated truth from beauty and goodness. The end result was the vehicle of science being used to crush all other truths, and Man becoming spiritually depraved, insolent to God, indiffer-ent to nature, and critical of himself and others. He asks the fundamental ques-

---

[65] Skrbina, D. (Ed.). (2015). Ethics For Life: Introductory Readings and Essays (Second ed.). Creative Fire Press. The relevant passages occur inside Dr. Skrbina's anthology on pages 9-18 in a work entitled "World Ethics" by Henryk Skolimowski

tion: "Was Aristotle responsible for derailing of western civilization? Or was western civilization, because of its peculiar mental makeup, bound to produce Aristotle and people like him who drove western people to the barren land of analysis"? This was what severed our quest for wholeness from the idea of wholeness as truth.

584. After Aristotle, the Hellenized world accepted an Epicurean ethos instead of a Stoic one, and this can be seen as directly caused from a lack of authority in the Christian traditions in securing a serious project for Ethics. However, the views of St. Francis were pushed aside for the harsh analytics of St. Thomas Aquinas that are an outright rejection of a more life affirming teaching, as shared by Jesus himself. Of course, the view of Justice and Goodness that was exchanged for one of Reason and Faith could not be institutionalized. In his work "The Participatory Mind"[66], Skolimowski more or less agrees with Kierkegaard that, "we are told that whatever our subjective makeup, truth is a different category. Truth is supposed to be sacrosanct, immune from our existential individual". Instead, Skolimowski sought to establish personal truths. He blames the popularly espoused correspondence theory of truth which completed the siphoning out of the individual from the range of truth. Truth was reduced to the correspondence between reality and its descriptions.

585. "Both descriptions and reality are doomed to be trans-subjective", hence the universal mind is assumed. Skolimowski asks us whether this instantiation of the universal mind, which is supposedly embodied in each of us to the same degree, allows us to operate as so-called "universal beings". If truth cannot be individuated, how can reality out there be knowable or accessible, or adequately described for that matter? Does furthermore, our mind not change historically or individually? Skolimowski writes, "It cannot be legitimately claimed that we all have the same universal mind". He goes on to say, "it is naive to assume now, after the revelations of quantum mechanics, that reality is independent of the nature of the mind. Further still, it is a gross oversimplification to assume that the mind has not changed evolutionarily, historically, culturally. In consequence: as the knowing mind has changed, so have our descriptions of reality changed, so has our truth changed". This replaces the tautological, circular, and unchanging universal truth for a personal truth, which has not only continuity, but also ebbs and flows. Truth naturally arises in us as a personal revelation. This has little to do with both external stimulus, and detached reflection. Truth fills the bearer of truth with a joy and confidence.

586. He carefully identifies the viewpoints that tend to hold us back. He points out, "the legacy of Platonic/Aristotelian metaphysics reinforced and legiti-

---

[66] These quotes are taken from the work "The Participatory Mind' by Henryk Skolimowski and were reprinted in a coursepack for Dr. David Skrbina for his course on Philosophy of Mind

mized by the metaphysics of Thomas Aquinas" as the background of western thought. The world is now read to us by Plato, Aristotle, Aquinas, Descartes, and Newton. Out of these thinkers, the views of Plato are perhaps the most benign, but also the furthest removed from us. While Plato separated form and matter, Aristotle created a view of perfectibility and teleology. Aquinas separated faith from reason. Descartes separated mind from matter, and Newton and Galileo made Nature into a secondary category based on observable mechanisms. The belief that Man was separate from the world still has consequences from the way we view the world. Newton's portrayal of a mechanized universe of dead matter full of fixed and unchanging laws, stultified our view of a living and changing world. Skolimowski writes, "From Aristotle on, we have inherited the correspondence theory of truth or the classical theory of truth, which claims that truth is the correspondence between reality and its faithful description", but this view, "presupposes the existence of an objective unchanging reality out there". We should question these assumptions. Only the truth can sober us. The truth will set us free. Yet the truth is nuanced and the universe has a way of course correcting. Truth has to be adopted tentatively because we can no longer wait for all the information to come in. We must act on what we know. Don't ask why if you know what is wrong. Reality cannot be formed outside of us because we are active participants in Truth. Truth must be a living truth and a "happening".

587. We can no longer believe with Wittgenstein that the limits of our language are the limits of our world. This view also presupposes that the language we have can accurately judge our concomitant circumstance. We must remember that the word is not the thing as Indian philosopher Jiddu Krishnamurti said. However, each one of us possesses a unique understanding, and much of what we experience is simply beyond description. Reality is not transparent. If there is no consciousness, then there is no truth. As Skolimowski said, "For our truths are only the distilled fragments of our own unfolding knowledge". Our Truth cannot simply dwell up above inert, but it must come down to Earth and participate. The Church saw a fixed and unchanging universal law of God, and this was continued by scientific laws in the view of a mechanistic understanding of the world, as the world was devoid of Spirit.

588. Although we do not agree with the evolutionary mindset or the philosophy of being and becoming as we presently demonstrated, we look to Skolimowski in his "Ecotheology"[67] to gain a positive view of what direction we can take. We cannot be stuck in the past, and nor can we rely on messianic expectation which imbues with a frail minded faith in the future that waits for change. Still we have to consider the aims of Christianity in the context of Western Civilization where they have had a unique development. The work begins with an important question: "To what degree has traditional (Newtoni-

---

[67] These quotes are taken from Henryk Skolimowski's work "Ecotheology"

an) Science undermined our quest for spirituality? In what sense is New Physics encouraging us to consider spirituality and our religious quests seriously?".
He also asks us to consider: "What is the structure of wholeness? And how can
it be justified in human terms?".

589. We can no longer believe in "narrow minded scientists and technologists
who have promised us salvation through material gratification", or the arro-
gance and anthropomorphism of the secular humanists. The question of
wholeness and the meaning of life must be addressed by an ultimate frame of
reference for which only religion is suited. This comes with a recognition of
the fallibility of human knowledge, and the realization that the scope of what
we know changes the way we perceive the world around us that is not separate
from ourselves. Skolimowski writes, "Newtonian physics is in the image of
Jehovah of the Old Testament. Protestant Ethics is an extension of both". The
combination of these three layers of development adequately encapsulates our
spiritual malaise.

590. This consisted in a matrix of separation between the inner and outer
realms, and of the physical from the human, but if we are to convey a broader
vision then our imagination, conception, and perception must be brought back
into one channel of connectivity, without which communication becomes impossible. Skolimowski wants a shift from the redemption driven mindset to
one that focuses on creation or the creative elements of divine nature, which
are also the nurturing elements not interested in saving Man from himself.
Akin to his vision of the participatory mind, Skolimowski states that, "The
process of frame making is the process of mind making", and "Only when the
world is given to us, and is brutish and nasty, and we are helpless in it, only
then we must be saved from it, we must be redeemed". It is perhaps all too true
as Skolimowski states, "Creativity is a gift, but it is also a curse". The tools we
use to shape and mold reality are concepts and processes which are transient
and can often all too easily end up defining what we set out to build and create.

591. Skolimowski criticizes Marx: "If the root of Man is Man himself then our
roots are not very deep". As Man thinks so he becomes: There are no static
notions; no realm of thoughts. As Paul Tillich argues for ontic self-affirmation
by abolishing fatalism as a rule of contingency, neither the resignation of the
stoics or the not too dissimilar contemplation of Aristotle can suffice. Tillich
argues in his "Courage to be", that one must view faith as courage.
Skolimowski declares that we have to build an ethic around the frugality of
"grace without waste" and friendship. Grace radiates harmony and hope and
imbues us with an individual responsibility. As Skolimowski puts it, "Grace is
a flower". If the entire point of existence were the creation of the most marvel-
ous and beautiful and unique flower, then who could object to it? The joy
would not be found in waiting for such a marvel but in the moment, one takes
to experience it.

592. Skolimowski discusses how neither the mending of contradictory eschatology, that is both of a Christian and Evolutionary thought seen in Teilhard de Chardin, or an outright dismissal and scapegoating of the Bible in our own worldview seen in thinkers like Lynn White, seem to be a solution, because the Western culture itself is intricately developed and held up by Christian values. What we need instead is a reappraisal of these Christian themes that have been ignored for others in battle between revelation and salvation mindsets that have removed the personal and participatory realm in religious ethics. For this Skolimowski proposes an 11th commandment implicit in the first ten: "THOU SHALT NOT DESPOIL THE EARTH, NOR DESTROY LIFE THERE ON, FOR THE EARTH IS THE LORDS AND IS A FULNESS UNTO ITSELF, IN WHICH ALL LIFE SHARES". We must ask ourselves as Dr. Skrbina asks an audience at South by South West: How much technology is necessary to live a good life? Our ethic must include Oicos as it relates to Theos. Oicos is a Greek word for family, economics, and environment. From a religious standpoint, all three are inextricably linked. As Skolimowski so eloquently states, "Wholeness is this place within which connects us to the sacred but at the same time attunes us perfectly to our own body". Thus, as the existential and theological are mixed so are the environmental and the theological. "Ecotheology is part of Ecocosmology".

593. The opposite range of thoughts is one found in Christians that find support in a pseudo-eschatology arrived at through Western progress, which suggests that the Kingdom of God or the salvation of mankind will be brought about by universal values reflected in Democratic thinking which are brought to us through the advancement in learning. In the ideas of thinkers like Wolfhart Pannenberg we see a view both conditioned by Protestant Ethics and the supranational tendency found in democratic modes and classical liberalism that were erected in Europe. This idea is closely related to the Kabbalistic idea of Tzim Tzum, the idea of God coming to know himself in the Hermetic tradition, the birth of a New Man in Paul, and the singularity of the Transhumanists. The idea is brought out in a work by Pannenberg entitled "Faith and Reality"[68]. While we agree that this development of European Christianity as founding the secular tradition is essential in understanding the eschatological scope, we do not agree that this development has been to the greater benefit of humankind. Like Buber, Pannenberg brings out the most stunning claims of those who are adherents of the soteriological and eschatological scope of the Pauline style Christian teaching, that force the conclusion that the European Christians are the central components in a scheme that promises salvation for the entire world through a utopian style model that would be too ideal for even the dreams of Plato, who is perhaps often seen as the head of all utopian thought.

---

[68] Pannenberg, W. (1977). *Faith and Reality*. Westminster Press. We cite the work by Pannenberg for sections 593-611 by page number.

This brings us to the political significance of the Pauline message as we see it today.

594. Pannenberg follows Hegel in claiming that "reality is the unity of essential being and existence". He also gives special importance to the thoughts of St. Paul who put an emphasis on the end of the world and the coming of a New Earth (pg. 20). This emphasis is not seen as much in the Gospels and Johannine writings. Yet and still, there is God's entrance into history and the playing out of this drama on the stage of world-history (pg. 9). The interpretation of how the Word or Spirit of God moves through history has been blended with the Aristotelian teleology to suggest that God is moving everything to its particular end through the process of history. Hence, Teilhard de Chardin represents a perfect blend of Aristotelian and Pauline notions as reflected in current European thought which has come to influence Modern Scientific dreams of a technological singularity, and so clearly underline our concerns.

595. While the Jewish God represents an ultimate reality, the Greek God represented the ground of being or the cosmic order (pg. 10). The Pauline synthesis of these two forms is essential to the understanding of the concept of world-history. This is also understood through the Messianic expectation of the Jews in the Eschatology of national restoration that will bring peace to the entire world by restoring the faith of Jerusalem (pg. 15), which is seen as the heart and center of world events. Now there is the Pauline view of a New Heaven and New Earth to atone for the Sin of Mankind. According to Paul, "Creation was subjected to futility, not of its own will but by the will of the one who subjected it, in hope that the creation itself will be set free from its bondage to decay" (Rom 8:20-21). Hence, all of creation was to be renewed which reflects the fact that this eschatological scheme views evil to be a part of the very fabric of existence, especially in the world which is now ruled by the devil, which is also incidentally the reason why people are subjected to sin, not of their own will as Paul states. We contest that it matters not whether Man is chained to fate or linked in to the process of contingency that is open to the future when one is no longer free to affirm what is there now in the fullness of creation. We simply cannot believe that God has somehow left something out. But in the Pauline view, not only does Earth become renewed, but also Man becomes a New Man as the Second Adam Jesus. This view is seen in 1 Cor 15:45, that the first man was given a living soul that was wasted on sin, but the New Man will be a life-giving spirit responsible for the salvation of the entire world in the age to come (pg. 20).

596. Pannenberg all but proves that this is not a radical interpretation with his own synthesis. Both the life-giving spirit which is the "breath of life" which God breathes into human beings, seen as the Pneuma, and the quickening elements that give form and house spirit, seen as the Soma, are to be linked through the ephemeral and ethereal stages of world-history (pg. 21). Pannen-

berg cites both Anaximenes and Psalms. It ties to the realization of life everlasting and the bestowal of an immortal soul in the life to come, which stresses
a unity with God above other three western religious traditions and non-
Pauline versions of the Christian message. Pannenberg chooses a historical
view of Spirit in the Hegelian sense and contrasts it to the subjectivist trend of
Spirit seen in Descartes (pg. 25). We object that while the idealist and subjectivist experience-based mode of Spirit as apart from matter leave one in a detached higher realm, the view of world history eclipses the human element and
individual responsibility by making Man temporally dislodged and having to
seek salvation in the future or in modes that are outside of himself.

597. Hence, we feel that thinkers like Pannenberg set up the false dialectic that
is the perpetual fault line of Pauline theology. This would be the dialectic between "self-determination" and collective salvation. Like Skolimowski, Pannenberg puts the dialectic in terms of the disagreement between the respective
philosophies of Paul Tillich and Teilhard De Chardin. He further explicates the
problem in terms of "the relation between ecology and genetics", linked with
Tillich's ideas of an "ecstatic nature" and Teilhard's Omega Point, which is a
moment of main thrust of the culmination of the entirety of existence in which
"becoming" realizes its final goal (pg. 25-35).

598. Another issue is the notion of Man overcoming his sinful nature through
self-transcendence, but also being paradoxically made in the image of God.
Pannenberg feels that being made in the image of God reflects Man's ability to
master the forces of nature, however being made in an image does not convey
capacity or end but merely constitutes similarity of shape and form with none
of the actual meaning or status of being like a God (pg. 39-40). We furthermore detest this interpretation because it has led to a gross materialism and
anthropocentrism which treats nature as a secondary category in the experience
of Man, even though Man originates from and is part of the natural world.

599. It also ties into the fundamentally Greek conception of "prosopon" or
persona (pg. 43). In order for there to be self-transcendence there must first be
a conception of a self, which is the primary tool used in the medium between
the symbolic world which emanates from the spiritual backbone, and the cultural and political world, which for the Hegelian world historical map is a stage
of primary importance for the supposed self-actualization of Man (and God for
that matter). We note that it has been observed by many intelligent folks that
the institutions of Man harbor Man's darkest element, and the true necessity of
these social implements is often all too easily evaded by the practice of mutual
trust. This is hard to come to when these very same institutions are imbued
with a divine decree and the mandate of heaven.

600. Since the Pauline conception of a New Man, reborn to fit the New Age in
the world to come, who Man is now best corresponds to the Old Testament,

and thus the entire message of the New Testament only applies to the world to come. The Greek conception of Man as a "rational animal" is also closely tied in, especially as represented in the philosophy of Boethius (pg. 44). Pannenberg talks of the significance of God's entrance into history in terms of Man and says, "God has also united himself with humanity as a whole, because by his unity with God this one human being has manifested true human perfection", and says, "The goal of this history of Man's becoming has already appeared in Jesus" (pg. 45).

601. Pannenberg notes that the point of futurism in Paul is already made by 15th century Cardinal Nicolas of Cusa, who defined Man's likeness to God in terms of creative production, especially of technical products, much like Philo, who called the Logos or "creative reason" the first-born son of God (pg. 46). Even the dialogue of becoming or self-improvement in Nietzsche too readily offers itself to the Christian scope (pg. 47). As Pannenberg says, "The longing and struggle for this coming to be of man as man form the hidden theme of history of religion", in quite a perennial outburst (pg. 49).

602. He notes that the main link between the Jewish and Greek conception of God was born of a humanism which reasons from God's actions and activities on, or in, the world. This is brought out especially by Paul in 1 Cor 15, whereby in Jesus' resurrection Man's future is already fulfilled. The resurrection, in short, is fully symbolized in the end of history depicted in Jesus' resurrection from the dead which is a promise made of eternal life in a future kingdom. This is also the hermetic notion of self-transformation and self-revelation. Finally, there is the doctrine of universality of Christ addressed to every Man's conscience in 2 Cor 4:2, and also apparent in the mission to the Gentiles (pg. 61).

603. We have focused on two critical stages. One is the championing of Greek philosophy which they used to prove the existence of God, and the other is the Kantian severing of the metaphysical domain from the function of external laws. Pannenberg makes the emphatic statement that, "faith always has to do with the future" (pg. 65), however we feel it is precisely this type of faith in the future, and justification by faith alone, that is really at the crux of the issue. This is because it presents Man with a temporally dislodged horizontal dualism, that matches the vertical dualism of being removed from the ascended realm. The temporal dualism of Hegel does not solve the separation of form and content seen in Kant, because it paradoxically assigns value to the present only in what it is to be made for, and eventually must surpass, so all of reality becomes nothing more than a transient phase. As Paul states in 1 Cor 15:17: "If Christ has not been raised, your faith is futile, and you are still in your sins". This knowledge is about a physical event existing in time that is the promise for all of mankind. Here the terminology of a collective salvation arriving in the future is exhausted. It is, for us, both the empiricism and futurism

that is to be doubted and questioned and has most influence on the current view of the West.

604. Furthermore, it has become apparent to us that this knowledge of Christ's resurrection is not available to the layman, scientists, or historians. This is part due to a lack of evidence from an event dating back to ancient times, and partly due to the ideological and dogmatic restraints that bind experts in any field that we have taken great care to describe. It is also suggested to us in a quite contradictory fashion that knowledge is not the same as faith, and Paul preaches salvation by faith alone. Suffice it to say we neither regard this an adequate definition of faith, nor do we succumb to the doctrine of salvation by faith alone, which we consider thoroughly irreligious. It is perhaps not hard to see how collective salvation of the future that is to be awaited and the doctrine of salvation by faith alone seems to put no emphasis on either the nature of Man's responsibility and the greater ecology which represents the vital currents of existence that appear to us now and sustain us fully. This removes God from Nature and Man from his present mode of existence which he is chosen to live.

605. As history begins with Israel, the meaning of salvation of the entire world coming about through Israel is exchanged for the physical reign of Jesus (pg. 73). As Pannenberg declares that the central motif of Christ as truly man figures into the greater picture and says, "the God of Israel is not tied to the world-order but confronts the world in freedom". But here Pannenberg makes an important proclamation: "All Western historical thinking stems from biblical understanding of the world as history". This not only accounts for the particularity of European society but also the modern period secularization (pg. 75).

606. In this world historical view (that was perhaps best explained in the second part of the book) the main intellectual and spiritual force began in the Middle East with the Jewish Kingdom, then passed to the Persian and Greek, which morphed into the Hellenistic, Alexandrian structures which are the crux of Pauline thought, and finally the spread of Christianity to Europe. As Pannenberg states, "after the fall of Jerusalem, the mandate of the world dominion formerly linked with the Davidic Kingdom first of all passed to Babylon (pg. 80). Later it was assigned to the Persians, then to the Greeks and Hellenistic state structures. This succession of world-kingdoms however, according to Daniel, forms a merely transitional period which will soon be superseded by a final kingdom". He goes on to say, "unlike the land once promised to Israel, the salvation which took place in Jesus has to reach all men'.

607. In an almost racially motivated shrill that is quite opposed to the notion of a world-historical movement, Pannenberg sees Europe in particular as playing a special role (pg. 85). Accordingly, Hegel and Pannenberg see the salvation of Man as derived from the Jews, brought through the pre-eminence of the European. On this note he remarks that as a result of the Enlightenment, "Europe

was preserved as a spiritual unity despite denominational conflicts. Western civilization and the Christian heresy of Communism have spread more successfully throughout the world than the mission of the churches. Here too there are opportunities for a Christianization of their mission. God preserved his aim of universal Christian mission through the West and it is from Europe particularly in modern times that the world has grown into a unity". He admits that this has not been accomplished directly by Church efforts but indirectly by spreading science and technology.

608. We object to the notion that everything is moving toward an ultimate end or divine purpose, not because we find it irreligious, but because it discounts for the fact that every act of the all-powerful God is self-sufficient. In our view, suffice it to say, God does not have to do something for something else to happen. This doctrine also holds that God is distinct from the world. Quite plainly, this Pauline notion denies God as the ultimate source, and that God is the sole basis for reality. Instead of God being the totality of existence, God has manufactured becoming through the void in a quite Aristotelian fashion.

609. Finally, the notion of universality figures heavily in the Pauline message and in Greek thought. The division of churches and the separation of national and religious spheres supported the rise of secularism. As Pannenberg notes, "total equalization of reciprocal human relations would dissolve all community" (pg. 102). The supra-national tendency of democratic ideas seem to match with the two kingdoms approach of Christianity, which represents one rule preparing one for the rule to come in a New Earth, and another Earthly rule (pg. 105). Pannenberg points out that both Eusebius and Origen felt that the ending of national division would lead to a spread of the Christian doctrine (pg. 107). Instead of a Stoic ideal of equality in terms of constitution and essential nature, the Christian equality is an equality in regards to tenets of faithfulness in preparation for the coming of a future Kingdom of God.

610. To sum it up, as Pannenberg writes, "the individualism of a wholly private piety and traditional Christian authoritarian morality consciously or unconsciously help to maintain existing structures of dominion" (pg. 123). This is coupled with the fact that Jesus seemed to reject the political messianism of his people that was exchanged for the Pauline notion of collective salvation. A nominal agreement arises between us and Pannenberg in discovering the fact that the eschatological interpretation of the Christian message bears much significance to Paul's message focused in a personalized experience which was individual and direct but was manifested through the coming of a universal and collective salvation available to each and every person. It was an ethic of transformation and penance, becoming and change.

611. In the current drive toward Universalism there is again the onslaught of the syncretistic element, which in today's world seems to find novel views and

interpretations of Eastern doctrine in light of the various claims of Western science, seeking a viable alternative to religion. One such contender is what we will collectively refer to as "Techno-Buddhism" which has been drummed up by the intellectual elite of the West. In a recent article written by Tenzin Gyatso, the current Dalai Lama of Buddhism, he poses an interesting query[69]:

"What is a Buddhist monk doing taking such a deep interest in science? What relation could there be between Buddhism, an ancient Indian philosophical and spiritual tradition, and modern science? What possible benefit could there be for a scientific discipline such as neuroscience in engaging in dialogue with Buddhist contemplative tradition?"

His answer to the question is quite puzzling but also quite informative on the various aspects of the intellectual elite and their fascination with the combination of spiritual aims of Buddhism to their own transhumanist and scientific ends. He states:

"Although Buddhist contemplative tradition and modern science have evolved from different historical, intellectual and cultural roots, I believe that at heart they share significant commonalities, especially in their basic philosophical outlook and methodology. On the philosophical level, both Buddhism and modern science share a deep suspicion of any notion of absolutes, whether conceptualized as a transcendent being, as an eternal, unchanging principle such as soul, or as a fundamental substratum of reality. Both Buddhism and science prefer to account for the evolution and emergence of the cosmos and life in terms of the complex interrelations of the natural laws of cause and effect. From the methodological perspective, both traditions emphasize the role of empiricism. For example, in the Buddhist investigative tradition, between the three recognized sources of knowledge - experience, reason and testimony - it is the evidence of the experience that takes precedence, with reason coming second and testimony last. This means that, in the Buddhist investigation of reality, at least in principle, empirical evidence should triumph over scriptural authority, no matter how deeply venerated a scripture may be."

[69] Gyatso, T. (2005, November 12). *Science at the Crossroads | The 14th Dalai Lama (a talk given by the Dalai Lama at the annual meeting of the Society for Neuroscience)*. Dalai Lama. Retrieved April 28, 2022, from https://www.dalailama.com/messages/buddhism/science-at-the-crossroads

612. One may wonder why anyone who holds their religious beliefs to such a low standard would continue to practice. Some are all too ready to seek what is foreign in a sort of frantic escapism, and tourist style voyeurism. One rather cheap attempt is seen in a BBC documentary entitled "Jesus was a Buddhist Monk"[70]. Whatever could such a proclamation mean in terms of history and philosophy? While popular Neoconservative spokespersons like Sam Harris promote practices of Buddhist meditation like mindfulness as an alternative to Christian faith, is the hype real? What explains the current hyperactivity around the suggestions of Buddhist doctrine being superior or equivalent to Christian teaching? Is it because of its inclusivity, and its apparent affinity for the methods and views of science? There is also the rise in Perennial Philosophy for those seeking to democratize, syncretize, and conflate various religious views to their own desired ends.

613. Writers like Astrotheologist Jordan Maxwell, or Jungian mythicist Joseph Campbell most famously (but also seen in works by Aldous Huxley, Huston Smith, and C.S Lewis), is the drive to claim that archetypal themes across a variety of faiths suggest similar meanings. Some mythicists like Acharya S. actually adopt Buddhist titles to go with their new style of beliefs. Are these traditions that have centuries old practice like Islam and Christianity or are they quite recent inventions? Christianity and Buddhism have often been linked, but is this link justified? While sharing a similar pacifist ethic, dualistic metaphysics (of individuated soul and unified essence or spirit), and ascetic practice, certain claims have been made over the veracity of various similarities within the two belief systems. We will first look at some of the views of Buddhists and compare them to Christian teachings, but then we will explore how certain of those beliefs have been conflated by scholars of religious history.

614. In "Buddhism as Philosophy" by Mark Siderits[71], he says that people often wonder if it could be a coincidence that Greek and Indian philosophical traditions started around the same time but arose independent of one another. Now we know of trade contacts between the two countries and find that they even reach "strikingly similar conclusions" (pg. 5). Many may not realize that the same Greek tradition is the basis for a lot of philosophical stances concerning the Christian doctrine. The Soteriological concerns of Buddhism match that of later Christian sects in many respects. To begin with, both assume a default Nature of Man. Many are aware of the expression, originally thought of by St. Augustine, of hating the sin and not the sinner. Indeed, we find in St. Paul in Romans 7:17, that it is not us that sin, but the sin living in us. In Bud-

---

[70] Roos, B. (date unknown). *Jesus was a Buddhist Monk BBC Documentary*. YouTube. Retrieved April 28, 2022, from https://www.youtube.com/watch?v=qB4pe9BDGmE

[71] Siderits, M. (2007). *Buddhism as philosophy : an introduction*. Ashgate. We rely on this text for the next few sections to provide key facts about doctrines and beliefs that influenced the Buddhist doctrine and make sure to include page numbers where the particular facts are cited.

dhism as well, Man's suffering is brought about by his own inherent nature, and by no fault of his own. Life is suffering. Similarly, for both, the world is just a clever distraction.

615. We do not choose to be saved but are chosen. All that is really necessary is acceptance of our own limited nature. In Buddhist practice there is a notion of reaching sudden enlightenment. Siderits says this is different from Christianity, because there is no doctrine of salvation by faith alone, but many Christians do not believe one can really choose to be saved and believe in predestination which is sometimes attributed to Paul (Romans 9:19). The problem of free will does not seem to be resolved in Buddhist teaching. While some Buddhists disagree over the meaning of enlightenment, and enlightenment and salvation cannot be said to be precisely the same, the same can be said about the views of God in the West. God is seen as a detached God of Nature to some in a Deist manner, but to others as a highly personalized being of Christian and Sufi mystics.

616. A remarkable fact of Buddhism, however, is its being totally unconvinced with higher powers and realms, but more about knowledge of self and personal liberation. To this end, Buddhism offers an ascetic practice for the attainment of Moksha or Liberation, but generally does not regard a belief in a higher deity. One obvious similarity is the ascetic practice Christian Monks and Buddhist Lamas. Both Christianity and Buddhism retain ascetic practices and monastic orders. Some Western Mystics referred to Indian spiritual practices as the "Oriental Kabbalah".

617. Another similarity is that stories about the founder of the religion were bolstered over time (pg. 17). Many claim that like Christianity, the view of Buddists is unduly pessimistic about the affairs of the world (pg. 26). A most fundamental similarity that ties in all of these is the dualistic split used by both systems of Essence and Existence, or the numerical and the qualitative (pg. 33). There is an allusion to a hidden order that defies selfhood, and material existence in general (Romans 1:20). The doctrine of dependent origination can be seen in Christianity in the Logos that existed with God for eternity. Some Christians have taken this to suggest that Name and Form arise together (pg. 42, 66) . The separation, but arising together of Nama and Rupa, or Name and Form is a fundamental dualism that separates the uncreated and created, however neither are first in the order of Existence.

618. This doctrine can be seen in the debate between Buddhist philosopher Nagasena in his questions to the Greek King Milinda. The text is known as the Milindapanda or "Questions of King Milinda". In the Nyasa school that influenced later Buddhist Doctrine but also challenged it, we find them to posit Universals. Both Buddhists and Western Atomists like Democritus believed in a mereological reduction of parts from a whole. The rejection of the whole or

relation of parts to the whole was seen as a necessary starting point for both Indian and Western philosophy. For the Nyasa school, A tree is equally present in its leaves and branches. This sounds like John 15:4, where we read "No branch can bear fruit by itself. It must remain in the vine". Nyasa was trying to establish the existence of a self, contrary to Buddhist doctrine. The radical Hindu school of Advaita Vedanta practiced a form of Radical Monism which treated all as self. There are three ways to look at the relation of name and form: 1. Name is something that exists along with form since before the beginning of creation or its formulation into matter. 2. Name is something that is brought into existence along with form at the beginning of creation or the formulation of matter. 3. Name or the Self is all of existence and is uncreated.

619. As Indian Philosophers can be seen talking to Greek Kings, this is largely due to the effects of Hellenization spreading to India. We see that during Alexander the Great, Egypt to India became involved in Greek culture, which also occurred to a lesser degree in the Persian Empire. The belief in reincarnation was accepted by Plato, who had most likely borrowed it from Pythagoras. Empedocles and other Pluralist thinkers were known to espouse beliefs similar to Eastern thought, including the belief in the four elements. In the "Jesus was a Buddhist Monk" BBC documentary, there is an account much like the account that is important to certain Gnostics about Mary Magdalene traveling to France. These accounts are legendary and have almost no basis in anything that can be historically verified, but some are willing to stretch these similarities.

620. One of the main scholars interviewed in the "Jesus was a Buddhist Monk" documentary is Elaine Pagels. In the introduction of her book "The Gnostic Gospels"[72] she cites the claim made in the documentary, that the disciple of Jesus named Thomas went to India to start a ministry. The claim is that the Greco-Roman trade routes of years 80-200 were when the Jewish-Christian heresy of Gnosticism first arose. Pagels adds that Hippolytus mentions a heresy espoused by Indian Brahmins being twisted up by those who philosophize. It seems a number of outside influences, like Neoplatonic and Zoroastrian views, can be seen in the Nag Hammadi Gnostic Library as well. There could very well be a range of influence as is seen from the eastern practices of Zoroastrianism. But can this be sought out in the doctrines of either faith?

621. Similarly Robert M. Price is seen promoting Buddhism[73]. The scholar of Christian history asks about Buddhism as a world religion. "What if some major faith places demythologizing at the fore-front of its missionary efforts?", he writes in a recent article entitled "Bultmann and Buddhism". He states there

---

[72] Pagels, E. H. (1989). *The Gnostic Gospels.* Vintage Books.
[73] Price, R. M. (2009). *Bultmannism and Buddhism by Robert M. Price.* Robert M. Price. Retrieved April 28, 2022, from
https://www.robertmprice.mindvendor.com/art_bult_budd.htm

that the appeal of Buddhism is its promotion of self-reliance and self-understanding in order to be saved. It also saw as irrelevant previous Vedic faith systems which often challenged it (another pattern we see is the constant conflating of Hindu and Buddhist practices). However, it can also be said that the offering of prayers and sacrifices in order to be saved from the sinful world was also cancelled by Paul's message in Galatians 2:19, where he says, "For through the law I died to the law, so I might live in God". Similarly, Buddha does not claim to have rejected the Vedic teaching but to have surpassed it, and sidestepped it, by figuring out its real meaning, and thereby breaking the cycle of reincarnation. Even Bart Ehrman spuriously makes the claim that one man's orthodoxy is another man's heresy. What is quite odd is the fact that Buddhism and Gnosticism function as a kind of "true interpretation" of the traditions that they are based on. Buddhism presents itself as a solution to Hinduism and the cycles of reincarnation. Buddha referred to himself as a reformer of Hinduism, just as Jesus referred to himself as a reformer of Judaism. While Judaism rejects Christianity, and Christianity rejects Gnosticism, similar to Buddhism being the true meaning of Hindu doctrine, Gnosticism considers itself to be the true meaning of the Christian message. While Buddhists and Gnostics are willing to accept and subsume their predecessors of Hinduism and Christianity, both Hindu and Christian thought firmly reject Buddhist and Gnostic views.

622. A similar writer who conflates the views of heretics with religious orthodoxy is Joseph Campbell who is renowned for his views on Myth and Archetype and the Jungian outlook. He regularly conflates Buddhist and Gnostic views. In his "Inner Reaches of Outer Space"[74] on pg 41, he explains the term Bodhisattva only to relate it to Ramakrishna, Dalai Lama, and Jesus Christ. First of all the term applies specifically to the Buddhist tradition, but then one has to wonder how to jumble up these various types of religious followers in the same group. Ramakrishna was a Hindu mystic. The Dalai Lama is the equivalent of Buddhist Pope. No one of the three big western religions agree on who Jesus was or what his purpose was on this planet. On pg 53 he equates the liberation of Prince Gautama Shakyamuni from fear and desire to the saying of the Gospel of Thomas which states "the Kingdom of God is within". While this message is devoid of eschatological view present in Orthodox Christianity formulated in 325 AD, it should also be noted that Gnostics were generally regarded as heretics by most Christians and Jews, and even viewed as deranged by Plotinus (Enneads).

623. Yet and still, certain Gnostic and syncretistic views have come to influence Christian and Buddhist doctrine. The Ascetic or Encratite view seen in some Gnostic texts, like the Gospel of Thomas, is also seen as similar to the practice of Buddhist Monks. A most bizarre fascination exists in theosophical

---

[74] Campbell, J. (2012). *The Inner Reaches of Outer Space: Metaphor as Myth and as Religion*. New World Library.

and perennial views on the link between Buddhism and Christianity. The "channeling" of the "Aquarian Gospel of Jesus Christ" by Levi Dowling includes the tales of Jesus as a young boy in India during the missing parts of his childhood (birth to age 30). While there, he instructs a Vedic priest named Ravana on the meaning of the law. Founder of the Theosophical Society Helena Blavatsky writes, "Maitreya Buddha (the last Bodhisattva, or Visnu in the Kalki Avatar) the tenth "messenger" expected on earth. But this will be the One wisdom and will incarnate itself into the whole humanity collectively"[75]. This combines Hindu, Christian and Buddhist teachings into a pseudo-eschatology that then involves progress on a world stage. Similar beliefs started the New Age movement.

624. Dr. Kelley Ross[76] correctly points out that Gnosticism is much more like Advaita Hinduism than Buddhism, and Pagels seems to promote Gnostic views above Christianity. She wrongly connects the view of being saved by Reason as a belief in inclusivity, and a belief in women becoming like men as some kind of feminism. What it actually seems to suggest is the strict hierarchy and rigor of ascetic practice. In Gnostic sects only a select few were given the real meaning behind certain beliefs. Also present is the Gnostic separation between Male and Female energies, where Male is seen as the creative nature, and the Female as the passive material nature. This can be seen in the writings of many Gnostics like Jung. One of his views seems to suggest that feminine energy within a person is exemplified by female characters one encounters in a dream state, or male characters for women. The view that one has to combine the feminine and male aspects within oneself to bring continual rebirth, by giving birth to oneself, is a concept employed in hermaphroditic cults and fertility cults of many varieties. This was not a doctrine of inclusion but one of transcendence. I suspect that this view is not so coincidental with Elaine Pagels belonging to the Lindisfarne Center. The center regularly promotes techno shamanism and techno Buddhism, while applying the doctrine of scientific progress and scientific method to explore spirituality and a merging of the concept of doctor and priest. The philosophy of A.N. Whitehead and pseudo-eschatology of Jesuit priest Teilhard De Chardin which merges Darwinian Evolution and Christian Eschatology are regularly employed by such groups to support a transhumanist agenda.

625. While the skittish and nervous world of escapism employed by the western philosophical tradition in trying to disown its own roots, we see a consid-

---

[75] *Maitreya in the Light of Real Theosophy.* (2015, June 2). THEOSOPHY. Retrieved April 28, 2022, from https://blavatskytheosophy.com/maitreya-in-the-light-of-real-theosophy/. According to the article, the quote mentioned above is from H. P. Blavatsky, "Lamas and Druses," "H. P. Blavatsky Theosophical Articles" Vol. 3, p. 288
[76] Ross, K. Elaine Pagels - Gnostic Gospels. Friesian School. Retrieved April 28, 2022, from https://www.friesian.com/pagels.htm. An insightful article by Dr. Kelly L. Ross (a retired philosophy professor) on work of Elaine Pagels

erable lack of substance provided on any real links between Buddhist and Christian thoughts, other than the links we have described. These are most readily expressed by Nietzsche in Beyond Good and Evil (Section 61), where we read, "Christianity and Buddhism is as venerable as their art of teaching even the lowliest how to place themselves through piety in an illusory higher order"[77]. This he saw was the most dangerous, subtle, and powerful element of Christian and Buddhist beliefs, that believe it or not make for a perfect soldier. This is the one who is castrated of will, and stripped of emotions: in short the perfect killing machine. The denial of life is, after all, the ultimate rebellion. Those who feel Buddhism and Christianity are about peace should read about the Crusades, or the Zen Buddhist support for Fascism in WWII. The book "Zen at War" by Brian Victoria is a fascinating explanation of the link between Zen Buddhism and fascism, as was also pointed out by author Arthur Koestler in his book "The Lotus and the Robot". One can quite readily point to the violence between Buddhists in countries like Myanmar and Sri Lanka and Muslim communities[78], where Buddhists have taken great care to segregate their communities from their Muslim neighbors and even terrorize them with violence and forbid their children to associate with them. All we have to say is that religious alternatives are sometimes haphazardly espoused. The grass is always greener on the other side. Sometimes the best way to understand one another is to be ourselves. On the other end, if we are to understand the value of religious traditions the approach of the Dalai Lama seems too broad and not enough of a challenge to the methods of science to be considered pure in any sense. The Buddha talked about the unity of all life, a reality that is constantly threatened by the hubristic views of science and technology that have caused an existential threat pitting Man against Nature.

626. The real Buddhism proceeds by negation to a state of non-dualism brought forth perfectly in the story of Mahakasyapa, the Buddha's chief disciple. Mahakasyapa smiled at the Buddha when he held up a flower instead of delivering a sermon. Even to say nothing is to affirm something. Even the act of destruction is a creative act. To be silent is to act and to attempt to do nothing is to strive. Granted this, non-violence is just as violent as overt violence. The attempt to bring about non-violence has led to many deaths. Silence can be violent and indeed words can kill.

627. The Occultist Helena Blavatsky founded the Theosophical Society headquarters in Madras India, and developed the myth of Shambhala and the Orien-

---

[77] Nietzsche, F. W. (1989). *Beyond good and evil* (W. A. Kaufmann, Ed.; W. A. Kaufmann & H. Zimmern, Trans.). Vintage Books.

[78] *Persecution of Muslims in Myanmar*. (n.d.). Wikipedia. Retrieved April 28, 2022, from https://en.wikipedia.org/wiki/Persecution_of_Muslims_in_Myanmar. The list of references to this Wikipedia article should yield tons of information on the persecution of Muslims in Myanmar which is a well-known fact

tal Kabbalah[79]. The myth of Shambhala was that a Eurasian caste of a sacred race of the inhabitants of Atlantis had survived in the Xinjiang province of China by hiding the remnants of an ancient civilization deep within the mountains. The province is known for the Chinese government's poor treatment of Uyghur inhabitants. Another Occultist who was fascinated with the myth of Shambhala as the origin of the Oriental Kabbalah was Swedenborg. In the 13th century Kabbalists like Abraham Abulafia used tantric techniques such as meditation on colors and repetition of divine names to reach "the ascent of the soul".

628. The Occult schools of Alexandria referred to the philosophers of India in their tantric and ascetic practice as "gymnosophists". Relying on various "Left-hand Tantra', which taught the "holiness of sin", similar to a belief of Frankist style Messianics, that everything was permitted and a reversal of values was necessary to bring about the coming of a New Age. These beliefs rather focused on the heretical "Vamachara", where the doctrine of "sacred marriage" helps one attain unity with the divine. Elements of Tibetan Buddhism are based on these practices, but also contain elements of the heterodox faction of Buddhism called "Bon" practiced around Tibet, a prominent symbol of which is the Swastika. Parts of "Bon" are seen to derive from pre-Buddhistic shamanism. The sexual and tantric practices which involve the withholding of orgasm to increase "spiritual energy" from the Mahayana path of Vajrayana is promoted by the Tibetan Buddhists. Mahayana doctrine itself is most notably a third century C.E phenomenon, akin to Roman Catholicism and Gnosticism, and is an amalgam of Greek culture and Buddhism. As noted, Alexandrian and Hellenistic influence had spread to India much earlier.

629. The link between Greek Philosophy and Buddhism can be readily found in the Greek inspired Kushan Empire. As late as the 8th century C.E, the furthest removed doctrine from traditional Buddhist practice appeared in the "Sahaja" or Sahajayana and Kalachakra schools. It was primarily in these schools of thought that we see the incorporating concepts of Messianism through the return of the Buddha and the use of various astrological and alchemical views jointly regarded as neo-Pagan. In the Sahajayana according to Swami Ananda Cooraswamy, "There is then no sacred or profane, spiritual or sensual, but everything that lives is pure and void."[80], and Kalachakra literally means "dark energy". These are most famously seen to develop into Kundalini Yoga practices which involve the cosmic serpent, or the male energy aspect of the universe, rising through the chakra system and reaching the thousand petal lotus,

---

[79] Livingstone, D. (2013). *Black Terror White Soldiers: Islam, Fascism & the New Age*. Sabilillah Publications. We use the research of Livingstone on the "Oriental Kabbalah" and information on many interesting facts such as the connections of the Dalai Lama to the Nazi party and Gandhi to the Theosophical society.

[80] Coomaraswamy, A. K. (1985). *The Dance of Śiva: Essays on Indian Art and Culture*. Dover Publications. Pg. 103

which represents the divine feminine principle. Occultists linked the Kundalini to the Caduceus of the Greek god Hermes. These practices are often combined with apotropaic magic offered to a plethora of spirits and demons which function as correspondences. The many novel practices were conglomerated and appropriated by Westerners into Oriental and Mystical Eastern Wisdom, and especially exploited by those who wanted an alternative to Western religion to match their new so-called quantum cosmology.

630. The most recent form of heterodox and perennial modes is taught by the visionary experiences of Sri Ramakrishna and spiritual methods of G.I Gurdjieff. The disciple of Sri Ramakrishna was Swami Vivekenanda, who coined the term "Hinduism", and is quoted at length in William James famous essay "Will to Believe". He paradoxically also taught the unity of all religions. His work and speeches had an influence on Annie Besant, and pedophile and occultist Charles Leadbetter, who while heading the Theosophical Society claimed to have discovered the New Messiah or Matreiya in a young Indian boy named Jiddu Krishnamurti. Much to his greatest credit Krishnamurti disbanded a group of followers assigned to him to assist him in fulfilling his role as "world teacher" and declared that he was not a guru. Most notably, Besant and Blavatsky were said to have met with Gandhi where they first introduced him to the legendary writing known as the Bhagavad Gita. A lesser-known fact is the tantric sex practices of Gandhi which included sleeping in a bed with his young nieces to overcome his sexual desires. This radical approach, and quite disgusting turn of events, seems to correlate with the Left-hand path methods of embracing sin in order to overcome it and even master it.

631. Gandhi had a theosophical approach to his reading of the Gita. It may surprise some to know that teachers like Gandhi and Vivekananda who export Hindu themes to Westerners are often seen as experts but often conflate these themes into Western values to make them more appealing. These tactics are the very same used by those who always style themselves as none other than religious reformers and perennial philosophers but are actually occultists attempting to subvert religion and use it to goals such as those of the Lindisfarne Institute who wish for a "planarization of the esoteric". This is just as those who traveled East in search of sacred knowledge often in an attempt to update their occult practices sought the most universalizing and abstract and distant ideologies. Lama Dorjieff or George Gurdjieff was linked to Russian intelligence and was family friends with Joseph Stalin. His idea of Man as "spiritual machine" in a perpetual state of waking sleep that could only be improved by his syncretistic practices to reach an awakening have had a profound influence on New Age thinking. Gurdjieff also helped to popularize the myth of Shambhala and was quite innovative in combining the scientific method with religious practices.

632. Carl Jung, a widely known Gnostic thinker whose foundation was linked with the discovery of the Nag Hammadi Gnostic Library according to Elaine Pagels, said about Freudian psychoanalysis and the theories of Freud that, "one would have to take a deep plunge into the history of the Jewish mind. This would carry us beyond Jewish orthodoxy into the subterranean workings of Hasidism". Freud's essential project was a reworking of the concept of Sin into a mastery of repressed sexual energy which was the driving force of human interaction. This hidden psycho-sexual order had much import for the theories of tantric methods that relied on double bind techniques to increase duration of altered states. These consisted of periods of intense stress followed by periods of complete surrender. Freud also wrote of equating the several tendencies that are usually regarded as sin as finding its origins in a concern with sex and incest. The repression of these drives led ultimately to the tools of the State.

633. According to historian Paul Johnson in his book "Modern Times", both Marxian and Freudian theories which regarded a hidden order to things were based in Jewish mysticism. Freud met with William James in 1909. James' father was a disciple of Swedenborg, and the work of William James is said to have contributed immensely to the views of Freud. Annie Besant, who was a Fabian Socialist, held correspondence with Edward Aveling who was one of the first to translate Marx into English. Together they helped to propel a Freud-Marxian synthesis that became predominant in Postmodern philosophy.

634. Fabian Socialists believed in the philosophy of gradualism in social change. Atheists such as Bertrand Russell openly espoused such aims. The details of how Fabian Socialists wish to create a utopia or "archaic revival" whereby Man's technology is both the problem and solution. Fabian socialists felt that change could only come about, "without breach of continuity or abrupt change", and believed in the inevitability of change and progress, which would be brought about through the existing social institutions and designs of power. This was based on a pseudo-spiritual value of evolution brought by the mathematics of Prigogine which suggest that change happens when chaotic elements derive far from equilibrium. Bertrand Russell promoted a society ruled by science and technology that would advance programs of Eugenics that were put forward by experts in pharmacogenomics. The theories of Symbolic Logic put forward by Bertrand Russell and A.N. Whitehead were used to develop cybernetics. Russell invited his protege, Engineer and Philosopher Ludwig Wittgenstein, to join his secret society called the "Cambridge Apostles". They advanced ideas of "platonic love" and engaged in various homosexual relationships. The group was linked to the Metaphysical society of which William James was a member.

635. The philosophy of William James and Henri Bergson influenced Italian Fascism, and Gandhi also met with Mussolini. Poets like Ezra Pound and Tristan Tzara continued a long tradition of fascination with the occult, much like

W.B Yeats and Willaim Blake. Pound even wrote for publications that were run by Oswald Mosely of the British Union of Fascists, and Blake was influenced by Emmanuel Swedenborg who used terms like "Oriental Kabbalah" to describe the practices of ancient mystics. Theosophist Nicholas Roerich, purportedly a student of both Blavatsky and Gurdjieff, had inspired not only Igor Stravinsky's Rites of Spring, but also Vice President Henry A. Wallace in using the eye on the pyramid on the back of the dollar bill. Bosnian Serb mystic Dimitric Mitrinovic anticipated the theories of transhumanism and viewed the universe as a great mind in the process of becoming, much like Whitehead in his idea of process theology. They combined the views of Pantheism where the universe is equated with God with the immaterial God of Plato, and finally a quasi-religious pseudo-eschatology based on the scientific world view and belief in progress.

636. Mitrinovic claims, as does Hegel, "there is no doubt that this divine function is performed by Europe. Europe is chosen...both by providence and by destiny and must be finally chosen also by the will of humanity", reflecting the view of secular humanism and the universal goal of democratic values. He goes on to say that the 'will of humanity" must "become the body of man". He also says, "the Jews or Israel, was 'chosen' for the 'mission' of becoming white". Mitrinovic corresponded with H.G Wells, Pablo Picasso, and Henri Bergson. He also approached several thinkers like Martin Buber, who was a relative of Karl Marx, to achieve his various aims which included working with the notorious Black Hand group responsible for murdering Archduke Ferdinand. In the words of Hegel in his Reason in History, in a section entitled "The Idea of Freedom", he states, "world history is the exhibition of spirit striving to attain knowledge of its own nature. As the germ bears in itself the whole nature of the tree, the taste and shape of its fruit, so also the first traces of Spirit virtually contain the whole of history. Orientals do not yet know that Spirit". He says that freedom expressed in Oriental terms is the freedom of an Asian Despot, but the concept of freedom "first arose among the Greeks". He goes on to say, "Only the Germanic peoples came, through Christianity, to realize that man as man is free and that freedom of Spirit is the very essence of man's nature. This realization first arose in religion, in the innermost region of spirit; but to introduce it in the secular world was a further task which could only be solved and fulfilled by a long and severe effort of civilization". It is not hard to see how this racial and hermetic and kabbalistic outburst went on to fuel Nazi sentiments but was ultimately seen in the story of the world-historical importance of the Jews who were seen to play a special role in the world to come. He says that while Orientals discovered that a Man can be free only on his own terms, this freedom was limited to the individual. The Greeks discovered how this could be practiced by a group of men, and finally the modern age will come to recognize it on Universal terms. The Hegelian concept that the abstract negation seeks its own negative impulse as its own reso-

lution as the engine of world history has had a considerable effect on those who espouse evolutionary or transcendental aims.

637. A major influence on the thoughts of the Nazi party was seen in the Occult society known as Thule. Thinkers like Dietrich Eckhart, Rudolph Hess, Lanz von Liebenfels, and Rudolph Sebottendorf (the founder of the Thule Society) were Nazi sympathizers used the ideas of the Occult and Blavatsky's ideas of the Aryan Race to craft their racial ideology. One such member was Karl Haushofer, who supposedly was advised by Gurdjieff in Tibet to adopt the symbol of the Swastika. Haushofer was the teacher of Rudolph Hess. The current Dalai lama was not only connected to Dr. Bruno Berger in his expedition to Tibet led by Ernst Shaefer to discover the remnants of an Aryan civilization but was also tutored at a young age by S.S officer Heinrich Harrer, who wrote about the account in his book "Seven Years in Tibet". The legend of Shambhala came to parallel the search for Zion or Holy Land seen in the Jewish tradition just as the Oriental Kabbalah was also seen to parallel Jewish mysticism.

PART IV

LOGOS DETHRONED, PART 2 / PAUL'S REVALUATION OF VALUES

Chapter 22
The Rejected Stone is Now the Cornerstone

638. In order to succeed, the Pauline message has subsisted alongside classical Greek and Roman (in other words Pagan) value systems. Paul's revaluation of values is a three-step process in terms of his philosophical approach. The first was the view that the Soul passed on into various forms of life and a variety of stages of existence. The pre-Socratic philosophers and the Orphic and Vedic mythologies that were prominent at the time share this with Platonic philosophy and predate it in several respects. However, it is important to note that in their view God was properly involved in all of existence, similar to the Hebrew God. The second step was the ascended realm or the removed plane of existence, where God was only in charge of the Universal. This was the Platonic/Pythagorean framework where God was seen as transcendental and not concerned with the particular aspects of the world. The third step was God coming down from the transcendental realm to partake in his creation. This is the entrance of God into history which culminates in the Pauline message. This was justified by the teleology of Aristotle. Note that Paul needed God to be far removed from existence in the Platonic view to then have him come into existence. The spirit had manifested in flesh. God was brought down from the higher plane of existence where he had been banished and Logos was dethroned from its heavenly reign. Then this heavenly reign could only take place in a New Earth for a New Man that was to exist in the future as the culmination of world events. Both God coming down to this realm and the entrance of God into history represent the same basic concept: in order for Man to become like God, God had to first become a Man.

639. While figures like Moses and Jesus reflect historical epochs dealing with the institutional fabric of certain ancient systems of Laws and how they relate to a people, figures like Plato and Paul serve as the interpreters of how the development of ancient symbols have come to be recognized. If all of "Western Philosophy" is a footnote to Plato, then all of Western Civilization is a footnote to Paul. The edifice of artistic, philosophical, and cultural technics has undoubtedly informed the development within a Platonic/Pauline melding within European society. Jewish and Roman elements were purged. Plato dealt with Athens on the terms of a subversive vengeance. Paul dealt with Romans with a sort of hostile vengeance. His goal was to both subvert Judaism and take control of the Gentile. Jewish teachings were subverted and used for the purpose of the destruction of Rome. This Roman system and the power of the Church landed into the hands of Europeans who used it for Empire building. Their philo-Semitism was based on a belief in the Pauline message of a dual path of salvation. The mixture of Platonic cosmology with Pauline Soteriology is a

factor. The mixture of Aristotelian metaphysics of teleology with Pauline eschatology is a factor. Gnostics, Mystics, Philosophers, Artists, Revolutionaries
have been swept up in the disinterested idealism that is manifest in the Pauline
message. One of the least touched on topics in Western scholarship is the re-
education of classical Greek and Roman scholarship in light of Paul. During
the secular mood of the day and the celebration of the achievements of European civilization, not much is said about the debt owed to Pauline views,
which after all, have been rarely questioned and largely taken for granted in
their relation to mainstream Christianity.

640. It was Paul who finally created a dialectic between grace and salvation
that would actually reach beyond its historical age, of which Hegel was only a
reformer. Paul's message teaches that life is suffering and sin, the new covenant is fulfilled in the world to come, and that the road to salvation and grace is
simple. One can reach salvation only by faith alone. A secular analog of Paul's
message can be found in the belief that man is flawed and comes from lowly
origins, that his success will be through the progress of a new age, and all that
has to be done to achieve this is to believe in humanity and faith in one's fellow man. The Darwinian natural progression of species from a lowly origin to
the pinnacle of the hierarchy of being was Heraclitean and Aristotelian. The
Freudian division of the mind into the three parts was a reflection on the trinity, and on the tripartite soul of Plato. Marx affirmed the view of Hobbes, that
Man is ill-natured and defined by savage impulses, and affirmed the Lockean
view that the summation of Man's efforts lies in the subsistence derived from
labor and material goods. Both are projected into a pseudo-eschatology
through the fun house mirror of Hegelian philosophy in so-called Postmodern
thinking. Man had to be collectively redeemed. The technique is one of assimilation. Why conquer when one can assimilate? Liberalism is compatible with
Christian teaching, and this has been made possible by the Pauline supersession. This supersession exists in the New Covenant that will be fulfilled with
the coming of the Lord. A faith in the future is a natural result. A tubular ag-
gression against one's present state is necessarily entailed. Moreover, even if
these things are not directly shown and or implied for Pauline teaching, it also
matters how they have been employed within a historical and philosophical
context. We see that Gnostic thinkers like Marcion, Powerful figures like Constantine, and unscrupulous fellows like Martin Luther have influenced Christian teaching in their promotion of the views of Paul, sometimes over the
views of Christ. The result is that Christians today do not follow Jesus but follow Paul. The fact that Paul's views are not in line with Jewish teaching should
not come as a surprise; Jewish scholarship has rejected Pauline teaching. The
fact that the views of the Pauline Epistles does not even square well with the
teaching of the Gospels is a fact even lesser known to many Christians.

641. We also cannot simply ignore our modern situation. In the lead up to today, we will give the shortest account possible of the historical misrepresenta-

tion of Pauline theology as it relates to Christian teaching. Paul's letters appear before the Gospels. Paul was an early hater of Christians, and we are told by his followers that he worked for the high priest to eliminate the Christian heresy. Soon he taught his own version of Christianity, and most notably disagreed with some of the other Church leaders. What is the Christian message before Paul? The followers of Jesus, and Jesus himself, spoke Aramaic, but the New Testament as we see it today was compiled after the writing of the Pauline letters, which comprise more than half of the New Testament, is written in Greek. The words of Paul play a more pivotal role to the narrative of the Gospels than the sayings of Jesus and those teachings had the most impact on the Gentile whom they were addressed to but also attach them to the prophecies of Israel which their own philosophy was put in the service of. Paul does not mention the life of Jesus. He breaks down rather than building up. He refers to himself constantly. He uses Greek concepts of Pagan philosophy to influence his listeners. The concept of the Logos is not the same as the Word. The concept of the Ruach Elohim, or breath of God, is not the same as the Pneuma or vital force. While Greek views were most fervently adopted by the Hellenized Jews, it also soon had an effect on Paul's target audience. These were the Gentile, or the rabble of Rome. If anyone could be enlisted to Judaize Rome, then it was them. Rome soon converted to Christianity and collapsed. Christianity survived and spread to Europe.

642. While in Europe, Christianity was melded with the scholastic tradition and divorced from the political stage. The impetus for this could be found in the Pauline doctrine. Christians sought an other-worldly Kingdom. European Christian scholars sought to reform the Christian doctrine. Luther's literalist interpretation gave new life to the idea that when Christ returns, he will convert the Jews. This affirmed the belief in a dual road of salvation that could include each and every person, which in the word of Paul continually said by him in Romans, "for the Jew first, but also for the Gentile". European Jews and Christians made a push towards secularism. A similar push was made in Islamic society but it was outright rejected, but today the result is the same with Muslims refusing to ask serious questions. Moreover, there is a growth in attempts to undermine the religious experience by promoting a "religion of science". There is yet another tendency to reduce all science and religion to artful speculation. There is the Apollonian drive which promotes Logos theology, and the Dionysian distinction which promotes a Perennial philosophy. The bifurcation of religious modes is vastly apparent. Split the truth in two pieces and only those who truly love it will surrender it in order to keep it whole. Even among prominent atheists there are those who try to banish religious forms into the hands of the rule of experts maintaining that religion is a historical superstition, while there are others who seek to recombine the aspects of several religions with the scientific worldview. We cannot simply settle for brute technological efficiency, or pure epicurean sensitivity, because we cannot forsake a sense of divine purpose.

643. Indeed our humanity seldom allows for it. The somber complexities of inner struggle awaken us all. Even in the praise of Science and Technology as the saviors of mankind, we observe a general impulse for the spiritually driven life. Regardless of the machinations of technological society, the drive to reduce the religious experience to pharmacological intervention has not been successful. It may have even been a surprise to some that such things are being proposed, but not for us. It has become all too apparent that Christianity has come to us from a nexus of various expressions of God that it first had to contend with. Based on the various conflicts, we can do no more than to view these as corruptions and contradictions on the original message that was brought forward by Christ in a period of political turmoil. These were later assimilated by Paul's message. There is firstly the Jewish God, whose expression was in a unification of imageless and cosmic superiority. Secondly there was the Roman God, whose expression was in the "god-emperor", the ideal of the State and the apex of power. Already there was a Jewish Temple opposed to a Roman State. The antithesis of the Roman form was the Greek form, which was based on the spirit of the laws in attunement with Nature in the more democratic aspects. There was the Republic of Rome, whose achievement was of might, was brought about by organization of the State and not by its artistic and cultural achievements also focused on pleasure brought by cultural refinement. The Polis of Athens was rather based on cultural enrichment and the plight of the citizens and the Laws of Solon. Finally, there was the Jewish Zealot view of political salvation and the promise of an earthly kingdom and eternal throne. This view sought power in land and blood relations. Not all Jews agreed with this view.

644. Some like Paul, seemingly agreed, but wished not to oppose the rule of Rome by force. The Goddess or Great Mother of the Temple of Ephesus was a final expression. This was a wholly pagan expression verging on the occult. We have the Jewish "God the father", The pantheistic Greek expression of the Spirit, the Roman expression of the "son of God" or half-human half-god, and the great vessel or Mother Mary, which was called forth to bring out the divine incarnation representing the material world (or the Shekinah in Jewish Mysticism and Isis in Hermeticism). We are not alleging or even concerned with whether or not these things were knowingly or unknowingly affirmed by either Paul or someone trying to invent the character of Paul. Our discussion is not about whether Paul was a historical figure. Our discussion is on the greater effects of Pauline theology so that someone can begin an appropriate analysis on the value of Paul as a historical figure. Many of the views we represent have been previously ignored, but we will challenge how certain of these views have been used to subvert, transform, hijack, and extort those original traditions in a game of intellectual and spiritual revenge. The effect of the Pauline message on the Gospel narrative cannot be ignored. Also, the fact that we read "the Word", a Jewish concept, instead of "Logos", a Greek one, is

largely thanks to these same changes which seem to obfuscate the true origin and effect of Pauline teaching. The way the Bible has come to be viewed presents us with a popular translation. If we want to reach Jews, Christian, and Muslims, then we must take an honest look at the Bible. We have to deal with the Christian message on its own terms. We cannot simply assume that Christians should be convinced by anything other than this. Does Paul contradict the words of Jesus? This final test should give Christians some pause. Can we see Paul's message apart from all other entanglements as it really is on its own terms so we can assess the true impact and range of the Pauline narrative? Those who are strong in their faith should not be afraid to challenge it, for it is precisely those who would be so sure that a strong faith can withstand any challenge. We then move to analyze the stories presented in the Gospels, leaving out the variations that can be seen in the "Passion" narratives. What primarily concerns us are not the historical facts and minute details, or the minor and major differences in Christological doctrine, but to extract from these, as much as we can the teachings of Jesus, so we can compare them to the teaching of Paul. Since there are hundreds of examples, to conserve time we have made a few selections of key themes.

Chapter 23
Let He Who is without Sin Cast the First Stone

645. While the ultimate sin is one of hypocrisy, no Man is without sin according to Paul. If the passage above is to be taken seriously, no one is anyone's judge. According to Scholars Dr. Bart Ehrman (atheist) and Dr. Daniel Wallace (Christian), the above verse from John cannot be found in the earliest manuscripts[1]. This Pauline message was added into the Gospels later. One of the longest and earliest accounts can be found in the Gospel of Matthew. Even though, in terms of chronology, the Gospel of Mark shows up before, we will begin with the Gospel of Matthew as to cover the largest swath possible of Jesus' teachings found in the New Testament. Paul makes very light mention of these traditions and sayings, so it can be useful to contrast the views of Jesus with that of Paul at least in some very nominal sense or in a way where the average Christian reader can easily cross-reference.

The Gospel of Matthew

646. When we open up the Gospel of Matthew, we see that an Angelic being appears to Joseph and tells him to protect Mary. Holy men or Magi come from the East and predict the birth of a baby boy. The Magi, for some reason or another, appear before Herod, and explain to him the Holy birth. Magi began to worship Jesus. It is a notable fact that Magi originate from Zoroastrian religion, and not Jewish faith. Why were these types of Holy men used instead of a Jewish rabbi? Joseph takes Mary to Egypt to protect the birth of the newborn child from the wrath of Herod. Herod is an enemy of Jesus from day one apparently but not in Paul's letters. Afterwards they are warned not to go to Judea, but to Nazareth, a small port city off of the Sea of Galilee. At this time John the Baptist is the harbinger of Christ, preaches in the wilderness, and admonishes the Pharisees. He warns that as he baptizes in water, another one will come to baptize in fire. This is quite an ominous prediction. Jesus does not come to bring peace on Earth, but a sword. Simply put, it is not a message of coming together, but of cleaving apart. John however, does teach a message of coming together. Those who are united for the good must also be united against evil.

647. Jesus, instead, faces the devil alone in the wilderness. While he is tempted, he overcomes it by fasting and praying. The exchange is interesting on

---

[1] Ehrman, B. D. (2015, February 26). *Bart Ehrman & Daniel Wallace Debate Original NT Lost?* YouTube. Retrieved April 28, 2022, from https://www.youtube.com/watch?v=wyABBZe5o68

many levels. Yet and still, it can be noted that nowhere in common Christian practice do you see any reason for why Jesus has to pray to God, about how going into the wilderness away from society can be a restorative measure, or any directive on marathons of fasting and praying alone. Should not this be a means of ritual practice in closeness with God? In another sense, if you believe that Jesus is here represented as God, then it presents a stark dualism between God and Devil, almost putting both on an equal footing. Jesus recommends to us not to tempt the lord and not to curse one's own station in life. When he is purged through ritual purification, he is baptized by John. Perhaps this was some sort of ritual purging before Baptism? Either way, during the Baptism ceremony an angel descends on Jesus. Whether it is an Angel, Spirit of God, the Holy Spirit, a nominal spiritual force or exuberance, or some combination of all four, is anyone's guess. In all four Gospels the fact remains that Jesus' ministry and healings begin after this angelic being descends on him in his Baptism ceremony. It is therefore hard to notice that Jesus begins his ministry because of, and during, and after, either his Baptism ceremony, or the persecution of John. After John is killed by Herod, Jesus goes to Galilee where he finds some of his earliest disciples. This could mean that in this particular Gospel Jesus was seen as a disciple of John the Baptist. We see the character of John become more of a follower of Jesus later. Jesus finds Peter, and the sons of Zebedee, John and James become his followers in the local town of Galilee. The town is seemingly shown to be a quite unremarkable setting.

648. Jesus does not seek out the powerful and the wealthy authority figures, or even the learned men of his day. He rather preaches to the local people and his own Jewish community. He tells them, "Do not think I have come to abolish the law, but to fulfill it". He follows it up with the statement warning his followers unless your justice exceeds that of the Pharisees you will not enter the Kingdom of God. It is quite clear from this statement that Jesus did not wish to amend or abolish the Law of Moses, but to improve it by re-establishing the true intent of the original law. He wished to do this in a rather extreme capacity that exceeds the standards. He willed to demonstrate a mastery of the tenets of Jewish Law. If the Law says do not kill, then Jesus says do not get angry, for hatred and ignorance and anger are the root of violence. Jesus tells his followers to not hold divisive relations in the community and to reconcile with brothers. He exceeds the law of adultery by telling his followers that lust, and not adultery, is the true cause of covetousness. Bad family relations make people an occasion to sin. This form of divisiveness has to be surmounted for the health of the community. He implores others not to swear on anything, even the Earth, and even ourselves. Jesus is not afraid to put the realm of the sacred into material circumstance on Earth, and even honoring the children and humanity in general. He puts Earth and Humanity on equal terms with God. Jesus most notably does not discuss man's lowly earthly abode. He wants us to give ourselves up to the world to embrace it, and even give the shirts off our back if

we must. Embrace with love our enemies, and do not hold a contest. Violence begets violence, and competitiveness breeds envy.

649. Jesus tells the people to forgive and be merciful, as the Lord is merciful. Mercy is indeed better than kindness. "Where your treasure is there your heart will be also". "A man cannot have two masters". Nothing can be gained by worry. Jesus extolls the awakened heart that has knowledge of self, and links knowledge and desire. Man must have a unified will. A man that is split between two worlds, in constant dualism and indecision cannot be awakened to the unified will. A person who the devil no longer has power over is not afraid or worried, or having split emotions. Those who seek to exploit others always seek what is outside of themselves. Do not judge lest ye be judged. Do unto others as you would be done by yourself. Be wary of deceivers and "wolves in sheep's clothing". Jesus warns us that false prophets will come and speak in his name. Given the contradictory nature of proposals made in the name Jesus Christ, we would at least have to mark this a true prediction.

650. When he heals a man of leprosy, he tells him not to spread the news. A deed should have no more recourse than what is offered in the deed itself. Let the dead bury their dead because Jesus preaches to the living. He rests not until a deed is finished. No midday pauses, and no breaking off and starting again. Do not stop your journey for bad weather. Rebuke the waves and the storm and move on. Forward. Jesus performs an exorcism on a man. He casts several demons living in the man into a herd of wild pigs. The pigs fall off a cliff and die. Jesus does not just transfer evil into something less evil. The object is to banish evil altogether. Jesus also declares, "the Son of Man has the authority to forgive sins". This phrase Son of Man is found in the Book of Enoch. It may either mean that Jesus, as God, can forgive sins, but also may mean that Man's saving power rests in himself. Man may have the power to judge Angels.

651. When Matthew the tax collector begins to follow Jesus, he declares that he is not sent to the righteous, but to the sinners. If everyone were already sinful as Paul declares, then this would be a puzzling statement. Rather it is the prophets who are sent to Israel when they become sinners. Jesus says to a blind man he heals not to tell anyone. Jesus is not concerned with spreading the news about himself. Jesus repeatedly tells others that it is their own belief that has healed them. This follows other stories related to Gospels, because apparently others who also believe are able to perform miracles as well, such as the followers of Jesus. Therefore, within the context of the Bible narrative, miracles don't incur any special status towards the one who performs them. Jesus heals through the Holy Spirit or Angel that descended on him. When Jesus gives authority to the apostles to preach on his behalf, he warns them to not go among the Gentiles or the houses of the Samaritans. He also instructs his disciples not to carry money or extra possessions. "Be as shrewd as snakes and innocent as doves". He also warns that those who follow him most earnestly

will face the most persecution and hardship. Ridicule will befall them. Jesus proclaims that he has not come to bring peace, but a sword. The truth will be brother to the light. He speaks highly of John and lowly of Herod. He even proclaims that miracles are not enough to convince the people who are often too hardhearted to even be aware of the simple signs in contrast to Paul who tells us to believe on the basis of visions and miracles.

652. Jesus thanks the Lord that the things of truth are hidden from the wicked adults but proclaimed to the righteous children. This means that people grow weary of truth over time. We begin in purity, not in sin. God desires us to have mercy, and not that we sacrifice ourselves. Jesus condemns the Jewish Temple as mere stone and mortar. He declares that the Sabbath was made for Man, and not Man for the Sabbath. Religion must serve the purposes of Man, and not Man serve the statutes of those who practice Religion. When asked by the Pharisees to show how he heals, Jesus says that it is through the Holy Spirit. The Pharisees compare Jesus to Beelzebub, and call him a sorcerer. They also criticize John. Jesus tells them that a house divided against itself cannot stand. Divisiveness breeds faction, faction breeds hatred, hatred breeds ignorance, and finally ignorance breeds fear and violence. Jesus tells them that their blasphemy against the Spirit will not be forgiven and makes no mention of his own status. There is also a dialectic created between John and the Pharisees, Jesus and Herod. Jesus proclaims that every generation since Jacob and Solomon has grown further away from God. There is a coming discord and disintegration. This is not a message of progress. When Jesus' mother and brother come to visit him, he says he is everyone's mother and brother. Although he does not dismiss his own family, he includes all mankind into his own family. However, there is also the verse where Jesus tells his disciples to not go among the Gentiles.

653. Jesus never emerges from his own people or goes out to seek a new class of believers. His conflict is clearly with the other learned scholars of the Jewish people. Those who possess lots of faith will be given more, while those who sow only a little will have what little they have taken away. Faith is something that builds exponentially, but often one must risk everything in order to discover it. If one wagers only a little, one can only gain little. Those who hedge their bets will end up on the losing side. You can see with eyes, hear with ears, and understand with the heart, but the dumb, deaf, and blind cannot. When Jesus returns to Nazareth, he complains that a lack of faith of the people is unable to allow him to heal them. You cannot force faith on the blind or hard of heart. Jesus feeds five thousand people and admonishes the Pharisees for caring more about the law than the people. He tells his followers, "beware of the yeast of the Pharisees". Paul on the other hand generally is proud of his status as a Pharisee and affirms his connection to Herod. Jesus is hesitant to heal a Gentile woman's child because she is not a practicing Jew. He declares Peter the rock of the Church. The name Peter or Petra, incidentally, means

rock. When Jesus walks on water, it is Peter that, through his belief, walks with him, although briefly. We see here that Peter is given a high status. Paul later declares himself as more knowledgeable than Peter, whom Jesus gives a high role. What the various Gospels say about the teachers and disciples who followed Jesus or preached with him is reflected in the variety of views held by the followers of Jesus. Yet and still, Jesus says he came to fulfill the law, not abolish it. He did not wish to go among the Gentiles and had no mission for the Gentiles. He tells us to beware the yeast of the Pharisees. He says children are pure. He makes Peter the rock of the Church. All these ways we see marked differences from the claims of Paul.

654. Next thing that Jesus does, curiously enough, is that he orders the disciples not to inform anyone that he is the Messiah. It seems that this continued secretiveness seems to suggest that Jesus did not wish to inform the world of his coming. He goes to Jerusalem knowing what fate that will befall him. Jesus does not wish to be saved by his friends or trouble them in this regard. There is a parallel in Socrates. What good is it to gain the world at the price of one's soul? Jesus becomes transfigured and talks to two figures. These figures are Moses and Elijah. This may have more to do with who Jesus is talking to while he is transfigured, rather the fact that he is transfigured. Either way, it is noted that Peter who is Jesus' top disciple does not understand what is happening. It seems these two particular figures have a lot to say about the practices of Judaism. Elijah was a prophet that God performed miracles through and who ascended to heaven. Moses was a figure that represents the fortification of the covenant made with God by the people of Israel coming to fruition in the Law, after the promise made to Abraham.

655. Moses of course deals with the Law of the Nation of Israel while Elijah deals with otherworldly concerns. At this point we see a pivotal switch in the narrative, much the same way we saw after in the Baptism of Christ. He now begins to lay down some of his most fundamental teachings. He tells the disciples, unless they change and become like little children, they will not enter the Kingdom of God. He again forbids divorce and encourages strong family relations. Jesus goes to Judea followed by crowds of people. He declares that it is easier for a camel to pass through the eye of a needle than for a rich man to enter into heaven. Jesus refers to 12 thrones, for 12 tribes, for 12 disciples. This may refer to 12 nations, 12 tribes of Jewish people, or 12 schools of thought of Christianity. Either way it is quite a cryptic passage. Mythicists have even proposed that it refers to the 12 Houses of the Zodiac. If anything, these lines are subject to interpretation. There is also the statement, "the first shall be last and the last shall be first". What can this possibly mean? In its simplest form, it seems to suggest that there is a finality to the world, but that it does not suggest an inherent progress. It will be in the beginning, as it will be in the end. There is one big cycle coming to completion and culminating in restoring itself to where it began. There is no linear growth. There is not com-

ing to pass. One simply returns to the source; one returns back to that which one emerged from.

656. Jesus enters the Temple. He turns over the table of the money changers. When the minting of coins was done, there were no graven images allowed, but the currency exchange had to be equal. Jesus tells the Pharisees they have made God's house a den of thieves. This must have meant that the money that was being exchanged was not an equal amount for an equal amount. This system of usury was exposed by Jesus. In the process of committing a holy deed of removing graven images, they were concealing their wicked sin, of taking a little for themselves. One cannot mask one's sin with good deeds or visible acts of faith, removing only what is on the surface. Give to Caesar what is Caesar's, and to God what is God's. Only those who can fully make this distinction are worthy of their praise of God. The Jewish laws forbid interest and usury. This was yet another attempt by Jesus to reaffirm and re-enliven the Law. Making money on money was forbidden. Taking something that was naturally fruitful in order to use it for something that extorts wealth was using natural abundance to create artificial strife. It may be seen today that most of the wealth in the world is ruled by interest. It may come as no surprise to many, that in this very same age, there are human faces adorning the various forms of currency issued by the State. All that is necessary to show what is in one's heart is the first two commandments, and not a complex set of laws. The Pharisees make complicated what is relatively simple. They fix up heavy burdens for others to lift and do whatever pleases the people who see them. This is all for show. Banquets, sacrifices, and temples, cannot proclaim what is in one's heart. There can be no Rabbi, for there is only one teacher. All men are brothers under the second commandment. Pharisees not only close doors to others, but they do not enter themselves. The price of the blood of Zacharia is the Temple, which will be brought down if the teachers and Pharisees remain in obstinacy and continue on the way of rejecting God by murdering his prophets.

657. Jesus warns that many will come in his name proclaiming to be Messiah. There will be wars and rumors of wars. There will be natural disasters and open persecution of the faithful. In the Holy Place will stand the "abomination of desolation". Jesus says that if anyone says to us that they have seen the Messiah in the inner rooms of the Temple, do not believe them. The Messianic fervor and apocalyptic teaching serves as a warning of coming strife, and not an invitation to some golden age. The symbolism of Messianism is dismissed as a placated deception waiting to unfold. Christ proclaims that none, even himself, knows the hour of the end of days. All he knows are the signs. That is also all we can expect. The sign of the time may be upon us and we can certainly feel the pressure, and in a very practical sense we also know that things cannot go on the way they are now for eternity. The situation is one where God accompanied by divine forces brings judgement upon the Earth.

658. When this great historical shift will take place, the meaning of Christ or Messiah will be at the forefront. Through declaring himself Messiah, Jesus is soon condemned by the High Priest Caiaphas. Some of the disciples begin to grow weary of the more questionable people that begin to arise in Jesus' ministry. In one particular instance they protest at him having perfumed oils massaged into his feet by a poor woman. He tells them that while they criticize him, she offers him the best of what she has. Jesus becomes aware of plots against him. He shares a Passover meal with his disciples. Here he explains to them of a betrayer in their midst. Judas sells out his friends, confirming what Jesus said about people who will sell out their souls for a bargain price. Either way, the Jews take credit for the condemnation of Jesus. When guards come to try to arrest Jesus, he offers no resistance. He asks why they bring swords as if he is leading a rebellion. Jesus is adamant that he is not setting up new places of worship, or vying for power in Rome, so he should not be apprehended in this way. Peter wishes to defend Jesus, but Jesus warns "those who live by the sword will die by the sword". Jesus tells Peter he will deny he knows him. Peter understands that Jesus is making a sacrifice for the greater good of the message prevailing. Judas regrets what he has done and goes to hang himself after giving back the silver he gained for selling out his friend and teacher. The Jews choose a criminal, Barabbas, over Jesus, their Messiah. The line "Eli Eli Lama Sabachtani" appears in Hebrew. It is perhaps quite odd that this phrase "God, why have you forsaken me" is the only verse in Hebrew. Why not other Hebrew phrases, or even Hebrew prayers? The Arch-Angel Gabriel is also seen over Jesus' grave. Other Gospels contain varying accounts of this sequence of events. Since they don't tell us much about what Jesus taught, we leave those for now.

The Gospel of Mark

659. Indeed, the Gospel of Mark is significantly shorter than the other three. Whoever composed it might have had an earlier account, or they just may have been trying to select the most important details. It is attributed to Mark, who travelled along with Paul for part of his journey but was a disciple of Peter. Mark is not known to have been a direct disciple of Jesus. This Gospel begins with Jesus Baptism, instead of information about his birth and lineage. This reaffirms that the Baptism was perhaps the most significant event for early Christians, and not Jesus' birth or crucifixion. It also alludes to the fact that the Baptism ceremony connected with John the Baptist was somehow related to the ministry of Jesus. Jesus was unable to enter the towns, because of the large audiences gathered at the healings. He was attempting to keep a low profile. He was forced to stay along the outposts to hide his identity. As a result, it is the outsiders and rebels that he usually finds company with. He accepts this as a good opportunity, because the major religious institutions of his day have already sold out to the powers. Certain attacks on the Pharisees are repeated.

Phrases like "the Son of Man has the authority to forgive sins", and "The Sabbath was made for Man, and not Man for the Sabbath", are used to attack
them. When the Pharisees accuse Jesus of using sorcery to drive out demons,
he asks them how it is that evil can drive evil out. In order for evil to be driven
out, the good must be used. He says again that "a house divided cannot stand".
When a woman is healed by touching Jesus' cloak, he notices that energy has
left him. This may mean that Jesus requires some external power source in
order to heal others. To explain further, the scene does not seem to mirror
other sorts of instantaneous miraculous occurrence but seem to suggest that
Jesus is not the source of the miracle and some of his healing power is both
externalized and able to be depleted.

660. He proclaims to the woman, "daughter of God, your faith has healed
you". He clearly does not object to others being called children of God other
than himself, and assures that he does not heal by himself, but by a power that
flows through him. Jesus talks about it as if it is a power external to him. His
power to heal is apparently not only mediated by God, but also by the faith of
the person being healed, which is then inspired through Jesus to take the form
of healing. As Jesus travels through the villages, he is amazed by the lack of
faith of the townspeople. Jesus sends his disciples to go and preach in the
towns. Herod compares Jesus to John. Jesus feeds a crowd of people, and
walks on the water, but this time Peter does not walk with him. Jesus goes to
Bethesda to pray alone.

661. Jesus tells the Pharisees that they have let go of God and follow human
traditions. The conflict with the Pharisees grows over time. Jesus tells them
that nothing coming from outside can harm them, but only what is in their
hearts. Not what you consume, but what comes out of your mouth is a reflection of your heart. He accuses the Pharisees of making their own laws. The
idols we erect in our hearts in the form of methods to judge others are traps.
This can also mean that we reap the seeds of our own destruction, and nothing
coming outside of us can truly harm us. Jesus says nothing about abolishing
the dietary restrictions mentioned in the laws of Moses. Jesus also again hesi-
tates to heal the child of Gentiles. Jesus calls Peter Satan for questioning why
he lets himself die. Jesus criticizes Peter for having only human concerns. As
mentioned before, the treatment of Peter becomes several times harsher, as
does the lowered status of John the Baptist, whose role is totally eclipsed by
Jesus in this Gospel.

662. Again, Jesus is critical of Adultery, and forbidding of divorce. Again, he
appears transfigured and talks to Moses and Elijah. The disciples begin healing
and ministering in the name of Jesus. Jesus tells them "whoever is not against
us is for us". Jesus radicalizes the ten commandments. He tells the Pharisees to
only have one cloak and to sell all their possessions. He tells disciples that no
one of them is chosen after him. He tells them not to be like the Romans and

Gentiles who fight among themselves for honor and respect. Jesus curses the fig tree which represents the seeds of the Pharisees and the Temple. Again, he turns over the tables of the money changers and says to give to Caesar what is Caesar's. In quite a strange tradition, Jesus says that when the dead rise they will not marry, but will be like the angels in heaven. The views of Jesus become more philosophical and abstract, and less Jewish. He says that the first two commandments contain the whole of the law. In admonishing the Pharisees, Jesus proclaims that a poor widow gives more in the sight of God than a rich man. He begins to warn of the destruction of the Temple, and of the end of days. He warns of famines, earthquakes, wars, and the young and the old turning against one another. He also talks about the destruction of family relations. Christians, it seems, no longer concern themselves with these things. Only a small portion remain who can read the signs.

663. There are similar stories from the Gospel of Matthew, about deceivers coming and performing wonders in the last days to perform wonders in the name of Christ. The Moon and the Sun will darken, and stars will fall from the sky. The world will end says Jesus. Says nothing about a New Earth or Kingdom. Jesus is given perfumed oil from a poor woman who rubs it into his feet using her hair. Again, Jesus sees it as a blessing, and the disciples are confused. This is again when Judas Iscariot turns on him. Jesus tells Judas he is aware of his deceit when he offers his disciples bread. Peter has to deny he knows Jesus. Jesus prays to God. Says the spirit is willing but the flesh is weak. Jesus is crucified but his body is not found by his female disciples as in the Gospel of Matthew.

The Gospel of Luke

664. In the Gospel of Luke we see a much different beginning. Luke was supposedly a chief student of Paul. He is also the writer of Acts in the Gospel. That so much space is given to Paul and his secretary and student Luke, it is obvious that if there were in fact factions in the early Church then it is Paul and Luke who won the day. While the Gospel of Matthew opens with patriarchal lineage of Christ, tracing him back to King David, Mark skips the birth. In Luke, we see it begin with the life of Mary. While the Gospel of Matthew may have been more concerned with establishing Jesus as the Messiah by tracing his lineage to King David, the Gospel of Luke is focused on the immaculate conception. The writer acknowledges that many other accounts have already been written on the subject. He identifies himself as someone who has learned from others, but not witnessed the events himself. He addresses the account to a certain Theophilus, which sounds like a Gentile name. It is often considered that, since Acts in the Gospel is addressed to the same Theophilus, these accounts must have been part of a unified work appearing earlier. He goes before the birth of even Jesus, to the birth of John, showing that the two were con-

nected from an early age. In the beginning the Angel of the Lord appears to Zechariah.

665. The Angel tells Zechariah that his son John will be filled with the Holy Spirit, and bring many to God. The angel declares himself to be Gabriel of the Old Testament. Zechariah was unable to speak about what he had seen. His wife Elizabeth, who was barren, became pregnant as Zechariah went into a silent seclusion. Next, God sent Gabriel to Mary. The angel told Mary that the Spirit of God will overshadow you. We see this referring to the Angel Gabriel who had taken Mary into a curtain of light. The spirit of Gabriel was used to overshadow Mary because Mary's spirit was pure enough to abide the complete obliteration of self when standing in the shadow of God. Mary is shaken up by the encounter and goes to the house of Elizabeth. Elizabeth assures Mary that everything will be okay. When Elizabeth gives birth to John, all take it as a really good sign, and Zechariah breaks his silence. A census is issued by Rome. Mary goes to the Temple in Jerusalem to offer a ritual sacrifice to thank God for the birth of a son. A man named Simeon gives a prophecy concerning the child. Another prophetess named Anna is mentioned. At the age of 12, Jesus attended the Passover festival and told some Rabbis the meaning of the law. Meanwhile, Herod begins to take notice of John as prophecy comes to him in the wilderness.

666. John criticizes the Jews. He says, say not to yourselves that we are the children of Abraham, but out of the stones God can make new children of Abraham. John told people to give up worldly possessions and not seek entitlement in land and power and family relations. He repeats the statement from the Gospel of Matthew, that says Christ will baptize with fire. Jesus is baptized by John just like any regular person. The spirit descends on him. Again, we are not sure if this is The Spirit, or just a spirit, or the Angel Gabriel as mentioned before. Jesus says to the devil that one must not put God to the test. He gives people the advice, "do not curse and you will not be cursed". The mouth speaks what the heart is full of. While we perceive harshness against the Jews, Jesus is not at all hesitant to heal the son of a Roman Centurion while in Matthew he offers a quite different response to the request of healing from a Gentile woman (Matthew 15:21-28). He proclaims that no one in Israel possesses the faith of the Centurion after hearing his plight. In this Gospel we hear more about Jesus' female followers.

Chapter 24
"I saw Satan fall like Lightning from Heaven"
(Luke 10:18)

667. Luke has the benefit of the other narratives that came before, as he mentions. Luke's view is also colored by the movement of the Christian message,
and the famous speeches of Peter and Paul, that are reconstructed by him in
Acts. He includes most of the miracles mentioned in Mark and Matthew. He
includes the parable of the farmer sowing seeds, the exorcism of a demonic
plague named Legion, the young lady who touched Jesus' cloak, and Jesus
being transfigured in front of Peter appearing with Moses and Elijah. He says
foxes and doves and birds have nests, but the Son of Man has nowhere to lay
his head. He tells a boy to follow him, but the boy declares he has to bury his
father first. Jesus tells the boy to let the dead bury the dead. No man who lays
his hand on the plow and looks back is fit for service in the Kingdom of God.
He sends men out in groups of two to spread his teaching. The story of the
good Samaritan appears for the first time. People outside of Judea are being
commented on. Centurions and Samaritans are held in high regard. This is
perhaps being done at the expense of the Jews. A more liberal or all-inclusive
message of salvation is shared. Ask and it will be given, seek and find, knock
and open. The truth is available to all as per the doctrine of inclusivity or universal call for salvation that is touted by most Christians. The Pharisees and the
Jews are accused of ignoring the truth, not caring for the poor, killing their
prophets, and laying up heavy burdens for others to carry. Jesus again warns
his followers to "Beware of the yeast of the Pharisees". Jesus admonishes
Pharisees for caring too much for possession and tells them to learn from the
birds who go here and there but find no fixed habitation. This is another attack
on finding entitlement and settlement in land and power.

668. There is also more talk of nature. Jesus warns against worrying and striving. Worrying will not help you, for every hair on your head is numbered.
Look at the flowers and learn, because they do not labor in order to grow. This
is quite antithetical to the keeping your head down message, to strive diligently
to proclaim a quiet work-a-day existence. These lines ask one to imitate nature.
Where your treasure is, there your heart will be also. We see the familiar predictions of the end of days. The Son of Man will come in a yet unexpected
hour. Christ does not come to bring peace, but a sword. He says to not interpret
the weather, which is a small change, but contemplates the sign of the times.
The end is near. All that is necessary to enter the Kingdom of God is the faith
of a mustard seed.

669. The Pharisees complain of Jesus and he ends up in the crosshairs of Herod for his teachings, like the one forbidding divorce. Jesus brings Lazarus back from the dead. This could be the same Lazarus from the book of John but is purported to be a different person. Jesus heals many people, but only one, a foreigner, thank him. Jesus seems pretty relaxed, even though the Pharisees talk about killing him. No man can serve two masters. Better to stay loyal to the real power. A man named Zacharias climbs a tree to get a view of Jesus in a crowd. Jesus is surrounded by a crowd of followers but walks up directly to the man and asks to stay at his house. The man gives up his possessions to follow Jesus. Jesus talks to his disciples at the Mount of Olives (seen in every Gospel). He rides into Jerusalem on a donkey as corroborated by other Gospels. When he comes into town the Pharisees swarm him. The stone the builders rejected is now the cornerstone. Nowadays, the devil is in charge of the world. Jesus tells the people to give to Caesars what is Caesars. The Temple is owned by Satan. Some of the Sadducees rejected the belief in an afterlife. Jesus tells them that God is not the God of the dead, but the God for whom all are alive. Angels do not have to marry. The encouragement of celibacy and forbidding of divorce is repeated.

670. False Messiahs will abound. The righteous will be heavily persecuted near the ending of the age. There will be great distress, especially for pregnant and nursing mothers. The world to come will not be a world that is conducive to life. Jerusalem will be trampled by Gentiles, until the time of the Gentile is fulfilled. Jesus gives a cup and bread to disciples at the Passover meal. Peter informs Jesus that he wishes to die with him. When the guards come to retrieve Jesus, Peter lashing out is not specifically mentioned. There is less talk of the Holy Spirit and Jesus has more direct authority. The Disciples and fellow Jews are put down in favor of strangers. Non-Jews and Gentiles begin to incur more honor. For example, less blame is given to Pontius Pilate in the Gospel of Luke and Gospel of John.

The Gospel of John

671. John has been thoroughly seen to be a quite different narrative than the other three Gospels just mentioned, however it has also been the most impactful in delivering the Pauline view. In this Gospel, Jesus is more like a Zoroastrian or Buddhist Philosopher than a slightly off-tone Jewish rabbi who is limited to a Jewish community in Galilee. This Jesus has almost cosmic and universal implications. The entirety of what sets it apart is mentioned in the first few lines. It presents a staunchly dualistic view. In the beginning was the Logos and the Logos was with God, and the Logos was God. God is beside himself. What is the word Logos doing here? Is this a clear influence of Logos Theology prevalent in the second century? Can the "Word" be equated with "Logos"? Does this make God bound by the very act of creation, which not only issues from the creator, but creates itself from eternity? The implications

have been debated for centuries. This is the first place that the view is mentioned that Christ existed alongside God from the beginning of creation, which is the modern interpretation. Not only is it not clearly understood who John was, but it is also noticed that this Gospel is ninety percent different from the other three Gospels. It follows roughly the same line of narrative but does not contain the same content. Was this a competing narrative along with the other three Gospels? It seems to be competing with the rest of the entire Old and New Testament in its casual rewriting of the most fundamental strands of Biblical theology. It rewrites Genesis.

672. The status of Jesus is raised in this Gospel. Jesus is life everlasting, and the light of all mankind. This light is akin to the divine spark of Reason, which darkness cannot comprehend. John the Baptist comes not only to testify about this light but is not a bearer of the light himself. John was only a witness to the light and not a light unto himself. This is quite a lowered status for John. John's sole business is to declare how the Logos became flesh so that Man can know it. John begins his preaching as preaching of Jesus. Law was given to Moses, but Grace comes by Jesus Christ. This reflects the new covenant theology of Paul. John is not even fit to make sandals for Jesus. John is more emphatic in his claim of Christ's superiority over him, whereas in other Gospels he is almost seen as a teacher of Jesus. He proclaims that Jesus will take away the sins of Man. This further reflects a message of salvation by faith alone.

673. There are a variety of characters that show up in Galilee, like Philip and Nathaniel, that are not highlighted in other Gospels, perhaps indicating that a different host of sources was used to compose this text. The story about Jesus attending a wedding ceremony and turning water into wine, which is a popular tale in relation to Christianity, shows up in this work as well. Apparently, God saves the best for last! Jesus stops in Jerusalem and overturns the tables of the moneychangers; however, this part of the story is moved to the beginning of the tale. This event is repeated in every Gospel. Jesus refers to the Temple as his own body, saying it will be destroyed and raised in three days. He proclaims a heavy dualism to Nicodemus, who is portrayed as a regular Jew, that flesh is given to flesh and spirit to spirit. He instructs him that God has given the world his only begotten son. Whoever simply believes in him will have everlasting life. He now travels to Samaria. The story of Jesus in Samaria instead of in Galilee is an interesting exchange.

674. While in Samaria he sits down at Jacob's well. He meets a woman there that sees he is a Rabbi. She apparently informs him that Jews and Samaritans don't associate. He tells the woman he is the Jewish Messiah and stays there to preach. Christ has no problem roaming far from home and going far and wide to people outside of Judea to proclaim his message. His going to Samaria after Judea is evidence that the writer of John felt, even more than Luke, that the Messiah had to be portrayed as the savior of all mankind. Christ is very open

to share miracles and knowledge with Samaritans. He makes no exceptions for Jews and non-Jews. Yet he makes the problematic statement that the Son can do nothing without seeking permission from the Father. Jesus says that the Father sent him. He is still adamant that he does come of his own accord. Whatever the Father does the Son also does.

675. Primarily based on statements like these, a lengthy debate begins to unfold with the Pharisees. Jesus says to the Jews, your accuser is Moses. He begins doing more miracles, which gets him some unwanted attention. He tells them that he is the bread "mana' that has come down from heaven to sustain Israel on its long quest. Man must not live on bread alone, but this time Christ declares that the real bread is his flesh. The Spirit gives life and the flesh counts for nothing. The Disciples plead for Jesus to reveal who he is to the masses, but Jesus prefers to stay hidden. His time has not yet come he tells them. Jesus tells people not to judge on appearances, and that everyone who sins is a slave to Sin. Only the truth can set you free. He says he has not come of his own accord but was sent from God. Before Abraham was, "I Am", he declared. The Jewish leaders were enraged. They told others to go around and spread lies and propaganda about Jesus. He speaks of the good shepherd who gives his life to preserve his flock and does not let even one sheep stray: a clear criticism of the Jewish leadership.

676. Jesus walks into the temple courts and says he and God are one. The Jews proclaim that it is better for one man to die than for a nation to perish, in a grave contradiction of the law of Moses. The woman identified as putting perfumed oil on Jesus' feet, much to the distaste of some of the Disciples, is identified as Mary. Whether this is Mary of Bethany or Mary of Magdalene, as has been charged with both this scene and the scene where Jesus saves an adulterous woman from stoning, it could be meant to show a more relaxed attitude towards women, which could be used to point to the fact that this Gospel is not written by your average Jew but one with a more Gentile attitude towards women in general. Judas in particular takes offence to the display of Jesus being anointed by this woman. Jesus' female followers that show up more in the Gospel of Luke and John are usually employed in Gnostic texts (mentioned in part 1 of this book). This is quite a surprise, because in the other texts it says the same woman is a "woman of sin" but is here mentioned as a follower of Jesus. There were definitely varying accounts over the role of this woman.

677. Jesus rides into town on a donkey. He constantly refers to the Father that sent him. Says to Thomas, "I am the way, the truth, and the light". In quite a pantheistic sentiment he says he is a tree, the Father is the gardener, and the believers are the vines. He thus proclaims himself the prince of the world, and the spirit of truth. Jesus is the root of goodness through which nourishment and grace enter the world. He tells Pilate that his Kingdom is not of this world. Pilate, who cleans his hands of the murder and proclaims Christ innocent, de-

nies Truth altogether, and so has no way to verify the statements of Jesus. On that note, we can safely say that we ourselves have no way to testify to any of these events. If Jesus and Pilate are talking alone then who is witnessing this exchange? If Christ is on the cross alone, then who is witnessing his words to God? These are no doubt allegorical accounts, and we see in Paul that the suffering and sacrifice of Jesus play a central role. How could anyone accurately report what Christ or Pilate or a crowd of Jews rambled together in these brief moments? Who could be said to oversee and account for all events? All Paul needs is Christ crucified. Quite paradoxically, for Paulinists the death and resurrection of Jesus are more important than his teachings. It does not help that each Gospel contains a different account of what happened at this stage. We are not interested in the purifying aspect of suffering for reasons that we hope have been made abundantly clear.

678. In John 12:31 we read a startling message. This repeats the sentiment of Luke 10:18, that the devil is, not only active in the world, but is somehow embodied in the suffering of the world in general. This seems to suggest that the world is cursed. In John, Satan is the prince of the corporeal and carnal (John 5:19). In the Book of Revelation, purported to be written by the same author, we see echoes of this belief. Satan is identified with worldly power, similar to Paul's view. This encourages the anarchistic and antinomian interpretations of the Christian faith that arose in the second century. This later view seemingly drew from an influence of Greek and Persian religion, especially in their Orphic and Zoroastrian expression. The Devil is usually not connected with the fall of man in Jewish Literature. We read in the "Wisdom of Solomon", that the Devil was the chief of Angels and was demoted because of his pride (Wisdom 2:24)[2]. The snake in the garden is purported to be another entity altogether but again where is the proof? Surprisingly enough, Paul makes no mention of the Devil or Lucifer in his fall of man, or of fallen angels in his explanation of Sin but mentions "The accuser" of the Gentiles, the son of perdition, and even the "spirit of the air" and elemental forces.

679. What lesson can be gleaned from these varying accounts? We find several. Firstly, there is the keen strategy of laying oneself open for attack to expose the motive of one's attackers. A second view is that Christ was dead but was brought back three days later. Could be. But of course, there is the view related to that, which suggests that Christ was freed of his material casing and now dwells in some sort of transcendent state, as he always has (at least according to John). A fourth view could be that Christ never died, and had quite miraculously but not supernaturally, escaped. This would mean that Christ lived out the rest of his life elsewhere. Related to this possibility, is a fifth view, that

---

[2] Riley, G. J. (2001). *The River of God : a new history of Christian origins*. HarperCollins. Pg. 99-119. The ideas here are roughly sourced from various verses laid out by Gregory Riley in his excellent and unique book on Christianity

another person was crucified in his place and made to look like him. Of course, there is a sixth view, espoused by a few Mythicists, that Christ was made up by Paul or the Romans, or that even Paul and Peter were manufactured by early Christians. Paul's letters show up before the Gospel of accounts and to what extent Pauline doctrine had already influenced the teachings found in the Gospels is unclear, especially since there is evidence that the information contained in the Gospels tends to vary depending on, not only which Gospel is being referred to, but also the information is organized differently within various manuscripts, some of which also contain apocryphal writings.

Unique Aspects of the Pauline Doctrine

680. Indeed if one wants to find the messages of salvation by faith alone, the total depravity of the carnal state, the dialectic between the old and new covenant, the use of Greek concepts and pagan philosophy, and the coming of a New Age in the fulfilment of the Kingdom of God, then one has to turn to the Pauline Epistles. These beliefs are almost exclusively Pauline doctrines. Nowhere did we read Jesus saying that good works are not necessary for redemption, or that Christ was sent as a savior to all mankind including the Gentile. We don't hear of good tidings for ages and apostles that come after Christ to proclaim his name. Rather, we find that after Christ has left deceivers will show up in his name and so he warns us. We see a staunchly moral teaching. We find that children are seen as pure. We don't see any mention of building a Church. Not one jot or tittle shall be wiped away from the Law.

681. We don't see a resemblance to Gnostic or Hellenistic views (with the exception of the beginning passages of John). No special message for Gentiles. Mainly, Jesus addresses his message to his fellow Jews. No liberal message or liberalizing sentiment can be sought here. There is a distrust of religious authority, as well as worldly stations. There are no political prescriptions. There are no revolutionary dictums or maxims. Does Jesus say that God made a scripture uncorrupted for all times? If God would have wanted to, he could have made a scripture that was clear for all time. Is there any evidence in the Biblical text that this happened? What evidence do we find in the Gospel that Paul should be accepted as a teacher? In the Bible we find the opposite view; namely, that the Bible was corrupted, so that false prophets and teachers, hypocrites and idolaters lead the charge. This cycle of decay does not begin at some apocalyptic time, but directly after Christ's ministry is said to end.

Chapter 25
If your Right Eye offend Thee, Pluck it out and Cast it from Thee (Mt 5:29)

682. Of the twenty-seven books contained in the New Testament, over half consist of the writings of Paul. If there are troubling themes that seem to contradict the teachings of Jesus then we should reject some of their content, especially taking into consideration that some of the letters are purported by notable scholars to be attributed to Paul, but others are claimed to be forged by those who felt that certain views needed a polarizing figure such as Paul to be their mouthpiece. We can examine the Lost Books of the Bible, and other texts that appear around the same time, to provide some clues on what early Christian sects believed. We read in 2 Esdras that there were 70 books for advanced members of the Church, but only 24 were for the general public. These 94 books could have included the writings of Paul or could have been vastly different. There is likewise no evidence of God starting the canonization process.

683. The Gospels seem to contain mentions to books outside of the canonical sources, and corroborates some information found in the Lost Books, and even Jewish texts like the Dead Sea Scrolls and the Damascus Document. A variety of these texts were even widely accepted by early Christians. Since these books contain enough content to equal the whole of the Old and New Testament, we're afraid we do not have time to cover this large swath of material. Suffice it to say, it should give pause to anyone studying the subject. We should not, however, settle for the blatant contradictions that are found in the text. Contradictions within the very same text and presentation should present us with larger difficulties and more important issues that need to be addressed then establishing historical validity or counting the number or manuscripts and reproduction of the certain source materials. If something is wise, it matters not who said it. If something is mutually destructive then it matters little if it was authored by a saint. Jesus warned that false prophets will declare that great signs and wonders through Christ are being done, but if anyone says that they saw a vision out in the wilderness, don't believe them. This is precisely what Paul claims. Paul claims to have seen a vision of Christ in the wilderness. This is in direct contradiction to the Gospel of Matthew 24:23-26. What should we do? Why would Christ take the trouble of appearing alive to a select few if he could appear in visions? Instead, he explicitly warns not to believe such visions in his own words. Are we to believe the visions of Paul or the words of Jesus? If your right eye offends, pluck it out and caste it. The highest sin is a contradiction against oneself. If we are split between two ways, we must re-

move the part of ourselves that differs with the truth. According to other sources like Luke, Paul explains his conversion in three different ways.

684. The first narrative which appears in Act 9 is being narrated to us by Luke. In this account Paul is surrounded by light, and his companions hear a voice but can't discern where it originates. Only Paul is able to discern that the voice is of Jesus, who asks him "Saul, Saul, why do you persecute me?". Paul is blinded, but goes to Ananias, who makes the proclamation that Paul is to become the disciple to the Gentiles. This is quite puzzling. Why did Jesus not tell Paul himself? Also, why did Paul think it was so important to persecute Christians on behalf of Jews, especially when it is clear to us that Judea was more opposed by Rome then the fledgling Christian community? Either way, we hear a slightly different version of events in Acts 22. There Paul is talking to the Jews and defending himself. In the first story his disciples hear a voice and see no one. In the second version they saw the light but did not hear the voice. If we are not even sure what the right version of events are when Paul reports them, how can we be sure of what he saw? All we know is that since Paul is talking to the Jews, he needs to bring up Ananias as a witness to the events, mainly because he is a fellow Jew. In yet another story, where Paul talks to King Agrippa in Acts 26, the story changes again. This time all of the men Paul traveled with fell to the ground. Jesus teaches him directly this time. Paul's own role is stressed, and there is no mention of Ananias. In this version poor Paul is being persecuted by the Jews for being chosen by God.

685. Paul changes his tone depending on who he talks to. One can compare Paul in three different letters. In Paul's letter to the Romans, he seems to stress a dual road of salvation for Jews and Gentiles. A very conflicting message is read there in Chapter 9. God chooses beforehand who to curse and who to save. He gives his message to the Jew, but also makes those his people who are not his people. God's message is open to everyone, but then again it is only open to a select few. Among these were the specially elected Nation of Israel. Of them, only a remnant will be saved. These are saved by faith but not by any works of righteousness. In his letter to the Hebrews, we see him take a different line of attack. There he stresses the claim that Christ is a "high priest in the Order of Melchizedek". I have yet to hear this out of the mouth of any Jew or Christian. Who can explain the meaning of these words? Say, there wouldn't happen to be a high priest or "Melchizedekian" who can assist us? Malik means ruler or angel and "zedek" or saadiq means righteous in the Semitic languages but this does not seem to assist us. In Hebrews 9, we read him stress the "tent of meeting", and the blood of the covenant. In other words, here he wants to stress the material promise of God in the entitlement of land and honor.

686. Yet in Corinthians, when Paul is speaking to a more Gentile crowd, he stresses a middle path between the Law and Faith. There in Chapter 9 (verse 11) we read, "If we have sown spiritual things among you, is it too much if we

reap material things from you?". He begins the Chapter by saying how much better and more self-sacrificing him and Barnabas are, because they travel without wives and funds given to them by the Church. After all, "who plants a vineyard without eating any of its fruit?". He asks if him and Barnabas will have to struggle alone (verse 6). When one works, one should be able to reap the rewards of his effort! But the only way to get spiritual rewards is by material sacrifice. That is why Paul has given up so much! That's right. Not Jesus, Paul. Paul has no choice but to preach the Gospel that gives him "no ground for boasting". Yet he boasts. He says, "Woe to me if I do not preach the gospel!" (verse 16). He stresses that he has no choice but to preach his gospel free of charge. Here we see just to what length Paul will go, for he declares that in order to preach the gospel he had to "become all things to all men". Paul is a Jew with the Jew, and a Gentile with the Gentile. To win the Jews he abides by the Law, and to win the Gentiles he became "as one outside the law" (verses 20-21). Paul admits that he uses the law to his convenience, and that he has a different message, and even standards, depending on who he talks to. We do not have to infer this. This is stated in Paul's own words and actions, if we are to believe the text of the Bible holds true to its portrayal of these characters. Jesus apparently would not change his rhetoric for his mother and father and brother, but Paul changes it for any and all occasions (Luke 2: 41-52, Mark 3:31-34)

687. It is claimed by some that Paul taught the true meaning of the law and followed Jewish customs. Paul himself claims to be a Pharisee and a Roman citizen. Yet in other places it is stressed by Christians that Paul rejected Judaism and was persecuted by Jews, as he claims in his story to King Agrippa. It is hardly suggested that Paul could be intentionally turning various groups against one another by bolstering conflicting narratives or confusing people and trying to defend his own shifty character. Yet the possibility and probability is all too apparent. Assuming Paul was innocent, then only one view can be believed, and the others must be rejected. But then we must ask ourselves who doctored these other views that were put in the mouth of Paul. The possibility remains, and is amazingly overlooked by scholars, of Paul setting up a cozy relationship with two opposing sides, mainly to advance his own ulterior motives. In Galatians 1:11, Galatians 1:15, and 1 Corinthians 15:8, we read that no one taught Paul what he believes. Instead, Paul was set apart since his birth, and was taught directly by God. In 2 Timothy 2:8, and Romans 2:16, we read that Paul is teaching according to his Gospel. Not a Gospel given to him through traditions, but by direct experience with God and religious matters. No one else teaches what Paul teaches by his own admission. There may be evidence of similar beliefs, but this is Paul's own version and interpretation. Jesus warns against those who will claim to see visions of him in Matthew 24:26, as we have stated. Most times that these visions seem to appear is in defense of the Pauline message of death and resurrection. Here we see that, at least as claimed by Paul, such teachings originated from himself.

688. In Clementine Homily 17 Chapter 13 and 14, Simon the Magi claimed a similar vision. If a false prophet can claim the same thing, and was rejected on the same basis, then how can we believe Paul? Simon claims, "He who hears anyone with his own ears is not altogether sure of the truth of what is said". Peter's response is quite scathing. He tells Simon that it cannot follow that, because our senses are mistaken often, an apparition can appear to be clearer than we hear with our own ears. After all, when soldiers came to take Jesus away, Peter defended him with his life and sword in hand, while Paul teaches that his sacrifice was necessary for the forgiveness of sins and formulation of a new covenant. Paul went to the house of Judas after his conversion. Some take this to believe that he was a replacement for Judas.

689. In another sense it could be a sign that Paul was to be a betrayer of Christians. In Matthew 16, Jesus tells us to beware of the "yeast of the Pharisees". In Acts 23:6 Paul tells us that he is a proud Pharisee from the Tribe of Benjamin. The insignia of the Tribe of Benjamin is the wolf. He also readily admits in several instances that he was a persecutor of early Christians. In Acts 22 we learn that Paul is a proud Roman Citizen as well. In fact, Paul greets Herodian as his kinsman. Paul had close ties to Herod who was the enemy of both Christ and John the Baptist (Romans 16:11). For starters, it is quite odd that every group that is cursed by Christ in the Gospel find patronage by Paul in order to garner support. Paul is nonetheless a member of the very same groups that were challenged by Christ and involved in his persecution, during which time Paul was likely working for the High Priest to stomp out the Christian community, according to Acts and the Epistles. Since this was happening before Paul's supposed conversion, we can likely assume that Paul was persecuting the Church during Christ's ministry, but as soon as he died, he converted in order to win Christians over to his own unique interpretation of the Christian message, which was taught to him directly by Christ. It certainly stretches credulity to believe Paul's goals were sincere, or that his true purpose was suddenly revealed to him at such a critical stage. Paul not only claims that he was set apart to preach HIS Gospel, but that he works harder than all the other apostles. While claiming to be chosen above them, he continually extolls his own humility and being made weak and low in the service of God.

690. So what is Paul selling us? Buy into a Jewish morality and he'll deliver the Roman Empire with the whole system attached at no expense. Buy into the promise of the next life and get this life half off. Buy into the promise of a willful sacrifice and attain eternal salvation. Paul is selling a shoddy piece of goods at a high price. Paul claims in Galatians 2:18 that he has torn the law down. He has replaced the old system of laws with his new covenant. He has commenced the revaluation of values. Jesus said he came not to abolish the law. Paul makes some questionable interpretations regarding the law. He says that those who follow dietary restriction have weak consciences (1 Cor 8:10).

Paul claims to have superior knowledge about what God means in reference to the treatment of animals. God is not concerned with the treatment of animals according to Paul (1 Cor 9). Paul not only claims superior knowledge but criticizes those who wish to be in keeping with the law, which forbids eating meat sacrificed to idols. Paul is especially concerned with this because of his regular banquets with Gentile followers which were recruited by him. This is why Paul travels to those synagogues that have mixed congregations.

691. In Matthew 23:9 we read Jesus say to not address anyone on earth as a teacher or father. For we have but one teacher, and one spiritual father in heaven. Paul, however, instructs his followers to look at him as a teacher and spiritual father (1 Cor 4:15, 16). He urges people to imitate him as he is their spiritual father in Christ. Here again is a clear contradiction with the teaching of Christ. We have to ask Christians: Who is your daddy? Is it the Father up above, or Paul, down below? Naturally, nobody who knew Jesus claimed this, or any of the other Pauline beliefs. Another one of Paul's interpretations of scripture is that Sin had come into the world through Adam and was mended by the blood sacrifice of Jesus (Hebrews 9:22). This concept of Original Sin, or the depraved nature of Man as a whole, is nowhere found in the Old Testament or the Gospels. It is interesting to note that the Pope is referred to as the spiritual father of the Church in Catholicism, following Paul. In Philemon 1:19, we see Paul telling Philemon that he owes him his very soul. This doctrine, that upon saving someone in the name of Christ, they owed you their soul, is quite a novel teaching. One of Paul's most overlooked claims is his claim of being the so-called "apostle to the Gentiles". The fulfilment of this role is not described in the teachings of Jesus. By what standards of proof are we to accept that others approved this role for Paul? According to Paul, God gave him the decree and that he was directly chosen, yet elsewhere in Acts it is also claimed that this authority was given to him by leaders of the Church who were known as some of Christ's disciples.

692. This claim can be found in Romans 11:13, Galatians 2:7, and Acts 15:7. There is another issue. If Peter and James were the early leaders of the Church, known as the Jerusalem Council, wouldn't they have authority over what Paul was preaching? Were the Disciples, who were aware of Paul, in agreement with the teaching that Man is born naturally sinful, and must seek salvation by faith alone that is described in Romans 7:17? Statements such as these are why Luther rejected both religious works and contemplative reason as tools of religious insight (Luther's Works Vol 35 pg 395-398). To this end, he felt that certain parts of the New Testament, like the Epistle of James, should be burned for teaching that one is saved by good works. He says, "James does nothing more than drive to the law and its works". While James called the Law a law of liberty, Paul called it a law of slavery. Quite ironic, because Paul is the creator of the dastardly slave morality that has taught slaves to behave for centuries. It is clear to many, including Luther, that if it is true that James wrote

these things, he must have contradicted Paul. Are we rather to believe that different ages and epochs contain different standards of redemption, but that salvation is always of the Jews? In Christianity, we can be as tainted and ill-mannered, begrudging, and sinful as we want to, as long as we believe that we can be saved from our misgivings. We rather believe, as does James, that faith without works is dead, until we see some proof in the other direction.

693. The view that Man is justified by faith, without the deeds of the law, is found in Romans 3:28, Romans 4:6, Galatians 2:16, Ephesians 2:8-9, 1 Timothy 1:9, and Titus 3:5. It is clear that throughout the Gospels both Jesus and his disciples refute this doctrine. This is the doctrine of "easy believism", or salvation by faith alone. When we compare Romans 3:28, that a person is justified by faith without the works of the law, and James's view in James 2:24, that by works a man is justified and not by faith only, we have to ironically agree with Luther, but we come to the opposite conclusion and say Paul should be rejected. Christ clearly tells us that unless our righteousness EXCEEDS that of the Pharisees and scribes, we will not enter the Kingdom. He nowhere proclaims the Pauline doctrine of justification. For both of these statements to appear in the Bible today means that we must pick which one we are to follow. Paul's all inclusive, passive/ascetic, individualistic view, which is not actively opposed to sin, smacks of Gnosticism. What happens in the world is secondary to what happens in the world of the spirit. In 1 Corinthians 9:20- 21, Paul says he follows the law of whoever he is preaching to but is not subject to the law. In James 4:11 it says not to judge others and not quibble over whether the law applies. Our job is to follow the law, and not to interpret it. This is almost precisely what Christ accused the Pharisees of doing; finding novel interpretations of the law is strictly forbidden in Christ's own words. Yet Paul judges others harshly by a law that no longer applies to him, putting on heavy burdens for others to carry.

694. The justification of one act of righteousness for all men, makes no more sense than the entrance of sin into the world through one man, seen in Romans 5:18-19. This doctrine either accuses God of immorality by programming sin into the nature of man, or of being flawed by not being able to solve the problem of man's error by any other means. It not only demotes God, but it disparages mankind. In the Bible and the Quran we see that those who are believers in God and do good works are of the highest praise. Next are those who do good works but have no knowledge of the scripture, so cannot attain knowledge of the details of the doctrines of faith. The next best are those who are not faithful, and do no good deeds. This group is, at the very least, honest. The last group is the hypocrites. These are those who attain knowledge of faith, but are still heedless in their ways. These are ones that believe that faith gives them justification to commit all sorts of sinful deeds. They perfect the art of lying in a holy manner. This is what the doctrine of justification by faith alone recommends. That this lowest type of believer too will be saved through

justification by faith alone, and atonement in the blood sacrifice of Jesus Christ.

695. In Clementine Homilies 11:35, we read that early Christians regarded James as a leader and declared to us to "remember to shun the apostle or teacher who does not first accurately compare his preaching with that of James". In Romans 4:4-8, Paul condemns the Law and calls it a punishment. The only way to follow the Law is to have no law at all. Those who gain for-giveness without works of the law and are lawless are better than those who have to work for forgiveness. In Ephesians 2:8-12 we read how Christ broke the law by giving us grace and forgiveness from sins, so that there is no more difference between Gentile and Jew. Just who is it that is affirming that one can be a believer in the flesh, just as one can be a Jew in spirit? It is Paul that says these things. In 1 Cor 15:10, Eph 3:9, Gal 2:6 and 1 Cor 9:1, Paul tells us about how hard he works. In Gal 2:6, he adds that the leaders of the Church (The Jerusalem Council) had nothing to add to his preaching. In Jude 4:16 we read that certain people have found a way into the Church by preaching the lie that God's grace gives us immortal life and is a license for immorality. It warns that they flatter others and brag loudly to get what they want. In Gala-tians 3:24-26 we read that Paul declares that the law is no longer guardian of the people. In Matthew, we read that the things of God are hidden from those wise and learned people but revealed to children. This is because in 11:30 we read Jesus declare for God, "My yoke is easy and my burden light". The law is liberating not oppressing. Easier to perform for the sincere and pure, than for those quibblers who argue about doctrines of salvation and grace as a mediation for righteousness and sin, all to evade doing good works. In the Damascus Doc-ument we read about "the man of mockery" who "looks for gaps in the law".

Chapter 26
"For I do not do the Good I want, but the Evil I do not want is what I keep on Doing" (Romans 7:19)

696. The books of the apocrypha find use in the New Testament. When Jesus criticizes the Pharisees for rescuing one of their animals if it fell into a well on the Sabbath, it is referring to the Damascus Document, which states a similar prohibition. Paul is however, no longer interpreting the law the way Jesus did, in order to justify his good works. He is saying that what he has is better than the law. Paul tears down instead of building up. This is the mark of his passive aggressive personality. Paul shows animosity towards his companion Mark and stops traveling with him (Acts 15:36-41). Even though the next time Paul saw Mark, Mark and Barnabas wanted to travel together, but Paul still held his grudge. This could be an allusion to the fact that Mark is a disciple of Peter, whom Paul seems to have a feud with, or just a testament to the fact that Paul is a deeply resent-filled personality. Even though Christ tells us not to hold a grudge against our brothers, to forgive one another, and not to backbite against others, Paul regularly employs these tools, while saying that he is chosen above other men.

697. Paul tells us in 1 Cor 10:27 to eat whatever is offered to you without raising questions of conscience. His lax treatment of dietary restrictions and eating food sacrificed to idols shows his contempt for the law. In Clementine Homily 13 Chapter 9, Peter refuses for a woman to eat with her sons because she was unclean. He told the woman to fast for a day and then had her baptized. This was not to repel people who were not Jewish, but to encourage others to be in keeping with the law as much as they could tolerate. Both James and Peter were known to be vegetarians. Hegesippus the Historian and Clementine Homily comment on this. James did not eat meat or drink alcohol. Peter lived on a diet of bread and olives, rarely used potted herbs, and owned only one cloak (Clementine Homily 12 Chapter 6). In 1 Cor 8:7-10 Paul judges the weak consciences of those who follow dietary restrictions. He says in verse 11 that those of "superior knowledge" are thus harmed by their knowledge.

698. On the surface it appears Paul is practical and simply stating a fact that false gods cannot harm the true and living God. However, what it actually seems to suggest to Jew and Gentile alike, is that observance of the law, knowledge of scripture, and an abiding will and a strong conscience in remaining in obedience to the commands of scripture, is utterly useless. In 1 Tim 4:4 it declares that whatever God created is good, so we should not reject anything

but simply accept it in "thanksgiving". In Acts 15:13-21 we read the words of James. Especially in verse 20, we read "write to them to abstain from the things polluted by idols, and from sexual immorality, and from what has been strangled, and from blood" in regard to the Gentiles who follow God. Clementine Homilies 9:9 and 9:10 condemn food sacrificed to idols as food consumed in the presence of Satan. Corruption of food and corruption of sexual relations is mentioned together, as is hording up of wealth and possessions that turn brother against brother. If anything, Christ told his followers to lead a simple life. It can be said that many of his followers executed this command in various ways but using one's own humility as a platform to attack others through not being humble is a unique stance of Paul.

699. Paul teaches in 1 Cor 7:9-16 that divorce and remarriage is allowed, even though Christ's sayings forbid this in the Gospels. He also comes up with the idea that mixed marriages between Christians and non-believers make the children clean and open the door of redemption for the non-believing spouse. This seems like a belief made up by Paul; it is nowhere found in the teachings of Jesus. He says in 1 Cor 12:3 that no one ever pronounces Jesus Lord, except by direct influence from the Holy Spirit. This doctrine of once saved always saved, combined with the new covenant theology, and salvation or justification by faith alone, provides a fairly liberal scope in a loose-fitting doctrine of redemption. It functions as a sort of very minimal requirement necessary for the function of a community.

700. Peter not only denies this doctrine of once saved always saved but also points out that Christ himself complained that people referred to him as Lord but did not do as he says. Even upon seeing and witnessing miracles being performed in front of them, the hard hearted were still not ready to sacrifice for the truth. When Simon Magus tried to buy his way into apostleship, Peter withholds the gift of the Holy Spirit from him. The Holy Spirit is such that you can receive it from someone who already has it, but once you have it, you can also deny others of it. No special preparation is needed to receive the Holy Spirit because this happens by faith, but once received it is good deeds and faith which nurture this gift. In the Epistle of Peter to James he says, "I beg and beseech you not to communicate to anyone of the Gentiles the books of my preachings which I sent to you". He tells him to withhold some teachings and teach them to a group of serious followers, so they are not "rent into many opinions". He says that some have accepted lawlessness and given themselves over to "the trifling preaching of the man who is my enemy". He says that this man's goal is doing away with the law of God, which God spoke to Moses. Peter is explaining this to James in this text that purportedly displays the views of early sects.

701. According to us, Paul seems to have invented the doctrine of Original Sin by explaining how sin entered the world through one man, but it seems that sin

actually entered the world more by the aid of Women. When compared with the other belief or tenet of faith, that humanity was made in the image of God, this view can hardly be found in the teaching of Jesus. This still does not address the issue of Paul's harsh treatment of women. In 1 Tim 2;11-15 he explains that Adam and Eve were deceived by Satan, and while faith can restore Adam, Eve and Women must be saved by childbearing. He also thinks women should not speak very often and remain silent to their male counterparts. Men don't have to follow religious restrictions like being circumcised, which is recommended by Jewish law, according to Paul, however women are held responsible by the old law. This is a double standard. It is often mentioned that Christ was criticized and his influence was partly curtailed by him having large amounts of women followers, who were supposedly not often women of very high status in society. Instead, Paul taught that Men can remarry, don't have to be circumcised (Gal 5:2), don't have to follow law, and should have women play a secondary role in religious affairs. Christ puts a strong emphasis on women and children.

702. Many mentions are made to Isaiah that were used to justify the Messianic fervor of the Jews. Paul and his new covenant theology sought to capitalize on this trend in Jewish theology. But what about Zechariah 11:10? There we read, "Then I took my staff called favor and cut in two (recall Solomon and the baby, and the splitting of the red sea), showing that I had revoked the covenant I had made with all the nations". This is God saying he had revoked his covenant with the people of Israel, but there is no mention of a new covenant being formed at a later stage. Suffice it to say, if we really believe about God what we say then a covenant made with God can be broken or renewed. There are many instances in the Biblical text that show us that once God makes a covenant there is no obligation on God to fulfill that covenant for all time, and God can break his covenant. Why did Christ never mention the sins of Adam if this was the only reason he had come into the world? As we have discussed, this view is particularly dangerous because it gives way to justification of the turmoil in the world; this is the view that the turmoil in the world is being used to bring about the Kingdom of God. It reflects utopian thinking and the beliefs of futurism/transhumanism on the inevitable progress of history and belief of New Age theology. It is a belief that all one has to do to attain salvation is to wait and quietly endure the suffering of this world to await heaven on earth. In Zechariah it warns that one can lose favor with God if we are not proactive in our faith. This is like the parable of the seed and weeds. We have to plant and nourish. God only judges what we produce. Sin can only harm itself. Neither God or Man is bound by sin. We cannot settle for a God which treats the world and nature as a mere accident: for this binds God and shackles Man.

703. For those looking for their salvation in an earthly kingdom, Jesus points to the political turmoil of the coming days. There is a storm at the sea of Galilee, on the border between Syria and Israel and Jesus cuts through the man-

made structures that were built to overcome the storm, by working with the forces of nature. And make no mistake, that he does not address religious and political institutions, but only warns his followers to be weary of the trials of the last days. He speaks of the collusion of nation-states, corruption of the food and sexual relations, and natural disasters causing those who inhabit Judea to flee. Finally, the abomination of desolation will sit upon the throne in Jerusalem. The Book of Revelations further details that the Church and the Synagogue are to be corrupted during the last times, and the persecution of the faithful will be a regular occurrence.

704. The message of a judgement being brought upon the world which tested the character of Man meant that Man had to be put to the test, first purifying themselves by regaining and renewing spiritual practices to prepare for a literal battle between good and evil, which would then culminate in the coming of the Messiah. No less important was the proclamation of the primordial battle taking place within each one of us. This was inverted into the foreknowledge of God which promoted the building of a Church to prepare the world for an earthly kingdom, and the coming promise of a life without sin. Paul is no doubt using some of the existing Christian doctrine to formulate his own version. This cleans one's hands of the suffering in the world by a veiled moral superiority. However, it does not answer the question of why Paul's teaching differs so much with other Christian sects and early Christian sources.

705. Paul's teachings were rejected in Asia. In 2 Timothy 1:15 we read Paul say, "You are aware that all who are in Asia turned away from me". Paul's teachings were rejected in Ephesus in Asia. It states in the Book of Revelation to John where Christ says about the Church of Ephesus, "I know your works, your labor, and your patience, and that you cannot bear those who are evil. And you have tested those who say they are apostles and are not and have found them liars". Many have suggested that since Paul's teaching differs with so many notable early Christians, that this passage and others which refer to false apostles actually refer to Paul. In Acts 21:27, we read Jews from Asia complain against Paul, "This is the man who teaches all men everywhere against the people, the Law, and this place (the synagogue), and furthermore he also brought Greeks into the temple and defiled this holy place". In 1 John 5:3 we read from a verse attributed to the same author as the apocalyptic revelations, "For this is the love of God, that we keep his commandments. And his commandments are not burdensome". Apparently, this author's views differed from that of Paul, at the very least in his views on the commandments of God and did not see the law as burdensome. He had cozy relations with those who rejected Paul, if we are to believe that these same named authors wrote the material that is attributed to them today. Unfortunately, this is rarely and hardly seen to be the case.

706. The dialectic was perfectly staged by Paul, about the old law and the new covenant, of legalism against faith, of spiritual unity versus political divisions. The goal was the reversal of the current order of things in a revaluation of values. These are loosely drawn from the teachings of Christian groups that formulated their own doctrines and culminated in the assemblage of the so-called synoptic texts. In Galatians we see the brunt of these misappropriations rendered to us by someone who was supportive of the Pauline line, if not Paul himself. In it we read "For by the work of the law no flesh shall be justified" (Gal 2:16), "no one is justified by the law" (Gal 3:11), and "Christ has redeemed us from the curse of the law" (Gal 3:13). He also states that God shows no personal favoritism to any man, but this is quite ironic because Paul was chosen over all other men to preach the Gospel of Christ, and to make known the true meaning of Christ, especially to the Gentile.

707. He says against the leaders of the Church, "For those who seemed to be something added nothing to me. But on the contrary when they saw the gospel for the uncircumcised had been committed to me, as the gospel of the circumcised was to Peter...and when James, Cephas, and John who seemed to be pillars, perceived that grace that had been given to me, they gave me and Barnabas the right hand of fellowship, that we should go to the Gentiles and they go to the circumcised". Paul is undermining others who have given him the authority to preach in their name. We urge Christians to deal honestly with these facts and information. In Acts 25:9-12 Paul is asked by a woman if he is prepared to go to Jerusalem and be judged. Paul replies, "I stand at Caesar's judgement seat, where I ought to be judged". This is quite an odd response. While Christ wanted to improve his own people and did not meddle in the affairs of Caesar or Gentiles, Paul chose to admonish his own fellow Jews. Jesus called himself the Jewish Messiah. Paul conversely ties his allegiance and calls for rebellion against Rome. Paul sees no reason to appeal to the Jews but wants to appeal to the Gentiles, because after all his battle is against Nero and the Romans. His only wish is to escape the influence of the Jerusalem council, and to somewhat curtail their influence in order to mask his goals behind the Christian agenda as a perfect cover against Rome. Such a philosopher will love the TarTar at the expense of his own neighbors.

708. Many like Laverne Gooding at "Trustin JC" youtube channel, or Pastor Ray Hagins[3] are adamant about the false teachings of Paul. However, number one on their list of problems is the teaching of forgiveness of all sins as a sign

---

[3] Many aspects of what was said in paragraphs can be seen discussed by many Christians and former Christians alike. Here are a couple views that we find especially informative: 1. Christian evangelist channel TrustinJC playlist on Paul: TrustinJC. (2020, November 20). *Apostle Paul is a Ravening Wolf*. YouTube. Retrieved April 29, 2022, from https://www.youtube.com/playlist?list=PLBF08FA4E9D6A8BF5 2. Former Christian Pastor Ray Hagins: Hagins, R. (Unknown). *The False Teachings of Apostle Paul*. Youtube. https://www.youtube.com/watch?v=Vgig9LRRjrs&t=3323s

of moral cowardice. The unconditional forgiveness of all sins, and lack of choice or free will in defining one's own character through good works, causes one to exhibit a sort of moral passivity. As seen in recent studies, the belief that we have true responsibility and choice on what type of moral decisions we make actually does have an effect on the way we behave. In other words, we tend to make moral choices more often when we feel that our choices make a real difference. This relates to the Pauline view of those in power. In the Pauline view, all sorts of power are naturally evil and are expected to have a certain level of corruption and moral ailment. As a result, this power is justified, and tolerated, but underhandedly opposed by God's work. One does not directly oppose those in power but uses the power that is there in order to turn it towards God's work. This view has made the Church a veritable middleman between the people and those in power. The Church is seen as the "bride of Christ", and so ephemeral change is channeled through worldly institutions. This seems quite paradoxical. God is using worldly power in order to anoint those who are of low status, while worldly power is itself an escape from God. While power is chosen by God, one is to "make it your ambition to lead a quiet life: you should mind your own business and work with your hands, just as we told you," says Paul (Thessalonians 4:11). This is a new level of docility in the formulation of the herd mentality. It is an almost Buddhist or Hindu sort of compliance and passivity. One is told to act as a normal person, rely on oneself, but regard those in power as chosen by God, and an opportunity to spread one's faith. One can show one's humility by serving those in the highest rungs of power. One must become all things to all men. The best way to do it is by hiding in plain sight (Acts 9:15).

709. If the poor are blessed and the rich man is cursed, what has one to do with the poor in preaching God's word? One must preach to those who are sick: namely, to the rich and powerful. This may seem paradoxical, but if power and wealth is already assured beforehand then one must maintain his station and go where our preaching will have the most impact. It is a fact that Paul continually went to wealthy and educated Jews, and corrupt Roman officials, mainly so he could target and exploit both sides, even by his own admissions. This is why we read in Thessalonians, that the rulers of this world are men of wickedness, but in Romans 13 that we have to obey them. The best way to oppose them is to appear weak. Appear weak to serve those in power while not getting your hands dirty with the actual responsibility of carrying out decisions. Don't hide your faith but pronounce it to the world. Remember, those in power are not perfect, and all power is transitory. Earthly power is ultimately chosen by God. In 2 Corinthians 3:12 we read how to get the job done: "we use great boldness of speech, unlike Moses who put a veil over his face". This opposes leadership, opposes the law, but emboldens the one who still wishes to be an agent of change. It belittles Moses but seeks to emulate him. This is quite a feat of craftiness. One has to show one's face and be distinguished among the people.

710. While the essential faithlessness in purpose and hope brings us to the whims of randomness and contingency where all choice is impossible, the other side of the dogmatic coinage is the Pauline foreknowledge of God that dwells on fatalism instead of faithfulness. The whole underlying thrust of Pauline theology is not an assurance of good works, but of a preparation for the return of Christ in a kingdom of earthly reign. Paulinists do not reject earthly power, in fact they justify it, while never directly getting involved. We are told only to endure and not be proactive in our faith. As it says, "may he strengthen your hearts so that you will be blameless and holy in the presence of our God and father, when our Lord Jesus comes with all his holy ones" (Thessalonians 3:13). "For there must be factions among you in order that those who are genuine among you may be recognized" (Cor 11:19). It does seem rather striking upon first notice that Jewish literature like the Book of Jubilees ascribes this same role to Satan. Paul tells us that he was summoned by the high priest to aid in the persecution of Christians, but could it be that Paul simply found another way to use factions within Judaism to attack the Roman elite? Many things suggest that when Paul came among the Christians he had double agent status, while being rogue.

711. This would explain Paul being rescued in the Synagogue by Roman soldiers. Flavius Josephus refers to a man named Saulus who was a "kinsman of Agrippa", and as noted earlier this was who Paul explained his conversion story to. Paul's story was not believed by other Christians, who thought of it as rather benign because it was seen as challenging the Jews, while his real goal must've been to avoid Jews, use Christians as pawns and deceive them, all in the effort of weakening Rome. His efforts to attract Jewish followers to his cause went rather slowly, so he mainly relied on Greeks (Rom 3:22, 1 Cor 12:13). Paul is "running the race to win" (1 Cor 9:19). He is in a rush to gain as many Gentile followers as possible with Rome clamping down on Judea. He is in a race to gain friends and influence. In a race against who we must ask ourselves? As Paul says in the first two chapters in his Letter to Romans, he wants salvation "for the Jew first, but also for the Gentile". He repeats this claim in many different respects. He uses a Jewish message to bring salvation to the non-Jew. What better way to evade authority than to mix one's Jewish philosophy into a Greek packaging? This included the use of anti-Jewish and pro-Roman views, that were pro-religious (and covertly pro-Jewish) but anti-State (and therefore anti-Roman) formulation. The Romans had previously assimilated other forms of religious practice into the Roman cult. The Roman system was susceptible to emendations of the religious sort. All one had to do was become weak. Furthermore, the decadence of Rome was attractive to certain Hellenized Jews. The other two options were to evacuate Rome or join in the resistance. It was Paul who understood that the first will be last and the last will be first. At the end of a long fight, it is the last one standing who will be declared victor, and not the one who displays the most might.

712. All of those who are part of the axis of worldly powers are the "dominion of Satan" (Acts 26:18), the "authority of darkness" (Col 1:13), under the control of the work of the spirit who controls the "children of disobedience" (Eph 2:1). The world is ruled by Satan, but most people are not aware who is really in charge of the affairs of the world, at least according to Paul. How can this world be both cursed and the place for the highest abode of salvation to ever come into existence? How is Christ only a spiritual being, which demands nothing more than immaterial faith, assured to us by a physical blood sacrifice? According to Paul, the powers of the world are synonymous with the Devil (2 Cor 4:4). Paul knew that ideology was more important than military force, that organization was more important than argumentation, and collusion and subversion more successful than force and aversion. The diplomacy of love and obedience was more long lasting than efforts of spreading fear and resentment for immediate gain. Paul used a Jewish morality for social organization, a Greek philosophy for intellectual appeal, and a Roman theology to supplant the "son of god" mythos.

713. The actual facts about virgin birth or the manner in which Christ ended up missing and or died is of no relevance to what we are saying about the teachings of Paul. Paul knew that the Roman cult tied together the religious and political establishment, but it also kept the priestly class separate from political business. While the cult of Rome was part of supra-religious duty, their main aim was to serve the Emperor, who was taken as the figure-head of the religious establishment. Paul's use of political terminology, while cleaving the political and theological, then paradoxically maintaining the re-emergence of this union in some future state of affairs where God comes to rule on earth, but only in the eschatological sense through the Kingdom of God, is a way of both opposing worldly powers, while using them to accomplish one's ends. This is why Paul can be seen being protected by Roman soldiers in Acts 21:31, extolling his status as a Roman citizen and Jew, but then putting down the Roman system and the Jewish law. Paul is of the Tribe of Benjamin, a Kinsman of Herod, a Pharisee, and even a Roman citizen (according to Luke in Acts, but scholars dispute this). Even though he tells us these things, and continually assures us that he does not lie, he stresses that it does not mean he is chosen above others. In fact, it is because Paul has made himself so low and rejected his high-born status that he was given such high honors. I assume if you are confused at this point it may not be accidental. Paul may have, or at the very least someone pretending to be Paul, spun up different diversions on the road to reaching his true aims to deliberately obfuscate the truth. Paul is either inspired by God and then changed to fit the ends of the early Church, woefully ignorant of scripture and Jewish laws, or smarter than we think and subverting the true message. The problem is that we are clearly not sure which one.

714. We venture to say that it is the third option. Paul could not have been both ignorant of the views of Jewish teachers, nor can we affirm that Paul was directly chosen by God to preach these things against the scripture or to enliven and awaken people to the true meaning of scripture. We argue also that Paul could not only have been deceptive, but extremely cunning. We give as proof of this the success of Pauline doctrine being used for the revolutionary means of causing factions to separate the wheat from the chaff. The Pauline view is the single most significant view determining world events other than the views of Muhammad (p.b.u.h) the prophet of Islam, and Paul's conversion is the single most significant religious conversion in history. This simply cannot be an accident. Paul is either inspired or an ingenious deceiver. The problem today is that most scholars claim neither. They see Paul as either a benign interpreter, or a second-rate Jewish scholar.

715. Modern Christian teachers like Douglas Coe remarked, "the more you make your organization invisible the more influence you will have"[4]. The best method of planning is a methodology of non-organization. The best way to hide is to be hidden in plain sight. Take the burden off of yourself and put it on the cross. Go where you will have the most impact. Accept one's faults and dissolve oneself in the suffering of Christ. All that is necessary is the Cross. All other forms of loyalty, whether it be to one's family or country, should be used for service to the Lord. The bigger the lie, the more people will believe it. In his Christian Fellowship we see how the designs and aims of Pauline theology can be weaponized. But this is just yet one modern example. There are yet many unresolved issues like the membership of the Council for National Policy and its sponsoring of Evangelical and Zionist backed positions.

716. We hope that those of you will study the Bible with us to show and understand other parts of these conflicts. There are several issues like Jesus' praying to God in several instances that are not honestly addressed by Christians. There is a considerable modern coloring of past events which does not honestly address certain historical markers, and which continues to merge doctor and priest in a technocratic and totalitarian game of material reductionism. Undoubtedly wealth and education replace the traditions of family and old age, and with it we have sacrificed the rites and rituals that raised up our various religious traditions. As a result, we have fell prey to priests and politicians, doctors and lawyers, media moguls and international banks. Though we are far removed from the traditions of the past there is a great importance in preserving these simple truths. To this end, we must discuss what made the Pauline message so successful. The achievements of Paul and Muhammad (p.b.u.h) dwarf those of almost any intellectual.

---

[4] Sharlet, J. (2009). *The Family: The Secret Fundamentalism at the Heart of American Power*. HarperCollins.

717. We find that it is these two views that have faced the most turmoil and attention in the establishment of current methods of political subversion and a central aspect of this is the spread of Christianity to the Roman Empire. We now turn to examine the travels of Paul and their historical relevance. Granted our current viewpoint and late stage in this discussion, we should not exclude this as a possible explanation of events in order to supplement our views. Paul did not confine himself to Judea and Rome, but his preaching in Greece and Europe was far more influential and helped propel the Pauline message to a new stage of history. In his role as Apostle to the Gentiles, Paul used both the Synagogue and the Forum to advance his newfound message of redemption that was seemingly taught exclusively by him. There is also the important point that leaders of Gnostic sects like Valentinus claimed they had received a secret doctrine from none other than the apostle Paul. This secret revelation taught him that the God that Jews worshipped was really the image of the real God who was worshipped actually only by the followers of Paul. This paints a different picture since the Pauline message predates these second century groups. As a result, the Pauline view seems to have influenced Gnostic views and not the other way around.

Chapter 27
"Crafty Fellow that I am, I caught you by Trickery" (2 Cor 12:16)

718. As a writer claiming to be Peter states in 2 Peter 3:16, "In all of Paul's letters there are some things which untaught and unstable people twist to their own destruction, as they do also the rest of the scriptures". Was Paul understood? If he was, who understood Paul the best? One person who claimed to understand Paul the most was Marcion, the son of a second century bishop. He most notably wished to do away with any connections between Judaism and Christianity. He put forward the idea that the writings of Paul were perhaps a most fundamental aspect in understanding Christianity. To this end, he both edited and collected the books of Paul. His interpretation of Christianity was branded heretical.

719. There were many antinomian factions that felt that the spirit of the laws is above the letter of the law. Constantine purged Jewish influence from Christian practices. He mixed Christianity with the Roman cult and made Christianity a version of certain pagan mystery cults. He formulated the Church, approved the Christian sect that won out in a debate over fundamental tenets of Christian doctrine, and oversaw the canonization of scripture. It is a notable fact that more Christians were persecuted after Constantine's conversion than before it. Differing versions of the Christian message were stamped out. Both Paul and Constantine saw visions of light from above upon conversion. Their conversion stories seem to parallel one another. He called an imperial edict that was discriminatory against certain Jewish practices and accused Jews of parricide against the Lord. He changed Passover to Easter. He separated Jewish and Christian Holy Days. St. Augustine also affirmed Paul's teachings.

720. The mix of Hellenistic Jewish thought and Neoplatonic philosophy produced the Trinity. Many scholars have noted that the Trinity was never mentioned by Paul. It is clear that Paul thought Christ was the Spirit of God. Later, the Trinity was devised through Neoplatonic philosophy to obtain a defense for the Pauline message. This was all hastened by the fall of Rome and Christianity's arrival in Europe. There, many sought to reform Christian teaching. One of the most notable reformers was Martin Luther, who defended Paul, and used his teaching to polarize law and gospel. He opposed the use of good works as mentioned by us before. He used the teaching of Paul against the Catholic Church. The Church itself was cleverly devised through the several modes of Paul's views. Luther used the teachings of Paul to make the claim

that Jews would convert to Christianity before the return of Jesus. Paul wrote to a mostly Gentile Church in 1 Corinth 11:1 to "imitate me as I imitate Christ". Paul claims to have superseded understanding of the laws and scriptures by his understanding of Christ's death and resurrection, and the blood sacrifice of Jesus Christ, who was also seen as the Jewish Messiah.

721. Paul's journey ends in Rome[5]. The burial place that is said to contain him was also said to be the burial place of Emperor Nero. In it there is a depiction by Paul by Caravaggio that is a personal favorite. It is one of two attempts by Caravaggio in painting Paul's conversion. In the painting Paul is seen wearing a Roman tunic. We find it a rather apt depiction for our current analysis. Not only is Paul seen as a symbol of Roman power, singularly shown the light, and set apart, but he is also shown falling off of his horse, flailing in agony. This embarrassing moment was actually a moment of empowerment. The roles of power were reversed, the revaluation of values was at hand. In short, Logos had been dethroned. The symbols used to describe heavenly ascension were now used to define earthly power. In Acts 9:1 Paul is asking the High Priest to enlist him in the cause of ridding him of the Christian faction after he was emboldened by witnessing the stoning of Stephen. Paul then supposedly went on the road to Damascus where the famous conversion took place. In Galatians 3:28 Paul declares, neither Jew nor Greek, neither male nor female, for all are one in Christ Jesus. Many scholars allege (such as Paula Fredriksen, N.T Wright, and Bart Ehrman) that Paul was a binitarian, who taught an extreme form of Judaism though this seems highly unlikely. But Paul's travels suggest another story. All roads lead to Rome, and in Rome, all roads lead to Paul. The figure of Paul was restyled as a figure of Roman power.

722. Paul was born in Tarsus in the Roman Province of Cilicia near Ephesus and the Aegean Sea. At the time of Paul it was a powerful center of the arts and commerce. The schools of Tarsus were well renowned for Greco-Roman learning and rivaled those of Athens and Alexandria. Paul was a Roman by birth, fluent in Hebrew and Greek, and learned in Greek philosophy. This is a highly rare list of expertise. Even learned Jews like Philo who had a Hellenistic education did not know Hebrew. He was also supposedly schooled under the top Rabbi at the time in the religious practices of the Jews. In Philippians 3:4-6 Paul declares that he is of the stock of Israel, of the tribe of Benjamin, and a Pharisee in regards to the Law. Cyprus, Phoenicia, and Antioch in Syria became main places for the operations of the early Church. Antioch was a major seaport, as well as the capital of Rome in Syria. At the time there were many types of people you could find in a Synagogue due to the Jewish diaspora.

---

[5] Adler, D. (Producer). *Quest for the Real Paul* [Film]. Vision Media Productions. https://www.youtube.com/watch?v=9kfXXnrUWp0. We rely on the information about Paul's travels from this documentary on Paul featuring scholars like Paula Fredriksen and Paul Tabor in the next seven sections.

There were regular diaspora Jews, Proselytes or converting Gentiles, and "God-fearers" or interested Gentiles who were curious about the new faith, according to certain scholars who promote Noahide Christianity, claiming that Christianity was an attempt to understand new evolutions in Jewish teaching. Interestingly enough, Paul never used the word Christian and felt that his views could be regularly assimilated within Jewish teaching. Paul and Barnabas sailed to Salamis in Cyprus. Wherever Paul went he first went to the synagogues, and then to address the Proselyte Gentiles. While in Cyprus, Paul moved west towards Paphos and met with the Roman Governor Sergius Paulus.

723. From Paphos they may have sailed to the southern coast of Turkey in Perga, and from there arrived in Antioch, another prominent Roman city, to meet with local Jews. Paul visited a mixed community of Jewish and Gentile followers. They soon left for Antioch in Syria, where Paul gained a new travel partner Silas. It was with this traveler that Paul went to some far-off lands, including Europe. They began by traveling to Philippi in Macedonia. Romans had conquered Macedonia in 68 B.C. They built the Ignatian Way which connected the Adriatic and Aegean Sea. The city spoke Latin and was often referred to as a miniature Rome. Paul had a notable meeting here with a god-fearing Gentile woman from Thyatira who was a sower of purple cloth named Lydia. Next, they went to Thessalonica, capital of the province of Macedonia. The cult of the emperor thrived in the city. Some Jews had raised an allegation against Paul and Silas and claimed that Paul taught others to serve Jesus instead of Caesar. They soon had to leave for Berea. There was a town with a large Jewish congregation which was more amenable to Paul's message, so he set up a mixed congregation there. However, soon some Jews began to take notice of Paul's preaching, so he left and Paul finally arrived in Athens, Greece.

724. Paul was surprised by a number of statues in the temples there. Paul capitalized on the situation and began teaching against "idolatry". In Paul's time Athens had declined in importance from its classical phase. Paul went to the marketplace or agora. This had become an intellectual and cultural center with much renown. In the Forum, Paul conversed with many Epicurean and Stoic philosophers. This area was filled with statues and temples. When the people heard Paul's preaching, they mistook him for a philosophical babbler that sought to do away with the many gods. When they took him to the Areopagus, or the official court of Athens (Acts 17:19), he came upon an altar to the "unknown God". He assimilated this "unknown God" as his Jesus character and proclaimed that all other gods were man-made. Paul next traveled to Corinth. This was a commercial capital and port city that contained a temple with many prostitutes that were paid for by the city. Corinth was a decadent society known for commerce and trade. Paul equates the Passover ritual with his own Eucharist ritual, which clearly promotes the drinking of blood, as well as eating flesh. If these are meant to be symbols, then why use them to persuade Jews? It was clear that Paul was maneuvering to invent an iconography that

was suitable to Gentile crowds, while still doing it in the context of the pro-
nouncements of Jewish scriptures.

725. It was here that Paul penned his famous statement of faith as a testament
to Corinth: "For I received from the Lord that which I also delivered you; that
the Lord Jesus on the same night in which he was betrayed took bread and
when he had given thanks he broke it and said, Take, eat; this is my body
which is broken for you" (1 Cor 11:3). He declares a new covenant in the
blood of Jesus Christ, and says, "as often as you eat this bread and drink this
cup, you proclaim the Lord's death till he comes". Yes, because naturally
when someone you love dies you want to proclaim their death fervently and as
many times as possible, especially by drinking their blood. Wouldn't you also
like to pretend to eat that person's flesh and blood to gain their power and
commune with their spirit? It is quite obvious there is no parallel belief to this
mentioned in Jewish scripture. There is also reflected in this Paul's new covenant. It is important to note that this covenant, although restored by faith, is
brought about by a blood sacrifice of the Jewish Messiah. Either way, after
laying this on Corinth Paul arrived in Ephesus, back in Turkey. Mentioned
earlier was the strange fact of the praise of Ephesus as a premier Christian
community, along with their rejection of Paul's message.

726. Ephesus was known for its beautiful religious temple which honored the
Goddess Artemis in Greece or Diana in Rome. Paul lived and taught there for
a few years as he did on most of his major stops. Paul traveled according to the
Jewish Holy Days. Again he turned to the philosophers and Gentiles when
rejected by the Synagogue. Paul made an additional stop in Greece and in Philippi. In Ephesians 1:5 and 1:11 we see Paul's view of predestination, which he
also uses in Romans 9. The doctrine is still divisive, and original sin is wholly
rejected by certain well known Christian denominations. According to Ben
Witherington, "Paul was celebrating the Passover or perhaps a Christianized
version". Which one is it? Are we to believe that Paul kept Jewish traditions to
himself and then made different practices amenable to Gentiles? Scholar John
D. Garr argues this was Paul's way of making the Gentile a "commonwealth
of Israel". Although his view is that Christians should return to their Jewish
roots, which would be hard to do with Paul's teaching, we agree with his general premise that Paul's motives include Judaizing Romans and Gentiles. During Paul's travels he was imprisoned twice and eventually ended up in Rome
where legends say he was beheaded on Nero's orders and left to suffer the
same fate as some of the other early martyrs of the Church. Some mention
Paul being buried in Rome with Peter, even though there is no evidence that
Peter ever went to Rome. We also see that Peter was from the small town of
Galilee and probably did not possess a similar upper-class education that Paul
had to spread his message.

727. While many scholars go so far as to say that Paul was not the founder of a new religion and simply trying to update Jewish teachings in light of his own faith and certain transpiring of events, we are not so sure. Others say Paul could not have been a Pharisee. Whoever wrote the Book of Acts claims Paul was a practicing Jew, but nearly all practicing Jews today reject his practices and can find no support for much of what he said in the Old Testament. Rather they see that Paul either knowingly or unknowingly distorted the views and opinions of practicing Jews. We ourselves have to allege that Paul knowingly accomplished this. Rabbi Tovia Singer claims that Paul corrupted the scripture. He finds it odd that Paul claimed he was a Pharisee but went around persecuting Christians at the order of the High Priest. Firstly, this does not square well with a religious life. Secondly, the historical setting of Jews in the first century precludes any possibility of there being special persecution of a Jewish minority or heresy, mainly because Jews were involved in a mortal struggle with Rome which held more salience. Jews at the time were planning on either fighting or fleeing from Roman rule. Why would the High Priest who was a Sadducee, employ Paul who was a Pharisee and religious teacher in order to persecute a fledgling group within Judaism? This confluence of events seems highly unlikely.

728. Why would the High Priest in Judea have any authority to persecute Christians in Syria?[6] There is, of course, another aspect of the story which was just presented, and it asks us to examine the travels of Paul. If Paul was interested in winning over Jews to his real message and interpretation, then why did he travel to centers of Greco-Roman learning? Not only was he well trained in philosophical discourse, unlike the disciples of Christ, but he seems to have employed it in just the same places where such a learning would find good use. Paul, by his own admission, became as one not under the law to serve the purposes of preaching to Gentiles. It was Paul, after all, who had the means to do so as well as the motive. The reason Paul most likely claimed he was a Pharisee was to make himself seem plainer to the Jews who would have readily rejected his message. The Book of Acts is about Paul's Christological framework winning out over Peter and James view, in the opinion of Rabbi Singer. He points to Romans 7 where Paul is speaking to the Jews and is rather uncharacteristically bringing the law into the discussion. He says that when he discovered the law, sin came into his life. How exactly does one "discover the law"? According to the law, there were prohibitions concerning the ethical

---

[6] For the next five sections we rely on the following material by Rabbi Tovias Singer from his official youtube channel: 1. Singer, T. (2018, January 9). *Paul Corrupted the Hebrew Scriptures and Could Not have been a Pharisee, Explains Rabbi Tovia Singer*. YouTube. Retrieved April 29, 2022, from https://www.youtube.com/watch?v=g0J2ZJTzuro. 2. Singer, T. (2017, January 3). *Was Paul a Rabbi, an Ignoramus, or a Charlatan? Rabbi Tovia Singer Responds*. YouTube. Retrieved April 29, 2022, from https://www.youtube.com/watch?v=XtgfS40f0w4

treatment of animals. Paul seems to have reversed some of these views by employing philosophical notions.

729. Not causing pain and suffering, prohibition of the use and consumption of
blood and eating of live animals, and prohibitions against the waste of food
could all be seen in Jewish law. The practice of keeping an animal alive while
cutting off one limb, using a tourniquet to stop the bleeding to save the rest for
later, was strictly forbidden. This was done to minimize suffering of the animal, as was the prohibition against blood. There were laws on how to slaughter
animals. Some even interpreted Genesis 9:4 as saying that God intended us to
be vegetarians, or at the very least minimize the consumption of meat. Certainly, some of the early Christians seem to have felt as much, such as Peter and
James. Paul took a different view to appeal to his Gentile followers. In Deuteronomy 25:4 the prohibition against muzzling animals is clearly to give mercy,
or "Rochmana" in Hebrew and "rahmat" in Arabic, to the animal. In 1 Cor 9:9,
Paul reverses the law of Moses. He questions whether God cares about the
animals suffering. He explains that it is entirely for our sake that God says
these things, even though this seems to contradict other considerations in scripture about the ethical treatment of animals. Paul's views are not dissimilar
from the Epistle of Barnabas which also question certain dietary restrictions,
like the one's forbidding pork. Barnabas is shown in the epistle saying that the
law concerns not behaving like a pig and not about what we consume. I myself, have chosen by and large to not engage in the consumption of meat. I am
often stunned to hear some of my Christian friends who upon hearing this confess that they could not live without bacon. Pigs are smarter than dogs. When
being prepared for slaughter, many of them are aware of their fate and begin to
panic, have a heart attack and die. Pigs are meant to be wild animals. Pigs and
goats are generally smarter than dogs. James was known neither to drink alcohol or eat meat according to early Christian sources. Peter was said to have
relied on a diet of bread and olives and owned one coat.

730. Now when Paul speaks of the Passover lamb being Jesus, there is clearly
nothing that suggests that blood has any purifying nature for the atonement of
sins in Jewish scripture. How can anything in Jewish teaching resemble drinking the blood of the Messiah? There is no possible way of deriving the Eucharist from any Jewish teaching. The mere eating of alive flesh and drinking of
blood is forbidden by Jewish law but is a well-known practice in pagan cults.
Gaining power by drinking the blood of the vanquished is still practiced in
indigenous population of Papua, New Guinea. When researchers came upon
such tribes they found it best to leave them undisturbed. Gaining the powers of
Jesus Christ by drinking his blood is what is preached by Paul. "In Christ we are
saved", and so we are to partake in the suffering and sacrifice of Christ. Paul
claims that he was directly taught this by Jesus himself. There is no way to verify
this claim. What we do know is Paul taught against the law in several instances.

731. We see this in Deuteronomy 30:10-14, which states that the command-ments of God are easy to follow, is reversed by Paul in Romans 10:6-8, where Paul adds to the verse that we are redeemed by faith, emitting the passage which says God's law is easy to follow. Similarly in Corinth, Paul is asked about the resurrection of the dead. This view was rejected by Greeks who saw that the physical body was a decayed substance apart from immaterial Nature or Spirit. Paul seems to have combined these two concepts and morphed them into the idea that in heaven we will possess "spiritual bodies". It is perhaps not hard to tell that Paul arrived at this belief through a merging of Greek philoso-phy and Jewish eschatology. This belief is even refuted by the Gospel of John, where the doubting Thomas asks to see the resurrected body of Jesus, and up-on inspecting him even touches his wounds. Greeks obviously did not believe in the resurrection of the dead at the end of days, mentioned in Daniel and Isai-ah in the Old Testament. Furthermore, the word for Gentile and Pagan is the same word in Greek. It is not a stretch to believe that Paul was using Pagan views to persuade Gentiles. While this is claimed by certain Mythicist schol-ars, none have come to the conclusion that Paul knowingly invented these myths, but rather that he was drawing on other views and creating his own mixed bag of myth and heresy. It is clear to us that Paul may have had much larger views in mind.

732. In 1 Cor 15:3-4 we read Paul say that Christ died for our sins in accord-ance with the scriptures. He was buried but rose on the third day. This is highly regarded by Christians to be a statement of faith. But what already existing scripture is Paul referring to? Some Bibles will cite verse 5:14 of Hosea. This verse is not about redemption from sins. It is about a people that are facing a heavy retribution from the Lord as repayment for sins. The verse is about be-ing punished by God but not being able to turn away from God, because after all God is the only place that one can be fixed. Nowhere in the verse is there any mention of the Jewish messiah or about a collective salvation and all-inclusive forgiveness of sins. The verse is referring to the retribution visited upon Ephraim, which was the name of the Jewish tribes of the Northern part of the Kingdom of Israel. Paul also seems to directly alter the text of the Bible in Galatians 3:16. So Rabbi Tovias Singer wonders if Paul was an ignoramus or charlatan and comes to the unfortunate conclusion that he was just innocently unaware of scripture and playing fast and loose with the text of the Bible. However, this completely and utterly discounts the fact that Paul was using Jewish scripture to accomplish a project that was clearly much bigger than reforming Judaism as some scholars have rather conveniently suggested by obfuscating the full range of options. We cannot assume that Paul was simply unaware of scripture, no more than we can deny the propulsion of the Pauline synthesis to insane heights throughout the chapters of history. It should be at least clear to us to have a small inkling that either something directly sinister or perplexingly major is afoot.

733. Who can deny the logical absurdity of the doctrine of Original Sin. Why would a physical death atone for spiritual sin, especially when works of the flesh are useless and utterly defiled? There is also the schizophrenia of what is assumed in the Christ figure. Christ has a dual purpose as pointed out by Scholar Gregory J. Riley, in which he is a vessel through which the world can be saved, but also the vanquisher and destroyer of the wicked armies of Satan (compare John 3:17 and 1 John 3:8). Referring to this world as degraded and deprived material after-effect was common coin for Pagan and Gentile believers. In Ephesians 2:2 we read that the spirit at work in those who are disobedient is "the ruler of the kingdom of air". Evil is permeated throughout material existence. In 1 Cor 10:10 we read about the "destroyed of the destroyer". These passages suggest that death, suffering, and sin are part of existence in Paul.

734. Paul readily used such Pagan concepts to justify his own views. In a most stunning passage, we read Paul describe what he wants people to believe about Christ:

> "He is the image of the invisible God, the firstborn of all creation. For by him all things were created, in heaven and on earth, visible and invisible, whether thrones or dominions or rulers or authorities-all things were created through him and for him. And he is the head of the body, the church. He is the beginning, the firstborn from the dead, that in everything he might be preeminent. For in him all the fullness of God was pleased to dwell, and through him to reconcile to himself all things, whether on earth or in heaven, making peace through the blood of his cross. And you, who once were alienated and hostile in mind, doing evil deeds, he has now reconciled in his body of flesh by his death, in order to present you holy and blameless and above reproach through him, if indeed you continue in faith, stable and steadfast, not shifting from the hope of the gospel that you heard, which has been proclaimed in all creation under heaven, and of which I, Paul, became minister." (Col 15-23)

We also read in Col 2:8, "See to it that no one takes you captive by philosophy and empty deceit, according to human tradition, according to the elemental spirits of this world, and not according to Christ". There are a number of conflicting views in these chapters and verses which needs exploration. The first line clearly seems to draw from some Greek concepts and is not readily found in Jewish teaching. Terms like "the image of God", "the invisible God", and "the fullness of God" cannot be readily understood within the framework of Jewish monotheism. Here God is shown as both immaterial and unseen. God creates through his own image, which is a reflection and medium that God uses in order to create, similar to the Demiurge of Plato. In the second line we see that, although God created the world through the power he delineated to his firstborn son, the thrones and dominions of the world were created through him (not by him), and for him. This would reverse the earlier thought that the rulers and dominion of this world was partially given over to the dark power at work in the world. Furthermore, since Paul preaches a dualism between flesh and spirit, should there not be a distaste towards the things of this world that are now created through Christ, but in other instances employed by Satan? God wishes to reconcile himself in all things. It is almost as if we are witnessing a struggle between God and himself. This is only reconciled by God's death in the flesh, so we can remain hostile in mind, and doing evil deeds, but are no longer alienated by God and held accountable for the wickedness of sin. Then we see that, while Paul uses Pagan philosophy, he degrades it and says it is concerning the elemental spirits of this world, and not with Christ. Yes, but you just said that this world was created through Christ. This view, and Paul's view of predestination seen in Romans 9, appear to attribute immorality and sin to God. There is also most notably no mention of the Holy Spirit in this equation of salvation.

735. This points to another issue with Greek philosophy that has been debated by dualists, idealists, philosophers, mystics, Gnostics and others who employ such thinking. The question that many have posed asks whether God is the totality of all existence (matter included), separate from existence and prior to existence as a whole, identical to reality and immaterial, or a deistic and necessary being. Either of these several views that are highly conflicting and hotly contested are possible extrapolations from this apparent dualism of Paul. God is seen firstly as pure essence, and secondly as form. He is thirdly the substance, history, and happenings of the world. God, however, is not to be equated with the material world. So, Paul both uses this as a starting point for his belief system but seems to contradict it.

736. Hence it can be said that no one mobilizes, popularizes, exploits, and highlights the tension between Jewish and Greek beliefs than Paul himself. This remarkable fact is not appropriately addressed, although we have attempted to make some small contribution to a starting point for analyzing the real scope and influence of Paul. A false line is drawn between Classical Greece, the Christian Medieval European period, and the period known as the Scientific enlightenment, but we see a clear line of development embodied in the Pauline view. What needs to be done in the Pauline view? Are we to use flattery, silence, and negativity to understand God? Are we to use asceticism, dualism, and suffering to reach God? How conducive are these beliefs to our happiness?

737. We read Peter say:

> "Therefore, from among the men who have accompanied us
> during the whole time the Lord Jesus went in and out among
> us— beginning from the baptism of John until the day he was

taken up from us—from among these, it is necessary that one
become a witness with us of His resurrection. So they proposed
two: Joseph, called Barsabbas, who was also known as Justus,
and Matthias. Then they prayed, You, Lord, know the hearts of
all; show which of these two You have chosen to take the place
in this apostolic service that Judas left to go to his own place.
Then they cast lots for them, and the lot fell to Matthias. So he
was numbered with the 11 apostles." Acts 1:21-26

These are the requirements to become a disciple of God. Paul was not a disciple of God that met any of these requirements. Instead, he was the, largely self-
appointed, "apostle to the Gentiles". Paul mentions that he shares his role with
Barnabas. There is, however, not a huge mention by other notable members of
the Church that Paul operates in this capacity. Paul is seen by the modern
Church as being chosen above the other apostles. The Church itself was seemingly formulated by Paul in its initial stages. If reformed Christians question
the teachings of the Church, then why not question the teachings of Paul who
formulated the practices of the Church? Paul himself seemed to have a conflict
with the leaders of the Christian movement in its early stages. Paul cannot be
authorized by James and Peter because he claims that he is better than Peter
and James. Since he has surpassed them in knowledge, how can these people
have given him the authority to preach to the Gentiles?

738. In Galatians 2:11-14 we read,

"But when Cephas came to Antioch I opposed him to his face,
because he stood condemned. For before certain men came
from James, he was eating with the Gentiles; but when they
came he drew back and separated himself, fearing the circumcision party. And the rest of the Jews acted hypocritically along
with him, so that even Barnabas was led astray by their hypocrisy. But when I saw that their conduct was not in step with the
truth of the gospel, I said to Cephas (Peter) before them all, "If
you, though a Jew, live like a Gentile and not like a Jew, how
can you force the Gentiles to live like Jews". We ourselves are
Jews by birth and not Gentile sinners"

This confrontation cries out for explanation. First we are to suppose that Peter
had nothing to say for himself. All we hear is Paul's side and Paul's own version of events. Paul is also once again attacking the two main leaders of the
Jerusalem Council. These leaders were chosen by Jesus or led by merit. What
right has Paul to challenge their views? Paul accuses Peter of creating two different standards, one for Jews, and another for Gentiles, but then not adhering
to his own standards. But we ask Christians, who is it really who creates two
different standards for Jews and Gentiles? Paul is the apostle of the Gentiles.

Only he was imbued with the special responsibility of preaching to the Gentiles. Paul himself gives different messages to Gentiles and Jews. He makes special rules for how Gentiles are to be saved and included in salvation. Paul even refers to James as the "circumcision party" and claims that they are the ones setting up two different standards.

739. Paul could just as easily be accused of doing the same thing he accuses others of doing. The fact that he even includes Barnabas in this accusation means that even Paul's fellow apostle to the Gentiles was willing to engage in this so-called hypocrisy. Since Paul is not in regular communication with these people and only appears a few times during these travels, Paul seemed to be looking for an opportunity to show up Peter. He confronts Peter before them all, more like a rival than a friend. He wants to prove Peter wrong in front of an audience. He does not pull him aside and ask him what the situation was. And what is his claim? That he is humbler than all of the other apostles in his unique understanding of the scriptures. Paul uses a false humility in order to slander Peter. One should also note, at the end Paul still refers to Gentiles as sinners.

Chapter 28
Through a Mirror Darkly

740. Many will not be pleased with our synthesis. Our job is not to amuse and enrich ourselves, or to distract from scholarly efforts or theological quests. We are far from these. There is a laughing God that brings joy through life. There is a hollow mockery that teaches escape through death. Neither Jews, Christians, or Muslims are ready to answer these claims. We have provided just a glimpse into some of the apparent sources for Western thought. What has been missing for us is a critical examination on the doctrines that most widely accepted and least frequently questioned. For those who believe the things outlined in these pages and reject our characterization, we hope that you can provide solid grounds for why you find our arguments to be misplaced and our claims to be spurious. We cannot but humbly invite you all to discuss with us. As far as I have looked, no one had provided any substantive critique of Paul, both acknowledging the possibility of a subversive ideology derived from Pauline thinking, but also showing the historical relevance of such views, other than our friend Dr. David Skrbina. His close reading of Nietzsche, and honesty in dealing with the facts provided by historians and scholars on the development of Jewish thought in the 1st century was an essential starting point.

741. We find it rather odd that in our many discussions with Dr. Skrbina over Religious Epistemology, Metaphysics, Environmental issues, Classical Greek texts, and many other topics, that we would become concerned with this particular issue. There is one indelible fact that has become apparent to us: that no other issue has the impact, academic clout, or intellectual and monetary manpower than the accomplishments of the West. Many are however often deluded as to what these accomplishments are based on. In our view, the Modern world did not appear on the scene through spontaneous evolution. Certain seeds were already put in place, and a certain mechanism was already put in motion, this was the underlying thrust of the Church. The inability of secular scholarship to give credence to religious and spiritual values for the development of certain philosophical tastes is an inherent obstacle for modern views only recently being discussed.

742. No one has had more influence over history and philosophy than the Son of Mary. No one has been more established as the interpreter of Jesus than Saul of Tarsus. According to data from Google in 2020, 29 percent of the world adheres to Christianity, 24 percent follow Islam, and 15 percent are Atheist/Secular. Being a member of either of these three groups suggests that one surely has an opinion over whether Jesus existed, how Jesus lived, and what his claims must have been concerning himself. For over half of the

world's population, the teaching of Paul is directed primarily at you. Of course, one cannot casually dismiss over half of the world's population. Jewish polytheism is mentioned in the Bible. The Jews make a golden calf, Moses throws down the tablets. A covenant can be broken, a law can be renewed by faith. This is not at issue, at least for us. Political solutions to religious problems and ethical problems are squarely condemned in religious teaching of the Bible taken in its full context, but so is the legalistic and the ascetic. The Bible tells us that those who inherit the Holy land will be a people of righteousness and justice in interpreting God's law. These are preconditions for political rule.

743. Paul most notably sought the opposite. In an obstinate rejection of the law, he sought a political solution based on cultural defacement and religious subversion. He capitalized on both the decadence of Rome, and the Hellenized Jewish population, to turn against the throne, and the religious orders. The Bible was an entirely Jewish document. Christianity has been used to bolster aspirations of Zionism. In the Bible Jesus is referred to as Rabbi by his followers. Jesus prays to God and keeps the Jewish law. He refers to himself as the Messiah, mentioned in the Jewish scripture. A large portion of Jews rejected Jesus. Paul tried to convince other Jews and even Gentiles that the Jewish scripture referred to Jesus as God. This began a new movement. The movement spread through Rome to Europe. The conversion of Rome to Christianity coincided with its collapse. The modern scientific enlightenment grew out of the Christian reformation. Notable Christian thinkers like St. Augustine and Martin Luther, while attacking Judaism as a form of religious practice, extolled the value of Jewish scripture and the preservation of the Jewish people, who were left in the world as a sign for the coming of the Lord. A Judeo-Christian alliance was formed in the West, primarily through cultural and religious reforms occurring in Europe.

The Antagonism Thesis
744. Paul claims that one can become Jewish by flesh or become Jewish by faith, and that these can be properly distinguished, but overall, both are favorable in the sight of God. Today in Israel, Judaism is not determined by a monolithic definition of what the Jewish faith represents, but by genetic tests. However, a person being a Jew refers to two distinct characteristics. One of them is coming from a background of people who are ethnically linked to the practice of Judaism within their history, and the other characteristic is a practice of Judaism as described in the earliest sources that related this practice to us. The use of the term "Jew" as a racial designation only applies in quite recent affairs when biological markers for racial categories were developed. Ancient Man was not concerned with such categories on a large scale, and it does not appear prominently in the text of the Bible either. Abraham was a Chaldean, and Moses assimilated peoples of many tribes, including the tribe of his wife, who was an Ethiopian. Jewish religion is unique for its emphasis on monotheism. While this claim includes certain Muslim and Christian groups it is not limited to them.

745. Many Christians, Jews, and Muslims are starting to find certain false traditions among them. Conversely, most heretics were true believers who grew disillusioned with the message of faith. We are not ones to reconcile tragedy and comedy in the abyss of skepticism. Nor should we let faith mean the credulity of compromise. Faith means action. Anything that mediates between you and God is an idol. Saul was not a disciple of Christ. He did not cite the messages in the Gospels or the events of Jesus' life. He changed his name to the Romanized "Paul". He seems to have reconstructed certain Jewish teachings to help delude the Christian sect, and to "judaize" Rome. In order to accomplish this, Paul had to point to some of his competition as "judaizers". Paul turned his energy against the Jews and Romans. Works like the Gospel of Luke and the Letters of Paul are written in a first-person account, unlike the rest of the Biblical texts. As noted by Dr. Skrbina in "The Jesus Hoax", the Christians began to resent Jews the more Christianity spread. As the Christian movement grew it had to defend against attacks from Jews. Tacitus writes about Christianity that the superstition had spread, "not only in Judea the first source of the evil, but even in Rome, where all things hideous and shameful from every part of the world find their center and become popular". This remark criticizes the Jews for letting their communities be subverted, but also criticizes the expansionist and assimilationist attitude of Rome, which led to a cultural disintegration. These were the two aspects which Paul had capitalized on in his capacity as "apostle to the Gentiles". Throughout Jewish history, as brought forward in the Biblical texts, the Jews have been caused by God in many instances to become a nation among nations.

746. We believe that "whoever knows the right thing to do and fails to do it, for him it is a sin", as stated by James. Paul's message taught that no Man can be redeemed by works of righteousness, but only by faith alone. Today Messianic Jews do not have a different belief system from Paul. The recent quote by Rabbi Yosef, that Goyim were made to serve the Jews, waits for God to provide earthly rule. Paul's message emphasized the rule of God on earth and the Kingdom of Heaven, brought forward on a spiritual plane of new bodies and a new earth. Paul became "all things to all men" in order to achieve his ends. Christians that claim to turn the other cheek discount the violence of Christian history. The tendency to justify the State, and use Jewish teaching was to subvert Judaism, and combat Roman rule.

Exegesis of Epistles
747. All of our discussions look clearer when we look at the words that Christians purport to be written by Paul. We don't want to skimp the reader of the precious details contained within the various plots and narratives derived from our present subject of inquiry. Up until now we have researched the various implications of the Pauline synthesis in historical, political, and philosophical terms. Now we move to find proof for what we have researched in the essen-

tial themes and concerns of the Christian doctrine that seems to be entirely based on Paul as its central figurehead. More significant than the origins of the Christian message which people hardly have the ability or capacity to research, the historical and political extension and development in terms of the application of Christian doctrine, or the ghosts of philosophical past, present, and future, is the carefully crafted and extremely tenacious words of the self-styled apostle to the gentiles. In our opinion, Paul shows himself to be both a master of rhetoric and dialectical thinking and his words as they appear to us even in the plain English of the King James Version (most popularly read and most widely available and accessible) contains fundamental concepts of a man who in spite of himself and to spite himself is raised to be lowered for the sake of all mankind. It is a tale of alienation, redemption, and self-sacrifice that has captivated the world. Concepts like Original Sin, Salvation by faith alone, faith in the future and the Kingdom of God (the world to come or the new age), false humility, and grace through suffering are all first described in Paul's letters, as is the formula for eternal rebirth of Man in a new body through the grace of the Lord, and an individualistic path of salvation through universal decree. Here we see the first notable utterance of the statement that Christ who was seen by Christians as the Messiah, sent by God on behalf of the Jewish people but rejected by Jewish leadership and dying for the sins of all mankind as a blood sacrifice, similar to ones performs by Jews in their holy altars.

Romans

748. Paul's letter to Romans opens by referring to Paul as a slave of Christ whose news has been promised through the holy scripture. It is clear that this refers to the Messiahship of Jesus according to the prophets of the Jews. It goes on to say that Christ is Son of God by both being sprung from the line of David but also by being miraculously appointed Son of God by Holy Spirit through resurrection.

749. Firstly, we see that Christ was dually made Son of God, on the one end through his lineage and the other end through the appointment of the "spirit of holiness". Whether this "spirit of holiness" refers to God the Father or an intermediary between the human and divine is unclear, but we see nonetheless a clear dialectic between flesh and spirit even in the first couple of verses. It strikes us as odd that there is no mention of Christ's incarnation as "God in the flesh" but instead we see Christ made divine through several factors and being appointed. Here we see a "binitarian" formula of two aspects of God instead of three. In Pauline cosmology, while God the Father reigns in heaven, the world is being prepared for the rule of God's only son. Jesus is the Lord of mankind, as God rules in heaven but now the world is prepared for the rule of Christ who will reconcile the rule of heaven with the rule of earth.

750. The formula is repeated in Romans 1:7, where Paul invokes God our Father but also the Lord Jesus as he says in Romans 1:9, "Your faith being

known worldwide, since, as God is my witness, whom I serve at the core of my being in service of the news of his son". We see here that while Jesus prescribes the method, he does so on God's authority. Paul declares his mission is unique and that he has been made in debt to barbarians and savages as well as the wise. Paul declares salvation to "first, of course, the Jew, and also to the Greek". This is where the confusion begins: If Paul's preaching is for the world, wise and savage alike, then why make this sort of distinction between Jew and Gentile? Furthermore, Paul is clear that the call of salvation to the non-Jew is made available through what has already been promised to the Jew. On the one hand Paul gives preference to the Jew because he declares himself to be one and constantly references the promise that God made to the Jews, on the other end he preaches to the Gentiles of a New Covenant superseding Jewish law.

751. Still, Paul declares citing scripture, "The righteous man will live off faith", describing his view of salvation by faith alone. Paul also however exhorts Christians to ponder and contemplate God's signs through the invisible attributes in the things he made (Romans 1:20). Paul also prescribes directives on those who are led astray by their own disobedience turning to carnal pleasure. While these dictates towards contemplation and sexual purity are to be taken seriously by any community wishing to gain some semblance of practice and a continuity of tradition, how do they match up with a life of faithfulness apart from the works of the law? We assume Paul wishes to weed out hypocrites as in Romans 2:3 where he warns hypocrites that God knows what they really do. The veracity of his preaching against hypocrites become apparent in his stance against the Torah. The only possible conclusion one could reach is that although Paul wishes to use the Torah as proof of his own teaching, he would not like his followers to rely on it exclusively or follow it.

752. In Romans 2:9-12 Paul explains that those who commit sin whether Jew or Gentile will be visited by tribulation and no partiality is to be found with God, but he declares the Jew is first in incurring both God's wrath and glory. In Romans 2:12 he declares, "Everyone who sinned outside the reach of the Torah will also perish without reference to the Torah", but those who sin from the Torah will be held accountable by the Torah. Ultimately, we must ask how no partiality can be found in the fact that some are held accountable by the Torah and some not, yet elsewhere Paul declares that the Torah was given on behalf of transgressions. How can this be possible when Paul says in verse 2:14 in Romans that the Torah is toilet paper; He states, "For when Gentiles who do not have the law, by nature do what the law requires, they are a law to themselves". Paul strikes down the law with three counts: 1. The law holds accountable those who are under it. 2. The Torah can be given two ways; it can be passed down by the flesh by traditions or it can be "written on the heart". 3. One can arrive without the Torah and be a "law unto themselves".

753. To emphasize the point, the Torah according to Paul holds those account-able who read it and is valid, yet it cannot save you as it says it can. We must legitimately ask if the Torah is not the source or cause of one's salvation then how can the words "according to scripture" be conflated with this doctrine. Or do Paul's words against hypocrisy now seem a little piece of projection as he asks, "you then who teach others, do you not teach yourself?" (Romans 2:21).

754. Providing a fake solution is sometimes worse than not helping. Here Paul brings in one of his main concepts that explores how he reconciles an appar-ently dual path of salvation: one can be circumcised in the flesh but if you vio-late the torah still you are a revert despite your circumcision, yet one can have a "circumcision of the heart" which is the essence of the act of circumcision and not a physical trait or action taken on your part. Paul introduces this term in Romans 2:29.

755. In the same verse we read "a Jew is one inwardly", and we know from earlier verses that invisible attributes and not the things seen up front are more important. The attributes of the invisible Jew are here described. The method of being a secret Jew or inward Jew are here prescribed. Paul describes the advantages of being a Jew who are vouchsafed revelation and says that God does not go back on his promises. "Let God be true and every man be a liar" (Romans 3:4), but Paul plays devil's advocate with the concept that God al-lows sin to prevail. We are not justified by deeds of the flesh (Romans 3:20-24), but by the blood of the covenant here shed by Christ for all mankind (Ro-mans 3:35). Evils works cannot tarnish what is already forlorn, and no good can come by our own effort. This is why Paul states in Romans 3:8, "And why not do evil that good may come as some people slanderously charge us with saying? Their condemnation is just"!

756. We must also remember that God is not only the God of the Jews but also God of the Gentiles (Romans 3:29). This fact is made true by the fact of salva-tion by faith alone which guarantees salvation to all mankind not by the law of the Torah but by the view of faith and guidance through the supernatural. However, the question remains: is Paul upholding the law or putting the Torah on a new footing? We must also ask if Gentiles are now held accountable by the Torah or Jews free from it? It would seem for now the mystery only deep-ens but we uncover more of Paul's stance in the next few chapters.

757. God gave commands to Abraham and even tells him to circumcise him-self and to take up the sword for God. Paul argues that since Abraham had not received the law of the Torah he was not bound by it. But can this really mean that all God demanded of Abraham was faith? True, God relied on faith by reading the heart of Abraham but was not this faith proved through some dras-tic means that consisted of complete self-sacrifice? Can we really allege that our great forefather in faith was saved by the merit of this faith alone and not

through his character that was like a firm rock on shifting sands? Here Paul makes his main point in Romans 4:15: "For the Law brings wrath, but where there is no law there is no transgression". Where is the law that just was written on the heart? Are even these being dismissed here? Apparently, it doesn't matter if one reaches the Torah by what is written through traditions or receives it by circumcision of the heart, but just having faith is now enough. What about reason being the bridge between faith and scripture as we are told by preachers and apologists? None of these views can abide Paul's teaching as we will see.

758. Since the Law is given on behalf of transgression, there must have been no sin before law but this is not technically true according to Paul because it is through Adam that sin first entered the world. Paul's philosophy seems to treat the father of humanity with a unique disdain, blaming him for the sin of all humankind. Paul writes, "Just as sin came into the world through one man, and death through sin, and so death spread to all men" (Romans 5:12), but not to worry because as he also writes, "God shows his love for us in that while we were sinners, Christ died for us. Since therefore we have now been justified by his blood, much more will be saved by him" (Romans 5:8-9). God sent his son as a second Adam, but we must ask, was not Adam also a son of God?

759. Paul seems to support the notion of blood sacrifice quite readily. Of course, there are several issues left to explore. The first issue is that while death is the penalty of sin, the death of Christ provides life everlasting. This means that this everlasting life promised comes through the blood sacrifice and animal sacrifice performed by Jews at the temple which Paul has already delegitimized, except apparently in this unique instance in which it was used to wipe away the sins of all of humanity. The other issue is that Christ is a second Adam sent to correct the mistakes of the first. This notion of "sins of the father" is a paradoxical concept in Christian teaching that blames Adam for the lowly status of mankind when it was our father Adam who, through his prayers of forgiveness placed mankind on the lofty status that he now enjoys. In Paul, it is also God the Father who not only lets humanity suffer in sin by testing and cursing Adam, but humanity had to also wait for the entrance of the Lord into the historical scheme, who by means of sacrificing his own son by blood sacrifice finally redeemed Man and saves, "much more, now that we are reconciled" (Romans 5:10). But an obvious question must be asked about all these sons of Adam that came before; were they cursed for simply being born?

760. This brings us to the basic question in the problem of Original Sin that makes for paradoxical theodicy and an ominous soteriological scope. It may seem that God is directly responsible for sin and immorality. If that is not true then we have to ask which fact is heavier on the scale of redemption and grace: that we are quite naturally sinful or that we are born in the image of God? The

polarity between the two is mired in the confusing rhetoric of Paul who seeks to emphasize man's sinful nature to promote salvation by faith alone.

761. Another puzzle is presented in the fact that our analysis of the New Testament shows us nowhere that Jesus makes the emphatic claim that he was sent to die for the sin of all mankind or that Man is conceived in sin. This might mean that the human nature of Jesus also predisposed him to sin, as Paul reported earlier about Christ lineage from the Davidic line. A concept that creeps up in Paul is a sort of false humility, as Romans 5:3 says, "we rejoice in our suffering, knowing suffering produces endurance". Wearing your suffering as a badge and a general sense of quietude in anticipation of salvation and grace is in one way the recounting of all your failures as successes and it almost takes no effort to point out that this is also carried out by the wicked. On the one end, you are a humble servant bearing the burdens of others, on the other end it is by these very means that you are made whole and boast on the account of accepting your station and calling. This is Paul's concept of being raised to be lowered. Hence, the suffering and the persecuted and meek are children of God, but the joyful and liberated and sensual are chosen to fulfill that role. At least to our mind, this constitutes a grotesque form of spiritual materialism, and playing the role of the victim constitutes a hallmark of liberal values.

762. In Romans 5:6-9 we see that the problem of sin is built right into the promise of redemption. In Romans 5:11 Paul says he rejoices in God through the Lord Jesus who was sent for our reconciliation. Jesus was sent by God as it plainly declares, so Jesus is not all powerful but under the decree of the Almighty God. We also clearly see the state of the law in Romans 5:20 where Paul declares, "the law came in to increase the trespass". Essentially, as sin increased based on the transgressions of the law so did the grace of God. In this clearly devised statement of rhetorical genius the law is both a gift and a curse on the righteous.

763. Although one who believes in Christ should not continue in sin as Paul says at the opening of Romans 6, such a declaimer is necessary to clarify the previous statement, where the logical conclusion would seem to be that law plus sin equals grace. It is not the case that Christians, as clarified by Paul in Romans 6:2-9, should actively sin, but that having restored their belief in Christ they are now no longer under the effect and persuasion of sin. Christians are dead to sin and have everlasting life, but those who still live in sin pay the penalty of sin which is death. For Christians, their old human nature is destroyed so they are excluded from paying the penalty of sin. However, we must also remember that through suffering and endurance one reaches grace and one can see that the path of reaching grace seem to be a treacherous one but lo and behold if we come to believe we suffer no more on account of sin.

Christians are "no longer under law but under grace (Romans 6:14) so have no longer to do with sin.

764. Paul claims that Christians are no longer at liberty to sin because they have been released by the law of the Torah in Romans 6:15 but can this really be true because as we just read sin entered the world by one man and all are subject to it since birth, but those who come to believe are affecting continual grace and no longer subject to it? This either means that Christians are no longer affected by their sinful nature or now free from it. In Romans 7 the mystery deepens when Paul declares that sin does not have agency but issues automatically and without agency from the sinful nature of the sinner. This autonomic version of sin is more like blinking, breathing, masticating, and defecating. In Romans 7-9 the arguments and rhetorical tricks of Paul become extremely tightly wound and the complexity of several terms and relations in Paul's soteriological message is charted out. Anyone with a little time to investigate will find the arguments leveled especially in Romans 9 to be debated and hotly contested by various Christian groups who have all arrived at different interpretations of these verses.

765. Paul claims that the Torah or law governs Man's conduct only as long as he is alive but this obfuscates a final judgement into an eschatological redemptive state occurring neither in the balance of sin or in the penalty of sin whose wage is death. Paul declares in Romans 6:6: "we know that our old self was crucified with him in order that the body of sin might be brought to nothing so that we no longer would be enslaved to sin", and in Romans 7:6: "we are released from the law, having died to that which held us captive". Yet, Paul does not say that law is sin even though he says that the law was given on account of transgressions, but that sin caused the law itself to bear the wrath of God through its own covetousness which makes it obsolete (Romans 7:7-9). We take this to mean that those who followed the law with pridefulness caused it to become a tool to slander others, but the message is still unclear.

766. Paul now Platonizes sin and says that the law is holy and righteous and good. The law is basically good but has been hijacked by sin which is practically synonymous with human nature. Paul's dialectic between law and sin is similar to the dialectic between flesh and spirit. Paul draws a dialectic also between the law of the inner being, which is righteous and the law of the flesh which is "the old way of written code". Hence there is external retribution for sin because the cause of sin is merely linked to the flesh and does not correspond to the inner being, for Paul still declares, "I delight in the law in my inner being" (Romans 7:22). This sin is manifest in the flesh and works of the flesh and only purifies by the blood of Christ, hence no one who commits fleshly sin bears on the inner being which is only manifest through works of righteousness through the spirit. Paul makes it abundantly clear that even he cannot go beyond the sin of fleshly existence, but it is not him that is to blame

but rather the sinful nature in which he was conceived. Paul writes in Romans 7:14-21: "For we know that the law is spiritual, but I am of the flesh, sold under sin. For I do not understand my own actions. For I do not do what I want, but I do the very thing I hate. Now if I do what I do not want, I agree with the law, that it is good. So now it is no longer I who do it, but the sin that dwells within me. For I know that nothing good dwells in me, that is, in my flesh. For I have the desire to do what is right, but not the ability to carry it out. For I do not do the good I want, but the evil I do not want is what I keep on doing. Now if I do what I do not want, it is no longer I who do it, but sin that dwells within me. So I find it to be a law that when I want to do right, evil lies close at hand".

767. Finally, Paul states "Wretched man that I am! Who will deliver me from this body of death (Romans 7:24) proving that no one is good on their own accord at least according to Paul. Paul states this in his usual self-deprecating manner. Since the formula for redemption precludes sin and suffering, the most miserable and most wretched are saved by the most grace, because no one is outside the call for salvation of all mankind, but no one is saved on their own accord. We are all saved in spite of our own corrupt nature. No one is truly exempt. Paul exhorts us to "walk not according to the flesh but to the spirit" (Romans 8:4). Paul introduces a new "spiritual law" and defines it in Romans 8. Paul says in Romans 8:12 that we are debtors but not according to the flesh and already dead but those who live according to the spirit you put to death the deeds of the body and so cannot experience the accidents of sin and flesh.

768. The "spirit of adoption" seen in Romans 8:15 is the one that prompts our own spirit so that we may become children of God. For we are co-beneficiaries of a new covenant not made in the flesh by dead words but in the spirit through the suffering and glory shared with Christ (Romans 8:17). In Romans 8:18 Paul bids us to ignore our present suffering that we endure only for a future glory. This establishes a unique role for the eschatological and teleological scope of Paul in his faith in the future. The present and the past have no relevance for Paul as the present is about quietude and suffering. This utilitarian sort of use of the notion of suffering for future reward is a cornerstone of the ethic that is built into western thinking, as Paul states, "For the creation was subjected to futility but because of him who subjected it in hope" (Romans 8:20). This establishes the two poles of Pauline thinking: a internal and external dualism of flesh and spirit and a push and pull between present and future in a temporal dualism that battles between suffering and grace.

769. We are quite sympathetic to the notion that those who are loved by God can be more than conquerors but must point out that Paul derides the political power in the world in favor of a spiritual connection. Paul says he has transcended the power active in the world and states, "neither death, nor life, nor angels, nor rulers, nor things present, nor things to come, nor powers, nor

height, nor depth, nor anything else in all creation will be able to separate us from the love of God" (Romans 8:38-39).

770. In Romans 9 it is hard to tell if Paul is talking about the promise God made to Israel, the Gentiles and Nations being saved through the promise of Israel, a brand-new path of salvation under a New Covenant that invites Jews as well, or a dual path of salvation for Christians and Jews. Furthermore, we cannot suppose that Paul is speaking of a message according to his own Gospel, according to the old scriptures and traditions, or according to a prophecy foretold in the old scriptures that transcends the old covenant and transforms it into a message of salvation for all mankind. Lastly, we must ask who God saves at the end of the day and does Paul actually see himself as a convert to a new religion or simply a fulfiller of old tradition. Paul laments, "For I wish that I myself were accursed and cut off from Christ for the sake of my brothers, my kinsman according to the flesh". He reports with anguish in his heart and implies that Israel is accursed. What he says next is that "to them belong the adoption, the glory, the covenants, the giving of the law, the worship, and the promises" (Romans 9:3-4). Paul tells us, "It is not as though the word of God has failed. For not all who are descended from Israel belong to Israel" (Romans 9:6). So in the first instance Paul is cut off from his brothers in salvation for Christ, but it is through them that this promise was fulfilled as it is through the patriarchs that Christ was brought forwards (Romans 9:5). Ultimately, however, not all who call themselves Israel are Israel as we just read. It is not hard to see how taken side by side these statements are rather confusing, and it may stand to reason that Paul is not making any consistent point on Judaism.

771. He states, "It is not the children of the flesh who are the children of God, but the children of promise are counted as offspring" (Romans 9:8). This could only mean that one is no longer a Jew in the flesh but only in the spiritual sense through adoption of God. In Romans 9:16 we read, "it depends not on human will or exertion, but on God, who has mercy". This reiterates the point that we are not saved because of our own effort or works. And on who does this salvation rest? Paul tells us it is, "not from the Jews only but also from the Gentiles" in Romans 9:24. But we must also remember that salvation comes to the Jew first but eventually also to the Greeks, gentiles, and pagans who are not part of the nation of God.

772. Paul says Israel is blessed, but only some of Israel is truly blessed. He employs the verse "the elder shall serve the younger' in an eschatological scheme which means that God chose Israel in order to give salvation to the world, almost reversing the original meaning of the verse. According to Paul, one is hated or blessed only by God's decree. Those blessed and hated ones are chosen by God in advance yet still put through trials. Then Paul cites Hosea in Romans 9:25 and claims that God changes who he hates and blesses. After all this, we are somehow to believe that God's salvation is now open to all people.

This is due to the staggering claim made by Paul that God brings in Nations who are not Jews to serve the ones who he once cursed. We fail to realize how such a decision to come to faith could ever be achieved given these various stipulations. St. Paul removes that option unless he means that God blesses those he once cursed by getting ahead of the sinner in a sort of guidance that is synergistic union of human and divine. Ultimately, one cannot possibly believe that the Jews were tested by God and cursed by God but eventually blessed the whole world even in their state of disobedience. Furthermore, in a paradoxical twist, this law has now been superseded and fulfilled, and is both the source of the knowledge and proof of that which has superseded it.

773. We see that Paul is the source of the view that Jesus is predicted in the Old Testament. Paul says that "Christ is the end of the law" and the fulfillment of the law and Torah (Romans 10:4). Paul now declares that there is no distinction between Jew and Greek (Romans 10:12). Finally, Paul derides Greeks in favor of Jewish salvation and says, "did Israel not understand? First Moses says, 'I will make you jealous of those who are not a nation; with a foolish nation I will make you angry'" (Romans 10:19).

774. On whose authority can Paul claim this? Well Paul reassures us at the opening of Romans 11 that God has not rejected his chosen people and declares that he is from the Tribe of Benjamin. God saves only a remnant (Romans 11:5), but here it is unclear if the remnant that is saved are part of the Jews while others are not saved, the Jews who come to believe in Christ, or the Gentiles that have newly become grafted into the promise of salvation along with the Jews. In Romans 11:13-14 we read a strange admittance by Paul who says, "Inasmuch as I am an apostle to the Gentiles, I magnify my ministry in order to somehow make my fellow Jews jealous and thus save some of them". Again, it is unclear if Paul's ministry is on behalf of Jews or Gentiles. Then we read that while Gentiles are not part of the original message of salvation they are "grafted in" (Romans 11:19). Not only are Jews to be made Christian so they are saved, but Gentiles are grafted into the call of salvation predicted by the prophets of Israel. Thus, Paul both has his proverbial cake and eats it too. It is no feat for God to restore those once fallen but in what covenant will those ones be grafted in if the old one is delegitimized? The rhetoric becomes quite complex. In a quite dispensationalist passage Paul declares, "a partial hardening has come upon Israel in part, until the fullness of the Gentiles has come in". Here we see a dual road of salvation, and one that has to wait for Israel. In a quite ambiguously phrased conclusion Paul states, "As regards to the Gospel they are enemies for your sake. But as regards election, they are beloved for the sake of their forefathers" (Romans 11:28).

775. Paul says, "How unsearchable are his judgements and inscrutable his ways!" (Romans 11:33). Yes, how unsearchable indeed. In addition to abandoning reason, Paul adds, "Do not be conformed to this world" (12:2). Quite

conversely however, Paul also preaches a sort of quiet conformity and says bless your persecutors, share the joy of the fortunate and the tears of weepers, live in harmony and do not be haughty. Christians are not supposed to cause a stir. We certainly do not disagree with Paul's exhortations to feed the hungry but find it contradicts his earlier command to "rejoice with those who rejoice" and not challenge power or dwell on material good (Romans 12:14-20). Now at the beginning of Romans 13 Paul preaches extreme conformity and promulgates to his followers to, "Let every person be subject to the governing authorities. For there is no authority except from God and those that exist have been instituted by God" (Romans 13:11).

776. Not only does Paul teach humans are born into the curse of the law through the flesh and cannot affect their own salvation, Paul also states that no one try to change their own station in life or question those in power to affect change in the world. The only option one is left is to wait for the future salvation that exists in the Kingdom of God. Just like those works of the flesh, those powers of the world are used in a sort of cosmic utilitarianism for the world to come that prepares us for the Kingdom of God. Whoever resists authorities resists who God appointed but how does this square with "blessed are the meek"? Paul tells us to obey the authorities only insofar as we can escape their judgement (Romans 13:3). Paul also says the rulers do not "bear the sword in vain" (Romans 13:4). Now we read, "whoever loves one another has fulfilled the law" but we must remind the reader that this is referring to the law of the Torah that Christ has freed us from already (Romans 13:10). The sword of the authorities is from God but we should have no fear because love is the fulfillment of the law. To this end we must don Christ like a "second skin" and as an armor of light to wait to receive our new bodies in the world to come.

777. Paul declares in Romans 14 that "the weak person eats only vegetable" but when nearly a fifth of the earth is stables of pigs and chickens and cows to make hamburger fillets for the mass of humanity that doesn't question what it takes to procure their food sources we must relegate this statement to the realm of absurdity and give it no credence. Suffice it to say that Paul's diatribe on going beyond dietary restrictions is strange for several reasons. In Genesis 9:4 we read, "But you shall not eat flesh with its life, that is, it's blood", but Paul also allows meat sacrificed to idols. Either way all dictates in Paul are according to one's internal state and inner consciousness about how he chooses to follow the law that is not in the written law itself. To this end Paul's teachings are highly individualistic and he says, "It is good not to eat meat or drink wine or do anything that causes your brother to stumble. The faith you have keep between yourself and God" (Romans 14:21-22).

778. Paul finally smuggles in the Holy Spirit at the end of the letter in Romans 15:13-16. The Holy Spirit is connected with the hope of future salvation and the completion of God's plan in time according to historical events mentioned

in the Bible where his spirit acts through history itself. This is significant for the two poles of redemption in Rome and Jerusalem, for Gentile and Jew. It is notable that Paul appears to have established the first Church in Rome that would later align with Roman power, but also that Paul talks extensively about the promise God made to Israel and to the Jews that is used by Christian Zionists and Jewish Messianists to usher in a New Age. Finally, Paul declares what we suspected all along in saying, "and this I make it my ambition to preach the gospel. Not where Christ has already been named, lest I build on someone else's foundation". Paul does not teach what has already been taught where it was already said and what was already said but brings a brand-new message of salvation. He also states, "This is the reason why I have so often been hindered from coming to you". Romans 16 contains notable mentions of figures associated with the Pauline ministry. What cannot be easily explained away is Paul's connections to elite Roman Jews. This may help explain why the Pauline corpus had so much range is because of these backers with immense resources. Paul greets Herodian as his Kinsman in Romans 16:11. Here we see Paul greet the enemies of Christ and John the Baptist who had John the Baptist killed and attacked both Jesus and his family treated on equal and friendly terms by Paul.

1 Corinthians

779. As we move to Paul's letter to Corinthians, we sense that Paul is probably speaking to the same type of crowd of Hellenized Jews and Pagan Greeks. Rome, Corinth, and Athens are the Hellenized capitals of the world where Paul ventures. We do not believe this detail to be accidental but quite readily find it can be very well conjoined to his purpose and end of bringing the gentiles into the Jewish message of salvation. Paul wishes to declare a solid message without schism, without devolving into the mystical or the philosophical, but he knows that the crowds he wants to reach are inundated with the theological scope of the Jews and the worldly sort of wisdom of the Greeks. Paul wants to teach that his simple message of Christ's crucifixion and resurrection is beyond all theological and cultural schism.

780. What is interesting is that there are already schisms and divisions with the early Church even though Paul seems to be the first instance of any communications between the Church and its cultural centers in Rome and Corinth. Two options seem available: either Paul was dealing with schisms within the message he already taught others or that he was actively trying to subvert a message that was already in existence but differed from Paul's version. Paul has female leaders like Phoebe and Chloe who report to him apparently. In Corinthians 1:11 some of those connected with leadership roles in the early church are raising concerns about schisms. According to 1 Corinthians 1:12 Paul states, "each one of you says, "I follow Paul or I follow Apollos or I follow Cephas, or I follow Christ". This verse is highly indicative of the types of divisions existing in the early Church. Some followed Paul's teaching which had its own flavor apart from Peter's or Cephas as he was also known, who as we

have seen was seen to have a kind of adversarial or parallel relationship with Paul. There is no clarification of who "Apollos" could be but sounds especially Greek to contrast with Christ who could appear to be a fundamentally non-Greek concept. This could mean that there were a variety of views in the early Church but one of the factions led by Paul came to dominate.

781. Paul declares, "Christ did not send me to baptize but to preach the Gospel". Paul does not admit to eloquent wisdom but seems most bashful as we have seen and is otherwise quite subtle and masterful in employing rhetorical tricks. What good are debates? For Paul they are useless. "Where is the debate of this age?", Paul asks and says, "Has not God made foolish the wisdom of the world?" (1Cor 1:20). He goes on to say, "Jews demand signs and Greeks seek wisdom" (1 Cor 1:22). God chose, however, what is nonsense to shame the sophisticated, and the weak to shame the strong. All expectations one has of God should be dispensed with quite neatly. The reason God employs this method is in order that no one should boast (1 Corinthians 1:27-29).

782. Here Paul explains why he does not preach about miracles or wisdom but only the mystery of the cross when before in Romans he did not seem very afraid to engage in complex theological debates. He proclaims, "I decided to know nothing among you except Jesus Christ and him crucified" (1 Corinthians 2:2). Paul makes clear what he says is not based on scripture or reason, but a mystery imparted to him of secret wisdom decreed before the ages (1 Corinthians 2:7). Paul received these "mysteries" through the spirit (1 Corinthians 2:11). Let no one deceive themselves that they are wise (1 Corinthians 3:18). For the righteous ones are but a spectacle to the world who persecutes them (1 Corinthians 4:9). Here we see the apex of the "raised to be lowered" theme. Those who suffer in the world are blessed, and true wisdom is an uncommon sort of knowledge that does give us status in the world. One should quite readily exchange pleasure for pain, and wisdom for ignorance. One is guaranteed status by having none, and almost made full by being emptied. One is blessed by having nothing but finds no need to boast. Essentially every situation can be perceived as a win-win. But aren't these humble brags really boasts about proceeding to a destination beyond mere mortals? Again, we see the characteristic false humility of Paul rendering every success an appointment from the lord and every peril a chance for grace through suffering.

783. A key passage is in 1 Corinthians 4:20 where Paul states, "For the Kingdom of God does not consist in talk, but in power. What do you wish? Shall I come to you with a rod, or in love with a gentle spirit?". The formula here is quite simple to decode. The Kingdom of God is the world to come since the power of this world is worth nothing in the present age. But if God chose what is weak to shame the strong how does it square with the passages in Romans that God did not dole out authority in vain? While we can't readily provide an answer to that question, we can see what Paul is basically telling his followers:

If you choose love now instead of power you will be given the rod in the world to come because the Kingdom of God consists in actual power in the world to come. At that time all roles will be exchanged so in anticipation Christians are to walk lightly but carry a big stick. A staff for protection and rod for correction is what Paul recommends. We can see, however, that this resembles the rule of Pharoah more than the rule of Moses. We see that throughout the years Jewish nationalism has shifted the role of what a Jew is from a religious statement to a national statement but this conflicts with the call of God who wishes Israel to be a nation of priests. Paul's view seems to separate the ruling power in the world from the spiritual law of the world to come in an almost complete separation of Church and State. Furthermore, Paul seems to be one of the first to make a distinction between what it means to be a Jew at heart and not necessarily a physical descendent of Semitic people.

784. In Corinthians 5:9-12 Paul tells his followers not to associate with sexually immoral, greedy and untrustworthy people or idolaters but only inside the Christian community meaning that one is still allowed to associate with such people when not engaging in one's religion. Paul places the religious life over and above common relations but does not obfuscate the role of these lesser bonds, but what is troubling is that one is not really sure what activity is a religious activity and what is not one when all things are brought to fruition for the Kingdom of God and the world to come. Inside the Christian community one is able to caste away immoral people, the lustful and greedy, and idolators but outside of the Christian community with the filth of the world and all this is just the price of doing business and besides one cannot be expected to leave this earth. Paul says, "For what have I to do with judging outsiders?". Outside the Christian community Christian can associate with all types of people that are not conducive to Christian teaching because God judges all those who are outside but inside the Church you are to "purge the evil one from among you" (1 Corinthians 5:13). This simply does not match the situation in passages like those of Galatians where Paul supposedly accused Peter to his face for associating with some Gentiles exactly on the same basis. Those inside the Church are apparently only judged by others inside the Church. In 1 Corinthians 5:5 Paul states, "that he handed over the accuser for the destination of the flesh in order that the spirit may be saved in the day of the Lord Jesus". Paul seems to teach that Satan governs over the flesh and is the ruler of death.

785. In Corinthians 6:1-6 Paul pleads to those who are in the Church to set up their own laws to hold others accountable instead of going before the law of the unrighteous. He tells them to settle all matters of the Church within the Church. No wonder it is so easy for Paul to obey the rulers as he says in Romans 13. This would come very easily if there were two sets of laws: one dealing with matters of this world and another dealing with matters inside the Church. How and when one applies each is, we would suppose, according to the discretion of each one that enacts such a statute. In Romans 6:12-14 we

read exactly these views where Paul says, "All things are lawful to me but not all things helpful. All things are lawful for me, but I will not be dominated by anything". Paul now goes in length to discuss his views on marriage in which he conflates having faith in God as being joined in the spirit of the Lord and being married to the flesh as akin to being joined in flesh to a prostitute.

786. Before we return to our analysis on 1 Corinthians, we should point out that, taken as they are, The Pauline letters present some absurd views on women. Since some of these views seem contradictory it may be hard to establish what Christians who followed the teaching of Paul would have practiced. Without reference to either views of women in ancient times or the views of modern secular liberals on the liberation of women, we present some of these views in an honest fashion. We should point that certain orthodox Jews that say a prayer after waking up that thanks God they are not born women or goyim (refers to "nations" or non-Jews) and the patriarchal format of Islamic society, means that neither Judaism, Christianity or Islam have views on women that align with the modern secular values of today. Still, this is not a book on views on women through the ages but rather a book about Paul's views.

787. In 1 Corinthians 11 Paul tells his followers "Be imitators of me, as I am of Christ", but also says, "the head of everyman is Christ, the head of a wife is her husband, and the head of Christ is God" (1 Corinthians 11:3). This would mean that in the spiritual hierarchy Christ is subordinated to God, Man is subordinated to Christ, and Woman is subordinated to Man. Women are at the very bottom of spiritual hierarchy and the cosmic totem pole. Men should remove head coverings and pray but women need to cover their heads while praying or be punished by having their hair cut off. Paul says Women were made from Men and not Men from Women which seems medically untrue since a woman requires less input from the gonadotropins of the sperm cell and a body without adequate resources of testosterone by default creates a female. Thus, the female is more readily conceived than the male but we admit nothing is outside the grasp of the almighty so we can readily concede this point which is not strongly argued anyways on the basis of biology alone. We don't want to be misunderstood as claiming that Paul understood it in any biological sense but rather in the spiritual sense which is a much more relevant and significant domain in Pauline theology. This spiritual hierarchy is also made reference to in Ephesians 5:22-24. In an almost parallel message Paul writes, "wives submit to your own husbands, as to the Lord. For the husband is the head of the wife as Christ is the head of the Church, his body, and is himself its savior. Now as the Church submits to Christ, so also wives should submit in everything to their husbands".

788. Women are also readily equated with the entrance of Sin into the world and the deeds of the flesh. In 2 Corinthians 11:2-3 we read, "For I feel divine jealousy for you, since I betrothed you to one husband to present you as a pure

virgin to Christ. But I am afraid that as the serpent deceived Eve by his cunning your thoughts will be led astray". In 1 Timothy 2:11-15 we read, "Let a women learn quietly with all submissiveness. I do not permit a woman to teach or to exercise authority over a man; rather she is to remain quiet. For Adam was formed first, then Eve; And Adam was not deceived and became a transgressor. Yet she will be saved through childbearing". How exactly did sin enter the world through one Man who is Adam the father of all mankind if he was the one who was deceived? Apparently, sin has a complex relationship with the feminine gender in Pauline theology.

789. One has to really ask if Eve incurs such blame, then how could Romans 5 have made any sense. Another puzzle and or conundrum seems to lie in the fact that woman are to be saved by child bearing when Paul says it is better not to marry, as he has said. We return now to 1 Corinthians 7 where in the opening line Paul says, "It is good for a man not to have sexual relations with a woman". Paul's view of extreme asceticism almost cancels out his previous statements about women being saved by the act of childbearing, because how else is a woman to bear a child other than in the lawful union of marriage? Paul goes on to say, "I wish all were as I myself. But each has his own gift from God, one of one kind one of another. To the unmarried and the widows, I say it is good for them to remain single as I am" (1 Corinthians 7:7-8). Apparently, Paul still implores husbands and wives who are together to stay together but encourages that those who are married to live an ascetic life not narrowly focused on sexual relations.

790. Paul mentions a strange new teaching in 1 Corinthians 7:14 that seems to be his own invention. He states, "For the unbelieving is made holy because of his wife, and the unbelieving wife is made holy because of her husband, otherwise your children would be unclean, but as it is, they are holy". The fact that unbelieving spouses and children are automatically made "clean" by union with a Christian is quite a strange doctrine. Even more confusion exists when we read in 1 Corinthians 7:16, "For how do you know wife, whether you will save your husband? Or how do you know, husband, whether you will save your wife?" Indeed, how do you know? If you marry a Christian, you are saved automatically but if you separate you are back to not being saved? This is quite a confusing picture and we are actually not so sure what Paul is teaching here. This could be linked to the Pauline view that once one is saved there is no way that one can outrun the salvation of God.

791. In 1 Corinthians 7:19-22 we read the explanation for the chores of the body like eating food sacrificed to idols, participating in the lawful union of marriage, or the ritual practice of circumcision where Paul states, "For neither circumcision counts for anything nor uncircumcision but keeping the commandments of God. Each one should remain in the condition in which he was called. Were you a bondservant when called? Do not be concerned about it.

But if you gain freedom avail yourself of the opportunity. For he who was called in the Lord as a bondservant is a freedom of the Lord. Likewise he that was free when called is a bondservant of Christ". These passages are interesting for two reason we shall mention. For one Paul says to keep the commandments of God which he said was not the be all and end all of our relationship with God previously in Romans. Secondly, Paul's view of being a bondservant: if you are a slave don't complain but if your free and believe you're a slave to Christ. We are to remain in what condition we were called and not try to change our station but also under the rule of Christ all roles are reversed.

792. We read a key passage in 1 Corinthians 7:23-31 where Paul says, "let those who have wives live as though they had none, and those who mourn as though they were not mourning, and those who rejoice as though they were not rejoicing, and those who buy as though they had no goods, and those who deal with the world as though they had no dealing with it. For the present form of this world is passing away"! This passage most elegantly underlines Paul's view of faith in the future. No one has to change their stations or do anything for God's kingdom to arrive. Everything and everyone is in their right place in their appointed stations in preparation for the Kingdom.

793. Paul says that having so called advanced knowledge can trip someone away from the path of self-restraint and spiritual purity, but instead one should employ love. The view that God is love fairs quite heavily in Paul, but we personally are not limited to this understanding. We agree that love is able to unlock some serious depths of emotional energy and passes certain barriers for the development of our ultimate potential, but we venture to say that God is more than love whose subtle gifts are mysterious and profound. Love is akin to wisdom in that it finds beauty in the mysterious, but wisdom also encompasses an order that requires a simplicity far beyond the duality and reflection seeking tendency of love. Wisdom seeks a beauty beyond relation.

794. Paul extends his arguments about having knowledge instead of love with his attack on the notion of unclean foods. Paul says concerning food sacrificed to idols that all have knowledge, but the knowledge tends to "puff up" while love builds up (1 Corinthians 8:1). The argument that Paul presents next is quite concerning. Paul seems to argue that food and meat sacrificed to idols is pure because the god that the idol represents has no real existence or power (1 Corinthians 8:4). However, one could also pray to the true God in jest so how relevant are these arguments to theology? Truly it must be the case that once one reduces ones worship to a single form and makes that the mediator between oneself and God one creates an idol which is a stand in for divine power. This would also mean that there is no one way to ritual perfection which begs the question why one should prescribe any doctrinal barriers. Paul seems to imply that other forms of worship should be subsumed under the worship of Christ for an expectation in the coming of the Kingdom of God.

795. Paul complains that those who take precautions for exact ritual purity and those on who it has no bearing having already given up ritual worship of idols possess weak consciences that are too easily offended (1 Corinthians 8:7-10). Paul is obviously here referring to Christians who keep dietary restrictions as prescribed by the Law of Moses that have been shown by medical experts to-day as being far more sanitary and ethical then those practices in ancient times (we will cite some examples of these later). What is clear to us is that Paul seems to be creating new rules when he already said to obey commandments in order to appease his Gentile following. It is not hard to see how eating food sacrificed to idols might still be a common practice among Gentile converts, who apparently, as even mentioned by Paul did not see the worship of many gods as creation of a new faction within their newly adopted Christian faith being availed of Roman henotheism.

796. Paul makes it clear that here he refers to the other leaders of the Church as being of weak conscience for criticizing those who eat at the table of those who eat food sacrificed to idols when he directly refers to them in 1 Corinthians 9. 1 Corinthians 9 contains some rather strange utterances from Paul that can be only taken in a way that seems to be a subtle way of deriding others by magnifying one's own hardship. We call this lack of sincerity and a stealing of one's own gifts to be a sort of false humility. Here however, Paul unveils another tactic that will clarify some of his previous stances which seem to change depending on the circumstances and who he is apparently talking to or about.

797. Paul complains, "Do we not have the right to eat and drink? Do we not have the right to take along a believing wife, as do the other apostles and the brothers of the Lord and Cephas? Or is it only Barnabas and I who have no right to refrain from working for a living?". Later Paul states, "Do I say these things on human authority? Does not the law say the same?" (1 Corinthians 9:8). Paul is apparently teaching the higher aspects of Law and is made better by his secret knowledge, which is exactly what he derided in Romans 8. Paul clearly thinks he is better than others for following the law in a superior sense especially when he complains against the disciples of Jesus for having wives, using dietary restrictions on Gentile worshippers, and not working for a living. One must accept that Paul is all humility, but then why compare your suffering to others and if Paul can prove his suffering is more than others than he is after all more blessed. Why then does Paul complain about a lack of funds? Paul is better than others because he does not live off the substance of the Church and suffers more than others on account of his poverty but then how can he complain and magnify his own suffering and demand funds? Paul would like to say he is more capable than others for having done more with less but elsewhere Paul preaches his way of life as the standard.

798. Paul tells others it is better to stay unmarried as he has but also complains against the disciples and brothers of the Lord for having wives. What is most interesting is that when others don't share Paul's stance on marriage, and Paul claimed his way is more conducive to his spiritual practice, Paul still gets to use his so-called humility and asceticism to complain against others. We see that there is also some tension between Paul and the other leaders of the Church. Paul earlier mentioned factions within his Church that choose to follow Cephas or Peter.

799. Paul now wants recognition for his effort. He asks, "If we have sown spiritual things among you, is it too much if we reap material things from you?" (1 Cor 9:11). It is funny how the dialectic between flesh and spirit collapses here when it is time to get paid. Yet Paul is adamant that he does not boast. He states, "For if I preach the gospel, that gives me no ground for boasting. For necessity is hard upon me. Woe to me if I don't preach the Gospel! For if I do this of my own will, I have a reward, For if not of my own will, I am still entrusted with a stewardship". Paul confesses that he preaches the Gospel for free.

800. In a stupefyingly breathtaking act of rhetorical mastery Paul shows how one can be invited to every party on earth by being as a sort of celestial or cosmic janitor or maintenance man. Paul states in a most famous passage, "For though I am free from all, I have made myself servant to all, that I might win more of them. To the Jew I became as a Jew in order to win Jews. To those under the law I became as one under the law. To those outside the law I became one outside the law (not being outside the law of God but under the law of Christ) that I might win those outside the law. To the weak I became weak, that I might win the weak. I have become all things to all people, that by all means I might save some" (1 Corinthians 9:19-22). Since the passage is self-explanatory, we merely point out a few things. Firstly, we note it is a feat of rhetorical and poetic genius. Secondly, we note that Paul says he is not under the law. Thirdly we note that Paul is under the "law of Christ" that bids him to be all things to all men. Lastly, this singular passage may be able to explain why Paul changes his views so many times throughout the epistles and depending on who he is talking to.

801. Almost reaffirming our last point we see a vastly different treatment of the Jews in Corinthians than in Romans. Here the Jews are painted as disobedient idolaters whose appropriate home is to be left wandering in the desert and in the wilderness. At first glance it would seem that Paul feels comfortable making these claims now that he is in a more mixed congregation and has already admitted to posing as a Gentile to win those not under the law. Now he states that God was displeased with the Jews (1 Corinthians 10:5) and that they desire evil (1 Corinthians 10:6).

802. Paul admits his stance on the law is ultimately as he states, "All things are lawful but not all things are helpful. All things are lawful but not all things build up" (1 Corinthians 10:23). It will be increasingly hard to keep up with such a standard that not only changes rules and shifts gears depending on who it talks to and with pragmatism and dissimulation applies different rules at different times. The difficulty will fall upon the followers of Paul who he exhorts to "Imitate me as I imitate Christ" (1 Corinthians 11:1). Paul says that even factions are signs of strength because it helps one discover the true members (1 Corinthians 11:18-19). Paul finally alludes to a teaching found in the Gospel about the last supper which both portrays his suffering of the body as purification given as the bread of Passover and the cup of the blood of Christ given as the blood of a new covenant. The view of blood sacrifice seems to color the Gospel narrative which appears also later in Hebrews. What is most striking is that it is the first time Paul mentions any portrayal of any information or teaching passed down to him as was passed down through Jesus to his disciples in Jesus' own lifetime, but it does not seem like it is viable for any biographical information about Jesus himself because it is shrouded by metaphors. Three things are accomplished by this ritual according to Paul: 1. Proclaiming the death of the Lord (1 Corinthians 11:26). 2. Proclaiming the blood of the new covenant. 3.Examining if you are in judgement of yourself truly or in judgement with the world that is condemned for the death of the Lord.

803. Paul says that the eating of the bread and drinking of the cup proclaims the death of the Lord "until he comes". The anticipation of the world to come is based on a faith in the future. Another factor we see is where Paul states, "For anyone who eats and drinks without discerning the body eats and drinks judgement on himself" (1 Corinthians 11:29). This demonstrates a stark duality also between spirit and flesh as we have previously described. To reiterate, these are the two main poles of Pauline theology (not devised through experts but by our own plain reading). One is the temporal dualism between the present suffering and future life of glory within the Kingdom of God. The second factor is the duality of flesh and spirit which is magnified by the spatial dualism of suffering and grace.

804. Paul's theology is also highly individualistic. His Church or doctrine operates on each according to his need. In 1 Corinthians 12:4-6 we read, "Now there are varieties of gifts, but the same spirit, and there are varieties of services but the same Lord; and there are varieties of activities, but it is the same Lord who empowers them all in everyone". Even further down we hear the type of all for one and one for all message that verges on the democratic and perennial. Paul writes, "For just as the body is one and has many members of the body, though many, are one body, so it is with Christ. For in one Spirit we are all baptized into one body, Jews and Greeks, slaves or free, and all were made to drink of one spirit. For the body does not consist of one member but of many". Paul prescribes a veritable "E Pluribus Unum". Paul teaches that

each member of the Churches is part of the body of Christ (1 Corinthians 12:27).

805. In 1 Corinthians 13 Paul states that love never runs out like prophecies but surely Paul prophecies and shares knowledge. It is rather convenient at this juncture to state that love is better than prophecy but not when you are in the prophecy business. Paul however admits, "now we see in a mirror darkly but then face to face" (1 Corinthians 13:12). In 1 Corinthians 14 Paul now raises prophecy above charismatic actions like speaking tongues and says, "the one who prophecies is greater than the one who speaks in tongues" (1 Corinthians 14:5). We would ask the reader to take facts laid out here upon further investigation, but it seems that the speaking in tongues bit is quite elusive, but we can only say here that it has been the laughing stock of religious experiencers along with talismans and gurus that charge you for their services of ritual purification. Of course, in 1 Corinthians 14:8-9 we see that not all prophesying and speaking in tongues is equal but context matters. Between receiving visions, prophesying and receiving revelation, but also incurring inspiration from the Spirit and speaking in tongues, Paul sets up a relation between the body, mind, and spiritual sensibilities in Man. In 1 Corinthians 14:13-17, "Therefore one who speaks in a tongues should pray that he may interpret. For if I pray in a tongue my spirit prays but my mind is unfruitful. What am I to do? I will pray with my spirit but I will pray with my mind also; I will sing praise with my spirit, but I will sing with my mind also. Otherwise, if you give thanks with your spirit, how can anyone in the position of an outsider say 'Amen' to your thanksgiving when he does not know what you are saying? For you may be giving thanks well enough, but the other person is not being built up". It is not enough to give the Church service your spirit but also needs your mind. Visions supersede the law of the body. The spirit can cause one to gain revelation, but the mind must follow it there. Finally, there is clearly an issue with people claiming new schisms, factions, and revelation.

806. In 1 Corinthians 15:3-7 we read an almost doctrinal statement of faith for Christians where Paul states, "For I delivered to you as of first importance what I also received: that Christ died for our sins in according with the scriptures, that he was buried, that he was raised on the third day in accordance with the scriptures and appeared to Cephas and the twelve. Then he appeared to more than five hundred brothers at one time, most of whom are still alive, though some have fallen asleep. Then he appeared to James, then to all the apostles". Paul follows this statement with the utterance, "Last of all, as to one untimely born, he appeared also to me". Paul also admits in the next verse that he formerly persecuted the Church (1 Corinthians 15:8-9)

807. Paul says Christ is the first fruits of resurrection of the dead prophesied by the Hebrew prophets as he states, "And if Christ has not been raised then our preaching is in vain and your faith is in vain" (1 Corinthians 15:14). Paul re-

peats the statements made in Romans 5 about the original sin of Adam and death entering into the world through Adam. In 1 Corinthians 15:21-22 he states, "For as by a man came death, by man also has come the resurrection of the dead. For as in Adam all die, so also in Christ all shall be made alive. But each in his own". In 1 Corinthians 15:25-29 we read a very important passage which states that in conquering death all things were subjected to God, but by God Paul clearly is not referring to Jesus because in verse 28 he states, "When all things are subjected to him, then the Son himself will also be subjected to him who put all things in subjection under him". This affirms not even a binitarian view much less a trinitarian one. Instead, what we have is a basic formula of Christ rule on earth and God rule in heaven but Christ's rule on earth is reserved for the world to come (1 Corinthians 15:51-53).

2 Corinthians

808. 2 Corinthians opens with Paul affirming his formula of grace through suffering. In 2 Corinthians 1:5-8 it reads, "for we share abundantly in Christ's sufferings, so through Christ we share abundantly in comfort too. If we are affected it is for your comfort and salvation". Paul also stresses that Christ is conqueror over death which entered the world through Adam according to Paul (2 Corinthians 1:9-10). In 2 Corinthians 3 Paul begins a polemic against the Torah using the character of Moses who he diminishes quite considerably. The resulting rhetoric is really quite amazing.

809. Paul begins by citing his visual dialectic between flesh and spirit by declaring, "And you show that you are a letter from Christ delivered by us, written not with ink but with the spirit of the living God, not on tablets of stone but on tablets of human hearts" (2 Corinthians 3:3). Paul declares himself minister of a New Covenant (2 Corinthians 3:6) and says, "the letter kills but the spirit gives life". In 2 Corinthians 3:7-8 Paul states, "Now if the ministry of death, carved in letters on stone, came with such a glory that the Israelites could not gaze at Moses' face because of its glory which was being brought to an end, will not the ministry of the spirit have even more glory?". Paul also says in 2 Corinthians 3:13, "Not like Moses who put a veil over his face so that the Israelites might not gaze at the outcome of what was being brought to an end". Paul now derides his people who previously he honored and wished sometimes even to be cut off from Christ for the sake of his people and announces that the law of the Old Covenant of Moses is really no better than toilet paper. Again, we must ask if this is true then what law is Jesus a fulfilment of as Paul has continually employed the words according to scripture. Unlike Moses, Paul uses boldness to convey the message of his New Covenant.

810. Paul now launches a complex dialectic between flesh and spirit and reduces the body to playing no role in man's salvation. Paul says we must not store our treasure up in "jars of clay" (2 Corinthians 4:7). Paul bids us to look not to what is on the surface but to the things that are unseen to reiterate a point

found in Romans 1. For the things that are seen are transient, but the things that are unseen are eternal" (2 Corinthians 4:18). Paul also embeds faith in the future in the coming salvation of the eternal Kingdom of God. In 2 Corinthians 5:2 Paul states, "For in this then we groan, longing to put on our heavenly dwelling", and that in 2 Corinthians 5:17, "Therefore, if anyone is in Christ he is a new creation. The old has passed away; behold, the new has come". Paul sets forth a formula of spirit plus reason in 2 Corinthians 5:13, where he says, "For if we are besides ourselves, it is for God; if we are in our right mind, it is for you", leaving to God the incomprehensible, and to Man what is in the bounds of reason.

811. Finally in 2 Corinthians 7 Paul declares that the flesh is polluted. He states in the opening verse, "Let us cleanse ourselves of every defilement of body and spirit". Since the spiritual realm is the domain of God, only the accursed body or what is in Man's control must be subjected to God to be purified. When Paul quotes scripture in 2 Corinthians 6:17 it tells the followers of God to "touch no unclean things" which seems like an obvious reference to ritual purity. Since Paul places no importance in the works of flesh it is strange for him to make such statements imploring his followers to keep the body in a state of purity when such a state is always connected with sinfulness.

812. Paul now establishes a "principle of liberality". It can be summarized in a statement he makes in 2 Corinthians 8:15 where he states, "As it is written, 'whoever gathered much had nothing left over, and whoever gathered little had no lack". He goes on to say in 2 Corinthians 9:6, "The point is this: whoever sows sparingly will also reap sparingly, and whoever sows bountifully will also reap bountifully". In 2 Corinthians 9:9 it states, "As it is written, 'He has distributed freely, he has given to the poor; his righteousness endured forever". In 2 Corinthians 9:7 Paul states, "God loves a cheerful giver". The principle of liberality or philanthropy encourages others to fit the bill of those less fortunate, but this is neither to uplift the condition of the poor or for some ritualistic or system or form of giving, but rather given freely as a gift.

813. In 2 Corinthians 10:3-5 we read Paul say, "For though we walk in the flesh, we are not waging war according to the flesh. For the weapons of our warfare are not of the flesh but divine power to destroy the strongholds. We destroy arguments and every lofty opinion raised against the knowledge of God and take every thought captive to obey Christ". All of Paul's operations in the flesh are covert warfare on behalf of his view of Christ. Paul warns, "of those who boast in the flesh but says he has right to boast of much more" (2 Corinthians 10:18). He adds, "Indeed, I consider that I am not in the least inferior to those super-apostles. Even if I am unstilled in speaking, I am not so in knowledge; Indeed, in every way we have made this plain to you in all things". Yet Paul humbles himself while boasting in his classic false humility and says,

"or did I commit a sin in humbling myself so that you might be exalted, because I preached God's gospel to you free of charge?"

814. Paul boasts about his weakness. He says, "Who is weak, and I am not weak? Who is made to fall and I am not indignant? If I must boast, I will boast of the things that show my weakness". Paul also has reason to boast on account of many strange mysteries he presents to the audience like in 2 Corinthians 12:2-5 where he states, "I know a man in Christ who fourteen years also was caught up in the third heaven. Whether in the body I do not know, God knows…And I know this man was caught up into paradise…whether in the body or out of the body I do not know, God knows….And he heard things that cannot be told which man may not utter. On behalf of this man I will boast but on my own behalf I will not boast, except of my weaknesses…". Finally, Paul reports that it is just as the power of God has Christ live on as a token of his weakness so does Paul boast only of his weakness (2 Corinthians 13:4). Paul presents himself as affirming the ultimate gift.

Galatians
815. We gain some knowledge of those that Paul derides as "super-apostles" in his letter to Galatians. Paul begins the letter by thinking about the sacrifice of Jesus for the sins of the present age which is dominated by evil (Galatians 1:4). Paul holds to this strict view of salvation and bids his followers to excommunicate those who teach otherwise and states, "If anyone is preaching to you a gospel contrary to the one you received, let him be accursed" (Galatians 1:9). Paul admits that the gospel that he preaches he did not receive after humans but directly from Christ in Galatians 1:11. There we read, "For I would have you know, brothers, that the gospel that was preached by me is not man's gospel".

816. Paul challenges the leaders of the early Church. Paul now exposes those who preach of factions within the Church as those who are followers of Torah (Since we have mentioned the encounter between Peter and Paul in the first part of this book and at the end of the book and exegesis of the contents of the New Testament and the Pauline Corpus and will only point out certain themes that will aid in the flow of our present discussion). In Galatians 2:7 Peter is mentioned as having a parallel mission to the circumcised as Paul has to the uncircumcised. Here we get the sense from Paul's own words that the two men have been given a parallel mission when in the Gospels it seems that Peter is mentioned as Christ's first follower and chief disciple. This leads to another question: Was Paul self-appointed in his role as "apostle to the Gentiles"? In a previous statement we read Paul mention how what he teaches about Christ was not received by him through mere mortals but that he was given authority directly from God. As we still read, Paul was set apart since birth. If this is true such a title as "apostle to the Gentiles" could not have been given to Paul by the other leaders of the Christian movement like Peter and James. Paul seems to once again deride Peter and James but since in other places he mentions

them as authorities (like 1 Corinthians 15) it is hard to come to a conclusion about who gave Paul his authority to preach to Gentiles as it says in other places such as Acts and other Christian histories that such an authority was given by precisely these people. If this was an agreement given to him on authority of those he now derides on whose account does he challenge them for colluding with Gentiles which is part of his very same mission? The false apostles mentioned by Paul in Romans and Corinthians in conjunction with Paul's rejection of the so-called old covenant appear to be the disciples of Christ and seem to present some serious problems within the early Church. Since Paul's letters are canonized as scripture, we don't have to guess much who won such a dispute. As Paul said earlier, he is running the race to win, and he must gain more followers in order to win the race against the others as is implied.

817. We must also remember that Paul formerly persecuted the Church and must have found that in his dealing with them they had a certain organizational structure and certain doctrinal beliefs. We find it hard to believe then upon joining the Christian organization he would not think of using some this information to organize his own faction within the already existing church based on the new revelation he had received. There is almost no other conclusion that can be had that this meeting is an early legend or example of some of those factions developing. Of course, every faction appears as a fifth column within the original that fashions itself as the core of the movement and all others as the heretics.

818. Paul also shows the classic characteristics of a passive aggressive personality. His view of changing his views based on who he is talking to is apparent in his confrontations. Paul also seems to continually speak on his own misfortunes and hardships and seems to relish all of his failures as a grand attempt to adjust him or derail him by either angelic or demonic forces. The way of making one's failures as the universe or the nefarious one's working against you is a characteristic of one under a spell of egoic madness. We try not to psychologize these almost historical tomes, but they seem to us quite odd and out of place for religious works that are canonized as scripture. Paul seems to psychologize himself as we see in 2 Corinthians 10:1, "I who am humble when face to face with you but bold toward you when I am away". Are we really to believe here that Peter the leader of the Church did not have anything to say in his defense? This is highly unlikely as one might come to suspect.

819. In accusation that Paul makes to Peter is that he refused to dine with Gentiles fearing the reprisal of James who had a party of men with him all who had arrived from Antioch along with Peter (Galatians 2:11-13). Paul says to Peter in his confrontation, "I said to Cephas (Peter) before them all, 'If you though a Jew, live like a Gentile and not like a Jew, how can you force the Gentiles to live like a Jew; we ourselves are Jews by birth and not Gentile sinner" (Galatians 2:14-15). The confrontation presents several clear problems which we

will summarize in four points: 1. Paul himself creates two different standards, one for Jew and another for Gentiles yet accuses others for doing so 2. Paul is still proud of the fact that he is a Jew and not a "Gentile sinner", and Gentiles are only grafted into the Jewish message of salvation 3. Paul bases what it means to be a Jew with the following of the laws prescribed in the Torah but later says he tore the law down (Galatians 2:18) 4. Jews are still raised above Gentiles in the order of salvation but Gentiles who profess Christ Lord are somehow seen as equal to Jews. It stands to reason that all these views cannot be easily reconciled. In Galatians 2:16-19 we read, "yet we know a person is not justified by works of the law but through faith in Christ, so we have believed in Christ Jesus, in order to be justified by Faith and not by works of the law, because by works of the law no one will be justified but if in our endeavor to be justified in Christ, we too were found to be sinners, is Christ then a servant of sin? Certainly not! For if I rebuild what I tore down I prove myself to be a transgressor". After all this it is hard to reconcile why Paul still refers to himself and even Peter as Jews (or why he refers to Gentiles as sinners?). Paul also sometimes refers to himself as a Gentile or Greek along with his followers.

820. Paul shows that his dialectic between Spirit and Flesh is really a dialectic between the performance of law and the salvation of grace apart from the law in Galatians 3:2-3 where we read, "Let me ask you this: Did you receive the Spirit by works of the law or by hearing with faith? Are you so foolish? Having begun by the spirit, are you now being purified by flesh?". In Galatians 3:10-11 he declares those under the Torah as having been under the curse of God and says that Christ bought the freedom of Gentiles using the Torah's curse in Galatians 3:13-14. In Galatians 3:10-11 we read, "For all who rely on works of the law are under a curse; For it is written, 'cursed be everyone who does not abide by all things written in the book of the law, and do them. Now it is evident that no one is justified before God by the law, for the righteous shall live by faith". Paul also then paradoxically declares that the Torah was a schoolmaster that prepared the world for the salvation of Christ. In Galatians 3:24-28 we read, "so then the law was our guardian until Christ came", however he states in Galatians 3:18 we read that not even Abraham was prepared by law. He continues, "in order that we may be justified in faith. But now that faith has come we are no longer under a guardian. For in Christ Jesus you are sons of God, through faith. For as many of you were baptized into Christ have put on Christ. There is neither Jew nor Greek, there is neither slave nor free, there is no male and female, for you are all one in Christ Jesus" (Galatians 3:24-28). We find it very hard to discern that if all are made one in Christ why Paul still finds the need to make distinctions between Jew and Greek. What purpose would such distinctions serve in addressing the mixed congregation of Jews and Greeks?

821. In Galatians 4:1-4 Paul explains how man is born in complete bondage to the elements of the world. Man is in a battle against nature and the forces en-

demic in his own flesh. One passage reads, "the heir, as long as he is a child, is no different from a slave, though he is the owner of everything, but he is under guardians and managers until the date set by his father. In the same way we also, when we were children, were enslaved to the elementary principles of the world. But when the fullness of time had come, God sent forth his son, born of women, born under the law". So, we see that Man being held captive by nature is similar to his capacity under the law of the father, but now Paul turns against Pagan gods when in 1 Corinthians he tried to subsume them under the umbrella of Christ. Now he writes, "But now that you have come to know God, or rather be known by God, how can you turn back again to the work and worthless elementary principles of the world whose slaves you want to be once more?" (Galatians 4:9).

822. Paul states that Arabs are cursed. In Galatians 4:22-24 we read, "For it is written that Abraham had two sons, one by a slave woman and one by a free woman. But the son of the slave was born according to the flesh, while the son of a free woman was born through promise. Now this may be interpreted allegorically: these women represent two covenants, one is from Mount Sanai bearing children for slavery; She is Hagar or she corresponds to the present Jerusalem, for she is in slavery with her children. But the Jerusalem above is free and she is our mother (referring to Sarah)". Paul seems to ignore that Isaac and Ishmael were both children of promise. This verse could explain why western Christians and Europeans have historically persecuted Arabs who they see as inferior to Jews, seen here as the children of promise. Jews have been surrounded by Arabs since their conception among the Arab tribes and among the Canaanites who they mixed with many times, so it is clear that most of the time when the Old Testament refers to other nations and tribes that are not considered part of Israel then it is most likely referring to the surrounding Arab tribes that it does not always seem hostile towards. This is coupled with the confusing fact that some lump western, European, and Roman cultures and philosophies into a collective worldview that they conflate as Gentile, since Paul spread his message among some people who are nominally considered to be Europeans, such as Macedonians. However it is clear that since Jews and Christians openly reject the following of the Law of Moses, as some Rabbi claim that the dwelling in the Holy Land outweighs all the commandments of the Torah, and Paul says that his New Covenant theology supersedes the law, there is a nation of people who by and large are not rejectors of the Laws of Moses because of their general acceptance of the three western religions and these would be the Arabs that Paul has seemingly cursed. Instead, we read in Genesis 17:9-14,

> "And God said to Abraham, "As for you, you shall keep my covenant, you and your offspring after you throughout their generations. This is my covenant, which you shall keep, between me and you and your offspring after you: Every male

among you shall be circumcised. You shall be circumcised in the flesh of your foreskin, and it shall be a sign of the covenant between me and you. He who is eight days old among you shall be circumcised. Every male throughout your generations, whether born in your house or bought with your money from any foreigner who is not of your offspring, both he who is born in your house and he who is bought with your money, shall surely be circumcised. So shall my covenant be in your flesh an everlasting covenant. Any uncircumcised male who is not circumcised in the flesh of his foreskin shall be cut off from his people; he has broken my covenant"

It is clear that Paul seeks to reverse the covenant that God has made with his people with his special emphasis on the "circumcision of the heart" and allowing of foods being sacrificed to idols that the Bible says gives demonic spirits legal right to enter one's body. How does one keep such a covenant? By following the commands of God such as circumcision as one of those things which he prescribes to those who keep his covenant. What is more is that Paul seems to reverse the blessing made on Ishmael as the progenitor of the Arabs. In Genesis 17:19-20 we read the opposite of Paul's decree, where God apparently says, "your wife Sarah will bear you a son and you will call him Isaac. I will establish my covenant with him as an everlasting covenant for his descendants after him. And as for Ishmael, we have heard you: I will surely bless him; I will make him fruitful and greatly increase his numbers. He will be the father of twelve rulers, and I will make him into a great nation". It is clear that the covenant that God made with Israel is not unconditional and that along with the announcement of the covenant a parallel blessing is laid on the Patriarch of the Arabs, just as one was laid on Israel. Paul has clearly reversed the meaning of this blessing and turned it into a curse and the followers of Paul are today the most ardent supporters of the Arab Genocide perpetrated by European Jews and their Zionist backers that has found support among Christian Zionists, who have, as we just read, been grafted into the promise made to Israel but cursed Arabs via Paul in his reversing of the message of Torah. Do these people really not know how to read the books they claim to profess and follow? Rather it is all too clear that when the either and or of a situation cannot be forced there seems to be some duplicity at play, and that there is some sort of agenda at play that obfuscates the truth.

823. Now Paul relates a strange teaching that sometimes shows up throughout the epistles that the believers in Jesus constitute the real Israel and have taken the place of the Jews. In verses 4:28-30 we read Paul equate believers in Christ to the children of promise and Torah observant Jews to the children of slaves. Paul calls them slaves because they are still bondsman in relation to the law. In Galatians 4:28-30 we read, "Now you brothers, like Isaac, are children of promise. But just as at that time he who was born according to the flesh perse-

cuted him who was born according to the spirit, so also it is now. But what does the scripture say? 'Cast out that slave woman and her son, for the son of the slave woman shall not inherit with the son of a free woman". Surely the decisions of Abraham and their impact on future nations have more weight than how Paul presents matters to us here.

824. In Galatians 2:15 Paul confirms himself as a Jew from birth but now Paul considers all those who are under circumcision to be under the yoke of slavery in the beginning of Galatians 5. In Galatians 5:2-5 we read, "I, Paul, say to you that if you accept, Christ will be of no advantage to you. I testify again to every man who accepts circumcision that he is obliged to keep the whole law. You are severed from Christ, you who would be justified by the law; you have fallen away from grace. For through the spirit, by faith, we ourselves eagerly wait for hope of righteousness". Paul also inserts faith in the future in to his discussion or which also coincides with the notion he employs of salvation by flesh versus salvation by spirit. In Galatians 5:16 we read concerning flesh and spirit that gratifying one is loss of the other. In Galatians 6:2 we read of the "Law of Christ" but nowhere find details of its expression. Is this the spiritual aspect of the Jewish law or something more? We are given no clues. Paul still finds time to bless Israel in Galatians 6:16 as he says, "mercy be upon them (followers of Jesus who walk by a 'new creation'), and upon the Israel of God".

Ephesians
825. In Ephesians 1:5 Paul says that God predestined us for adoption. This was according to the blood sacrifices of Jesus mentioned in Ephesians 1:7. This plan will be brought to fruition in the "fullness of time" (Ephesians 1:10) and not in the present mode of the world. No passage better expresses Paul's view of faith in the future and the age to come in the Kingdom of God than the letter to Ephesians. In Ephesians 1:20-21 we read, "that he worked in Christ when he raised him from the dead and seated him at this right hand in the heavenly places. For above all rule and authority and power and dominion, and above every name that is named, not only in this age but also in the one to come". This eventual unification of the world and the current dominion of the world being a rule of evil and darkness is a recipe for utopian thinking. While being excused from seeking power in the world one covertly prepares to become a ruler in a world where all is subsumed under the promise of faith which you now profess. The view of separation of Church and State, where the spiritual rule of the world to come is represented by the Church and the Divine Right of rulers in the present age which is consequently fading away. In Paul's own day this power that is fading away can be represented by Rome and it is on this oath that Paul tells his followers to obey the ruling authorities which is really call to treat the rule of this present age as if it were no doubt passing away and predisposed to evil. However, it is clear that Paul cannot be outright insisting that one does this if the authorities of the present age are actually ruled by spir-

itual wickedness hiding out in high places. Paul says the "prince of the power of air" (the devil?) influences mankind in his present state (Ephesians 2:2). What is near and dear should be locked away in the inner sanctum while what is stored in clay jars is the spoils of this world that is already set to decay but put on display for the drama of creation whose endnote is the reflection of true power and wealth and not what passes away.

826. Furthermore, the coming world is concerning a specific claim to salvation and that salvation is a message brought to us by the Jewish scripture and prophets that were sent to the Jews who broke their covenant with God after murdering his prophets and creating a hermeneutical and arcane system of temple worship in order to delude and control the masses. In Galatians we read how those who are followers of Torah, and the laws of the old prophets and scripture are under a curse, but now we read Paul mention his other idea, seen in Romans of Gentiles grafted into the already existing message of salvation promised to the Jews, and we pair this with the emphasis we have already seen on the age to come and eschatological schemes of Paul. In Ephesians 2:8 we read that salvation was given to those now saved by faith as a gift from God. In Ephesians 2:11-12 we read, "Therefore remember that at one time you Gentiles in the flesh, called 'the uncircumcision' by what is called the circumcision, which is made in the flesh by hands, remember that you were at a time separated from Christ, alienated from the commonwealth of Israel, strangers to the covenant of promise". In Ephesians 2:15 Paul says, "by abolishing the law of commandments expressed in ordinances, that he might create himself one new man in place of the two, so making peace". We get the picture that Paul has done away with all distinctions between Jew and Gentile in the previous statements, along with the reliance on the old traditions and prophets. This is until Paul states in Ephesians 2:19 to Gentiles that, "so then you are no longer aliens, but you are fellow citizens with the saints and members of the household of God". What saints and prophets? What household of God? Surely not Adam or Moses or Abraham whose deeds were already minimized or dismissed. Why praise their works and status when they were turned around by faith alone?

827. Paul repeats the claim in Ephesians 3:1 that he was given a special mission on behalf of the Gentiles and made "apostle to the Gentiles". In verse 3:5 Paul explains the mystery of Christ, "which was known to the sons of men in other generations as it has now been revealed to his holy apostles and prophets by the spirit" is available now to all men, however in just the next verse declares, "the mystery is that the Gentiles are fellow heirs, members of the same body, and partakers of the promise in Christ Jesus through the Gospel". However, this again begs the question if such a message or mystery had always been declared by the prophets, saints, apostles than what need is there now for Paul's special role as apostle to the Gentiles? If such a mission had always been declared it could not be now needed, and if Paul declares a new message,

then the old one stands to perish. The universalism of Paul becomes apparent in Ephesians 4:16-18 where Paul writes of a sort of spiritual economy and says, "From whom the whole body, joined and held together by every joint with which it is equipped, when each part is working properly, makes the body grow so that it builds itself up in love. Now this I say and testify in the Lord, that you must no longer walk as the Gentiles do, in the futility of their minds". Here not only is the Gentile recast as one of futile mind and darkened under-standing but this is only to reiterate the point that distinction between Jew and Gentile are now moot according to Paul and a Gentile can become a full-scale Jew through the promise of Christ. In verse 4:27 Paul points out that divisions and an abused and angry heart are opportunities for the devil to create strife and misery among the followers of God.

828. This is due to Paul's eschatological scheme which is detailed by the mys-terious figure known as the "Holy Spirit". The devil in verse 4:27 and the "Ho-ly Spirit" in verse 4:30 play a significant role in the world scheme arriving at the end of days where Satan is the accuser of Gentiles but Christ their advocate through the "Holy Spirit". Just as Christ paves the way for redemption through the "Holy Spirit", the devil paves the way for torment through the "Son of Per-dition", who appears in Thessalonians. In Paul's eschatological scheme which develops the concept of faith in the future he writes, "And do not grieve the Holy Spirit of God, by whom you were sealed for the day of redemption" (Ephesians 4:30). The "Holy Spirit" is really the "spirit of history" as God's will is brought to fruition through time securing the rule of God at the end of history when God and Jesus will become all in all in the day of grace and re-demption in eternal rule.

829. The view of Christ's rapture is described, and the "Holy Spirit" is men-tioned as the agent of time. The "Holy Spirit" is what secures for now what is to come in Pauline cosmology. In Ephesians 5:8 we read, "For at one time you were darkness but now you are light in the Lord. Walk as children of light". It is a little difficult to determine who these ones in darkness are. Are these the unrighteous or the ones who have not come to accept Christ? Also, light in the Lord seems to be available in the present age but prepares us only for the fu-ture. The present time however is ruled by Satan and the present age is the enemy. In Ephesians 5:16-18 we read Paul evoke his followers in "making the best use of time because the days are evil". One has to quietly accept but ig-nore the present state of the world and not engage in idleness. A similar view is found in Romans 13 as well as 1 Thessalonians 4. The light versus darkness motif has similarities with Orphic-Pythagorean and Zoroastrian cosmology.

830. The follower of Christ has nothing to do with power in the world but is only concerned with a kind of "spiritual warfare" in which he or she is covertly involved on behalf of the Holy Spirit which seeks to bring about the rule of Christ on Earth and God in heaven. This is seen in Pauline cosmology which

assumes a sort of hierarchy of being. In Ephesians 5:20-23 the husband is chief of the wife, just Christ is chief of the Church, and just as God the Father is chief over all things to outline the true structures of power in the world. In Ephesians 6:11-13 Paul describes this covert spiritual warfare in quite subversive terms using and employing the imagery of preparing for a bloody battle. Here we read, "put on the whole armor of God, that you may be able to stand against the schemes of the devil. For we do not wrestle against flesh and blood but with the rulers, against the authorities, against the cosmic powers over this present darkness, against the spiritual forces of evil in heavenly places. Therefore, take up the whole armor of God, that you may be able to withstand in the evil day, and having done all, stand firm". Paul is confronting the present age and its rulers of darkness by conducting warfare on the spiritual plane as these earthly forces in the age of darkness are controlled by spiritual forces of wickedness. So Paul conducts spiritual warfare on a hidden plane to bring about the future rule of God having already charted out a course that brings the promise of universal salvation and ascension. "And take the helmet of salvation and the sword of the spirit, which is the word of God", says Paul in Ephesians 6:17. Finally we see that this is towards a secret plan. Paul states in Ephesians 6:19-20: "that words may be given to me in opening my mouth boldly to proclaim the mystery of the Gospel on behalf of which I serve as ambassador". This "mystery" is the secret plan of redemption that will bring about the coming salvation.

Philippians

831. In Philippians or Paul's Letter to Philippi, we see a more developed relationship between the various members of the Church and Paul's apostleship including his unique relations to members of the elite like Epaphroditus. Paul is apparently sent a gift from Epaphroditus while in house arrest under Rome, and some sources mention that such a figure is also mentioned in a dedication of the antiquities of Josephus (Paul's 'Comrade-in-Arms' Epaphroditus and the First Gospels by Robert Eisenman, Published by The Jerusalem Post August 26, 2013). Paul's cozy relations with those elite Jews in power and the Temple authorities can only help to suggest that he made such connections to further his covert methods of which we can only assume because further information cannot be gathered. Since we have already taken care to mention many forms of which Paul adopts various methods and dual standards for those inside and outside the Church so if the reader would only pay attention, we find no need to repeat them here. In the opening verse of the Letter to Philippians, Paul mentions that he writes the letter in conjunction with Timothy mentioned in other letters and that he shares Church leadership with several overseers and deacons. Paul declares that through the Church all fates have changed. Paul opts for death as any real believer in an afterlife should, but this is not for the sake of his own righteousness or martyrdom but instead because of a life of faithfulness in anticipation of the world to come. In Philippians 1:20-22 we read, "as it is my eager expectations and hope that I will not be at all ashamed, but that with full courage now as always Christ will be honored in my body,

whether by life or by death. For to me to live is Christ, and to die is gain. If I am to live in the flesh, that means fruitful labor for me. Yet which I shall choose I cannot tell".

832. Followers of Christ are expected to live a quiet life in expectation of things to come. He implores his followers to, "complete my joy by being of the same mind, having the same love, being in full accord and of one mind", and also to, "Let each of you look not only to his own interests but also to the interests of others" (Philippians 2:2-4). Paul pens the doctrinal statement known as the Philippians hymn in Philippians 2:6-11 which reads, "who though he was in the form of a God, did not count equality with God a thing to be grasped, but emptied himself by taking the form of a servant, being born in the likeness of men. And being found in human form he humbled himself by becoming obedient to the point of death, even death on the cross. Therefore, God has rightly exalted him and bestowed on him the name that is above every name, so that at the name of Jesus every knee will bow". Notice that Paul says to whom every knee "will bow", again putting things in the future tense with a continual sense that the truth of the matter has not yet arrived. He continues, "And every tongue shall confess that Jesus Christ is Lord, to the glory of God the Father". In the meantime, Paul evokes his followers to, "work out your own salvation by fear and trembling, for it is God who works in you, both to will and to work for his good pleasure".

833. A few things seem to stand out. One is the notions of God-form and human-form which are combined in Jesus. This is linked with the concept that Jesus is the image of God while those who pray to God the Father are worshipping only the invisible image of God. As one might assume, these concepts are Greek sounding and find no parallel in the reflections of Jewish theology as attested to by Jewish theologians for centuries. Only until we tread on the Kabbalistic and the Mystical Christian beliefs of Giovanni Pico della Mirandola and Jacob Bohme, which themselves obtain influence from Neoplatonic thought. Since we discussed these influences on the development of Christian thought, we find no reason to repeat them here. Another factor is Paul's motif of raised to be lowered that is exemplified by the lowering of Jesus to the earthly plain and God taking on human form, which is again a concept readily available to the Greek audiences but not a hallmark of the Jewish theology which worshipped an unseen God and considered images of gods to be idols. Secondly, we find in Pauline theology that Christ subordinated to God through his obedience but not because of his not being equal with God, but also not by his own decision and decree but only through the sovereign will of the creator. We also find that Jesus is only equal to God as the form of God or in essence and not in his own particular expression which is in limited human form into which Jesus is lowered. Finally, we see that about Jesus, it is written that he is Lord and to him every knee will bow. That every knee "will" bow as was mentioned means that this is referring to a future state as we recall Paul continu-

ously mentioned the coming age of the Kingdom of God. Paul refers not to the rule of the present age as was previously mentioned all throughout Ephesians for example as we just read. Also, as we have noted, Christ is Lord by the glory of God the Father and not God by virtue of his own nature. Paul's synergistic view of Jesus as both human and divine outlines most clearly the dialectic between spirit and flesh that we have continuously mentioned which finds its final resolution in his conception of Jesus Christ.

834. In Philippians 3:3 Paul reaffirms this teaching by saying, "For we are the circumcision who worship by the Spirit of God and glory in Jesus Christ (again not directly saying he worships Jesus) and put no confidence in the flesh". Yet Paul elaborates on his Jewish ancestry and his following of the law almost contradicting his previous statements saying that he considers himself having entered a new covenant and the old title of being a Jew should have no meaning because of the resurrection of Jesus. If there is no distinction between Jew and Gentile, then does a Jew still have to follow the commandments of the law? These are issues we have hitherto discussed in great detail, and we leave the reader to discern. In Philippians 3:4-8 we read Paul say, "though I myself have reason for confidence in the flesh also. If anyone else thinks he has no reason for confidence, I have more: circumcised on the eighth day, of the people of Israel, of the tribe of Benjamin, a Hebrew of Hebrews; as to the law a Pharisee; as to zeal, a persecutor of the church; as to righteousness under the law, blameless. But whatever gain I had, I counted as loss for the sake of Christ...I have suffered the loss of all things and count them as rubbish in order that I may gain Christ". First of all, it seems strange that Paul would be persecuting Christians, some of whom would be indistinguishable from Jews in the early stages of the church. Secondly, if Paul is a Pharisee then why would he go around persecuting Christians who elsewhere in Acts is claimed to be a job given to Paul by the temple authority known as the High Priest. It would seem strange for the temple authorities to employ their religious men for the task of weeding out Christians. Thirdly, Paul considers himself a Pharisee when Christ says in Gospel of Mathews to "beware the yeast of the Pharisees". Fourthly if the Torah points to the universal redemption of humankind, then why should this have been news to the Jew since it is a fulfillment of their prophecy? Paul says he has reason to boast but considers it rubbish, but it is because he has given up his lofty status that he boasts. This is a perfect description of Paul's false humility as well which is another topic we have amply explored. Naturally, if one has no reason to boast then why should one boast of not boasting.

835. We must ask what Paul's relationship is to the centers of the Alexandrian and Hellenistic worldview which he frequents. He travels to those places frequented by Gentiles and to the areas where Greek learning has spread just as his origin from the town of Tarsus suggests. Paul also conveys an understanding of scripture that seems fundamentally Greek in its tone meaning that it may

not be simply by some divine jurisdiction that Paul receives his post as apostle to the Gentiles but also by being predisposed to the pagan or Greek worldview. In Philippians and Colossians, we see this view both in Paul's view of "The invisible image of God" and the form or image of God which is represented by Jesus being two distinct entities is nowhere seen in the Old Testament literature. This is related to his views of the dialectic between flesh and spirit, and his view of the resurrection in new spiritual bodies or a "new body" in the world to come. Many Jews interpreted the scripture as saying that Man being resurrected in the world to come and the coming of the Son of Man only meant the restoration of Israel that would come to dominate over the nations of the world. In rejecting the Jewish message, the Prophet Muhammad (p.b.u.h) taught that all bodies would be resurrected in their physical form when the bone at the end of the spine is recreated, and their body brought before the creator to be judged according to their deeds at the end of time. Paul claimed neither that Christ's Kingdom would be of this world but also that believers will be raptured up and this would be made possible by their resurrection in a "spiritual body" not made of flesh. The concept of "Spiritual body" is a paradoxical one when framed within the aforementioned dialect between flesh and spirit. Since the body is subject to impermanence and change, degradation and sin, but also the Spirit can only abide in the pure Nature or Essence of God, the concatenation of these too is wildly paradoxical and is a classic Pauline melding of two contradictory notions into a third way.

836. In Philippians 3:20-21 we read, "But our citizenship is in heaven, and from it we await a savior, the Lord Jesus Christ, who will transform our lowly body to be like his glorious body, by the power that enables him even to subject all things to himself", in which we see mention of the rapture and transformed spiritual body of the adherent of Christ. This New Body theology lends itself to the evolutionary and transhumanist scope in obvious ways. The formula that one has to die while still alive to give birth to a new and better version of oneself is a familiar motif. Imam Ghazali once argued against the view of Neoplatonist thinkers in Medieval times who believed that the resurrection of the body was meant in spiritual or immaterial form or essence and not the physical body by pointing to the carnal delights of heaven against them. Such Natural Philosophers and theologians came to argue that since the physical was subject to impermanence and change, such a body could not endure the eternal life of a heavenly body and they argued that God would resurrect only in the non-physical or spiritual. Although this view describes Paul's eschatology and cosmology in a unique fashion, we must also note that it is quite strange that the Holy Spirit is wholly absent.

837. Paul does not however conflate spirit and body in any sense and does not say we will be resurrected in a spirit-body or any such concatenation, because Paul considers the spirit and flesh to be utterly distinct. Paul instead feels that our current body will be exchanged for a body that is not flesh ruling over spir-

it, but spirit ruling over flesh and hence indestructible and undying. Our "new bodies" will be eternal and so abide in spirit and be able to dwell in the Kingdom of God for all eternity where the true believers will become one body with Christ, which is to say find their permanent dwelling with the Lord as is Christ the first fruits of the resurrection.

838. We also have made note of the fact that Paul colludes with the Jewish Roman elite whenever it is convenient for his covert ends. He states in Philippians 4:22, "All the saints greet you, especially those of the Caesar's household". This can be compared with Romans 16:11 where Paul refers to Herod who is the enemy of Christ and John the Baptist (who are mentioned in the synoptic gospels) as his kinsmen. For someone who is part of a fledgling sect that represents itself as the religion of the downtrodden, Paul sure seems to collude with some powerful figures that suggest a more covert means and ends. These utterances or power relations with elite Jews cannot be easily explained away and most Christians are simply not aware of them.

Colossians
839. In Colossians 1:15-20 we read a doctrinal statement of Christian belief issuing from Paul. He states, "He is the image of the invisible God, the firstborn of all creation. For by him all things were created, in heaven and on earth, visible and invisible, whether thrones or dominions or rulers or authorities, all things were created through him and for him. And he is before all things, and in him all things hold together. And he is the head of the body, the church. He is the beginning, the first born from the dead, that in everything he might be preeminent. For in him all the fullness of God was pleased to dwell and through him to reconcile to himself all things, whether on earth or in heaven, making peace through the blood of his cross". There is firstly the issue the Paul is saying that all authorities and rulers were created through Christ but in the previous verses in Ephesians we read that the rulers of this age are the rulers of the age of darkness. This could only mean that this present rule is only in preparation for the age to come as we have previously stated which is the only way one could really reconcile the two points of view into one coherent theology. Nowhere in this doctrinal statement or in the Hymn in Philippians do we read of the Holy Spirit mentioned in Ephesians. Instead, we see a binitarian formula which parallels John 1:1. We also see terms like "the Invisible Image of God" and "the fullness of God" which exemplify a fundamentally Greek or mystical tone which appears rather odd in the midst of a discourse largely organized around Jewish themes.

840. In Colossians 1:21-22 we hear Paul paint the picture clearer in elaborating the well-known dialectic of flesh and spirit as he writes, "And you who were once alienated and hostile in mind, doing evil deeds, he has now reconciled in his body of flesh by his death, in order to present you holy and blameless and above reproach before him". We see the deeds of the flesh which are funda-

mentally wiped away by Christ who took on his spiritual body to aid in the ascent of Man. Paul still seems to warn against Pagan philosophy and theology even though he seems to use emanations of God whereby God functions in various degrees and forms throughout history that seem to be to some extent borrowed from a Greek or Alexandrian cosmology. In Colossians 2:8 we read, "See to it that no one takes you captive by philosophy and empty deceit, according to human tradition, according to the elemental spirits of this world, and not according to Christ". But we must ask, since Paul rejects the Jewish law and traditions and seeks to be apostle to the Gentiles, does he not now employ a fundamentally Greek tone and vision all while maintaining his elite status as a Jew? Paul repeats his denigration of Pagan Philosophy in Colossians 2:20-23. In Colossians 4:14 Paul mentions his secretary Luke who supposedly wrote the Gospel of Luke as well Acts of the Apostles which includes a tale about how Paul was supposedly given authority by the leaders of the early Church known as the Jerusalem council to preach to Gentiles.

1 Thessalonians

841. In Thessalonians we read that Paul's actions have been considered subversive by some. He states, "For our appeal does not spring from error or impurity or any attempt to deceive". Why would Paul say this if no one had charged him? Paul claims this again and again and repeats that his message is not man-made in 1 Thessalonians 2:13. Paul charges Jews with having murdered Jesus but extols them in many parts of the epistles and even refers to himself as a Jew when it is convenient. In Thessalonians 2:14-15 we read, "For you, brothers, became imitators of the character of God in Christ Jesus that are in Judea. For you suffered the same thing from your own countrymen as they did from the Jews, who killed both the Lord Jesus and the prophets, and drove us out, and displease God and oppose all mankind". Here it seems Paul is not especially interested in winning those under the law by becoming as one under the law now that he is in front of a mostly Greek audience in Thessalonica (which is located in Macedonia). Thessalonians marks a Pauline epistle delivered to those who are today now considered to be Europeans.

842. Paul states in 1 Thessalonians about his travels in Athens confirming the narrative laid down by Luke in Acts. He says, "Therefore when we could bear it no longer, we were willing to be left behind at Athens alone" (1 Thessalonians 3:1). We must ask why Athens has to play such a pivotal role for Paul's ministry when it can be readily identified as the origin of Hellenistic views? Since Paul neither follows the Jewish traditions or rejects pagan rituals on the same basis he must seek to incorporate unsuspecting Greeks into his strange interpretations of Jewish prophecy. And since this mode of healing does not prescribe much in terms of enforcing or rejecting certain practices, Paul exhorts his followers to, "aspire to live quietly and to mind your own affairs and to work with your hands" (1 Thessalonians 4:11). The verse seems to exemplify Paul's view of a detached and individualistic style of life where idle hands

are kept busy in anticipation of a future salvation. This level of complacency, docility, and conformity has been rightly criticized by many. The injunction to work with one's hands we can only say is much needed in a post-industrial age where most cannot match their subsistence with the basic tools of survival and the main functions of human society are left to experts. Paul must have foreseen that those who don't produce the means for their own subsistence are more likely to be controlled. Do Christians today realize this and make the tools necessary for their own communities?

843. In 1 Thessalonians 4:16 Paul informs us of the rapture and says, "For the Lord himself will descend from heaven with a cry of command, with the voice of an archangel, and with the sound of the trumpet of God. And the dead in Christ will rise first. Then we who are alive, who are left, will be caught up together with them in the clouds to meet the Lord in the air, and so we will always be with the Lord". A quite literal view of ascension is presented. Various roles as ascribed to Archangel Metatron (descending from heaven) and Israfel (the blowing of the trumpet that summons the end of the age) are given to Jesus himself who is seen taking his followers up into the clouds. We also see that before the end of days Jesus will remove all those who follow him to an ascended plane here described in quite abstract terms. Paul also says in a famous passage that the day of the rapture secretly quickens its arrival and is deceptively near and will come upon those who least expect it as a big surprise. Paul writes in 1 Thessalonians 5:2, "For you yourselves are fully aware that the day of the Lord will come like a thief in the night". Paul repeats his verses about donning the breastplate of faith and the helmet of salvation in 1 Thessalonians 5:8 (also seen in Ephesians 6).

844. Paul seems to dwell on his exhortations against laziness to a great extent in Thessalonians. This could be because the congregation there had a proclivity for passivity and enjoyment. He says in 1 Thessalonians 5:14, "And we urge you brothers, admonish the idle, encourage the faint hearted, help the weak, be patient with them all". The same type of thoughts are continued in 2 Thessalonians which tends to complete some of these previous reflections of tending to oneself.

2 Thessalonians
845. In 2 Thessalonians 3 we hear a similar call. There Paul says in verses 11-12, "For we hear that some among you walk in idleness, not busy at work, but busybodies. Now such persons we command and encourage in the Lord Jesus Christ to do their work quietly and to earn their own living. Paul again stresses a life of quiet conformity. We also hear an expansion of the rapture narrative and the coming rule of the Kingdom of God as we did in 1 Thessalonians.

846. In 2 Thessalonians 1:5-9 we read, "This is evidence of the righteous judgement of God, that you may be considered worthy of the Kingdom of God

for which you are also suffering...and to grant relief to you who are afflicted as well as to us, when the Lord Jesus revealed from heaven with his mighty angels in flaming fire, inflicting vengeance on those who do not know God...they will suffer the punishment of eternal destruction". Paul describes the appearance of false apostles and even false letters allegedly written by his hand. Paul warns, "not to be quickly shaken in mind or alarmed, either by a spirit or a spoken word, or a letter seeming to be from us" (2 Thessalonians 2:2). Paul mentions that the source of such deception is the "Son of Perdition".

847. Paul states in 2 Thessalonians 2:3-4 writing about the "Son of Perdition", "Let no one deceive you in any way for that day will come, unless the rebellion comes first and the man of lawlessness is revealed, the son of destruction". Here we see that the son of darkness and the man of destruction and lawlessness appears to show up right before the return of Jesus. It is important to note the appearing of the coming age of destruction with the rapture just as the notion of sin entering the world is paired with the law and the physical man-made law is rejected for the spiritual law. In 2 Thessalonians 2:7-9 we read, "for the mystery of lawlessness is already at work. Only he who now restrains it will do so until he is out of the way. And then the lawless one will be revealed, whom the Lord Jesus will kill with a breath of his mouth and bring to nothing by the appearance of his coming. This coming of the lawless one is by the activity of Satan with all powers and false signs and wonders". This is a Jewish eschatology except for some passages about the rapture and the resurrection of man in a new body on an ascended plane.

1 Timothy

848. Paul continues with his imagery about war in the Pastoral epistle entitled 1 Timothy. In 1 Timothy 1:18-19 he says to Timothy, "in accordance with the prophecies previously made about you, that by them you may wage the good warfare, holding faith a good conscience". The demotion of Christ in a narrative totally bereft of the trinitarian scope is what we read in 1 Timothy 2:5, where Paul states, "For there is one God, and there is one mediator between God and Men, the man Christ-Jesus". Paul does not say that Christ is God but distinct from God but somehow also superior to humanity in being a total representation of humanity and Paul even calls him a man. This follows from Paul's formula in many places as we discussed that as God is to Christ, Christ is to mankind, but those having died in Christ remaining eternally alive (having escaped the death of the world brought about by the sins of Adam) forming one body with the body of Christ which is the Church.

849. In 1 Timothy 2:13-14 we read Paul curse women with the statement we discussed before which reads, "For Adam was formed first, then Eve; and Adam was not deceived, but woman was deceived and became a transgressor". This does not square well with the fact that in Romans 5, Paul claims that sin entered the world by one man Adam who is the father of all mankind with no

discussion on Eve. In Romans 8:20 Paul says, "For the creation of the world was subjected to futility", but says in 1 Timothy 4:4, "For everything created by God is good". Of course, Paul offers qualifiers after those statements where the overall picture one gets is that nothing is good because of its own inherent nature but only by its instrumental use by the creator of all things to bring about the best. This is the cosmic utilitarianism of Paul which is linked to the idea of faith in the future and coming Kingdom of God.

850. Paul's tone for the rest of the letter is quite managerial and gives the vibe of a boss trying to humanize himself to his workers and not have them feel too pressed. Paul recommends wine in 1 Timothy 5:23 and says, "No longer drink only water, but use a little wine for the sake of your stomach". In 1 Timothy 6:14-16 we read an interesting passage where Paul states, "the appearing of our Lord Jesus Christ which he will display at the proper time, he who is blessed and only sovereign, the king of kings and Lord of Lords, who alone has immortality, who dwells in unapproachable light, whom no one has ever seen or can see". It is clear that Paul is not referring to Jesus making himself appear, but rather Jesus bringing about the appearance of the Lord of Lords who is the Lord of Christ as well. If this was not clear then the fact that such an entity exists in unapproachable light hitherto unforeseen, that no one has ever laid eyes on makes no sense. Clearly many had seen and witnessed Jesus according to Paul's own statements in 1 Corinthians 15, so Paul must again be referring to God the Father making his glory known to all through Jesus, where all who have died in Christ remain with the Lord in unapproachable light meaning that this state of being can hardly be described in our mortal frames. No one has up until the day of the return of the Lord been able to behold the glory of the true God whose image and form is Jesus.

2 Timothy
851. In 2 Timothy Paul announces more divisions in his ministry. In 2 Timothy 1:15-16 we read Paul state that all those in Asia have broken from his ministry. Paul invokes more warlike passages in 2 Timothy 2:3-4 and says, "share in suffering as a good soldier of Christ Jesus. No soldier gets entangled in civilian pursuits, since his aim is to please the one who enlisted him". In 2 Timothy 3 Paul warns of the trials of the last days which will be on the increase even according to the words of the Old and New Testament. Paul talks about the compartmentalization of knowledge and the obfuscation of truth which are real dangers. We can find very little objectionable nor in the signs of the last days mentioned here in 2 Timothy 4:3. In 2 Timothy and Titus, Paul seems to warn against the argumentative and exhorts his followers to encouraging decency and simplicity and abide by laws whenever practical.

Titus
852. In Titus Paul warns against rebels and deceivers and those of the circumcision faction in Titus 1:10. He further tells his followers to turn away from

"Jewish myths" which will come to seem strange when we address his heavy use of the temple ritual of the Jews in Hebrews. He writes in Titus to tell his followers to "rebuke them sharply, that they may be sound in the faith, not devoting themselves to Jewish myths and the commands of people who turn away from the truth" (Titus 1:13-14). Yet Paul also says in Titus 1:12-13 about the Greeks, "One of the Cretans, a prophet of their own said 'Cretans are always liars, evil beasts, lazy gluttons'. This testimony is true". It is for this reason that one must rebuke the Greeks to stay away from Jewish myths because of their obstinacy making them most susceptible to the sly peddlers of Jewish myths of the circumcision party. This would seem to be a document meant for internal circulation among the leadership because of the way Paul seems to divulge his tactic of going against both Jewish traditions and the earthly sort of wisdom of the Greeks. In Titus 2:9 Paul bids slaves to be obedient to masters and in Titus 3:1-2 he bids his followers to be law abiding citizens displaying the utmost conformity. Paul bids his followers to pay no attention to arguments of complex genealogies or the laws of scripture in Titus 3:9.

Philemon

853. In 1 Corinthians 4:15 Paul tells his followers that he has become their spiritual father through Christ Jesus even though in the Gospels Jesus tells his followers to call no man father except for God the Father in heaven (Matthew 23:9). In 1 Corinthians 11:1 Paul tells his followers to imitate him as he imitates Christ. We also hear that Paul was set apart since birth to preach the Gospel to Gentiles and to act as a vessel for the fulfillment about the law of the prophets. Paul's lofty status can be paired with the line from Philemon 1:19 where he says to Philemon that he owes him his life and soul while asking him for a favor. It seems that just as Christ acts as a mediator for the Lord in heaven so does Paul act as a mediator of Christ.

Hebrews

854. Although some authors claim that the Epistle to the Hebrews was never penned by Paul, we feel that not only does this information not matter for our present course of discussion but also that Hebrews displays the most succinct aspects of Pauline theology that can be found within the Pauline corpus and brings to the forefront the most important issue which is to square the fact of whether Paul is concerning himself with Jewish theology at all. Paul is said to be writing to a primarily Jewish audience so now we can appropriately reappraise some of his main belief systems as they relate to Jewish theology. Paul addresses specific Jewish themes and now concerns himself with the mysteries of Jewish theology.

855. Paul has to prove to the average Jewish listener in a more watered-down aspect of his beliefs what a mainstream version of Christian thought can be extracted and taught among the Jews, where previously we see that while Paul sees his theology as a completion of the message given to the Jews and an ex-

tension of the covenant that God made with the Jews, he does not see his mission as exclusively Jewish or concerning the practices of the Jews. Finally, as we have seen, while Paul considers himself a Jew, he does not consider himself beholden to some of the most fundamental aspects of Jewish law. Paul draws on the more mystical and mysterious elements of Jewish thought for his interpretations. Since Paul is not now supposedly addressing himself to a mixed or Gentile crowd and as we have seen he uses Judaism as a proof of his teaching, his views presented in Hebrews contain reiterations of some themes found in the other letters that are now being explained via Jewish mysteries and reinterpretations of Jewish scripture.

856. Paul uses a fundamentally Jewish cosmology and the tales of Jewish prophets to make room for his version of Jesus as it were. Whether or not we believe it is Paul writing these words, many Christians do, and therefore those Christians must feel apart from religious Jews who are not aware of Paul's visions or openly reject them that Paul's message represents a true form of instruction based on the Torah. Paul begins the letter by mentioning what Jewish elders have received in the past through the prophets. In Hebrews 1:2-3 we read, "But in these last days he has spoken to us by his son when he appointed the heir of all things, through whom he also created the world. He is the radiance and the glory of God and the exact imprint of his nature, and he upholds the universe by the world of his power. After making purification for sins, he sat down at the right hand of the Majesty on high".

857. It is interesting that God has once again appointed Jews and created the world through Jesus who sits at Gods right hand side in obedience and said about him, "You are my Son, today I have begotten you" (Hebrews 1:5). But why should God make anyone who was his son like an angel and say today I have begotten you? Wouldn't that be obvious, and would not such a being be unlike an angel existing before all time? After all, angels are also created beings. Anyone who was the son of God from the outset would not need to obtain such information from their own father on a certain day and time with the proclamation "today I have begotten you". According to Paul, God also proclaims, "I will be to him a father, and he shall be to me a son" (Hebrews 1:5). Will be? Shall be? Why use such disclaimers?

858. Paul also says, "Of the angels he says, 'He makes his angels winds and he ministers a flame of fire'" (Hebrews 1:7), but in other places says that elemental spirits are synonymous with demonic forces, which are like inborn limitations on mankind because of sin. Paul here is not so keen on Man's fallen nature in this letter but talks about the heights that Man is able to attain. He says in Hebrews 2:5, "For it was not to angels that God subjected the world to come, of which we are speaking". This clarifies things if only a little. Elemental spirits rule in this age but in the world to come even angelic may subject themselves to the rule of Man taken to be sons of God through Christ. Paul

says in Hebrews 2:8, "At present we do not yet see everything subjected to him", affirming the current rule of evil and the coming age of good for which one must have faith. Again, Paul employs a faith in the future to captivate his audience into waiting for a future salvation as we have previously mentioned.

859. He goes on to say, "But we see him who for a little while was made lower than angels, namely Jesus, crowned with glory and honor because of the suffering of death" (Hebrews 2:9). This is the formula for the "raised to be lowered" motif. In Hebrews 2:14 we read quite a strange introduction of the concept of blood sacrifice and even human sacrifice. There Paul states, "Since therefore the children share in flesh and blood, he himself likewise partook of the same things, that through death he might destroy the one who has the power of death, that is, the devil". The power of Jesus in the world is contrasted with the power of the devil in the world.

860. Paul presents himself as the sustainer of a new covenant far better than the one presented by Moses based on laws. In Hebrews 3, similar to 2 Corinthians 3, he uses Moses as a metaphor for the law of the prophets. In Hebrews 3:3 Paul states, "For Jesus has been counted worthy of more glory than Moses". In Hebrews 3:16 Paul states, "For who were those who heard and yet rebelled? Was it not all those who left Egypt led by Moses?". In Hebrews 4 Paul seems to speak of a progressive revelation in respect to his interpretation of the Holy Sabbath and the phrase that "God rested on the seventh day". Paul takes this to mean that humanity will collectively come into "God's rest" (Hebrews 4:3-4). In Hebrews 4:10 Paul states, "For whoever has entered God's rest has also rested from his works as God did from his". This could only mean that God anticipated that the Law of Moses would be superseded. The designs of a progressive revelation mean that God has to base his commandments on a sort of cosmic utilitarianism used to bring about desired results.

861. Paul unleashes the epitome of his dialectical and dualistic thought in Hebrews 4:12 where he states, 'For the world of God is living and active, sharper than any two-edged sword; piercing to the division of soul and spirit, of joints and marrow, and discerning thoughts and intentions of the heart". Paul now employs the same line of thought and states that there are two high priests operating at any one time. One is beset with weakness having to offer sacrifices as Aaron did, while the other high priest is a "high priest forever after the order of Melchizedek" (Hebrews 5:6). Just what is a priest of the Order of Melchizedek and what a strange mystery Paul has introduced. Such a "higher understanding" is apparently not available to layman.

862. Paul goes on further to explain to his own followers the difference between the exoteric or surface meaning and the esoteric or hidden meaning. He admonishes his listeners, "About this we have much to say, and it is hard to explain, since you have become dull of hearing" (Hebrews 5:11). He further

states, "You need milk not solid food. For everyone who lives on milk is un-skilled in the world of righteousness since he is a child. But solid food is for the mature, for those who have powers of discernment trained by constant prac-tice to distinguish good from evil". We see those who live on milk are the initi-ates and receive only the surface meaning while those who have completed the trials of faith are true adepts who live on solid food of esoteric meaning which he uses to refer to the mystery he presents to us about the hidden high priest.

863. In Hebrews 6:6 Paul mentions those who have fallen away from enlight-enment and cannot restore themselves to the original state, so it is very im-portant for the learned to not turn back on their teachings. In the beginning of Hebrews 7 Paul unveils the mystery of Melchizedek who is the King of Salem, but the descriptions seem mired in all sorts of anagrams and allegories. First, the name Melchizedek itself is a combination of the word Malachi meaning messenger or angel or lord all depending on the context in which it is used. In Arabic the word "Malik" means ruler. Zedek or Saadiq in Arabic means right-eous. Put all together the name means righteous ruler or divine king or some-thing of that sort. The word Salem which is one half of the word Jerusalem means "peace" similar to its translation in Arabic where it means connection, surrender, and peace summarized in the acknowledgement or greeting Salaam in Arabic and Shalom in Hebrew. In Hebrew, Schlomo is similarly a name of God.

864. In Hebrews 7:3 Paul says that King Melchizedek is an immortal and therefore maintains his post as high priest forever, unlike the descendants of Levi also known as the priestly clan mentioned in Hebrews 7:5. Paul now claims that those under the authority of the High Priest Melchizedek follow a different law and are beholden to an eternal rule unlike the Levitical priests mentioned in Hebrews 7:11-12. In Hebrews 7:14 Paul connects this to the fact that Jesus is descended from the tribe of Juda although such relations of the flesh should have no bearing on the order of sainthood in this new covenant. Paul's claims here about Jewish heirs seems almost paradoxical when matched with previous statements.

865. In Hebrews 7:19 we read, "For the law made nothing perfect; but, on the other hand, a better hope I introduced through which we draw near to God". This hope is described in Hebrews 7:22 where Paul says, "This makes Jesus the guarantor of a better covenant". This covenant should, as it stands to rea-son, exist in the future to be hoped towards. However, how can this be if this priestly order is an ancient one that has been in existence already since the time of Abraham? What would be the impetus to renew such a command when it has already existed all along? In Hebrews 7:28 Paul writes, "For the law ap-points men in their weakness as high priests, but the word of the oath, which came later than the law, appoints a son who has been made perfect forever". Earlier Paul stated the Order of Melchizedek existed since before Abraham through a man who knew no mother and father and is immortal. Now we read

that this promise came after the Levitical law adopted by Moses" I guess we are not sure what Paul is saying at this point.

866. In Hebrews 8 Paul derides Moses by referring to the tent of meeting in which Moses spoke to God. In Hebrews 8:5-6 Paul explains that priestly factions are but a shadow and copy of heavenly functions and Moses erected a tent according to what God showed him on the mountain, "But as it is Christ has obtained a ministry that is much more excellent than the old as the covenant he mediates is better". This leads to the inevitable question: was not Gods covenant made between him and his people with God as mediator of his own covenant? Here the covenant is instead presented as being between God, the people, and the mediator of the covenant as some sort of extraneous legal party involved. In Hebrews 8:10 Paul declares that the new covenant will be written on the heart, however, still declares this covenant to be linked with the restoration of Israel. Paul finally explains, "In speaking of a new covenant, he makes the first one obsolete" Hebrews 8:13), but if the last covenant was about the restoration of Israel and made obsolete then how is the new covenant about precisely the same order of business? We reiterate that Paul is apparently speaking to the Jews here.

867. In Hebrews 9:11 Paul says, "But when Christ appeared as a high priest of the good things that have come, then through the greater and more perfect tent (not made with hand, that is not of this creation". He now moves to address the temple sacrifice of the Jews in Hebrews 9. He states in Hebrews 9:12-14: "For if the blood of goats and bulls and the sprinkling of defiled persons with the ashes of a heifer, sanctify for the purification of the flesh, how much more will the blood of Christ, who through the eternal spirit offered himself without blemish to God". Paul sometimes mentions that the temple sacrifices of the Jews were allegorical works of the flesh which were meant to imitate heavenly power but sometimes states that the flesh is purified by blood. Are those temple sacrifices really delegitimized? If this is true then why does the abrogation of the law of flesh also require a blood sacrifice?

868. Now giving the example of Moses which was previously dismissed as the old covenant Paul declares, "Indeed, under the law almost everything was purified by blood, and without the shedding of blood there is no forgiveness of sins" (Hebrews 9:22). What a strange doctrine! Besides employing blood sacrifice, it is human sacrifice and at that it is the sacrifice of the Messiah of the Jews and the drinking of his blood in order to forgive the sins of humanity. It should be obvious to many that no teaching of the Old Testament closely resembles this or even alludes in the faintest sense to such a teaching and most people are not aware of this most fundamental of Christian beliefs.

869. In Hebrews 9:28 Paul clarifies that, "he has appeared once and for all at the end of all ages to put away sin by the sacrifice of himself", and finally,

"will appear a second time, not to deal with sin but to save those who are eagerly waiting for him" (Hebrews 9:28). However, one must really ask if the sin of this age or the rule of this age has to completely pass away in order for there to be no more sin which is synonymous with the works of the flesh, then how has Jesus already dealt with the problem of sin with his sacrifice on the cross? Does not the true salvation only come upon those in the future who have eagerly awaited it in faith?

870. In Hebrews 10 Paul comes back to his dialectic between law and faith. Now Paul states in Hebrews 10:3-4, "But in these sacrifices there is a reminder of sins every year. For it is impossible for the blood of bulls and goats to take away sins". Paul now presents the sacrifice of Christ as an allegorical completion of the temple ritual. In Hebrews 10:19-22 he states, "Therefore brothers, since we have confidence to enter the holy place by the blood of Jesus, by the new and living way he opened for us through the curtain, that is, through his flesh, and since we have a great priest over the house of God, let us draw near with a true heart in full assurance of faith; without hearts sprinkled clean". Paul uses this to reinterpret the Jewish Nationalism of the Jew at the time that some have conflated with their religion, similar to the temple sacrifices in Hebrews 11.

871. Paul recounts all the successes of the Jews throughout history as the success of faith and not in the "chosenness" of the Jews, but instead asserts that the Jews were not chosen for their exemplary character but by an unshakeable faith in the works and blessings of divine favor. In Hebrews 11:1 Paul states, "Now faith is the assurance of things hoped for, the conviction things not seen" as he mentioned in Romans 1. Paul describes faith as evidence of things unseen, but we have challenged this definition throughout the course of this work. Purpose or faith must come before one begins and does not concern themselves with the tangible results. Faith comes after knowledge before receiving results as faith comes to test one's beliefs even under the uncertainty of failure out of never reaching truth. Faith rests on the idea that the truth is out there and not a conviction or hope or faith in the future. Faith is an attitude that believes and has the conviction to act on one's beliefs come what may.

872. As we were saying however, Paul ascribes all the victories of the Jewish prophets to what we feel that he wrongly terms faith as he sees it as a kind of contemplative resignation. By faith we understand the creation of the universe (Hebrews 11:2), the ascension of Enoch (Hebrews 11:5), and the promise of Isaac and Jacob (Hebrews 11:20-21). Paul mentions the nationalism of the Jews as being one with otherworldly goals and not narrowly focused on this present age as he says in Hebrews 11:16, "they desire a better country, that is, a heavenly one". Paul also says to the Jews that they, "through faith conquered kingdoms, enforced justice, obtained promises, stopped the mouths of lions". Are we really to believe that these were by faith alone and not by actions of the flesh as they clearly demonstrate? Furthermore, if Israel kept faith through all

these actions, then what need would there be for the new covenant that Paul speaks of?

873. Paul makes some interesting statements about God in the close of Hebrews. He firstly states that "Our God is a consuming fire" (Hebrews 12:29). This description of God does not seem allegorical or contain the words "appearing to us" or "appearing as". Taken as it is and with the unfamiliar backdrop of unacceptable interpretations that verge on the arcane the utterance seems demonic. Paul also claims in Hebrews 12:8 that, "Jesus Christ is the same yesterday and today and forever". If this is true then why should the message of God change for different people in different ages and have a new dispensation or a new covenant? Should not God have a consistent message of salvation for all mankind since the beginning of his creation of mankind since it is our lot to serve God and not for God to serve us? These and other questions we have presented seem to remain in the balance. We have attempted to provide an honest summary and exegesis of Pauline thought bringing up some of the main principles, problems, and concerns. We hope to share many dialogues with Christians who attempt to sincerely address these issues to provide both answers and or solutions.

Epilogue
Positive Aspects of Pauline Teaching

874. When the light shines in the darkness, the darkness knows it not, as we read in the Gospel of John. We may have our little light of Reason, but even our ignorance is not aware of what it illuminates. Light and dark cannot be on equal terms, yet they co-exist. Indeed, the more we illuminate with our light of Reason, the more it illuminates what Reason itself has hidden in the form of our own ignorance. So we ask: what is the relationship between "is" and "ought", and between the Speculative Reason, which pertains to our experience of what is, and the Practical Reason of our moral "oughts"[7]? These ideas were explored by John Locke, who provided the instruments of Democratic Society. In light of his views, we contrast the work of another Christian Theist, C.S. Lewis, to illuminate some tension and agreement in their views pertaining to Faith and Reason.

875. In the spirit of civil discourse, we must appreciate the debt paid to Locke in his use of Nature's Law of the preservation of life to defend human rights as the very basis for our debate. But we must understand that however much we are indebted to Locke, Locke himself saw the progress of human knowledge as not being in a stasis. We are therefore allowed by Locke to challenge his views. One thinker who did exactly this was C.S Lewis, who while accepting Locke's idea of Practical Reason, rejected the Lockean notion of the "Blank Slate" or "Tabula Rasa"[8]. Locke did not feel that we had innate speculative principles outside of those discovered by Reason. But as C.S Lewis recants, "the head rules the belly through the chest". This notion derived from Plato, is the Spirited Nature or Passion. In order for us to practice the principle of "love of one's own", we must first feel that we are right in doing so. This is the beginning of going beyond love of one's own to a true understanding of one another and of humanity, whose highest expression is intrinsic love. Love is a high elevation of understanding.

876. Lewis relies more on Natural Instinct than the progress of Reason and ingenuity. He warns that man's power over nature has often come to mean man's power to use nature against other men. But Lewis is quite radical in his

---

[7] Locke makes these styles of arguments in a work entitled "An Essay Concerning Human Understanding". As a book which attempts to link on Epistemology and Morality or Ethics it had a profound influence on thinkers like Immanuel Kant as well as others.
[8] In the work "Abolition of Man" by C.S Lewis he uses Plato and Taoism as well as a dialectic between science and morality to put into question the notion of a Lockean Blank Slate.

view, sometimes suggesting that no new ethic can be invented or derived. There is nothing new under the sun, and inventing a new ethic is like placing a new sun in the sky. "We never start from a Tabula Rasa. If we did, we should end, ethically speaking, with a Tabula Rasa" he writes. This comment was probably meant for Atheists like Sigmund Frued, and not for men like Locke, yet it provides quite a contrast, and also brings us to the final issue: How much do those underlying values converge between different belief systems as Lewis suggests?

877. In his Letter on Religious Toleration, Locke says we should accept those who have differing beliefs because this allows us the very basis to have our own[9]. But Toleration is preferred over a convergence of values. In this both Locke and Lewis agree that alteration from within, is more conducive to truth, than alteration from without. Lewis mentions that, as the Tao or "The Way" in Chinese Philosophy stands for "the way things are" or "the true call", and "only by such shreds of the Tao as he has inherited is he able to attack it". This type of man rejects there is such a thing as underlying value. We must not let our drive for Reason push us so far as to reject the call for our Faith in underlying values. Faith and trust in our fellow man is necessary to build any type of community.

878. To do this is to forsake what makes us truly human and fall into the the abyss of nihilism, skepticism, and moral subjectivity. Every man who claims that each man has a right to decide for himself, and judge only what is best for himself, loses the ground he stands on to make the very claim. As G.K Chesterton wrote, "the madman is not the man without Reason, but the man who has lost everything except Reason"[10]. So, we cannot fall into moral paralysis or paralysis by analysis, but the simplest aspect of faith is practicing what we preach and acting on what we know.

New Attempts at Defining the Christian Narrative
879. The Accelerationist Philosopher Nick Land influenced by thinkers like cyberpunk author William Gibson, Nihilistic philosopher Georges Bataille, Deleuze and Guatarri in their work "Anti-Oedipus", and many others, has recently cosigned the so-called political theology of a blogger who calls himself Mencius Moldbug. The blog is a penname of Curtis Yarvin who is an Ashkenazi Jew whose real profession is as a computer programmer but makes a pretense that he is just a layman or a blogger or a sort of political dissident (the term political dissident is usually applied to those who are defanged revolutionaries who feed off their own cleverness). The use of psychology or medical

---

[9] Locke agrees that all forms of religion are tolerable for stressing a basic sense of community and family except for Atheism which he says should be vigorously opposed by all people.
[10] This quote is from the "Orthodoxy" by G.K Chesterton

science and economic or evolutionary theory as a replacement for the philosophical and political scope is visible in such thinkers as Yarvin, who also draws from those of the Chicago School of Economics like Milton Friedman and Ludwig Von Mises. While Yarvin pretends to draw from such thinkers as Thomas Carlyle and Niccolò Machiavelli, it is clear that if the breadth of these thinkers' views were applied to the thoughts of Yarvin it should produce utter confusion. Machiavelli was as critical of science as he was of religion, noting that politics neither regards measured and planned outcomes nor moral restraints, and that the political actor should maintain shrewdness and coldness when judging such matters for success. As for Carlyle, Yarvin seems to miss his criticisms of the machine and the modern age where as Yarvin recommends such measures as internet crowdsourcing and digital currency to bring about a neoliberal hellscape where pseudo-governmental corporations create pirate utopias to entrap citizens within a profit-sharing venture in lieu of extracting taxes. This sounds no different from the present reality where corporations already control the State, especially via private weapons contractors.

880. Yarvin's view that the "Einsteinian" or the Atheistic liberal view of the modern world is a recasting of Christian values taken to their logical endpoint is a bootleg version of Nietzsche's claim in "Beyond Good and Evil" that liberal values are nothing more than secularized Christian values. While this is blatantly obvious, Yarvin never acknowledges any debt to Nietzsche in his writing and makes an almost deceptive claim and pretense to originality. Yarvin makes these claims in his work "How Dawkins Got Pwned" where he whines and gripes about Dawkins, who creates the concept "memes" in his work "Selfish Gene" to refer to the part of an idea that can join with other ideas to recombine and form ideas that have an entirely new existence. Yarvin employs such terms as Christian Atheism which he describes as a "memeplex" or structure of memes. Yarvin styles his arguments as an internal critique of leftism that looks for viable alternatives to the leftist project whose implosive nature is doomed for self-sabotage. What are some of Yarvin's recommendations? He recommends a return to the 16th century that would quite paradoxically seem to mean the collapse of scientific atheism as well as focus on the State as the main project of humanity which is an outgrowth of scientific humanism. The main factor in Yarvin's push for the 16th century seems to be not a reversal of science and technology, but instead a return to the foundations of Classical Liberalism in pre-Puritan England. A true return to the 16th century would mean not only the collapse of scientific atheism as we have described but Yarvin also does not seem to explain the genesis of ideas like inherent equality between all mankind and the endemic progress of human learning as a fundamental belief, where these ideas arise in Christian teaching or adequately chart their development in western thought. Properly understood, these ideas if conflated with Christianity cannot be 400 years old but 2,000 years old. For example, the idea of the hierarchy of being as well as the teleological and eschatological scope had combined to form both the notions of evolution and

inherent progress of man and the arts (techniques). The idea that Man can transcend himself, to a better version of himself and is driven by an inner potential, is not either religious or scientific as we have noted but does issue from a Western and European perspective that stems quite readily from Christian teaching that was first promulgated by the Apostle Paul. Yarvin lazily overlooks these various themes which have been claimed by several notable scholars as we have shown.

881. Or perhaps his obfuscation of truth is all too obvious and based on a clear agenda. Many cannot ask simple questions like how a regular blog can receive such attention positive and negative. In a podcast entitled "The Filter" with Matt Asher, on episode 60 (February 7, 2022), Yarvin admits that both of his parents are part of the "deep state". Yarvin is always Neoconservative in his views and attempts to present an anti-Liberal critique of history, but a much closer look at his views on European history can be shown to be based on said history as it treats the Jews of Europe. Such themes are often presented in his writing with no reference to Jews and Judaism. We find this odd, not only because Yarvin seems to collude with White Nationalists and others but also because Yarvin is, at least ethnically speaking, a Jew. It is quite puzzling then why Yarvin labels essays such titles as "Why I am not an Antisemite". Yarvin always pays homage to such evil men as Bertrand Russell and second-rate thinkers like Sam Harris, who he presents as a non-dogmatic thinker. In "Why I am not an Antisemite", he states that anyone with negative views on Jews as a whole should be considered an Antisemite, but it should be clear from our present analysis that such a phrasing is much too broad and can be used to apply to anyone critical of Judaism in general or any aspirations that are considered nominally Jewish. In the writing Yarvin is apparently responding to the claim that he blames Christianity but overlooks the intellectual and political influence of Jews in Europe that was vastly apparent at certain phases of the history of Great Britain such as the Cromwell protectorate. This was during the rise of Protestantism that greatly benefited such sects of religious minorities. Yarvin claims that it is hard to get from massacring the Midianites to a support for open borders, but this is clearly oversimplification. Hence historical development does not function as 'memetic" propagation as those ideas are never divorced from their historical context, just as genes cannot gain their particular expression without epigenetic signals from their environment. Yarvin denies the role of any Jews in, for example, Cromwell's rescinding of Jewish expulsion but key links can be found on the views and actions of thinkers like Manasseh Ben Israel and Hayyim Samual Falk and others. Yarvin himself draws a distinction between reformed and socialist Jews and Zionist or Hasidic ones. For someone who makes the claim that Catholicism is Conservatism and Protestantism is Liberalism, how can one really not see one important minority of Jews swaying the tide on each side with both reformed and orthodox views on either side? What about the term Judeo-Christian that is being touted by some

now on what is termed the "alt-right" which explores alternative conservative criticisms of liberalism?

882. Another thinker who poses as an intellectual critic of the implosive or regressive leftist crowd, as they are referred to by "alt-right" thinkers who are also called "Dark Enlightenment" or Neoreactionary, is Jordan Peterson. He also exemplifies the projects of showing that the progress of the enlightenment values is being curtailed by a radical leftism overly focused on identitarian schemes. To this end Peterson embarks on a parallel mission to Yarvin and even employs terms like Christian Atheism which he uses as a natural aid to Classical Liberalism, which like Yarvin, is also a worthwhile solution. Also like Yarvin, he does not shy away from the extreme example of Adolf Hitler. Peterson is overly focused on preserving the intellectual achievement of Ash-kenazi Jews just like Yarvin is as well, but this is especially strange for an atheistic type. In a Spring 2018 article entitled "On the 'Jewish' Question" he explains that Ashkenazi Jews generally possess a higher I.Q score than most Europeans and their intellectual achievements have dwarfed almost any other group. In May 18, 2017, Peterson spoke in Ontario in celebration of the cen-tennial of the Balfour Declaration which established the State of Israel. What would a so-called promoter of Christian Atheism achieve from celebrating the Jewish return to their Holy Land after 2,000 years? Peterson also worked for the U.N, which was another organization that is responsible for bringing about the State of Israel and recognizing it on a world stage. In 2009-2012, Peterson worked for Jim Balsillie, a protégé of George Soros, who he helped at the U.N in drafting a plan for the redistribution of world resources. This is strange since Peterson never mentions these to his audience where he presents himself a conservative guru giving self-help advice based on the Bible and a push for a traditional life, intellectual pursuits, and a critique of feminism. Peterson para-doxically supposes that radical individualism of thinkers like the Frankfurt School can be used to offset a postmodernist and cultural Marxist drive for identity politics, but many experts have pointed out that Peterson does not ade-quately understand Postmodernist or Marxist theory.

883. However, like Yarvin, Peterson has not adequately identified the source or origin of these views. Peterson employs Logos theology, or a belief that the Platonic and so-called western notion of Human reason being the middle point between the human and divine is seen in the outline of the Christian message. What is quite confusing is that, while not having the success at it as a Joseph Campbell level thinker, he focuses his thoughts through the Jungian system. While Jung openly declared himself a Gnostic in an inversion of the views of conventional religion, Peterson also haphazardly employs the philosophy of overcoming or "Becoming" seen in Nietzsche, who paradoxically rejected all forms of Christian and Platonic morality. Like Yarvin, Peterson also employs a psychological and economic framework, as he is a mixed psychiatrist and uses psychology and self-help to mask political prescriptions. Peterson directs his

psychological aid to disenchanted young white males who he hopes to move away from the prodding of leftists who he complains are awakening the beast in the conservative male voice which ultimately leads to Hitlerism. To this end, Peterson offers a path to getting one's life in order, cleaning one's room, and becoming a productive member of society. Unfortunately, Peterson does not address the industrial revolution, feminism and women in the workplace, or the extended adolescence of males in developing countries to any satisfactory degree. It is clear that a lack of a religious outlook is what is crippling the view of the traditional life and these problems and issues cannot be properly addressed from a secular viewpoint which is instead responsible for their outgrowth.

884. On the podcast "The Joe Rogan Experience" in an appearance with evolutionist Bret Weinstein, Peterson makes several interesting statements regarding his views on religion. 18 minutes in he reports to us that he likes to read Hitler for his own edification as he relates to his Jewish friend. A little later Peterson employs the metaphor of pharmacogenomics, similar to Yarvin, who employs the metaphor of developing immunity and evolutionary integrity by constructing parasitic memes that anticipate new viruses before they are spread and, as one reader said, beats the metaphor to death in his "How Dawkins Got Pwned". Peterson quotes Hitler's Table Talk just as Yarvin cites Carl Schmitt, the political philosopher of Hitler's regime. At 56 minutes in the interview, Peterson says that prophets are sent to discover the limitations of Nature and offer it as a corrective for the people. Peterson compares himself to a prophet but does not give an accurate job description here of what a prophet is. A prophet is given information he does not comprehend from a source unknowable and unseen and must comprehend the opportunity he is given to offer a service to humanity that requires great sacrifice of one's own goals and aspirations, which places them usually in direct opposition to those who are the manufacturers of symbols and idols that propagate through Man's catalyzation of himself as divine, reconstructing his own image as idol. The prophet is a smasher of idols and not a purveyor of memes. At 57 minutes in the interview, Peterson claims that the Bible is the document of the emergence of the divine individual. This occultic and esoteric understanding of the Bible does not explain the sometimes-misanthropic viewpoint of the Bible. At 58 minutes, Peterson mentions "Christian Atheism", as does Yarvin and in 1 hour and 13 minutes mentions the collective Judeo-Christian values as being responsible for western progress and excludes Islam.

885. One scholar who finds the synthesis of Greek Philosophy and Jewish theology in Christianity is E. Michael Jones, who also sees the establishment of the modern period located in the Protestant Reformation that occurred in Europe from roughly the 15th-18th century. He is a foremost proponent of Logos theology that has been hijacked by secular types like Peterson. While Heraclitus used the term Logos to refer to the ordering principle of the universe, Plato used it to refer to Reason, and the Sophists like Gorgias relegated it to human

speech. E. Michael Jones conflates the concepts of God's word or the Breath of God, in which God uses speech to create (God said…and then there was) within his concept of Logos, while saying Logos collectively represents speech, Reason, and the ordering principle of the cosmos. In truth the views of Heraclitus, Plato, and Gorgias cannot be conflated with any Jewish conceptions however E. Michael Jones claims that the term Jew can mean nothing other than a rejector of Logos, which first came to fruition in their selection of Barabbas over Jesus in the Gospel of John. The Gospel of John does not define Jews as a racial group but a religious group and does so in a critical fashion or in a way that is a negative response to the Jewish religion. It was at this stage that, being expelled from the synagogue, St. Paul sought to spread the religion of Christianity to the non-Jews which culminated in the spread of Christianity to Europe after the fall of Rome and the unification of Europe. It was there that proto-Protestant forces and supporters of Napoleon's liberation of Jews in Europe that took the authority away from the Church that the people of Europe became subject to the revolutionary and oppositional tendency of the Jews.

886. In a debate with Christopher Jon Bjerknes on Know More News with Adam Green which occurred on December 8, 2020, Bjerknes challenges some of the foundational aspects of Christian teaching and alleged that Christianity was a plot of spiritual revenge by Jews who fooled Gentiles into taking on the sins of the Jewish people in a scapegoat ritual, outlined by both the Yom Kippur ritual and the Ransom Theory of Atonement put forward by Proto-Christian thinker Origen. Bjerknes claims that Jesus praying to the father is actually Satan in disguise as Yahweh offers Jesus the throne of David, but he rejects it. This was all decided because of the Age of Pisces which is the time of the Gentiles which must be fulfilled until the Age of Aquarius which is the age of the world to come in which the birthright of Israel will be fulfilled in Jewish World Domination. To this end, Greek themes were employed to fool the Gentile. Elements from the Orphic Pythagorean religion which was seemingly a Hermaphroditic cult existed within Christianity according to Bjerknes, as well as the heretical concept of the Logos, borrowed from Heraclitus, and developed in the Neoplatonism of Plotinus. Bjerknes says that the Logos is the belief in the Monad of Panentheism and such a belief precludes belief in the emanations of God and is fundamentally derived from Gnosticism (compare these views with the Mythicism and Astrotheology mentioned in the first part of this book). In Paul, he refers to Satan as "the accuser" of the Gentiles quite mysteriously as we have pointed out. The debate breaks down when Bjerknes misidentifies the Logos of John as the Father when Jones corrects him and says it is the second person in the trinity. Apparently, Bjerknes does not do well in terms of understanding Christian doctrine on its own terms and instead relies on radical theorists like Walter Bauer and others influenced by the Tubingen School.

887. Bjerknes is of course reflecting on the line "The Word was God" or Logos was Theos is actually seen as all three members of the trinity and not just The Father. E. Michael Jones further alleges that to say Jews created Christianity is preposterous and that Christianity was born out of a conflict between Christians and Jews. By rejecting Jesus, Jews became a new religion. The Gospels and St. Paul reject the fact that what makes Jews chosen is because they are descendants of Abraham. Abraham existed before Moses and did not follow the Laws of Leviticus or anything similar. Bjerknes instead says that Jesus never existed contrary to the Antagonism thesis and the majority of scholarly opinions, but that he was based on Phanes Protagonos of the Orphic Pythagorean hymns. Jews made up a religion to make Romans worship Saturn or Satan. The Jews had already broken their covenant before Jesus and did not need to reject Jesus in order to lose God's covenant, and besides, the Jews still believe they are chosen, as is shown by them about themselves in the Talmud and Zohar, which contains a unique interpretation of the verses in Isaiah 53, Psalms, and other places that mention a "suffering Messiah". In the Talmud and the Zohar traditions of Jews like Isaac Luria, there are two Adams, two Eves, and two Messiahs, as well as a dual nature of God that includes a feminine aspect that is labeled the Shekinah. While Jews represent vessels of light of the tree of Sephirot, the Gentile represents the polar negative Qliphot or inversion of the universal order. Gnosticism led to the Kabbalah. Bjerknes alleges that Christianity came from these forms of Jewish mysticism but does not explain why the Talmud does not show up until after Gnosticism or the Lurianic Kabbalah until the 15th century and beyond, and furthermore claims that the plot to exterminate the Gentile is located in a plot to eradicate Edom or Amalek which is the ancient enemy of Israel represented by Greek or European culture. This not only does not explain why Greek attitudes were used to construct the Gnostic views or why such views did not appear until the second century and seem to present some sort of reaction to the Pauline epistles which appear much earlier. Furthermore, it is more likely that Edom are other Semitic people like Arabs or Eurasians since they would be closer in genetic and geographical proximity to the Ancient Jews as we have already discussed. E. Michael Jones says the Demiurge of Christianity is not the same as that of the Gnostic but is the Platonic "Worker of the People". Jewish sin is not the cause of Christian salvation he says, and the Church is the true Israel. These views consist of the furthest application of the contents of this book. We are confident to the degree that we have armed you with what culminates in a wider understanding of those terms employed here and the various forms of argumentation.

888. Jon Swinn and others at Exposetheenemy.com have provided a significant amount of research into the workings of certain deep state actors who are using Zionism and religious fundamentalism as a cover for their actions. According to retired Colonel Paul E. Vallely who is author of an important essay entitled "From PsyOp to Mindwar: The Psychology of Victory", he states that, "The advantage of MindWar is that it conducts wars in nonlethal, noninjuri-

ous, and nondestructive ways. Essentially you overwhelm your enemy with argument. You seize control of all of the means by which his government and populace process information to make up their minds, and you adjust it so that those minds are made up as you desire. Everyone is happy, no one gets hurt or killed, and nothing is destroyed. Ordinary warfare, on the other hand, is characterized by lack of reason". Paul Vallely writes most authoritatively on subjects such as psychological operations because of his unique role in Delta Force, Alternative Media, and spreading of misinformation during the Iraq War. In his book "Blueprint for Victory in the War on Terror" he advocates for regime change in countries like Iran and Syria. Paul Vallely served as committee chairman for Frank Gaffney's Center for Security Policy which is in turn connected to top Defense contractors like Raytheon, Boeing, Lockheed Martin, Northrup Grumman, and General Dynamics. Also connected are groups like "Stop the Islamization of America", the Council for National Policy, and the Family Research Council headed by the family of former Blackwater CEO Erik Prince. Alternative Media personalities like Steve Bannon and other Zionist groups regularly promote a so-called "Judeo-Christian" vision and claim that there is a war between Islam and Judeo-Christianity. A number of anti-Islam and anti-Muslim networks are funded by groups like Donors Capital Fund, Richard Melon Scalfe foundations, Lynde and Harry Bradley Foundation, The Russell Berrie Foundation, Becker Foundations, Anchorage Foundation, William Rosenwald Family Fund, The Fairbrook Foundation, and have several million in funding groups like Frank Gaffney and the Center for Security Policy, Daniel Pipes at the Middle East Forum, David Yerushalmi at the Society of Americans for National Existence, Robert Spencer at Jihad Watch, and Steve Emerson's Investigative Project on Terrorism. Such groups allege that Muslims around the world are waging a stealth Jihad in preparation for the coming of or rise of an eventual Caliphate that will enact Shariah Law and render the constitutions of western countries inactive is really based on the fears in Europe that Jews in Europe had two sets of books and were awaiting the day when Gentiles will become their slaves. Supported by groups like Prager University these organizations pretend to fight for Christianity but are really responsible for a Zionist infiltration in America.

Epilogue
This leads us to the "apocalyptic paradox" where religion as well as the basic science of entropy or empiricism suggest a constant devolution and unification of the contents of the world, while the scientific and occultic view suggests a utopian yet collectivized ethos of man as a microcosm of the macrocosm that is reified through chaos and change. While the religious impulse finds unity through the one at the beginning of time and sees all creative process determined by chaos without change, the futurist seeks change in the future emerging through chaos and transcendence from Nature.

Hence, the religious ideal seeks a return of the unity of the past in the future that is not man-made and science and the occult seeks to achieve transformation in the future through the man-made. This is partly why the New Age Spiritualist seeks a merger of all religious sects in the future while the religious ideal seeks a return to a direct and primordial connection with God existing at the beginning of time apart from human contrivance. Although science cannot predict the future according to its own epistemological framework, it contemplates future as the ideal, while religion prophesied about the future but contemplates Nature as ideal which existed at the beginning.

A false dialectic exists in the modern age between religion and science as the modern is itself a dialectic between science and art. This dialectic can be summed up in seven points, support for which can be found throughout this work. The seven main points where science and religion form a false dialectic are as follows: 1.) Science does not mean free inquiry but is ordered and structured with rules and experts and a hierarchical organization similar to religious orders. 2.) Science arbitrarily chooses where to direct its focus and does not exist in a vacuum of objective analysis but is really driven by human concerns. 3.) Science and magic are similar, (a) in their manipulation of Nature, and (b) in posing a similar dialectic to the one formed between science and religion. 4.) Science ascribes a pseudo-eschatology to the progress of human knowledge. 5.) Science is not antithetical to the practice of religion: (a) religious people have made scientific discoveries that are important in scale and are not wholly divorced from their religious motivations; (b) certain types of religion have an affinity for the scientific method. 6.) Innovation can be used by anyone and does not necessarily lead to improvement as the belief in progress suggests and moral and ethical considerations must be made in interpreting the relevant methodology that is necessary to proceed given a scientific or religious endeavor or any endeavor at that rate. 7.) One has to rely on instinct to a certain extent: (a) decisions made only on the basis of science never yield complete results; (b) waiting for the results to come in often takes too long; and (c) a world ruled by science is highly ordered but very selfish.

www.ingramcontent.com/pod-product-compliance
Lightning Source LLC
Chambersburg PA
CBHW020428130626
46549CB00001B/38